ISBN 978-1-5284-7147-3
PIBN 10928737

This book is a reproduction of an important historical work. Forgotten Books uses
state-of-the-art technology to digitally reconstruct the work, preserving the original format
whilst repairing imperfections present in the aged copy. In rare cases, an imperfection in
the original, such as a blemish or missing page, may be replicated in our edition. We do,
however, repair the vast majority of imperfections successfully; any imperfections that
remain are intentionally left to preserve the state of such historical works.

1 MONTH OF
FREE
READING

at
www.ForgottenBooks.com

By purchasing this book you are eligible for one month membership to ForgottenBooks.com, giving you unlimited access to our entire collection of over 1,000,000 titles via our web site and mobile apps.

To claim your free month visit:
www.forgottenbooks.com/free928737

English
Français
Deutsche
Italiano
Español
Português

www.forgottenbooks.com

Mythology Photography **Fiction**
Fishing Christianity **Art** Cooking
Essays Buddhism Freemasonry
Medicine **Biology** Music **Ancient
Egypt** Evolution Carpentry Physics
Dance Geology **Mathematics** Fitness
Shakespeare **Folklore** Yoga Marketing
Confidence Immortality Biographies
Poetry **Psychology** Witchcraft
Electronics Chemistry History **Law**
Accounting **Philosophy** Anthropology
Alchemy Drama Quantum Mechanics
Atheism Sexual Health **Ancient History**
Entrepreneurship Languages Sport
Paleontology Needlework Islam
Metaphysics Investment Archaeology
Parenting Statistics Criminology
Motivational

INVESTIGATION OF UN-AMERICAN PROPAGANDA ACTIVITIES IN THE UNITED STATES

HEARINGS

BEFORE A

SPECIAL
COMMITTEE ON UN-AMERICAN ACTIVITIES
HOUSE OF REPRESENTATIVES

SEVENTY-SIXTH CONGRESS

THIRD SESSION

ON

H. Res. 282

TO INVESTIGATE (1) THE EXTENT, CHARACTER, AND OBJECTS OF UN-AMERICAN PROPAGANDA ACTIVITIES IN THE UNITED STATES, (2) THE DIFFUSION WITHIN THE UNITED STATES OF SUBVERSIVE AND UN-AMERICAN PROPAGANDA THAT IS INSTIGATED FROM FOREIGN COUNTRIES OR OF A DOMESTIC ORIGIN AND ATTACKS THE PRINCIPLE OF THE FORM OF GOVERNMENT AS GUARANTEED BY OUR CONSTITUTION, AND (3) ALL OTHER QUESTIONS IN RELATION THERETO THAT WOULD AID CONGRESS IN ANY NECESSARY REMEDIAL LEGISLATION

VOLUME 13

APRIL 11, 12, 19, 23, 24, 25, MAY 6, 8, 9, 21, 1940

AT WASHINGTON, D. C.

Printed for the use of the Special Committee on Un-American Activities

INVESTIGATION OF UN-AMERICAN PROPAGANDA ACTIVITIES IN THE UNITED STATES

HEARINGS

BEFORE A

SPECIAL
COMMITTEE ON UN-AMERICAN ACTIVITIES
HOUSE OF REPRESENTATIVES

SEVENTY-SIXTH CONGRESS

THIRD SESSION

ON

H. Res. 282

TO INVESTIGATE (1) THE EXTENT, CHARACTER, AND OBJECTS OF UN-AMERICAN PROPAGANDA ACTIVITIES IN THE UNITED STATES, (2) THE DIFFUSION WITHIN THE UNITED STATES OF SUBVERSIVE AND UN-AMERICAN PROPAGANDA THAT IS INSTIGATED FROM FOREIGN COUNTRIES OR OF A DOMESTIC ORIGIN AND ATTACKS THE PRINCIPLE OF THE FORM OF GOVERNMENT AS GUARANTEED BY OUR CONSTITUTION, AND (3) ALL OTHER QUESTIONS IN RELATION THERETO THAT WOULD AID CONGRESS IN ANY NECESSARY REMEDIAL LEGISLATION

VOLUME 13

APRIL 11, 12, 19, 23, 24, 25, MAY 6, 8, 9, 21, 1940

AT WASHINGTON, D. C.

Printed for the use of the Special Committee on Un-American Activities

UNITED STATES
GOVERNMENT PRINTING OFFICE
94931   WASHINGTON : 1940

CONTENTS

III

INVESTIGATION OF UN-AMERICAN PROPAGANDA ACTIVITIES IN THE UNITED STATES

THURSDAY, APRIL 11, 1940

House of Representatives,
Committee on Un-American Activities,
Washington, D. C.

The committee met at 10 a. m., Hon. Martin Dies (chairman), presiding.

The CHAIRMAN. The committee will come to order. The committee will act this morning as a subcommittee composed of the chairman, Mr. Mason, and Mr. Voorhis.

The first witness is Elmer Johnson. Will you please take the witness stand? Will you raise your right hand and be sworn?

Mr. ELMER JOHNSON. I would like to say, Mr. Chairman, I am expecting my attorney here any minute, and I would rather wait until he appears.

The CHAIRMAN. That is perfectly all right. We want you to have the benefit of counsel. You can be sworn in the meantime, however.

Mr. ELMER JOHNSON. I would rather wait until the attorney is here. Here he is now.

Mr. COHN. I had understood we were to convene at 10:30. I apologize for being late.

My name is Sol H. Cohn.

The CHAIRMAN. Raise your right hand, Mr. Johnson. You solemnly swear to tell the truth, the whole truth, and nothing but the truth, so help you God?

Mr. ELMER JOHNSON. I do.

The CHAIRMAN. Have a seat, Mr. Johnson. Will you try to speak loudly and as distinctly as possible, so we may hear you? The acoustics in this room are rather bad and we have difficulty in hearing the witnesses unless they speak loudly and distinctly.

Mr. COHN. Mr. Chairman, may I say for the record Mr. Johnson appeared here yesterday prepared to testify. We were advised there were no committee hearings.

It appears from the newspapers this morning that there was no committee hearing yesterday because no witnesses had appeared. Now, I wish to make clear on the record that Mr. Johnson had been here.

The CHAIRMAN. All right. Proceed.

TESTIMONY OF ELMER LAWRENCE JOHNSON, SECRETARY OF THE COMMUNIST PARTY OF THE STATE OF MICHIGAN

Mr. MATTHEWS. Please give your full name for the record.

Mr. JOHNSON. My full name is Elmer Lawrence Johnson.

The CHAIRMAN. Wait just a minute. Mr. Thomas is here and the subcommittee is now composed of the chairman, Mr. Mason, Mr. Thomas, and Mr. Voorhis. You may proceed.

Mr. MATTHEWS. Where were you born?

Mr. JOHNSON. I was born in Illinois, Wheeling, Ill.

Mr. MATTHEWS. Wheeling, Ill.?

Mr. JOHNSON. That is right.

Mr. MATTHEWS. When?

Mr. JOHNSON. 1904.

Mr. MATTHEWS. Have you ever gone by any other name than that of Elmer Lawrence Johnson?

Mr. JOHNSON. I have always used the name "Elmer Johnson" and have been known by that name by all of my acquaintances at all times. However, I did use the name of Elmer Carr for self-protection.

The CHAIRMAN. Elmer Carr?

Mr. JOHNSON. That is right.

The CHAIRMAN. C-a-r-r?

Mr. JOHNSON. C-a-r-r; that is right. C-a-r-r. For the reason I had occasion one morning about 4 o'clock in the morning when a number of people smashed the door of the home in which I was living and ransacked the entire place.

When these men grilled me I did not feel obligated in any way to give them my right name.

The CHAIRMAN. All right.

Mr. JOHNSON. Later on I found out that these gentlemen actually were F. B. I. men.

Mr. THOMAS. In what year was that?

Mr. JOHNSON. That was recently—during the Detroit raid.

Mr. THOMAS. What year?

Mr. JOHNSON. This year.

The CHAIRMAN. You mean outside of this year you never used any other name except Elmer Johnson?

Mr. JOHNSON. That is right.

The CHAIRMAN. And you used that on the occurrence which you have just described? It was after this occurrence that you have just described that you used the name of Elmer Carr?

Mr. JOHNSON. Only for that moment.

The CHAIRMAN. Only on that occasion?

Mr. JOHNSON. Only for that moment.

The CHAIRMAN. All right.

Mr. MATTHEWS. How long have you been a member of the Communist Party?

Mr. JOHNSON. Well, let me see— about 7 or 8 years.

Mr. MATTHEWS. Will you please give us the date when you joined?

Mr. JOHNSON. It was in the early part of 1932. I don't remember the exact date.

Mr. MATTHEWS. Where did you join?

Mr. JOHNSON. I joined in the city of Chicago.

Mr. MATTHEWS. What positions have you held in the Communist Party, beginning from the time you joined down to the present time?

Mr. JOHNSON. Well, I was county secretary in Chicago.

Mr. MATTHEWS. When?

Mr. JOHNSON. That was approximately 2½ years ago, I believe. It was for a period of about a year.

Mr. MATTHEWS. And after that?

Mr. JOHNSON. And after that I became field organizer in Illinois.

Mr. MATTHEWS. How long did you occupy that position?

Mr. JOHNSON. Several months.

Mr. MATTHEWS. What was your next position?

Mr. JOHNSON. Came to Detroit.

Mr. MATTHEWS. When did you go to Detroit?

Mr. JOHNSON. I think it was a year ago last January.

Mr. MATTHEWS. And what is your position in the Communist Party in that State?

Mr. JOHNSON. State secretary.

Mr. MATTHEWS. You are State secretary for the Communist Party in Michigan?

Mr. JOHNSON. That is right.

Mr. MATTHEWS. Does the territory under your jurisdiction include anything more than the State of Michigan?

Mr. JOHNSON. It does not include the Upper Peninsula.

Mr. MATTHEWS. It does not include the Upper Peninsula of Michigan?

Mr. JOHNSON. That is right.

Mr. MATTHEWS. Does it include any territory outside of the State of Michigan?

Mr. JOHNSON. No.

Mr. MATTHEWS. Who was your predecessor in the State secretaryship in Michigan?

Mr. JOHNSON. Well, prior to that there was a committee of three that assumed the leadership of the party there.

Mr. MATTHEWS. What were their names—it is a matter of public record, I take it.

Mr. JOHNSON. I am not sure exactly who they were, at the present time.

Mr. MATTHEWS. Was one of them William Weinstone?

Mr. JOHNSON. No.

Mr. MATTHEWS. One of them?

Mr. JOHNSON. I believe that was before my time.

Mr. MATTHEWS. Well, who were they from your own recollection?

Mr. JOHNSON. Well, I recall Earl Reno.

Mr. MATTHEWS. Is that R-e-n-o?

Mr. JOHNSON. That is right. I don't remember the others because it is rather vague in my memory.

Mr. MATTHEWS. How long had that trio occupied the secretariat?

Mr. JOHNSON. It was for a very brief period of time—just a few months.

Mr. MATTHEWS. Do you know who the secretary was prior to this period when the three men were in charge?

Mr. JOHNSON. William Weinstone, I believe.

Mr. MATTHEWS. William Weinstone. Now, do you know how long William Weinstone was State secretary for Michigan?

Mr. JOHNSON. I don't know.

Mr. MATTHEWS. Approximately.

Mr. JOHNSON. I couldn't say.

Mr. MATTHEWS. Where are the headquarters of the Communist Party in Michigan—what is the address?

Mr. JOHNSON. 5969 Fourteenth Street.

Mr. MATTHEWS. What is the size of the membership under your jurisdiction or in the State of Michigan?

Mr. JOHNSON. Well, a little over 2,000.

Mr. MATTHEWS. How do you arrive at that figure?

Mr. JOHNSON. It is an approximate figure.

Mr. MATTHEWS. How do you approximate it?

Mr. JOHNSON. Reports, reports from the various congressional districts, and so on.

Mr. MATTHEWS. How often are those reports made?

Mr. JOHNSON. Well, once a year and then in between times there is a check-up.

Mr. MATTHEWS. Is there an annual check-up of the membership from your office?

Mr. JOHNSON. Yes.

Mr. THOMAS. Will you speak louder, Mr. Johnson? We can't hear you?

Mr. JOHNSON. Yes. There is an annual check-up.

Mr. MATTHEWS. When was the last membership report made to your headquarters from the branches or districts or congressional districts?

Mr. JOHNSON. Repuorts are still coming in.

Mr. MATTHEWS. Have you ever traveled abroad?

Mr. JOHNSON. No; I haven't. I have been in Canada.

Mr. MATTHEWS. Have you ever been anywhere else outside of the United States?

Mr. JOHNSON. Outside of Canada for a day or two at the most. I think I was there 4 days in 1926.

Mr. MATTHEWS. You were not a member of the Communist Party at that time?

Mr. JOHNSON. That is right.

Mr. MATTHEWS. You have never been in Canada since you became a member of the Communist Party?

Mr. JOHNSON. Yes. Been there once to deliver a radio broadcast.

Mr. MATTHEWS. Under what auspices?

Mr. JOHNSON. Under the auspices of the Communist Party.

Mr. MATTHEWS. Where was that?

Mr. JOHNSON. Right across the river from Detroit.

Mr. MATTHEWS. Windsor?

Mr. JOHNSON. It is a Detroit station.

Mr. MATTHEWS. Did you bring with you the records of the Communist Party of the State of Michigan as called for in the subpena which was served on you?

Mr. JOHNSON. What records, specifically, are you referring to?

Mr. MATTHEWS. The ones called for in the subpena which was served on you.

Mr. JOHNSON. Would you be more specific, because it refers to quite a number of records?

Mr. MATTHEWS. Do you have a copy of your subpena with you?

Mr. JOHNSON. My attorney has it in his possession, I believe.

Mr. COHN. I think—I don't have it in my possession. Just a moment, Mr. Chairman; I do have it, I think. No; I am sorry.

Mr. MATTHEWS. Well, Mr. Johnson, did you bring with you any records of correspondence of the Communist Party in Michigan?

Mr. JOHNSON. We have no correspondence at the present time in the office.

Mr. MATTHEWS. What did you do with it?

Mr. JOHNSON. It is destroyed from day to day as it is received.

Mr. MATTHEWS. You have no letters on file of any kind pertaining to the work of the Communist Party?

Mr. JOHNSON. Not in the office.

Mr. MATTHEWS. Where are they?

Mr. JOHNSON. We haven't them anywhere, as far as I know.

Mr. MATTHEWS. When were they destroyed?

Mr. JOHNSON. Each day as——

Mr. MATTHEWS. Yes; but up until a certain period, I take it, you did have correspondence filed consisting——

Mr. JOHNSON. We did.

Mr. MATTHEWS. Consisting of back correspondence in your office; is that correct?

Mr. JOHNSON. Well, sometimes we permitted it to accumulate.

Mr. MATTHEWS. When you took over the office a little more than a year ago there was back correspondence in the files in the office, was there not?

Mr. JOHNSON. There was a lot of material that was in many respects not of immediate service and——

The CHAIRMAN. He is asking you about correspondence. Was there any correspondence—letters at the time you took over the office?

Mr. JOHNSON. Yes, there was.

The CHAIRMAN. Letters?

Mr. JOHNSON. Yes.

Mr. MATTHEWS. When did you destroy that?

Mr. JOHNSON. That was destroyed during a process—during a period of a number of weeks—a number of months.

Mr. MATTHEWS. Who ordered this correspondence destroyed?

Mr. JOHNSON. Well, I did.

Mr. MATTHEWS. Who gave instructions that all correspondence should be destroyed from day to day?

Mr. JOHNSON. I did.

Mr. MATTHEWS. Did you receive any suggestions or instructions from anyone else to that effect?

Mr. JOHNSON. No.

Mr. MATTHEWS. You acted entirely on your own responsibility?

Mr. JOHNSON. That is right.

Mr. MATTHEWS. In instituting the procedure of destroying all correspondence from day to day?

Mr. JOHNSON. That is right.

Mr. MATTHEWS. What is the purpose of the destruction of the correspondence from day to day?

Mr. JOHNSON. Well, we generally act upon the correspondence immediately as we receive it and there is, in most cases, no need to keep it on record. Sometimes it can serve to fall into the hands—that is, names of people, innocent people fall into the hands of those who are trying to smear these innocent people who communicate with the Communist Party.

Mr. MATTHEWS. What is the approximate number of letters which you receive from day to day—that is each day?

Mr. JOHNSON. Well, I would say, of course, newspapers we receive in the mail. I don't think you were referring to them.

Mr. MATTHEWS. No; I am referring to letters.

Mr. JOHNSON. Personal correspondence?

Mr. MATTHEWS. Yes.

Mr. JOHNSON. Sometimes an average of one per day; sometimes two; sometimes we don't receive any for a day or two. I think that is an approximate estimation.

Mr. MATTHEWS. Do you keep any carbon copies of any of your out-going mail?

Mr. JOHNSON. No.

Mr. MATTHEWS. Did you bring with you any records of the names and addresses of branch functionaries—branch or unit functionaries in the State of Michigan?

Mr. JOHNSON. No; I cannot. I cannot deliver or give such material as names and addresses of members or branch organizers of the party to this committee for the reason that the chairman——

The CHAIRAMN. What he asked you was, if you brought with you any of the records showing the secretaries of the branches. That is the question he asked you.

Mr. JOHNSON. That is right.

The CHAIRMAN. You did not bring those records?

Mr. JOHNSON. No; I understood the question but I would like to given a reason.

The CHAIRMAN. The question now to you is whether you brought the records. Did you bring them or not?

Mr. JOHNSON. No.

The CHAIRMAN. You did not bring the records?

Mr. JOHNSON. But I would like to get the reason——

The CHAIRMAN. Well, wait until we ask you one or two questions. Do you have any such records?

Mr. JOHNSON. No; we don't.

The CHAIRMAN. Then there is no use to talk about reasons if you have no records. You couldn't bring something that you don't have.

Mr. JOHNSON. It would be unlawful——

The CHAIRMAN. But you say you have no records. Of course, you can't bring them.

Mr. JOHNSON. It would be unlawful to give this committee such names.

Mr. THOMAS. You haven't got any records, so how could you bring them?

Mr. JOHNSON. That is true.

The CHAIRMAN. Then what is the use of giving a reason?

Mr. JOHNSON. There is an additional reason.

Mr. THOMAS. The only reason you want to give a reason is to use this committee now as a sounding board, just like all the rest of you Communists.

Mr. COHN. I object to the statement on the record. I move it be expunged from the record.

The CHAIRMAN. All right; let us proceed.

Mr. JOHNSON. I think it was important to submit a reason.

The CHAIRMAN. You have said you have no records. How can you give a reason for not producing records that you don't have, according to your statement?

Mr. JOHNSON. Because I believe that this committee has no power to ask for such records.

The CHAIRMAN. That is not going to be permitted. Proceed.

Mr. MATTHEWS. Do you have a Communist Party organization in each of the congressional districts of the State of Michigan?

Mr. JOHNSON. Not all of them.

Mr. MATTHEWS. Now, how many congressional districts do you have an organization in?

Mr. JOHNSON. Well, it would be hard to answer that question accurately because in certain congressional districts we have only a few members, and then it would be hard to the—it would be difficult to say whether that would be characterized as an organization, and of course in other congressional districts we have——

Mr. MATTHEWS. Approximately in how many do you have organizations to the extent that you have functionaries who supervise the work of the party in any respect in those districts?

Mr. JOHNSON. Well, let us see. In a majority of the congressional districts of Detroit and several out of the city.

Mr. MATTHEWS. How many would that be? Ten or twelve in all?

Mr. JOHNSON. Not quite that many.

Mr. MATTHEWS. Eight, perhaps?

Mr. JOHNSON. Yes, sir.

Mr. MATTHEWS. About eight congressional districts you have party organizations in?

Mr. JOHNSON. That is right.

Mr. MATTHEWS. Will you please give the titles of the functionaries who have charge of the affairs of the congressional districts in the Communist Party?

Mr. JOHNSON. [No answer.]

Mr. MATTHEWS. What do you call the officers of the organization in a congressional district?

The CHAIRMAN. While you are conferring with your attorney I want to make the announcement that the committee has a quorum present and is operating now as a full committee. The quorum is Mr. Casey, Mr. Voorhis, the chairman, Mr. Mason, and Mr. Thomas. Now proceed. What was the question?

Mr. MATTHEWS. I asked the witness what the title of the functionaries are who served in the congressional district organizations for the Communist Party.

The CHAIRMAN. All right.

Mr. JOHNSON. Well, we call them "section organizers."

Mr. MATTHEWS. Each congressional district that has an organization has a section organizer?

Mr. JOHNSON. That is right.

Mr. MATTHEWS. In addition to the section organizer what other functionaries are there in each congressional district?

Mr. JOHNSON. Well, there is an executive committee.

Mr. MATTHEWS. How many members are there on the executive committee?

Mr. JOHNSON. Approximately from five to nine.

Mr. MATTHEWS. In addition to these what other functionaries are there?

Mr. JOHNSON. Well, there are the branch organizers.

Mr. MATTHEWS. The branch organizer would be a subdivision of the congressional district?

Mr. JOHNSON. That is right.

Mr. MATTHEWS. For the district itself do you have a membership director?

Mr. JOHNSON. Yes; we have a membership director.

The CHAIRMAN. Will you speak a little louder, if you can, please, sir?

Mr. MATTHEWS. Do you have a treasurer or financial secretary in each district?

Mr. JOHNSON. In each congressional district?

Mr. MATTHEWS. Yes.

Mr. JOHNSON. Yes; we do.

Mr. MATTHEWS. What do you call that person. Financial secretary?

Mr. JOHNSON. That is right.

Mr. MATTHEWS. What other functionaries can you think of?

Mr. JOHNSON. Well, we have educational directors and, of course, there are educational directors in the unit as well.

Mr. MATTHEWS. I am speaking of the districts. Do you have literature?

Mr. JOHNSON. Yes, sir; literature—Daily Worker—literature agent, Daily Worker agent.

Mr. MATTHEWS. Literature agent?

Mr. JOHNSON. Daily Worker agent.

Mr. MATTHEWS. Is the Daily Worker agent in addition to the literature agent?

Mr. JOHNSON. It is sometimes true.

Mr. MATTHEWS. Are there any other functionaries in the districts?

Mr. JOHNSON. Well, there are in many cases, but it is not uniform all the way through.

Mr. MATTHEWS. What would be some of the others that would not be uniform?

Mr. JOHNSON. Well——

Mr. MATTHEWS. Do you have a man in charge of trade-union matters in some of the districts?

Mr. JOHNSON. Well, sometimes we have commissions—commissions to give study to certain problems or phases.

Mr. THOMAS. Do you always speak as quietly as you are speaking now, Mr. Johnson?

Mr. CASEY. I think it is getting to be a colloquy. You both have lowered your voices.

The CHAIRMAN. Speak a little louder, gentlemen. It is difficult to hear. The question was whether or not you had anyone who is in charge——

Mr. MATTHEWS. In charge of trade-unions or labor-union matters in the districts. Now, what was your answer to that?

Mr. JOHNSON. The answer is "no."

The CHAIRMAN. You have no one in charge of trade-union matters?

Mr. JOHNSON. That is right.

The CHAIRMAN. Have you had in the past anyone in charge of trade-union matters?

Mr. JOHNSON. Not since I have been there. As far as I know, we have never had any such.

Mr. MATTHEWS. Now, in the State organization itself, in addition to yourself, what officers are there in the party?

Mr. JOHNSON. (No answer.)

Mr. MATTHEWS. You are State secretary?

Mr. JOHNSON. That is right.

Mr. MATTHEWS. Do you have a State administrative secretary in addition to yourself?

Mr. JOHNSON. We have a financial secretary and we have a campaign manager in the coming elections.

Mr. MATTHEWS. Do you have an administrative secretary?

Mr. JOHNSON. No; we don't. We have an organizational secretary which takes in that class.

Mr. MATTHEWS. Would he be called a district organizer?

Mr. JOHNSON. He would be called an organizational secretary.

Mr. MATTHEWS. Is there a membership director for the State?

Mr. JOHNSON. Well, the organizational secretary also assumes that capacity at the present time.

Mr. MATTHEWS. Now, what are the subdivisions of the party within the congressional districts?

Mr. JOHNSON. Well, the subdivisions of the party within the congressional districts are branches.

Mr. MATTHEWS. Is that the smallest of the subdivisions in the districts?

Mr. JOHNSON. That is right.

Mr. MATTHEWS. And there are no intermediate subdivisions between the branches and the district organization?

Mr. JOHNSON. Between the branches—well, there is a section—a section and its committee.

Mr. MATTHEWS. The section is a subdivision of the congressional district, is it?

Mr. JOHNSON. That is, the section leadership is the congressional leadership.

Mr. MATTHEWS. Congressional district leadership?

Mr. JOHNSON. Yes, sir.

Mr. MATTHEWS. Now, is the congressional district the same as the section in the territory covered?

Mr. JOHNSON. I think so; yes.

Mr. MATTHEWS. Well, the branch is the smallest subdivision within the congressional district or section; is that correct?

Mr. JOHNSON. That is right.

Mr. MATTHEWS. How many branches of the Communist Party are there in your jurisdiction?

Mr. JOHNSON. Well, I would have to give an approximate figure; perhaps about 60.

Mr. MATTHEWS. How many of these 60 branches are in the city of Detroit?

Mr. JOHNSON. About half, I would say.

Mr. MATTHEWS. In what other center is there a number of branches?

Mr. JOHNSON. Well, in the outlying towns, I think.

Mr. MATTHEWS. Is there any other city in Michigan that has a number of branches—three, four, five, or six?

Mr. JOHNSON. Scattered.

Mr. MATTHEWS. Branches in one city?

Mr. JOHNSON. Scattered; yes.

Mr. MATTHEWS. What are those cities?

Mr. JOHNSON. We have a party in Flint.

Mr. MATTHEWS. How many branches are there in Flint?

Mr. JOHNSON. I am not certain exactly just about how many.

Mr. MATTHEWS. Well, what would be the approximate number?

Mr. JOHNSON. Well, I would not like to give any estimation because I am afraid it would not be accurate.

Mr. MATTHEWS. A half a dozen or a dozen?

Mr. JOHNSON. Approximately.

Mr. MATTHEWS. You get regular reports from them, do you not?

Mr. JOHNSON. Reports are coming in as I indicated.

Mr. MATTHEWS. Is this the first time that reports have come in from these branches during your secretaryship in Michigan?

Mr. JOHNSON. They are not completed yet. No; it is not the first time they have been coming in.

Mr. MATTHEWS. How many branch reports have you up to date from the city of Flint?

Mr. JOHNSON. I don't remember.

Mr. MATTHEWS. Would Flint rank next to Detroit in the number of branches of the Communist Party in Michigan?

Mr. JOHNSON. I think so.

Mr. MATTHEWS. What city or center of population would come after Flint?

Mr. JOHNSON. Well, I believe the rest of them are more or less evenly divided.

Mr. MATTHEWS. Now, as to the location of the membership. You say you have something more than 2,000 members in the State of Michigan. How many of those members are within the Detroit area?

Mr. JOHNSON. Approximately half or a little more.

Mr. MATTHEWS. A little more than half?

Mr. JOHNSON. Approximately, I think so.

Mr. MATTHEWS. Is the membership increasing?

Mr. JOHNSON. Yes.

Mr. MATTHEWS. Has there been a dropping off in membership at any time during your secretaryship in the State of Michigan?

Mr. JOHNSON. Well, it works both ways. It drops off and they come in.

Mr. MATTHEWS. As to the composition of the membership, what professions or occupations predominate in the membership in the Communist Party in Michigan?

Mr. JOHNSON. Well, the membership is in the industries of Detroit—in the building trades, in the steel, rubber, auto industry—in the agricultural region.

Mr. MATTHEWS. Approximately how many members do you have in the steel industry in Michigan?

Mr. JOHNSON. I cannot give you an exact figure on that or even an approximate figure because the reports are still coming in, Mr. Chairman.

Mr. THOMAS. Mr. Chairman, the witness has gotten down to the whispering stage again. Isn't there some way we can get him to talk louder?

The CHAIRMAN. Speak a little louder, please.

Mr. JOHNSON. I say that the reports are coming in now during this period of check-up on membership.

Mr. THOMAS. Then you do have some records?

Mr. JOHNSON. We get reports, verbal reports.

Mr. THOMAS. You get reports. Don't you consider those reports as records?

Mr. JOHNSON. Mental records; yes.

Mr. THOMAS. But are the reports coming in verbally or written?

Mr. JOHNSON. They come in verbally.

Mr. THOMAS. No written report?

Mr. JOHNSON. We don't have any written reports.

Mr. MATTHEWS. You receive no written reports?

Mr. JOHNSON. No.

Mr. MATTHEWS. When do you expect this reporting to be completed?

Mr. JOHNSON. Well, of course, we want it to be completed as soon as possible.

Mr. MATTHEWS. When did it begin?

Mr. JOHNSON. (No answer.)

Mr. MATTHEWS. When were the district branches instructed to make these reports?

Mr. JOHNSON. Around the first of the year.

Mr. MATTHEWS. Were they given any time limit on reporting?

Mr. JOHNSON. No. We expect the reports to be completed within the next few weeks.

Mr. MATTHEWS. Did you have all the functionaries throughout the State assembled to receive these instructions or did you write them letters?

Mr. JOHNSON. They received letters as well as verbal instructions on the matter—discussions on the problem.

Mr. MATTHEWS. Were they given a blank to indicate what type of information was required in these reports?

Mr. JOHNSON. Dues paying members.

Mr. MATTHEWS. Was that all they were asked for, was dues paying members?

Mr. JOHNSON. That is right.

Mr. MATTHEWS. They were not asked about the occupations or professions of the individual members?

Mr. JOHNSON. Well, we expect a verbal report on that.

Mr. MATTHEWS. Were they asked to give that kind of report?

Mr. JOHNSON. Yes; verbal reports.

Mr. MATTHEWS. In addition to asking for the number of dues paying members they were asked also for occupational information of members? What other types of information were required?

Mr. JOHNSON. Well, we required, of course, we wanted to know dues payment, and we wanted to know where they work—what industries they worked in. Wanted to know the age, nationality, and so on.

Mr. THOMAS. Mr. Chairman, I would like to ask a question there.

The CHAIRMAN. Mr. Thomas.

Mr. THOMAS. Mr. Johnson, if you don't keep a record of all these reports that come in, who is it that keeps all this in his mind? Who is the one who has got this exceptional memory and can retain all this information that you receive?

Mr. JOHNSON. Well, I do.

Mr. THOMAS. You remember all that?

Mr. JOHNSON. That is right.

Mr. THOMAS. Then, Mr. Matthews, I think you ought to ask him questions on just what all the reports show at the present time?

Mr. MATTHEWS. Yes. To date, then, what is the complexion of the membership with respect to nationality?

Mr. JOHNSON. We have not completed that report.

Mr. MATTHEWS. Well, you have it in your mind up to date, you just stated.

Mr. JOHNSON. You see, we expect to have a convention——

Mr. MATTHEWS. Yes—all right.

Mr. JOHNSON. And at the convention we will receive all these reports and then we will have a general view of the status of the party.

Mr. MATTHEWS. Well, never mind what you are going to learn. What do you have in your mind now with respect to that information?

Mr. JOHNSON. I don't know; I cannot say definitely outside of an approximate figure that I have given you—2,000.

Mr. MATTHEWS. That is the number of members. Now, I am asking you about the nationality of the membership as it has been verbally reported to you and retained by you in memory up to the present time.

Mr. JOHNSON. Well, the vast majority of the workers in our party, of course, are American-born workers in shops in the industries that I have indicated.

Mr. MATTHEWS. Is that the only form in which you have retained that information?

Mr. JOHNSON. That is the only form.

Mr. MATTHEWS. What about the age groups of the party? You say that you required that information—you received verbal reports with respect to the ages of the members, and you said that you are the person who remembers that. Now, what is the situation in the party with respect to age?

Mr. JOHNSON. But, Mr. Chairman, I explained on the age limit or on the age composition, and so on, these other details, we will be able to complete this general outlook and report which the convention——

The CHAIRMAN. Well, he means up to date.

Mr. JOHNSON. That is what I say. I cannot give you figures on age limits.

The CHAIRMAN. You don't know, in other words?

Mr. JOHNSON. That is right.

Mr. THOMAS. Mr. Chairman, if he keeps it all in his mind, how is he ever going to be able to complete it if he doesn't know at this date where it stands?

Mr. JOHNSON. I will know at the time of the convention. I will know all these things very definitely.

Mr. THOMAS. Even though you don't know now, you will know at the time of the convention?

Mr. JOHNSON. That is right.

Mr. THOMAS. In other words, your memory fails you now, but it will not fail you at the time of the convention?

Mr. JOHNSON. No; that is not true.

Mr. MATTHEWS. Have you already received any reports at all with respect to the age composition of any fraction of the members of Michigan?

Mr. Johnson. I have not; not for this year.

Mr. Matthews. Have you received any reports at all with respect to nationality of any of the party members in the State of Michigan?

Mr. Johnson. I have not.

Mr. Matthews. Have you received any reports at all with respect to occupations of the members of the party in Michigan?

Mr. Johnson. I have received some reports on occupations; yes.

Mr. Matthews. All right; now, what are the figures on that?

Mr. Johnson. Well, the figures are still coming in, and, as I indicated in my previous remarks, the great majority—the great majority of workers in the industries of Michigan—in the industries of Michigan in the——

The Chairman. Well, you have professional people in there, don't you?

Mr. Johnson. Yes; we have—yes; we have professional people.

The Chairman. Doctors?

Mr. Johnson. Well, the professional people are in the minority, I would say.

The Chairman. But you do have some lawyers and doctors and teachers; is that correct?

Mr. Johnson. We have some.

The Chairman. All right; proceed.

Mr. Matthews. Do you know the names of the section organizers in the congressional districts?

Mr. Johnson. Yes; I know their names.

Mr. Matthews. How many such persons are there?

Mr. Johnson. I gave you an approximate figure previously in which I think it is eight; is that right?

Mr. Matthews. Yes. Do you know who those eight persons are?

Mr. Johnson. I do.

Mr. Matthews. Who are the section organizers whose districts are within the Detroit area? Will you please name them?

Mr. Johnson. I cannot submit any names of any individuals to this committee.

The Chairman. You decline to give them?

Mr. Johnson. On the ground that the chairman of this committee has stated in the record to the effect that workers in the shops should be laid off—should be discharged by the employers, and I don't want to submit any names to a blacklist because it is unlawful.

Mr. Thomas. There it goes. That is the same old story.

The Chairman. You decline to answer the question?

Mr. Johnson. On that ground.

The Chairman. All right, you have given the grounds. The Chair directs you to answer. Do you still decline to answer?

Mr. Johnson. I decline on the grounds——

The Chairman. Well, you have already stated the grounds. Do you decline to answer even though the Chair directs you to do so?

Mr. Johnson. I decline to answer.

The Chairman. All right.

Mr. Matthews. Who is the financial secretary of the party in the State of Michigan?

Mr. Johnson. He is a worker.

Mr. Matthews. What is his name?

Mr. JOHNSON. That depends upon a living on the industries of Detroit.

Mr. MATTHEWS. What is his name?

Mr. JOHNSON. I cannot give his name for the same reason.

The CHAIRMAN. Now, isn't that, as a matter of fact, a public record, your financial secretary? Haven't you had that printed on your literature?

Mr. JOHNSON. But I do not want to——

The CHAIRMAN. I am asking you, Isn't it a fact that his name has been printed on literature of the party?

Mr. JOHNSON. That is true.

The CHAIRMAN. Isn't it true?

Mr. JOHNSON. Yes.

The CHAIRMAN. And you decline to tell us what his name is?

Mr. JOHNSON. For the reasons I have given.

The CHAIRMAN. You have already stated your reasons. The Chair directs you to tell us what his name is. Do you still decline?

Mr. JOHNSON. Yes, sir; because I believe I would like——

The CHAIRMAN. You have stated your reasons.

Mr. JOHNSON. I would like to state another reason.

The CHAIRMAN. The Chair has been fair to you in permitting you to state your reason.

Mr. COHN. Will the Chair permit the witness to state his additional reason?

The CHAIRMAN. With reference to this particular man?

Mr. COHN. With reference to his declination to state any name.

The CHAIRMAN. With respect to this name—confine it to this name.

The WITNESS. Because, in addition to the reasons that I have already stated, the political beliefs of an individual and his affiliations to political parties are of his own—are his own private business. It is a private matter and that the Constitution grants every individual that right to belong to any political party.

The CHAIRMAN. All right, proceed.

Mr. THOMAS. Well, I want to get one point cleared up there. Mr. Johnson, in other words, you believe that the Communist Party——

Mr. JOHNSON. I would like to give an additional reason.

Mr. THOMAS. Wait a minute.

Mr. JOHNSON. Just a moment.

Mr. THOMAS. You believe that the Communist Party is a political party?

Mr. JOHNSON. I would like to complete my answer, Mr. Thomas.

Mr. THOMAS. Well, now, just answer that question. In other words, you believe the Communist Party is a political party?

Mr. JOHNSON. Of course.

Mr. THOMAS. You do believe that, don't you?

Mr. JOHNSON. Why, of course, I believe it is a political party, legally recognized as such by the Government of the United States.

Mr. VOORHIS. Well, if so, Mr. Johnson, then don't you believe it should operate in an open and aboveboard manner. If so, then why shouldn't the names of the leaders of the party, the men who are responsible in these various sections, why shouldn't that be a matter of public knowledge?

Mr. JOHNSON. The party operates in an above, open, legal manner the same as every other political party. There is nothing secret about our organization in the least. If I decline to give names of individuals I stand on my constitutional rights and I stand on the basis of experience that the people of Detroit have had with the committee here.

Mr. VOORHIS. Well, what I mean is, if people who are responsible for the conduct of a political organization, if their names are secret, then I don't see how you can say that it is all open.

Mr. JOHNSON. But their names are not secret.

Mr. VOORHIS. They are not?

Mr. THOMAS. You are keeping them secret. We have asked for certain names and you refuse to divulge the names.

Mr. JOHNSON. On the basis of the reasons I have submitted to this committee.

The CHAIRMAN. All right.

Mr. MATTHEWS. Mr. Johnson, do you know Joseph Kowalski?

Mr. JOHNSON. I decline to discuss any names—any individuals for the same reasons mentioned.

The CHAIRMAN. You decline to answer the question, in other words, for the reasons heretofore stated, is that correct?

Mr. JOHNSON. That is right.

The CHAIRMAN. The Chair directs you to answer the question. Do you still decline?

Mr. JOHNSON. Will you repeat that question more clearly?

Mr. MATTHEWS. I asked you if you know or are you personally acquainted with Joseph Kowalski?

Mr. JOHNSON. Well, I decline to answer that question on the ground that his name or any other name brought into this committee and made public in the papers, may have a discriminatory effect upon him—may hinder his opportunity of getting a job.

The CHAIRMAN. All right, the Chair directs you to answer the question and you decline to do so, is that correct?

Mr. JOHNSON. On the reasons submitted.

The CHAIRMAN. All right, let us proceed.

Mr. MATTHEWS. It is true, is it not, that Joseph Kowalski is the financial secretary?

Mr. COHN. Excuse me just a minute.

Mr. MATTHEWS. It is true, is it not, that Joseph Kowalski is the financial secretary of the Communist Party in the State of Michigan?

Mr. JOHNSON. For all of the reasons stated before, I cannot answer that question.

The CHAIRMAN. The Chair directs you to answer the question. Do you decline to answer the question, is that correct?

Mr. JOHNSON. That is right.

Mr. MATTHEWS. What is the name of the campaign manager in the State of Michigan in this presidential election year?

Mr. JOHNSON. For the same reasons, Mr. Chairman, I decline to answer.

The CHAIRMAN. The Chair directs you to answer and you decline to do so, is that right?

Mr. JOHNSON. Yes.

Mr. MATTHEWS. Has the name of the campaign manager in the State of Michigan been announced already?

Mr. JOHNSON. It is being announced at the present time.

Mr. MATTHEWS. Well, has it been announced?

Mr. JOHNSON. Well, in some places it has.

Mr. MATTHEWS. In some places in the State of Michigan?

Mr. JOHNSON. That is right.

Mr. MATTHEWS. In what way has it been announced?

Mr. JOHNSON. Through public meetings.

Mr. MATTHEWS. Now, when did you last see Roy Hudson, Mr. Johnson?

Mr. JOHNSON. I think that is a personal question and——

The CHAIRMAN. Let me ask you this: Do you know Roy Hudson?

Mr. JOHNSON. Yes; I know Roy Hudson.

The CHAIRMAN. You know Roy Hudson?

Mr. JOHNSON. Yes.

Mr. MATTHEWS. What is Roy Hudson's position in the Communist Party of the United States?

(No answer.)

Mr. MATTHEWS. You know, Mr. Johnson, that Roy Hudson is the executive secretary of the Communist Party of the United States?

Mr. JOHNSON. I did not know that, Mr. Chairman.

The CHAIRMAN. Well, what is his position in the Communist Party?

Mr. JOHNSON. To be frank with you, Mr. Chairman, I don't know.

Mr. MATTHEWS. You knew that Jack Stachel was the executive secretary of the Communist Party in the United States, did you not, for a number of years?

Mr. JOHNSON. Yes; I think he still is, if I am not mistaken—I am not sure.

Mr. MATTHEWS. Have you seen Roy Hudson in Detroit within the past month?

Mr. JOHNSON. No.

Mr. MATTHEWS. Have you seen Roy Hudson in Detroit during the present year of 1940 at any time?

Mr. JOHNSON. I will try to——

Mr. MATTHEWS. In other words, you have sometime in the——

Mr. JOHNSON. I don't remember.

Mr. MATTHEWS. Not distant past seen Roy Hudson in Detroit but you don't remember the date exactly?

Mr. JOHNSON. I saw him in New York, Mr. Matthews, some time ago.

Mr. MATTHEWS. What were you seeing Roy Hudson for or about?

Mr. JOHNSON. I attended a national committee meeting of our party in the city of New York.

Mr. MATTHEWS. Well, what was your hesitation about stating if you had seen him in Detroit during the year 1940?

Mr. COHN. May I say for the record there was no intentional hesitation on the part of the witness.

The CHAIRMAN. Did you see him in Detroit during 1940?

Mr. JOHNSON. No; not during 1940.

Mr. MATTHEWS. When did you last see him in Detroit?

Mr. JOHNSON. I believe it was—I can't remember or give you the exact month, last year some time.

Mr. MATTHEWS. It was toward the end of the year, was it not?

Mr. JOHNSON. No; it was not.

Mr. MATTHEWS. When did you last see Jack Stachel, and where?

Mr. JOHNSON. I saw him at the national committee meeting, the one held, the one preceding the recent one.

Mr. MATTHEWS. You haven't seen him recently?

Mr. JOHNSON. I haven't.

Mr. MATTHEWS. Has Jack Stachel been in Detroit, to your knowledge, recently?

Mr. JOHNSON. Not to my knowledge.

Mr. MATTHEWS. Do you know John Schmies?

Mr. JOHNSON. Yes; I know John Schmies.

Mr. MATTHEWS. And you know him as a member of the Communist Party, do you not?

Mr. JOHNSON. Yes.

Mr. MATTHEWS. You have known him for a number of years, have you not?

Mr. JOHNSON. Yes, sir.

Mr. MATTHEWS. As a member of the Communist Party?

Mr. JOHNSON. That is right.

Mr. MATTHEWS. John Schmies is quite well known as a member of the Communist Party, is he not?

The CHAIRMAN. I wonder if we may have some order and quiet in the room.

Mr. JOHNSON. That is right.

Mr. MATTHEWS. I did not get the witness' answer. You said "I think so"?

Mr. JOHNSON. I think he is.

Mr. MATTHEWS. Is John Schmies in Detroit at the present time?

Mr. JOHNSON. Not to my knowledge.

Mr. MATTHEWS. Has he been there recently?

Mr. JOHNSON. Not to my knowledge.

Mr. MATTHEWS. Who is the organizational secretary for the State of Michigan?

Mr. JOHNSON. For the same reasons and all of the reasons I have stated prior, I cannot give this committee that information.

The CHAIRMAN. You decline to answer the question asked you?

Mr. JOHNSON. That is right.

The CHAIRMAN. The Chair directs you to answer the question, and you decline to do so?

Mr. JOHNSON. For all the reasons mentioned.

The CHAIRMAN. All right, proceed.

Mr. MATTHEWS. Will you please explain the operations of the national control commission, Mr. Johnson.

Mr. JOHNSON. I have never been a member of that committee and therefore I would not be in a position to speak about its functions or its operations.

Mr. MATTHEWS. You know there is a national control commission in the Communist Party, do you not?

Mr. JOHNSON. Well, I am not so sure at the present moment.

Mr. MATTHEWS. You mean you think it may have been abolished since you had——

Mr. JOHNSON. I am not sure.

Mr. MATTHEWS. Intimation about it?

Mr. JOHNSON. That is right.

Mr. MATTHEWS. When did you last know of its existence?

Mr. JOHNSON. I don't know whether it is in existence or whether it is not in existence. I never participated in any of its sessions and was never there, so I couldn't tell you.

Mr. MATTHEWS. When the national control commission was in existence, according to your information, what were its functions?

Mr. JOHNSON. To hear complaints and grievances, and so forth— to settle these complaints and grievances.

Mr. MATTHEWS. Who is the head of the national control commission of the Communist Party of the United States?

Mr. JOHNSON. I don't know.

Mr. MATTHEWS. Have you ever known who was the head at any time of the national control commission?

Mr. JOHNSON. No; I don't.

Mr. MATTHEWS. Do you know Charles Dirba?

Mr. JOHNSON. No; I don't.

Mr. MATTHEWS. You do or you do not?

Mr. COHN. He said, "No; I don't."

Mr. MATTHEWS. Did you ever hear of Charles Dirba?

Mr. JOHNSON. The name is unfamiliar.

Mr. MATTHEWS. You never heard the name to your recollection?

Mr. JOHNSON. That is right; to my recollection.

The CHAIRMAN. Do you know Nicholas Dozenberg?

Mr. JOHNSON. No.

The CHAIRMAN. You never heard of him?

Mr. JOHNSON. The first time I ever heard of him was when I saw his name in the paper.

The CHAIRMAN. You never met him?

Mr. JOHNSON. That is right.

The CHAIRMAN. All right.

Mr. MATTHEWS. As a member of the Communist Party, Mr. Johnson, you are acquainted with the constitution of the party, are you not?

Mr. JOHNSON. Yes.

Mr. MATTHEWS. That is the constitution of the American Communist Party?

Mr. JOHNSON. I am.

Mr. MATTHEWS. You have read that document more than once in your life?

Mr. JOHNSON. I did.

Mr. MATTHEWS. Are you familiar with its contents?

Mr. JOHNSON. I am.

Mr. MATTHEWS. Don't you know that the functions of the national control commission are set forth rather explicitly in the constitution of the Communist Party?

Mr. JOHNSON. That is what I explained, that its reasons are to settle grievances and to make adjustments of it in dealing with personal matters of the party.

Mr. MATTHEWS. I understood you to have some doubts as about whether it now exists.

Mr. JOHNSON. I have. I am not certain.

Mr. MATTHEWS. Have you heard rumors that it had been abolished?

Mr. JOHNSON. No; I didn't.

Mr. MATTHEWS. Has anyone suggested to you it might have been abolished then?

Mr. JOHNSON. No.

Mr. MATTHEWS. Then the doubt about its existence is something that has arisen exclusively——

Mr. JOHNSON. I am not sure about its existence. I don't want to say anything I cannot definitely confirm.

Mr. MATTHEWS. On the same general principle that you could not prove that Detroit still exists since you are here?

Mr. COHN. I object to this line of questioning as argumentative.

Mr. MATTHEWS. I want to know what the reason is why the witness doesn't know about the National Control Commission, if he has any valid reason other than the fact he isn't——

Mr. COHN. I object to the question as improper.

The CHAIRMAN. Why did you say you had a doubt about the existence of the National Control Commission when provision is made in the constitution for it as a permanent adjunct to the party?

Mr. JOHNSON. When I used the term "doubt" I meant it in the sense that I was not certain that it was in existence now. I am not certain— I am not sure because I haven't participated in any of its sessions. I haven't received any communications from it. I have had no dealings with it.

The CHAIRMAN. All right.

Mr. MATTHEWS. Have any members of the Communist Party been expelled in your jurisdiction during the past 12 or 13 months?

Mr. JOHNSON. Yes, sir. We have expelled some stool pigeons— agents in our ranks.

Mr. MATTHEWS. How many have been expelled from the party in your jurisdiction?

Mr. JOHNSON. I am not prepared to give an exact figure on it, but we have expelled a number of them, people who have collaborated with the employers trying to wreck the union.

Mr. MATTHEWS. Have you expelled a hundred or so?

Mr. JOHNSON. No; that figure would be much too high.

Mr. MATTHEWS. Fifty?

Mr. JOHNSON. That figure would also be high. I would say approximately a half a dozen.

The CHAIRMAN. Were their cases handled by the Control Commission?

Mr. JOHNSON. They were handled by the branches of the party.

The CHAIRMAN. Was the matter referred at any time to the National Control Commission?

Mr. JOHNSON. The matter was referred to the State executive committee.

The CHAIRMAN. State executive committee?

Mr. JOHNSON. That is right.

The CHAIRMAN. Did they in turn refer it to the National Control Commission?

Mr. JOHNSON. We sent—that is the one who is in charge of the disciplinary committee in our own party in the State of Michigan, refers these matters to the Control Commission of the party.

The CHAIRMAN. What did you do? The branch offices refers it to you?

Mr. JOHNSON. The branch acts on it.

The CHAIRMAN. And refers the matter to the State committee?

Mr. JOHNSON. That is right.

The CHAIRMAN. And the State committee refers it to some local official in the State who is connected with the Control Commission?

Mr. JOHNSON. No.

The CHAIRMAN. Who is he after the State committee?

Mr. JOHNSON. The State control commission refers the matter to the National Control Commission.

The CHAIRMAN. Control commission?

Mr. JOHNSON. That is right. I should use the term "State disciplinary committee."

The CHAIRMAN. And the National Control Commission has the final say?

Mr. JOHNSON. That is right.

The CHAIRMAN. All right; proceed.

Mr. MATTHEWS. Who reports from your State to the National Control Commission in such cases involving expulsion?

Mr. JOHNSON. For the reasons previously stated, I cannot divulge the name.

The CHAIRMAN. He asked you what official; is that right?

Mr. MATTHEWS. Yes.

Mr. JOHNSON. The head of the disciplinary committee.

The CHAIRMAN. What is his title? "Chairman of the disciplinary committee"?

Mr. JOHNSON. That is right.

Mr. MATTHEWS. Has anyone been expelled from the party in Michigan during the month of April 1940?

Mr. JOHNSON. I don't think so.

Mr. MATTHEWS. During the month of March 1940?

Mr. JOHNSON. Not this year, to my knowledge.

Mr. MATTHEWS. You don't recall anyone who has been expelled during the year 1940?

Mr. JOHNSON. No; I don't.

The CHAIRMAN. I did not get this very clear. Mr. Johnson, you say you have been in the party since what year? Was it 1900 and what?

Mr. JOHNSON. 1932.

The CHAIRMAN. 1932?

Mr. JOHNSON. Yes. I would like to have—1932.

The CHAIRMAN. What has been your occupation during that period? Where have you worked?

Mr. JOHNSON. Well, during that period?

The CHAIRMAN. Yes.

Mr. JOHNSON. Of course, during the time I was county secretary at Chicago——

The CHAIRMAN. Of the party?

Mr. JOHNSON. That is right.

The CHAIRMAN. I am talking about in any industry or any other work outside of the party work. Have you done any work outside of the party work since 1932?

Mr. JOHNSON. Yes.

The CHAIRMAN. What was that work?

Mr. JOHNSON. I am a painter by trade.

The CHAIRMAN. You are a painter by trade?

Mr. JOHNSON. That is right. I was secretary of one of the largest painters' local unions in the country.

The CHAIRMAN. Largest?

Mr. JOHNSON. That is right.

The CHAIRMAN. What was that?

Mr. JOHNSON. 637.

The CHAIRMAN. What?

Mr. JOHNSON. Painters' Local Union 637.

The CHAIRMAN. That is in Chicago?

Mr. JOHNSON. That is in Chicago.

The CHAIRMAN. How long were you secretary? From what year to what year?

Mr. JOHNSON. I think it was 1934.

The CHAIRMAN. 1934. During that one year you were secretary of that local?

Mr. JOHNSON. That is right.

The CHAIRMAN. Well, did you receive a salary as secretary of the local?

Mr. JOHNSON. I did as secretary of the local.

The CHAIRMAN. And that was your work during that particular year?

Mr. JOHNSON. Well, it was not a salary. I had to work in the shop in addition to that.

The CHAIRMAN. During that time did you have a position with the Communist Party?

Mr. JOHNSON. No. I was a member of the Communist Party.

The CHAIRMAN. Just a member, but you had no position with the Communist Party at that time?

Mr. JOHNSON. That is right.

The CHAIRMAN. Did you hold any office in the Communist Party at that time—during 1934?

Mr. JOHNSON. No; I did not hold any office.

The CHAIRMAN. Now, during 1934 how did you supplement your income? Did you do that painting?

Mr. JOHNSON. That is right. I worked in the shop.

The CHAIRMAN. What shop did you work in?

Mr. JOHNSON. Well, I have worked in practically all the big shops in the city of Chicago.

The CHAIRMAN. Have you worked——

Mr. JOHNSON. In the union shops.

The CHAIRMAN. Have you worked fairly steadily during the period from 1932 to the present time in the shops as a painter?

Mr. JOHNSON. Well, as you know the painters don't work steadily, all the year round.

The CHAIRMAN. I mean insofar as painter's work is concerned.

Mr. JOHNSON. That is right.

The CHAIRMAN. You have worked steadily during that period?

Mr. JOHNSON. I did.

The CHAIRMAN. At no time have you depended wholly upon your salary from the Communist Party for a living?

Mr. JOHNSON. Well, not at that time. I was not getting a salary from the Communist Party.

The CHAIRMAN. Well, I mean since you started getting a salary from the Communist Party you have continued to work in the shops whenever you could get a job, is that right?

Mr. JOHNSON. No; I don't.

The CHAIRMAN. You don't do any outside work now?

Mr. JOHNSON. All of my time is devoted to the Party.

The CHAIRMAN. To the Communist Party?

Mr. JOHNSON. That is right.

The CHAIRMAN. Were you employed by the W. P. A. during any of this period?

Mr. JOHNSON. During what period?

The CHAIRMAN. Since the W. P. A. started. Have you ever been employed by the W. P. A.?

Mr. JOHNSON. Let me see. Employed on the C. W. A. as a union painter.

The CHAIRMAN. You haven't been employed since the W. P. A. was formed to take the place of the C. W. A., have you?

Mr. JOHNSON. No.

The CHAIRMAN. Now, since you were secretary of this large local, what other position have you held in any union?

Mr. JOHNSON. In any union?

The CHAIRMAN. In any union; yes?

Mr. JOHNSON. Well, I was delegate to the painters' district council and to the Chicago Federation of Labor.

The CHAIRMAN. Delegate selected by the local union?

Mr. JOHNSON. Elected by the local union.

The CHAIRMAN. I mean elected by the local union of which you were at one time secretary?

Mr. JOHNSON. That is right.

The CHAIRMAN. You were the delegate elected by that union to what convention? What year was that convention?

Mr. JOHNSON. Well, I was elected in the local union—in the local union during the period of elections when they take place every June.

The CHAIRMAN. About what year was that when you were a delegate?

Mr. JOHNSON. I believe it was in '33 or '34.

The CHAIRMAN. Now, did you hold any other position with the exception of delegate and secretary in any union?

Mr. JOHNSON. Well, I was also secretary of the committee for unemployment insurance and relief.

The CHAIRMAN. For what union?

Mr. JOHNSON. For quite a large number of local unions in the city of Chicago—approximately 60 or more.

The CHAIRMAN. What year was that, sir?

Mr. JOHNSON. During the same time—1933 to 1934.

The CHAIRMAN. You mean that all of the unions had a committee for unemployment and what was the other—insurance?

Mr. JOHNSON. Yes. We had a committee that would promote the movement for unemployment insurance and relief; a committee that sponsored or, the committee that supported the unemployment insurance bill that was introduced by Congressman Lundeen.

Mr. Matthews. Was that organization known as the American Federation of Labor rank and file for unemployment insurance?

Mr. Johnson. That is right.

The Chairman. But it was selected, as I understand, the members of the committee were elected——

Mr. Johnson. Duly elected by the local union.

The Chairman. By some 60 unions in Chicago?

Mr. Johnson. That is right.

The Chairman. And then the committee elected you as its secretary, is that correct?

Mr. Johnson. Correct, at a conference.

The Chairman. Now, outside of that connection or position, have you held any other position in any union?

[No answer.]

The Chairman. You have got three positions, as I recall it: Delegate, secretary of this local, and secretary of this committee. Now, have you held any other positions in any union?

Mr. Johnson. I don't believe so, Mr. Chairman.

The Chairman. Well, do you have any doubt about it, or is your memory somewhat hazy on the question or are you fairly certain?

Mr. Johnson. Our local union called quite a number of conferences, and I participated in these conferences and was elected on the committee.

The Chairman. You mean conferences on different union matters?

Mr. Johnson. That is right.

The Chairman. And those conferences were over a period of years?

Mr. Johnson. That is right.

The Chairman. No particular year. You mean from time to time?

Mr. Johnson. Right.

The Chairman. Your union has conferences and you have participated as a delegate or representative on the conference?

Mr. Johnson. That is right.

The Chairman. Elected by the members of the union?

Mr. Johnson. That is right.

The Chairman. All right.

Mr. Matthews. Mr. Johnson, is this A. F. of L. rank-and-file committee an official A. F. of L. organization?

Mr. Johnson. It was an official A. F. of L. organization in the sense that local unions elected their representatives to represent them and it was supported by the local unions. Of course, the committee was not recognized by William Green. Nevertheless the local unions recognized the committee and carried on the fight for unemployment insurance.

Mr. Matthews. You no doubt know that the Federal Trade Commission issued a cease and desist order prohibiting this organization from using the name "A. F. of L." on the ground that it was a Communist organization?

(No answer.)

Mr. Matthews. You know that, don't you?

Mr. Johnson. That was not true, that it was a Communist organization.

Mr. MATTHEWS. I am asking you if you know the Federal Trade Commission issued a cease and desist order prohibiting you from using the name "A. F. of L."?

Mr. JOHNSON. That—that——

Mr. MATTHEWS. Well, is that true or not?

Mr. JOHNSON. They did, that is true, but I am not sure, Mr. Chairman——

The CHAIRMAN. You are denying—you admit they issued the order, but your statement is that it was not predicated upon facts. In other words, it wasn't a Communist organization, is that what you would say?

Mr. JOHNSON. I would like to consult with my attorney for one moment.

Mr. Chairman, I recall a statement by the Federal Trade Commission making such—having contained within it some remarks as Matthews indicated, but whether or not the Federal Trade Commission ordered this committee to not use the name, I don't remember.

The CHAIRMAN. But at any rate you continued to use it, didn't you?

Mr. JOHNSON. We did. It was officially disbanded.

Mr. MATTHEWS. Mr. Chairman, I would like to ask permission to introduce the cease and desist order into the record at this point.

The CHAIRMAN. All right.

(The Federal Trade Commission cease and desist order referred to by Mr. Matthews was made a part of the record.)

UNITED STATES OF AMERICA

BEFORE FEDERAL TRADE COMMISSION

In the Matter of A. F. of L. Trade Union Committee for Unemployment Insurance and Relief, Louis Weinstock, Abraham Baskoff, Richard M. Kroon, Frank Mozer, J. P. Anderson, A. Allen, Elmer Johnson, Robert C. Brown, Harry Bridges, David Gordon, Elmer Brown, Ben Gerjoy, Dora Zukor (or Zucker), C. Taylor, Luigi Genovese, M. Manes (or Manis), T. L. Major, A. Edwards, G. Alston, M. Balya, G. Spagnol, A. W. McPherson, Karl Maisus (or Masis), A. Weiner, William Thacker, E. Crews, F. Phillips, A. Fleming, and Charles B. Killinger. Docket No. 2531

COMPLAINT

Pursuant to the provisions of an Act of Congress, entitled "An Act to Create a Federal Trade Commission, to define its powers and duties, and for other purposes", the Federal Trade Commission, having reason to believe that the A. F. of L. Trade Union Committee for Unemployment Insurance and Relief, hereinafter referred to as respondent association, Louis Weinstock, Abraham Baskoff, Richard M. Kroon, Frank Mozer, J. P. Anderson, A. Allen, Elmer Johnson, Robert C. Brown, Harry Bridges, David Gordon, Elmer Brown, Ben Gerjoy, Dora Zukor (or Zucker), C. Taylor, Luigi Genovese, M. Manes (or Manis), T. L. Major, A. Edwards, G. Alston, M. Balya, G. Spagnol, A. W. McPherson, Karl Maisus (or Masis), A. Weiner, William Thacker, E. Crews, F. Phillips, A. Fleming, and Charles B. Killinger, hereinafter referred to as respondent individuals, have been and now are using unfair methods of competition in commerce as "commerce" is defined in said Act, and it appearing to the Commission that a proceeding by it in respect thereof would be in the public interest, hereby issues its complaint, stating its charges in that respect as follows:

PARAGRAPH ONE: Respondent association, A. F. of L. Trade Union Committee for Unemployment Insurance and Relief, is an unincorporated, voluntary association of persons, having its principal office and place of business at 1 Union Square, New York City, in the State of New York. Respondent individuals, Louis Weinstock, Abraham Baskoff, Elmer Brown, Ben Gerjoy, Dora Zukor (or Zucker), all of the City of New York, State of New York; Richard M. Kroon, A. Allen, G. Alston, all of the City of Detroit, State of Michigan; Frank Mozer, A. Fleming, both of the City of Philadelphia, State of Pennsylvania; E. Crews of the City of Pittsburgh, State of Pennsylvania: Robert C. Brown of the City of Butte, State of Montana; Harry Bridges, of the City of San Francisco, State of California; J. P. Anderson of the City of Washington, District of Columbia; Elmer Johnson of the City of Chicago, State of Illinois; C. Taylor of the City of Cleveland, State of Ohio; David Gordon of Middle Village, Long Island, State of New York; Luigi Genovese of the City of Rochester, State of New York; A. W. McPherson of the City of Clairton, State of Pennsylvania; Charles B. Killinger of the City of Flint, State of Michigan; and M. Manes (or Manis), T. L. Major, A. Edwards, M. Balya, G. Spagnol, Karl Maisus (or Masis), A. Weiner, William Thacker and F. Phillips, whose addresses are unknown, are members of the respondent association and compose a "national committee" for the purpose of supervising and directing all of the activities of the respondent association, including the publication and distribution of the "A. F. of L. Rank and File Federationist".

One of the principal purposes for the organization of the respondent association by the respondent individuals was and is the publication each month of a magazine entitled "A. F. of L. Rank and File Federationist". The publication of this magazine began in the month of January, 1934, and has, with a few exceptions, continued monthly.

PARAGRAPH TWO: In the course and conduct of the business of publishing the magazine, "A. F. of L. Rank and File Federationist," hereinbefore mentioned, the respondent individuals, acting through and by the aforesaid respondent association, sell and solicit the sale of the aforesaid magazine between and among the various states of the United States and in the District of Columbia, and cause copies of the aforesaid magazine when sold, to be transported from the place of business of the respondent association in New York City to the purchasers of such copies, some located in the State of New York and others located in various other states of the United States, and there is now and has been for more than one year last past a constant current of trade and commerce by the respondent association and respondent individuals in such magazine between and among the various states of the United States

In the course and conduct of their business the respondent association and respondent individuals are now and for more than one year last past have been in substantial competition with other associations and individuals, and with corporations, firms and partnerships engaged in the sale of magazines between and among the various states of the United States. Among such competitors is the American Federation of Labor, hereinafter described, which now and for more than one year last past has published a monthly magazine known as the "American Federationist," hereinafter described.

PARAGRAPH THREE: In 1881 an unincorporated association was organized in the United States under the name of "Federation of Organized Trades and Labor Unions of the United States and Canada." which name was, in the year 1886, changed to "American Federation of Labor." This organization consists of local, national, and international unions, and directly affiliated with it are approximately 482 federations with approximately 725 central boards and approximately 1,350 local unions. The aggregate number of persons affiliated with the American Federation of Labor is approximately 3,000,000.

The initials "A. F. of L.", through their use by the American Federation of Labor and by its local, national, and international labor unions, its affiliated federations, central boards and local unions, are now and have been for more than one year last past known and understood by the American Federation of Labor, its local, national, and international labor unions, its affiliated federations, central boards and local unions, and by the general public, as initials for the aforesaid American Federation of Labor, and as a designation of the aforesaid organization.

The American Federation of Labor has since 1894 published monthly as its official magazine the "American Federationist", which has a circulation throughout the various states of the United States to more than 110,000 subscribers. Through and by its use since 1894 of the term "American Federationist" by the American Federation of Labor for its aforesaid magazine, the word "Federationist", when used as a designation of a magazine, has become known to the American Federation of Labor, its local, national and international labor unions, its affiliated federations, central boards and local unions, and to the purchasing public as an abbreviated designation for the magazine "American Federationist".

PARAGRAPH FOUR: The use by the respondent association and respondent individuals of the name "A. F. of L. Trade Union Committee for Unemployment Insurance and Relief", and of the name "A. F. of L. Rank and File Federationist", has the capacity and tendency to mislead and deceive members of the American Federation of Labor and the purchasing public into the beliefs that the respondent association, A. F. of L. Trade Union Committee for Unemployment Insurance and Relief, is a committee of the American Federation of Labor, and that the said publication is a publication of the American Federation of Labor, and to purchase the aforesaid "A. F. of L. Rank and File Federationist" in such erroneous beliefs; thereby trade is diverted by respondent association and respondent individuals from their competitors who do not by the use of names for their publications or by the use of names for associations, mislead and deceive the purchasing public, and thereby substantial injury is done by respondent association and respondent individuals to substantial competition in interstate commerce.

PARAGRAPH FIVE: The above alleged acts and practices of the respondent association and the respondent individuals are to the prejudice of the public and to the competitors of the said respondents, and constitute unfair methods of competition in·commerce within the intent and meaning of Section 5 of an Act of Congress entitled "An Act to Create a Federal Trade Commission, to define its powers and duties, and for other purposes", approved September 26, 1914.

WHEREFORE THE PREMISES CONSIDERED, the Federal Trade Commission, on this 30th day of August, A. D., 1935, now here issues this its complaint against respondents.

NOTICE

Notice is hereby given you, A. F. of L. Trade Union Committee for Unemployment Insurance and Relief, respondent association, and Louis Weinstock, Abraham Baskoff, Richard M. Kroon, Frank Mozer, J. P. Anderson, A. Allen, Elmer Johnson, Robert C. Brown, Harry Bridges, David Gordon, Elmer Brown, Ben Gerjoy, Dora Zuzor (or Zucker), C. Taylor, Luigi Genovese, M. Manes (or Manis), T. L. Major, A. Edwards, G. Alston, M. Balya, G. Spagnol, A. W. McPherson, Karl Maisus (or Masis), A. Weiner, William Thacker, E. Crews, F. Phillips, A. Fleming, and Charles B. Killinger, respondent individuals, that the 4th day of October, A. D., 1935, at 2:00 o'clock in the afternoon, is hereby fixed as the time, and the offices of the Federal Trade Commission in the City of Washington, D. C., as the place, when and where a hearing will be had on the charges set forth in this complaint, at which time and place you shall have the right, under said Act, to appear and show cause why an order should not be entered by said Commission requiring you to cease and desist from the violation of the law charged in the complaint.

You are notified and required, on or before the twentieth day after service upon you of this complaint, to file with the Commission an answer to the complaint. If answer is filed, and if your appearance at the place and on the date above stated be not required, due notice to that effect will be given you. The Rules of Practice adopted by the Commission with respect to answers or failures to appear or answer (Rule V) provide as follows:

(a) In case of desire to contest the proceeding, the respondent shall, within 20 days from the service of the complaint, file with the Commission an answer to the complaint. Such answer shall contain a short and simple statement of the facts which constitute the ground of defense. Respondent shall specifically admit or deny or explain each of the facts alleged in the complaint, unless respondent is without knowledge, in which case respondent shall so state, such statement operating as a denial. Any allegation of the complaint not specifically denied in the answer, unless respondent shall state in the answer that respondent is without knowledge, shall be deemed to be admitted to be true and may be so found by the Commission.

(b) In case respondent desires to waive hearing on the charges set forth in the complaint and not to contest the proceeding, the answer may consist of a statement that respondent refrains from contesting the proceeding or that respondent consents that the Commission may make, enter, and serve upon respondent an order to cease and desist from the violations of the law alleged in the complaint, or that respondent admits all the allegations of the complaint to be true. Any such answer shall be deemed to be an admission of all the allegations of the complaint, to waive a hearing thereon, and to authorize the Commission, without a trial, without evidence, and without findings as to the facts or other intervening procedure, to make, enter, issue and serve upon respondent:

(c) In cases arising under Section 5 of the Act of Congress approved September 26, 1914, entitled "An Act to Create a Federal Trade Commission, to define its powers and duties, and for other purposes" (The Federal Trade Commission Act).

* * * * * * *

—an order to cease and desist from the violations of law charged in the complaint.

* * * * * * *

(f) Failure of the respondent to appear or to file an answer within the time as above provided for shall be deemed to be an admission of all allegations of the complaint and to authorize the Commission to find them to be true and to waive hearings on the charges set forth in the complaint.

IN WITNESS WHEREOF, the Federal Trade Commission has caused this, its complaint, to be signed by its Secretary, and its official seal to be hereto affixed at Washington, D. C., this 30th day of August, A. D., 1935.

By the Commission.

[SEAL]   OTIS B. JOHNSON, *Secretary.*

UNITED STATES OF AMERICA

BEFORE FEDERAL TRADE COMMISSION AT A REGULAR SESSION OF THE FEDERAL TRADE COMMISSION, HELD AT ITS OFFICE IN THE CITY OF WASHINGTON, D. C., ON THE 18TH DAY OF NOVEMBER, A. D. 1936

Commissioners: Charles H. March, chairman; Garland S. Ferguson, Jr., Ewin L. Davis, William A. Ayres, Robert E. Freer.

In the Matter of A. F. of L. Trade Union Committee for Unemployment Insurance and Relief, Louis Weinstock, Abraham Baskoff, Richard M. Kroon, Frank Mozer, J. P. Anderson, A. Allen, Elmer Johnson, Robert C. Brown, Harry Bridges, David Gordon, Elmer Brown, Ben Gerjoy, Dora Zukor (or Zucker), C. Taylor, Luigi Genovese, M. Manes (or Manis), T. L. Major, A. Edwards, G. Alston, M. Balya, G. Spagnol, A. W. McPherson, Karl Maisus (or Masis), A. Weiner, William Thacker, E. Crews, F. Phillips, A. Fleming, and Charles B. Killinger. Docket No. 2531.

FINDINGS AS TO THE FACTS AND CONCLUSION

Pursuant to the provisions of an Act of Congress approved September 26, 1914, entitled "An Act to create a Federal Trade Commission, to define its powers and duties, and for other purposes", the Federal Trade Commission, on August 30, 1935, issued and served its complaint in this proceeding upon respondents A. F. of L. Trade Union Committee for Unemployment Insurance and Relief, hereinafter referred to as respondent association, Louis Weinstock, Abraham Baskoff, Richard M. Kroon, Frank Mozer, J. P. Anderson, A. Allen, Elmer Johnson, Robert C. Brown, Harry Bridges, David Gordon, Elmer Brown, Ben Gerjoy, Dora Zuckor (or Zucker), C. Taylor, Luigi Genovese, M. Manes (or Manis), T. L. Major, A. Edwards, G. Alston, M. Balya, G. Spagnol A. W. McPherson, Karl Maisus (or Masis), A. Weiner, William Thacker, E. Crews, F. Phillipps, A. Fleming, and Charles B. Killinger, hereinafter referred to as respondent individuals, charging them with the use of unfair methods of competition in commerce in violation of the provisions of said Act. After the issuance of said complaint, and the filing of respondents' answers thereto, testimony and other evidence in support of the allegations of said complaint were introduced by Edward L. Smith, attorney for the Commission, before John W. Norwood, an examiner of the Commission theretofore duly designated by it (Harry Sacher, attorney for the respondents, having waived the introduction of testimony and other evidence in opposition to the allegations of the complaint), and said testimony and other evidence in support of the allegations of the complaint were duly recorded and filed in the office of the Commission. Thereafter the proceeding regularly came on for final hearing before the Commission on the said complaint, the answer thereto, testimony and evidence, briefs in support of the complaint and in opposition thereto, but without oral argument, respondents having waived oral argument; and the Commission having duly considered the record and being now fully advised in the premises, finds that this proceeding is in the interest of the public, and makes this its findings as to the facts and its conclusion drawn therefrom:

FINDINGS AS TO THE FACTS

PARAGRAPH ONE: Respondent association, A. F. of L. Trade Union Committee for Unemployment Insurance and Relief, is an unincorporated, voluntary association of persons, having its principal office and place of business at 1 Union Square, New York City, in the State of New York. Respondent individuals, Louis Weinstock, Abraham Baskoff, Elmer Brown, Ben Gerjoy, Dora Zukor (or Zucker), all of the City of New York, State of New York; Richard M. Kroon, A. Allen, G. Alston, all of the City of Detroit, State of Michigan; Frank Mozer, A. Fleming, both of the City of Philadelphia, State of Pennsylvania; E. Crews of the City of Pittsburgh, State of Pennsylvania; Robert C. Brown of the City of Butte, State of Montana; Harry Bridges, of the City of San Francisco, State of California; J. P. Anderson of the City of Washington, District of Columbia; Elmer Johnson of the City of Chicago, State of Illinois; C. Taylor of the City of Cleveland, State of Ohio; David Gordon of Middle Village, Long Island, State of New York; Luigi Genovese of the City of Rochester, State of New York; A. W. McPherson of the City of Clairton, State of Pennsylvania; Charles B. Killinger of the City of Flint, State of Michigan; and M. Manes (or Manis,) T. L. Major, A. Edwards, M. Balya, G. Spagnol, Karl Maisus (or Masis), A. Weiner, William Thacker and F. Phillips. whose addresses are unknown, are members of the respondent association and compose a "national committee" for the purpose of supervising and directing all of the activities of the respondent association, including the publication and distribution of the "A. F. of L. Rank and File Federationist".

One of the principal purposes for the organization of the respondent association by the respondent individuals was the publication each month of a magazine entitled "A. F. of L. Rank and File Federationist". The publication of this magazine began in the month of January, 1934, and continued through October, 1935.

PARAGRAPH TWO: In the course and conduct of the business of publishing the magazine, "A. F. of L. Rank and File Federationist", hereinbefore mentioned, the respondent individuals, acting through and by the aforesaid respondent association, sold and solicited the sale of the aforesaid magazine between and among the various states of the United States and in the District of Columbia. and caused copies of the aforesaid magazine when sold, to be transported from the place of business of the respondent association in New York City to the purchasers of such copies, some located in the State of New York and others located in various other states of the United States. and there was from January, 1934, to and until October, 1935, a constant current of trade and commerce by the respondent association and respondent individuals in such magazine between and among the various states of the United States.

In the course and conduct of their business the respondent association and respondent individuals have been in substantial competition with other associations and individuals, and with corporations, firms and partnerships engaged in the sale of magazines between and among the various states of the United States. Among such competitors is the American Federation of Labor, hereinafter described, which now and for more than one year last past has published a monthly magazine known as the "American Federationist", hereinafter described.

PARAGRAPH THREE: In 1881 an unincorporated association was organized in the United States under the name of "Federation of Organized Trades and Labor Unions of the United States and Canada", which name was, in the year 1886, changed to "American Federation of Labor". This organization consists of 110 national and international unions, 1154 local unions, and about 3,615.000 members.

The initials "A. F. of L.", through their use by the American Federation of Labor and by its local, national, and international labor unions, its affiliated federations, central boards and local unions, are now and for more than one year last past have been known and understood by the American Federation of Labor, its local, national and international labor unions. its affiliated federations, central boards and local unions, and by the general public, as initials for the aforesaid American Federation of Labor, and as a designation of the aforesaid organization.

The American Federtion of Labor has since 1894 published monthly as its official magazine the "American Federationist", which has a circulation throughout the various states of the United States to more than 110,000 subscribers. Through and by its use since 1894 of the term "American Federationist" by the American Federation of Labor for its aforesaid magazine, the word "Federationist", when used as a designation of a magazine, has become known to the American Federation of Labor, its local, national and international labor unions, its affiliated federations, central boards and local unions, and to the purchasing public as an abbreviated designation for the magazine "American Federationist".

PARAGRAPH FOUR: Respondent association was not a committee of the American Federation of Labor nor was the aforesaid A. F. of L. Rank and File Federationist, a publication of the American Federation of Labor. The use by the respondent association and by respondent individuals of the name "A. F. of L. Trade Union Committee for Unemployment Insurance and Relief" and of the name "A. F. of L. Rank and File Federationist" was without the authority or permission of the American Federation of Labor.

PARAGRAPH FIVE: The use by the respondent association and respondent individuals of the name "A. F. of L. Trade Union Committee for Unemployment Insurance and Relief", and of the name "A. F. of L. Rank and File Federationist", has had the capacity and tendency to mislead and deceive members of the American Federation of Labor and the purchasing public into the beliefs that the respondent association, A. F. of L. Trade Union Committee for Unemployment Insurance and Relief, was a committee of the American Federation of Labor, and that the said publication was a publication of the American Federation of Labor, and to purchase the aforesaid "A. F. of L. Rank and File Federationist" in such erroneous beliefs; thereby trade has been diverted by respondent association and respondent individuals from their competitors who do not mislead and deceive and who have not misled and deceived the purchasing public by the use of names for their publications or by the use of names for associations. Thereby substantial injury has been done by respondent association and respondent individuals to substantial competition in interstate commerce.

CONCLUSION

The aforesaid acts and practices of the respondent association, A. F. of L. Trade Union Committee for Unemployment Insurance and Relief, and respondent individuals Louis Weinstock, Abraham Baskoff, Richard M. Kroon, Frank Mozer, J. P. Anderson, A. Allen, Elmer Johnson, Robert C. Brown, Harry Bridges, David Gordon, Elmer Brown, Ben Gerjoy, Dora Zukor (or Zucker), C. Taylor, Luigi Genovese, M. Manes (or Manis), T. L. Major, A. Edwards, G. Alston. M. Balya, G. Spagnol, A. W. McPherson, Karl Maisus (or Masis), A. Weiner, William Thacker, E. Crews, F. Phillips, A. Fleming, and Charles B. Killinger, are to the prejudice of the public and of respondents' competitors, and constitute unfair methods of competition in commerce, within the intent and meaning of Section 5 of an Act of Congress, approved September 26, 1914, entitled "An Act to create a Federal Trade Commission, to define its powers and duties, and for other purposes".

By the Commission.

[SEAL] CHARLES H. MARCH, *Chairman.*

Dated this 18th day of November, A. D. 1936.

Attest:

OTIS B. JOHNSON, *Secretary.*

UNITED STATES OF AMERICA

BEFORE FEDERAL TRADE COMMISSION AT A REGULAR SESSION OF THE FEDERAL TRADE COMMISSION, HELD AT ITS OFFICE IN THE CITY OF WASHINGTON, D. C., ON THE 18TH DAY OF NOVEMBER, A. D. 1936

Commissioners Charles H. March, Chairman, Garland S. Ferguson, Jr., Ewin L. Davis, William A. Ayres, Robert E. Freer.

In the matter of A. F. of L. Trade Union Committee for Unemployment Insurance and Relief, Louis Weinstock, Abraham Baskoff, Richard M. Kroon, Frank Mozer, J. P. Anderson, A. Allen, Elmer Johnson, Robert C. Brown, Harry Bridges, David Gordon, Elmer Brown, Ben Gerjoy, Dora Zukor (or Zucker), C. Taylor, Luigi Genovese, M. Manes (or Manis), T. L. Major A. Edwards, G. Alston, M. Balya, G. Spagnol, A. W. McPherson, Karl Maisus (or Masis), A. Weiner, William Thacker, E. Crews, F. Phillips, A. Fleming, and Charles B. Killinger.   Docket No. 2531.

ORDER TO CEASE AND DESIST

This proceeding having been heard by the Federal Trade Commission upon the complaint of the Commission, the answers of the respondents, testimony and other evidence taken before John W. Norwood, an examiner of the Commission theretofore duly designated by it, in support of the allegations of the complaint, (Harry Sacher, attorney for the respondents having waived the introduction of testimony and other evidence in opposition to the allegations of the complaint), and briefs filed herein, and the Commission having made its findings as to the facts and its conclusion that the respondents herein have violated the provisions of an Act of Congress approved September 26, 1914, entitled, "An Act to create a Federal Trade Commission, to define its powers and duties, and for other purposes";

It is hereby ordered that the respondent association, A. F. of L. Trade Union Committee for Unemployment Insurance and Relief, and respondent individuals Louis Weinstock, Abraham Baskoff, Richard M. Kroon, Frank Mozer, J. P. Anderson, A. Allen, Elmer Johnson, Robert C. Brown, Harry Bridges, David Gordon, Elmer Brown, Ben Gerjoy, Dora Zukor (cr Zucker), C. Taylor, Luigi Genovese, M. Manes (or Manis), T. L. Major, A. Edwards, G. Alston, M. Balya, G. Spagnol, A. W. McPherson, Karl Maisus (or Masis), A. Weiner, William Thacker, E. Crews, F. Phillips, A. Fleming and Charles B. Killinger and their respective agents, servants and employees, in connection with the sale and offering for sale of magazines in interstate commerce or in the District of Columbia, do forthwith cease and desist from the use of the name "A. F. of L. Trade Union Committee for Unemployment Insurance and Relief" and of the name "A. F. of L. Rank and File Federationist" and of any other name indicating or suggesting that the said respondent association or any of its members constitute a committee of the American Federation of Labor, or that any publication by them or by any of them so sold and offered for sale is a publication of the American Federation of Labor.

And it is hereby further ordered that the aforesaid respondent association and respondent individuals shall, within sixty (60) days after service upon them of this order, file with this Commission a report in writing setting forth in detail the manner and form in which they have complied with this order

By the Commission.

[SEAL]

OTIS B. JOHNSON, *Secretary.*

Mr. COHN. I will object to its introduction unless I have an opportunity to examine it and find out what——

Mr. MATTHEWS. The witness testified that he recalls there was such a cease and desist order issued.

The CHAIRMAN. You can offer the order and show the counsel the order if you have it.

Mr. MATTHEWS. Do you know Lewis Weinstock?

Mr. JOHNSON. Yes; I know him.

Mr. MATTHEWS. He is also or has been rather prominent in the Painters' Union, has he not, in the New York local?

Mr. JOHNSON. I knew him at that time.

Mr. MATTHEWS. Local 9?

Mr. JOHNSON. During that period I knew him. As a secretary of the Painters' Local Union 637, I knew of Lewis Weinstock.

The CHAIRMAN. What position did he hold in the union?

Mr. JOHNSON. Well, he was secretary of the Painters' District Council No. 9 at one time in New York, and it was in that capacity that I had relations with him.

Mr. MATTHEWS. Were you openly known as a member of the Communist Party when you occupied the position of secretary of Local 637—as secretary of the painters' local?

Mr. JOHNSON. I was known by many members of the union as a Communist.

Mr. MATTHEWS. But you were not known by the union as a whole to be a member of the Communist Party, were you?

Mr. JOHNSON. Well. they called me a Communist. I never denied it.

Mr. MATTHEWS. You never denied being a Communist during your secretaryship?

Mr. JOHNSON. I never had an occasion to make an issue of that.

Mr. MATTHEWS. You know Lewis Weinstock as a member of the Communist Party, do you not?

Mr. JOHNSON. No: I don't know him as a member. I knew him as a secretary of District Council No. 9.

Mr. MATTHEWS. Mr. Johnson. the Communist Party is a revolutionary party, is it not?

Mr. JOHNSON. Yes; in the best traditions of American revolutionary.

Mr. MATTHEWS. It is also revolutionary in the sense as set forth by the teachings of Marx. Engels, Lenin, and Stalin, is it not?

Mr. JOHNSON. That is true.

Mr. MATTHEWS. That is, part of your revolution is based on the teachings of those four men, is that correct?

Mr. COHN. May I say——

The CHAIRMAN. Wait a minute. Mr. Counsel, let him answer the question.

Mr. COHN. I wish to state that probably the best authority would be the leading authorities in the Communist Party.

The CHAIRMAN. Well, he has a right to ask this witness that question. He already answered as I understand the question.

Mr. JOHNSON. Will you repeat that again?

The CHAIRMAN. Have you not answered the question—the three questions that he asked you?

(No answer.)

The CHAIRMAN. You have already answered.

Mr. JOHNSON. But there was one question that he asked here I didn't get.

The CHAIRMAN. Well. the same question was answered by the witness two times. Proceed.

Mr. MATTHEWS. The Communist Party being, as you say, a revolutionary organization, it is revolutionary as interpreted in the sense in which Marx, Engels, Lenin, and Stalin stated it. Isn't it true, Mr. Johnson, that the reason you don't want to give the names of anyone in or associated with the Communist Party, is that it is a conspiratorial organization which aims at a revolution to displace the capitalist system in the United States with a soviet form of government?

Mr. JOHNSON. Mr. Chairman. I object to that question. It is not based on any facts at all. I object to it because our party is not a conspiratorial organization and all facts and evidence prove the contrary.

The CHAIRMAN. Your answer is that it is not a conspiratorial organization?

Mr. JOHNSON. That it is a legal, open organization that carries on its activities before all.

The CHAIRMAN. All right; proceed.

Mr. JOHNSON. And there is nothing to hide.

Mr. MATTHEWS. Are the teachings of Lenin and the others who have occupied positions of leadership in the Communist movement such that illegal actions are barred from the work of the Communist Party?

Mr. COHN. I must ask that the question, unless it is made more specific, is meaningless.

The CHAIRMAN. Wait just 1 minute, if you don't mind.

We have a number of witnesses here on another phase of this matter and let us conclude with this witness.

Mr. MATTHEWS. Well, I would like to ask the witness if he doesn't know that Lenin stated that the revolutionaries, if they are to be worthy of the name, must employ or must combine both illegal and legal methods——

Mr. JOHNSON. Where did you get that statement from?

Mr. MATTHEWS. I got that from Lenin.

Mr. JOHNSON. Well, I don't want to discuss anything taken out of a text as you are doing it now. I would rather see the document. I would rather examine the document, and then I would have to discuss it in the period that it was said, at the time it was mentioned. I would have to take many things into consideration.

Mr. MATTHEWS. In other words, you are not prepared to repudiate categorically that statement?

Mr. JOHNSON. No; that is not the answer at all. The answer is as I have given it.

Mr. MATTHEWS. In the event of a war between the United States and the Soviet Union, Mr. Johnson, where would your allegiance lie?

Mr. JOHNSON. Mr. Chairman, I object to that question on the ground that I think it is a war-mongering question.

The CHAIRMAN. You decline to state?

Mr. JOHNSON. I want to answer that question, Mr. Chairman, on the grounds——

The CHAIRMAN. But you object to it. You are not answering.

Mr. COHN. He wishes to state his objections.

Mr. JOHNSON. I object on the ground I think it is a war-mongering question.

The CHAIRMAN. Just a minute. Do you decline to answer the question?

Mr. COHN. The witness declines.

The CHAIRMAN. We have been very lenient in giving him an opportunity to state reasons. He has asked a question, and do you decline to answer the question?

Mr. JOHNSON. On the grounds, and I want the reasons for my failure——

The CHAIRMAN. I am asking you now do you decline to answer the question?

Mr. JOHNSON. For the reason, Mr. Chairman——

The CHAIRMAN. All right.

Mr. JOHNSON. That I consider this question a war-mongering question that possibly will whip up war hysteria between two countries whose people, the people of our own country and the people of the Soviet Union, want peace and that this question on that basis, in my opinion, it is a war-mongering question.

The CHAIRMAN. All right. In other words, as I understand you, you decline to state whether or not you would support the United States in the event of war between the United States and the Soviet Union?

Mr. JOHNSON. I would say that.

The CHAIRMAN. For the reason that you decline to answer that for the reasons stated, is that right?

Mr. JOHNSON. For the reasons stated.

The CHAIRMAN. All right, proceed.

Mr. MATTHEWS. Mr. Johnson, when Mr. Browder was on the stand here he stated that if the United States entered this so-called "imperialistic war" against the Soviet Union, that he would try to turn it into a civil war in the United States. Do you accept that view?

Mr. JOHNSON. I don't recall seeing that statement, and I don't want to discuss it.

Mr. MATTHEWS. Will you repudiate that view?

Mr. JOHNSON. Because I would have to see the statement, Mr. Chairman, and I would have to see it in an official document, and then I would have to consider that statement in the light of the period in which it was written.

The CHAIRMAN. When you say "official document" do you mean you would not accept the hearings of this committee as an official document—his statement as recorded in the hearings?

Mr. COHN. No. I think what the witness means is that he was not accepting Mr. Matthews' recollection as to what any witness said as being the text of any document.

The CHAIRMAN. Assuming that Earl Browder made the statement, would you repudiate the statement?

Mr. JOHNSON. Well, I would have to consider the period in which he made that statement.

The CHAIRMAN. Well, the period was last year.

Mr. JOHNSON. Then it would have——

The CHAIRMAN. Before the pact between Russia and Germany.

Mr. MATTHEWS. Just after the pact.

The CHAIRMAN. Just after the pact; that is right.

Mr. JOHNSON. This is a hypothetical question, Mr. Chairman.

Mr. MATTHEWS. Mr. Johnson, you are familiar with the constitution and program of the Communists' International—you have seen this, have you not [exhibiting pamphlet to the witness]?

Mr. JOHNSON. I have.

Mr. MATTHEWS. I read you from page 84:

The fundamental slogans of the Communists' International must be the following: "Convert imperialistic wars into civil war, defeat your own imperialist government, defend the U. S. S. R. and the colonies by every possible means in the event of imperialist war against them."

Mr. COHN. Are you through?

The CHAIRMAN. He has read it.

Mr. COHN. I would like to know the date on which that was written?

Mr. MATTHEWS. This is the constitution of the Communists' International.

Mr. COHN. I did not ask that. I asked the date on which it was written?

Mr. MATTHEWS. July 1928. Adopted by the Sixth Congress of the Communists' International and is still in force, according to the witnesses who have been before the committee.

This particular document was printed by the Workers Library of Publishers in February of 1936 [handing pamphlet to Mr. Cohn].

Mr. JOHNSON. Mr. Chairman, I don't think that it is within the scope of this committee to probe into my opinions.

The CHAIRMAN. But you are a representative of this party and this is the constitution of the International. Mr. Matthews is asking you whether you subscribe to this. You certainly can say whether you subscribe to it or not.

Mr. JOHNSON. But this document was written in a period unlike the period now and it would have been considered under those circumstances.

The CHAIRMAN. Regardless of the period under which it was written, do you subscribe to it now under this period?

Mr. JOHNSON. I would have to read the entire document.

Mr. MATTHEWS. Mr. Johnson, how many world congresses have there been since this was adopted?

Mr. JOHNSON. I think there were six.

Mr. MATTHEWS. No, since this was adopted. This was adopted at the Sixth World Congress in 1928. How many world congresses of the Communists' International have there been since that time?

Mr. JOHNSON. Well, there have been 7 world congresses, of course.

Mr. MATTHEWS. No, there has been one. You know there has only been one world congress since 1928, is that right?

(No answer.)

Mr. MATTHEWS. The Seventh World Congress held in Moscow in 1935, in August, is the only world congress of the Communists' International held since 1928. You know that is correct?

Mr. JOHNSON. That is correct.

Mr. MATTHEWS. Did the Seventh World Congress abolish this constitution or in any way amend it?

Mr. JOHNSON. Well, I am not an authority on this question.

Mr. MATTHEWS. Well, as a member of the Communist Party and one of the State secretaries, you must know a matter like that, don't you?

Mr. JOHNSON. It further developed the thesis contained within that document.

Mr. MATTHEWS. You know that the Seventh World Congress did not in any way amend this constitution, don't you?

Mr. JOHNSON. It further developed the political perspective.

The CHAIRMAN. Did it amend it? Did it change it in any respect?

Mr. JOHNSON. It did change it in some respects.

The CHAIRMAN. Did it change it in the respect that we have been talking about? Did it make any alteration in the pronouncements that Mr. Matthews read to you?

Mr. JOHNSON. They made certain changes corresponding to the new situation.

Mr. MATTHEWS. Mr. Chairman, I would like to ask the witness if he realizes he is testifying under oath when he says the Seventh

World Congress "made certain changes in the constitution." I would like to know that he is aware he is testifying under oath when he makes that statement?

Mr. Cohn. I will say for the witness he is aware he is testifying under oath.

The Chairman. All right; let the witness answer the question.

Mr. Casey. Let me ask the witness one question.

Mr. Thomas. Wait a minute.

The Chairman. Let us get this developed. Do you say that the Seventh World Congress made changes in the constitution of the International?

Mr. Johnson. I am not sure.

Mr. Matthews. He already stated they did.

The Chairman. Let us proceed.

Mr. Thomas. Let us have the matter cleared up first. He said they did and now he says he is not sure. Now, what is the answer? What is your answer to the question?

Mr. Cohn. Are we being asked concerning the constitution of the Communists' International, or are we being asked for the extract from the preamble or the introduction to the program of the Communists' International?

The Chairman. The question is clear, whether or not the Seventh World Congress made any changes in the constitution that was adopted in the Sixth World Congress.

Mr. Cohn. The extract that Mr. Matthews read has nothing to do with the constitution.

The Chairman. We are talking about the constitution.

Mr. Cohn. If he knows, answer it.

The Chairman. He says he is not sure whether they did or not; is that correct?

Mr. Johnson. That is right. I thought Matthews was referring to the political perspective.

The Chairman. We are talking about the constitution. It is the constitution itself.

Mr. Thomas. Did they make any changes or didn't they?

Mr. Casey. Wait a minute; let counsel ask the questions. I wanted to ask a question a moment ago and you objected.

Mr. Matthews. The follow-up question I wanted to ask was, Were any changes made by the Seventh World Congress in the so-called preamble or program to the constitution, as incorporated in this volume, if the witness knows the answer to that question?

Mr. Cohn. If he knows.

Mr. Johnson. I am not sure.

The Chairman. All right.

Mr. Casey. Do you subscribe to the constitution of the Communist Party as a member of the Communist Party?

Mr. Johnson. I subscribe to the constitution of the Communist Party of the United States; yes, sir.

Mr. Casey. Do you consider the United States an imperialistic nation?

Mr. Cohn. May I say if you are asking for his opinion, his opinion is not properly before the committee. It is beyond the scope of your authority to examine into the opinions of people.

Mr. Casey. We are inquiring as to un-American activities and the whole crux of the matter is whether this is, as they claim, a national party or whether it owes allegiance to somebody outside of this country.

Mr. JOHNSON. I will say this in that respect, that there are certain forces in this country who have imperialist designs and who would like to draw this country into the imperialist war in Europe; that would like to defeat the wishes of the great majority of the American people who want peace; who don't want to be drawn into this war for profits and this war for spheres of influence that is going on in Europe now.

The CHAIRMAN. Now, he asked you if you considered this country an imperialist country. Is that right?

Mr. CASEY. That is correct.

Mr. COHN. And my objection is that it calls for the opinion of the witness.

The CHAIRMAN. He gave the opinion.

Mr. COHN. In violation of his constitutional rights under the fourth and fifth amendments.

Mr. JOHNSON. My opinion is that there are forces in this country who have imperialistic designs.

The CHAIRMAN. But you don't consider the country an imperialistic country as used in the constitution?

Mr. COHN. I object to the opinion of the witness.

The CHAIRMAN. The witness voluntarily gave them.

Mr. COHN. I move to expunge them as not properly before the committee.

The CHAIRMAN. Including——

Mr. COHN. Including any answer given in his opinion.

The CHAIRMAN. I would suggest you and your client get together on the proposition.

Mr. COHN. My client and I will get together.

The CHAIRMAN. He voluntarily gave his opinion. Now, you object to his stating that opinion that he gave, is that right?

Mr. COHN. You may have the answer with respect to that opinion. I will object to any future opinions called for by you.

The CHAIRMAN. All right, you may proceed.

Mr. COHN. And I am advising my client not to answer any questions calling for his personal opinions.

The CHAIRMAN. All right, who is the next witness?

Mr. COHN. Mr. Chairman, are you through with this witness?

The CHAIRMAN. Yes; we are through with him.

Mr. COHN. May I ask him a few questions?

The CHAIRMAN. No. The committee cannot permit that procedure.

Mr. COHN. May I call your attention——

The CHAIRMAN. I want to ask one other question. Did you bring any records with you of the Communist Party?

Mr. JOHNSON. I did bring some records; I did bring some material here on un-American activities in the city of Detroit—Coughlin—Smith——

The CHAIRMAN. I asked you if you brough any of the records of the Communist Party—any of the official records.

Mr. JOHNSON. We have records of un-American activities——

The CHAIRMAN. I am asking you if you brought——

Mr. JOHNSON. In the city of Detroit——

The CHAIRMAN. Of the official records of the Communist Party? Did you or did you not?

Mr. JOHNSON. For the reasons previously stated, I did not.

The CHAIRMAN. That is all I am asking you. That is all.

Mr. COHN. Mr. Chairman, may I call your attention to the following statement of Mr. Felix Frankfurter, now Justice Frankfurter, which appeared in the New Republic?

The CHAIRMAN. We are not interested in Judge Frankfurter's statements in the New Republic. Is that since he has been on the Supreme Court bench?

Mr. COHN. No. That is prior to the time.

The CHAIRMAN. And is that a judgment of the judge?

Mr. COHN. It is his opinion.

The CHAIRMAN. No.

Mr. COHN. May I say with respect to the right of counsel to examine a witness, that Mr. Frankfurter said, as follows—I would like to read this.

The CHAIRMAN. Well, the committee will not permit that because the committee is not interested in Judge Frankfurter's opinions unless they are opinions as a Justice on the Supreme Court.

Mr. COHN. I am asking for the right to question the witness.

The CHAIRMAN. Well, that right is being denied you.

Mr. COHN. May I argue the point?

Mr. THOMAS. No.

The CHAIRMAN. No.

Mr. COHN. May I state to you the reasons why I believe——

The CHAIRMAN. Have you any decisions of the court saying that counsel has a right to ask questions?

Mr. COHN. No; but I wish to read——

The CHAIRMAN. Then if you haven't a decision that concludes the matter.

Mr. COHN. May I read to you the political science textbook?

The CHAIRMAN. No; we are not interested in the political science textbook. Who is the next witness?

Mr. COHN. I respectfully—I object and I wish to enter an exception on the record.

The CHAIRMAN. All right; the next witness is Mr. McKenna.

Mr. McKenna, will you raise your right hand and be sworn?

Mr. THOMAS M. McKENNA. Yes, sir.

The CHAIRMAN. Do you solemnly swear to tell the truth, the whole truth, and nothing but the truth, so help you God?

Mr. THOMAS M. McKENNA. I do.

TESTIMONY OF THOMAS M. McKENNA, WARD COMMITTEEMAN OF FIFTH WARD ORGANIZATION OF THE COMMUNIST PARTY, CHICAGO, ILL.

Mr. MATTHEWS. Please give your full name to the committee?

Mr. McKENNA. My name is Thomas Morrison McKenna.

Mr. MATTHEWS. Where were you born?

Mr. McKENNA. In Pittsburgh, Pa.

Mr. MATTHEWS. When?

Mr. McKENNA. January 27, 1907.

Mr. MATTHEWS. How long have you been a member of the Communist Party?

Mr. McKENNA. For approximately 4 or 5 years.

Mr. MATTHEWS. When did you join?

Mr. McKENNA. I joined the Communist Party in about 1935.

Mr. MATTHEWS. Where did you join?

Mr. McKENNA. In Chicago, Ill.

Mr. MATTHEWS. Who recruited you?

Mr. McKENNA. On the question of names of individuals, I feel that this is an improper question, because in giving such names I would be divulging the political opinions of other people—membership in political organizations of other people—and I think this is a private matter of individuals and that I would not have the right to bring before a committee of this kind the names of people or the political affiliation by the people. That is their private concern.

The CHAIRMAN. All right; for that reason you decline to answer his question?

Mr. McKENNA. For that reason I decline to answer.

The CHAIRMAN. The Chair instructs you to answer the question. You still decline to do so?

Mr. McKENNA. For the reasons stated.

The CHAIRMAN. All right; proceed.

Mr. MATTHEWS. Under what name are you a member of the Communist Party?

Mr. McKENNA. My name in the Communist Party is Thomas Morrison McKenna.

Mr. MATTHEWS. Have you ever gone under any other name since you became a member of the Communist Party?

Mr. McKENNA. I have used another name since I became a member of the Communist Party; yes.

Mr. MATTHEWS. What was that name?

Mr. McKENNA. The name I used was Thomas M. Stanley.

Mr. MATTHEWS. Under what circumstances did you use that name?

Mr. McKENNA. I was seeking employment in about 1937, I think it was, and it happened that there is in Chicago, there is in many cities, a blacklist where persons are deprived of their right to a job to earn a livelihood for themselves and their families because they—because of their political beliefs—because of their political affiliations. It happened that my political beliefs and affiliations were matters of public record. They had appeared in the newspapers on various occasions and in order to obtain a job I used the name "Thomas M. Stanley."

Mr. MATTHEWS. Do you spell that S-t-a-n-l-e-y?

Mr. McKENNA. That is right.

Mr. MATTHEWS. Have you ever traveled abroad?

Mr. McKENNA. Yes, sir.

Mr. MATTHEWS. Where have you traveled abroad?

Mr. McKENNA. I lived abroad for 2½ years between the years 1929 and 1931—the spring of 1929.

Mr. MATTHEWS. That was before you became a member of the Communist Party?

Mr. McKENNA. Yes.

Mr. MATTHEWS. Before you became a member of the Communist Party had you traveled abroad?

Mr. McKENNA. I have not.

Mr. MATTHEWS. Have not been out of the United States?

Mr. McKenna. No.

Mr. Matthews. What is your position?

Mr. McKenna. Ward committeeman of the fifth ward organization in the Communist Party in the city of Chicago, county of Cook.

Mr. Matthews. How long have you held that position?

Mr. McKenna. I have held that position for, let me see, about, approximately—not by that name. I formerly was the organizer, ward organizer, and we established a fifth-ward organization of the Communist Party.

Mr. Matthews. How long have you held that position?

Mr. McKenna. I have held a position of that sort for about 3 years—2½ years.

Mr. Matthews. Does that position make you a member of the city committee of the Communist Party?

Mr. McKenna. No; it does not.

Mr. Matthews. What other positions have you held in the Communist Party?

Mr. McKenna. I held for a brief time a position as chairman of a branch of the—I don't know whether it was called the fifth-ward branch of the Communist Party—I think it was.

The Chairman. At this point the Chair designates as a subcommittee the Chairman, Mr. Mason, and Mr. Thomas, and Mr. Voorhis.

Mr. Matthews. Are you a member of a trade union?

Mr. McKenna. I have been a member of a trade union of the American Newspaper Guild.

Mr. Matthews. How long have you been a member of the Newspaper Guild?

Mr. McKenna. Well, I was a member of that organization during the time that I was circulation manager of the Daily Record, a Chicago publication.

Mr. Matthews. That was the Mid-West Daily Record?

Mr. McKenna. It was known, when I was circulation manager, as the Daily Record; not the Mid-West Daily Record.

Mr. Matthews. But later renamed?

Mr. McKenna. No; formerly named the Mid-West Daily Record. The name was changed to Daily Record.

Mr. Matthews. It was a publication of the Communist Party in the city of Chicago?

Mr. McKenna. No. That was not a publication of the Communist Party.

Mr. Matthews. Despite the fact that Earl Browder said it was a Communist Party publication, you would deny that?

Mr. McKenna. That is not a publication of the Communist Party.

Mr. Matthews. Was Louis Budenz editor of the Daily Record?

Mr. McKenna. It is obvious the question of the editorship, of the editor of the paper, is a matter of public record and the only reason I object to answering that question is that I think although there is no question of political association—I reconsider. Mr. Budenz was the editor of this paper.

Mr. Matthews. And he is publicly known as a member of the Communist Party, is he not?

Mr. McKenna. For the reasons I stated earlier, I do not feel that I have the right, or the privilege, or duty to divulge to this committee the political affiliations and opinions——

The Chairman. In the case where this man is publicly known——

Mr. McKenna. It isn't for the sake of secrecy. It isn't a question of secrecy at all. The names and addresses—even the official positions——

The Chairman. Do I understand you to decline to answer whether or not this individual is a member of the party?

Mr. McKenna. I want to state that the questions are already—the party is not a secret organization. The names of large numbers of members are published in all sorts of documents issued by the Communist Party—addressed public meetings, and so forth. However, for the purpose of this committee, I do not think that I have the right to divulge the names of any members.

The Chairman. You have stated that reason. Now, what I am asking you is, do you decline to state whether or not this individual is a member of the Communist Party?

Mr. McKenna. I do.

The Chairman. Do you know whether he is a member of the Communist Party?

Mr. McKenna. I decline to answer that question.

The Chairman. You decline to say whether you know?

Mr. McKenna. Yes, sir.

The Chairman. Whether he is a member of the Communist Party?

Mr. McKenna. Yes, sir.

The Chairman. The Chair instructs you to do so and you decline to do so for the reasons you stated?

Mr. McKenna. I do.

The Chairman. All right, proceed.

Mr. Matthews. Do you still deny the Daily Record or the Mid-West Daily Record——

Mr. Cohn. Just a second.

Mr. McKenna. Just one moment.

Mr. Matthews. Do you still deny that the Daily Record or the Mid-West Daily Record was a publication of the Communist Party?

Mr. McKenna. I deny it. I do; yes.

The Chairman. The purpose of asking the political affiliations of the members of the staff becomes even more pertinent in view of the witness' denial.

Who are some of the other members of the staff of the Mid-West Daily Record?

Mr. McKenna. There is William L. Patterson.

Mr. Matthews. Is he a member of the Communist Party?

Mr. McKenna. For the reasons I previously stated and also for additional reasons that the Communist Party is a legal party, is a party that—legal political party and also for the reason that there is an attempt on the part of a large number of people, and I think that this committee is participating in this attempt and doing a great deal to bring this about, and the Chairman of the committee has said, has advocated blacklists of people who belong to the Communist Party—this political party, and for those reasons as well as the ones that I already stated, I decline to discuss the political affiliations of any individual.

Mr. MATTHEWS. You know that both William L. Patterson and Louis Budenz are members of the Communist Party?

(No answer).

The CHAIRMAN. You stated your reasons?

Mr. McKENNA. Yes, sir.

The CHAIRMAN. And you decline to answer whether or not William L. Patterson is a member of the Communist Party?

Mr. McKENNA. I do decline.

The CHAIRMAN. The Chair instructs you to answer the question and you decline to do so?

Mr. McKENNA. Yes, sir.

The CHAIRMAN. The Chair asks you a question: Do you know whether William Patterson is a member of the Communist Party? Do you decline to answer that question?

Mr. McKENNA. For the reasons stated I do.

The CHAIRMAN. Although the Chair directs you to do so?

Mr. McKENNA. Yes.

The CHAIRMAN. Proceed.

Mr. MATTHEWS. You know that both William L. Patterson and Louis Budenz——

Mr. COHN. Just a second. Would you excuse me?

The CHAIRMAN. All right, proceed.

Mr. MATTHEWS. You know both Louis Budenz and William Patterson are members of the International Committee of the Communist Party of the United States, don't you?

Mr. McKENNA. I think this is the line of questions that I declined to answer.

The CHAIRMAN. He declined to answer those questions.

Mr. MATTHEWS. Have you ever belonged to any other trade union than the American Newspaper Guild?

Mr. McKENNA. No, I never have.

Mr. MATTHEWS. Have you ever held any office in the American Newspaper Guild?

Mr. McKENNA. No, I have not.

Mr. MATTHEWS. Have you ever been employed by the Government?

Mr. McKENNA. I have been employed by the Government and I am employed by the Government at the present time.

Mr. MATTHEWS. What is your present position in the Government?

Mr. McKENNA. It is not a position in the Government. My position is as a noncertified worker on the W. P. A. project—the monthly report of employment—unemployment, a survey that is being conducted throughout the country with its national office in Chicago. I am engaged there as a principal research interviewer.

Mr. THOMAS. I did not get the last answer.

The CHAIRMAN. Engaged in what capacity?

Mr. McKENNA. As a principal research interviewer.

Mr. THOMAS. Under the W. P. A.?

Mr. McKENNA. It is under the P. W. A. but it is a noncertified project. That is to say that the persons who work on that project, although they receive a salary less than the nonsecured.

Mr. THOMAS. Who do you get your salary from? Who pays you?

Mr. McKENNA. My checks are from the W. P. A. It is a project that is connected with the W. P. A.

Mr. MATTHEWS. How long have you held that position?

Mr. McKENNA. Since December of 1939.

Mr. MATTHEWS. What is your salary?

Mr. McKENNA. My salary is 73 cents an hour.

Mr. MATTHEWS. How many other members of the Communist Party are employed on this project?

Mr. McKENNA. For the reasons that I have stated, I do not feel that I have the right to discuss the political affiliations of other people. I think that the question of membership——

The CHAIRMAN. You have stated your reason. Do you decline to answer that question for the reasons heretofore given?

Mr. McKENNA. Yes.

The CHAIRMAN. The chair instructs you to do so and you continue to decline?

Mr. McKENNA. I do.

Mr. THOMAS. Mr. Chairman, I would like to ask Mr. Matthews if he will ask the witness to describe the duties. Will you do that, Mr. Matthews—under the W. P. A. work?

Mr. McKENNA. I will be glad to do that. The purpose of the project is to secure an estimate of the amount of employment and unemployment throughout the country as it varies from one month to the next. And in Chicago there are some eight or nine hundred households that are included in the survey. These are chosen by sampling methods in various parts of the city. They are supposed to represent a cross section of the population of the city.

The work that I have is to take a card that has included in it some of the questions—the question of age and the question of the employment status of individuals, and to use this card on which to inscribe information, information for the purpose of this survey, and I interview during—for 1 week, approximately 1 week each month, and during that period I visit about 100 families and get this information from them.

Mr. THOMAS. Mr. McKenna, who is the head of your project?

Mr. McKENNA. Well, I don't—there is a Mr. Wattenberg that is in the Chicago office.

The CHAIRMAN. How do you spell that name, do you know?

Mr. McKENNA. I am not certain of the spelling. I think it is W-a-t-t-e-n-b-e-r-g or W-o-t. I don't know what—I don't know which it is.

The CHAIRMAN. Is he the head of the whole thing?

Mr. McKENNA. He is in Chicago.

Mr. THOMAS. What is he the head of? Your particular project?

Mr. McKENNA. Yes, sir. He is the head of this project there.

Mr. THOMAS. What is the address of the headquarters of that organization?

Mr. McKENNA. Room 1175 Merchandise Mart.

Mr. MATTHEWS. What is his first name or initial?

Mr. McKENNA. I don't know.

Mr. MATTHEWS. Have you ever been to Moscow?

Mr. McKENNA. No, I never have.

Mr. MATTHEWS. When you obtained your present employment, Mr. McKenna, what name did you use on your application blank?

Mr. McKENNA. I used the name that was on my Social Security

number, the name under which I had held previous positions—I held a position at, for Walgren & Co. Mr. Walgren——

Mr. MATTHEWS. What name did you use?

Mr. McKENNA. I used the name "Thomas Stanley."

Mr. MATTHEWS. That is not your correct name?

Mr. McKENNA. This is the name under which I work. According to the laws of the State of Illinois a person has a right to choose or use a name or whatever names he desires to use.

Mr. MATTHEWS. Did you have that name registered with the courts of the State of Illinois?

Mr. McKENNA. No. It is not required that names be registered.

Mr. MATTHEWS. In other words, in making your application for employment with the United States Government you also thought it necessary to use a false name?

Mr. McKENNA. I continued to use the name that was on my Social Security number.

Mr. MATTHEWS. You had given a false name in your Social Security registration?

Mr. McKENNA. I had given the name "Thomas Stanley," which is the name I used in order to secure employment for the purpose of supporting my family. I have a wife and child and at the time I secured employment my wife was about to have a child. It was necessary that we—that I secure employment. I secured employment.

The CHAIRMAN. All right, I think you have made a full answer.

Mr. MATTHEWS. Mr. McKenna, have you ever seen a copy of the Democratic Front, by Earl Browder?

Mr. McKENNA. I have.

Mr. MATTHEWS. You are acquainted with the document?

Mr. McKENNA. I am.

Mr. MATTHEWS. I read you from page 65, and you may follow as I read:

> It is in the circulation of our most important newspapers however, that we are alarmingly backward. The Daily Worker, Sunday Worker and Daily Record, and People's World are already of a quality sufficiently high, notwithstanding all needed improvements, to justify a circulation ten times that which they now have.
> All the conditions are present to justify us in demanding from every State organization the rapid expansion of the circulation of these papers.

Do you understand Mr. Browder to include the Daily Record as one of the Communist Party publications?

Mr. McKENNA. Not by that statement.

Mr. MATTHEWS. In that statement?

Mr. McKENNA. No, I certainly could not. I understand Earl Browder to have said there, and we all recognize this, that the question of building a paper in Chicago, particularly that would be a voice of the labor, whole labor, and progressive movement, was a need of the people of Chicago and that the people of this whole country, and that the Communist Party was interested, very much interested in developing this—in helping to give the people of Chicago an opportunity to read the real news about what was happening in the world and about what was happening in regard to the needs of the people—the various legislation that was proposed, and to assist the people in organizing their—strengthening their trade-union movements, and so forth.

I think when Mr. Browder used it, spoke of the need of developing this and the need of the Communist Party doing everything in its power to increase the circulation, he was speaking in the interests of all the people, that it is not only the task of the Communist Party to do that, but of all progressives to do this.

The CHAIRMAN. All right, I think that is pretty full.

Now, let me ask you a question or two. During the period that you have been a member of the Communist Party, have you engaged in any union activities outside of the Guild?

Mr. McKENNA. No. I was not—as a matter of fact I was not an active member of the Newspaper Guild.

The CHAIRMAN. Any organizations that you have belonged to other than the Guild and the Communist Party?

Mr. McKENNA. Since the time—I probably have belonged to, let me see what organizations—my chief activity was in the Communist Party. I have held—I think I—I think that I have joined certain organizations, certain other organizations.

The CHAIRMAN. Will you state what organizations they are?

Mr. McKENNA. First, I want to make this clear, the fact that the organization I would belong to, when I mention the name of the organization or those organizations, the fact that I am a member of the organization should not be used in any way against that organization.

The CHAIRMAN. I am just merely asking you what organizations you have belonged to.

Mr. McKENNA. I want to say, for example, I am on the register list of precinct voters. That doesn't make the rest—make any other person a Communist.

The CHAIRMAN. I just merely asked you what organizations you belonged to.

Mr. McKENNA. I am a member of the Labor Non-Partisan League in the fifth ward in the city of Chicago.

The CHAIRMAN. All right, what others?

Mr. McKENNA. At the present time I think that is the only organization other than the Communist Party to which I belong.

The CHAIRMAN. Did you belong to the American League for Peace and Democracy?

Mr. McKENNA. I did belong to the American League for Peace and Democracy.

The CHAIRMAN. Did you belong to the International Workers Order?

Mr. McKENNA. No.

The CHAIRMAN. Never joined?

Mr. McKENNA. No.

The CHAIRMAN. Do you have any affiliation with International Labor Defense?

Mr. McKENNA. None.

The CHAIRMAN. The only two organizations—the only three organizations to which you belong are Labor Non-Partisan League, the Guild, and the Communist Party?

Mr. McKENNA. That is during the period of my membership in the Communist Party.

The CHAIRMAN. All right.

Mr. MASON. May I ask a question now, Mr. Chairman? What was the last date that you worked as circulation manager of the Daily Record? That is, when did you sever your connection there?

Mr. McKENNA. It was July—I think it was July of this last year. 1939.

Mr. MASON. July 1939?

Mr. McKENNA. Yes, sir.

Mr. MASON. Then you were circulation manager of that Daily Record when they got out a special edition of 50,000 copies to circularize in the city of Rockford just previous to the 1938 election in which they majored on a lot of lies about me to try to defeat me for my reelection?

Mr. McKENNA. I question very seriously whether there would be any statements that were not exact facts printed in the Daily Record, knowing it.

Mr. MASON. Well, there were many statements in that special edition circulated in Rockford, supposedly 50,000 copies, about me and my personal affairs, which were lies absolutely.

Mr. McKENNA. Well, now, and I think that there are many occasions on which it appears that certain statements are or feel that certain statements are lies. Some are matters of opinion. I think that the Daily Record did take a stand relating to legislative questions, relating to individuals running for political office.

Mr. MASON. This had nothing to do with legislative questions.

Mr. McKENNA. People running for political office. I think that was the time you were running for political office and I think the Daily Record did publish—I think I do remember that occasion, the Daily Record did publish material and information about your record, about your activities, and I think that it urged the progressive people not to vote for you. I think that was true; it did take a stand against your candidacy and told why it took a stand.

Mr. MASON. The point I want to make is that these lies were furnished to the editorial staff of the Daily Record, and they accepted them without verifying them and published them.

Mr. McKENNA. I was in the circulation department. All I know is that in my opinion our paper was a very fine paper, a paper that gave facts that could be found in no other papers; that all the information where I had a chance to see whether it was true or not was true, and I don't know the particular instances—I did not travel in Rockford—I don't know what the situation is there, but I feel it would be correct.

Mr. MATTHEWS. Have you been employed on any other projects on W. P. A.?

Mr. McKENNA. No; I haven't.

Mr. MATTHEWS. Your only connection with W. P. A. has been since December?

Mr. McKENNA. That is right: or in December—not since.

The CHAIRMAN. Did you ever do any organizing work for any union?

Mr. McKENNA. No: I never have.

The CHAIRMAN. Never had any of that?

Mr. McKENNA. No.

Mr. MATTHEWS. In the event of a war between the United States and the Soviet Union, where would your allegiance lie?

Mr. COHN. That is an objectionable question, Mr. Chairman.

The CHAIRMAN. Do you decline to answer?

Mr. COHN. That is an objectionable question calling for the opinion of the witness, a question that is incompetent and irrelevant and immaterial.

The CHAIRMAN. All right.

Mr. COHN. And that question is not within the scope of this examination.

The CHAIRMAN. Do you object to the question on these grounds?

Mr. COHN. I do.

The CHAIRMAN. Do you decline to answer the question?

Mr. McKENNA. On the grounds stated by my attorney, I do.

The CHAIRMAN. The Chair directs you to answer, and you refuse to do so?

Mr. McKENNA. On the grounds previously stated I do.

The CHAIRMAN. In connection with your office in the Communist Party, I believe you said you were—what are you now?

Mr. McKENNA. Ward committeeman of the fifth ward organization of the Communist Party.

The CHAIRMAN. How many members of the committee are there?

Mr. McKENNA. Of the ward committee?

The CHAIRMAN. Yes.

Mr. McKENNA. There are about—oh, I think about 10 is the number.

The CHAIRMAN. Do you know them all?

Mr. McKENNA. I do.

The CHAIRMAN. State who they are.

Mr. McKENNA. For the reasons that I have previously objected—objections I have previously raised—I will not divulge the names of any persons who belong to my political party.

The CHAIRMAN. You stated your reasons, and do you decline to answer that question?

Mr. McKENNA. I decline to answer the question.

The CHAIRMAN. For the reasons given?

Mr. McKENNA. For the reasons I gave, that I don't want—I want to make this clear——

The CHAIRMAN. You have already stated your reasons.

Mr. McKENNA. I don't think I have the right to discuss the political——

The CHAIRMAN. You have stated that two or three times.

Mr. McKENNA. To discuss the political opinions of other people.

The CHAIRMAN. The Chair directs you to answer the question, and you decline to do so for the reasons stated?

Mr. McKENNA. I do.

The CHAIRMAN. All right, any other questions? Call the next witness. His name is Mr. Lightfoot.

Mr. CLAUDE LIGHTFOOT. Mr. Chairman, I would like to postpone this until I have time to discuss it with my counsel; I arrived in town this morning and haven't had time to discuss it with my counsel.

The CHAIRMAN. Weren't you discussing this with your counsel a moment ago?

Mr. Claude Lightfoot. No.

The Chairman. Then suppose you go out there and discuss it, but we want to get through so we can let you go home.

Mr. Cohn. Mr. Chairman, I had stepped away for a half a moment. I note that you have terminated the examination of Mr. McKenna. Now, I want to ask Mr. McKenna some questions.

The Chairman. And we will give you the same ruling.

Mr. Cohn. I would like to read into the record a new text that I think has not yet come to your attention, called The Developments of Congressional Investigative Power, by Professor McGerry, of——

The Chairman. The Chair declines you that right. You have your exception in the record.

Mr. Cohn. I would also like to read to you a statement made by Felix Frankfurter prior to the time that he became Justice of the United States Supreme Court.

The Chairman. You have stated that and the ruling is the same as before.

Mr. Cohn. Note an exception.

The Chairman. All right.

Mr. Cohn. My theory is that I have a right to cross-examine for the purpose of completing the record after there is a direct examination which may not have given the witness a full opportunity to bring out what he desires to relate to the committee.

The Chairman. All right, you have made your statement and now will you confer with your client?

Mr. Cohn. I would like to have an opportunity, an hour to confer with Mr. Lightfoot.

The Chairman. The witnesses who have been subpenaed and who are present. Tony DeMaio, Milton Wolff, Fred Keller, and Gerald Cook. They are witnesses who have been subpenaed and they will remain here subject to the call of the committee. You will let the clerk of the committee know where you are located and he will advise you when we will hear you. We will hear you as soon as possible.

Mr. Schwab. Mr. Chairman, I am attorney for the witnesses you have just named. My name is Irving Schwab, 551 Fifth Avenue, New York.

Now, I would like to ask this body to consider my convenience and see if we can set the hearing for some definite time.

I left a case to come down here. I have another matter with the Federal court tomorrow morning. My clients want me present and I feel sure——

The Chairman. How many clients do you represent?

Mr. Schwab. I represent the four you have just named. Now, if you expect to call them tomorrow I will appreciate it if you will let me know or give me an idea when they will be called.

The Chairman. You say you have a case pending in the Federal court tomorrow?

Mr. Schwab. Yes. Now, I could postpone it. It is a writ of habeas corpus, but I prefer not to.

The Chairman. Suppose we set the hearing at 10 o'clock tomorrow morning. Would that be convenient to you? Can you arrange to postpone your case in New York so as to be here?

Mr. Schwab. Well, will we finish by tomorrow?

The CHAIRMAN. We will be finished with these four but as I understand it, there are a number of witnesses in connection with this matter that will have to be heard and you might want to be present when the other witnesses are examined.

Mr. SCHWAB. I prefer Monday. I did not consult my clients.

The CHAIRMAN. Would Monday be more convenient to you? But we better set it for in the morning and with these four witnesses we can conclude the hearing in the morning as far as they are concerned, I am satisfied.

Mr. SCHWAB. Will the committee understand that is subject to my calling New York and arranging an adjournment. I don't think I will have any trouble but should there be trouble——

The CHAIRMAN. We want to accommodate you——

Mr. SCHWAB. No chance of being heard this afternoon?

The CHAIRMAN. No, because the members have to be on the floor. We have sat here all morning and it is rather difficult to sit in the afternoon. As I understand a postponement was arranged for these witnesses once.

Mr. SCHWAB. That was not their fault. They were on trial as everybody knows. I arranged it specifically with the understanding I thought we would be heard today.

The CHAIRMAN. Suppose we set it for tomorrow morning at 10 o'clock.

Mr. SCHWAB. Well, if I can't get it adjourned, can I get in touch with anybody?

The CHAIRMAN. You get in touch with us, and let us know.

Mr. SCHWAB. Mr. Chairman, I suppose it is understood the witnesses are here right in the hearing room now. You understand, Mr. Chairman, the witnesses are here now.

The CHAIRMAN. That is what I understand and that is the reason I announced the hearing will be tomorrow morning at 10 o'clock.

Mr. COHN. We are ready, Mr. Chairman.

The CHAIRMAN. All right, raise your right hand. Do you solemnly swear to tell the truth, the whole truth, and nothing but the truth, so help you God?

Mr. CLAUDE LIGHTFOOT. I do.

The CHAIRMAN. Have a seat.

TESTIMONY OF CLAUDE LIGHTFOOT, ORGANIZER FOR THE COMMUNIST PARTY IN THE SOUTH SIDE OF CHICAGO, ILL.

Mr. MATTHEWS. What is your full name?

Mr. LIGHTFOOT. Claude Lightfoot.

The CHAIRMAN. May we have order, please. The Chair announces that the committee is proceeding as a subcommittee with the chairman, Mr. Mason, and Mr. Voorhis present. Proceed.

Mr. MATTHEWS. Where were you born?

Mr. LIGHTFOOT. I was born in Lake Village, Ark.

Mr. MATTHEWS. When?

Mr. LIGHTFOOT. January 10, 1910.

Mr. MATTHEWS. How long have you been a member of the Communist Party?

Mr. LIGHTFOOT. About 9 years.

Mr. MATTHEWS. And what is your present position in the Communist Party, if any?

Mr. LIGHTFOOT. I am the organizer of the Communist Party in the south-side community of Chicago.

Mr. MATTHEWS. How long have you held that position?

Mr. LIGHTFOOT. Well, I held that position about 3 months.

Mr. MATTHEWS. Have you held other positions in the Communist Party prior to the one you now hold?

Mr. LIGHTFOOT. I was the educational director of the party in the State of Illinois.

Mr. MATTHEWS. Educational director for the entire State of Illinois?

Mr. LIGHTFOOT. Yes, sir.

Mr. MATTHEWS. For how long did you hold that position?

Mr. LIGHTFOOT. One year.

Mr. MATTHEWS. And prior to that?

Mr. LIGHTFOOT. I was the State chairman of the Young Communist League.

Mr. MATTHEWS. How long did you hold that position?

Mr. LIGHTFOOT. About 3 years.

Mr. MATTHEWS. You held that position about 3 years?

Mr. LIGHTFOOT. Yes.

Mr. MATTHEWS. Have you held any other positions than these?

Mr. LIGHTFOOT. Well, I have held various positions in functional capacity.

Mr. MATTHEWS. Were you a member of the Young Communist League before you joined the Communist Party?

Mr. LIGHTFOOT. No; I was a member of the Communist Party.

Mr. MATTHEWS. Are you a member of both?

Mr. LIGHTFOOT. I was a member of both.

Mr. MATTHEWS. Did you join at the same time?

Mr. LIGHTFOOT. No. I joined the Young Communist League later.

Mr. MATTHEWS. Are you a member——

The CHAIRMAN. Will you speak a little louder, please?

Mr. MATTHEWS. Are you a member of a trade-union?

Mr. LIGHTFOOT. I am a member of no trade-union.

Mr. MATTHEWS. Have you ever been a member of any union?

Mr. LIGHTFOOT. No.

Mr. MATTHEWS. Have you ever engaged in any trade-union organization or activities?

Mr. LIGHTFOOT. No; I haven't.

Mr. MATTHEWS. Did you bring the records which were specified in the subpena?

Mr. LIGHTFOOT. I have no records.

Mr. MATTHEWS. With you?

Mr. LIGHTFOOT. I have no records.

Mr. MATTHEWS. You have no records?

Mr. LIGHTFOOT. I have no records.

Mr. MATTHEWS. Of any kind?

Mr. LIGHTFOOT. No.

The CHAIRMAN. You mean you kept no records?

Mr. LIGHTFOOT. Destroyed all records we had.

The CHAIRMAN. You destroyed all the records? When did you destroy the records?

Mr. LIGHTFOOT. Destroyed them as rapidly as we get them.

The CHAIRMAN. You destroy records as rapidly as you get them?

Mr. LIGHTFOOT. Yes.

The CHAIRMAN. All right, proceed.

Mr. MATTHEWS. You have no financial records?

Mr. LIGHTFOOT. I have no records at all.

Mr. MATTHEWS. Mr. Lightfoot, in the event of a war between the United States and the Soviet Union, where would your allegiance lie?

Mr. LIGHTFOOT. I think that question is irrelevant and I decline to answer.

The CHAIRMAN. The Chair instructs you to answer and you decline to do so?

Mr. LIGHTFOOT. I decline.

The CHAIRMAN. All right, proceed.

Mr. MATTHEWS. I have no more questions to ask him.

Mr. THOMAS. I would like to ask the witness a question. You state you were State chairman of the Communist League—Young Communist League in Illinois?

Mr. LIGHTFOOT. I was.

Mr. THOMAS. What year?

Mr. LIGHTFOOT. For a period of about 3 or 4 years—that was up until the last year.

Mr. THOMAS. That covered the whole State?

Mr. LIGHTFOOT. Yes.

The CHAIRMAN. What other organizations do you belong to besides the Young Communist League and the Communist Party?

Mr. LIGHTFOOT. At present I am a member of no other organization.

The CHAIRMAN. Have you been a member during the time that you were a member of the Communist Party of any other organization?

Mr. LIGHTFOOT. I have been a member of various civic organizations in my community.

The CHAIRMAN. Now, your position is director of education, I believe you said?

Mr. LIGHTFOOT. My former position was.

The CHAIRMAN. Your present position is what?

Mr. LIGHTFOOT. Organizer.

The CHAIRMAN. How many organizers do you have? Are you the only one in your particular section?

Mr. LIGHTFOOT. About 25.

The CHAIRMAN. Do you know those 25?

Mr. LIGHTFOOT. Yes.

The CHAIRMAN. Will you state the names of the 25?

Mr. LIGHTFOOT. For the reasons that I have already explained, I decline to answer.

The CHAIRMAN. The Chair instructs you to do so and you decline to answer?

Mr. LIGHTFOOT. I decline to answer.

Mr. COHN. May I state in full the objections to questions of this type, Mr. Chairman?

Mr. LYNCH. Just a minute.

The CHAIRMAN. The objections that have previously been stated?

Mr. COHN. May I state in full what the objections are?

The CHAIRMAN. You have already stated the objections. We will carry those same objections with this unless you have some additional.

Mr. COHN. Are you referring to the previous witnesses?

The CHAIRMAN. Yes.

Mr. COHN. For all the reasons stated by the previous witnesses, this witness likewise declines to answer.

Mr. LIGHTFOOT. Mr. Chairman, could I state my reasons aside from the reasons——

The CHAIRMAN. Do you have any additional reasons?

Mr. COHN. Yes.

Mr. LIGHTFOOT. I have this reason. I believe that if any names are submitted here they will be used as a black list for jobs.

The CHAIRMAN. That has been given.

Mr. LIGHTFOOT. And my people are blacklisted from the right to vote in Texas and I don't want them blacklisted from jobs in Chicago.

The CHAIRMAN. All right; any other witnesses?

Mr. LYNCH. What other occupations have you had except as organizer or educational director for the Communist Party?

Mr. LIGHTFOOT. I have had no other occupation in the last 9 years other than functionary of the Communist Party.

Mr. LYNCH. For the 9 years, what was your occupation then?

Mr. LIGHTFOOT. I was a student.

Mr. LYNCH. Where?

Mr. LIGHTFOOT. High school.

Mr. LYNCH. What high school?

Mr. LIGHTFOOT. And college.

Mr. LYNCH. What high school?

Mr. LIGHTFOOT. Wendell Phillips High School.

Mr. LYNCH. Chicago?

Mr. LIGHTFOOT. Chicago.

Mr. LYNCH. You went right from high school into the Communist Party work, is that correct?

Mr. LIGHTFOOT. About a year later.

Mr. LYNCH. During that year you engaged in no occupation?

Mr. LIGHTFOOT. I worked part-time.

Mr. LYNCH. Where?

Mr. LIGHTFOOT. Pullman Co.

Mr. LYNCH. As a porter?

Mr. LIGHTFOOT. No, car cleaner.

Mr. LYNCH. Where?

Mr. LIGHTFOOT. Chicago.

Mr. LYNCH. Doing what at the Pullman Co.?

Mr. LIGHTFOOT. Car cleaner.

Mr. LYNCH. Have you been employed at any time on any Federal or State relief project?

Mr. LIGHTFOOT. I have been employed on no Government project.

Mr. LYNCH. On both?

Mr. LIGHTFOOT. On none.

Mr. LYNCH. Are you a member of the Workers' Alliance?

Mr. LIGHTFOOT. I am not a member of the Workers' Alliance.

Mr. LYNCH. Have you ever been a member of the Workers' Alliance?

Mr. LIGHTFOOT. I have never been a member of the Workers' Alliance.

Mr. LYNCH. How long did you work for the Pullman Co.?

Mr. LIGHTFOOT. Oh, about 6 months.

Mr. LYNCH. You quit your job and went to——

Mr. LIGHTFOOT. Went to school.

Mr. LYNCH. What is that?

Mr. LIGHTFOOT. Went to school.

Mr. LYNCH. And after school you went right in to the work——

Mr. LIGHTFOOT. I remained unemployed.

Mr. LYNCH. For how long?

Mr. LIGHTFOOT. Well, about 6 months or a year almost.

Mr. LYNCH. Then you went to work with the Communist Party?

Mr. LIGHTFOOT. That is right.

Mr. LYNCH. How much is your salary now?

Mr. LIGHTFOOT. $20 a week.

Mr. LYNCH. And who pays your salary?

Mr. LIGHTFOOT. Financial secretary.

Mr. LYNCH. And who is the financial secretary?

Mr. LIGHTFOOT. I decline to answer for the reasons enumerated before.

The CHAIRMAN. You are instructed to answer the question and you decline to do so?

Mr. LIGHTFOOT. I decline.

Mr. LYNCH. Now, in the records, as organizers, you come in contact with the new members who are secured, don't you?

Mr. LIGHTFOOT. Yes, I do.

Mr. LYNCH. And if a new member is secured, say like John Smith, he is issued a card; isn't he?

Mr. LIGHTFOOT. Issued a card?

Mr. LYNCH. Yes.

Mr. LIGHTFOOT. No.

Mr. LYNCH. No card is issued.

Mr. LIGHTFOOT. No card is issued.

Mr. LYNCH. How does he know he is a member—what credentials does he have?

Mr. LIGHTFOOT. He has no credentials.

Mr. LYNCH. How does he know he is a member? How does he know he is being accepted and can attend a branch meeting?

Mr. LIGHTFOOT. After he pays his dues.

Mr. LYNCH. Does he get a receipt?

Mr. LIGHTFOOT. No.

Mr. LYNCH. Don't you put a stamp in his book?

Mr. LIGHTFOOT. No.

Mr. LYNCH. Don't you have any party books?

Mr. LIGHTFOOT. No.

Mr. LYNCH. Well, who knows whether he is a member when he comes to a meeting?

Mr. LIGHTFOOT. The members know each other.

Mr. LYNCH. And how many members do you have in Chicago?

Mr. LIGHTFOOT. Oh, I don't know exactly in Chicago.

Mr. Lynch. Approximately.

Mr. Lightfoot. About 5,000.

Mr. Lynch. In Chicago alone?

Mr. Lightfoot. Yes.

Mr. Lynch. How many do you have in the entire State of Illinois.

Mr. Lightfoot. Oh, about 6,000.

Mr. Lynch. And do you send the names of the new members to the headquarters in New York?

Mr. Lightfoot. We do not.

Mr. Lynch. What?

Mr. Lightfoot. We do not.

Mr. Lynch. What is your social-security number, under what name?

Mr. Lightfoot. I haven't got my number on me.

Mr. Lynch. What?

Mr. Lightfoot. I haven't got my number with me, and I can't recall it by memory.

Mr. Lynch. You don't have it with you?

Mr. Lightfoot. No.

Mr. Lynch. Is it under your name?

Mr. Lightfoot. It is under my name.

Mr. Lynch. Well, if there are no lists kept how do you determine that there are approximately 5,000 members in Chicago?

Mr. Lightfoot. We determine that on the basis of dues.

Mr. Lynch. And you make your reports of those dues to New York, don't you?

Mr. Lightfoot. Well, we send a certain percentage of our dues money to New York.

Mr. Lynch. Do you send that by check or cash?

Mr. Lightfoot. Send it through various methods. I am not familiar.

Mr. Lynch. Do you send it by check or cash?

Mr. Lightfoot. We send our money from the community I am working in to the State and the State to New York. Whether they send it by cash or check, I don't know.

Mr. Lynch. Where is the State headquarters?

Mr. Lightfoot. In Chicago.

Mr. Lynch. Where in Chicago?

Mr. Lightfoot. 208 North Wells Street, room 201.

Mr. Lynch. Who is in charge there?

Mr. Lightfoot. Morris Childs.

Mr. Lynch. What is his position?

Mr. Lightfoot. State executive secretary.

Mr. Lynch. And you give him the money that is collected from your particular organization?

Mr. Lightfoot. I don't; the financial secretary handles it.

Mr. Lynch. And then he in turn turns it over to New York?

Mr. Lightfoot. New York. I presume he turns it over to the State financial secretary.

Mr. Lynch. And who in turn turns it over to New York at the national headquarters?

Mr. Lightfoot. Perhaps.

Mr. LYNCH. And if you submit say $100 to that particular party, you have to let him know what it is for, don't you, whether for dues or Earl Browder's defense fund, don't you?

Mr. LIGHTFOOT. Of course.

Mr. LYNCH. And do you write a letter on that?

Mr. LIGHTFOOT. Do I write a letter to who?

Mr. LYNCH. The man you sent the money to.

Mr. LIGHTFOOT. It is carried downtown—a very simple process—streetcar and automobile and you get there.

Mr. LYNCH. Do you have a list what it is for, whether for dues?

Mr. LIGHTFOOT. We have a list for dues specified.

Mr. LYNCH. Don't you keep a record of that for your own information?

Mr. LIGHTFOOT. I don't keep a record.

Mr. LYNCH. Does anybody keep a record in your office?

Mr. LIGHTFOOT. I don't keep a record and no one else keeps a record.

Mr. LYNCH. You destroy all records?

Mr. LIGHTFOOT. Destroy all records.

Mr. LYNCH. How long have you had the practice of destroying records?

Mr. LIGHTFOOT. Since our offices and homes have been invaded by people.

Mr. LYNCH. How long ago was that?

Mr. COHN: Will you allow him to finish, Mr. Lynch?

Mr. LYNCH. What time was that?

Mr. LIGHTFOOT. That started about October.

Mr. LYNCH. October what year?

Mr. LIGHTFOOT. Last year.

Mr. LYNCH. Was your home ever invaded?

Mr. LIGHTFOOT. My home personally was not.

Mr. LYNCH. Have you been instructed from New York to destroy all records?

Mr. LIGHTFOOT. I have been receiving no instructions from New York.

Mr. LYNCH. Who told you to destroy the records?

Mr. LIGHTFOOT. My State secretary.

Mr. LYNCH. Who is the State secretary?

Mr. LIGHTFOOT. Morris Childs.

Mr. LYNCH. He gave you that information last October?

Mr. LIGHTFOOT. Yes.

Mr. LYNCH. That is all.

Mr. LIGHTFOOT. Mr. Chairman, I would like to raise a question before the committee. It is not relevant to the investigation——

Mr. LYNCH. Then I submit he hasn't any right to raise it.

The CHAIRMAN. If it isn't relevant to the investigation we can't hear it.

The committee will stand adjourned until tomorrow morning at 10 o'clock.

(Whereupon, at 12:40 p. m., the hearing was adjourned until 10 a. m., Friday, April 12, 1940.)

INVESTIGATION OF UN-AMERICAN PROPAGANDA ACTIVITIES IN THE UNITED STATES

FRIDAY, APRIL 12, 1940

House of Representatives,
Special Committee on Un-American Activities,
Washington, D. C.

The committee met at 10 a. m., Hon. Martin Dies (chairman) presiding.

The CHAIRMAN. The committee will come to order. The Chair is sitting as a subcommittee of one under the regulations, until the other members arrive.

Mrs. Selby is your first witness. Mrs. Selby, will you raise your right hand. Do you solemnly swear to tell the truth, the whole truth, and nothing but the truth, so help you God.

Mrs. WALTER OWENS SELBY. I do.

TESTIMONY OF MRS. WALTER OWENS SELBY, CHESTERTOWN, MD.

Mr. LYNCH. Your name is Mrs. Walter Owens Selby?

Mrs. SELBY. Yes.

Mr. LYNCH. And your home is in Chestertown, Md.?

Mrs. SELBY. Yes, sir.

Mr. LYNCH. On the Eastern Shore?

Mrs. SELBY. Yes.

Mr. LYNCH. And, Mrs. Selby, your son, Vernon, went to Spain in May 1937, did he not?

Mrs. SELBY. No; September.

Mr. LYNCH. September 1937?

Mrs. SELBY. Yes.

Mr. LYNCH. And thereafter did you receive letters from him from time to time?

Mrs. SELBY. Yes; beginning October 14.

Mr. LYNCH. Until when did you receive your last letter from him, Mrs. Selby?

Mrs. SELBY. February 27, 1938. That is, it was dated February 27, 1938. I received it about 4 weeks later.

Mr. LYNCH. And this is the letter here, is it not?

[Handing letter to the witness.]

Mrs. SELBY. Yes.

Mr. LYNCH. And he says in here that he received your letter of January 22 and was glad to hear from you.

There is very little I am able to tell you except that I am well and getting along okay. There could be more to tell you but the censorship prohibits it so I will have to save all that for a later date.

7727

And there are some other matters which are not pertinent. Were there other occasions when some of his letters were not received, Mrs. Selby?

Mrs. SELBY. I don't think I missed more than two or three, probably four, at the most.

Mr. LYNCH. Did there come a time when you were advised that he was missing?

Mrs. SELBY. Yes.

Mr. LYNCH. And did you take the matter up with the State Department?

Mrs. SELBY. At once.

Mr. LYNCH. Through Congressman Goldsborough who was your Congressman?

Mrs. SELBY. Yes. I had the notice April 8 that he was missing April 1. That is when I received the notice but he was missing April 1.

Mr. LYNCH. Missing April 1, 1938?

Mrs. SELBY. Yes, sir.

Mr. LYNCH. You did not know that he was going to Spain until after he had left, did you?

Mrs. SELBY. No, I didn't have any idea until I received his first letter.

Mr. LYNCH. Now, did you receive this letter from Simon Leinoff, dated March 23, 1939, from Los Angeles, Calif., sent to you at Chestertown, Md.?

Mrs. SELBY. Yes.

Mr. LYNCH. I would like to read this letter into the record. It is on the letterhead of the Friends of the Abraham Lincoln Brigade, 617 Union League Building, Los Angeles, Calif. The letter is dated March 23, 1939.

DEAR MRS. SELBY: It grieves me very much that you are taking your son's absence so hard. I'm sure he would not like you to worry so much.

I have made inquiries concerning your son and cannot get anything definite, but regardless of where he is, or what happened to him, you must understand that he went to Spain because he believed in democracy, and he knew he was on the side of justice. He had the courage of his convictions which really puts him on a part with Washington and Lincoln. Please remember that worrying yourself to a nervous breakdown will not do you or anybody else any good, only harm. You should accept the fact that he is missing and, of course, if he is able to write to you he would, as I surmise from your letter.

I have asked about Mr. Honecombe, but evidently he is not in this city at the present time.

Am extremely sorry you have gone through so much distress, Mrs. Selby, but remember that by worrying you are merely doing what your son would not want you to do, so try to keep yourself under control, or else you will be a case for a doctor.

Sincerely yours,

SIMON LEINOFF.

And on this letterhead the officers and sponsors, which the reporter can copy into the record, appear together with the national sponsors.

(The officers, sponsors, and national sponsors referred to by Mr. Lynch, are as follows:)

Officers: C. H. Jordan, chairman, Secretary American Radio Telegraph Association; Mrs. Alice Eaton, honorary chairman and Morris Lappin, treasurer, and Sophie Feider, executive secretary.

Sponsors: Rube Boroughts, Harold Buchman, James Cagney, Supervisor John Anson Ford, Leo Gallagher, Lee E. Geyer, J. W. Gillette, Lillian Hellman,

Judge Robert W. Kenny, Carey McWilliams, Assemblyman Ben Rosenthal, Judge Lester W. Roth, Frank Scully, Assemblyman Jack B. Tenny, Oliver Thornton, Charles L. Upton, and Clara Weatherwax.

National sponsors: Congressman John T. Bernard, Muriel Draper, Louis Fisher, Henry Hart, John Houseman, Archibald MacLeish, Jack R. Miller, Wallingford Reigger, William Rollins, Jr., and Upton Sinclair.

And also this letter of July 30, 1938, was received by you, was it not, Mrs. Selby?

[Handing letter to the witness.]

Mrs. SELBY. Yes.

Mr. LYNCH. And on the official letterhead appear the names of the national officers, sponsors, Maryland branch, executive secretary, and executive committee. The reporter will copy these into the record.

(The national officers, sponsors, Maryland branch chairman, executive secretary, and executive committee, are as follows:)

National officers: David McKelvy White, chairman; Wm. D. Leider, treasurer; Phil Bard, executive secretary; and Jack R. Miller, national organizer.

Sponsors: Helen Arthur, Ralph Bates, Congressman John T. Bernard, Clyde Beals, Asa Bordages, James Cagney, Abram Chasins, Muriel Draper, Louis Fisher, Francis J. Gorman, Henry Hart, Lillian Hellman, Langston Hughes, Fred Keating, Julia Church Kolar, Arthur Kober, Archibald MacLeish, Carl Sandburg, Wallingford Reigger, Isabel Walker Soule, Upton Sinclair, Donald Ogden Stewart, and Paul Strum.

Maryland branch: Chairman, Frederick Arnold Kummer, Sr.

Executive secretary: Coleman Blum.

Executive committee: Margaret Baker, Dr. Albert E. Blumberg, Alphonse Butrow, Michael Gallo, Gregory Krause, Frederick Arnold Kummer, Jr., Rev. Joseph S. Nowak, Jr., C. A. B. Shreve, Dr. Ross Thalheimer, Fanny Tuomi, and Charles Williams.

Mr. LYNCH. The name of Dr. Albert E. Blumberg appears among the names of the executive committee.

This letter is dated July 30, 1939. It reads:

My DEAR MRS. SELBY: I trust you will pardon my seeming neglect in not answering you sooner as I have been busy moving and have spent little time at the office.

I take pleasure in enclosing a couple of tickets from the last meeting in Baltimore as per your request. We hope to have another like it next month.

Hereafter kindly write to your son in care of the following address: "Friends of the Abraham Lincoln Brigade, care of Comite Internationale d'Aide de Peuple Espagnol, 1 Cite Paradis, Paris, France," who will then attempt delivery of all mail addressed through them.

Kindly address any checks to Friends of the Abraham Lincoln Brigade, Maryland Branch.

I hope to get to New York soon and will do my utmost there to find out some news of interest to you. In the meantime I hope you will continue to "keep your chin up" and hope for the best. I am sure the mystery will be solved soon. May I extend my kindest personal wishes to you and your family, and suggest you feel free to call on me at any time.

Cordially yours,

COLEMAN BLUM.

And I think, Mrs. Selby, you said that in April 1938 you were officially advised through Congressman Goldsborough, who had taken the matter up with the State Department, that your son was evidently missing at that time?

Mrs. SELBY. Yes, sir.

Mr. LYNCH. And you have never been able to find out what really happened to him, have you?

Mrs. SELBY. No.

Mr. LYNCH. That is all.

The CHAIRMAN. Thank you, Mrs. Selby.

Mr. LYNCH. May the witness be excused, Mr. Chairman?

The CHAIRMAN. Yes, the witness is excused.

The next witness is Maxwell M. Wallach.

The CHAIRMAN. Will you raise your right hand and be sworn. Do you solemnly swear to tell the truth, the whole truth, and nothing but the truth, so help you God?

TESTIMONY OF MAXWELL M. WALLACH, DETROIT, MICH.

Mr. WALLACH. I do.

Mr. LYNCH. Mr. Wallach, will you give the reporter your full name, please, sir?

Mr. WALLACH. Maxwell M. Wallach.

Mr. LYNCH. And your address, Mr. Wallach?

Mr. WALLACH. Hotel Imperial, Detroit, Mich.

Mr. LYNCH. And, Mr. Wallach, did you have a son who went to Spain?

Mr. WALLACH. I did.

Mr. LYNCH. What year did he go to Spain?

Mr. WALLACH. In the year 1937, the early part.

Mr. LYNCH. And any particular month? Can you fix it more definitely?

Mr. WALLACH. Well, to the best of my knowledge it was about February or March of 1937.

Mr. LYNCH. And kindly give us his age at that time.

Mr. WALLACH. At that time Al was 23 years of age.

Mr. LYNCH. And his full name, please, sir?

Mr. WALLACH. Albert M. Wallach.

The CHAIRMAN. May I announce a subcommittee of the chairman, Mr. Voorhis of California and Mr. Thomas of New Jersey. You may proceed.

Mr. LYNCH. Mr. Wallach, was he employed at the time he left or was he attending school?

Mr. WALLACH. He was engaged in the advertising business in the city of New York.

Mr. LYNCH. Do you know anything about the method in which he was recruited?

Mr. WALLACH. Upon investigation last year I ascertained the method.

Mr. LYNCH. Will you kindly state it for the benefit of the committee, please, sir?

Mr. WALLACH. I found that he was given a sum of money in the city of New York by the so-called International Workers Order at No. 80 Fifth Avenue, and that he, together with another gentleman, was to go across to Spain, and there he had on his person the sum of $3,000, which was to pay the individual expenses of the boys as they were needed.

Mr. LYNCH. Did you receive letters from him after his arrival in Spain?

Mr. WALLACH. There were just one or two letters that came from him as late as July 1937.

Mr. LYNCH. And after the last letter was received, did you make any inquiry or any investigation as to what occurred?

Mr. WALLACH. As soon as I definitely knew that he was in Spain I contacted the State Department in Washington and made repeated appeals for them to intercede and obtain his release and discharge from Spain.

Mr. LYNCH. And did you receive any information as to what he was doing or his whereabouts and condition?

Mr. WALLACH. Yes; through the American consul in Spain the State Department was able to notify me from time to time just what was taking place there.

Mr. LYNCH. Did you have any particular letter of importance that would indicate at any particular time what was occurring?

Mr. WALLACH. First I had a telegram here January 6 from Cordell Hull.

Mr. LYNCH. Stating that the matter would be investigated?

Mr. WALLACH. That is right.

Mr. LYNCH. Did you have any letters from your son in which he described the conditions over there and what he was doing?

Mr. WALLACH. No.

Mr. LYNCH. Did he say anything as to whether or not there was a strict censorship on the information he was able to get to you?

Mr. WALLACH. I had no direct contact with him setting any such thing forth.

Mr. LYNCH. Did you receive any information thereafter from anyone else?

Mr. WALLACH. I did. I received a card from a salesman out of Switzerland who had, in his travels in Spain, contacted and spoken to my boy and my son had asked him to write to me so that I should be able to do what I can to get him released and discharged from Spain.

Mr. LYNCH. So apparently from that letter your son was unable to write you direct asking that you secure his release?

Mr. WALLACH. That is what I understood.

Mr. LYNCH. And did you continue your efforts to get him released thereafter?

Mr. WALLACH. I did. I sent that card together with my letter to the State Department and again appealed to the State Department as an American citizen to do all they could through the Americn consul to have him discharged and sent out of Spain.

Mr. LYNCH. And they did, of course——

Mr. WALLACH. Finally on March 6, 1938, I received a telegram from the State Department stating: "Your son has been discharged and released and is being sent out of Spain," but he never showed up.

Mr. LYNCH. Did you ever check to determine what happened to him after that date in March 1938?

Mr. WALLACH. I did.

Mr. LYNCH. What happened?

Mr. WALLACH. After receiving that telegram I waited a reasonable time and then when he failed to show up I took sick and I was in the hospital for a period of about 10 weeks, but when I finally came to myself I came to Washington, made inquiries and found that they had no further word concerning the whereabouts or welfare of my son.

I then went on to New York to investigate and contacted several of the boys who had succeeded in coming back alive from Spain, and from them I ascertained the facts, which I forwarded, not only to the State Department but to the Department of Justice and asked Attorney General Murphy, at the time, to cause his Department to check up on my investigation and to have these men who were responsible for the killing of my son brought to the bar of justice for prosecution here.

Mr. LYNCH. And what did that investigation show, Mr. Wallach?

Mr. WALLACH. It showed that after several efforts had been made to kill my son they finally succeeded in the month of July 1938.

Mr. LYNCH. And the efforts were made by whom to kill him?

Mr. WALLACH. By the, as I understand it, these people in charge of the affairs of the Abraham Lincoln Brigade. This happened in a so-called prison camp or jail known as Castle de Fells, which I understand is about 25 kilometers south of the city of Barcelona and that it was done under the supervision of the officer known as Captain Gates, and that the man in charge of this prison was a fellow by the name of Tony de Maio, who I understand was the actual killer, not only of my boy but of six other American boys whose remains to this very moment are in the courtyard of this prison camp, Castle de Fells.

Mr. LYNCH. And was there any intimation that they were killed because they had sought their release from service on the side of the Loyalists in Spain?

Mr. WALLACH. It was because it was known that efforts were being made in his behalf to have him released that they took a dislike to him and decided that the best thing that they could do was to kill him rather than have him come back to America and let the people here know what these Communists were doing in Spain.

Mr. LYNCH. Do you recall any information or any conversation when you speak about other Americans, about a young American from the west coast—I think from Seattle, named Summers, who was a student at one of the large universities out there and was taken and enlisted and recruited in the last year?

Mr. WALLACH. Of course, in my conversations with these returned soldiers names were mentioned—Summers, a fellow by the name of Norris, I think another boy by the name of Keller, but, frankly, I didn't take particular notice of them. Maybe you will call that a selfish interest. I was interested in knowing what happened with my boy and that was what I was concerned with.

Mr. LYNCH. I will show you the name of your son, Mr. Wallach, "Mr. Albert Wallach," on the passenger list [handing paper to the witness].

Mr. WALLACH. Of the steamship *Paris*.

Mr. LYNCH. Of the steamship *Paris* of March 1937?

Mr. WALLACH. That is a correct sailing list showing my son sailed on that ship to Spain.

Mr. LYNCH. These fellows that you contacted up in New York, Mr. Wallach, gave you the information which you diligently sought out. How did they describe the conditions existing over there with relation to these American boys?

(No answer.)

Mr. LYNCH. Do you recall any of the conditions they described existing in Spain that you can give to the committee?

Mr. WALLACH. My general reaction to the stories I obtained from the four or five that I interviewed in New York was a dissatisfaction with the personnel in charge; that the entire movement they found upon arrival in Spain was a selfish one in that those in charge were trying to receive all the benefits they could out of the movement and that the men themselves were treated like—worse than dogs.

Mr. LYNCH. And when you speak about receiving benefits from the movement, did it also include financial benefits?

Mr. WALLACH. Such things as supplies that were sent over instead of being distributed among the men were even sold by these so-called officials in charge so that they could have the cash to use upon themselves selfishly.

Mr. LYNCH. You mean the officials of the Abraham Lincoln Brigade?

Mr. WALLACH. That is right.

Mr. LYNCH. Do you have any letter there particularly, Mr. Wallach, that describes conditions in Spain?

Mr. WALLACH. I have a letter in addition to the five former soldiers of Spain that I interviewed. I received a letter from the Department of State on May 11, in which they enclosed a letter from one Edward Palega, out of the Chicago office of the Friends of the Abraham Lincoln Brigade, at 3111 North Sacramento Avenue, Chicago, Ill., dated May 3, 1939, which reads as follows:

SECRETARY CORDELL HULL,
Department of State, Washington, D. C.

DEAR SIR: If the father of Albert Wallach, formerly of the 15th Brigade International of the Spanish Loyalist Army is seeking information about his son, please ask him to communicate with me as I may be able to aid him.

Very truly yours,
EDWARD PALEGA.

I then, upon receiving this letter, contacted Mr. Palega. He wrote to me on August 26, 1939, as follows:

MY DEAR MR. WALLACH. Your son Albert made me promise to let you know of his condition if and when I got out of Spain alive.

I don't know what happened to him. For that reason I hate to say anything, but he and I were in prison together in the International Brigade prison of Castle de Fells, about twenty-five kilometers south of Barcelona. The prison was in the Castle. Castle de Fells on a hill top overlooking the town.

We were there together in June and July 1938. He was arrested in Barcelona in June while wearing civilian clothes and while carrying alleged forged papers from the American Consul, stating he was under protection of the United States Government.

For that reason he was suspected of being a spy. One day he was taken out of our cell. Two days later, due to a murderous intent of the prison commander, I was beaten up and thrown into the black hole No. 6. Albert was already there. He had really been given a beating. They had nothing against me so my beating wasn't bad, as I was all right in a few days. But Albert was quite ill and was hardly able to speak.

About a week after I entered that cell Albert was taken out in the nighttime. Though I inquired everywhere I could never learn what happened to him, but I am afraid he may have been killed that night.

I must ask you not to show this letter to any one and above all not to use my name or quote me. I want no one to know I was in prison and I write this only because I promised Al I would. But you now know he was alive until sometime in July 1938. It may be the clue that will tell you the whole story or it may lead you to the truth. I don't know which.

Consul Flood in Barcelona may be able to give you more of the story. I don't know. But he knew Albert personally during May and June of 1938.

Also Colonel Fuqua, American Military Attaché, at the Barcelona Consulate now.

May I say by way of explanation that even though the writer asks me not to use his name and not to show the letter, I feel it is my duty in an exposé of this kind to present the facts and I hope I am not regarded ill as a result of reading this letter into the record, because I believe the American people here will give this man sufficient protection that the Communists won't be able to retaliate against him for revealing what he knew to have taken place.

Mr. THOMAS. It is not clear to me why your son and these other boys were in prison. Would you please tell the committee what you know about that? You probably have told it.

Mr. WALLACH. The only reason I could ascertain was because selfish motives of these individuals in charge of the brigade prompted the arresting of these boys who were fighting and agitating against their selfish conduct, and because they were afraid that if they returned alive to America the people in this country would know the facts, they decided to do away with them on the wholesale basis.

Mr. LYNCH. Mr. Wallach, in that letter which you have just read it refers to the fact that your son was carrying papers which showed that he was under the protection of the American Government. Now, it was a fact that before that time you had endeavored and had succeeded, through the State Department, in getting him the protection of the American Government over there, hadn't you?

Mr. WALLACH. I had made direct contact with the American consul through the State Department.

Mr. LYNCH. So when they speak about having found these papers upon your son and which they regarded as forgeries, and thought he was a spy, the fact was that through your efforts with the State Department they were actually genuine papers, weren't they?

Mr. WALLACH. Absolutely.

Mr. LYNCH. And, of course, you never heard any—there never was any question of any trial of anybody over there on matters of that sort, was there?

Mr. WALLACH. How could there be a trial? What Government did they represent? They were not connected with the Spanish Army or the Spanish Government. They were a bunch of guerrillas that went to Spain together and took unto themselves the law. They created law for themselves—an irresponsible group.

Mr. LYNCH. Mr. Wallach, are there any other facts or information that you have on this inquiry that you feel would be helpful to the committee?

Mr. WALLACH. Well, the only thing is that I know that when Judge Murphy was the Attorney General and head of the Department of Justice he had promised me that an investigation would be made and if the facts justified there would be indictments for the recruiting of American boys to be sent over on this foreign mission, and though a long time did take place eventually indictments were presented in Detroit, and I know that the grand jury, the Federal grand jury in New York, was holding sessions and conducting its investigations with the hope that indictments there, too, would be lodged against those responsible.

Unfortunately, Judge Murphy was promoted and a new man came in and the first thing I heard through the press was that on February

16 the new Attorney General issued a statement that he would have the indictments thrown out and the investigation stopped because he claimed no public injury was done.

Now, I say this: A greater public injury than murdering American citizens, no matter where it took place, could not possibly happen.

Now, where is the justification on the part of the Attorney General in saying that no public injury was done, and I feel that this committee, representing the legislative branch of government, is performing a public duty in arousing the public interest to call upon the head of the law-enforcement agency of our Government to reinvestigate and take this matter up anew against those responsible for taking American lives in this irresponsible way in Spain.

Mr. THOMAS. Mr. Chairman, I would like to say right there, this committee has called upon the Attorney General and the Department of Justice for cooperation right from the start and I have yet to see a scintilla of cooperation from the Department of Justice, particularly the present Attorney General.

This matter of quashing those indictments is just typical of the kind of things he stands for and does and I am getting sick of it.

Mr. WALLACH. After all I feel the so-called Communist interest in this country is rather a very small minority, and while protecting civil rights of these minorities who are trying to tear the insides out of us may be in place, yet at the same time where it is demonstrated that human life has been taken and a great public injury has been done, the least the Attorney General of the United States can do is to see that where the laws have been violated prosecutions should take place. Let the American juries pass upon the guilt of those responsible.

Mr. THOMAS. That is right.

Mr. LYNCH. Anything further, Mr. Chairman?

Mr. VOORHIS. I would like to ask a question.

Mr. Wallach, so far as you know when your son enlisted what did he think he was doing? What I mean is, What were the motives that he had when he first enlisted to go to Spain?

Mr. WALLACH. Well, let me make this plain to you. I did not know that he was enlisting. I did not know for months later that he had actually enlisted and gone to Spain. But what I did ascertain from others he thought he was going into a movement that had behind it the highest human impulse, human ideals, like a great many others that went into it, only to find out when they got there that it was nothing but a racket operated in this country by a handful for their own personal selfish gain.

Mr. VOORHIS. One other question. Don't you think that one thing that motivated—I don't know whether it motivated your son, but other people—was the fact that they felt that on the other side of that struggle that there was support being given by foreign governments?

Mr. WALLACH. That probably was the reason as I have ascertained from investigation and talking with those that lived to return.

The CHAIRMAN. You have made a very extensive investigation?

Mr. WALLACH. I spent several weeks personally contacting men. It was hard to get them to talk. They were afraid of their lives even when they returned here, for fear these Communists, if they knew they were revealing the facts, would kill them here.

Mr. VOORHIS. Do you know of any case where anything like that happened?

Mr. WALLACH. No, I don't because, frankly speaking, this is the first opportunity in a public way that we have had a chance to present the evidence.

The CHAIRMAN. Any other questions, gentlemen?

Mr. LYNCH. That is all, Mr. Chairman. Thank you very much, Mr. Wallach.

Mr. WALLACH. If you want the picture of Albert for the purpose of tying him up with those that returned, I will gladly let you have it.

The CHAIRMAN. How old was he when he went to Spain?

Mr. WALLACH. When he enlisted he was 23 years of age.

The CHAIRMAN. A graduate of a high school?

Mr. WALLACH. No, but he was—I might as well put that in the record, too. He had attempted to enter West Point and he had prepared for entrance to West Point and subsequently received a commission as a lieutenant in the Reserve of the American Army and was connected with the Three Hundred and Sixth Infantry in New York City.

The CHAIRMAN. Was he an idealistic young man? Was he a young man with high ideals?

Mr. WALLACH. Very.

The CHAIRMAN. And believed in democracy?

Mr. WALLACH. He certainly did.

The CHAIRMAN. The type that would be misled into believing that he was fighting for a good cause?

Mr. WALLACH. That is right.

The CHAIRMAN. You don't think he would ever have gone to Spain if he had thought or if he had known what the situation was?

Mr. WALLACH. Why, of course not. He was American born. His interests were those that we, you and I, have received as a result of attending American institutions of learning.

Mr. THOMAS. Mr. Chairman, this is just one more instance and illustration of the idealism of the American youth being capitalized by these subversive elements.

Mr. WALLACH. And that is why it is more important that this Government protect our youth against its own indiscretions.

Mr. THOMAS. That is right.

Mr. LYNCH. The next witness is Mr. Honeycombe.

The CHAIRMAN. Raise your right hand, Mr. Honeycombe. Do you solemnly swear to tell the truth, the whole truth, and nothing but the truth, so help you God?

TESTIMONY OF JOHN G. HONEYCOMBE, FORMER MEMBER OF THE ABRAHAM LINCOLN BRIGADE

Mr. HONEYCOMBE. I do.

Mr. MATTHEWS. Will you please state your full name for the record?

Mr. HONEYCOMBE. John Gordon Honeycombe.

The CHAIRMAN. Mr. Counsel, before we go on with the examination of this witness the Chair has received information—I don't know how authentic it is—that one of the witnesses here to testify was beaten up last night; that a group practically kidnaped him and inflicted bodily injury upon him. I don't know whether there is any foundation for that or not, but this committee must protect the witnesses who appear here.

I think there ought to be some determination of that fact and immediate means should be made to protect all witnesses, regardless of who they are, when they attend this committee. They are entitled to the protection of the Government of the United States, so I think that it might be well for us to go into that phase of it if you can, as soon as possible.

Mr. LYNCH. Very well.

Mr. MATTHEWS Mr. Honeycombe, what is your address?

Mr. HONEYCOMBE. 223 North Oxford Street, Los Angeles, Calif.

Mr. MATTHEWS. Where were you born?

Mr. HONEYCOMBE. Ilion, N. Y.

Mr. MATTHEWS. Were you ever a member of the Communist Party?

Mr. HONEYCOMBE. I was.

Mr. MATTHEWS. Where?

Mr. HONEYCOMBE. Los Angeles.

Mr. MATTHEWS. Did you hold any positions in the Communist Party or its subsidiary organizations?

Mr. HONEYCOMBE. I did.

Mr. MATTHEWS. Will you please enumerate them?

Mr. HONEYCOMBE. I was the field organizer for the southern California district of the Friends of the Soviet Union.

Mr. MATTHEWS. When was that?

Mr. HONEYCOMBE. 1933 to 1936.

Mr. MATTHEWS. Will you please state briefly for the record at this time what you found to be the facts with reference to the Communist Party's control of the Friends of the Soviet Union?

Mr. HONEYCOMBE. They were the creators of the organization for the purpose of the recognition of the U. S. S. R. and the United States Government recognition of the U. S. S. R. Government in 1933.

Mr. MATTHEWS. Were the activities of the Friends of the Soviet Union in general under the control of the Communist Party?

Mr. HONEYCOMBE. They were.

Mr. MATTHEWS. Did you receive instructions or orders to engage in the work of the Friends of the Soviet Union from the Communist Party?

Mr. HONEYCOMBE. I did.

Mr. MATTHEWS. Did you, while you were organizing for the Friends of the Soviet Union, receive directives from time to time with reference to the way you should carry out the work of the Friends of the Soviet Union from the Communist Party?

Mr. HONEYCOMBE. I did.

Mr. MATTHEWS. Can you give some of the specific details that indicate that?

Mr. HONEYCOMBE. The furthering of the propaganda by motion pictures and the lecture platform about the development of the socialist economy form of government, how it functions; the difference between the autocracy of the Czars against the new democratic form of the Soviets, the workers and peasants and soldiers deputies.

Mr. MATTHEWS. Was there a Communist Party fraction working or functioning in the Friends of the Soviet Union?

Mr. HONEYCOMBE. Controlled the Friends of the Soviet Union.

Mr. MATTHEWS. Will you please state as briefly as possible how a Communist Party fraction operates in such an organization as the Friends of the Soviet Union?

Mr. HONEYCOMBE. They are called upon for a meeting with the political bureau of the general section of which the organization happens to be located. They receive the directives from the committee in New York, which in turn receives their instructions from the Communist International at Moscow. They are applied to the local conditions and sections and activities with respect to fraternal organizations, labor organizations, democratic groups generally and an infiltration of the democratic processes of those groups.

Mr. MATTHEWS. Now, Mr. Honeycombe, when did you volunteer for enlistment in the Loyalist Army in Spain?

Mr. HONEYCOMBE. 1937, in August.

The CHAIRMAN. Wouldn't it be well to find out more of his activities in California for the Communist Party before you lead up to that?

Mr. MATTHEWS. Mr. Chairman, my thought in that respect was that Mr. Honeycombe had a great deal of experience in the Communist Party work in California and that would take a good deal of time to develop that testimony, and since he has first-hand knowledge with reference to this Spanish recruiting situation, that we would bring that out at this time.

The CHAIRMAN. Well, bring that out at a later date but you will have to keep him here for us to hear it.

Mr. MATTHEWS. Now, will you please state the facts with reference to your enlistment in the Loyalist Army in Spain, Mr. Honeycombe?

Mr. HONEYCOMBE. I enlisted in the city of Los Angeles on August 5, 1937. I arrived in La Havre, France, on August 21; was transported over the Pyrenees Mountains—on foot rather, we hiked over— and was received at Figueras on September 1, 1937.

There we entrained 3 days later to Albacete, the international base training headquarters and receiving depot.

Mr. MATTHEWS. Before you go further into Spain, I would like to have you go back to the period before you sailed. Did you travel on an American passport?

Mr. HONEYCOMBE. I did.

Mr. MATTHEWS. Was that passport issued in your own name?

Mr. HONEYCOMBE. It was.

Mr. MATTHEWS. Were there any notations on your passport with reference to your entry into Spain?

Mr. HONEYCOMBE. Nothing other than it was marked "Not valid for travel in Spain."

Mr. MATTHEWS. Were American passports at that time generally so marked?

Mr. HONEYCOMBE. I understood they were.

Mr. MATTHEWS. But yours was marked "Not valid for travel in Spain"?

Mr. HONEYCOMBE. That is right.

Mr. MATTHEWS. Where did you obtain your passport?

Mr. HONEYCOMBE. San Francisco.

Mr. MATTHEWS. Did the party, the Communist Party, have anything to do with your enlistment?

Mr. HONEYCOMBE. They had everything to do with it—all arrangements.

Mr. MATTHEWS. Will you please state the facts, how were you approached or by whom?

Mr. HONEYCOMBE. By former members of the Communist Party whom I had known and associated with for years.

Mr. MATTHEWS. And what was the idea that was in their minds about your enlistment?

Mr. HONEYCOMBE. Because they felt because of my previous World War service, both in the Army and Navy, that I should go over and do my part.

Mr. MATTHEWS. Was enlistment in the State of California in the hands of communists or the Communist Party to your first-hand knowledge?

Mr. HONEYCOMBE. It was.

Mr. MATTHEWS. Will you please describe more in detail the method as to how you were enlisted, what was said to you, and so on?

Mr. HONEYCOMBE. I was approached by——

Mr. MATTHEWS. And what you were told about your passport, if anything.

Mr. HONEYCOMBE. Well, I was instructed to make the formal application for passport in the Pacific Electric Building at Sixth and Main in Los Angeles, at the commissioner's office.

I made out an affidavit to the effect that I was going over to England to my ancestral home for a 4 months' visit. These were our instructions.

Mr. MATTHEWS. You were instructed to do that?

Mr. HONEYCOMBE. That is right; not to reveal the intent or purpose of our trip.

I so made out the application and swore to the affidavit. Three days later I received my passport in San Francisco and I reported back to the office at the recruiting bureau, operated by one John Lightner, under the alias of Mr. West, and received my further instructions to report the following day with my ticket and transportation, to New York where further arrangements would be made for my sailing.

Mr. MATTHEWS. Now, was it a Communist Party member who actually signed you up for Spain?

Mr. HONEYCOMBE. It was.

Mr. MATTHEWS. Who was that Communist Party member?

Mr. HONEYCOMBE. Mr. Lightner, alias Mr. West.

Mr. MATTHEWS. Do you know what his first name was?

Mr. HONEYCOMBE. John, I believe.

Mr. MATTHEWS. John Lightner?

Mr. HONEYCOMBE. I am sure.

Mr. MATTHEWS. Alias West. You mean he was known as West in the Communist Party?

Mr. HONEYCOMBE. That is correct, and in the recruiting bureau.

Mr. MATTHEWS. And in the recruiting bureau?

Mr. HONEYCOMBE. That is right.

Mr. MATTHEWS. Were you examined by a physician for service in Spain?

Mr. HONEYCOMBE. I was.

Mr. MATTHEWS. What physician examined you?

Mr. HONEYCOMBE. I don't know whether I can think of the name now.

Mr. MATTHEWS. Was it Dr. Leo Beegleman?

Mr. HONEYCOMBE. Beegleman, that is correct.

Mr. MATTHEWS. Were you instructed by the Communist Party to go to Dr. Beegleman for this examination?

Mr. HONEYCOMBE. I was.

Mr. MATTHEWS. Were you given the money for your passport?

Mr. HONEYCOMBE. I was.

Mr. MATTHEWS. By whom?

Mr. HONEYCOMBE. Mr. Lightner.

Mr. MATTHEWS. By Mr. Lightner, the member of the Communist Party whose alias was West?

Mr. HONEYCOMBE. That is correct.

Mr. MATTHEWS. Did you receive any funds or tickets for travel to New York.

Mr. HONEYCOMBE. I did.

Mr. MATTHEWS. From whom and in what sum?

Mr. HONEYCOMBE. The same man, Mr. Lightner, in the amount of $37.50 plus $5 to eat on.

Mr. MATTHEWS. And what were the instructions with reference to your reporting in New York?

Mr. HONEYCOMBE. To report to a certain address in New York City on Forty-first.

Mr. MATTHEWS. Do you recall the exact address on Forty-first Street?

Mr. HONEYCOMBE. I think it is 371 West Forty-first—I am quite sure.

Mr. MATTHEWS. Whom did you meet there?

Mr. HONEYCOMBE. The disbursing agent for the party who arranged all the sailings.

Mr. MATTHEWS. What party was that?

Mr. HONEYCOMBE. Communist Party.

Mr. MATTHEWS. Communist Party?

Mr. HONEYCOMBE. That is correct.

Mr. MATTHEWS. Did you find that these headquarters to which you were instructed to report in California were under the direction of members of the Communist Party?

Mr. HONEYCOMBE. That is right.

Mr. MATTHEWS. In New York?

Mr. HONEYCOMBE. That is correct.

Mr. VOORHIS. What was that question?

Mr. MATTHEWS. Did he find when he arrived in New York that the headquarters to which he was instructed to report were under the control of the Communist Party and his answer was "Yes."

How did you know that, Mr. Honeycombe?

Mr. HONEYCOMBE. By the form of instructions I received—the responsibilities I had for the transportation of three other men with me.

Mr. MATTHEWS. You were placed in charge, were you?

Mr. HONEYCOMBE. That is correct, from Los Angeles to New York.

Mr. MATTHEWS. Now, when you left for France what instructions did you receive from these members of the Communist Party in New York?

Mr. HONEYCOMBE. Practically identical instructions that I received in Los Angeles, going to New York with the address to report to in Paris, and how to proceed between New York and Paris, both on board ship and upon arrival in Havre and to the committee at Paris.

Mr. MATTHEWS. How many men went over in your charge?

Mr. HONEYCOMBE. There were only four under my charge and five under another man. There were two of us in charge of that contingent.

Mr. MATTHEWS. You sailed on the same ship?

Mr. HONEYCOMBE. Steamship *Champlain.*

Mr. MATTHEWS. The date of your sailing?

Mr. HONEYCOMBE. I believe August 14, on Saturday, 12 o'clock noon.

Mr. MATTHEWS. 1937?

Mr. HONEYCOMBE. That is correct.

Mr. MATTHEWS. And you arrived in——

Mr. HONEYCOMBE. Havre, France, on the 21st of that month.

Mr. MATTHEWS. Were you met at Le Havre?

Mr. HONEYCOMBE. No, I was not.

Mr. MATTHEWS. Were you met in Paris?

Mr. HONEYCOMBE. That is right, in Paris.

Mr. MATTHEWS. By whom?

Mr. HONEYCOMBE. By a member of the Control Commission of the Syndicate of the Union.

Mr. MATTHEWS. What is the Control Commission of the Syndicate of the Union?

Mr. HONEYCOMBE. Well, that is the party fraction in charge of the receiving bureau in Paris. It has the location of their office in the Union Syndicate.

Mr. MATTHEWS. Are they the headquarters to which you reported?

Mr. HONEYCOMBE. That is correct.

Mr. MATTHEWS. Do you recall the address in Paris?

Mr. HONEYCOMBE. Offhand I cannot recall. It is a very famous spot in Paris. It is the location of all the labor unions. It is a syndicate of unions.

Mr. MATTHEWS. Syndicate of unions roughly equivalent to the American Federation of Labor?

Mr. HONEYCOMBE. Correct.

Mr. MATTHEWS. For the French trade unions?

Mr. HONEYCOMBE. Correct.

Mr. MATTHEWS. Now, what instructions did you receive at these headquarters on your arrival in Paris?

Mr. HONEYCOMBE. To stand by for further orders, which was a 3-day period. On the third day, at night, I was approached with tickets to board a train with the men and proceed to Narbonne in southern France.

Mr. MATTHEWS. And how many of you proceeded to go?

Mr. HONEYCOMBE. The same contingent, nine.

Mr. MATTHEWS. Nine of you?

Mr. HONEYCOMBE. Yes.

Mr. MATTHEWS. Now, will you give in detail what you started to give a moment ago about your arrival at the Pyrenees and how you were conducted across the border?

Mr. HONEYCOMBE. We were detrained in Béziers in southern France to rest for a period of a day and night. At 12 o'clock in the evening on the second day we received a committee member with instructions to proceed to the foothills of the Pyrenees Mountains, I believe below Carcassonne, and from there we were to meet a French guide, Communist guide to lead us over the Pyrenees Mountains.

Mr. MATTHEWS. And what did you do with your American passports or what was done with your American passports when you crossed into Spain.

Mr. HONEYCOMBE. We surrendered those upon arrival at Albacete upon filling out the questionnaire as to our social history and political background.

Mr. MATTHEWS. To whom did you surrender your American passports?

Mr. HONEYCOMBE. I believe an adjutant or aide to one Bill Lawrence who at that time was the commissar—receiving man in charge.

Mr. MATTHEWS. Was Bill Lawrence an American?

Mr. HONEYCOMBE. I understand he is. I don't know.

Mr. MATTHEWS. Was there any agreement with you as to receiving your passports back?

Mr. HONEYCOMBE. Well, the understanding and the agreement, both prior to sailing and at the point of enlistment in Los Angeles, was that after 6-months' service in Spain every man was entitled to automatic repatriation.

Mr. MATTHEWS. Were you so promised?

Mr. HONEYCOMBE. I was so informed on both ends.

Mr. MATTHEWS. You know from others that they received like promises?

Mr. HONEYCOMBE. I do.

Mr. MATTHEWS. That they would be repatriated after the end of 6 months if they desired to return to the United States?

Mr. HONEYCOMBE. That is correct.

Mr. MATTHEWS. The man to whom you surrendered your American passport was not an American official of any kind, was he?

Mr. HONEYCOMBE. No; he was not. You mean by that a member of the American Government?

Mr. MATTHEWS. Yes.

Mr. HONEYCOMBE. No; I am sure he was not.

Mr. MATTHEWS. Did he have any authority from any governmental agency to receive your passport?

Mr. HONEYCOMBE. He did not.

Mr. MATTHEWS. But you were required to surrender your passport, is that correct?

Mr. HONEYCOMBE. I would use the word "compelled" because I wished to retain mine against any eventuality.

Mr. MATTHEWS. Were the Americans traveling with you likewise compelled to surrender their passports?

Mr. HONEYCOMBE. It was advisable under the circumstances; although we didn't overenjoy the idea of surrendering the only method of exodus.

Mr. MATTHEWS. Did you learn from other members of the fighting units in Spain who were Americans that they were also compelled to surrender their passports?

Mr. HONEYCOMBE. Some of the men were very careful and shrewd in that they claimed they lost theirs in the hike over the mountains and retained them. That was quite an excellent idea.

Mr. MATTHEWS. But it was the rule that passports had to be surrendered.

Mr. HONEYCOMBE. That is right.

Mr. VOORHIS. I would like to find out a little more in detail about what happened. How were you compelled to give up the passports? What was told you?

Mr. HONEYCOMBE. Well, for example, Mr. Voorhis, supposing you were the receiving committee at Albacete and I was the recruit arriving at the base. Your job was to surrender or rather have me surrender any means of identification and establish my qualifications as to your requirements, whether I am a fit man to be applied or designated for any certain task in Spain according to my history and my political background and my political activities in America. You were the judge of that and by surrendering my passport automatically I was under your control.

That was my only means of escape or exodus in the event of any eventuality, and you had complete control over me when I surrendered the passport. It was obligatory on my part to do so—compulsory.

Mr. VOORHIS. Suppose you said, "I don't want to give it up"?

Mr. HONEYCOMBE. I did not advise that, and I thought better of it under the circumstances. One doesn't do that when he is surrounded by arms in the time of war.

Mr. MATTHEWS. How soon did you go to the front, Mr. Honeycombe, after you arrived in Spain?

Mr. HONEYCOMBE. I was in Albacete about 8 hours when I was transferred into a uniform from civilian clothing, and proceeded——

Mr. MATTHEWS. Before you go on to that, were you met by Spanish Communists anywhere?

Mr. HONEYCOMBE. Over the Pyrenees we were met by a Spanish Communist guard and the border guard, of course, in uniform.

Mr. MATTHEWS. Was there any welcoming committee anywhere along this route?

Mr. HONEYCOMBE. In the first village we were received and received rations. In going over the mountains most of us failed to carry water.

Mr. MATTHEWS. Were you expected?

Mr. HONEYCOMBE. Yes; it was all arranged for on arrival. The camions were there. We had our lunch, or rather breakfast or lunch, between 10:30 in the morning when we arrived and left France that night. It is a 13-hour hike over the mountains.

Mr. MATTHEWS. Did you go direct to the front?

Mr. HONEYCOMBE. I went to Fort Figueras and from there—we were detained some 2 or 3 days to await transportation to Albacete. They had difficulties in arranging the transportation of troops owing to the extreme demand on transportation service. And following my change into uniform I proceeded to the American base at Quintanas, the training base, and I was there about 7 days, and because of my previous military service, I had charge of drilling a section and was recommended to go to Pozo Rubio, the officer's school, and I was sent to Pozo Rubio, where for 3 weeks I was under Russian instructors in the art of mapping, scouting, and observing.

Mr. MATTHEWS. You had a Russian instructor?

Mr. HONEYCOMBE. That is correct.

Mr. MATTHEWS. Was he a soldier from the red army?

Mr. HONEYCOMBE. That is correct; Colonel Melinkoff.

Mr. MATTHEWS. That is the army from the Soviet Union?

Mr. HONEYCOMBE. That is correct.

Mr. MATTHEWS. What was his name?

Mr. HONEYCOMBE. Colonel Melinkoff.

Mr. MATTHEWS. And how long did that instruction under Colonel Melinkoff last?

Mr. HONEYCOMBE. Twenty-one days—3 weeks, day and night.

Mr. MATTHEWS. Was that the usual period of training before going to the front?

Mr. HONEYCOMBE. Well, at that time because of the urgency and necessity for replacing some men following some action, that was responsible for the rush.

Mr. MATTHEWS. Were there any others, to your knowledge, than you who received a shorter period of training before going to the front?

Mr. HONEYCOMBE. Some of the men, I understand, never handled a rifle until they were put into the front lines at the last.

Mr. MATTHEWS. You mean they were put there without military experience?

Mr. HONEYCOMBE. That is correct.

Mr. MATTHEWS. And were taken to Spain and put in the front lines with less than 21 days of training?

Mr. HONEYCOMBE. I would say in less than 2 days.

Mr. MATTHEWS. Will you give for the record the exact record of military service which you have had in the United States?

Mr. HONEYCOMBE. United States Navy, between May 8, 1917, and June 21, 1921; the United States Army, Eleventh United States Cavalry, Presidio of Monterey, 1922 to 1925, and my service in Spain.

Mr. MATTHEWS. Did you find in Spain that the Communist International had been able to recruit men from all parts of the world for this war in Spain?

Mr. HONEYCOMBE. Practically all parts of the world. I think I even saw one or two Chinese, if I recall correctly, in the medical units.

Mr. MATTHEWS. Now, will you please describe how and where you went to the front after your period of training?

Mr. HONEYCOMBE. I left Pozo Rubio, without trying to give an exact date from memory, on September 21. I was transported with a contingent of some 550 men under the command of Captain Davis and Lieutenant Bill Titus to the front at Quinto. That was some four and a half days and nights riding trains. When we arrived at the front at Quinto we were quartered at the demolished cemetery upon a rise near the church on the hill at Quinto.

There we prepared for front-line duty and entered the trenches at Fuentes De Ebro on the evening of October 11.

Mr. MATTHEWS. How long did you have front-line service?

Mr. HONEYCOMBE. Altogether from the time of my arrival, from October 11 until April 2, when I crossed the Ebro after the retreat at Gandesa.

Mr. MATTHEWS. Now, during this period of your service in Spain, did you ever see Earl Browder?

Mr. HONEYCOMBE. I did once.

Mr. MATTHEWS. Where did you see Earl Browder in Spain?

Mr. HONEYCOMBE. About 26 kilometers east of Teruel, after we were withdrawn from Teruel. That would be approximately February 27 or 28, 1938.

Mr. MATTHEWS. And what were the circumstances under which you saw Browder on February 27 or 28? That would be 1938?

Mr. HONEYCOMBE. We were being evacuated, presumably, to Valencia for a rest. The train broke down some 8 kilometers west of Mora station and the men were ordered to quit the train and take to the hillsides, owing to the airplanes overhead in close proximity to Teruel, and Earl Browder addressed the men at that time.

Mr. MATTHEWS. What was the content of Earl Browder's speech to the men on this occasion?

Mr. HONEYCOMBE. The usual pep talk and propaganda about the attitude of America and the continued pressure of the nonintervention committee and the effect of the immense victory—the taking of Teruel by the all-Spanish brigade and the general encouragement to attempt to lift the morale of the men, but he was not overwell received by some of the men.

Mr. MATTHEWS. Did Browder specifically take up the question of the length of service of the Americans in Spain?

Mr. HONEYCOMBE. He did. He pointed out it would be necessary to maintain us there until the end of the war.

Mr. MATTHEWS. Did he in effect state that the promise of repatriation after 6 months was abrogated?

Mr. HONEYCOMBE. Well, not in so many words. Inferentially he gave us to understand that.

Mr. MATTHEWS. That no one would be repatriated until the end of the war?

Mr. HONEYCOMBE. Words to that effect, along that line—we were expected to stay there until the end of the war as real anti-Facists.

Mr. THOMAS. May I interrupt there? He told you that you people should stay there until the end of the war but he came home shortly after that, didn't he?

Mr. HONEYCOMBE. And how! And many of the men would like to have joined him, I assure you.

Mr. MATTHEWS. How was his announcement received by the men?

Mr. HONEYCOMBE. Not overly well received by some men that had been over there a year and had already started for home and were sent back to the lines. Many of the men were denied permission to return who had well served their period of time. Many of them in very poor health and run-down condition.

Mr. MATTHEWS. Did you observe any actual discontent?

Mr. HONEYCOMBE. I did.

Mr. MATTHEWS. Among the men at that time?

Mr. HONEYCOMBE. I did.

Mr. MATTHEWS. Because of the speech of Mr. Browder?

Mr. HONEYCOMBE. The reactions were not very complimentary to his propaganda talk over there.

Mr. MATTHEWS. Did the officers take any special precautions following the speech for self-protection?

Mr. HONEYCOMBE. To a degree, they did. Some of them required Spanish guards to go around with them, armed, at all times.

Mr. MATTHEWS. Did you hear a good number of men who were entitled to repatriation because they had served 6 months, express themselves as determined to go?

Mr. HONEYCOMBE. I did, in undertones generally, of course. They did not do it openly because they would be marked men.

Mr. MATTHEWS. You spoke of 550 men going up to the front, I believe, a moment ago. Were they all Americans?

Mr. HONEYCOMBE. I would say practically all Americans in our battalion.

Mr. MATTHEWS. Was there an Abraham Lincoln brigade in Spain?

Mr. HONEYCOMBE. That was the nom de guerre, I would call it here in America, for the purpose of exploiting the sympathetic people to the Spanish cause and that of the men and relatives of the men serving over there for the purpose of raising funds. It was simply a convenient slogan adopted to shake the people down here.

Mr. MATTHEWS. Do you mean to say there was not in Spain any unit known as the Lincoln brigade?

Mr. HONEYCOMBE. It was known as the Lincoln-Washington Battalion, the Fifteenth International Brigade.

Mr. MATTHEWS. Did you make any efforts to get repatriated after this speech of Browder?

Mr. HONEYCOMBE. No. Sometime later I wrote a letter out to the brigade commander requesting informally that I be repatriated and stating my reasons, and I turned that over to John Gates when he joined us southeast of Belchite prior to the action there on March 9. This letter was addressed to the brigade commander, and we were under the command of Capt. Dave Rees who was killed at Albacete.

Mr. MATTHEWS. Was the morale of the American boys diminished or increased as a result of Earl Browder's speech?

Mr. HONEYCOMBE. To a degree. You see I would estimate 40 percent of those men were non-Communists that went to Spain—at least that much, who knew little or nothing about the mechanization or mechanics of the Communist Party or its theories or policies, who had by one means or another come in contact with one or another group affiliated and became in sympathy with the cause by the intense propaganda disseminated by them.

Mr. MATTHEWS. Now, will you please go ahead with the description of your own efforts at repatriation? What was the reaction to you as a result of your efforts to be repatriated?

Mr. HONEYCOMBE. Well, frankly, at that time I could not say, but following the Belchite retreat there is a chain of events there that must be explained to answer your question correctly.

The following morning about 2:30 we moved up into the lines, presumably as was what to be our front line held on the previous day by the Sixth Spanish Brigade. It was occupied by the Facists that evening. Prior to our moving up, and we were ordered into action that night at midnight and moved up at 3 o'clock, and the hike was about 7½ kilometers, and there is a monastery that was known as the second-line ridge—a highway going out toward Teruel, north. We were ordered to proceed, and about daylight we were caught between the presumable front and second lines, which were no longer the front lines but the Fascist lines. We were caught in no man's land some four or five hundred meters beyond what was our front-line trenches due to the wrong orders. So we retreated back to what had been designated properly as the first line which was now the monastery line and we held that until 2 o'clock in the afternoon when we were forced to retreat under terrific fire and that retreat continued back to practically into Caspe and eventually into Cambrils. I began March 9, the general retreat, that was practically a rout, on March 9, back to Hijar and Castellote, where they tried to reorganize us but were constantly driven back to Alcañiz and finally to Caspe and into the Gandesa Valley, day and night.

Mr. MATTHEWS. Now, what happened to you as a result of your efforts to get repatriation?

Mr. HONEYCOMBE. I was one of the last men to leave the monastery ridge with the following men: Milton Sills, the commissar—the Communist commissar, I should say—and our young battalion clerk, I can't think of his name now, Vernon Selby, Romaro Bloom (?), the commissar of the second company; one more man that I can't recall— a new man. We carried Commander Parker's body—Commander Rees' body—about 450 meters behind the monastery and discovered the man was dead and we let him go under terrific fire and each man to himself to make the retreat.

Mr. MATTHEWS. Did you ever make a formal request for repatriation?

Mr. HONEYCOMBE. I did. I am coming to that point. Following our reorganization and meeting of the remnants of the battalion at Hijar, I requested permission to return to Barcelona. I had a very badly injured knee—swollen, and I could hardly walk—had to drag it—stiff, and Vernon Selby had a shrapnel wound in the shoulder.

Mr. MATTHEWS. Is that Vernon Selby, whose mother appeared on the stand this morning?

Mr. HONEYCOMBE. It is. He requested permission to go to the base hospital in the rear and was granted permission by the brigade commissar attached to reorganize the remnants of the battalion. That was on the dawn of March 12, just before they crossed the creek at Hijar.

I went back to Barcelona for the purpose of verifying the story that we would not be entitled to repatriation and were expected to remain there for the duration of the war, and went to Lerida. Selby had attention at the hospital here and I had my knee dressed and I continued on to Barcelona.

When I arrived in Barcelona I proceeded to the Ministry of War to ask the following question: Was the International Brigade responsible to the Spanish Government or the Spanish Army, and the answer was: "No; you have complete autonomy and you are under the control committee of the International Communist Party." That is the Third International under the direction of Andre Marty.

Andre Marty is the former French Deputy. He was in charge of the French contingent and a representative of the Secretariat of the Third International at Moscow. In fact, a member of it, Robert Minor, was in charge of the American contingent of the International

Brigade and the Lincoln-Washington Battalion of that brigade, the Fifteenth. Commander—Captain Kay's brigade at Barcelona, his headquarters there, was assisted by Lieutenant Cohn. These were aides of Mr. Minor and representatives of the secretariat, Andre Marty, at Barcelona.

I asked the Minister of War if it was true that we were expected and demanded by the Spanish Government to remain until the end of hostilities, and he said "No." He said: "That is entirely up to the brigade command for the International command or their representative; that repatriation would be passed upon by them."

Mr. MATTHEWS. Was this the War Minister of the Spanish Loyalist Government that you asked the question of?

Mr. HONEYCOMBE. That is correct.

Mr. MATTHEWS. And he said the Spanish Loyalist Government did not have authority over the International Brigade?

Mr. HONEYCOMBE. That is correct; only insofar as it did not conflict with the military orders of the Army corps or divisions we happened to be in line with.

Then I asked why it was that these men who had served their period—I explained of course the promises made and many men were thoroughly demoralized and sick and disgusted and they wanted to go home, and why they were not allowing them. He said: "Frankly," he said: "I would like to see you all get out of here." He said: "You have caused us more trouble than good because they help the International Brigades, largely, with the Communist divisions of Spain had continued the war. The Spanish people were fed up with it, including the Government, and the sooner it ended the better and they held us largely responsible for its continuation."

Events later proved that statement to be true. Catalonia did not raise a shot when they walked in on them. So I reported to headquarters at Barcelona and was immediately placed under arrest with Mr. Selby and we were kept under arrest for 10 days and returned to the front under guard on March 25. We were taken back to Batea.

Mr. MATTHEWS. What charges were formally placed against you when you were arrested?

Mr. HONEYCOMBE. No charges whatsoever. Only threats were made that I would be taken to General Gomez and thrown into the dungeon, so I demanded to be taken before General Gomez and demanded a military trial of my own comrades—the men I served with, if there were any charges against me.

Mr. MATTHEWS. Now, Selby was arrested with you at that time?

Mr. HONEYCOMBE. That is right.

Mr. MATTHEWS. And you were taken under guard to the front?

Mr. HONEYCOMBE. Some 8 or 10 days later. We were arrested on March 17 and returned to the front lines at Batea, some 22 of us, on March 25, exactly, about 5 days before the Gandesa action. We went into the lines at dawn on April 1.

Mr. MATTHEWS. You mean there were 22 of you under arrest who went into action?

Mr. HONEYCOMBE. Under guard; prisoners without arms.

Mr. MATTHEWS. Were you armed?

Mr. HONEYCOMBE. I was unarmed from the day I returned from Hijar into Barcelona.

Mr. MATTHEWS. Was Selby armed?

Mr. Honeycombe. He was also unarmed.

Mr. Matthews. Unarmed?

Mr. Honeycombe. He was also unarmed.

Mr. Matthews. Were any of the 22 prisoners who were taken to the front allowed to have arms?

Mr. Honeycombe. They were not.

Mr. Matthews. In other words, under arrest the 22 of you were placed at the front?

Mr. Honeycombe. That is correct.

Mr. Matthews. Entirely helpless to protect yourself as far as arms were concerned?

Mr. Honeycombe. That is quite true.

Mr. Matthews. Do you know whether that occurred on any other occasions with respect to prisoners?

Mr. Honeycombe. Well, I can't speak for the other battalions. Some of their officers were under arrest with me. I can give you the names of several of the men.

Mr. Matthews. Yes.

Mr. Honeycombe. Lieutenant Skinner of the all-Canadian Battalion, Lieutenant Anderson, Lt. Hank Basko—Basakowski, and a lieutenant of the brigade machine gunners. I can't think of his name offhand now.

Mr. Matthews. Well, that will be all right for their names.

Mr. Honeycombe. And Lawrence McCullough was placed incommunicado. He was under arrest there. Vernon Selby was released on the night, I think, of March 29, or the 30th, the last day before he went into that action, presumably to go back to the hospital for attention, but I later heard he was sent up in the lines with the entire battalion. No one was allowed to go back for rest or hospitalization because of the urgency of the situation.

Mr. Matthews. Now, Mr. Honeycombe, how did you and your associates who were under arrest understand this action of the authorities in sending you up to the front unarmed?

Mr. Honeycombe. Well, I would like to go into detail on that because there is a man here who will testify later, whom at the time I warned of the very thing that is happening today would happen.

While a prisoner under arrest I went to our battalion headquarters and talked to Fred Keller, who is the commissar for the battalion——

Mr. Matthews. What do you mean by "commissar"?

Mr. Honeycombe. That means he was in complete command of the political control of the battalion.

Mr. Matthews. You mean he was the political commissar?

Mr. Honeycombe. That is correct.

Mr. Matthews. Representing what political party?

Mr. Honeycombe. Well, representing the Communist International.

Mr. Matthews. Did each of the units or battalions of the International Brigade have political commissars?

Mr. Honeycombe. They did. Each company, each battalion, each brigade, and each division.

Mr. Matthews. A commissar for each?

Mr. Honeycombe. Yes, sir.

Mr. Matthews. Can you state what their functions were?

Mr. Honeycombe. Well, they were varied. First of all to ascertain the proper transports and supplies in time of action; see that food and all organized facilities and auxiliary units of the battalions and brigades are functioning properly, and to assist in maintaining the morale of the men, encourage them, both by example and by understanding the abilities to explain situations or apologies as the case may demand for mistakes, and generally to be a pet boy—propagandizing, having the same authority and responsibility with the commander of the battalion.

Mr. MATTHEWS. Did you have meetings at which the political commissars made speeches?

Mr. HONEYCOMBE. Yes; several.

Mr. MATTHEWS. And Fred Keller was the political commissar at the time that you are now speaking when you went to the front under arrest?

Mr. HONEYCOMBE. That is right; yes, sir.

Mr. VOORHIS. Just one minute. Suppose there was a conflict between the military commander and the commissar, if there ever was one, whose word would be final?

Mr. HONEYCOMBE. Well, now, that would depend, Mr. Voorhis, upon the situation, but usually the commissar had the supreme authority.

Mr. MATTHEWS. Do you have reason to know—at this point I would like to ask this question, Mr. Honeycombe, whether or not Robert Minor was the head political commissar for the American Communist Party attached to the International Brigade?

Mr. HONEYCOMBE. He was the chief.

Mr. MATTHEWS. Was Minor's word final?

Mr. HONEYCOMBE. It was.

Mr. MATTHEWS. In all matters respecting the American boys who were fighting?

Mr. HONEYCOMBE. It was.

Mr. MATTHEWS. You are sure of that?

Mr. HONEYCOMBE. I am positive of that.

Mr. MATTHEWS. And Robert Minor is an American?

Mr. HONEYCOMBE. I don't know. You could not prove it by me.

Mr. MATTHEWS. Do you know whether or not Robert Minor is a leading member of the Communist Party of the United States?

Mr. HONEYCOMBE. I know he is.

Mr. MATTHEWS. Well, now, will you go on with what happened when you were taken up to the front under arrest with Fred Keller acting as your commissar?

Mr. HONEYCOMBE. We were taken up to the front at Batea. We were kept out in an olive grove in the rain for 2 days and nights under Spanish guard, improperly clothed, men ill, sick, and wounded; denied water to drink, denied fire or cover, denied food, and reduced to rations within a day's period of only one ladle of lentil soup, very watery, I assure you, a little mule-meat flavor and two small pieces of bread. While under arrest the most terrific sadistic pressure was brought to bear on those prisoners. I have witnessed some crucial and cruel conditions under which men have sometimes had to exist.

But I charged Fred Keller the day would come when I would reveal to the world just what type of men and what form of sadism would be practiced upon men who went over there, presumably as previously explained by the past witness who believed in ideals of the highest type.

Mr. MATTHEWS. What happened at the end of this period at the front when you were under arrest?

Mr. HONEYCOMBE. The Fascist assault on the morning of April 1 was so terrific that my Spanish guards were removed or rather they evaporated, I should say, and some of my comrades of the McKenzie Battalion, men whom I had known in other activities, were placed over us as guards and they in turn were forced to return. So the former adjutant and myself found ourselves alone in a sort of a no-man's land between the brigade and what was left of the remnants of the battalion.

We were sent up under their control by the brigade guards, the all-Spanish guards which were taken out, and about 2 o'clock in the afternoon—no, I would say earlier than that, I would say high noon after a terrific artillery and heavy arms bombardment and strafing and bombing and grenading, we managed to crawl back to the brigade pill box where we were prisoners.

We took cover as much as possible. Two of the men returning gave us each three grenades which we stuck in our belts for self-defense in case we didn't get out. These men, of course, knew we were prisoners and unjustly treated under the circumstances.

We had the sympathy of the men.

I think my chief grievance or, rather, the chief grievance of the command against me was that I spoke very frankly and freely to the men and I sympathized with their condition and I felt they were entitled to repatriation and I made that demand in Barcelona and this was why I was a marked man largely. I know of no other reason.

Certainly my military conduct was anything else but discommendable.

Mr. MATTHEWS. What do you know about the fate of Vernon Selby?

Mr. HONEYCOMBE. What I know of Vernon Selby would be simply inferential hearsay evidence. All I know is what Lawrence McCullough told me.

Mr. MATTHEWS. Who was he?

Mr. HONEYCOMBE. An observer on the staff with me.

Mr. MATTHEWS. What did McCullough tell you as to what happened to Vernon Selby?

Mr. HONEYCOMBE. He told me that he had heard from one Reed—Bill Reed, a guard at Barcelona, that Vernon Selby was taken out of his cell at night and executed or, rather, killed. I would say murdered is the proper term, by these sadists while a prisoner under their control in Barcelona.

Mr. MATTHEWS. In what prison?

Mr. HONEYCOMBE. Castle de Fells was the understanding I received.

Mr. MATTHEWS. Castle de Fells. Who was in charge of the prison at Castle de Fells at that time?

Mr. HONEYCOMBE. I don't know, no.

Mr. MATTHEWS. Do you know anything of the fate of Albert Wallach, whose father appeared here this morning?

Mr. HONEYCOMBE. No, I do not know of his fate, but I know of him.

Mr. MATTHEWS. Do you know of other cases where men were executed or as you have termed it, murdered by the men in charge?

Mr. HONEYCOMBE. It would be very difficult because those things were hushed up and generally the men in fear for their own lives and in self-preservation would try to ignore any incidents which might involve them and put them in the same jeopardy.

The CHAIRMAN. I just want to make this statement, that Mrs. Selby is not required to stay here unless she wants to do so. She is not a witness under the committee's jurisdiction any longer. You are excused.

Mr. MATTHEWS. Mrs. Selby says she prefers to stay.

The CHAIRMAN. All right.

Mr. MATTHEWS. Now, how did you get out of Spain from the time that you found yourself in this no man's land between the Fascists' lines and what was left of the retreating Loyalists' forces?

Mr. HONEYCOMBE. As I previously pointed out, upon my arriving in Spain, I was slightly skeptical of the intents and purposes of the surrendering or the compulsion to surrender our passports.

I have learned in my struggles and experiences in life to always be on the safe side and prepare for the unexpected. So I maintained this document.

Mr. MATTHEWS. This is your seaman's passport?

Mr. HONEYCOMBE. That is correct. I used that as a visa and ran the gantlet of the guard and immigration and came out on a train. I ran the blockade.

Mr. MATTHEWS. Was some one else with you?

Mr. HONEYCOMBE. No one; I came alone.

Mr. MATTHEWS. You escaped alone?

Mr. HONEYCOMBE. That is right.

Mr. MATTHEWS. How long did it take you to get from the spot where you were at the time the rout occurred and the French frontier?

Mr. HONEYCOMBE. Five days and nights.

Mr. MATTHEWS. Five days and nights. And when you got to the border you used your seaman's transport?

Mr. HONEYCOMBE. That is correct.

Mr. MATTHEWS. To enter France?

Mr. HONEYCOMBE. That is right. It is stamped where I came out and the date itself all on there by immigration officials.

Mr. MATTHEWS. Yes; the French visa.

Mr. HONEYCOMBE. Spanish visa.

Mr. MATTHEWS. Yes. It is the 8th of April 1938.

Mr. HONEYCOMBE. Yes; that is correct.

Mr. MATTHEWS. Now, what difficulties did you encounter after you reached France, if any, from the Communist Party of France?

Mr. HONEYCOMBE. I found no difficulties until I arrived in Havre.

Mr. MATTHEWS. And what was that difficulty?

Mr. HONEYCOMBE. But other men who followed me out, some 12 or 13 others who needed medical attention, food, and care, why, they were denied by the control committee in Paris after they had sent a delegate, a spokesman for them to the Internationale Brigade office in Paris to representatives of the Lincoln Brigade office, demanding attention and care and transport for the men that came over the hill who were forced out in the big retreat.

Mr. MATTHEWS. Was any attempt made on your life while you were in France after your escape from Spain?

Mr. HONEYCOMBE. There was an attempt to beat me up in Havre but they chose the wrong man. I was coming out of a cafe one night in Havre and I was being accompanied by Hank Bosco, a big Pole, six footer, and we usually went together for self protection as we knew what to expect sometimes in things like this, and some other man was badly beaten up and practically at the point of death, you might say. He was sent to the hospital in France and recovered some 3 months later—a terrific beating.

Mr. MATTHEWS. Were any of your fellow soldiers stranded in France?

Mr. HONEYCOMBE. Many of them were until I released the news of the actual conditions over there and demanded that——

Mr. MATTHEWS. Did you give out a release of this story?

Mr. HONEYCOMBE. I did.

Mr. MATTHEWS. Some parts of it from France?

Mr. HONEYCOMBE. I did when I came over to France.

Mr. MATTHEWS. Were there any efforts made to prevent your returning to the United States aboard ship?

Mr. HONEYCOMBE. There was.

Mr. MATTHEWS. Will you please state the facts with reference to that?

Mr. HONEYCOMBE. The American consul had arranged for my transportation on the steamship *Manhattan* but it happened that the delegate of the steamship *Manhattan*, who was later killed, a Communist Party fraction member, obviously received instructions to call the men off the ship on strike if they attempted to carry me. In other words, I was boycotted.

Mr. MATTHEWS. How did you eventually return to the United States?

Mr. HONEYCOMBE. Through the efforts of the United States consul on a United States Maritime ship. An able-bodied seaman took sick in Havre and I replaced him, being a seaman, and I worked back.

Mr. THOMAS. Mr. Matthews, I think it is advisable to develop more of the actions in regard to the steamship *Manhattan*. I would like to know whether the strike actually took place; whether the officials on the steamship *Manhattan* told Mr. Honeycombe that he could not sail on that ship, and whatever else took place in regard to it.

Mr. MATTHEWS. Mr. Honeycombe, will you give the committee the facts?

Mr. HONEYCOMBE. Yes. sir; I will answer the gentleman. The consul took me over to the first officer but the word obviously got to the first officer from the delegate of the ship that if he carried me he would call the men off in protest, so he told the consul in order to avoid the trouble he would rather not carry me. So then he took me to the commander——

Mr. MATTHEWS. Who was the consul?

Mr. HONEYCOMBE. Mr. Donaldson, vice consul.

Mr. THOMAS. Do you recall the name of the first officer of the ship?

Mr. HONEYCOMBE. I can't do that.

Mr. THOMAS. You are sure he was the first officer?

Mr. HONEYCOMBE. I am positive of that, first mate. And the captain, of course. flatly refused when he heard the story.

Mr. MATTHEWS. Refused to carry you?

Mr. HONEYCOMBE. That is correct.

Mr. MATTHEWS. The captain of the *Manhattan?*

Mr. HONEYCOMBE. That is right.

Mr. MATTHEWS. Are there any questions, Mr. Chairman?

The CHAIRMAN. Well, I want to ask, Do you have any information that the Communist Party is now seeking to recruit for service in Mexico?

Mr. HONEYCOMBE. Well, I was down in Mexico some 4 weeks ago. I know there was a great deal of activity, but what they are doing now on that point I am not qualified to say.

The CHAIRMAN. Did you observe activity in Mexico while you were there?

Mr. HONEYCOMBE. I did.

The CHAIRMAN. With reference to the matter of preparing for revolution?

Mr. HONEYCOMBE. Well, what little Spanish I speak I know there is something going in Mexico. That is obvious. I was in Chihuahua 3 weeks ago.

The CHAIRMAN. Did you see any Communist activity there?

Mr. HONEYCOMBE. It would be very difficult for me to say whether I did because all I could go by was what I read in the papers and the little snatches of conversation I heard here and there between the various union people I happened to meet.

The CHAIRMAN. Did you see any American Communists there?

Mr. HONEYCOMBE. No; I did not.

The CHAIRMAN. I want to get this general idea. How long were you active in the Communist Party of California?

Mr. HONEYCOMBE. Four years.

The CHAIRMAN. About what was the membership in California of the Communist Party during the time you were a member?

Mr. HONEYCOMBE. I think our peak membership was 5,600. That was in 1936.

The CHAIRMAN. Did you keep records of the membership then?

Mr. HONEYCOMBE. They have the complete records. Every section organizer or its secretary has complete records of all party members.

The CHAIRMAN. And all dues paid?

Mr. HONEYCOMBE. That is right.

The CHAIRMAN. Were you fairly well acquainted with many Communists in California?

Mr. HONEYCOMBE. Oh, yes; know practically all of them.

The CHAIRMAN. Were they active in various organizations, unions, and other organizations?

Mr. HONEYCOMBE. That is the roll of the Communist Party, to be active, to get control of all these organizations.

The CHAIRMAN. You know of your own knowledge that many Communists had strategic positions in other organizations in California?

Mr. HONEYCOMBE. I do.

The CHAIRMAN. We will take that up later and develop that.

Mr. LYNCH. Mr. Honeycombe, approximately how many Americans were there in Spain engaged in military activities?

Mr. HONEYCOMBE. I can merely base my judgment on that on the amount of men killed or wounded or missing in action and the amount of replacements at each action.

Mr. LYNCH. How many would you estimate as the full number of Americans who were there for military service?

Mr. HONEYCOMBE. I would estimate anywhere from five to six thousand as a minimum in all forms of service. I don't mean front line, but auxiliary, and so on.

Mr. LYNCH. How many would you estimate actually served in the fighting lines?

Mr. HONEYCOMBE. Well, the actual brigade strength was only 2,500.

Mr. LYNCH. How many would you estimate were either lost or killed or murdered?

Mr. HONEYCOMBE. Well, my best estimation would be based upon the various actions I was involved in. I think at Quinto the report was 364 killed and wounded and missing. That was prior to my first arrival in the lines. I went in the lines following the Quinto action. At Fuentes De Ebro I understand they lost approximately 240. At the Teruel action, from frost bite, cold, sickness, and so on, sporadic sniping, I imagine our losses were the least there of any place to my knowledge, I would estimate that about 105 wounded, sick, dead, and injured, and so no.

At Séguro the action was our greatest—I think—no; I believe not Séguro. I don't believe our casualties ran much over 140, if that much, or 150, approximately. That was a dawn attack at Séguro. We had a fortified hill to take. And let me see, at Belchite, this is where we had our terrific losses. The actual count of the men left in the battalion, the Lincoln Battalion, to my knowledge, on the morning we assembled, was about 65 men out of 550.

Mr. LYNCH. In other words——

Mr. HONEYCOMBE. That gives you an estimate.

Mr. LYNCH. You lost almost 500 there?

Mr. HONEYCOMBE. Dead, wounded, missing, or wounded.

Mr. LYNCH. That amounted to about 1,350 during the entire period—just that period, either lost, killed, or otherwise?

Mr. HONEYCOMBE. Wounded, missing, or otherwise. It is pretty difficult to determine.

The CHAIRMAN. Mr. Hurley desires to ask a few questions.

Mr. HURLEY. Going back a little bit, Mr. Honeycombe, the volunteers who traveled to France with you, were they members of the Communist Party?

Mr. HONEYCOMBE. All but three, six out of the nine.

Mr. HURLEY. Do you know whether or not the recruiting of those comrades was part of a pattern here in the United States and was not centered in any one particular city or any one——

Mr. HONEYCOMBE. Do you mean was that the general rule?

Mr. HURLEY. Yes.

Mr. HONEYCOMBE. Yes; that was throughout the country.

Mr. HURLEY. Do you know whether or not they followed the same procedure you did, that is with regard to securing passports?

Mr. HONEYCOMBE. Yes.

Mr. HURLEY. And also the medical examination?

Mr. HONEYCOMBE. Same thing.

Mr. HURLEY. And after you arrived in Spain were you given a pep talk by anybody? I am not speaking of Browder now.

Mr. HONEYCOMBE. Yes; by Bill Lawrence.

Mr. HURLEY. And who is Bill Lawrence?

Mr. HONEYCOMBE. He was the commisar in charge of the base at Albacete.

Mr. HURLEY. Were you also spoken to by Gates?

Mr. HONEYCOMBE. Yes.

Mr. HURLEY. And who is he?

Mr. HONEYCOMBE. He was the commisar for the brigade at the last.

Mr. HURLEY. John Gates?

Mr. HONEYCOMBE. John Gates.

Mr. HURLEY. And with regard to these pep meetings that were held, were you required at the termination to sing the Communist song?

Mr. HONEYCOMBE. International.

Mr. HURLEY. As I understand it the training conducted in Spain was in large part conducted under the auspices of officers of the Red Army, is that correct?

Mr. HONEYCOMBE. That is correct.

Mr. HURLEY. After you returned to the United States you became aware of the fact that in the United States during the time that you were over there that there was an extensive campaign for the raising of money?

Mr. HONEYCOMBE. That is right.

Mr. HURLEY. To support the Spanish Loyalist cause?

Mr. HONEYCOMBE. That is correct.

Mr. HURLEY. Can you recite from your own personal experience what proportion of that money you comrades in Spain received?

Mr. HONEYCOMBE. I would estimate not over 20 percent and probably much less.

Mr. HURLEY. Twenty percent or less?

Mr. HONEYCOMBE. That is right.

Mr. HURLEY. And in your judgment where did the rest of that money go?

Mr. HONEYCOMBE. Propaganda and the building up of the party apparatus here and paying off the racketeering functionaries.

Mr. HURLEY. Then it is your judgment the Communist Party in the United States utilized this cause as a lucrative racket for the perpetration of their own policies in the United States?

Mr. HONEYCOMBE. That is right, propaganda I think and spreading it and recruiting.

Mr. HURLEY. From your long experience in the Communist Party would you state that the Communist Party is the vanguard of the working class or just a political clique playing upon international emotions.

Mr. HONEYCOMBE. Well, I have a new phrase for them. I would call them "political Capones," and a thousand times more vicious, parading under the guise of an ideal and appealing to the highest social and moral feelings of men to prostitute it for their own selfish ends. That is exactly my opinion of them. Where at least a gunman will stick you up and he has an avowed purpose and intention and that is to rob you without any high sounding phrases of idealism and sophistries.

Mr. HURLEY. That is all, Mr. Chairman.

The CHAIRMAN. You will remain under subpena until we can hear you further in regard to California and the west coast.

Mr. HONEYCOMBE. Yes, sir.

The CHAIRMAN. Who is your next witness?

Mr. MATTHEWS. The next witness is Fred Keller.

The CHAIRMAN. Come around, Mr. Keller. Raise your right hand. Do you solemnly swear to tell the truth, the whole truth, and nothing but the truth, so help you God?

TESTIMONY OF FRED KELLER, COMMISSAR, ABRAHAM LINCOLN BATTALION

Mr. KELLER. I do.

The CHAIRMAN. Have a seat, Mr. Keller. You are represented here by your attorney, Mr. Schwab? Do I have your name correctly?

Mr. SCHWAB. Schwab; Irving Schwab, 551 Fifth Avenue, New York City.

The CHAIRMAN. You are a regularly licensed practicing attorney?

Mr. SCHWAB. Duly admitted to practice law in the courts of the State of New York and the Federal courts there.

The CHAIRMAN. All right, proceed.

Mr. MATTHEWS. Will you please give your name for the record?

Mr. KELLER. Fred Keller.

Mr. MATTHEWS. Where were you born?

Mr. KELLER. New York City.

Mr. MATTHEWS. When?

Mr. KELLER. June 4, 1914.

Mr. MATTHEWS. Are you a member of the Communist Party?

Mr. KELLER. I was never a member of the Communist Party, and I am not now.

Mr. MATTHEWS. Have you ever used any other name than that of Fred Keller?

Mr. KELLER. I never have.

Mr. MATTHEWS. Have you ever been a member of the Young Communist League?

Mr. KELLER. I was never a member of the Young Communist League.

Mr. MATTHEWS. What was your employment before you went to Spain?

Mr. KELLER. I was an organizer for a union.

Mr. MATTHEWS. What union?

Mr. KELLER. Building Service Employees International Union, Local 32-B.

Mr. MATTHEWS. Affiliated with——

The CHAIRMAN. Will you speak a little louder?

Mr. KELLER. American Federation of Labor.

The CHAIRMAN. You were an organizer for what union?

Mr. KELLER. Building Service Employees International Union, Local 32-B. It is in New York City and affiliated with the American Federation of Labor.

The CHAIRMAN. All right.

Mr. MATTHEWS. What other positions did you hold before you went to Spain?

Mr. KELLER. I can't say that I—in what respects?

Mr. MATTHEWS. Was that the only job you ever had?

Mr. KELLER. No, it isn't.

Mr. MATTHEWS. What other?

Mr. KELLER. I worked at a great many things before that.

Mr. MATTHEWS. What was your trade or profession?

Mr. KELLER. At present I am a longshoreman.

Mr. MATTHEWS. And what other jobs have you held, that is prior to your going to Spain?

Mr. KELLER. Well, I worked in the trade of the union in which I got to be an organizer.

Mr. MATTHEWS. How long did you hold that position as union organizer?

Mr. KELLER. I would say approximately 6 months.

Mr. MATTHEWS. Was that immediately prior to your sailing to Spain?

Mr. KELLER. It was.

Mr. MATTHEWS. What positions did you hold——

The CHAIRMAN. Just one second, Mr. Matthews. I want to make an announcement that the committee is sitting as a quorum; present are Mr. Dempsey of New Mexico, Mr. Voorhis of California, Mr. Mason of Illinois; and the chairman. Proceed.

Mr. MATTHEWS. Now, what positions did you hold in Spain?

Mr. KELLER. I was a sergeant in a machine-gun company. I was a lieutenant in a machine-gun company. I was commissar of war of the Lincoln Battalion.

Mr. MATTHEWS. Commissar of what?

Mr. KELLER. Commissar of war.

Mr. MATTHEWS. You were commissar of war?

Mr. KELLER. Yes.

Mr. MATTHEWS. For the Lincoln Battalion?

Mr. KELLER. Yes.

Mr. MATTHEWS. When did you go to Spain?

Mr. KELLER. I left New York on June 5, 1937.

Mr. MATTHEWS. Did you travel on an American passport?

Mr. KELLER. I did.

Mr. MATTHEWS. Issued in your own name?

Mr. KELLER. I did.

Mr. MATTHEWS. Was it stamped "not valid for travel in Spain"?

Mr. KELLER. I don't believe it was. I never noticed it.

Mr. MATTHEWS. In your application for this passport did you state that you intended to go to Spain?

Mr. KELLER. No; I didn't. I said I was traveling in Europe.

Mr. MATTHEWS. What was the exact spelling of the name under which you got your passport?

Mr. KELLER. K-e-l-l-e-r.

Mr. MATTHEWS. And your first name?

Mr. KELLER. Fred, F-r-e-d.

Mr. MATTHEWS. And any initial?

Mr. KELLER. P.

Mr. MATTHEWS. Fred?

Mr. KELLER. Paul.

Mr. MATTHEWS. Fred P., or Fred Paul?

Mr. KELLER. Well, I couldn't be positive, but my middle name is Paul and I used my exact name.

Mr. MATTHEWS. Where was it issued?

Mr. KELLER. New York City.

Mr. MATTHEWS. What were the duties of the commissar of war for the Lincoln Battalion, which position you say you held?

Mr. KELLER. I will have to explain a little of the situation in Spain.

Mr. SCHWAB. Don't answer a question unless he gives you an opportunity to state all the facts.

Mr. LYNCH. Just a minute. I submit counsel is not controlling the committee as to what the witness should answer or not answer.

Mr. SCHWAB. I am advising my client.

The CHAIRMAN. Do you want to confer with your client?

Mr. SCHWAB. I merely told him he should not answer the questions fully.

The CHAIRMAN. Well, proceed. What was the question?

Mr. MATTHEWS. The question was, What were the duties of the commisar of war, which position Mr. Keller has stated he held in Spain, as a commisar of war in the Lincoln Battalion.

Mr. KELLER. The popular-front government of Spain was a government composed of some 30 political parties. There was a rule at the beginning of the war that no officer was permitted to be a member of any political party. He had to resign his rank in any political party, if he held one before he took any position. In order that the orders of the government was carried out the duties as set down by the popular-front government, the office of commissar, commissar of war—in Spanish, the commissar de guerra, and we can say it literally translated is commissar of war—was established.

The commissar of war had to do with coordinating the services of a battalion, see that a battalion was fed, ammunition arrived on time, and that the fronts were generally coordinated.

It is a lengthy subject and I could speak at it to some great length.

The CHAIRMAN. I would like to know in connection with this, was that a position or an office simply in this particular brigade?

Mr. KELLER. No. That was throughout the entire Spanish Republican Army. This office existed in all units from sections up.

The CHAIRMAN. All right.

Mr. MATTHEWS. Had you had any previous military experience before going to Spain?

Mr. KELLER. I never had any military experience in my life.

Mr. MATTHEWS. Will you proceed to outline the duties of the commissar of war? You said to coordinate the activities, to see that food arrived and so forth, and what else?

Mr. KELLER. To explain to the troops the latest developments that the government was doing, the activities of the government. You have to understand that Spain was a government that was formed after the Fascist government or Franco government deserted and it was a very fast, swift-moving scene, and my job was to tell the troops the position of the government. It was a democratic army in which men, in which men expressed themselves to the government and the men had a right to express themselves back through my particular office and I in turn relayed that to my superior and he could relay it up to the government. In this way the great democracy of Spain functioned.

The CHAIRMAN. A political office as well as a military office?

Mr. KELLER. Yes. It was military in a sense.

The CHAIRMAN. I mean you had both duties, both military duties and political duties?

Mr. KELLER. No; I didn't have any directly military duties.

Mr. MATTHEWS. Only political duties?

Mr. KELLER. Yes, sir. My office was supposed to be one in which— it was an honor to arrive at such an office.

Mr. VOORHIS. How were you selected for that office, Mr. Keller?

Mr. KELLER. I was elected by the troops.

The CHAIRMAN. What body of troops, a company or what?

Mr. KELLER. Whatever you represented.

The CHAIRMAN. What did you represent?

Mr. KELLER. In the end I represented the Lincoln Battalion. Therefore, I was elected——

The CHAIRMAN. You first started out as a commissar for a smaller unit?

Mr. KELLER. No. I was sergeant at first of a machine-gun company.

The CHAIRMAN. When you became commissar you were commissar of the entire——

Mr. KELLER. Battalion.

Mr. MATTHEWS. Were a majority of the members of the Lincoln Battalion members of the Communist Party?

Mr. KELLER. That is not true.

Mr. MATTHEWS. You know that Mr. Browder has published in his book that 60 percent of the members of the Lincoln Battalion were members of the Communist Party, don't you?

Mr. KELLER. I don't know that.

Mr. MATTHEWS. And that he also testified before this committee that 60 percent of them were members of the Communist Party?

Mr. KELLER. Can't be responsible for what Mr. Browder says.

Mr. MATTHEWS. At any rate you deny that as being a fact; is that your testimony?

Mr. KELLER. It is difficult to say what the percentage were of the battalion at different times, but to give you an impression that the Lincoln Battalion was entirely communistic——

The CHAIRMAN. He asked you if a majority of them were Communists. That was the question.

Mr. KELLER. No; I don't believe, to the best of my knowledge at any one time, and you have to remember that the number in our battalion changed over the 9 months in which I was in office, and at different times the percentage was probably different, but 60 percent to me, if I may express an opinion, seems to me not correct.

Mr. MATTHEWS. You would say Mr. Browder was wrong, in other words?

Mr. KELLER. I don't know. I am not responsible.

Mr. MATTHEWS. Are you willing to state that that is a wrong statement?

Mr. KELLER. I don't know if Mr. Browder said it.

Mr. MATTHEWS. Never mind whether he said it or not.

Mr. SCHWAB. May the record note the difference in treatment here of this witness and the previous witness.

Mr. MATTHEWS. Will the witness answer the question.

The CHAIRMAN. Put it this way: Is the statement that 60 percent of those were Communists? Is that a correct statement regardless of who made it?

Mr. KELLER. Let me say this, Mr. Dies, that I can never say what percentage there were at any one time—nobody was ever asked for their political affiliations and they were not forced to say and so I can't say any particular number existed.

Mr. MASON. Would you say if you did express an opinion as to the proportion of Communists or non-Communists in the Lincoln Brigade, it would be just your opinion and an estimate because no definite check had been made, is that the idea?

Mr. KELLER. That is to the best of my knowledge.

Mr. DEMPSEY. Mr. Keller, you did say positively that a majority of the brigade were not Communists?

Mr. KELLER. I was anxious——

Mr. DEMPSEY. That is your unqualified statement. If that is true then a majority—certainly 60 percent could not have been.

Mr. KELLER. I was just anxious that I would not be asked to make—make any—ask to make any particular figure or compare my figures with anybody else.

Mr. DEMPSEY. When you stated the majority were not Communists were you stating your knowledge?

Mr. KELLER. Yes, sir; to the best of my knowledge the majority of the Lincoln Battalion was never communistic.

The CHAIRMAN. Now, we have a subcommittee, designated by the chairman as being composed of Mr. Dempsey, Mr. Mason, and the chairman until further announcement, and we are now proceeding as a subcommittee. Proceed.

Mr. MATTHEWS. Now, Mr. Keller, in Spain did you meet Robert Minor?

Mr. KELLER. Yes; on one occasion in Barcelona I met him.

Mr. MATTHEWS. What was the occasion of your meeting Robert Minor in Barcelona?

Mr. KELLER. It was in a restaurant or hotel lobby after dinner or something of that sort.

Mr. MATTHEWS. What did you confer with him about?

Mr. KELLER. Well, I don't exactly remember what it was. It wasn't anything of tremendous significance. He wasn't there very long, you know.

Mr. MATTHEWS. How long was Robert Minor in Spain?

Mr. KELLER. I could not say.

Mr. MATTHEWS. You said he wasn't there very long.

Mr. KELLER. Well, to the best of my knowledge, I don't believe he was there very long.

Mr. MATTHEWS. You know Robert Minor to be an outstanding member of the Communist Party of the United States, do you not?

Mr. KELLER. I have heard that.

Mr. MATTHEWS. Do you know it only from hearsay?

Mr. KELLER. What else can I base it on?

Mr. MATTHEWS. Did you know a man in the Lincoln Battalion whose first name was Ivan or Evon—I-v-a-n or E-v-o-n?

Mr. KELLER. Doesn't sound very familiar.

Mr. MATTHEWS. I-v-a-n. Did you have any relations whatever with a man who was familiarly known in the battalion as Ivan and known only by his first name as a rule?

Mr. KELLER. Evon.

Mr. MATTHEWS. Yes; E-v-o-n—I-v-a-n.

Mr. KELLER. Was that Evan—not Evan.

Mr. MATTHEWS. No; I-v-a-n.

Mr. KELLER. I can't speak for that.

Mr. MATTHEWS. You don't know any such man who worked in the——

Mr. KELLER. Over a year in the front, and meeting a great many people I cannot say positively I identify that name.

Mr. MATTHEWS. Did you know a man in the American contingent of the Loyalist Army by the name of Paul White?

Mr. KELLER. I did.

Mr. MATTHEWS. Did you know Paul White in the United States before you knew him in Spain?

Mr. KELLER. I may. He went over on the same ship that I did; that is correct.

Mr. MATTHEWS. Did you know him before you sailed together?

Mr. KELLER. No; I don't believe I did.

Mr. MATTHEWS. Under what name did you know Paul White?

Mr. KELLER. Never knew him under any other name.

Mr. MATTHEWS. You never knew Paul White under the name of John Adams?

Mr. KELLER. This is not particularly familiar to me.

The CHAIRMAN. Did you know a Johnnie Adams?

Mr. KELLER. No; I can't say that I did.

Mr. MATTHEWS. You know now, do you not, that Paul White's real name was John Quincy Adams, don't you?

Mr. KELLER. I do not.

Mr. MATTHEWS. And that he was a direct descendant of John Quincy Adams, a President of the United States?

Mr. KELLER. I do not. This is the first time I ever heard of that.

Mr. MATTHEWS. What happened to Paul White in Spain?

Mr. KELLER. I don't know. I understand he was missing in action.

Mr. MATTHEWS. Did you ever hear anything else about Paul White's state other than he was missing in action?

Mr. KELLER. No. At the time that I believed I would return to America—when I left Spain he was still O. K. I had seen him myself.

Mr. MATTHEWS. Did you see him in Spain?

Mr. KELLER. Yes.

Mr. MATTHEWS. Where did you last see him in Spain?

Mr. KELLER. I believe it was around the great retreat at Ebro, which occurred approximately in March of 1938.

Mr. MATTHEWS. And the only report you ever heard about his fate was that he was missing in action; is that correct?

Mr. KELLER. Yes. I don't know any other.

Mr. MATTHEWS. Did you know George Mink in Spain?

Mr. KELLER. Never heard that name before.

Mr. MATTHEWS. You have never heard the name of George Mink?

Mr. KELLER. To the best of my knowledge—I know a great many people's names, but I don't—I am not familiar with that.

Mr. MATTHEWS. Perhaps you knew him by the name of George Hirsch in Spain. Did you know George Hirsch in Spain?

Mr. KELLER. Doesn't sound immediately familiar to me.

Mr. MATTHEWS. Did you know Morris Pasternak in Spain?

Mr. KELLER. No; I didn't.

Mr. MATTHEWS. Do you know the name?

Mr. KELLER. I have heard the name since I returned.

Mr. MATTHEWS. In what connection did you hear his name?

Mr. KELLER. I know his mother. I have met her since I come back, and I understand that he was missing in action sometime before I arrived in Spain.

Mr. MATTHEWS. Is he still missing as far as you know?

Mr. KELLER. To the best of my knowledge that is so.

Mr. MATTHEWS. Did you know Sid Levine?

Mr. KELLER. Yes; I know that name.

Mr. MATTHEWS. Did you know him in Spain?

Mr. KELLER. I did.

Mr. MATTHEWS. In what connection did you know him in Spain?

Mr. KELLER. When I first arrived at the machine-gun company as a private, he was a lieutenant in charge of the same company.

Mr. MATTHEWS. Where is Sid Levine now?

Mr. KELLER. Well, I believe he is—well, I am not positive, but I believe he is in America.

Mr. MATTHEWS. Did you know him in any other connection in Spain than the one you just described?

Mr. KELLER. No; not to the best of my knowledge.

Mr. MATTHEWS. Did you know Phil Bard?

Mr. KELLER. I know him now. I did not know him in Spain or——

Mr. MATTHEWS. You had no contact with him in Spain?

Mr. KELLER. No.

Mr. MATTHEWS. None whatsoever?

Mr. KELLER. None whatsoever.

Mr. MATTHEWS. How many New York boys enlisted in the Abraham Lincoln Battalion, or the Fifteenth Division, Loyalist Army?

Mr. SCHWAB. May I consult my client just a moment.

Mr. KELLER. I must say in fairness that when volunteers came to Spain they came from all over the world. They came by every particular means—from Mexico, from South America, Americans who lived in Europe. There is no way of knowing, except by hearsay, and it is impossible to put a number of how many people came from New York City.

The CHAIRMAN. As long as you don't know, you can say you don't know.

Mr. KELLER. Yes, sir.

Mr. MATTHEWS. Was there any Abraham Lincoln Brigade in Spain?

Mr. KELLER. Positively.

Mr. MATTHEWS. There was?

Mr. KELLER. There was, positively.

Mr. MATTHEWS. A unit of the Loyalist Army known in Spain as the Abraham Lincoln Brigade?

Mr. KELLER. That is correct, and so identified, and it has been written about extensively.

Mr. MATTHEWS. Identified where?

Mr. KELLER. In the newspapers of Spain and the newspapers of America. I could say it is universally known. It is known all over the world by that name.

Mr. MATTHEWS. Well, I am not asking you how it was known all over the world. I am asking you if there was an Abraham Lincoln Brigade in Spain itself?

Mr. KELLER. (No answer.)

The CHAIRMAN. Is that the official title of the brigade?

Mr. KELLER. Official title.

The CHAIRMAN. Known in Spain as the Abraham Lincoln Brigade?

Mr. KELLER. The Premier of Spain addressed our battalion. He referred to us as the men of the Abraham Lincoln Brigade.

Mr. MATTHEWS. Did you know a man in Spain named Hikiss?

Mr. KELLER. Never heard that name before, to the best of my knowledge.

Mr. MATTHEWS. Were you ever discharged as the commissar of war?

Mr. KELLER. No.

Mr. MATTHEWS. How long did you retain that position?

Mr. KELLER. When I was discharged from the Army I was given an honorable discharge.

Mr. MATTHEWS. Did you retain that position as long as you were in Spain?

Mr. KELLER. I was wounded. I went to the hospital at that time. I still retained the title, but I didn't function in the office.

Mr. MATTHEWS. In other words, you mean to say that you never received a formal discharge from the office of commissar of war, as you describe it?

Mr. KELLER. I was given an honorable discharge by the Army when I left, that is all.

Mr. MATTHEWS. That is when you left the Army?

Mr. KELLER. When I left for—when I left Spain.

Mr. MATTHEWS. Then you never encountered any charges of any kind with respect to your carrying out of your functions as commissar of war?

Mr. KELLER. No; I think not. Even these——

Mr. MATTHEWS. Well, is that true or not?

Mr. SCHWAB. Let him answer the question.

Mr. MATTHEWS. I am asking for an answer.

Mr. KELLER. It is positively not true and I resent the question. My record in Spain was good.

Mr. MATTHEWS. Did you ever encourage your men to pillage houses in the occupied villages of Spain?

Mr. KELLER. That is not true.

Mr. MATTHEWS. Well, the answer is no; is it?

Mr. KELLER. The answer is no.

Mr. SCHWAB. Did anybody——

Mr. KELLER. Nobody did that. We had respect for the peasants and we done this thing, we preserved the sparse materials that the Government had.

Mr. MATTHEWS. Were you ever charged with lack of discipline?

Mr. KELLER. No; I never was.

Mr. MATTHEWS. Were you ever charged with encouraging drunkenness in your battalion?

Mr. KELLER. Your honor—your honor, I am sorry. If I can speak with a little bit of earnestness I resent these questions.

The CHAIRMAN. You won't have to answer——

Mr. KELLER. The answer is no.

Mr. MATTHEWS. Mr. Chairman, the witnesses here testified to incontrovertible facts and I am asking the witness for his——

Mr. Schwab. Do you call those "incontrovertible facts"?

The Chairman. You want to have an opportunity to deny any charges made against you, do you not?

Mr. Schwab. Mr. Chairman, I say this——

The Chairman. You want to have an opportunity to deny any charges made against you by other witnesses?

Mr. Schwab. Mr. Chairman, in amplifying that suggestion, not only would we like the opportunity of denying them, we would like the opportunity similar to the witnesses who have testified before, to explain these things, even though——

The Chairman. Well, he is explaining them. There has been no opportunity denied him. He has not been denied that.

Mr. Keller. As emphatically as I can I deny this as positively as I can deny this. I want the record that way. My record with the Army was good, and I was complimented for it when I left, and I am still proud of it.

Mr. Mason. There is nothing more emphatic in the English language than "no."

Mr. Keller. I agree with you.

Mr. Matthews. After your return from Spain, Mr. Keller, did you make a tour of the United States, a speaking tour?

Mr. Keller. Yes, sir; I did.

Mr. Matthews. In that speaking tour of the United States did you publicly take up the question of charges which had been made against you by certain persons who had been in Spain at the same time you were?

Mr. Keller. I don't understand the question.

Mr. Matthews. Well, you made speeches over the United States on a tour?

Mr. Keller. Yes.

Mr. Matthews. In those speeches did you answer or make reply to——

Mr. Keller. I spoke for Spain.

Mr. Matthews. Charges which had been made against you personally by persons who had known you in Spain?

Mr. Keller. I couldn't be so egotistical. I couldn't be so egotistical. I didn't do that.

The Chairman. Gentlemen, it is about——

Mr. Matthews. I want to ask the witness one more question. Have you ever been arrested in the United States, Mr. Keller?

Mr. Keller. I was arrested about 2 weeks ago when I attempted to picket the French consul in behalf of the Spanish refugees who were being repatriated to Franco, Spain, where it means certain death for them.

Mr. Matthews. Under what auspices were you demonstrating?

Mr. Schwab. He hasn't finished answering.

Mr. Keller. It was disorderly conduct charge that I was arrested under—arrested for, this attempted picket line at the French consul.

Mr. Matthews. Are you through?

Mr. Keller. I am.

Mr. Matthews. Under what auspices was this picket line in front of the French consulate?

Mr. Keller. Fifty-seven organizations in New York City that I represented—57 organizations in New York City got together and formed an organization of organizations.

Mr. MATTHEWS. What is the name of the association?

Mr. KELLER. Emergency Committee to Save the Spanish Refugees, and it was under their auspices the picket line was held.

Mr. MATTHEWS. Emergency Committee to Save the Spanish Refugees? Is that the exact title of the organization?

Mr. KELLER. Maybe a small deviation, but that is in essence.

Mr. VOORHIS. Did that organization authorize the picketing?

Mr. KELLER. They did. They publicized it in the newspapers beforehand.

Mr. VOORHIS. The whole organizations authorized it?

Mr. KELLER. It was a meeting at which 57 organizations were represented that this picket line was voted—that it was voted to take this action of attempting to picket the French consul.

Mr. MATTHEWS. Who is the head of this organization?

Mr. KELLER. Well, I can't be sure at the present moment. I didn't attend the meeting at which this went through and I can't say. It is a new organization.

Mr. MATTHEWS. Would the exact name of the organization be The Spanish Refugee Relief Campaign?

Mr. KELLER. No.

Mr. MATTHEWS. Is it a new organization which has been recently formed?

Mr. KELLER. Well, it is an association of all the organizations.

Mr. MATTHEWS. Is it a new organization which has recently been formed?

Mr. KELLER. Well, it is hardly an organization. It is an association of all the organizations that aided and supported Spain. By that I mean the democracy of Spain.

Mr. MATTHEWS. Has the association been recently brought about?

Mr. KELLER. Yes. That association was brought about I would say last month.

Mr. MATTHEWS. As a result in the split of the Spanish Refugee Relief Campaign?

Mr. KELLER. Well, I want to give exact answers and I don't know all the facts there. I am not very active in that and I would rather not——

Mr. MATTHEWS. Well, you know that there was some difficulty inside the organization known as the Spanish Refugee Relief Campaign, don't you?

Mr. KELLER. Yes; I know there was some disaffection among the people who worked there. Many of them seemed to be most interested in protecting the French Government from any embarassment and we who were in Spain and supported Spain and who know the Spanish people—we have many friends who have been sent back to Franco of Spain and have been shot there. We who felt the most bitter about this thing decided on this organization. I can't speak for the others.

Mr. MATTHEWS. What has been the disposition of the case under which you were arrested?

Mr. KELLER. Still in court.

Mr. MATTHEWS. Have you ever been arrested——

Mr. KELLER. I was never arrested in my life up until this occasion.

Mr. MATTHEWS. That completes my examination.

The CHAIRMAN. Gentlemen. we have to conclude with these witnesses this afternoon.

Mr. SCHWAB. I understood this witness was going to be given a full opportunity to answer these previous witnesses.

The CHAIRMAN. Do you want to?

The WITNESS. I would like that opportunity.

The CHAIRMAN. Then suppose we meet back here at 2 o'clock.

Mr. SCHWAB. Mr. Chairman, do you know whether we will be able to get through with these four witnesses today?

The CHAIRMAN. I think we can. We will make every effort to do so.

The committee will recess until 2 o'clock p. m.

(Whereupon at 12:25 p. m., a recess was taken until 2 p. m., the same day.)

AFTER RECESS

The CHAIRMAN. The committee will come to order.

The Chairman designates a subcommittee composed of the chairman. the gentleman from Illinois. Mr. Mason, and Mr. Voorhis from California.

You may call your witness. Mr. Matthews.

Mr. MATTHEWS. Mr. Keller.

The CHAIRMAN. Come around, Mr. Keller.

TESTIMONY OF FRED KELLER—Resumed

Mr. KELLER. My counsel has not arrived yet.

The CHAIRMAN. We will wait a few moments. You may proceed now. Mr. Matthews.

Mr. MATTHEWS. Mr. Keller, when you were arrested in New York recently, in connection with the picketing of the French consulate, were you taken before a magistrate?

Mr. KELLER. Yes; I was.

Mr. MATTHEWS. Did you testify before the magistrate that you used another name than that of Fred Keller at any time?

Mr. KELLER. I did.

Mr. MATTHEWS. In any connection?

Mr. KELLER. I did.

Mr. MATTHEWS. Then your testimony here this morning was false, was it. when you said that you had never used another name?

Mr. KELLER. No; that is not correct. I told them that I was a member of a union and in that union the book I carried did not have Fred Keller on the book.

Mr. MATTHEWS. What name does that union book have on it?

Mr. KELLER. Do I have to answer that?

Mr. SCHWAB. No.

Mr. MATTHEWS. What name does that book have on it?

Mr. KELLER. Unless the chairman insists I would rather not give that because that is how I make my living and I am not anxious to have that name used. I assure the committee it is of no cousequence.

The CHAIRMAN. Well, as I understand it, this morning you were asked the question if you had ever used any other name except Fred Keller?

Mr. KELLER. Yes.

The CHAIRMAN. And you said you had not. Now, as I understand your testimony you used another name in some union.

Mr. KELLER. Yes; I did.

The CHAIRMAN. The union that you are affiliated with?

Mr. KELLER. Yes, sir.

The CHAIRMAN. Well, what was the purpose of using the other name?

Mr. KELLER. It was just impossible for me to get a book in my own name. I needed work.

The CHAIRMAN. Why was it impossible?

Mr. SCHWAB. Do you want to answer the question?

Mr. KELLER. Well, it was not possible for me to use my own name in that union. I work as a longshoreman. A friend of mine offered to get me a book there and he proceeded—and he provided me with a book to work with.

The CHAIRMAN. You mean that the union would not have permitted you to join under your true name; is that correct?

Mr. KELLER. It would have cost me a lot of—more money—I couldn't afford it at the time.

The CHAIRMAN. Why would it cost you more money?

Mr. KELLER. Initiation fees and things of that type.

The CHAIRMAN. Well, you had that anyway when you joined under any name, didn't you?

Mr. KELLER. No. My friend gave me this book that I used.

The CHAIRMAN. It wasn't a real book?

Mr. KELLER. Yes, it was a genuine book.

The CHAIRMAN. It was a book of someone else and they let you use it?

Mr. KELLER. Yes, sir; that is correct.

The CHAIRMAN. In order to work?

Mr. KELLER. Yes, sir.

The CHAIRMAN. So you could avoid having to pay initiation fees and dues?

Mr. KELLER. Yes, sir.

Mr. LYNCH. In effect it was a fraud being perpetrated on the union, Mr. Keller?

Mr. KELLER. No; I wasn't—I didn't use another name.

Mr. SCHWAB. What has all this got to do, Mr. Chairman——

The CHAIRMAN. Now, be courteous. Nobody is excited here.

Mr. SCHWAB. I object to this whole line of testimony. It has nothing to do with the purposes of this committee.

Mr. MASON. It seems to me if the witness has testified under oath here to something that was not true, and the testimony that he gave before a magistrate contradicts the testimony that he gave today that in itself, it seems to me, is pertinent and is of interest to this committee and we should know those facts.

Mr. SCHWAB. He has already answered those questions, Mr. Mason. I object to going into this matter any further.

The CHAIRMAN. Now, what is your question? You are asking him to tell the name——

Mr. MATTHEWS. I want to know——

The CHAIRMAN. Under which he went into the union?

Mr. LYNCH. That is right.

Mr. MATTHEWS. I want to know now if he is employed at this time or has been employed recently under another name, quite apart from his union book. Is he using another name with his employer than the name of Fred Keller.

The CHAIRMAN. All right, you can ask him that question.

Mr. MATTHEWS. Under what name are you employed?

Mr. KELLER. I am not employed at the present time.

Mr. MATTHEWS. Have you been employed recently?

(No answer.)

Mr. MATTHEWS. When was your last employment?

Mr. KELLER. Approximately a month ago.

Mr. MATTHEWS. And under what name were you employed a month ago?

Mr. KELLER. I told you that I used another book in the industry in which I work.

Mr. MATTHEWS. I am not concerned about the union book but under what name did your employer have you listed?

Mr. KELLER. I used the same one as the one on the book.

Mr. MATTHEWS. What name was that?

The CHAIRMAN. Wait just a minute. Have you ever used any other name except the one name that you are talking about that was in the union book?

Mr. KELLER. That is correct, I never did.

The CHAIRMAN. That is the only name you ever used?

Mr. KELLER. Yes, sir.

The CHAIRMAN. You deny that you are a member of the Communist Party?

Mr. KELLER. I am not a member of the Communist Party.

The CHAIRMAN. You have never been a member of the Communist Party?

Mr. KELLER. I have never been a member of the Communist Party.

The CHAIRMAN. Have you ever been a member of the Young Communist League?

Mr. KELLER. I have never been a member of the Young Communist League.

The CHAIRMAN. Have you ever been a member of the International Workers Order?

Mr. KELLER. No; I am not.

The CHAIRMAN. Have you ever had any connection with the Communist Party?

(No answer.)

The CHAIRMAN. Been active in any of the work of the Communist Party?

Mr. KELLER. No, sir.

The CHAIRMAN. None whatsoever?

(No answer.)

The CHAIRMAN. Well, no one has testified that this man is a member of the Communist Party.

Mr. SCHWAB. Someone has testified, Mr. Chairman, about his activities in Spain and I understood you to say——

The CHAIRMAN. I am talking about the question of membership in the Communist Party.

Mr. MATTHEWS. There is a considerable line of questioning that has to do with whether or not this man is giving truthful answers.

The CHAIRMAN. I understand that is true. He has already contradicted his testimony this morning. He said he did not go under any other name, as I remember, and now he says he did. But the point I have in mind is that there is no testimony here that he is a member of the Communist Party.

Now, that being true, is it pertinent to require him to state under which name he was working in the union?

Mr. MATTHEWS. Then I would like to have the question held up for a moment until some more questions are asked.

The CHAIRMAN. All right.

Mr. MATTHEWS. You stated just now, Mr. Keller, that you were not a member of the International Workers Order; is that correct?

Mr. KELLER. No; I am not.

Mr. MATTHEWS. Have you ever been a member of the International Workers Order?

Mr. KELLER. No. I never attended one of their meetings.

Mr. MATTHEWS. I did not ask you if you ever attended a meeting.

Mr. KELLER. No; I have never been a member of the International Workers Order.

Mr. MATTHEWS. I ask you if this is your photograph? Is that a picture of yourself?

(Exhibiting photograph to witness.)

Mr. KELLER. That is.

Mr. MATTHEWS. This is a copy of The New Order, the official organ of the International Workers Order for July 1938. On page 16 there appears a photograph of Mr. Keller, which he just identified, and above the photograph is this caption: "Fred Keller, Spanish war hero, a member of order."

The CHAIRMAN. What about that?

Mr. KELLER. I can only say that if they said that that is a misquote; that I never joined that particular organization.

Mr. MATTHEWS. Did you ever address a communication to Max Bedacht?

Mr. KELLER. No, sir.

Mr. MATTHEWS. Never did? Were you ever known by any other title than that of commissar of war in the Lincoln Battalion?

Mr. KELLER. This morning I testified that I once was a sergeant in a machine-gun company, and I held the position in—two positions in a machine-gun company besides the title of commissar of war.

Mr. MATTHEWS. Were you ever known as the political commissar?

Mr. KELLER. Political commissar is not the correct term.

Mr. MATTHEWS. Well, were you ever known as the political commissar of the Lincoln Battalion?

Mr. KELLER. I can't say. I can only say what I was.

Mr. MATTHEWS. Did you ever sign yourself as political commissar of the Lincoln Battalion?

Mr. KELLER. Not to the best of my knowledge. My correct title was commissar of war, and I think in all official communications I must have used that.

Mr. MATTHEWS. When was that title conferred upon you?

Mr. KELLER. I think it was about October 15 in 1937.

Mr. MATTHEWS. And how long did you have that? Until the time you left Spain in 1938?

Mr. KELLER. Approximately June '38·

Mr. MATTHEWS. Mr. Keller, is that your signature?

(Exhibiting pamphlet to the witness.)

(No answer.)

Mr. MATTHEWS. Is that your signature? Never mind the letter, is that your signature?

Mr. KELLER. I can't be sure, but it probably is.

Mr. MATTHEWS. Mr. Chairman, here is a copy of the New Order, official organ of the International Workers Order for March 1938. On page 11 there is a letter dated January 31, 1938, addressed to Max Bedacht, whom the witness just testified he never wrote any letters to. This is on the letterhead of the Battalion Lincoln-Washington, Fifteenth Brigade International, from Spain. It is signed "Fred Keller, Battalion Political Commissar."

Now, did you write that letter, Mr. Keller?

(Handing letter to the witness.)

Mr. KELLER. I never remember that letter. I can say when we were in Spain that the office that carried on work in America for raising publicity sent out many letters when we were at the front. We have no opportunity to write letters, as I know I haven't written home in months because I was so busy.

The CHAIRMAN. You deny that you wrote that letter?

Mr. KELLER. Mr. Chairman, I want to say in fairness that I cannot be sure. I may have had somebody write such a letter for me. There were hundreds of such communications.

The CHAIRMAN. You said that you thought that was your signature.

Mr. KELLER. I am not sure that that is my signature. It doesn't look familiar. It looks like "Kelly."

Mr. MATTHEWS. I will show you a signature——

Mr. KELLER. I don't make my signature——

The CHAIRMAN. Read the letter so you can state whether or not you wrote the letter.

(Mr. Matthews handing letter to the witness.)

Mr. KELLER. I can say I never wrote the letter. I would not say I did not authorize somebody else to do the letter.

The CHAIRMAN. You would not have authorized somebody to sign your name?

Mr. KELLER. No. On occasions they would because——

The CHAIRMAN. I mean if you authorized someone to write the letter you would sign your name?

Mr. KELLER. I can't say whether that——

The CHAIRMAN. Doesn't that look like your signature, Mr. Keller?

Mr. KELLER. It has some similarity to my signature.

Mr. MATTHEWS. Mr. Keller, is that your signature?

(Handing paper to the witness.)

Mr. KELLER. That is; yes, sir.

Mr. MATTHEWS. This is a signature on a voucher which Mr. Keller just signed today. Do the signatures compare, Mr. Keller, as being the same signatures?

Mr. KELLER. I don't think it is of relative importance when I denied that I wrote——

The CHAIRMAN. Let us have some order.

Mr. KELLER. Mr. Chairman, when I deny that I wrote a letter to the International Workers Order or said I was never a member of the International Workers Order I meant that. That is exactly the way it was in my mind, and I never remember writing this letter to this thing. The fact that I may have authorized such a letter, I don't know. But I can say that at the front we never had any opportunity to write letters, and this letter was probably written from some place else.

The CHAIRMAN. You know whether that is your signature, to be frank?

Mr. KELLER. Yes; it does appear to be my signature.

The CHAIRMAN. But you don't recall writing the letter?

Mr. KELLER. And I don't recall signing the letter either.

The CHAIRMAN. What is the date of that letter?

Mr. MATTHEWS. January 31, 1938.

The CHAIRMAN. All right, read the letter.

Mr. MATTHEWS. The letter reads as follows:

January 31st, 1938.
Max Bedacht, I. W. O., 80 5th Avenue, N. Y. C.

Dear Comrade Bedacht:
The boys of the Lincoln Battalion wish to thank the I. W. O. for the wool sweaters we recently received.

They came in a time when they were very much needed—right into our trenches, while we were stationed in one of the coldest regions of Spain.

The moral and material aid that the I. W. O. has given to the American Brigade here, has been an important factor in our service to the Spanish Peoples Army. In recent weeks, during which we have been unusually active, no small concern of ours has been with the elements.

Your very necessary gifts will serve as a constant reminder of the great efforts the American workers are jointly waging in our fight against the Fascists.
Salud y Victoria.   Fred Keller.

and then in typewriting "Fred Kelly, Battalion Political Commissar" and below that the signature of "Frank Rogers" and below that in typewriting, "Frank Rogers, Party Secretary."

Who was Frank Rogers, Mr. Keller?

Mr. KELLER. He was in our battalion in Spain.

Mr. MATTHEWS. Of what party was he the secretary?

Mr. KELLER. I don't know that. I don't ever remember this letter. And the reason that I am pretty sure that I would never allow my signature to be put on the same letter with one from a political representative, because that was indirect contradictions to the orders of the Spanish Republican government.

Now, that I have heard the text of the letter I can say that I might have allowed or authorized this letter to be written in thanks to the people who sent these things. We often done that when people sent us gifts there, but the fact that the party secretary signs his name, also, to the letter, makes me believe that it is hardly possible, because that would have been in direct contradiction to my orders from the Spanish Republican government; that I never was to be identified with any political party.

Mr. MATTHEWS. Mr. Keller, I would like to ask you for a yes or no answer to the question. Is that your signature? [Handing pamphlet to the witness.]

Mr. KELLER. I say that I cannot be sure. I don't want to say that is my signature. I never remember the letter. I admit there is a possibility of my authorizing such a letter. I cannot say that that is my signature.

The CHAIRMAN. You said a moment ago it appears to be.

Mr. KELLER. It says "Fred Kelly" there, doesn't it? If I may say so, isn't that "Kelly"? That isn't my name at all. Well, it is obvious a line of fraud of some kind because the signature here says "Fred Kelly."

Mr. MATTHEWS. No; it doesn't.

Mr. KELLER. The typing under the thing said "Fred Kelly." My name is "Fred Keller." I think anybody I authorized to sign my name would at least have been correct in the spelling of it.

The CHAIRMAN. Does it have the signature? Let me see the signature.

Mr. KELLER. I am quite certain now that this letter was never with my knowledge or anything like that. I have never seen it before.

The CHAIRMAN. Then you deny that you wrote this letter and deny that this is your signature?

Mr. KELLER. I deny that I wrote the letter. The fact that I authorized the letter I am not willing——

The CHAIRMAN. You deny also it is your signature?

Mr. KELLER. Yes; I will deny that that is my signature and I will deny also that anybody who signed my name, typed or otherwise, and misspelled it, they certainly had no right to use my name.

Mr. MATTHEWS. Was it also a mistake to put the words "Political Commissar" on this letter?

Mr. KELLER. I told you in the beginning my title was commissar of war. I never authorized anybody to use any other title but that.

Mr. MATTHEWS. Did you know a Fred Kelly in Spain?

Mr. KELLER. No; never did.

Mr. MATTHEWS. Was there a Fred Kelly who was political commisar for the Lincoln battalion?

Mr. KELLER. No.

Mr. MATTHEWS. That is, you were the only one who occupied that post at this period, were you not? This is January 31, 1938?

Mr. KELLER. That is correct.

Mr. MATTHEWS. Have you ever seen Mr. Browder's The Peoples' Front. Mr. Keller, this book?

(Exhibiting book to the witness.)

Mr. KELLER. I have never read it.

Mr. MATTHEWS. On page 182 of Earl Browder's book, The Peoples' Front, which is already in evidence before this committee, appears the following statement by Mr. Browder:

And not the least source of our pride is the fact that over sixty per cent of the Lincoln Battalion members are members of the Communist Party.

Is Mr. Browder incorrect in that statement, Mr. Keller?

Mr. KELLER. I can say that I can give no definite figures on this. I am not concerned with what Browder or anybody else said about the Lincoln Battalion.

Mr. MATTHEWS. Did you meet Earl Browder in Spain?

Mr. KELLER. I heard him speak.

Mr. MATTHEWS. Did you personally talk to him?

Mr. KELLER. I never spoke to the man in my life.

Mr. MATTHEWS. Now, Mr. Chairman, I would like to raise the question of the other names under which Mr. Keller has stated to the magistrate in New York that he was employed, and the reasons why he told the magistrate he used other names.

The CHAIRMAN. Did you give another name before the magistrate's court?

Mr. KELLER. No; I did not. The magistrate said it wasn't necessary that I give it.

Mr. MATTHEWS. What was the reason you stated to the magistrate that you used another name?

Mr. KELLER. I told him that that was my means of making a livelihood.

Mr. SCHWAB. Just a moment. I object to this whole——

Mr. MATTHEWS. Did you tell the magistrate——

Mr. SCHWAB. Just a moment. I object to going any further into this line. It has nothing to do with the objects of this committee.

The CHAIRMAN. It is very much the object of this committee to find out whether or not people use other names. We have had quite a bit of evidence of members of the Communist Party who use other names.

Mr. SCHWAB. Nothing illegal about it.

The CHAIRMAN. Using other names?

Mr. SCHWAB. Yes; nothing illegal about it in the State of New York.

Mr. MATTHEWS. Did you tell the magistrate in New York that you used another name because you were known as a Communist under the name of Fred Keller?

Mr. KELLER. I did not. On the stand I was asked if I was a Communist, and I said I was not.

The CHAIRMAN. Mr. Keller.

Mr. KELLER. Yes, sir.

The CHAIRMAN. Did you hear the testimony of the previous witness?

Mr. KELLER. I did.

The CHAIRMAN. Did you know the previous witness in Spain?

Mr. KELLER. I did.

The CHAIRMAN. When did you first meet him?

Mr. KELLER. I first met him, I believe, it was about November 1937.

The CHAIRMAN. Where did you meet him?

Mr. KELLER. There was considerable—I was at the front at Fuentes De Ebro, and I had to travel several miles back, and he was in charge of some kitchen unit there.

The CHAIRMAN. State whether or not you deny the testimony he gave here.

Mr. KELLER. I emphatically deny everything he said—not everything he said, but most of the accusations are a thin tissue of lies. We speak with a lot of bitterness when we denounce him.

The CHAIRMAN. You don't undertake to deny the things when you were not present?

Mr. KELLER. He said he was at the front. This man was never 1 day at the front. I want that entered in the record, not even 1 day.

The CHAIRMAN. You deny that he was at the front?

Mr. KELLER. Yes. Could he speak of my activities, and if he were any witness, I think it can be asked throughout the battalion—I was known all over as a non-Communist. There was nothing in Spain—it was well known I was non-Communist throughout Spain. It is still well known in America, but he hatches some story of, I might call "control commission," that I was some stooge of Moscow or something. That is not true. The proof that the battalion was'nt a Communist institution was that men, who were never associated with any political party, as I was never before I went to Spain, rose to the ranks that I attained there.

The CHAIRMAN. How many times did you see him in Spain?

Mr. KELLER. I saw him on several occasions.

The CHAIRMAN. Two times?

Mr. KELLER. He was a disciplinary case about three times, and I saw him on all those three occasions.

The CHAIRMAN. You had control over him or he came within your jurisdiction?

Mr. KELLER. They were referred to me, yes. Mostly because he was a coward and wouldn't go to the front and many times he was spoken to.

Mr. LYNCH. Did your counsel just suggest that answer to you, that he was a coward?

Mr. KELLER. He did not. He said explain it to me.

Mr. SCHWAB. May the record show that I said "explain your answer."

The CHAIRMAN. Where did you see him outside of the three times? Did you see him any more?

Mr. KELLER. Oh, I have seen him more than three times, but I remember on three different occasions he was a disciplinary case.

The CHAIRMAN. You say he never went to the front and never——

Mr. KELLER. He never had one day at the front.

The CHAIRMAN. Never did engage in any actual combat?

Mr. KELLER. He never engaged in any actual combat.

The CHAIRMAN. How did he get out of it?

Mr. KELLER. He deserted. Our battalion had a minimum of deserters.

The CHAIRMAN. He was there for a year before he deserted.

Mr. KELLER. He was never there for a year.

The CHAIRMAN. How long was he there before he deserted?

Mr. KELLER. Well, I can't speak with very much authority. I would say approximately 8 or 9 months. I know that he came—he was the first—got near the front when he was in charge of a kitchen unit at a place called Quinto. That was about November 1937. It was in 1938, in March, that he deserted, so we can say that he had 5 months' associationship with our brigade.

The CHAIRMAN. And your statement is that during the 5 months he never was in actual combat?

Mr. KELLER. He never was in actual combat.

The CHAIRMAN. Do you know the the terms under which the men enlisted—the period for which they enlisted?

Mr. KELLER. There were never any terms of enlistment as far as I know. In my own case there wasn't.

The CHAIRMAN. Wasn't it understood that they were enlisting for a 6 month's period.

Mr. KELLER. I have never heard that—certainly I have never known of those terms or circumstances.

The CHAIRMAN. I say you never heard of that?

Mr. KELLER. There were arrangements by which a doctor declared a man unfit for front-line service.

The CHAIRMAN. I wasn't speaking about that. When they enlisted——

Mr. KELLER. For a 6 months' service—duty.

The CHAIRMAN. That is what I am talking about.

Mr. KELLER. I never heard of that.

The CHAIRMAN. You never heard of it?

Mr. KELLER. No, sir.

The CHAIRMAN. What were the conditions you enlisted for—what were the conditions or agreements under which you enlisted?

Mr. KELLER. No formal terms of agreement.

The CHAIRMAN. You had to sign something, didn't you?

Mr. KELLER. No, I never signed anything.

The CHAIRMAN. Did you take an oath?

Mr. KELLER. I never took an oath.

The CHAIRMAN. Never was any understanding about the length of time that anybody enlisted?

Mr. KELLER. No, there never was.

The CHAIRMAN. Well, they could do anything. They could quit any time they wanted to, couldn't they?

Mr. KELLER. We were under the regulations and discipline of the Spanish Republican Army.

The CHAIRMAN. What did that provide as the duration of enlistment?

Mr. KELLER. After an action was over and the troops retired they were taken to the rear guard. Men could take up with a certain commission, which I had something to do with, and give reasons why they would like to be repatriated to America if they were—if they wanted that.

The CHAIRMAN. In other words, there wasn't any regulation of the Army that prevented any of these volunteers from leaving any time they wanted to?

Mr. KELLER. They couldn't leave in the midst of a military action.

The CHAIRMAN. I understand that.

Mr. KELLER. They couldn't leave without permission and formal discharge from the International Brigade headquarters.

The CHAIRMAN. The point I am trying to clear up, since there wasn't any understanding or agreement when they joined, why was it necessary to get your permission to quit?

Mr. KELLER. The army is the highest type of organization. We can't have people that just walk out any time at all.

The CHAIRMAN. That is true, but you say there wasn't any oath required; they signed nothing, there was no agreement as to how long they were going to fight.

Mr. KELLER. There was never any such thing. When a man wanted to come back he went before the medical tribunal and if he was declared unfit for front-line service——

The CHAIRMAN. They would let him go?

Mr. KELLER. They would be automatically discharged just as soon as the Government could get around.

The CHAIRMAN. Was that the only reason they could assign?

Mr. KELLER. No, there were others. Family troubles, other things, and many people were sent back in America to speak in America and tell what they had seen in Spain.

The CHAIRMAN. Sent back by the brigade?

Mr. KELLER. Yes.

The CHAIRMAN. Who would send those back? Send them back for the purpose of enlisting more men?

Mr. KELLER. No.

The CHAIRMAN. For the purpose of——

Mr. KELLER. Nobody was ever sent back until such time as there were never any further need for enlistment. We had all the men that the Government wanted.

The CHAIRMAN. You never did attend a Communist meeting under the auspices of the Communist Party either in Spain or the United States?

Mr. KELLER. No, sir.

The CHAIRMAN. Any other questions?

Mr. LYNCH. Yes, I have a few questions.

The CHAIRMAN. All right.

Mr. LYNCH. Mr. Keller, you said if a person wanted to be relieved of responsibility of military duty and return to the United States that the matter would come up to you for consideration, is that right?

Mr. KELLER. On most occasions it would, yes. Not entirely—not for every——

Mr. LYNCH. All right, and you would decide whether or not you would give him permission to return to the United States, is that correct?

Mr. KELLER. No, I didn't have anything to say. There were many elements to be considered.

Mr. LYNCH. Who had the say?

Mr. KELLER. The Government.

Mr. LYNCH. What Government?

Mr. KELLER. Government of the Spanish Republic. I could only submit——

Mr. LYNCH. You would submit a recommendation?

Mr. KELLER. A statement or recommendation.

Mr. LYNCH. In other words, the Lincoln Brigade or the Washington-Lincoln Brigade was entirely responsible to the Spanish Republican Government?

Mr. KELLER. We were responsible directly to the headquarters of the International Brigade and from then—and they were responsible to the Government.

Mr. LYNCH. And a member or a person who had enlisted in the Lincoln Brigade was not permitted to return to America or leave the country or get out of the military service without the permission of the Spanish Republican Government, isn't that correct?

Mr. KELLER. That is correct.

Mr. LYNCH. And you would make the intermediate report and recommended whether they be retained or whether they be relieved of responsibility, is that correct?

Mr. KELLER. That is correct.

Mr. LYNCH. And what military experience did you have before you went to Europe?

Mr. KELLER. I had no military experience.

Mr. LYNCH. What was your age at that time?

Mr. KELLER. Twenty-three.

Mr. LYNCH. And what work had you done before you went to Europe?

Mr. SCHWAB. That has already been answered.

Mr. LYNCH. I submit not.

Mr. KELLER. I worked at many things—several things.

Mr. LYNCH. From 20 to 23 what was your primary work?

Mr. KELLER. Worked in a trade-union.

Mr. LYNCH. Trade-union as an organizer?

Mr. KELLER. Worked as an elevator operator. I worked as a laborer; worked at a great many things.

Mr. LYNCH. Laborer and elevator operator. Anything else of importance?

Mr. KELLER. Playground director. I once worked for the National Broadcasting Co.

Mr. LYNCH. What were you doing with the National Broadcasting Co.?

Mr. KELLER. I was an usher.

Mr. LYNCH. Now, when you received your passport what address did you give in New York?

Mr. KELLER. The address where I was living at that time.

Mr. LYNCH. What was it?

Mr. KELLER. I don't correctly remember where I was living at that time. I lived with my family.

Mr. LYNCH. Don't remember what the address was?

Mr. KELLER. No, I don't. That was 4 years ago or 3 years ago.

Mr. LYNCH. Can't remember where your family was living when you went to Europe?

Mr. KELLER. I think it is the present address, where I live now.

Mr. LYNCH. I am asking, can you remember that, to test your memory. You testified about so many things here. Can you remember that?

Mr. KELLER. I think it is the same address that I have at present.

Mr. LYNCH. What is that address?

Mr. KELLER. 1364 Sixth Avenue.

Mr. LYNCH. Did you ever live at 227 Sixty-eighth Street, New York City?

Mr. KELLER. What was that?

Mr. LYNCH. 227 Sixty-eighth Street, New York City.

Mr. KELLER. Not to my knowledge.

Mr. LYNCH. Did you ever know a fellow named Louis Stark?

Mr. KELLER. Stark—I don't think I remember his name.

Mr. LYNCH. All right. Did you give the name of Fred P. Keller, Jr., when you obtained a passport?

Mr. KELLER. I am not positive. I gave my correct name and that is my correct name.

Mr. LYNCH. Junior?

Mr. KELLER. (No answer.)

Mr. LYNCH. And what birth date did you give?

Mr. KELLER. I believe it was June 4, 1913.

Mr. LYNCH. And you gave here June 4, 1914. Which is correct?

Mr. KELLER. '13.

Mr. LYNCH. '13 is correct?

Mr. KELLER. Yes, sir.

Mr. LYNCH. Did you know that you gave '14 when you started your testimony here a few moments ago?

Mr. KELLER. I think I gave '13—I am not positive.

Mr. LYNCH. What did you say that you were going abroad for at the time you made your passport application?

Mr. KELLER. I don't think I gave any statement at all. I went there and I got it the following Wednesday. I got it very rapidly. I remember that. I remember the clerk making a point of it.

Mr. LYNCH. And you knew, of course, at that time you were going to Spain to fight in the cause of the Republican Government of Spain, didn't you?

Mr. KELLER. I did.

Mr. LYNCH. Sir?

Mr. KELLER. I did.

Mr. LYNCH. And didn't you say in your passport application that you were going for a 2-month pleasure visit to France and Germany?

Mr. KELLER. I don't remember that.

Mr. LYNCH. Will you deny it?

Mr. KELLER. I don't remember giving any statement of why I was going to Europe.

Mr. LYNCH. Will you deny that in your passport application you said you were going to France and Germany for 2 months' pleasure trip?

Mr. KELLER. I will not deny it because I don't remember giving any statement.

Mr. LYNCH. But you did know you were going to fight in the forces of the Spanish Government, didn't you?

Mr. KELLER. I did.

Mr. LYNCH. You sailed on what ship?

Mr. KELLER. An English ship.

Mr. LYNCH. *Laconia?*

Mr. KELLER. (No answer.)

Mr. LYNCH. Is that it?

Mr. KELLER. No; I don't believe it was.

Mr. LYNCH. Now, Mr. Keller, were you at the front all the time while you were in Spain?

Mr. KELLER. At the time my battalion was there I was there.

Mr. LYNCH. How long a period of time, let us say from November 1937 to March 1938, did you spend at the front lines?

Mr. KELLER. November. We were there in action about 15 days. We were there again from January until—through February.

Mr. LYNCH. Let us stop right there for a moment. You were there about 15 days in November. Then where would you go?

Mr. KELLER. We would retire to some place in the rear guard to give our people some rest.

Mr. LYNCH. And you stayed there in the rear until sometime in January or February?

Mr. KELLER. I would say about January. It was approximately that. We again went into action at Teruel.

Mr. LYNCH. You were there in action for what period of time?

Mr. KELLER. I would say about 35 days.

Mr. LYNCH. Then retired again?

Mr. KELLER. Just for a short while.   Then we were involved in a big action which the—big—first great blitzkrieg, it is known as, which took us about some 20 days with a short intermediate rest, and then back into action again.

Mr. LYNCH. It was your duty as the head of the brigade to know the important qualifications of the men, wasn't it?

Mr. KELLER. Well, correction, please.   I was not head of the brigade. I was in a position of leadership in the battalion.

Mr. LYNCH. The commissar of war?

Mr. KELLER. Of the battalion.

Mr. LYNCH. Does that require you to know the qualifications of the members of the Lincoln Battalion?

Mr. KELLER. That is correct.

Mr. LYNCH. Did you know Vernon Selby?

Mr. KELLER. Yes; I did.

Mr. LYNCH. Did you know that he was an engineer who spent 3 years in educating himself at the United States Military Academy at West Point?

Mr. KELLER. That is correct.

Mr. LYNCH. And what was his rank or position?

Mr. KELLER. He was a sergeant.

Mr. LYNCH. He was a sergeant and you were the commissar?

Mr. KELLER. Yes, sir.

Mr. LYNCH. And the commissar would rank with what position in the American Army, general?

Mr. KELLER. Major.   Don't promote me.

Mr. LYNCH. And who would decide whether a sergeant should be made lieutenant and finally a commissar?

Mr. KELLER. Well, the officers that worked directly with them.

Mr. LYNCH. The officers that worked directly with them?

Mr. KELLER. Yes, sir.

Mr. LYNCH. Were they all Americans who worked directly with you?

Mr. KELLER. No.   Americans and Spaniards, English, Canadians, and other nationalities too.   There were 57 nationalities represented throughout our brigade, although not all of them were immediately identified with our own battalion.

Mr. LYNCH. You knew that Vernon Selby had engineering experiences in Panama and South American countries, didn't you, or did you know that?

Mr. KELLER. I knew Vernon had some military experience.   I heard of his West Point experience and he was generally regarded as a very high type fellow.

Mr. LYNCH. And he was a sergeant.   Did he ever get promoted above a sergeant?

Mr. KELLER. I can't be sure, but I think he was a sergeant.

Mr. LYNCH. What employment have you been engaged in since you returned to this country?

Mr. KELLER. As was brought out previously I worked for Friends of the Lincoln Brigade.   I toured for about 9 months.

Mr. LYNCH. And what more recently?

Mr. KELLER. Worked as a longshoreman.

Mr. LYNCH. But under an assumed name?

Mr. KELLER. (No answer.)

Mr. LYNCH. That is correct, isn't it? You said that before?

Mr. KELLER. Yes. I would like to make the point that I didn't believe this morning when I was asked if I ever used another name, I didn't consider that and if it was necessary I would have stated it.

Mr. LYNCH. You have a Social Security number, don't you?

Mr. KELLER. I don't believe I ever had one. I didn't have one before Spain. It hadn't come into being.

Mr. LYNCH. And you don't have one now?

Mr. KELLER. I probably have one, but I haven't got it.

Mr. LYNCH. Do you know what name you are under?

Mr. KELLER. I don't know what it is.

Mr. LYNCH. Do you know what name you carried under the Social Security records?

Mr. KELLER. I don't believe I have one. I am not positive I have one—that I was ever registered under the Social Security.

Mr. LYNCH. Are you regularly employed?

Mr. KELLER. I haven't been regularly employed since I returned to this country.

Mr. LYNCH. Were you or were you not presented with a life membership by the Communist Party when you returned to this country?

Mr. KELLER. That is not true. I am very weary of denying it.

Mr. MATTHEWS. Mr. Keller, did you desert?

Mr. KELLER. I did not.

Mr. LYNCH. Did you know a fellow by the name of Edwin Rolf?

Mr. KELLER. I did.

Mr. LYNCH. Did you read his book?

Mr. KELLER. Yes; I have.

Mr. LYNCH. Do you remember on page 172, speaking about Commissar Fred Keller of the Lincoln Brigade:

Himself set a new note in military attire when he appeared in striped morning trousers, heavy riding boots, a service sheeplined coat and huge sombrero, a huge 38 caliber pistol swinging at his side completed the costume.

Correct?

Mr. KELLER. Essentially, that is correct.

Mr. LYNCH. Did you get those by pillaging some place or were they given to you?

Mr. KELLER. That is not true.

Mr. LYNCH. Which is correct?

Mr. KELLER. We never pillaged any place.

Mr. LYNCH. How did you get those?

Mr. KELLER. Have to understand that in Spain there were no clothes—no clothes for anybody.

Mr. LYNCH. Where did you get those clothes?

Mr. KELLER. Probably given to me by a government entendencia.

Mr. LYNCH. Do you know Eric Parker?

Mr. KELLER. Eric Parker. I met him. I didn't know him very well.

Mr. LYNCH. Dave Rees?

Mr. KELLER. Dave Rees—I met—yes; I knew Dave Rees.

Mr. LYNCH. Was Eric Parker a commissar or not?

Mr. KELLER. I went to—I had an ear injury and when I went to Barcelona to have it taken care of he took my place.

Mr. LYNCH. When did he take your place?

Mr. KELLER. Well, I can't be positive of the exact date but it was approximately March 1938.

Mr. MATTHEWS. Mr. Keller, was Mr. Honeycombe wounded?

Mr. KELLER. No. He was never wounded.

Mr. MATTHEWS. Was he hospitalized for any reason?

Mr. KELLER. I can't be sure of all the details of Honeycombe. The only thing was Honeycombe never was a respectable member of our battalion. He was never at the front. I wouldn't know about him. I only knew him—knew of him as a disciplinary case.

Mr. LYNCH. How many Americans were in France?

Mr. KELLER. In France?

Mr. LYNCH. I mean in Spain; excuse me.

Mr. KELLER. It is very difficult to estimate the exact number. The number fluctuated some place between 2,800 and 3,200.

Mr. LYNCH. And how many injured or killed or otherwise disposed of?

Mr. KELLER. I object to that. I wouldn't say that anybody else was disposed of. I will say that our men were killed in action. They died—they died very bravely.

Mr. LYNCH. How many were killed or missing?

Mr. KELLER. I can't say. I have no exact figures on the subject.

Mr. LYNCH. Have no records of it?

Mr. KELLER. There are records but I don't have them, and if I am being held exactly to the figures that I give I cannot give those figures.

Mr. MATTHEWS. Mr. Keller, was anybody executed who was a member of the Lincoln Battalion?

Mr. KELLER. I don't know.

Mr. MATTHEWS. Wasn't a notice of the execution of Paul White posted for the members of the Lincoln Battalion?

Mr. KELLER. I don't know that. I was—when I left Spain Paul White was functioning as a member of our battalion.

Mr. MATTHEWS. That is all.

Mr. LYNCH. That is all.

The CHAIRMAN. All right, who is your next witness?

Mr. MATTHEWS. Mr. Wolff.

Mr. KELLER. I want to, Mr. Chairman, refute one or two other things that Mr. Honeycombe said.

The CHAIRMAN. All right.

Mr. KELLER. If I may. It will only take a minute. I want to again repeat that only Honeycombe was never 1 day at the front.

The CHAIRMAN. You have made that statement.

Mr. KELLER. That he was a coward; that he never asked me or anybody else for repatriation. He was arrested once in Spain as a deserter. That was in the first days even before an action came up. When the action appeared imminent, Mr. Honeycombe went to Barcelona. Earlier in the day he called me a sadist. He said there was no food. I want to say there wasn't much food in Spain. There wasn't any food for anybody and our battalion went through and fought on no food or clothing. On any of these things if he didn't get food it was no fault of ours. Our people, all of them—many of them died very bravely in action. There were hundreds killed there and they suffered untold things.

The history of the American battalion will be an American history. Mr. Honeycombe will get the headlines or newspapers today with the things our men suffered. It is a shame they have to be sullied by this man whom I challenge to get five members of our brigade to say that he was a brave man; to say that he was anything but a disreputable character throughout the entire thing in Spain.

Mr. MASON. Mr. Chairman, the witness was given the privilege of refuting evidence that had been given by a former witness——

Mr. SCHWAB. I object to the interruption.

Mr. MASON. Statements of this kind are not refutation of a witness. It is simply one man under oath as compared to another man under oath and I don't consider that any method of refutation of any of these charges.

The CHAIRMAN. Confine yourself to refutation.

Mr. KELLER. I agree, Mr. Congressman. I wanted to make that point, that he had no respect among our men.

Mr. DEMPSEY. Mr. Chairman, his opinion doesn't mean a thing.

Mr. KELLER. I will comment on something else then. He said that the money raised by organizations here in America, that only 20 percent of it was used for the purpose of the men of the Lincoln Brigade.

We are registered under the State Department, and every cent of our money has to be accounted for by them, and is accounted for.

Mr. VOORHIS. Whom do you mean by "we"?

Mr. KELLER. The organizations that head our battalion—the Friends of the Lincoln Brigade—at that time when they were in operation, has strict accounting of all funds by the State Department, and their money was used to take——

The CHAIRMAN. Isn't that an overstatement? They don't have any accounting at the State Department. They require you to file a statement of the amount of money that you receive; isn't that it?

Mr. KELLER. That is correct; the money that is sent over, and what is the money used for.

The CHAIRMAN. All right.

Mr. KELLER. The Friends of the Lincoln Brigade have repatriated and taken care of wounded and crippled men—over 3,000. Their money was used, and the statement made here today that other than 20 percent of the money was just a lucrative racket is something which I don't have to deny. It is on the record.

I want to say another word about the Communist Party——

The CHAIRMAN. Confine yourself to denial of what he said.

Mr. KELLER. I deny this.

The CHAIRMAN. What are you denying?

Mr. KELLER. I deny the statement of his that other than 20 percent of the money that was collected for the Lincoln Brigade in America was a lucrative racket. Those words were used this morning.

Mr. MASON. Of course, right there, Mr. Chairman, that was his opinion of it as expressed as an opinion, and now we are getting your opinion as expressed as you saw it, and there again there is no evidence.

The CHAIRMAN. This witness has the same right.

Mr. MASON. Yes; I am not objecting to his right to make the statements.

Mr. KELLER. Mr. Congressman, the name of Vernon Selby has been mentioned here.

Mr. DEMPSEY. How much money was collected for the Lincoln Brigade?

Mr. KELLER. I can't be sure.

Mr. DEMPSEY. How much money was received in Spain?

Mr. KELLER. I can't be sure of that.

Mr. DEMPSEY. Then how do you happen to know anything about what percentage——

Mr. KELLER. I happen to be an officer, and worked for the organization.

Mr. DEMPSEY. If you don't know how much money was collected, and don't know how much arrived in Spain, you don't know anything about it, do you?

Mr. KELLER. I say an accounting of all this was made to the State Department.

Mr. DEMPSEY. But you have no knowledge of the situation as far as you are concerned?

Mr. KELLER. I am not authorized or prepared to present the figures here but I want to say——

Mr. DEMPSEY. If you don't know what was collected and what was received in Spain, then I think you are without knowledge to testify upon that.

Mr. SCHWAB. If the committee is interested in the figures, Mr. Chairman, we can produce witnesses to testify to the real figures.

The CHAIRMAN. Now, listen, Mr. Attorney. You have been treated with great courtesy, and you can treat this committee with courtesy. Now, proceed.

Mr. DEMPSEY. This witness states that it isn't true that only 20 percent arrived in Spain, yet he says he has no knowledge of how much was collected nor does he have any knowledge of how much arrived in Spain. If that is true, I don't think you are qualified to testify on this subject.

Mr. SCHWAB. Mr. Honeycombe wasn't——

Mr. DEMPSEY. He testified and apparently had knowledge.

The CHAIRMAN. All right. What else do you want to refute?

Mr. KELLER. The name of Vernon Selby has been mentioned here. Vernon Selby was a very good friend of mine in Spain. It is true that in one case in Spain Vernon Selby did—his conduct was not all that we expected of the men of the Lincoln Battalion, but Vernon Selby was a brave man and he died very bravely in action. He believed in what he was fighting for and I disagree and I want to say in front of his family, how sorry I am that his name is brought in in this disrespect.

The CHAIRMAN. How do you know he died in action?

Mr. KELLER. I was told by other members. When Mr. Wolff gets on the stand he can testify exactly to that.

The CHAIRMAN. You have no personal knowledge of it yourself?

Mr. KELLER. I was with Selby for a long time. I was not with him——

The CHAIRMAN. I am talking about with reference to his death. You are basing your statement upon what you heard just like the previous witness based his upon what he was told?

Mr. KELLER. Yes.

The CHAIRMAN. All right. Any other statement you want to make?

Mr. KELLER. That is all I can think of.

The CHAIRMAN. All right, the next witness.

Mr. MATTHEWS. Mr. Milton Wolff.

The CHAIRMAN. Raise your right hand, please. Do you solemnly swear to tell the truth, the whole truth, and nothing but the truth so help you God?

TESTIMONY OF MILTON WOLFF

Mr. WOLFF. I do.

The CHAIRMAN. Have a seat.

Mr. MATTHEWS. Please give your full name?

Mr. WOLFF. Milton Wolff.

Mr. MATTHEWS. What is your address?

Mr. WOLFF. 1794 West Twelfth Street, Brooklyn, N. Y.

Mr. MATTHEWS. Where were you born?

Mr. WOLFF. In Brooklyn.

Mr. MATTHEWS. When?

Mr. WOLFF. October 8, 1915.

Mr. MATTHEWS. Are you a member of the Communist Party?

Mr. WOLFF. I am not.

Mr. MATTHEWS. Have you ever been a member of the Communist Party?

Mr. WOLFF. I have not.

Mr. MATTHEWS. Have you ever been a member of the Young Communist League?

Mr. WOLFF. I have not.

Mr. MATTHEWS. When you went to Spain did you travel on a passport issued in your own name?

Mr. WOLFF. I did.

Mr. MATTHEWS. American passport?

Mr. WOLFF. Yes, sir.

Mr. MATTHEWS. Was there a notation stamped on it that it was not good for travel in Spain?

Mr. WOLFF. There was.

Mr. MATTHEWS. When you applied for that passport what reason did you give for traveling abroad?

Mr. WOLFF. I don't remember the reason.

Mr. MATTHEWS. But you did not state that you were going to Spain?

Mr. WOLFF. I did not.

Mr. MATTHEWS. When you applied for the passport was it your intention to go to Spain?

Mr. WOLFF. It was.

Mr. MATTHEWS. When did you sail for Spain?

Mr. WOLFF. February 1937, I believe. I am not sure of that.

Mr. MATTHEWS. On what ship?

Mr. WOLFF. It was a French ship. I don't remember the name.

Mr. MATTHEWS. *Champlain?*

Mr. WOLFF. No; I don't think so.

Mr. MATTHEWS. *Paris?*

Mr. WOLFF. Might have been.

Mr. MATTHEWS. How do you spell your last name, Mr. Wolff?

Mr. WOLFF. W-o-l-f-f.

Mr. MATTHEWS. When you arrived in France did you go directly to Spain?

Mr. WOLFF. I did.

Mr. MATTHEWS. Where did you cross into Spain?

Mr. WOLFF. Where did I cross into Spain?

Mr. MATTHEWS. Yes.

Mr. WOLFF. What point?

Mr. MATTHEWS. Yes.

Mr. WOLFF. I don't know the point. It was over the Pyrenees, and there is no way of establishing my location.

Mr. MATTHEWS. What did you do with your passport when you arrived in Spain?

Mr. WOLFF. I turned it over to some people there for safekeeping, because I did not want to have it on me while I was in action, because I was aware of the fact that there was a very real possibility of losing it. Later events proved the correctness of my reasoning because I lost all of my other personal belongings that I came to Spain with.

Mr. MATTHEWS. What was your position in the Spanish Loyalist Army?

Mr. WOLFF. When I first got there it was that of a soldier. When I left I was commander of the Lincoln Battalion.

Mr. MATTHEWS. When were you appointed to the position of commander of the Lincoln Battalion?

Mr. WOLFE. After a year and a half of fighting on the front line. I don't know the exact date.

Mr. MATTHEWS. Who appointed you to that position?

Mr. WOLFF. I was recommended by Colonel Valledor, who was the commander of the Fifteenth Brigade. I was recommended by him to the minister of defense, and the minister of defense appointed me commander of the battalion.

Mr. MATTHEWS. Was the minister of defense of the Spanish Loyalist Government?

Mr. WOLFF. He was commander of the Fifteenth Brigade.

Mr. MATTHEWS. You say you were appointed commander of the Lincoln Battalion. In what respect did the Lincoln Battalion differ from the Abraham Lincoln Brigade?

Mr. WOLFF. The Lincoln Battalion was one of five units in the Abraham Lincoln Brigade.

Mr. MATTHEWS. There was an Abraham Lincoln Brigade in France, was there?

Mr. WOLFF. Just as there was a Fighting 69th in France. It was known by that name. It had no official designation.

Mr. MATTHEWS. It was not officially designated in Spain: is that correct?

Mr. WOLFF. Not by the minister of defense. The name was applied to the Fifteenth Brigade just as the name the Lincoln Battalion was applied to the Fifty-eighth Battalion of the Fifteenth Brigade.

Mr. MATTHEWS. How long did you hold the position of commander of the Lincoln Battalion?

Mr. WOLFF. For a half year.

Mr. MATTHEWS. How old were you when you were appointed to that position?

Mr. WOLFF. 23.

Mr. MATTHEWS. What previous military training did you have?

Mr. WOLFF. None.

Mr. MATTHEWS. What was your previous education in this country?

Mr. WOLFF. High school.

Mr. MATTHEWS. Did you gradnate from high school?

Mr. WOLFF. I did.

Mr. MATTHEWS. Where was that?

Mr. WOLFF. In Brooklyn.

Mr. MATTHEWS. And what types of work had you done before you went to Spain?

Mr. WOLFF. I was an art student. I was in a C. C. C. camp and I worked in—as a shipping clerk at one time.

Mr. MATTHEWS. And you had been in Spain approximately a year and a half when you say you were made commander of the Lincoln Battalion?

(No answer.)

Mr. MATTHEWS. Now, how did you happen to join the Loyalist Army?

Mr. WOLFF. When the war broke out in Spain I recognized it, or it was my opinion at least, that it was a war of democracy against fascism. I understood that the regularly elected republican government of Spain was under attack by a rebellious army, much the same as the Southern Army attacked the regularly elected Government of the North during the Civil War.

I also realized that Italy and Germany had a very strong hand in on the Fascist side as against that of Republican Spain.

At that time in America we were already beginning to feel and see the actions of our own democratic breed of fascism—I am Jewish. and knowing that as a Jew we are the first to suffer when fascism does come, I went to Spain to fight against it. There were a chance to fight on the front——

The CHAIRMAN. Isn't it true that you also suffer under communism?

Mr. WOLFF. I have no idea of that at all. As far as my knowledge—as far as my knowledge goes. I know of no instances where Jews have suffered under communism.

The CHAIRMAN. Didn't you know that the Government of Soviet Russia was under a Communist dictatorship just as bad as a Fascist dictatorship?

Mr. WOLFF. I knew the Government of the Soviet Union, as far as I knew, was elected by the people. I knew that there was a strong Communist Party in the Soviet Union. I was not aware of the existence of any dictatorship in the Soviet Union.

The CHAIRMAN. Didn't you regard Stalin as a dictator just like Mussolini and Hitler?

Mr. WOLFF. Did I record him?

The CHAIRMAN. Didn't you regard him as a dictator like you did Mussolini as a dictator?

Mr. WOLFF. No; I did not.

The CHAIRMAN. You do now?

Mr. WOLFF. I do not.

The CHAIRMAN. You don't think he is a dictator?

Mr. WOLFF. I do not.

The CHAIRMAN. You don't think they have a dictatorship in Russia?

Mr. WOLFF. I do not.

The CHAIRMAN. Do you think that is a democracy?

Mr. WOLFF. I don't know what type of government it is, but I do know it is my opinion that it is not a dictatorship.

The CHAIRMAN. Do you think it is a democracy?

Mr. WOLFE. No; I don't think it is a democracy—I don't think it is a democracy, for instance, similar to—I imagine that you are referring to and your standard is based on American democracy. I don't think it is that type of democracy.

The CHAIRMAN. Is it any type of democracy?

Mr. WOLFF. I don't know.

Mr. VOORHIS. What do you think of the support of Germany by Russia?

Mr. WOLFF. What is that?

Mr. VOORHIS. What do you think of the support of Germany by Russia?

Mr. WOLFE. At this time I would like to ask the committee a question. I received a subpena in court last week asking me to appear before the House Committee Investigating Un-American Activities, headed by Martin Dies, of Texas. I would like to know what my opinion of Soviet support of Germany or alleged support of Germany has to do with the subpena that was served on me.

The CHAIRMAN. Well, you gave your opinion with reference to the democracy in Spain. I was trying to get your idea of what you meant by democracy.

Mr. WOLFF. I was more familiar with democracy in Spain than I was either in the Soviet Union, since I had never been there.

The CHAIRMAN. You had never been to Spain either.

Mr. WOLFF. When I got to Spain I was aware of it.

The CHAIRMAN. But at the time you joined——

Mr. WOLFF. There was no need for me to go to the Soviet Union to defend anything there. There was no struggle. All I knew there was in Spain a regularly elected government.

The CHAIRMAN. Let us proceed.

Mr. MATTHEWS. In the event of a war between the United States and the Soviet Union, which side would you support?

Mr. WOLFF. Is there such a war today?

The CHAIRMAN. You certainly would know. You went over and fought in Spain.

Mr. WOLFF. Is there such a war today?

The CHAIRMAN. If there were such a war.

Mr. WOLFE. Is there a war today between the United States and Soviet Russia?

The CHAIRMAN. If war should break out between the United States and the Soviet Union, would you support this Government?

Mr. WOLFF. If war should break out between the United States and the Soviet Government, I would be glad to give my answer.

The CHAIRMAN. All right; proceed. Any questions?

Mr. MATTHEWS. Who paid your way to Europe when you joined the Spanish Loyalist Army?

Mr. WOLFF. I, and I did. I raised the money from my friends, and I had some myself.

Mr. MATTHEWS. Were any members of the Lincoln Battalion or of the Abraham Lincoln Brigade in Spain ever executed by a firing squad under your command?

Mr. WOLFF. A firing squad under my command?

Mr. MATTHEWS. Yes.

Mr. WOLEF. I never commanded a firing squad.

Mr. MATTHEWS. Your answer is "no," is it, to the question?

Mr. WOLFF. I never commanded a firing squad. The answer is no. I commanded the battalion. Command of a firing squad is beneath my dignity.

Mr. MATTHEWS. Were any American boys ever executed in your presence?

Mr. WOLFF. No.

Mr. MATTHEWS. Were any executed to your knowledge?

Mr. WOLFF. American boys?

Mr. MATTHEWS. Yes.

Mr. WOLFF. No.

Mr. MATTHEWS. Was there any case that came within your knowledge of a court martial of any of the members of the Lincoln Battalion or the Abraham Lincoln Brigade?

Mr. WOLEE. Court martial? No.

Mr. MATTHEWS. No court martials?

Mr. WOLFF. Not that I know of. I want to state here——

The CHAIRMAN. You have answered.

Mr. WOLFF. That for 2 years I was at the front. On very rare occasions was I in the rear for rest or leave. On those occasions I didn't interest myself in the rear-guard activities. There were no court martials conducted at the front. There were no executions conducted at the front. Therefore, I know nothing of these things.

Mr. MATTHEWS. Did Paul White belong to your battalion?

Mr. WOLFF. He did.

Mr. MATTHEWS. Did you know him under the name of Jonnie Adams?

Mr. WOLFF. I knew him as Paul White in Spain.

Mr. MATTHEWS. Did you ever know him under any other name anywhere else?

Mr. WOLFF. No.

Mr. MATTHEWS. Did you know him personally?

Mr. WOLEE. No; merely as one of the soldiers in the outfit.

Mr. MATTHEWS. What happened to him?

Mr. WOLFF. He was reported missing in action.

Mr. MATTHEWS. Was that while you were still in command of the battalion?

Mr. WOLFF. That he was missing?

Mr. MATTHEWS. Yes.

Mr. WOLFF. No. I was not in command of the battalion at that time.

Mr. MATTHEWS. Where were you at that time?

Mr. WOLFF. At that time I was in command of the machine-gun company.

Mr. MATTHEWS. Did you ever have any connections or contacts with the Russian Secret Service?

Mr. WOLFF. No; I did not.

Mr. MATTHEWS. With the G. P. U.?

Mr. WOLFF. I did not.

Mr. MATTHEWS. With the Soviet Military Intelligence?

Mr. WOLFE. I did not.

Mr. MATTHEWS. Did you know a young man named Ivan at brigade headquarters?

Mr. WOLFE. I did not.

Mr. MATTHEWS. Did you have any contact with Robert Minor in Spain?

Mr. WOLFE. I met Mr. Minor on one occasion.

Mr. MATTHEWS. In what capacity did you meet him on that occasion?

Mr. WOLFE. Mr. Minor came to the front to visit the front line, as on other occasions Congressmen from America did. I remember once a nephew, I think, of President Roosevelt was up there; some members of Parliament from England, and a few authors and actors, and so on.

The CHAIRMAN. All right; you have answered the question.

Mr. MATTHEWS. Now, what were Robert Minor's duties or activities in Spain?

Mr. WOLFF. As far as I know Robert Minor had no—wasn't acting in no official capacity in Spain.

Mr. MATTHEWS. Did you know Lt. Sid Levine?

Mr. WOLFE. I did.

Mr. MATTHEWS. Was he in your battalion?

Mr. WOLFE. He was.

Mr. MATTHEWS. How long?

Mr. WOLFF. I remember him as being in the battalion on two different occasions. I knew Sid Levine when he was in command of a machine-gun company where I was serving as a machine gunner—a soldier. I knew Sid Levine in the action of Teruel where he was on the battalion staff and again—I was at this time, I was commander of the machine-gun company. The last occasion I saw Sid Levine he was in command of a special machine-gun company of the brigade, and I was in the command of the Lincoln Battalion.

Mr. MATTHEWS. Was he ever assigned to any later position that you knew about?

Mr. WOLFE. Not that I know of.

Mr. MATTHEWS. Or did any other work from that which you mentioned?

Mr. WOLFF. No; not that I know of.

Mr. MATTHEWS. Were you in command of the battalion during the Teruel action?

Mr. WOLFE. I was not.

Mr. MATTHEWS. Why not?

Mr. WOLFF. The commander at the beginning of the Teruel action was Phillip Detro. His assistant was Captain Lamb. And I was attached to brigade staff at that time as a captain.

Mr. MATTHEWS. What did you do as captain of the brigade staff?

Mr. WOLFE. I acted as a liaison man between the brigade and the various units of the brigade.

Mr. MATTHEWS. Where were you with respect to the fighting that was going on at Teruel?

Mr. WOLFF. During the action at Teruel I spent most of my time with the English battalion, which was in a most crucial position in that action.

Mr. MATTHEWS. Have you got your American passport?

Mr. WOLFF. It was taken from me when I arrived in America.

Mr. MATTHEWS. Now, what employment have you received since you returned to the United States?

Mr. WOLFF. I have worked for a Mr. Baruch on a cooperative enterprise which failed.

Mr. MATTHEWS. Have you ever used any other name than that of Milton Wolff?

Mr. WOLFF. I have not.

Mr. MATTHEWS. Have you ever been on relief?

Mr. WOLFF. I have not.

Mr. MATTHEWS. What is your position now?

Mr. WOLFF. As to employment?

Mr. MATTHEWS. Yes.

Mr. WOLFF. At the present time I am being paid by the Dies committee. I have no employment other than that.

Mr. MATTHEWS. How long have you been unemployed?

Mr. WOLFF. Well, irregularly. I don't know—every now and then we would renew this cooperative enterprise.

Mr. MATTHEWS. What is the name of the cooperative enterprise?

Mr. WOLFF. It was called Brico and Nico.

Mr. MATTHEWS. What is the nature of the enterprise?

Mr. WOLFF. One was the New York Cooperative Organization, and the other one was the Brighton Cooperative Organization. The nature of it was to bring dairy products to women at low prices.

Mr. MATTHEWS. Have you any title in the organization known as the Friends of Abraham Lincoln Brigade?

Mr. WOLFF. I have not.

Mr. MATTHEWS. Have you ever had?

Mr. WOLFF. I have not.

Mr. MATTHEWS. For the veterans of the Abraham Lincoln Brigade?

Mr. WOLFF. I am the national commander of the Veterans of the Abraham Lincoln Brigade.

Mr. MATTHEWS. Do you hold that title now?

Mr. WOLFF. I do.

Mr. MATTHEWS. Who appointed you to that position?

Mr. WOLFF. I was elected at our third national convention in December of 1939.

Mr. MATTHEWS. Was a majority of the membership of the Lincoln Battalion under your command members of the Communist Party?

Mr. WOLFF. I would not know about that, since I never had any occasion to investigate their political beliefs.

Mr. MATTHEWS. Do you receive a salary in connection with your position as national commander of the Veterans of the Abraham Lincoln Brigade?

Mr. WOLFF. I do not.

Mr. MATTHEWS. Do you have a copy of the bylaws of the organization known as the Veterans of the Abraham Lincoln Brigade?

Mr. WOLFE. With me?

Mr. MATTHEWS. Yes.

Mr. WOLFE. I have not.

Mr. MATTHEWS. Could you supply the committee with one?

Mr. WOLFE. We might be able to, if we have it. I don't know.

Mr. MATTHEWS. Does the organization which was known as the Friends of the Abraham Lincoln Brigade still exist?

Mr. WOLFF. It does not.

Mr. MATTHEWS. Were its affairs merged in with those of the Veterans of the Abraham Lincoln Brigade?

Mr. WOLFF. Might say that their affairs disappeared and the veterans took up from that point.

Mr. MATTHEWS. Did you take over their books?

Mr. WOLFE. We did not.

Mr. MATTHEWS. In what bank do you have your—the account of your organization, the veterans' organization?

Mr. WOLFF. I am not familiar with that phase of the activities of the organization.

Mr. LYNCH. Mr. Wolff, did you graduate from high school in Brooklyn?

Mr. WOLFF. In Brooklyn?

Mr. LYNCH. Yes.

Mr. WOLFE. Yes.

Mr. LYNCH. What was the name of it, please?

Mr. WOLFF. The Utrecht High School; I think that is it.

Mr. LYNCH. And I did not get the employment that you had after your high-school education and before you went to Spain.

Mr. WOLFF. How did I—I didn't hear you.

Mr. LYNCH. What was your employment after your high-school education and before you went to Spain?

Mr. WOLFF. Immediately that I left high school I went to art school and I studied commercial art for a few months. I don't know exactly how many. After which I was unemployed for a short period and then I—my family was on relief at that time, and I was sent to a C. C. C. camp for 10 months.

Mr. LYNCH. And then did you go from the C. C. C. camp over to Spain?

Mr. WOLFE. No. I came from the C. C. C. camp and again I was unemployed for a short time and I finally secured employment. I believe it was an importing and exporting house—millinery goods or something, where I was the shipping clerk.

Mr. LYNCH. And did you—what books did you read in the study that you had between democracy and fascism?

Mr. WOLFF. I beg your pardon?

Mr. LYNCH. That led you to your opinion that you have expressed here in your examination?

Mr. WOLFF. I didn't hear the beginning.

Mr. LYNCH. What books did you read on that subject of the struggle between democracy and fascism which led you to the opinion you expressed here a few moments ago?

Mr. WOLFE. I remember I read what particularly impressed me. was Jay Allen's account of what happened in Spain at the outbreak of the war. I don't remember reading any books. When Jay Allen described the massacre of Spanish people——

Mr. LYNCH. And did you read anything else?

Mr. WOLFF. No. I read in the newspapers at the time.

Mr. LYNCH. How many were in your battalion?

Mr. WOLFF. Well, the number varied. I think the highest number we ever hit was 700 and the lowest about 350.

Mr. LYNCH. And you spoke about losing—you lost all your personal belongings?

Mr. WOLFF. That is right.

Mr. LYNCH. Were you a prisoner?

Mr. WOLFF. No. I lost my belongings when I was—when the battalion was surrounded on one particular occasion and scattered and it was necessary for me to swim the Ebro River to get back to our lines.

Mr. LYNCH. And at the time you sailed, did you know that you were going to Spain to fight?

Mr. WOLFF. I did.

Mr. LYNCH. And what did you say in your passport application that you were going to Spain for?

Mr. WOLFF. I did not say I was going to Spain.

Mr. LYNCH. What did you say you were going to Europe for, or going abroad for?

Mr. WOLFF. I don't know. Perhaps to study art.

Mr. LYNCH. Did you not say you were going to Johannesburg, South Africa, to visit an uncle for 3 months?

Mr. WOLFF. That might have been it.

Mr. LYNCH. You knew that was a perjury at the time?

Mr. WOLFF. No; I didn't think it was.

Mr. LYNCH. You swore to the affidavit, didn't you, when you got your passport?

Mr. WOLFF. I don't know that I did.

Mr. LYNCH. Do you recall that you took an oath that you would not travel in Spain when you got your passport?

Mr. WOLFF. No; I don't recall such an oath.

Mr. LYNCH. But if you said that you were going—you don't have an uncle in Johannesburg, South Africa?

Mr. WOLFF. I have.

Mr. LYNCH. Did you have any intention of visiting him when you got that passport?

Mr. WOLFF. When I got the passport?

Mr. LYNCH. Yes.

Mr. WOLFF. No; I did not.

Mr. LYNCH. That is all.

Mr. MATTHEWS. That next witness is Tony DeMaio.

Mr. SCHWAB. Just a moment.

Mr. WOLFF. If the Chair pleases, I would like to further—what Fred Keller said about Vernon Selby. Vernon Selby on one occasion, I believe, deserted with Honeycombe and was brought back under guard to our battalion.

I had a talk with Selby at that time and he agreed that it was the wrong thing to do; that he had gotten panic-stricken because it did appear that at that particular time that as though the war was over. It was during the retreat on the Ebro and he was hot-footing it for the border. However, when Selby came back with the rest of the prisoners, and I want to state for the record in denial of what Honeycombe said, that we would have had no use for the prisoners at the front as unarmed men. There was no purpose in their coming up there if they were unarmed. And at that time all the prisoners were given arms.

Selby, because of his valuable experience and knowledge of injuries and so forth, was used by myself as an observer and a scout for the battalion.

When the battalion was surrounded and cut off 450 of us on a hill outside of Grandesa—when nightfall came it was Vernon Selby that led the battalion off that hill and through the Fascist lines up to a certain point. He was a very exhausted man at that time, as we all were. We had been on the run for several days. The battalion ran into a German auxiliary unit of the Fascist Army.

The battalion was scattered at that time and only 60 of the battalion got across the river. Vernon Selby was not one of those 60. Except for those who were captured and were spared by Franco and were imprisoned and have since returned, the rest are missing and considered dead, which is all we can do. And Selby was one of those.

Mr. MATTHEWS. I want to ask you one question. Mr. Wolff, you say Selby and the other men were arrested for an alleged desertion. They were given arms when they were brought back to the front?

Mr. WOLFF. When they returned to the front they were given arms, as every man at the front was given.

Mr. MATTHEWS. So that Honeycombe was at the front at that time, wasn't he?

Mr. WOLFF. He didn't stay there.

Mr. MATTHEWS. Well, was he or was he not?

Mr. WOLFE. All right, I will further exaggerate—I will further explain.

Mr. MATTHEWS. Was he at the front?

Mr. WOLFF. He was not. And may I explain—may I explain?

The CHAIRMAN. Explain what?

Mr. WOLFF. The time that these deserters came back we were outside of the town of Coberra. We were organizing our battalion. We had gotten new men from —— who had just recuperated from their wounds. These deserters were brought back and some hundred Spanish conscripts. None of the men had any arms at all at this time because they had all been lost in the previous retreat. A shipment of brand-new rifles came in—about 500 rifles, and every man who was in the battalion was given arms.

From that point we went up to the front. Honeycombe did not go up.

Mr. MATTHEWS. You just testified that Honeycombe did go to the front with arms.

Mr. WOLFE. I attest to the cleverness of the questioner, Mr. Matthews.

Mr. LYNCH. What was the rank of Mr. Selby?

Mr. WOLFF. What is that?

Mr. LYNCH. What was the rank of Mr. Selby?

Mr. WOLFF. Mr. Selby at that time was a sergeant.

The CHAIRMAN. All right, bring your next witness.

Mr. MATTHEWS. Tony DeMaio.

Mr. SCHWAB. Mr. Chairman, do you think we will be finished with both of these witnesses today?

The CHAIRMAN. I don't know. It depends on how long it takes.

TESTIMONY OF ANTHONY E. DeMAIO

The CHAIRMAN. Raise your right hand. Do you solemnly swear to tell the truth, the whole truth, and nothing but the truth, so help you God?

Mr. DeMAIO. I do.

Mr. MATTHEWS. Will you please give your full name?

Mr. DeMAIO. My full name is Anthony E. DeMaio.

Mr. MATTHEWS. Spell the last name?

Mr. DeMAIO. D-e-M-a-i-o.

Mr. MATTHEWS. M-a-i-o?

Mr. DeMAIO. That is right.

Mr. MATTHEWS. Have you ever used any other variations of that name?

Mr. DeMAIO. (No answer.)

Mr. MATTHEWS. Have you ever spelled it, for example, DeMayo?

Mr. DeMAIO. I just spelled that "D-i" because the committee in serving the subpena spelled it "D-i" and I didn't want to give the committee the reasons for raising any question of doubt. That is why I spelled it "D-i." "D-e" is the regular spelling.

Mr. MATTHEWS. Have you ever gone under any other name for any purpose other than the name of Anthony DeMaio?

Mr. DeMAIO. I would like to state, Mr. Chairman, that I have been called in here for testimony regarding my activities in the Abraham Lincoln Brigade, and that any questions involving my personal life be kept out of it.

That is not the purpose of this committee.

The CHAIRMAN. Well, he is asking you a question, whether you ever went under any other name besides the name that you have now. Is this your true name?

Mr. DeMAIO. That is my true name.

Mr. MATTHEWS. Where were you born?

Mr. DeMAIO. I was born in Hartford, Conn.

Mr. MATTHEWS. When?

Mr. DeMAIO. February 21, 1914.

Mr. MATTHEWS. When you went to Spain—did you go to Spain?

Mr. DeMAIO. I went to Spain.

Mr. MATTHEWS. Did you travel on an American passport?

Mr. DeMAIO. I did.

Mr. MATTHEWS. You did?

Mr. DeMAIO. I did.

Mr. MATTHEWS. Under what name did you get your American passport?

Mr. DeMAIO. I refuse to answer that question.

The CHAIRMAN. What is the question?

Mr. MATTHEWS. I asked the witness under what name he got his American passport when he went to Spain. He declines to answer.

The CHAIRMAN. Do you decline to answer?

Mr. DeMAIO. I do.

The CHAIRMAN. The Chair instructs you to answer that question. Do you still decline?

Mr. DeMAIO. I still decline.

The CHAIRMAN. All right, proceed.

Mr. MATTHEWS. Did you get your passport under the name of Anthony DeMaio?

Mr. DeMAIO. I decline to answer that question.

The CHAIRMAN. Do you decline to answer that question?

Mr. DeMAIO. I decline.

The CHAIRMAN. The Chair instructs you to answer the question.

Mr. DeMAIO. I decline.

The CHAIRMAN. You still decline?

Mr. DeMAIO. I decline.

Mr. MATTHEWS. But your testimony is that you did travel on an American passport, is that correct?

Mr. DeMAIO. That is my testimony.

Mr. MATTHEWS. Were you ever in any of the service branches of the United States Army or the Navy or Marine Corps or National Guard?

Mr. DeMAIO. Mr. Chairman, that is still going back into my own personal history, which has no bearing on this investigation.

The CHAIRMAN. Do you decline to answer that question?

Mr. DeMAIO. I decline to answer that question pertaining——

The CHAIRMAN. This particular question?

Mr. DeMAIO. I do.

The CHAIRMAN. The Chair instructs you to answer. Do you still decline?

Mr. DeMAIO. I still decline.

The CHAIRMAN. All right, proceed.

Mr. MATTHEWS. You did travel on a false passport when you went to Spain, didn't you, Mr. DeMaio?

Mr. DeMAIO. I still refuse.

The CHAIRMAN. You have covered that.

Mr. MATTHEWS. Are you a member of the Communist Party?

Mr. DeMAIO. I am not.

Mr. MATTHEWS. Were you ever a member of the Communist Party?

Mr. DeMAIO. I was.

Mr. MATTHEWS. When did you join the Communist Party?

Mr. DeMAIO. I don't recall the exact date. It was when I returned from Spain.

Mr. MATTHEWS. Were you a member of the Communist Party at any time before you went to Spain?

Mr. DeMAIO. I was not.

The CHAIRMAN. The Chair wants to make an announcement. We are sitting as a subcommittee with the chairman, Mr. Mason, of Illinois, and Mr. Voorhis of California.

Mr. LYNCH. Mr. Chairman, you will note from the time Mr. De-Maio commenced his testimony to this present moment we were sitting as a full committee.

The CHAIRMAN. A quorum was present. Proceed.

Mr. MATTHEWS. When did you get out of the Communist Party?

Mr. DeMAIO. I don't recall the exact time. It was just a dropping away process, that is all.

Mr. MATTHEWS. Quite recently?

Mr. DeMAIO. No. It is about 6 months at least.

Mr. MATTHEWS. Were you expelled?

Mr. DeMAIO. I was not expelled.

Mr. MATTHEWS. Were you given permission to drop out?

Mr. DeMAIO. No. I just dropped.

Mr. MATTHEWS. Were you ever assigned to work in any part of New Jersey for the Communist Party?

Mr. DeMAIO. I was not.

Mr. MATTHEWS. Did you ever do any work for the Communist Party in the State of New Jersey?

Mr. DeMAIO. I did not.

Mr. MATTHEWS. Weren't you an official of the Communist Party during the seamen's strike in the spring of 1936?

Mr. DeMAIO. I had no connection with the seamen's strike in New Jersey in 1936. I don't even recall if I was in New Jersey at the time.

Mr. MATTHEWS. Did you ever work as a merchant seaman?

Mr. DeMAIO. I never did.

Mr. MATTHEWS. Did you assist in the raising of funds for the strike committee in the strike of 1936?

Mr. DeMAIO. I don't recall whether I might have or not in one way or another, but not as any particular job.

Mr. MATTHEWS. Do you recall whether you had any official connection with the strike committee?

Mr. DeMAIO. I had no official connection with the strike committee.

Mr. MATTHEWS. Do you remember the names of any of the members of the strike committee?

Mr. DeMAIO. I don't remember any of their names.

Mr. MATTHEWS. Did you know two men by the names of Panchelli and Brown?

Mr. DeMAIO. I don't know.

Mr. MATTHEWS. Who were arrested in connection with that strike, and are serving terms in Trenton, N. J.?

Mr. DeMAIO. I never heard of the men before, and I never knew them.

Mr. MATTHEWS. It doesn't refresh your recollection to state that they are serving 15-year terms in the State prison at Trenton?

Mr. DeMAIO. Doesn't refresh my memory at all.

Mr. MATTHEWS. Did that case have anything to do with your leaving the State of New Jersey?

Mr. DeMAIO. Had nothing to do with my leaving the State.

Mr. MATTHEWS. When did you enlist for service in the International Brigade?

Mr. DeMAIO. Will you repeat that question?

Mr. MATTHEWS. When did you enlist for service in the International Brigade, in Spain?

Mr. DeMAIO. My service in Spain began in Albacete, January 6.

Mr. MATTHEWS. No. When did you enlist—when did you volunteer to go across from this side?

Mr. DeMAIO. I didn't volunteer from this side.

Mr. MATTHEWS. When did you go to Spain?

Mr. DeMAIO. Sometime in December 1936.

Mr. MATTHEWS. From what port did you sail?

Mr. DeMAIO. I sailed from New York.

Mr. MATTHEWS. On what ship?

Mr. DeMAIO. On the *Normandie*.

Mr. MATTHEWS. What was the date of the sailing?

Mr. DeMaio. I don't recall.

Mr. Matthews. December 1936 on the *Normandie?*

Mr. DeMaio. That is right.

Mr. Matthews. In what class?

Mr. DeMaio. Third class.

Mr. Matthews. Was your name listed on the passenger list?

Mr. DeMaio. It was.

Mr. Matthews. What was the name on the passenger list?

Mr. DeMaio. Mr. Chairman, this is bringing up the same question time and time again. I previously stated——

The Chairman. Do you decline to state what name you were listed under in the passenger list?

Mr. Schwab. That isn't the question.

The Chairman. What?

Mr. Schwab. That isn't what he declines to answer.

Mr. Matthews. I asked him what name he was listed under on the *Normandie* in December 1936 when he sailed to Europe?

The Chairman. You decline to answer that?

Mr. DeMaio. I decline.

The Chairman. The Chair instructs you to do so and you decline. Proceed.

Mr. Matthews. Was it the same name you used on the passport which you fraudulently obtained?

Mr. DeMaio. I don't know.

Mr. Matthews. You don't know whether it was the same name or not?

Mr. DeMaio. No.

Mr. Matthews. Under what name were you enlisted in the Loyalist Army in Spain?

Mr. DeMaio. Under my own name.

Mr. Matthews. What did you do with your passport when you reached Spain?

Mr. DeMaio. I turned it over to some one.

Mr. Matthews. Did you ever get it back?

Mr. DeMaio. The passport was lost at the front.

Mr. Matthews. To whom did you turn it over in Spain?

Mr. DeMaio. I don't recall his name.

Mr. Matthews. How did you apply for your passport as to the purpose of your going to Europe? Did you state that you were going to Spain in your application?

Mr. DeMaio. I refuse to answer that question.

Mr. Matthews. Was there a notation stamped on your passport that it was not valid for travel in Spain?

Mr. DeMaio. I refuse to answer that question.

The Chairman. Wait a minute. You decline to answer that?

Mr. DeMaio. I might add that at the time I went to Spain that there——

The Chairman. Isn't it a fact that all passports were marked "Not valid for travel in Spain"?

Mr. Schwab. Mr. Chairman, may I ask that the photographs—they have got enough pictures now. I think I can be unmolested for a minute.

The Chairman. All right, gentlemen.

Mr. Schwab. Never having been at the front, those things annoy me.

The Chairman. No question about that, is there, about all the passports being marked "not valid for travel in Spain"?

Mr. DeMaio. I don't know about all of them.

The Chairman. Do you object to answering that so far as you were concerned

Mr. DeMaio. I don't know anything about that. I refuse to answer the question.

Mr. Matthews. In what year was your passport issued?

Mr. DeMaio. I refuse to answer any questions pertaining to my passport on my constitutional grounds.

Mr. Matthews. When you sailed for Spain, was it your intention to join the Loyalist Army?

Mr. DeMaio. I hadn't that intention.

Mr. Matthews. That is, when you left the United States you had not intended to join the Loyalist Army?

Mr. DeMaio. I didn't.

Mr. Matthews. Did you go directly to Spain?

Mr. DeMaio. No; I didn't.

Mr. Matthews. Well, of course, you know the Spanish civil war did not break out until but a few months before that time.

Mr. DeMaio. That is right.

Mr. Matthews. You did not go directly to Spain?

Mr. DeMaio. I did not go directly to Spain.

Mr. Matthews. How long after you arrived in Europe before you went to Spain?

Mr. DeMaio. Very short time.

Mr. Matthews. How long would you say?

Mr. DeMaio. A matter of a couple of weeks about.

Mr. Matthews. Was it long enough to go to Moscow and then back to Spain?

Mr. DeMaio. I don't know what transportation is like to Moscow and back. I couldn't tell you that.

Mr. Matthews. Well, it depends on how you travel. You could get there in a few days if you went by air.

The Chairman. Did you go to Moscow before you went to Spain?

Mr. DeMaio. I did not go to Moscow and could not.

Mr. Matthews. In what countries did you travel in Europe before you went to Spain?

Mr. DeMaio. Just France and Spain.

Mr. Matthews. What occupation did you give on your passport application?

Mr. DeMaio. Refuse to answer the question.

Mr. Matthews. What was the date of your arrival in Spain?

Mr. DeMaio. I don't recall the exact date. It was sometime.

Mr. Matthews. What was the month?

Mr. DeMaio. It was January 1937.

The Chairman. I want to clear up one thing. You have refused to answer certain questions. Do you refuse on the ground to answer those questions might tend to incriminate you?

Mr. DeMaio. Not at all. I said that I do not recall the exact date that I landed in Spain.

Mr. LYNCH. That isn't an answer to your question.

The CHAIRMAN. I am asking you this: You have refused to answer certain questions heretofore about your passport. Do I understand that the reason for your refusal is it may tend to incriminate you?

Mr. DEMAIO. It is within my constitutional right to refuse to answer the question.

The CHAIRMAN. I am trying to get you to specify whether your refusal to answer is because you fear that it might tend to incriminate you? Is that the constitutional ground upon which you rely in your refusal to answer the questions?

Mr. DEMAIO. I am not giving any reasons beyond what I have given before, that it is within my constitutional rights not to answer any questions that I don't want to.

The CHAIRMAN. You mean in other words then, you don't put it on the ground that it might tend to incriminate you?

Mr. SCHWAB. May I discuss it with my client for a moment?

The CHAIRMAN. Go ahead.

(Inaudible discussion between Mr. Schwab and the witness.)

The CHAIRMAN. I am asking you, what is the constitutional ground? Is it that you fear that it may tend to incriminate you in any way?

Mr. DEMAIO. Yes; that is it.

The CHAIRMAN. Then he shall not be required to answer the question with reference to the passport.

Mr. LYNCH. Well, Mr. Chairman, I think he should be required to answer the question in regard to his passport because the statute gives him immunity.

Mr. SCHWAB. May I speak on that question, Mr. Chairman?

The CHAIRMAN. Yes. We are talking about the passport.

Mr. SCHWAB. I don't think in the first place it has anything to do with the purpose of this committee, but I don't think any committee can take away this man's constitutional right to refuse to testify on the ground that he has given. There is nothing in the statute— enabling statute dealing with congressional bodies which takes away that right. He stated it, and I don't believe we should waste any more time on it.

Mr. LYNCH. If the gentleman wants me to I will get him the law. I will send upstairs and get it. There is a statute of the United States which gives a right to a committee when a man refuses to answer to compel him to answer, and he doesn't have any right to refuse to answer on the ground his testimony might tend to incriminate him. He is still required to answer it. You have the same precise law before the Communications Commision and the Interstate Commerce Commission and other Government agencies.

The CHAIRMAN. Well, it may be that is true, that he has immunity when testifying before a committee of Congress, and that you could require him to do so. However, the committee has hesitated in the past to require any man to answer a question on that ground.

Anyway we will carry along. Go ahead.

Mr. MATTHEWS. Who furnished you with the funds to travel to Spain?

Mr. DEMAIO. I was working at the time just previous to that. I had my own money.

Mr. MATTHEWS. When you reached Spain, to what duty were you assigned?

Mr. DeMAIO. I was a soldier in the infantry.

Mr. MATTHEWS. Where did you go?

Mr. DeMAIO. Went to a training camp.

Mr. MATTHEWS. Which training camp was that?

Mr. DeMAIO. Villejara.

Mr. MATTHEWS. How long were you in the training camp?

Mr. DeMAIO. About a month.

Mr. MATHEWS. And then did you report at the front?

Mr. DeMAIO. Sent to the front.

Mr. MATTHEWS. How long were you at the front?

Mr. DeMAIO. We were at the front for the entire campaign.

Mr. MATTHEWS. How many days was that?

Mr. DeMAIO. The exact days. I think it was something like 120 days straight.

Mr. MATTHEWS. You were there at the front during the entire 120 days?

Mr. DeMAIO. That is right.

Mr. MATTHEWS. And then where did you go?

Mr. DeMAIO. Went on rest.

Mr. MATTHEWS. What was your rank in the army?

Mr. DeMAIO. Soldier at that time.

Mr. MATTHEWS. Were you ever promoted?

Mr. DeMAIO. I was.

Mr. MATTHEWS. To what rank?

Mr. DeMAIO. To sergeant.

Mr. MATTHEWS. Were you ever promoted beyond that?

Mr. DeMAIO. I was.

Mr. MATTHEWS. To what rank?

Mr. DeMAIO. To lieutenant, junior grade.

Mr. MATTHEWS. Was there any other promotion after that?

Mr. DeMAIO. Lieutenant, senior grade, or rather lieutenant, because the lower rank was cut out.

Mr. MATTHEWS. And did you hold that rank at the time you left Spain?

Mr. De MAIO. I did.

Mr. MATTHEWS: In what other engagements were you at the front?

Mr. DeMAIO. I was in the engagement of Brunete and the Ebro offensive.

Mr. MATTHEWS. Were you ever assigned to any duties behind the front?

Mr. DeMAIO. No permanent duties.

Mr. MATTHEWS. Any temporary duties?

Mr. DeMAIO. Well, I had been in the rear.

Mr. MATTHEWS. Were you ever assigned to Camp Lunkas?

Mr. DeMAIO. I was never assigned there; no.

Mr. MATTHEWS. Were you ever there?

Mr. DeMAIO. I was there.

Mr. MATTHEWS. What were your duties there?

Mr. DeMAIO. I was recuperating from a wound.

Mr. MATTHEWS. Was Camp Lunkas a concentration camp for prisoners?

Mr. DeMAIO. I never considered myself as a prisoner.

Mr. Matthews. Was it?

Mr. DeMaio. It was not.

Mr. Matthews. Were you placed in charge of the Anglo-American section?

Mr. DeMaio. No; I was not in charge of them.

Mr. Matthews. Did you know William C. McCuistion in Spain?

Mr. DeMaio. I heard of him.

Mr. Matthews. Did you ever meet him personally?

The Chairman. He asked you if you knew him?

Mr. DeMaio. I knew him.

Mr. Matthews Did you know him personally?

Mr. DeMaio. I knew him.

The Chairman. You knew him in Spain?

Mr. DeMaio. (No answer.)

Mr. Matthews. Did you have any conversations with him?

Mr. DeMaio. He was at Camp Lunkas with me at the time.

Mr. Matthews. He was with you at Camp Lunkas. What was your purpose at Camp Lunkas?

Mr. DeMaio. We certainly weren't there for the same reasons.

Mr. Matthews. Why was he there?

Mr. DeMaio. (No answer.)

The Chairman. You say McCuistion was in the same camp and for the same purpose with you?

Mr. DeMaio. I did not say that.

Mr. Matthews. He said a different purpose. Why was he there?

Mr. DeMaio. I never asked him.

Mr. Matthews. Do you know why he was there?

Mr. DeMaio. I don't know why he was there.

Mr. Matthews. How do you know his purpose was different from yours then?

Mr. DeMaio. He wasn't wounded. I know that.

Mr. Matthews. Wasn't he in charge of the military section of the Anglo-Americans there?

Mr. DeMaio. McCuistion?

Mr. Matthews. Yes.

Mr. DeMaio. Not to my knowledge.

Mr. Matthews. Was he to your knowledge demoted or disrated for assisting prisoners in the camp to escape?

Mr. DeMaio. Don't know anything about it.

Mr. Matthews. Were any of the inmates of Camp Lunkas placed there for the purposes of waiting for repatriation?

Mr. DeMaio. I don't know if they were sent there for that purpose or not.

Mr. Matthews. How long were you at Camp Lunkas?

Mr. DeMaio. About 3 weeks, I think.

Mr. Matthews. And was that entirely for recuperation?

Mr. DeMaio. For recuperation purposes.

Mr. Matthews. Were there any men at Camp Lunkas who were there because they were labeled as dangerous or destructive or disruptive?

Mr. DeMaio. I never inquired as to the reason why others were there. I was there myself for recuperation purposes and that is all.

Mr. Matthews. Now, don't you know of your own knowledge that the majority of the men at Camp Luukas were sent there because they objected to the tactics of the Communist Party in Spain?

Mr. DeMaio. I do not know of any such reason.

Mr. Matthews. Because they resented the interference of political commisars and other politicians in army affairs?

Mr. DeMaio. I repeat, Mr. Chairman, why I was at Camp Lunkas, and I do not know why others were there.

The Chairman. All right.

Mr. DeMaio. I think that answers the question on that sufficiently.

Mr. Matthews. Were any Americans at Camp Lunkas removed from there to Albacete?

Mr. DeMaio. I was.

Mr. Matthews. Did you know of any others who were removed?

Mr. DeMaio. I don't know of any others.

Mr. Matthews. Do you know of any who were removed from Camp Lunkas to Albacete for the purpose of execution?

Mr. DeMaio. I do not.

Mr. Matthews. Or Chinchilla for the purpose of execution?

Mr. DeMaio. I do not.

Mr. Matthews. Did you superintend the removal of any persons from Camp Luukas?

Mr. DeMaio. I did not.

Mr. Matthews. And did you know Maj. Allen Johnson?

Mr. DeMaio. I knew him.

Mr. Matthews. In what capacity did you know him?

Mr. DeMaio. Only that he was there. I never served with him or under him, so I don't know him personally. I know of him.

Mr. Matthews. Was he a former officer in the Regular Army of the United States?

Mr. DeMaio. I don't know.

Mr. Matthews. To refresh your memory don't you remember numerous speeches in which he talked of his experiences in the Fifteenth and Twenty-Seventh Infantries of the United States Army?

Mr. DeMaio. I never listened to any of his speeches.

Mr. Matthews. Did he make speeches?

Mr. DeMaio. I don't know if he did or not.

Mr. Matthews. At this time you were given an official position as brigade police officer for the American section of the fifteenth brigade, were you not?

Mr. DeMaio. That is not so.

Mr. Matthews. Do you know of any police officers who were assigned to special tasks of that sort?

Mr. DeMaio. I do not.

Mr. Matthews. Do you know Lieutenant Ehrlich?

Mr. DeMaio. I do not.

Mr. Matthews. You don't know any one in Spain by that name?

Mr. DeMaio. No.

Mr. Matthews. Captain Cohn?

Mr. DeMaio. I do not.

Mr. Matthews. Did you know any police officer by that name?

Mr. DeMaio. The only police officers that I can think of are Spanish police officers.

Mr. Matthews. Did you know Albert Wallach?

Mr. DeMaio. I do not.

Mr. Matthews. Did you ever hear the name of Albert Wallach?

Mr. DeMaio. I did not; never did.

Mr. Matthews. Were you in charge of the prison at Castle de Fells?

Mr. DeMaio. I was never in charge of the prison at Castle de Fells.

Mr. Matthews. Were you ever at the prison at Castle de Fells?

Mr. DeMaio. I was never at the prison at Castle De Fells.

Mr. Matthews. Did you ever see Albert Wallach?

Mr. DeMaio. I don't know. I might have passed him. I didn't know him so I couldn't say whether I saw him or not.

Mr. Matthews. Did you know Paul White?

Mr. DeMaio. I did not know Paul White.

Mr. Matthews. Did you ever hear of Paul White?

Mr. DeMaio. I heard of him.

Mr. Matthews. Did you read the notice given to the Lincoln Battalion of his execution?

Mr. DeMaio. I heard of it but I didn't——

The Chairman. What was his answer?

Mr. Matthews. That you heard of the execution?

Mr. DeMaio. I don't know whether it was termed "an execution" or what it was.

Mr. Matthews. Well, you said you heard of it.

Mr. DeMaio. I heard of him.

Mr. Matthews. Well, I asked you if you heard of his execution, or if you read the notice, and you said you heard of it.

Mr. DeMaio. Just a moment.

Mr. Matthews. You heard of Paul White's execution?

Mr. DeMaio. I did not hear of it in Spain.

Mr. Matthews. You heard of it after you came back to the United States?

Mr. DeMaio. I heard—some newspapers printed something to that effect. I never heard of it at that time.

Mr. Matthews. Where did you get that answer?

Mr. DeMaio. (No answer.)

Mr. Matthews. It differs from your previous answer.

Mr. DeMaio. It does not.

Mr. Schwab. I suggest Mr. Matthews, you don't start a personal altercation here.

Mr. Matthews. Do you recognize that photograph as being any person you ever saw in Spain?

(Handing photograph to the witness.)

Mr. DeMaio. It looks like Carey Grant, the movie actor.

Mr. Lynch. Ask him to answer the question.

Mr. DeMaio. No.

(Mr. Matthews handing the picture to the witness again.)

Mr. DeMaio. I don't know him.

Mr. Matthews. You don't recognize these pictures as being Albert Wallach?

Mr. DeMaio. I don't recognize him.

Mr. Matthews. And you never heard of the name of Albert Wallach in Spain, is that correct?

Mr. DeMaio. Never heard of him.

Mr. Matthews. How long were you in Spain?

Mr. DeMaio. About 2 years.

Mr. MATTHEWS. Did you know many of the men in the Abraham Lincoln Brigade, so-called?

Mr. DEMAIO. I didn't know all of them.

Mr. MATTHEWS. Now, in what capacity did you know Maj. Allen Johnson?

Mr. DEMAIO. I never knew him at the—in the Abraham Lincoln Brigade.

Mr. MATTHEWS. Did you know him in Spain?

Mr. DEMAIO. I knew him as an officer in Spain, that is all.

Mr. MATTHEWS. Did you ever deliver any prisoners to Maj. Allen Johnson in Spain?

Mr. DEMAIO. I never did.

Mr. MATTHEWS. Of what was Maj. Allen Johnson an officer? You said you knew him as an officer?

Mr. DEMAIO. At the base in Tarragona.

Mr. MATTHEWS. You did know him at Tarragona?

Mr. DEMAIO. I knew he was there. I didn't say I knew him there.

Mr. MATTHEWS. Did you see him in Tarragona?

Mr. DEMAIO. I saw him once, I believe.

Mr. MATTHEWS. What were you doing in Tarragona at the time you met Maj. Allen Johnson?

Mr. DEMAIO. I believe I was at Camp Lunkas at the time, and it was a short run over there, and I took a trip over there to see some of the men, and I saw him while I was there.

Mr. MATTHEWS. And you took prisoners from Camp Luukas to Tarragona and delivered them to Maj. Allen Johnson, did you not?

Mr. DEMAIO. I did not.

Mr. MATTHEWS. Did you know of any men who were executed in Spain?

Mr. DEMAIO. No, did not.

Mr. MATTHEWS. Were there any disciplinary cases that were of such seriousness that executions resulted, to your knowledge?

Mr. MEMAIO. Not to my knowledge.

Mr. MATTHEWS. Did you ever hear of any?

Mr. DEMAIO. Never heard of any direct cases of execution; no.

Mr. MATTHEWS. Except the one of Paul White to which you testified? Is that the only one?

Mr. DEMAIO. I did not testify that I knew he was executed.

Mr. MATTHEWS. No, only that you had heard of it. Did you know of any others who were executed?

Mr. DEMAIO. I did not.

Mr. MATTHEWS. In Spain?

Mr. DEMAIO. (No answer.)

Mr. MATTHEWS. Did you ever meet George Mink in Spain?

Mr. DEMAIO. Never heard of him.

Mr. MATTHEWS. You never heard of the name of George Mink?

Mr. DEMAIO. Never did.

Mr. MATTHEWS. Did you know George Hirsch in Spain?

Mr. DEMAIO. Never heard of him.

Mr. MATTHEWS. You never heard of that name either?

Mr. DEMAIO. No.

Mr. MATTHEWS. Did you know an American by the name of Moran?

Mr. DEMAIO. No, I don't.

The CHAIRMAN. Speak a little louder, please. It is very hard to hear.

Mr. DEMAIO. I never heard of him.

Mr. MATTHEWS. Were you ever in Barcelona?

Mr. DEMAIO. I had been there; yes.

Mr. MATTHEWS. Do you recall whether or not you were in Barcelona on May 2, 1938?

Mr. DEMAIO. (No answer.)

Mr. MATTHEWS. That was the day following the May Day celebration, to refresh your recollection.

Mr. DEMAIO. Then I wasn't there.

Mr. MATTHEWS. You were not in Barcelona on May 2, 1938?

Mr. DEMAIO. I was not there around any May Day.

Mr. MATTHEWS. Did you ever frequent the cafes on the Rambla de Catalonia in Barcelona?

Mr. DEMAIO. Mr. Chairman, may I ask just what all that this here is about. Certainly if a man went to Barcelona in time of war on leave he visited a cafe.

The CHAIRMAN. That is just what he was asking you. Go ahead.

Mr. DEMAIO. Then, but I ask what the purpose of this question is. Certainly, I visited some of these cafes but what has that to do with the investigation?

The CHAIRMAN. All right, proceed.

Mr. MATTHEWS. Did you meet George Mink or George Hirsch in any of the cafes.

Mr. DEMAIO. I told you previously I never heard or saw these individuals.

Mr. MATTHEWS. Did you ever sit on a court martial to try two Finnish-Americans in Spain?

Mr. DEMAIO. I never sat on a court martial in Spain.

Mr. MATTHEWS. Did you sit on a court martial to try a Canadian and Finn for drunkenness?

Mr. DEMAIO. This is getting ridiculous.

The CHAIRMAN. Wait a minute. You will find out how material it is later on. You are now being afforded an opportunity to answer certain questions.

Mr. DEMAIO. No; I don't know anything about that.

Mr. MATTHEWS. Do you know the name of Paul Oskar?

Mr. DEMAIO. I do not.

Mr. MATTHEWS. Did you ever hear that name in Spain?

Mr. DEMAIO. I never heard it in Spain.

Mr. MATTHEWS. Did you ever hear the name of George Niemin in Spain?

Mr. DEMAIO. I never did.

Mr. MATTHEWS. Did you ever hear the name of George Kulksinem?

Mr. DEMAIO. I never did.

Mr. MATTHEWS. In Spain?

Mr. DEMAIO. I did not.

Mr. MATTHEWS. You never heard of those three men?

Mr. DEMAIO. I never heard of those men.

Mr. MATTHEWS. Did you ever hear that two Finnish-Americans and one Canadian Finn were executed on the beach in Barcelona?

Mr. DEMAIO. I never heard of this.

Mr. MATTHEWS. Did you know a man by the name of Sullivan who was a political commissar in the Irish-American Battalion?

Mr. DEMAIO. I never heard of an Irish-American Battalion.

Mr. MATTHEWS. Did you know a man named Sullivan who was a political commissar connected with any of the sections of the Loyalist Army?

Mr. DEMAIO. I never heard of him.

Mr. MATTHEWS. Did you know Louis Oliver?

Mr. DEMAIO. The name sounds familiar. I can't place him.

Mr. MATTHEWS. Well, you placed him under arrest once, didn't you?

Mr. DEMAIO. I did not.

Mr. MATTHEWS. In Barcelona, didn't you place Louis Oliver under arrest?

Mr. DEMAIO. No.

Mr. MATTHEWS. Did you ever go aboard the American steamship *Oregon?*

Mr. DEMAIO. I don't recall ever having done so; I might have— I think I went aboard one American steamer there.

Mr. MATTHEWS. Where?

Mr. DEMAIO. In Barcelona.

Mr. MATTHEWS. In Barcelona?

Mr. DEMAIO. Yes.

Mr. MATTHEWS. Wasn't it the American steamship *Oregon?*

Mr. DEMAIO. I don't know whether that was the name of it or not. There were several American ships.

Mr. MATTHEWS. Who went with you when you went aboard the ship?

Mr. DEMAIO. I went alone.

Mr. MATTHEWS. Are you sure that George Mink and Cohn didn't accompany you when you went aboard that ship?

Mr. DEMAIO. They did not.

Mr. MATTHEWS. Well, what was your purpose in going aboard the steamship *Oregon* in Barcelona?

Mr. DEMAIO. It was along the same line as visiting a cafe. It was part of the time—of killing time while in Barcelona—possibly being able to pick up a pack of American cigarettes, that is all.

Mr. MATTHEWS. Now, Mr. DeMaio, didn't you go aboard the American steamship *Oregon* to place Albert Wallach under arrest?

Mr. DEMAIO. I did not.

Mr. MATTHEWS. In company with George Mink?

Mr. DEMAIO. I did not.

Mr. MATTHEWS. And Captain Cohn?

Mr. DEMAIO. I did not.

Mr. MATTHEWS. Did you ever have any acquaintance that you can now recall or any knowledge of Albert Wallach?

Mr. DEMAIO. No knowledge whatsoever.

Mr. MATTHEWS. Did you know Wayne Taine?

Mr. DEMAIO. No.

Mr. MATTHEWS. Lawrence McCullough, did you know him?

Mr. DEMAIO. No.

Mr. MATTHEWS. Did you know any one by the name of Frich?

Mr. DEMAIO. No.

The CHAIRMAN. Did you know Mr. Wolff in Spain?

Mr. DeMaio. I knew Mr. Wolff in Spain.

Mr. MATTHEWS. Did you ever know Virgil Morris?

Mr. DeMaio. No.

Mr. MATTHEWS. Did you ever hear the name in Spain?

Mr. DeMaio. Can't recall.

Mr. MATTHEWS. George Dempsey?

Mr. DeMaio. (No answer.)

Mr. MATTHEWS. Did you ever meet him?

Mr. DeMaio. I think George Dempsey was once our cook, but I don't know him.

Mr. MATTHEWS. Did you know them any time as prisoners—calling the name, reading the names?

Mr. DeMaio. No.

Mr. MATTHEWS. Did you ever see any prisoners in Spain who were members of the American section?

Mr. DeMaio. Never paid much attention to them. I wouldn't recall their names or faces.

Mr. MATTHEWS. Did you ever see any prisoners?

Mr. DeMaio. I saw the labor battalions but I never distinguished their faces or anything.

Mr. MATTHEWS. Were members of the labor battalion the same as prisoners? Is that what you mean to testify?

Mr. DeMaio. I don't know whether they were or not. I don't know anything about the disciplinary units in Spain.

Mr. MATTHEWS. Did you know Paul White?

Mr. DeMaio. I did not.

Mr. MATTHEWS. Did you ever hear the name of Paul White?

Mr. DeMaio. I can't recall the name definitely or the face.

Mr. MATTHEWS. You can't recall his face. Do you have a vague recollection of his face?

Mr. DeMaio. No.

Mr. MATTHEWS. Did you ever know him as Johnnie Adams in this country?

Mr. DeMaio. Never did.

Mr. MATTHEWS. But you now have some vague recollection?

Mr. DeMaio. I have a vague recollection of the name but the individual I have no recollection or knowledge of.

Mr. MATTHEWS. And you associate his name with the execution about which you say you have a vague recollection, is that right?

Mr. DeMaio. That is right. That is the only recollection I have.

Mr. MATTHEWS. Did you meet Robert Minor in Spain?

Mr. DeMaio. Robert Minor spoke to us a few times only in the capacity of a correspondent.

Mr. MATTHEWS. Was that the limit of his duties in Spain?

Mr. DeMaio. As far as I know. I never knew him personally.

Mr. MATTHEWS. Did you ever talk to him personally in Spain?

Mr. DeMaio. I never did.

Mr. MATTHEWS. Did you meet any of the members of the International Political Commission for the International Brigade in Spain?

Mr. DeMaio. What is the International Political Commission?

Mr. MATTHEWS. By whatever title it was known—the group of men——

Mr. DeMaio. Tell me exactly what you mean.

Mr. Matthews. Well, Andre Marty, for example. Did you ever meet Andre Marty in Spain?

Mr. DeMaio. I have seen him.

Mr. Matthews. Did you ever meet Harry Pollock from England?

Mr. DeMaio. I never saw him.

Mr. Matthews. You know he was in Spain, don't you?

Mr. DeMaio. I don't know.

Mr. Matthews. You know Andre Marty was in Spain?

Mr. DeMaio. I know Andre Marty was in Spain.

Mr. Matthews. Did you meet Earl Browder in Spain?

Mr. DeMaio. I never met him.

Mr. Matthews. Did you see him in Spain?

Mr. DeMaio. I didn't see him.

Mr. Matthews. But you did see Robert Minor there. How long was Minor in Spain?

Mr. DeMaio. I don't know.

Mr. Matthews. Did you ever make any reports to Robert Minor?

Mr. DeMaio. I told you I never spoke to Robert Minor.

Mr. Matthews. Did you ever make any reports to him?

Mr. DeMaio. Never did.

Mr. Matthews. About any matters?

Mr. DeMaio. About nothing at all.

Mr. Matthews. Pertaining to the Lincoln Brigade?

Mr. DeMaio. (No answer.)

Mr. Matthews. Do you know John Little?

Mr. DeMaio. I don't know him.

Mr. Matthews. John Little, of the Young Communist League?

Mr. DeMaio. I don't know him.

Mr. Matthews. You don't know him?

Mr. DeMaio. No.

Mr. Matthews. You did not meet him in Spain?

Mr. DeMaio. I did not meet him in Spain.

Mr. Matthews. How much time did you spend at the front altogether? Can you give us a rough estimate of that, Mr. DeMaio?

Mr. DeMaio. I think about 11 months, exclusive of a period that I spent convalescing.

Mr. Matthews. Eleven months at the front. And how much time would that leave? About 9 or 10 months when you were not at the front?

Mr. DeMaio. About that.

Mr. Matthews. Were you familiar with the details of the retreat to the Ebro in April 1938?

Mr. DeMaio. I am not.

Mr. Matthews. Did you know that a large number of the American soldiers preferred to surrender to the Fascists at the time of that retreat than to continue in the service of the International Brigade?

Mr. DeMaio. I never heard of it, and I don't believe it.

Mr. Lynch. Mr. DeMaio, when did you return to the United States?

Mr. DeMaio. Sometime in March 1939.

Mr. Lynch. And did you return on a passport or not?

Mr. DeMaio. I object; I refuse to answer.

The Chairman. You refuse to answer that?

Mr. DeMaio. I refuse to answer.

The CHAIRMAN. On what ground?

Mr. DeMaio. On the grounds previously stated.

The CHAIRMAN. It will tend to incriminate you?

Mr. DeMaio. That is right.

The CHAIRMAN. Is that right?

Mr. DeMaio. That is right.

Mr. LYNCH. What ship did you return on?

Mr. DeMaio. I refuse to answer that on the same ground.

Mr. LYNCH. At what port did you land?

Mr. DeMaio. I landed in the port of New York.

Mr. LYNCH. And where were you educated, Mr. DeMaio?

Mr. DeMaio. In Hartford, Conn.

Mr. LYNCH. Did you graduate from high school?

Mr. DeMaio. I did not.

Mr. LYNCH. Did you attend high school?

Mr. DeMaio. I did.

Mr. LYNCH. Which high school?

Mr. DeMaio. Mr. Chairman, may I ask what that has to do with this investigation?

The CHAIRMAN. Do you object to answering that question—what high school you attended?

Mr. DeMaio. (No answer.)

Mr. LYNCH. Do you know what high school you attended?

Mr. DeMaio. I refuse to answer that question.

The CHAIRMAN. All right.

Mr. LYNCH. Did you go under the name of Anthony DeMaio at that time?

Mr. DeMaio. I did.

Mr. LYNCH. And you spelled it D-e-M-a-i-o, is that correct?

Mr. DeMaio. That is correct.

Mr. LYNCH. And what was your address at the time you went abroad in this country?

Mr. DeMaio. I believe it was—I refuse to answer that question.

The CHAIRMAN. On the ground it tends to incriminate you?

Mr. DeMaio. That is right.

Mr. LYNCH. Did you have a witness to your passport application when you obtained a passport?

Mr. DeMaio. I refuse to answer.

Mr. SCHWAB. Mr. Chairman, in order to save time I would appreciate getting through with my last witness here so we could all leave. And I think the witness has indicated clearly that he won't answer any questions pertaining to the passport.

Mr. LYNCH. Now, Mr. Chairman, the section of the law, for the benefit of counsel who never heard of it, is section 103 of the Revised Statutes, says:

Mr. SCHWAB. Nothing in that statute, Mr. Chairman, that refers to a constitutional right that everybody in America knows about—nothing about refusing to testify on the ground that it may incriminate him.

Mr. LYNCH. Now, the next section:

No testimony given by a witness before either House or before any committee or by the Houses of Congress shall be used as evidence in any criminal proceeding against him in any court except in the prosecution for perjury committed in giving such testimony.

I ask the chairman, in view of these two statutes, to direct the witness to answer the questions which he heretofore refused to answer.

The CHAIRMAN. Well, that is a matter that the committee will have to forego for the time being. We will have to consider that.

Mr. MATTHEWS. I have one more question to ask the witness. Mr. DeMaio, did you know Bernard Ades in Spain?

Mr. DeMAIO. Spell that last name?

Mr. MATTHEWS. A-d-e-s—Bernard Ades.

Mr. DeMAIO. I did not know him.

Mr. MATTHEWS. Did you know Major Galleani?

Mr. DeMAIO. I heard of him; I don't know him.

Mr. MATTHEWS. What was his position in Spain?

Mr. DeMAIO. A major, that is all I know. He was never connected with any unit that I was connected with.

Mr. MATTHEWS. But you do know he was in Spain?

Mr. DeMAIO. I took that for granted.

Mr. MATTHEWS. The next witness is Major Galleani, Mr. Chairman.

Mr. SCHWAB. I was here all day yesterday—I had a matter on— there is one more of my witnesses here and I think as a courtesy to me, if for no other reason, you should not make me stay over or come back and I think——

The CHAIRMAN. Major Galleani.

Mr. SCHWAB. May I say this, I have to be back tonight. I was figuring on making the next plane.

Mr. DEMPSEY. You are not under subpena.

Mr. SCHWAB. I am an attorney, and I am asking a courtesy.

The CHAIRMAN. We have to proceed in order. We will take that up in a few minutes.

Mr. SCHWAB. Will you hear this witness today?

The CHAIRMAN. I will have to confer with counsel with reference to this witness. What witness is it you have?

Mr. SCHWAB. Jerry Cooke.

The CHAIRMAN. We will take that up in a few minutes.

TESTIMONY OF HUMBERTO GALLEANI, FORMER MAJOR, SPANISH LOYALIST ARMY

The CHAIRMAN. Raise your right hand. Do you solemnly swear to tell the truth, the whole truth, and nothing but the truth, so help you God?

Mr. GALLEANI. I do.

Mr. MATTHEWS. What is your full name?

Mr. GALLEANI. Humberto Galleani.

Mr. MATTHEWS. What is your address, Mr. Galleani?

Mr. GALLEANI. 2 West Fifteenth Street, New York.

Mr. MATTHEWS. Mr. Galleani, I show you a copy of Newsweek, dated July 24, 1937. On page 16 there is a photograph. Is that a photograph of yourself [handing magazine to the witness]?

Mr. GALLEANI. Yes, sir.

Mr. MATTHEWS. Under the photograph are the words: "Major Galleani, first United States volunteer." Was that the first United States volunteer to Spain?

Mr. GALLEANI. Yes, sir.

Mr. MATTHEWS. I show you a flyer or. throw-away with a photograph and ask you if that is a photograph of yourself [handing paper to the witness]?

Mr. GALLEANI. Yes.

Mr. MATTHEWS. At what meeting were you speaking when this photograph was taken?

Mr. GALLEANI. I was speaking at the meeting in the first anniversary of the conflict in Spain on July 19, 1937.

Mr. MATTHEWS. And there are other photographs on this throw-away. I ask you if you can identify this photograph [handing paper to the witness]?

Mr. GALLEANI. Earl Browder.

Mr. MATTHEWS. Earl Browder, the general secretary of the Communist Party of the United States?

Mr. GALLEANI. Yes.

Mr. MATTHEWS. And who is this?

Mr. GALLEANI. Angelo Herndon.

Mr. MATTHEWS. I show you a sheet which comes from Life magazine. Here is a picture taken in a field [handing exhibit to the witness].

Mr. GALLEANI. Yes.

Mr. MATTHEWS. Is that a photograph of yourself?

Mr. GALLEANI. Yes, sir.

Mr. MATTHEWS. Where was that taken?

Mr. GALLEANI. In Alabres, near Madrid.

Mr. MATTHEWS. In Spain?

Mr. GALLEANI. Yes; in Spain.

Mr. MATTHEWS. Now, Major Galleani, I show you a certificate. Will you please identify that certificate and state its significance?

Mr. GALLEANI. That is a certificate given by the Ministry of Defense—by the Defense Ministry of Spain, stating that I have served in the International Brigade as a major in defense of liberty of Spanish people.

Mr. MATTHEWS. Was this given you at the time you left Spain?

Mr. GALLEANI. Yes. And I have another one here.

Mr. MATTHEWS. This is dated Barcelona, 15th of November 1938.

Mr. GALLEANI. And I have another one here.

Mr. MATTHEWS. This is from the Minister of Defense.

Mr. GALLEANI. Yes; awarding the medal of the International Brigade to Major Galleani.

Mr. MATTHEWS. Is this an award for your services?

Mr. GALLEANI. Yes.

Mr. MATTHEWS. In Spain?

Mr. GALLEANI. Yes.

Mr. MATTHEWS (reading):

As a reward for his behavior during the second war for Spanish independence, His Excellency, the Minister of National Defense, has resolved to award to you the medal of the International Brigades, established by circular order of October 20, 1938, official journal of the Government No. 275, for non-Spanish combatants who have served in said brigades since their formation until the date of the said circular order.

This information I take pleasure in communicating to you in the name of His Excellency, the Minister, for your satisfaction and for all purposes.

Signed at "Barcelona, November 15, 1938," by the subsecretary, "Antonio Cordon." It is addressed to "Maj. Humberto Galleani."

What was your rank in Spain, Mr. Galleani?

Mr. GALLEANI. Well, I went to Spain on October 1, 1936, and as the International Brigades were in formation at that time, the first International Brigades were in formation, and as I am of Italian descent I was put in command of the Italian battalion of the International Brigade.

Mr. MATTHEWS. Did you see service at the front?

Mr. GALLEANI. Yes.

Mr. MATTHEWS. What length of service did you have at the front?

Mr. CALLEANI. Well, I was there from October 10, 1936, up to April 19, 1937. In 1937 the Spanish Government sent me to United States in a tour of propaganda. I went back to Spain in October 1937—in September, rather, 1937—and was there up to the last day. I left Spain on February 7, 1939.

Mr. MATTHEWS. Did you have as long a record of service in the actual front lines as——

Mr. GALLEANI. Yes, sir.

Mr. MATTHEWS. As any American who fought in the Spanish civil war?

Mr. GALLEANI. I was. When I came back—when I went back in October 1937 I was assigned to the general staff of the Fifteenth International Brigade, and I remained with the Fifteenth International Brigade until the end of March 1938, when I was transreferred to the regular Spanish army as the commander of a brigade.

Mr. MATTHEWS. Was there an Abraham Lincoln Brigade in Spain?

Mr. GALLEANI. Well, in Spain I never heard of the Abraham Lincoln Brigade. The name of the Abraham Lincoln Brigade was the Fifteenth International Brigade, and it was the English-speaking brigade—that is, a brigade composed of English—Battalion Fifty-seventh of the Lincoln-Washington, Battalion Fifty-eighth, Battalion Fifty-ninth—it was completely of Spanish people and of the Sixtieth Battalion MacKenzie-Papeneau.

Mr. MATTHEWS. Now, were you on the general staff of the International Brigade?

Mr. GALLEANI. Yes, sir.

Mr. MATTHEWS. Were your duties political or military?

Mr. GALLEANI. Military.

Mr. MATTHEWS. Had you had previous military experience?

Mr. GALLEANI. Yes. I was an officer in the Italian Army during the World War.

Mr. MATTHEWS. You were an officer in the Italian Army during the World War? What rank did you hold?

Mr. GALLEANI. I was lieutenant and became captain when the war dismissed.

Mr. MATTHEWS. Now, when you volunteered to go to Spain to fight with the International Brigade, were you a member of the Communist Party?

Mr. GALLEANI. I was.

Mr. MATTHEWS. How long had you been a member of the Communist Party?

Mr. GALLEANI. Well, I had been since the Communist Party started the policy of democratic liberty—of democracy in 1934 or 1935.

Mr. MATTHEWS. What was your purpose in enlisting for service in Spain?

Mr. GALLEANI. I enlisted—first of all, I went to Spain almost against the will of the party. The policy of the party at that time was not to send men to Spain. I made my application to the Spanish consul to go to Spain and was warned by the party if I insisted in my application I would be expelled, so I made many requests and finally told that if I asked, if paying my own fare to go to Europe, they will let me go.

Mr. MATTHEWS. Then is it correct, as stated in the Newsweek Magazine, that you were the first volunteer?

Mr. GALLEANI. Yes, sir.

Mr. MATTHEWS. To fight from the United States?

Mr. GALLEANI. Yes, sir. The other contingent—the first contingent of Americans arrived in Spain about the beginning of January 1937. I arrived in Spain October 10, 1936.

Mr. MATTHEWS. To what extent was your volunteering as the first volunteer from the United States to fight in the Spanish civil war motivated—by your experience—dislike of fascism as you had known it in Italy?

Mr. GALLEANI. Well, I was a political refugee in this country since 1924. I had been—was submitted by Fascists to mistreatment plenty of times. I had several times plenty of castor oil. I was beaten several times and then as a lawyer, I was not permitted to practice, and so I had to leave Italy in order to not be obliged to submit to persecution.

In this country I have always been a militant of the anti-Fascist Italians, and I have been foreign editor of the Italian anti-Fascist newspaper.

Mr. MATTHEWS. Was that what led you to join the Communist Party, your dislike of fascism, or shall I say your intense dislike of fascism?

Mr. GALLEANI. Well, there are many reasons.

Mr. MATTHEWS. When you were persuaded that the Communist Party had embarked on a program for the defense of democracy was that the reason you joined the Communist Party?

Mr. GALLEANI. Yes, sir.

Mr. MATTHEWS. Now, will you please state briefly and clearly and distinctly as possible what you discovered in Spain with reference to Russian control of the International Brigade, and I mean by that not simply Communist Party control, but control from the Soviet Union?

Mr. GALLEANI. When the International Brigades were formed, when the International Brigades were formed. in October 1936, there were not yet any Russians in Spain. The first Russian to arrive was General Kleber, who took command of what was at that time the only International Brigade, composed mainly of French, Italian, German, Polish, and a few more nationalities of the Balkan countries. After General Kleber arrived, General Lukacz, who had the command of the Second Brigade, that was called the Twelfth Brigade, the brigade commanded by General Kleber was the Eleventh Brigade, the brigade commanded by General Lukacz was the Twelfth Brigade, and these were the two brigades who helped a great lot in saving the city of Madrid from the Fascist invasion. At that time in the International Brigade there was really a regime of democracy.

I have explained this in many interviews to the press.

In 1937 I explained this in my lecture tour all over the United States. And I have said that, for instance, the political commissars at that time were elected by the rank and file. If the rank and file were not satisfied with an officer, the officer was exonerated before going to a combat. A report was called of all the battalion commanders, and they were exonerated, completely—what the action was to be, what the purpose of the action, how were the forces of the enemy, how many were the firearms that the enemy had at his disposal, and so on. Then the same thing would happen again in the battalion, who is the commander, the same thing would happen in the company, with the commander of section. That is, that there was really a debate how the combat had to be prosecuted and everyone had the right to criticize the plan of the command, to make propositions and to sometimes—it happens that even the proposition of a sublieutenant are accepted by the general command.

Mr. MATTHEWS. How long did that situation prevail?

Mr. GALLEANI. That situation prevailed until I left for America. And I have to tell very frankly that I never would have come over here to make propaganda if this was not the situation.

When I come back I found that in every International Brigade there was a great number of Russian officers who were the direct representatives of the Comintern, sent over there, I think, for two purposes: To establish the strictest connection between the leader of the Russians, who were in Spain, and also to make a little of experience on a real war because, of course, you know, there were many young officers who did not have any practice, in war.

Mr. MATTHEWS. You mean the Russian Government was training men for a future European war on the battlefields of Spain?

Mr. GALLEANI. Yes, sir. Of course, all the International Brigade at the time—at the time there were 5 International Brigades, from 11 to 15—all commanded by officers arriving from Russia—Eleventh by Kleber and Twelfth by Lukacz and the Thirteenth by an Italian man who bore the name of Krieger. The Fourteenth was under the command of Lt. Cole Dumont, a French Communist Party member, designated by Andre Marte, and the Fifteenth by Vladimir Copic, who was a former deputy in Yugoslavia—an exiled Russian since about 8 or 9 years.

Mr. MATTHEWS. Now, who was General Gall?

Mr. GALLEANI. General Gall was the first commander of the Fifteenth International Brigade, also Russian.

Mr. MATTHEWS. And that was the brigade in which the Lincoln Battalion——

Mr. GALLEANI. Yes. At that time the two battalions, Lincoln and Washington—it was afterward one, reduced to one battalion.

Mr. MATTHEWS. Now, I want to come back to that presently, Major Galleani, but I would like to ask you if you knew Tony DeMaio in Spain?

Mr. GALLEANI. Yes. I know—I have known Tony DeMaio. As a matter of fact I was in charge of the Fifteenth International Brigade in Grandesa around the 20th of March 1938, when a battalion arrived from the instruction base at Terregona. I saw the list of the men and I saw the name of this young Italian man, so I approached him and I asked him if he was Italian-born. He told me he was American born. I saw that he was a husky young fellow, and I told him, "Well, I hope you will do good here."

After about 5 or 6 days I went to inspect the Lincoln Battalion and I asked where DeMaio was. DeMaio, by the way, had the rank of sublieutenant at the time. So I learned DeMaio left the battalion on a special mission, and I protested with Copic and told him not right young man like DeMaio just arrived at the front sent out on a mission. The right way to send him to the trenches before and see what he could do in the trenches and then send him on special mission.

Later on I found out DeMaio had been put in charge of the International Brigade prison at Castle de Fells, near Barcelona.

Mr. MATTHEWS. Did you hear DeMaio's testimony?

Mr. GALLEANI. I did not hear it completely, the testimony.

Mr. MATTHEWS. But you testify that you learned that DeMaio was placed in charge of the prison for the——

Mr. GALLEANI. At Castle de Fells. And when I left Barcelona at the end of January, just a couple of days before the Fascists arrived in Barcelona, at the railroad station at about 15 kilometers from Barcelona, I don't remember the name just now, I met DeMaio with his prisoners—he had about, oh, I don't know—I can't estimate—180 or 200 prisoners——

Mr. MATTHEWS. In his charge?

Mr. GALLEANI. In his charge. And I talked to him, and as I know what military discipline is, I asked him the permission to see some of the Italian prisoners who had been in the formation of the Garibaldi Battalion. So I saw two or three of the prisoners—a man by the name of Ortega and a man by the name of Perogina and another man by the name of Oloca, and all the three complained to me about the brutal treatment that DeMaio was giving to the prisoners. But, of course, at the time the International Brigade was almost—there was no reason for making any way—we were where we could not take care of a matter of that kind any more.

Mr. MATTHEWS. How long was it between the time that you first learned that DeMaio had been placed in charge of the prison at Castle de Fells and the time you met him on this occasion?

Mr. GALLEANI. About—now, I will tell you, from the middle of April 1938 to the end of January 1939.

Mr. MATTHEWS. For a period of 8 or 9 months?

Mr. GALLEANI. Yes.

Mr. MATTHEWS. DeMaio was in charge of prisoners?

Mr. GALLEANI. Yes, sir.

Mr. MATTHEWS. In Spain?

Mr. GALLEANI. In Spain; yes, sir.

Mr. MATTHEWS. Did you learn of any individual cases which were handled by or under DeMaio which had to do with discipline—even with execution?

Mr. GALLEANI. Well, I can't say anything about execution. I don't know. I am told that several prisoners at Castle de Fells disappeared mysteriously, but I can't say by my proper knowledge anything about the disappearance of anybody.

Mr. MATTHEWS. Well, do you know——

Mr. GALLEANI. What I can tell, if you will permit me, what I can tell is this, that among the prisoners which, according to my information, were mistreated, there was a James Dougherty from Detroit, Mich.——

Mr. MATTHEWS. D-o-u-g-h-e-r-t-y?

Mr. GALLEANI. Yes. To whom DeMaio made the threat that he would never come back to the United States. I really don't know if Dougherty came back to the United States. Other prisoners who complained about the treatment by DeMaio were Frank Alexander, Paul Elliott, Robert Quinn, and, of course, these three Italian fellows whom I have named before.

I have been told also that the man whom I knew very well at the brigade by the name of Isenberg was put in the old—you have to know the prison was an old monastery and there was a little church, of course, with marble floor and this was the place where the prisoners were put who had to be punished—were put without anything to sleep in, even without a little straw. They were sleeping on the floor. They were having very little food. They were forbidden even if they had the means, of smoking, and so on.

This Isenberg was put in the church because it seemed he complained to DeMaio about the treatment he was receiving there and about the fact that the guards were selling tobacco to people who had money instead of putting the tobacco among the prisoners.

Mr. MATTHEWS. What other facts did you learn about the system of punishment or torture or inhumanity practiced against prisoners?

Mr. GALLEANI. Well, let me tell you, I am absolutely in disfavor of any physical punishment, so when another battalion where DeMaio belonged to come over to Alcañz, I was sent to meet this battalion and I was informed for the first time that by order of Maj. Allen Johnson the instruction base at Tarragona had a special police and the officer in charge of the battalion told me that he had about 16 or 17 prisoners, most of them guilty of getting drunk, you know, which was very easy in Spain because the wine is very heavy and a great alcoholic content. We were in a village which was dominated by anarchists, and the anarchists didn't like at all the International Brigade, so I was particularly zealous that nothing happened that gave to the anarchists any reason for showing this displeasure for the International Brigade. Instead when this little platoon of prisoners passed on, I didn't know myself for what reason the man in charge began to club them with the blackjack, and they never in any other brigade in Spain use the blackjack.

So I ran in among these men and this man in charge of the police, the chief of police was so excited that he tried to hit me too with the blackjack in spite I was in uniform and, of course, was a superior officer.

I can tell that they have been using rather brutal system against men from the physical violence to the universal system of threatening for any reason if a man made any criticism. The first thing they used to say was that he was a provocateur; that he was a defeatist and threatening to put him against the wall.

Mr. MATTHEWS. Now, was Maj. Allen Johnson in charge of this platoon of prisoners that you saw?

Mr. GALLEANI. He was not in charge of the platoon of prisoners. He was in charge of the battalion of the instruction base at Tarragona. He was not with this particular battalion. He was remain in Tarragona.

Mr. MATTHEWS. Did you know of the cases of men who were executed on the beach at Barcelona for drunkenness?

Mr. GALLEANI. Well, I heard of it, but I had no particular way—I have heard—what I am sure about is the execution of Paul White who was the quartermaster of the Lincoln-Washington Battalion.

Mr. MATTHEWS. Will you tell what you know about the execution of Paul White?

Mr. GALLEANI. Paul White tried to abandon Spain—he tried to leave Spain—we were volunteers of liberty—we had no engagement whatsoever with the Spanish Government and the Spanish Government has never made any difficulty to volunteer, for a volunteer who wanted to leave Spain because they didn't like it any more and didn't want to stay here. Instead, the policy of the International Brigade was that no volunteer could leave and, as a matter of fact, they were declared deserters, people who tried to abandon Spain.

Many, many time it happen that people to whom the International Brigade forbade to leave Spain, went to the Ministry of War there and they were immediately discharged from the army and sent back to their country.

So, in the case of Paul White, according to my information, he was arrested on the Pyrenees while he was trying to get out of Spain. There was, of course, a mock trial, you know—it was very easy to make mock trial in the International Brigade, and after a couple of days this rather ironical communication was made to the battalion, that for unanimous decision of the battalion the volunteer Paul White had been executed. This was communicated at the battalion who should have given the sentence and we didn't know anything about it.

Mr. MATTHEWS. Did you know that Paul White's real name was John Quincy Adams?

Mr. GALLEANI. I don't know his real name. I have no name but Paul White.

Mr. VOORHIS. Just a minute. It seems to me that is very important. As I understand your testimony it is that the men serving in the International Brigade had never taken any obligation to the Spanish Government?

Mr. GALLEANI. Never.

Mr. VOORHIS. That the Spanish Government's attitude was that whenever they wanted to leave they were free to do so?

Mr. GALLEANI. Sure.

Mr. VOORHIS. But that the policy of the International Brigade itself was quite the opposite?

Mr. GALLEANI. Yes, sir; quite the opposite.

Mr. VOORHIS. Well, who was responsible for that policy on the part of the International Brigade?

Mr. GALLEANI. Well, the International Brigade have been most of the time almost a autonomous formation in the Spanish Army, depending more by the political control of the Comintern than by the Government. There was a big political hierarchy that started at the top with the so-called International Commission of Control headed by a Russian woman, and where the representatives of the Communist Party of all the country were represented from the Commission of Control. The power was going to a so-called commission—political-military commission of the Spanish Communist Party, which, however, was a rubber stamp in the case of the International Commission of Control.

Then every party—every Communist Party there had a member of the central committee—a delegate of the central committee. In the case of the Fifteenth International Brigade the American Central Committee was represented by Robert Minor; the English Communist Party was represented by Rust, and the Canadian Communist Party was represented by Taylor.

Mr. MATTHEWS. Mr. Galleani, I want to make that perfectly clear. Are you sure that Robert Minor was in charge of the affairs for the American Communist Party?

Mr. GALLEANI. Well, I can tell you positively that no change in the high command of the brigade or in the political commissariat or brigade could take place without the consent of Robert Minor.

The CHAIRMAN. So that the International Brigade was completely controlled by the Communist Party?

Mr. GALLEANI. By the Communist Party; yes.

Mr. MATTHEWS. Now, did you finish with the information which you had on the execution of Paul White?

Mr. GALLEANI. This is all I know of the execution of Paul White.

Mr. MATTHEWS. Do you know where he was executed or by whom?

Mr. GALLEANI. He was executed in Marsan (?) and by whom, according to my information, by a New York young man who was known at the brigade by the name of Ivan.

Mr. MATTHEWS. I-v-a-n?

Mr. GALLEANI. I-v-a-n. Now, I have to tell that before leaving Spain no special police of the type of G. P. U. was existing in Spain. At the request of one of the Russian chiefs at the time the Defense Ministry of the Loyalist Government instituted the thing which was called S. I. M.——

Mr. MATTHEWS. What is the English equivalent of that?

Mr. GALLEANI. The Intelligence Service.

Mr. MATTHEWS. Soviet Intelligence Service?

Mr. GALLEANI. Yes.

Mr. MATTHEWS. Now, Mr. Galleani, would Robert Minor have anything to say about disciplinary cases or executions?

Mr. GALLEANI. I don't think an execution—I don't think he had ever been asked about the executions. The execution was made without even asking him, but he had supervising power, as I told you, in every change of superior officer and he was in contact with the International Commission of Control.

Mr. MATTHEWS. Now, did you find on your second period of stay in Spain——

Mr. GALLEANI. Well, I was talking—pardon me, if I interrupt—I was talking of this S. I. M., as we say in Spanish, this S. I. M., was a kind of intelligence service which required undoubtedly to be executed by some very responsible man. Instead of that the Fifteenth International Brigade was in charge of a young man about 21 or 22 years old. Very excitable and who tried to show that he was a tough guy, so this man, this Ivan, made the inquiry on the case of

Paul White and reported that Paul White had tried to desert and so on. And I have been told that he had been in command of the firing squad.

Mr. MATTHEWS. Did you know anything about the case of a man named Tachus?

Mr. GALLEANI. Well, these are two brothers, Joe and John, to whom DeMaio made threat that they would never come back to the United States.

Mr. MATTHEWS. DeMaio threatened them they would never come back to the United States?

Mr. GALLEANI. Yes. Now, I don't know if they returned or not.

Mr. MATTHEWS. Did you know a case of a man named Modesto?

Mr. GALLEANI. Well, Modesto. Modesto was one of the highest ranking officers of the Spanish Army. He was lately in command of the Army of the Ebro. He was the general even if he didn't carry the rank of general. He was a colonel, but he was the one who prepared the crossing of the Ebro in July 1938.

Mr. MATTHEWS. And did he return to Russia?

Mr. GALLEANI. He was a younger man who had been at the military school in Russia and he was put in charge of the command of one of the battalions of the Fifth Regiment, which was the communist formation of the First Spanish Militia.

Mr. MATTHEWS. Did you know Fred Keller in Spain?

Mr. GALLEANI. Yes; very well.

Mr. MATTHEWS. What did you know about Keller's activities?

Mr. GALLEANI. Well, to use a very mild expression, Fred Keller was a bad boy. He undoubtedly—he had no sense of responsibility necessary to be a political commissar of a battalion, and when I had Fred Keller under my command, particularly when we moved the brigade in train from near Teruel to Valencia, I had to complain about Fred Keller for several reasons, which we will explain, and after my report to the lieutenant colonel and the political commissar of the brigade, Fred Keller was exonerated from the charge by the political commissar of the battalion.

Now, I want to mention two cases. He was the one who was encouraging the men to do a little vandalism, you know. For instance, we arrived with the train near Segundo and the train was stuck in the field. There was a marvelous orange garden. There was the more severe order that we didn't touch anything of the fruit of the Spanish peasants. He released all the men of the battalion and they went to rob a great quantity of oranges which belonged to poor working men.

On the return to Barrajas we were waiting the order from the division where we had to go and there was in the office of the station master waiting for a telephone, one of the Spanish sergeants came over and complained to me that he was on guard of a wagon of a fruit train and that the political commissar with a bunch of men went there to rob 8 bottles of cognac and about 20 or 25 cases of corn beef—canned corn beef.

Mr. MATTHEWS. Was that political commissar Fred Keller?

Mr. Galleani. Yes, sir. So I called Keller and I told——

What is the matter, Keller? What do you think you are? What is this idea. This man has been put in charge of a guard over a wagon and, of course, he is responsible. How can he justify that political commissar of the International Brigade gave the order to rob these things from the wagon.

So I compelled Keller to give back the cognac but, unfortunately, the cognac was about 20 gallons and unfortunately 3 bottles had disappeared. A couple of hours later almost all of the men of the battalion were drunk. That was a big danger because we were at the front and we were near the enemy, and the battalion could have been called to action at any moment.

Mr. MATTHEWS. Did you say that Fred Keller had been discharged at one time?

Mr. GALLEANI. He was exonerated. The proof is this: This fact occurred on February 1938.

Mr. MATTHEWS. You used the word "exonerated." I think you mean the opposite?

Mr. GALLEANI. No; exonerated. He was taken away from the charge.

Mr. MATTHEWS. Well, that means the opposite?

Mr. GALLEANI. This is the Spanish expression—"exonerated."

Mr. MATTHEWS. You mean relieved of duty?

Mr. GALLEANI. Relieved of duty; yes. Now, as proof of this, later on, 15 days or a little more later, when the Belchite action took place and the commander of the Lincoln Battalion, the political commissar of the Lincoln Battalion were killed in action, the commander of the base was Dave Rees from Paterson, N. J., and the political commissar was Parker from Boston.

After the death of Parker the political commissar of the battalion for a few weeks was Johnnie Gates, political · commissar of the Lincoln Battalion, so this proved that Fred Keller had been relieved from his duty.

Mr. MATTHEWS. Well, now, was he relieved for the reason——

Mr. GALLEANI. He was relieved by order of Dave Doran, and as there was not a way in Spain in the International Brigade to send a man to a lower charge, he was put—he was assigned to the political commissariat staff of the brigade.

Mr. MATTHEWS. Did you know Milton Wolff?

Mr. GALLEANI. Yes.

Mr. MATTHEWS. What was his connection with you?

Mr. GALLEANI. I have a high estimation of Milton Wolff. Mr. Wolff is a young man. He has no great experience. He has been courageous. He has a show of good will at all times. The only thing that Mr. Wolff has is this, that he is a member of the Communist Party and as a member of the Communist Party, he has a sense of discipline and of obeyance to his party leaders, which many times make him commit great mistakes.

Mr. MATTHEWS. Did you know J. Gordon Honeycombe in Spain?

Mr. GALLEANI. Yes. He was a runner or a chief runner of the brigade.

Mr. MATTHEWS. Did you know him to have experience at the front?

Mr. GALLEANI. Yes. He had been at the front. He had been at the front. He had been at the front at Teruel and Belchite and other places.

Mr. MATTHEWS. You know that he was at the front in those actions?

Mr. GALLEANI. Yes, sir.

Mr. MATTHEWS. Do you know Phil Bard in Spain?

Mr. GALLEANI. Yes; but he didn't participate any longer in the brigade. He had been wounded and he had come back to the brigade just for a few days but didn't take any particular service.

Mr. MATTHEWS. Now, what were the activities of Browder in Spain, which came to your attention?

Mr. GALLEANI. Well, I saw Earl Browder in Spain when we left Teruel just to go to Valencia in that famous expedition where Fred Keller committed those abuses. Earl Browder spoke to the men of the Lincoln Brigade in a field near the station where we were stopping, and he told to the men—this is what I can't exactly remember, that he had to complain because he had heard that the American boys in Spain had taken the role of imperialists that was not in compliance with the direction of the Communist Party.

Mr. MATTHEWS. Did he say anything about American boys being required to stay in Spain until the end of the war?

Mr. GALLEANI. Yes; he did. He declared that they had to stay in Spain until the war was finished.

Mr. MATTHEWS. Do you know whether or not many of the American boys were promised they would be repatriated after 6 months?

Mr. GALLEANI. I don't know about this, because I was not in America when the engagement took place. I know, however, that this promise had been made to the English volunteers who came over to Spain and the English volunteers who came over to Spain had been promised that they would be released after 6 months. But in spite of their insistence, many of them who asked to be relieved were not relieved and I think there were two English boys, a sergeant and a soldier, tried to pass to the Fascist lines because they knew that this was the only way to get back to England, and they were surprised and they were executed immediately.

Mr. MATTHEWS. Do you know whether or not the Communist Party promised any volunteers for Spain who were in the United States illegally that if they went to Spain that the party would see that they got back to the United States?

Mr. GALLEANI. That is a very, very sad story—one of the stories which have prompted me to come here to tell the truth, because I think that the treatment of these boys has been a criminal one.

There were when we left the concentration camp, because I have been in the concentration camp in France—there were about 100 American residents who were illegally in this country.

The CHAIRMAN. The United States?

Mr. GALLEANI. In the United States. When they were sent to Spain the party knew that these men were illegally in this country and they guaranteed to them that they would take care of their return to the United States when the war in Spain would be finished.

The CHAIRMAN. How were they going to do that?

Mr. GALLEANI. Now, I don't know how, but they promised that. So when we were released from the concentration camp and brought over to Le Havre, really a step had been taken in order to see if it was possible to send back these people to the United States, but the step taken met with a refusal, and an absolute refusal on the part of the State Department and the Department of Labor, so these men were stranded in Le Havre and it cost the committee $1 a day.

Finances were very poor. The friends of the Lincoln Brigade decided that this man and the other one had to be disposed of and they were disposed in this way: If you were sent to Belgium, to Antwerp, or sent to Mexico; if you were sent to Cuba and if you were brought to the United States illegally with this particular order—

you go on such and such a boat. You hide yourself for a couple of days and after a couple of days you present themselves to the commander of the boat. You tell him that you were former volunteer in Spain and he will make you work and you will arrive at Ellis Island. When you arrive at Ellis Island we will take care of you.

When these people arrive at Ellis Island nobody took care of them and they remained at Ellis Island 5 or 6 or 7 months, while it was granted to them as they were anti-Fascist—most of them from Fascist country where their life would be in danger if they had to return. They were granted the right to be shipped away to another country but to ship them away to another country they had, of course, to have money—it required money and the party never wanted to spend 1 cent for these people.

Now, I want to make this clear, that friends of the Lincoln Brigade and now the veterans of Lincoln Brigade are completely identified with the Communist Party. When the party say: "We, the friends of the Lincoln Brigade," or "the veterans of the Lincoln Brigade," say they have no money that means that the party has refused to give them money, and they really thought at that time that the party had no money.

But when they found out, for instance, that after 10 or 15 days the party was paying a full-page ad in the New York Times for the New Masses, they found out they had money but they didn't want to pay the money for the men who sacrificed themselves in Spain.

Mr. MATTHEWS. Now, do you know anything about how passports were obtained for the men who went to Spain?

Mr. GALLEANI. That is a big mystery how the passports were obtained. I don't know. As I told you, I left when nobody had left.

Mr. MATTHEWS. Do you know any irregularities——

Mr. GALLEANI. I want to explain to you this, that, of course, the order from Russia to form the International Brigade was dated around the beginning of October.

Mr. MATTHEWS Do you mean there was an order from Russia to form the International Brigade?

Mr. GALLEANI. Yes; to form the International Brigade and the Communist Party—the Communist Party of France started to engage the volunteers but, of course, it was easy in France to engage volunteers because it cost only a few francs to send them to Spain.

Instead the Communist Party here had to spend about $150 for each person they were sending to Spain and they had to collect money before being ready to send the men over there. That is why the Americans started to leave only at the end of December.

Mr. MATTHEWS. Do you know anything about any passport irregularities?

Mr. GALLEANI. Well, I know that several of the American boys arrived there, who were American passports—the American passports were taken away from them at Figueras. That is a city near the French border. They say that this passport will be transferred to Albacete. Then went from the base of the International Brigade, move from Albacete to Barcelona when the Fascist forces were about to cut the road. They said: "These passports will be shipped on a truck from Albacete to Barcelona and that this truck had been captured by the enemy."

Well, the fact is that the passports were never found any more. I can tell you, however, that at the time the transfer of the base was made from Albacete to Barcelona, the base of the International Brigade had no transportation by railroad so it seems the capture was a little like a funny stuff.

Mr. MATTHEWS. Now, what happened to the passports?

Mr. GALLEANI. Well, they were never found any longer and when the boys asked for their passports they were told that the passports were lost during the retreat.

Mr. MATTHEWS. Will you please state whether or not you discovered that the Russian Army methods, including political commissars and party representatives and party propaganda meetings, educational methods, and so on, was completely incorporated in the International Brigade?

Mr. GALLEANI. Completely; completely; but as I told you, not at the very beginning.

Mr. MATTHEWS. But ultimately it was completely incorporated?

Mr. GALLEANI. Completely; completely. Now I will tell you, for instance, the political commissar, at least for the minor units like a company or battalion, should have been elected by the rank and file, but they were all the time elected by the top. That is, the battalion by the brigade commissar, who was naturally asking the advice of the secretary of the party that was acting in every unit of the International Brigade.

Mr. MATTHEWS. Mr. Galleani, are you now a member of the Communist Party?

Mr. GALLEANI. No.

Mr. MATTHEWS. How did you leave the Communist Party?

Mr. GALLEANI. Well, when I—I didn't continue my membership in the Communist Party in Spain because I saw that there was many, many faults. The proof is that I asked to leave the International Brigade and to go into the regular Spanish Army because in the regular Spanish Army there was not such a political machine as there was in the International Brigade. So my belonging to the Communist Party ended in November 1938.

The CHAIRMAN. You joined the Communist Party here in the United States?

Mr. GALLEANI. In 1935, I think; at the end of 1934 or the beginning of 1935.

The CHAIRMAN. What were you informed as to the membership in the party at that time?

Mr. GALLEANI. Well, I really didn't have much activity because of the fact I was a foreign editor of a daily and I was excused from the activity of the party.

When it came to this, only the last 3 or 4 months before going to Spain I was put in charge of the Latin Division of the American Committee for the Protection of the Foreign Born.

Mr. MATTHEWS. You were placed there by the American Committee for the Protection of the Foreign Born?

Mr. GALLEANI. Yes, sir.

Mr. MATTHEWS. Do you know who the head of the Committee for the Protection of the Foreign Born is—do you know who the national officers of that organization are?

Mr. GALLEANI. Well, at the time the chairman was Herman Reissig. The secretary was Dwight Morgan and later——

The CHAIRMAN. Was that organization in control of the Communist Party?

Mr. GALLEANI. Sure.

The CHAIRMAN. They directed the control of the Communist Party?

Mr. GALLEANI. Sure.

Mr. MATTHEWS. You were assigned by the party to that organization?

Mr. GALLEANI. Yes.

Mr. MATTHEWS. In Spain, did you see any Russian aviation units?

The CHAIRMAN. Pardon me. Is that the same organization that met here in Washington recently?

Mr. MATTHEWS. That is correct.

The CHAIRMAN. At the Annapolis Hotel?

Mr. MATTHEWS. I don't know what hotel.

The CHAIRMAN. And you say that the party was in complete control of that organization?

Mr. GALLEANI. Yes, sir; positively.

The CHAIRMAN. What was the purpose of the organization?

Mr. GALLEANI. Well, now, I will tell you. At the time the American Committee for the Protection of Foreign Born was really defending pitiful cases of aliens who were put under their protection and many of these cases were political cases of refugees who have been in danger if they were returned to their native country. It was taking care of those so as to obtain a way to transfer them to other countries.

Later on while the war in Spain, I have been told, that the main activity of the American Committee for the Protection of the Foreign Born is now to legalize the aliens who were illegally in this country—legalize them by sending them outside of the United States and making them reenter into the United States.

Mr. MATTHEWS. Did you ever see any Russian aviation in action in Spain?

Mr. GALLEANI. Yes.

Mr. MATTHEWS. Were they there from near the beginning of the war?

Mr. GALLEANI. Oh, yes. They arrived there—not at the very beginning of the war, but they arrived there around the middle of October or the end of October. As a matter of fact, they were there—there were Russian aviators there when the defense of Madrid took place in November 1936.

Mr. MATTHEWS. And still there in 1938 when the war was over?

Mr. GALLEANI. Yes. They were still Russians in 1938. But this is one of the things that we could never explain. Around the month of June 1938 all the high officers sent to Spain by Russia was returned to Russia. They were explaining that this way: A particular order of the Spanish Government who wanted all the units under command of the Spanish officers, but their explanation was denied by the fact that the commander of the Forty-fifth Division, who was a German, and the commander of the Forty-fifth Division was in retreat and in June 1938 the help of Russia to Spain began to become something very very inconsiderable.

Mr. MATTHEWS. How long were you in charge of the Latin-American Division or, was it the Latin Division?

Mr. GALLEANI. Latin Division of the American Committee for the Protection of Foreign Born. I was in charge about 4 or 5 months.

The CHAIRMAN. I think that is all.

Mr. MATTHEWS. That is all.

The CHAIRMAN. All right, thank you very much. Who is your next witness?

Mr. MATTHEWS. Mr. McCuistion.

TESTIMONY OF WILLIAM C. McCUISTION

The CHAIRMAN. Raise your right hand. Do you solemnly swear to tell the truth, the whole truth, and nothing but the truth, so help you God?

Mr. McCuistion. Yes.

Mr. MATTHEWS. Give us your full name?

Mr. McCuistion. William C. McCuistion.

Mr. MATTHEWS. You have been a witness before this committee previously, have you not?

Mr. McCuistion. Yes, sir. I testified as to how I went to Spain and why and et cetera.

Mr. MATTHEWS. Did you go to Spain to fight in the Loyalist Army?

Mr. McCuistion. Yes, sir.

Mr. MATTHEWS. Did you sail aboard the same ship with Albert Wallach?

Mr. McCuistion. We were jointly in charge of the group that went to Paris. Sailed on March 27, 1937.

Mr. MATTHEWS. Is this the passenger list of that sailing?

(Handing document to the witness.)

Mr. McCuistion. Yes, sir. The names marked are the men that were in the group, and the "X's" are the ones who are surely dead, and the others are the ones that have subsequently showed up.

Mr. MATTHEWS. I ask this be marked as an exhibit.

The CHAIRMAN. It is so ordered.

(The passenger list referred to by Mr. Matthews was marked "McCuistion Exhibit No. 1, April 4, 1940.")

Mr. MATTHEWS. How many men sailed aboard this ship under the charge of yourself and Albert Wallach?

Mr. McCuistion. Approximately 24 Americans and 11 Canadians.

Mr. MATTHEWS. This is your name on the passenger list [indicating]?

Mr. McCuistion. Yes, sir.

Mr. MATTHEWS. William McCuistion?

Mr. McCuistion. Yes, sir.

Mr. MATTHEWS. And the name of Albert Wallach?

Mr. McCuistion. In addition to a medical unit which we had nothing to do with, that was going to Spain.

Mr. MATTHEWS. In Spain did you ever see George Mink?

Mr. McCuistion. Only once.

Mr. MATTHEWS. Will you please relate the circumstances under which you saw George Mink in Spain?

Mr. McCUISTION. I saw George Mink and Tony DeMaio and Captain Cohn on May 2, 1938, in a little cafe—one of the nicer but small cafes on the Rambla de Catalonia. I saw Tony DeMaio kill 2 men in that cafe.

Mr. MATTHEWS. Will you please describe the circumstances?

Mr. McCUISTION. At that time they were having a round-up of stragglers, a general round-up of a few of us who were out of the brigade. I was in the International Brigade at that time. I was carrying a ministry of war letter that protected me somewhat from the International Brigade police, and we were circulating more or less freely, but there were several hundred members of the International Brigade that were living under cover in Barcelona, looking for a chance to get away on the ships, and through the help of some influential Spaniards we established a means of stowing these guys away in Barcelona and helping them get out of the country.

We helped a large number of French, English, Americans, and various others to get out of the country. Several—a number of Spaniards helped us. Especially we were being helped by the Spanish Federation of Labor, which is similar to the Mexican Federation of Labor and controlled largely by the anarchists.

On this occasion we were following DeMaio when he met the other two.

Mr. VOORHIS. Who is "we"?

Mr. McCUISTION. A group of us—some Spaniards and some Cubans and myself that were in this group helping guys out of the country that had legal papers to be in Barcelona.

Mr. MATTHEWS. Can you give the names of any of those people?

Mr. McCUISTION. Yes; I can give the names of several of them. One of them was George Heins. Another a boy from Buffalo called Kelke. Those are the only Americans that I can remember roughly by name. I think they are both alive.

Mr. VOORHIS. Were they with you at this time?

Mr. McCUISTION. Yes, sir. And we followed him into this cafe and just as we got into the cafe we heard the shooting and we naturally didn't want to be around there for fear we would get shot ourselves. We knew what was taking place because it was an everyday occurrence with other groups.

It hadn't been so frequent with the American groups, but the American that was killed at that time was going under the name of Matthews. He had a State Department passport issued under the name of Aronofski—I think that was his correct name, but he was using the name "Matthews" over there, and he was shot through the side—through the temple, right in here [indicating].

The other fellow wasn't quite dead. His name was Moran, an Englishman. He was taken away to the hospital. Whether he died or not, I don't know.

Mr. MATTHEWS. Who shot them?

Mr. McCUISTION. Tony DeMaio shot them.

Mr. DEMPSEY. Why?

Mr. McCUISTION. Because they were stragglers, and because they had evidently started an altercation or something when he tried to arrest them, probably. He used it as an excuse. That is what he later said to me personally, that he had to do it to save his own life, but it was ridiculous. There were four or five in his party, but only two of them.

Mr. VOORHIS. Did you actually see that?

Mr. McCUISTION. I actually saw it.

Mr. MATTHEWS. Was George Mink with him at the time?

Mr. McCUISTION. Yes; George Mink was with him at the time.

Mr. MATTHEWS. Was George Mink going under any other name?

Mr. McCUISTION. George Hirsch—frequently used that name.

Mr. MATTHEWS. Do you know whether Albert Wallach was able to get aboard the American steamship *Oregon?*

Mr. McCUISTION. Yes, sir. Albert Wallach was stowed away on board the American steamship *Oregon* with the assistance of several members of the crew. I think one of them was named Samuel Singer. He is at present a member of the sailors' union of the Pacific coast and is in San Francisco at this time. He was aboard the ship for 10 days. He got careless and he came out and was taken off the ship by Tony DeMaio and others, and placed in prison in Barcelona.

Mr. MATTHEWS. In what prison?

Mr. McCUISTION. He was placed in the military prison, either at Karl Marx Barracks or up on the hill or at San Sebastian. I don't know which one he was placed in.

Mr. MATTHEWS. Did you meet DeMaio on any other occasion than the one you describe?

Mr. McCUISTION. Yes. At one time I was placed in military charge of the Anglo-Americans at the concentration camp at Camp Luukas. They had some there for repatriation and some for disciplinary action. DeMaio was sent there as a political commissar, and I didn't want the job very bad anyway, and I had the full charge of issuing passes, so I issued everybody that wanted a pass and then I wrote myself out one and left.

Mr. MATTHEWS. You were trying to assist the men to get away— escape?

Mr. McCUISTION. Yes.

Mr. MATTHEWS. And DeMaio was there at the time, was he?

Mr. McCUISTION. Yes.

Mr. MATTHEWS. Was he there when you wrote your own ticket for leave?

Mr. McCUISTION. No.

Mr. MATTHEWS. When did he leave Camp Luukas?

Mr. McCUISTION. He left after they brought me back to Camp Luukas when all of us were transferred together to Tarragona and placed in the disciplinary company in Tarragona under Maj. Allen Johnson. And at that time Tony DeMaio went into Albacete with the other brass hats and got himself a job as brigade policeman.

Mr. MATTHEWS. Were you arrested after you attempted to get away on that pass?

Mr. McCUISTION. Yes.

Mr. MATTHEWS. And you were placed in prison?

Mr. McCUISTION. In Albacete.

Mr. MATTHEWS. Under Allen Johnson?

Mr. McCUISTION. No. In Albacete the prison was commanded by a younger brother of Colonel Copic. He was later arrested himself for theft from the Spanish Government.

Mr. MATTHEWS. What was the charge against you? Desertion?

Mr. McCUISTION. The charge was just a conglomeration of charges. They never read any official charges. They just threw you in jail, and you stayed there until you got out or were killed.

Mr. MATTHEWS. Do you know of any other cases where violence was used against American boys?

Mr. McCUISTION. Yes. In the case of Wallach. There was violence used against him a number of times at Camp Luukas. Why, one time Tony DeMaio slapped him around. That was after I had been relieved of any authority and a fellow by the name of Howe, that is sailing under the name of Jameson, now an active seaman, was also beaten up pretty badly and thrown into prison at Chinchilla and held there for 4 months under sentence of death.

Other cases of violence were against Virgil Morris. Just any number that I can name. Another one Fred Miller. He is over in Baltimore now. I think he was subsequently captured and spent a year in the Franco prison.

Mr. MATTHEWS. Do you know the cases of the court martial of two Finnish-Americans and one Canadian-Finn?

Mr. McCUISTION. Yes, sir.

Mr. MATTHEWS. Do you recall their names?

Mr. McCUISTION. Yes. I remember one was named Oskar and one was named Niemin, and the other was Kul——

Mr. MATTHEWS. K-u-l-k-s-i-n-e-m?

Mr. McCUISTION. Something like that. It was a Finnish name, I remember.

Mr. MATTHEWS. What do you know about those cases?

Mr. McCUISTION. They were at a stragglers camp just north of Tarragona on the beach. I forget the exact name of the camp, but they were bringing all the stragglers in there from Barcelona and other points of Spain, and putting them in this camp and determining whether they were to be sent to concentration camps, sent to prison labor battalions, or sent back to the front as ordinary soldiers.

In addition they had the normal brigades—parts of the brigades that had scattered, and they were re-forming the brigade at this place.

At that time these three fellows, in particular little Niemi, had one of the best records in the whole army over there. They went into Tarragona on a drunk, and they were a little bit late getting back, and the Spanish guard placed them under arrest, and they broke out of the Tarragona jail and came back and reported in to the military command themselves.

They were given a trial and given 30 days, and then at the instance of the political commissars, they were retired and sentenced to death.

They drew up some eight or nine hundred men that were there in a three-cornered formation facing the beach, and they selected 18 men at random from the English and Americans to act as an execution squad—as a firing squad.

Mr. MATTHEWS. Under whose command was that execution squad?

Mr. McCUISTION. Under the command of a fellow by the name of Sullivan. I don't know him very well. But that was the fellow that was commanding the squad. And the ambulance brought the three men up. They lined them up on the beach. All of us—we even thought at that time that it was just going to be a show and they were going to get a last-minute pardon or something like that. We couldn't possibly conceive of any men being killed for going out on an ordinary drunk.

And they lined them up with their backs facing the Mediterranean. And took three volleys from the firing squad to kill them. And Sullivan had to go up and shoot them in the head after that—after the first two volleys Niemi was still standing on his feet and holding his hands up in the Red front salute.

Mr. Voorhis. What was the motive for that?

Mr. McCuistion. At that time motives were taking place at the rate of 25 to 50 a day, and the object to terrorize the men so that they wouldn't attempt to desert or wouldn't disobey the military commands.

Mr. Voorhis. Did you see that happen?

Mr. McCuistion. I saw that happen personally.

Mr. Voorhis. About Tony DeMaio: Was that the same man that testified here today?

Mr. McCuistion. That was the same man. He knows me well. He admitted he knew me on the stand.

Mr. Matthews. Did you have any other contacts with Tony De-Maio at any time in Spain?

Mr. McCuistion. In the month of May in Barcelona, after this other thing happened, why, I was approached by Tony DeMaio and told that Bob Minor wanted to see me at the Majestic Hotel.

I went up to the Majestic Hotel and Bob Minor and Captain Cohn and one or two others were in there and made me a proposition if I would help round up the guys and break up desertions by ship, they would see I got sent home right away.

I refused it, and I went down the rear elevator and took out for the border.

Mr. Matthews. You testified as to how you got out of Spain?

Mr. McCuistion. Yes.

Mr. Matthews. That is all.

The Chairman. Any questions? All right, stand aside.

The committee is sitting now as a subcommittee composed of Mr. Voorhis, the chairman, and Mr. Mason.

Mr. Matthews. The next witness is Gerald Cooke.

TESTIMONY OF GERALD COOKE, FORMER MEMBER, ABRAHAM LINCOLN BRIGADE

The Chairman. Raise your right hand. Do you solemnly swear to tell the truth, the whole truth, and nothing but the truth, so help you God?

Mr. Cooke. I do.

Mr. Matthews. Give your full name, please.

Mr. Cooke. Gerald Cooke.

Mr. Matthews. Where were you born?

Mr. Cooke. United States.

Mr. Matthews. Where?

Mr. Cooke. St. Louis, Mo.

Mr. Matthews. When?

Mr. Cooke. April 30, 1916.

Mr. MATTHEWS. Have you ever gone under any other name than the name "Gerald Cooke"?

Mr. COOKE. I have not.

Mr. MATTHEWS. When you went to Spain did you travel on an American passport?

Mr. COOKE. I did.

Mr. MATTHEWS. Was it issued in your own name?

Mr. COOKE. It was.

Mr. MATTHEWS. Did it bear a notation it was not good for travel in Spain?

Mr. COOKE. It did.

Mr. MATTHEWS. When you applied for that passport, what did you state as the purpose for your traveling in Europe?

Mr. COOKE. I don't recall.

Mr. MATTHEWS. It did not include a visit to Spain, however. You did not state your purpose was to visit Spain for any reason?

Mr. COOKE. I did not.

Mr. MATTHEWS. You knew that you were going to Spain, did you, when you applied for your passport?

Mr. COOKE. I did.

Mr. MATTHEWS. Whatever reason it was that you gave them it was a false one; is that correct?

Mr. COOKE. I don't recall what I said.

Mr. MATTHEWS. How long were you in Spain?

Mr. COOKE. Nineteen months.

Mr. MATTHEWS. Are you a member of the Communist Party?

Mr. COOKE. I am not.

Mr. MATTHEWS. Have you ever been a member of the Communist Party?

Mr. COOKE. I have not.

Mr. MATTHEWS. Have you ever been a member of the Young Communist League?

Mr. COOKE. I have not.

Mr. MATTHEWS. What is your present position or occupation?

Mr. COOKE. I am—you mean what is my employment?

Mr. MATTHEWS. Yes.

Mr. COOKE. I am employed by the organization of which I am a member.

Mr. MATTHEWS. Now, what is the organization?

Mr. COOKE. Veterans of the Abraham Lincoln Brigade.

Mr. MATTHEWS. What is your position in the Veterans of the Abraham Lincoln Brigade?

Mr. COOKE. I am the national secretary.

Mr. MATTHEWS. Mr. Keller. I think it was, this morning testified about an association of some 57 organizations. I don't remember the exact name of the association. Can you give us the name of that association?

Mr. COOKE. What association is that?

Mr. MATTHEWS. It was an association of some 57 organizations which he said were the auspices for picketing in front of the French consulate in New York recently. Do you know the name of the organization?

Mr. COOKE. The Emergency Conference to Save the Spanish Refugees was set up and it consisted of some 50 organizations, of which the Veterans of the Abraham Lincoln Brigade is a part.

Mr. MATTHEWS. Do you have any position in that organization?

Mr. COOKE. No.

Mr. MATTHEWS. Or in that conference?

Mr. COOKE. I do not.

Mr. MATTHEWS. You were subpenaed to appear before this committee as an officer of the Veterans of the Abraham Lincoln Brigade, were you?

Mr. COOKE. I was.

Mr. MATTHEWS. Were you required by the subpena to bring any records of any kind?

Mr. COCKE. I believe the subpena read something about records in some organization. It did not name any organization.

Mr. MATTHEWS. Now, where were you served this subpena?

Mr. COOKE. In the doorway of the magistrate court in the city of New York.

Mr. MATTHEWS. You did not bring any records?

Mr. COOKE. I did not.

Mr. MATTHEWS. Of the organization with you?

Mr. COOKE. I did not.

The CHAIRMAN. Have you the subpena?

Mr. LYNCH. Yes.

(Mr. Schwab handing paper to Mr. Lynch.)

Mr. SCHWAB. Will that subpena be returned to me?

Mr. LYNCH. Certainly. Do you have record of the organization of which you are a member?

Mr. COOKE. Have I what?

Mr. LYNCH. Records of the organization of which you are a member?

Mr. COOKE. What do you mean?

Mr. LYNCH. Is that question plain to you, Mr. Cooke, or not?

Mr. COOKE. No; it is not.

Mr. LYNCH. What is your position?

Mr. COOKE. I am the national secretary of the Veterans of the Abraham Lincoln Brigade.

Mr. LYNCH. Do they have any records?

Mr. COOKE. They do not.

Mr. LYNCH. No records at all?

Mr. COOKE. No.

The CHAIRMAN. They have a record of membership?

Mr. COOKE. They do not.

Mr. MATTHEWS. Do you have a bank account?

Mr. COOKE. We do.

Mr. MATTHEWS. Do you have any financial records?

Mr. COOKE. We have.

Mr. MATTHEWS. Then you do have records?

Mr. COOKE. I misunderstood the question then.

Mr. MATTHEWS. He asked you if you had any records and you said "none at all."

Mr. COOKE. In my capacity I have no records; no.

Mr. LYNCH. Who has the records?

Mr. COOKE. The financial records?

Mr. LYNCH. Yes.

Mr. COOKE. The financial records are in charge of the bookkeeper.

Mr. LYNCH. Who is the bookkeeper?

Mr. COOKE. An employee of the organization.

Mr. LYNCH. What is her name?

Mr. COOKE. Miss Bunin.

Mr. LYNCH. First name?

Mr. COOKE. Vera.

Mr. LYNCH. Spell the last name.

Mr. COOKE. B-u-n-i-n.

Mr. LYNCH. What is her address?

Mr. COCKE. I don't know.

Mr. LYNCH. Address of the office?

Mr. COOKE. 55 West Forty-second Street.

Mr. LYNCH. Does she work there?

Mr. COOKE. Yes.

Mr. LYNCH. Paid a salary?

Mr. COOKE. Yes.

Mr. COOKE. 55 West Forty-second Street.

Mr. COOKE. We do.

Mr. LYNCH. Do you have a social-security number for her?

Mr. COOKE. No.

The CHAIRMAN. She has charge of the financial records of the organization; is that true?

Mr. COOKE. She handles the financial records—bookkeeper.

The CHAIRMAN. She keeps records—the records are in her custody; is that correct?

Mr. COOKE. As the bookkeeper; yes.

Mr. MATTHEWS. Do you conduct any correspondence?

Mr. COOKE. Occasionally; yes.

Mr. MATTHEWS. Do you receive letters?

Mr. COOKE. We do.

Mr. MATTHEWS. What do you do with the letters?

Mr. COOKE. Answer them.

Mr. MATTHEWS. Keep copies of them?

Mr. COOKE. No.

Mr. MATTHEWS. Do you file them?

Mr. COOKE. No.

Mr. MATTHEWS. Destroy them day by day?

Mr. COOKE. Yes.

The CHAIRMAN. You destroy all the correspondence you receive. You get a letter, answer it, and you destroy the original and the copy of your answer?

Mr. COOKE. As the letter is received and answered it is tossed in the wastebasket; yes, sir.

The CHAIRMAN. And you keep no records of the members? No written records anywhere of the members?

Mr. COOKE. No.

The CHAIRMAN. Does any one carry that in his mind—in his memory?

Mr. COOKE. Carry what in his memory?

The CHAIRMAN. The names of the members? Does anyone know who the members are?

Mr. COOKE. There are some fifteen hundred members, so therefore no one carries it in his mind.

The CHAIRMAN. No one knows, therefore who the members are?

Mr. COOKE. No, naturally.

Mr. MATTHEWS. How do you know there are fifteen hundred members.

Mr. COOKE. As the men returned home it is a matter of common knowledge from the passenger lists of all the ships that returned. We received national-wide publicity.

Mr. LYNCH. It is an estimate of fifteen hundred?

(No answer.)

Mr. LYNCH. Is there any reason why you destroy the papers and letters?

Mr. COOKE. None whatsoever.

Mr. LYNCH. You have no pride in the list of membership, so you don't have a name you can refer to?

Mr. COOKE. No.

Mr. LYNCH. You wouldn't know who they are?

Mr. COOKE. No.

Mr. MATTHEWS. How long have you been national secretary?

Mr. COOKE. Less than 4 months.

Mr. MATTHEWS. Were records destroyed from day to day? Was that the procedure when you took over the national secretaryship?

Mr. COOKE. I don't understand. Do you mean records destroyed? Do you mean correspondence destroyed daily?

Mr. MATTHEWS. Anything that came in.

Mr. COOKE. Correspondence, as I stated before, was destroyed.

Mr. MATTHEWS. Has that always been a custom of the organization since you were connected with it?

Mr. COOKE. Yes.

The CHAIRMAN. Were there any records when you took over the office of the secretary?

Mr. COOKE. There was not.

Mr. LYNCH. Are there any other employees other than the lady whom you mentioned a few moments ago?

Mr. COOKE. Myself.

Mr. LYNCH. You are the only two?

Mr. COOKE. That is correct.

Mr. LYNCH. Are you paid a salary?

Mr. COOKE. Am I paid a salary?

Mr. LYNCH. Yes.

Mr. COOKE. Yes, sir; I am.

Mr. LYNCH. Do you have a social-security number?

Mr. COOKE. I have.

Mr. LYNCH. But there isn't one for the young lady?

Mr. COOKE. I didn't say she didn't have one. I thought you meant is social security paid for her.

Mr. LYNCH. Is it?

Mr. COOKE. No; and for myself neither.

Mr. MATTHEWS. How many of the fifteen hundred members who are veterans of the Abraham Lincoln Brigade are members of the Communist Party?

Mr. COOKE. I couldn't say.

Mr. MATTHEWS. You have no idea about that?

Mr. Cooke. No, sir.

The Chairman. Do they pay dues? Do they have initiation fees or pay dues?

Mr. Cooke. Each post conducts its own collection of dues, and so forth.

The Chairman. How many posts do you have?

Mr. Cooke. There are some 10 posts.

The Chairman. Ten posts? Where are they located?

Mr. Cooke. Throughout the country in various cities.

The Chairman. And each post has a commander?

Mr. Cooke. That is true.

The Chairman. And each member pays dues?

Mr. Cooke. Yes.

The Chairman. What are the dues?

Mr. Cooke. What are the dues for each member?

The Chairman. Yes.

Mr. Cooke. Twenty-five cents a month for those employed.

The Chairman. Twenty-five cents a month for employed members?

Mr. Cooke. Yes.

The Chairman. What is the initiation fee?

Mr. Cooke. There is no initiation fee.

The Chairman. And when they pay their 25 cents what proportion of that goes to the national office?

Mr. Cooke. Well, technically 50 percent of the dues is supposed to come to the national office.

The Chairman. Fifty percent is supposed to go to the national office, and 50 percent is retained by the local post?

Mr. Cooke. Yes.

The Chairman. Does the local post keep any records?

Mr. Cooke. I couldn't say about that.

The Chairman. Do you belong to any local post?

Mr. Cooke. I do.

The Chairman. Which one?

Mr. Cooke. The New York Post.

The Chairman. Does your post keep any records?

Mr. Cooke. I couldn't say. I have no official position in the post other than a member.

The Chairman. Who is the commander of this post?

Mr. Cooke. Mr. Keller.

The Chairman. The man who testified here today?

Mr. Cooke. That is right.

The Chairman. He is commander of the New York Post?

Mr. Cooke. That is right.

The Chairman. How many posts do you have in New York?

Mr. Cocke. One.

The Chairman. You have a post in Chicago?

Mr. Cooke. Right.

The Chairman. Who is commander of that post?

(No answer.)

The Chairman. Do you know?

Mr. Cooke. I could not say—I don't know.

The Chairman. Do you have a post in Cleveland?

Mr. Cooke. I don't recall.

The CHAIRMAN. You don't know?

Mr. COOKE. It is possible. I don't recall offhand.

The CHAIRMAN. Give us the name of any other city where you have a post?

Mr. COOKE. There is a post in San Francisco.

The CHAIRMAN. Who is the commander there?

Mr. COOKE. I don't know the commander.

Mr. MATTHEWS. Do you have a list of these commanders in your office?

Mr. COOKE. No.

Mr. MATTHEWS. Any list of the posts?

Mr. COOKE. No lists at all.

Mr. MATTHEWS. Is there anybody in the national headquarters who knows where the posts are?

Mr. COOKE. No.

Mr. MATTHEWS. Nobody there knows who they are or where they are?

Mr. COOKE. No.

Mr. MATTHEWS. Nobody there knows where the commanders live?

Mr. COOKE. No.

Mr. MATTHEWS. If you wanted to get in touch with one of them you would not be able to?

Mr. COOKE. He would get in touch with us.

Mr. MATTHEWS. That is, you are cut off from getting in touch with them; is that correct?

Mr. COOKE. Yes. They would get in touch with us.

Mr. MATTHEWS. Is there a meeting celebrating the anniversary of some phase of the Spanish civil war this Sunday night in New York City?

Mr. COOKE. I don't know.

Mr. MATTHEWS. You haven't heard anything about any such anniversary celebration?

(No answer.)

Mr. MATTHEWS. You don't know General Vijar is speaking in New York City?

Mr. COOKE. I do not.

Mr. MATTHEWS. You know who General Vijar is, don't you?

Mr. COOKE. I do.

Mr. LYNCH. How much is your salary?

Mr. COOKE. $21 a week.

Mr. LYNCH. How much is the girl's salary?

Mr. COOKE. $21.

Mr. LYNCH. The same?

Mr. COOKE. $21; yes.

Mr. LYNCH. How much is your office rent?

Mr. COOKE. May I ask a question, Mr. Chairman. I would like to know what this has to do with the purpose of this organization?

Mr. LYNCH. Has a great deal to do with it, as you will see in a very few moments.

The CHAIRMAN. All right; let us proceed.

Mr. COOKE. Am I not entitled to an explanation of what it has to do with it?

The CHAIRMAN. You want an explanation?

Mr. COOKE. As to what our office rent has to do with the purposes for which this committee was formed.

The CHAIRMAN. Well, that is something for the committee to determine.

Mr. COOKE. And I have a right to know it.

The CHAIRMAN. Is your organization a front for the Communist Party?

Mr. COOKE. Is that it?

The CHAIMAN. Is it?

Mr. COOKE. No; it has no political affiliation whatever.

The CHAIRMAN. You are not a member of the Communist Party?

Mr. COOKE. I am not.

The CHAIRMAN. You went to Spain to fight for democracy?

Mr. COOKE. I did.

The CHAIRMAN. And you would fight for this country in a war against Russia, wouldn't you?

Mr. COOKE. The answer to that—I can think of no better answer than to quote Mr. Wolff, who answered that this afternoon.

The CHAIRMAN. That satisfies you; his answer?

Mr. COOKE. That satisfies me. There is no war at present between the United States and——

The CHAIRMAN. Is that the attitude of the members of your post?

Mr. COOKE. I could not vouch for the members of my post—what their attitude would be.

The CHAIRMAN. All right.

Mr. LYNCH. How much is the office rent, Mr. Cooke?

Mr. COOKE. $45 a month.

Mr. LYNCH. And do you have expenses such as postage and stationery, et cetera?

Mr. COOKE. That is all handled by the girl. I don't know anything about that.

Mr. LYNCH. There would be some expense, wouldn't there?

Mr. COOKE. Yes, sir.

Mr. LYNCH. And do all of the fifteen hundred members that you have pay dues? Are they all dues-paying at 25 cents a month or are some of them nonpaying members when unemployed?

Mr. COOKE. That is right.

Mr. LYNCH. About how many would you say are paying dues at 25 cents a month of the fifteen hundred members?

Mr. COOKE. I couldn't say—I have no idea.

Mr. LYNCH. Half or three-quarters?

Mr. COOKE. I have no idea whatsoever.

The CHAIRMAN. How much money did you get in last month?

Mr. COOKE. I don't know that.

The CHAIRMAN. Who knows?

Mr. COOKE. The bookkeeper knows that.

The CHAIRMAN. You know nothing about the finances?

Mr. COOKE. That is correct.

The CHAIRMAN. What does your office call for?

Mr. COOKE. To assist the national committee in conducting the business of the Veterans of the Abraham Lincoln Brigade nationally.

The CHAIRMAN. You know nothing about the records?

Mr. COOKE. I know nothing whatsoever about the financial records.

The CHAIRMAN. What business do you assist in?

Mr. Cooke. As I believe I answered before, I carry on communications with the posts, being the national secretary.

The Chairman. But you don't know where the posts are?

Mr. Cooke. I don't offhand; I don't know, no; but when I receive correspondence from the posts I answer it.

The Chairman. You answer it?

Mr. Cooke. Yes.

Mr. Lynch. But if you wanted to get hold of the post or to write to some man of a particular post you wouldn't know the address until he wrote to you first?

Mr. Cooke. I wouldn't be able to get in touch with any man in the country.

Mr. Lynch. I see. Now, Mr. Cooke, has anyone contributed to the organization other than the membership?

Mr. Cooke. Yes.

Mr. Lynch. Who?

Mr. Cooke. Quite a few American people—quite a few thousand.

Mr. Lynch. Do you have a list of the people?

Mr. Cooke. No; I have no idea. I have no list of these people.

Mr. Lynch. You have received contributions from them?

Mr. Cooke. Yes.

Mr. Lynch. And how much do those contributions amount to?

Mr. Cooke. I know nothing whatsoever of the financial records.

Mr. Lynch. Well, you know you got contributions?

Mr. Cooke. I know we received contributions, but I don't know the amount.

Mr. Lynch. Who told you?

Mr. Cooke. The bookkeeper.

Mr. Lynch. Are you reciving those contributions regularly?

Mr. Cooke. Yes.

Mr. Lynch. Every month?

Mr. Cooke. Every day.

Mr. Lynch. Contributions come in from citizens of the country?

Mr. Cooke. From citizens of the United States; yes.

Mr. Lynch. Do you answer those contributions with a letter of thanks?

Mr. Cooke. Yes.

Mr. Lynch. And then destroy the copy?

Mr. Cooke. There is no copy made to be destroyed.

Mr. Lynch. Nothing to be ashamed about that organization, is there?

Mr. Cooke. Nothing whatsoever.

The Chairman. About what?

Mr. Cooke. The finest body of Americans in this country.

The Chairman. What about this bookkeeper? Have you ever seen the books kept by the bookkeeper?

Mr. Cooke. Seen them? Inspected them?

The Chairman. Yes.

Mr. Cooke. No.

The Chairman. You never look at them?

Mr. Cooke. No; I have no interest in them.

The Chairman. Anyone else ever look at them outside of the bookkeeper?

Mr. Cooke. They are audited.

The CHAIRMAN. Who audits them?

Mr. COOKE. I don't know his name.

The CHAIRMAN. Is it a public accountant?

(No answer.)

The CHAIRMAN. You have been auditing them every year?

Mr. COOKE. I only know for the last 4 months.

The CHAIRMAN. How often does he audit them?

Mr. COOKE. I don't know that.

The CHAIRMAN. You don't know how often?

Mr. COOKE. No.

The CHAIRMAN. Who directs him to audit them?

Mr. COOKE. The bookkeeper.

The CHAIRMAN. The bookkeeper? The person in charge of the books?

Mr. COOKE. Yes.

The CHAIRMAN. Who pays him? The bookkeeper?

Mr. COOKE. The person in charge of the finances.

The CHAIRMAN. That is the bookkeeper?

Mr. COOKE. Correct.

The CHAIRMAN. When the bookkeeper wants the books audited the bookkeeper notifies the auditor?

Mr. COOKE. That is correct. That is the position of a bookkeeper and secretary.

The CHAIRMAN. All right.

Mr. MATTHEWS. Who pays you your salary check?

Mr. COOKE. The organization.

Mr. MATTHEWS. Who signs it?

Mr. COOKE. I do.

Mr. MATTHEWS. Do you investigate to find out if you have a bank balance before you sign checks?

Mr. COOKE. No.

Mr. MATTHEWS. You just sign the checks without regard to the balance in the bank?

Mr. COOKE. That is correct, because all of that—all that knowledge is known to the bookkeeper.

The CHAIRMAN. You don't know how much money you have in the bank? That is up to the bookkeeper?

Mr. COOKE. I could not say how much we have.

Mr. MATTHEWS. You ask her if it is all right to sign a check?

Mr. COOK. She gives me the check to sign so it must be okay.

Mr. LYNCH. Where do you bank—what bank?

Mr. COOKE. Amalgamated Bank of New York.

Mr. LYNCH. Where it is located?

Mr. COOKE. Fifteenth Street and Broadway, I believe.

The CHAIRMAN. Do you do any other kind of work? What is your trade?

Mr. COOKE. I have no trade.

The CHAIRMAN. Did you ever do any work?

Mr. COOKE. Yes; I did.

The CHAIRMAN. What did you work at?

Mr. COOKE. I worked as an office clerk, department-store clerk, shipping clerk.

The CHAIRMAN. Do you belong to a union?

Mr. COOKE. At the moment; no.

The CHAIRMAN. Have you ever belonged to a union?

Mr. COOKE. I have.

The CHAIRMAN. Which one?

Mr. COOKE. I belonged to Local 16 of the United Office and Professional Workers of America.

The CHAIRMAN. Did you hold any office in that organization?

Mr. COOKE. No.

The CHAIRMAN. You haven't been a member for some time?

Mr. COOKE. That is right.

The CHAIRMAN. At present your work is solely in connection with this organization?

Mr. COOKE. Solely with the veterans; yes, sir.

Mr. MATTHEWS. You know that Mr. Browder testified before this committee that a majority of the Veterans of the Abraham Lincoln Brigade were members of the Communist Party?

Mr. COOKE. I don't know that, no.

Mr. MATTHEWS. I will read you the testimony, first, from Mr. Browder's book, on page 182:

Not the least source of our pride is the fact that over sixty per cent of the Lincoln Battalion members are members of the Communist Party—

and then on page 4449, of the hearings of the Special Committee on Un-American Activities, Mr. Browder modified that slightly by saying:

I would say about fifty-five to sixty per cent—

and then he was quoted this passage from the book:

Not the least source of our pride is the fact that over sixty per cent of the Lincoln Battalion members are members of the Communist Party.

And Mr. Browder said, "Yes."

Would you say that Mr. Browder was incorrect in making that statement?

Mr. COOKE. Not being a member of the Communist Party myself I would say that I haven't the same sources of information as Mr. Browder. Therefore, I would say that I don't know anything about it. I have no way of knowing who is a Communist and who is not.

Mr. MATTHEWS. You don't challenge his statement?

Mr. COOKE. I do not challenge—I do not know.

The CHAIRMAN. The fact is that your organization is not concerned with whether a member is a Communist or not?

Mr. COOKE. That is correct. We have no committee to investigate them or anything like that.

The CHAIRMAN. You don't inquire into them at all?

Mr. COOKE. That is correct.

The CHAIRMAN. Any other questions? If not, you are excused. All your witnesses are excused, Mr. Attorney.

The committee will stand adjourned subject to call.

(Whereupon at 6 p. m., the hearing adjourned without date.)

INVESTIGATION OF UN-AMERICAN PROPAGANDA ACTIVITIES IN THE UNITED STATES

FRIDAY, APRIL 19, 1940

House of Representatives,
Special Committee on Un-American Activities,
Washington, D. C.

The committee met at 1:30 p. m., Hon. Martin Dies (chairman) presiding.

The Chairman. The committee will come to order.

The chair designates a subcommittee composed of the chairman. Who is your first witness, Mr. Matthews?

Mr. Matthews. Mr. Frantz.

The Chairman. Raise your right hand.

TESTIMONY OF LAURENT BROWN FRANTZ

The Chairman. Do you solemnly swear to tell the truth, the whole truth, and nothing but the truth, so help you God?

Mr. Frantz. Yes.

The Chairman. And what is the name of the attorney?

Mr. Fleischer. Fleischer—Louis Fleischer, 152 West Forty-second Street, New York.

The Chairman. Mr. Frantz, do you mind standing while the oath is administered to you, please?

(The witness standing.)

The Chairman. Do you solemnly swear to tell the truth, the whole truth, and nothing but the truth, so help you God?

Mr. Frantz. I do.

The Chairman. All right.

Mr. Fleischer. Mr. Chairman, before Mr. Matthews starts interrogating this witness, may I be permitted to make a brief statement on behalf of this witness who is sought to be examined before you?

The Chairman. With reference to what?

Mr. Fleischer. With reference particularly to the manner in which this witness was held incommunicado by representatives of the police department of the city of Birmingham, and by a representative of your committee.

The Chairman. Suppose you let him testify to the facts.

Mr. Fleischer. I think that if such was presented it might aid the committee here.

The Chairman. We will ask him because he is the witness, and naturally you cannot testify about this matter unless you were under oath and knew about it of your own knowledge.

7841

Suppose that we give the witness an opportunity to make a statement in that respect?

Mr. FLEISCHER. Very well, sir.

The CHAIRMAN. All right. I will ask the witness: What is your name?

Mr. FRANTZ. Laurent Brown Frantz.

The CHAIRMAN. Will you spell it so we can get it, please?

Mr. FRANTZ. The last name is F-r-a-n-t-z.

The CHAIRMAN. First name?

Mr. FRANTZ. L-a-u-r-e-n-t.

The CHAIRMAN. Where do you live, Mr. Frantz?

Mr. FRANTZ. Birmingham.

The CHAIRMAN. How long have you lived in Birmingham?

Mr. FRANTZ. Three months.

The CHAIRMAN. Three months?

Mr. FRANTZ. I mean 3 years.

The CHAIRMAN. What day was the subpena served upon you?

Mr. FRANTZ. On April 9, Tuesday.

The CHAIRMAN. Where were you at the time?

Mr. FRANTZ. No; I beg your pardon. The subpena was served on April 11. I was thinking of the date of my arrest. That was April 9.

The CHAIRMAN. Where were you at the time the subpena was served?

Mr. FRANTZ. In jail.

The CHAIRMAN. In what jail?

Mr. FRANTZ. The City Jail, Birmingham City Jail.

The CHAIRMAN. Were you in jail under some warrant that had been issued?

Mr. FRANTZ. No warrant, no, sir.

The CHAIRMAN. When were you placed in jail?

Mr. FRANTZ. I was placed in jail Tuesday afternoon, April 9.

The CHAIRMAN. Who put you in jail?

Mr. FRANTZ. City Detective Osborne of the Birmingham force.

The CHAIRMAN. What ground did he assign for arresting you?

Mr. FRANTZ. Held for investigation.

The CHAIRMAN. By the city authorities?

Mr. FRANTZ. He did not say. He said: "Held for investigation."

The CHAIRMAN. He did not tell you who was holding you for investigation?

Mr. FRANTZ. No.

The CHAIRMAN. Well, tell us what took place. Your attorney made some statement and I want to afford you an opportunity to say.

Mr. FRANTZ. All right, sir. It happened this way: Tuesday afternoon, April 9, at about 3 o'clock in the afternoon, I was in the office of Mr. Hall, who is an official of the Communist Party in Birmingham. I was in that office by myself. There was a knock on the door and I opened it and I admitted two officers—this city detective whose name is Osborne and a deputy United States marshal, whose name is Ellis.

These two officers questioned me about where Mr. Hall was, and I didn't know. I told them so. And they eventually told me, although not until after they questioned me for some time, that one of these officers was a deputy marshal and that he had a Dies Committee subpena for Mr. Hall.

After they had asked me a great number of times about where Mr. Hall was, and I continued to tell them that I did not know; that I only knew that he was out of the city on a trip of some kind, the detective, Osborne, told me that if I did not tell them immediately where Hall was that he would put me in jail and hold me until I did tell.

And I continued to insist that I did not know where he was.

So the detective then said: "Come on, I am taking you to jail."

I asked him: "Am I under arrest", and he said: "Yes".

Then the three of us, the detective, the deputy marshal and myself went to the police headquarters where I was questioned for about another thirty minutes.

I was then booked as a vagrant suspect and taken to the jail in a patrol wagon.

The CHAIRMAN. Now, is this an account of what happened, which I received in a wire from Raymond E. Thomason, United States marshal. I will read it to you and ask you, under your oath, whether this is true:

With reference to phone conversation, subpenas for Hall and Crouch received this office April 9, and assigned to Deputy Ellis. After search of city Deputy learned men had fled the district and were said to be in Knoxville, Tennessee. Returns made to Sergeant-at-arms on the morning of April 10 setting forth this information. On the afternoon of April 10 investigator Barker came to this office at which time he delivered to Marshal subpenas for Wirt R. Taylor, Laurent Frantz and Robert Hall, this being the second subpena for Hall. Upon investigation found that Frantz was in the custody of City of Birmingham having been arrested twenty-four hours prior to the time of the arrival of Barker in Birmingham. Marshal requested city authorities to advise him as to date and hour Frantz would be released. City authorities advised Marshal at one p. m., April 11th that Frantz would be released at 2 p. m., April 11. Deputy Ellis went to the city jail and served Frantz on his release by the city and return was made to this effect to the Dies Committee. On April 12 Hall returned to Birmingham and was served by Deputy Ellis in his office and a return to this effect has been made to the Dies Committee. There was no understanding between the Marshal and the City authorities in reference to Frantz being held by the city other than the Marshal would be notified when Frantz was released."

Is that true or is it false?

Mr. FRANTZ. I am not in a position to know whether that is true or false, because that took place while I was in the jail, held incommunicado.

The CHAIRMAN. I may say——

Mr. FRANTZ. I don't know anything about it.

The CHAIRMAN. I may say for your benefit the instructions of this committee were that a subpena be placed in the hands of the marshal to serve you, which of course is the legal power of this committee to do.

Now, Mr. Barker, will you raise your right hand and be sworn at this point?

TESTIMONY OF ROBERT B. BARKER, INVESTIGATOR, COMMITTEE ON UN-AMERICAN ACTIVITIES

The CHAIRMAN. Do you solemnly swear to tell the truth, the whole truth, and nothing but the truth, so help you God?

Mr. BARKER. Yes, sir.

The CHAIRMAN. You are an investigator for this committee, are you not, Mr. Barker?

Mr. Barker. Yes, sir; Mr. Voorhis is present, Mr. Chairman. Will you have the record show that?

The Chairman. The chair announces a subcommittee composed of the chairman, Mr. Voorhis, of California, and Mr. Mason, of Illinois. Mr. Barker, you went to the city of Birmingham, did you not?

Mr. Barker. Yes, sir.

The Chairman. For the purpose of serving subpenas upon or procuring the service of subpenas upon certain witnesses?

Mr. Barker. Yes, sir.

The Chairman. Did you deliver to the marshal a subpena for Laurent Frantz?

Mr. Barker. Laurent Brown Frantz.

The Chairman. Laurent Brown Frantz.

Mr. Barker. Yes, sir.

The Chairman. What day was it that you delivered this subpena to the marshal.

Mr. Barker. The date appears on the original; April 10, 1940.

The Chairman. What else did you do after you delivered to the marshal the subpena?

Mr. Barker. I delivered to him a subpena for Wirt A. Taylor and for Rob—or Bob Hall—Robert F. Hall.

The Chairman. All right. Were you present when the subpena was served?

Mr. Barker. No, sir.

The Chairman. Did you do anything further than to turn the subpena over to the marshal's office?

Mr. Barker. No, sir; I wasn't there when the subpena was served. I was in Tennessee.

The Chairman. I see. Was there anything said by anyone with reference to placing this man in jail?

Mr. Barker. Well, Mr. Frantz was in jail when I got to Birmingham.

The Chairman. He was in jail when you got to Birmingham?

Mr. Barker. He said he was arrested on April 9. Well, I didn't get to Birmingham until—I didn't deliver this subpena to the marshal until April 10.

The Chairman. You heard the telegram. In fact, the telegram is addressed to you by the marshal?

Mr. Barker. Yes, sir.

The Chairman. Is that substantially correct, insofar as you have personal knowledge of what he says here?

Mr. Barker. Yes, sir; that is from Mr. Raymond E. Thomason.

The Chairman. Was anything said with reference to serving the subpena while this witness was in jail?

Mr. Barker. No, sir; I requested the marshal not to serve the subpena upon Mr. Frantz until he had been released from jail, and I asked the city authorities when they were going to release Mr. Frantz from jail, and they said that they would release him as soon as the F. B. I. cleared his record. They had sent his fingerprints and photographs to Washington by air mail and said as soon as they received a wire from the F. B. I. clearing his record they would release him if nothing further was found against him.

The Chairman. Well now, of course you are not in position—any part of that you want to contradict?

Mr. FLEISCHER. May I be permitted at this moment on behalf of my client to ask Mr. Barker a few questions with reference to the matters which he has testified to?

The CHAIRMAN. Well, that is not customary, but in this particular case I see no reason to deny you the right to ask Mr. Barker several questions.

Mr. FLEISCHER. Thank you.

Mr. Barker, when did you first—when were you first advised that Mr. Frantz was in jail in Birmingham, Ala.?

Mr. BARKER. On the afternoon of April 9, about 4:30; I think it was about 4:30 p. m.

Mr. FLEISCHER. And how did you receive that advice or notification?

Mr. BARKER. I received it orally from E. F. Hollums, captain of detectives of the police department of the city of Birmingham, in his office.

Mr. FLEISCHER. Do you know who advised him to get in touch with you?

Mr. BARKER. He did not get in touch with me: I went to his office.

Mr. FLEISCHER. Were you in Birminghan on April 9, 1940?

Mr. BARKER. Yes, sir. I arrived on the Delta Airlines plane about 3 o'clock, I think, at the Birmingham Airport, and I was in his office sometime after 4—I think sometime after 4, between 4 and 4:30 that afternoon.

Mr. FLEISCHER. Before you left for Birmingham, Ala., did you know that Mr. Frantz was in custody?

Mr. BARKER. No, sir.

Mr. FLEISCHER. What brought you down to Birmingham?

Mr. BARKER. I went down to serve subpenas upon Bob Hall, also known as Rob Hall, or Robert F. Hall, and Paul Crouch.

Mr. FLEISCHER. So when was the first time that you knew Mr. Frantz was in custody?

Mr. BARKER. On April 9.

Mr. FLEISCHER. When you arrived in Birmingham, Ala.?

Mr. BARKER. Yes, sir.

Mr. FLEISCHER. Who told you that?

Mr. BARKER. I told you his name, the chief of detectives, Mr. Hollums. Now, if you will allow me I will clarify that a little bit for you. I went into his office and I said—he said: "Who do you want to see?" And I said, "I want to see Mr. Trion," really the chief of police, who was in the next office. I saw him at his desk and he said, "Well, wait a minute." He said, "You can see me," and I said, "Who are those two men out in the hall? Are they newspapermen?" And he said, "Not necessarily." Well, I said, "They are either newspapermen or they are not. I don't want to see any newspaper men, because I am investigator for the Dies committee." And in the meantime one of these men out in the hall had taken a chair and blocked the door so that I couldn't get out of the room and he said, "Oh," he said, "you are from the Dies committee." He said, "Come on in, men," and the two men came in, and the man that introduced himself as Osburn said, "So, your name is Barker." He said, "Can you identify yourself?" And I said, "Yes." "Well," he said, "I thought you was Bob Hall" He said, "We have been trying to find Bob Hall," so the marshal, a man by the name of Ellis, had　subpena in his pocket for Bob Hall and they thought I was Bob Halla

The CHAIRMAN. Have you any more material questions you want to ask?

Mr. FLEISCHER. Yes; quite a few questions, Mr. Chairman.

The CHAIRMAN. I can't agree to "quite a few questions." We want to get into this matter and dispose of it.

Mr. FLEISCHER. The type of questions I seek to ask I think will enlighten——

The CHAIRMAN. As to material questions, and let us hurry.

Mr. FLEISCHER. Now, the first time you found out Mr. Frantz was in custody April 9, was sometime in the afternoon; is that right?

Mr. BARKER. Yes, sir.

Mr. FLEISCHER. Now, at that time no subpena as far as you know it, was not—you had no subpena for Mr. Frantz; is that correct?

Mr. BARKER. No, sir.

Mr. FLIESCHER. And as far as you know, no subpena was to be issued for Mr. Frantz; is that correct?

Mr. BARKER. That is right, at that time.

Mr. FLEISCHER. At that time?

Mr. BARKER. Yes, sir.

Mr. FLEISCHER. Now, did you see Mr. Frantz at all from April 9 to April 11, 1940?

Mr. BARKER. Yes; I saw Mr. Frantz.

Mr. FLEISCHER. Where did you see him?

Mr. BARKER. At the city jail.

Mr. FLEISCHER. And what day was that?

Mr. BARKER. That was on April 10.

Mr. FLEISCHER. Did you have a subpena for him at that time?

Mr. BARKER. The marshal had the subpena.

Mr. FLEISCHER. On April 10?

Mr. BARKER. Yes, sir.

Mr. FLEISCHER. But he was not served until April 11; is that correct?

Mr. BARKER. That is right; yes.

Mr. FLEISCHER. And you were not present when the subpena was served on him?

Mr. BARKER. No, sir.

Mr. FLEISCHER. Were you told as a matter of fact that Mr. Frantz was served with a subpena while he was still in custody?

Mr. BARKER. Well, I left instructions with the marshal to serve him when he was released from the city jail. I don't know when he was served except by the return on the subpena, which shows it was executed on the 11th day of April of 1940, "Raymond E. Thomason, United States marshal, by Arthur M. Ellis, Jr., deputy United States marshal."

Mr. FLEISCHER. As a matter of fact, Mr. Barker, didn't you or someone associated with the service of subpenas or as an investigator for the Dies committee, leave specific instructions with the persons who had charge and control of the custody of this witness, that he was to be not released until a subpena was to be issued for him?

Mr. BARKER. No, sir.

Mr. FLEISCHER. You are sure of that?

Mr. BARKER. Oh, I am positive of that.

Mr. FLEISCHER. That is all.

The CHAIRMAN. All right. Now, the Chair wants to state that it is rather difficult to get some of the witnesses. Some of them have, I might say for the benefit of the attorney, too, in case he represents any more, that some of the witnesses who find out they are likely to be subpenaed, purposely leave the town or the state or hide out in order to avoid being served, and even when we get some of them, we get telegrams such as this telegram:

This is to inform you I will present myself in answer to your subpena at any time you desire on receipt of the necessary money for round-trip transportation by plane as well as per diem expenses. I must inform you that correspondence, membership lists of membership cards, financial records, and names and addresses of branch or unit functionaries requested in subpena are not in my possession, jurisdiction, or control.

And another one from the west coast:

House subpena dated April 6th has just been served upon me requiring me to appear forthwith before your committee in Washington and to bring with me documents and records pertaining to Communist Party or its activities which are in my possession or under my jurisdiction or control and specifying all correspondence, membership lists, membership cards, financial records and names and addresses of all branch and unit functionaries.

I wish to advise you that I have no such documents or records and therefore cannot bring anything. Under these circumstances, does the committee desire my presence even if I cannot contribute anything? If you require me I will be forced to close my dental office at great personal monetary sacrifice to myself, which I can ill afford and I therefore request that you advise me of a definite date when you desire to hear me and thus obviate the necessity of a long sojourn in Washington, which I am unable to undertake as I have a family to support. In such an event, of course, it will be necessary for you to defray all expenses and I estimate that a minimum of four hundred dollars will be required for this purpose, as the round-trip airplane fare alone will cost about two hundred seventy five dollars. I shall await further word from you. If I do not hear from you I will take it to mean that the committee does not require my presence and will accordingly forget about the whole matter.

Mr. VOORHIS. How many words in the telegram?

The CHAIRMAN. It was sent collect, and I may say that some of the witnesses have even been brazen enough to leave word where they have their headquarters to tell the Dies commitee agents that they were going on a long vacation for their health.

The instructions to the agents of this committee are to serve subpenas upon the witnesses—leave the subpena with him.

In El Paso at which place some four or five witnesses, if I remember correctly, were in jail and the question of serving the subpenas was involved, the chairman instructed that the subpenas be not served upon the witnesses while the witnesses were in jail. As a result of that, however, I understand that several of the witnesses when they got out of the jail disappeared across the Mexican border. I merely want to make that clear.

Mr. FLEISCHER. For the purpose of the examination of this witness, Mr. Chairman, I move to strike out any and all correspondence that you have just read into the record, on the ground that it is not binding on this particular witness.

The CHAIRMAN. Of course not. But the Chair wants to get this in the record independent and apart from this witness' testimony, and will not be used in connection with his testimony.

Mr. FLEISCHER. And I think the testimony of this witness will further indicate exactly the contrary as to what you, Mr. Chairman, just read.

The CHAIRMAN. That is what I want to inquire into.

Now, Mr. Frantz, were you seeking to avoid being served with a subpena?

Mr. FRANTZ. No, sir.

The CHAIRMAN. Do you know whether or not Bob Hall left Birmingham in order to prevent being served with a subpena?

Mr. FRANTZ. I don't know whether he did or not.

The CHAIRMAN. Do you know when he left Birmingham?

Mr. FRANTZ. He left Birmingham, I would estimate, about 10 days before I was arrested, which would have been right at or slightly before the 1st of April.

The CHAIRMAN. Do you know whether he returned at any time during those 10 days?

Mr. FLEISCHER. Now, Mr. Chairman, I will object to this line of questioning—if I respectfully may object to this line of questioning. I understand that this witness is sought to be examined as to un-American activities and as to his knowledge and what he has done or failed to do.

The CHAIRMAN. I am trying to find out with reference to Bob Hall because this is vital information the committee wants to know and when the subpena arrived there Bob Hall was not there, and as I understand—understood the witness you were in the office of Bob Hall.

Mr. FRANTZ. I was.

The CHAIRMAN. Are you associated with Bob Hall in any respect?

Mr. FLEISCHER. I press my objection on the ground this witness is to be questioned only on his own specific activities or his knowledge.

The CHAIRMAN. Your exception is duly noted, Mr. Attorney. Do you know Bob Hall to be an official of the Communist Party of Alabama?

Mr. FRANTZ. Yes, sir; I do.

The CHAIRMAN. Are you associated with him in any respect?

Mr. FRANTZ. For the past several weeks I have been doing some legal research for Mr. Hall.

The CHAIRMAN. Legal research work for him?

Mr. FRANTZ. Yes, sir.

The CHAIRMAN. Do you—are you a member yourself of the Communist Party?

Mr. FRANTZ. No; I am not.

The CHAIRMAN. Have you ever been a member of the Communist Party?

Mr. FRANTZ. Never.

The CHAIRMAN. Have you ever attended any fraction meetings or other meetings of the Communist Party?

Mr. FRANTZ. No.

The CHAIRMAN. You have never been present at any meeting under the auspices of the Communist Party?

Mr. FRANTZ. Well, I wouldn't go so far as to say I have never heard Communist speakers.

The CHAIRMAN. At what occasions were these Communist meetings at which you heard the Communist speakers?

Mr. FRANTZ. Mr. Hall conducted an election campaign at one time. I heard him speak.

The CHAIRMAN. Well, I wasn't speaking about a general meeting where everyone was present. I am speaking about a meeting under the auspices of the Communist Party.

Mr. FRANTZ. No.

The CHAIRMAN. You never have been present in such meeting as that?

Mr. FRANTZ. No, sir.

The CHAIRMAN. All right. Do you want to proceed?

Mr. BARKER. Yes.

Mr. VOORHIS. I would like to ask one or two questions.

Mr. Frantz, who arrested you when you were arrested in Birmingham?

Mr. FRANTZ. Detective Osborne.

Mr. VOORHIS. What were you arrested for?

Mr. FRANTZ. He told me that if I did not tell him where Hall was he would put me in jail and hold me there until I did tell him. I told him I didn't know where Hall was. He said: "Come on, we are going to the jail." I said: "Am I under arrest," and he said "Yes."

Mr. VOORHIS. That had nothing to do with this committee in any way, did it?

Mr. FRANTZ. Yes, sir; it did. They were trying to find Mr. Hall so they could serve him with your subpena.

The CHAIRMAN. You mean the marshal was trying to find Mr. Hall; is that what you are saying?

Mr. FRANTZ. The marshal and Detective Ellis were trying to find Mr. Hall. The marshal had the subpena.

Mr. VOORHIS. Must have given some reason for arresting you, didn't they?

Mr. FRANTZ. They arrested me because—that is the reason they gave. They instructed the desk sergeant to book me as a suspect of vagrancy. That is to say, Detective Osburne did. But he didn't give me any such reason. The reason he gave me was that he wanted to hold me until I told him where Hall was.

The CHAIRMAN. All right, proceed.

Mr. BARKER. Mr. Frantz, you are a graduate of the University of Tennessee?

Mr. FRANTZ. I am.

Mr. BARKER. Are you a member of the bar, and, if so, of what State?

Mr. FRANTZ. Tennessee and Alabama.

Mr. BARKER. Both States?

Mr. FRANTZ. Yes.

Mr. BARKER. What is your address in Alabama?

Mr. FRANTZ. 1421 Seventeenth Avenue, South.

Mr. BARKER. Are you married or single?

Mr. FRANTZ. Single.

Mr. BARKER. This article that appeared in the Daily Worker of April 17 on the front page, under the caption, "Ask Jackson to Probe Illegal Arrest by Dies in Alabama." That article was prepared after you arrived here in Washington to appear before the committee and you told your story to the reporter for the Daily Worker; is that right?

Mr. Frantz. Mr. Lapin got in touch with me and asked me questions about my experience; yes.

Mr. Barker. That is Mr. Adam Lapin, the correspondent of the Daily Worker over there?

Mr. Frantz. Yes.

Mr. Barker. Now, when you came up here to the office you were represented by Mr. Sol Cohn?

Mr. Frantz. That is right.

Mr. Barker. And is he still your attorney or is Mr. Louis Fleischer your attorney now?

Mr. Frantz. Both.

Mr. Barker. Both of them—both Mr. Cohn and Mr. Fleischer represent you?

Mr. Frantz. Yes, sir.

Mr. Barker. Now, this article states here on page 21:

Of the most interesting aspects of this whole case was that Frantz had not even been under a Dies Committee subpena at the time he was arrested. The Dies Committee apparently heard that he was in jail and sent down a subpena which arrived after he had been held for some time.

Is that correct?

Mr. Frantz. I think that is a reasonable inference. There was nothing said to me about a subpena when I was arrested.

Mr. Barker. Now, when City Detective Osbourne came up there to your office, did you admit him and this deputy marshal, Ellis, to the office?

Mr. Frantz. It was not my office. It was Mr. Hall's office. I admitted them, yes.

Mr. Barker. Where is that office located, Mr. Frantz?

Mr. Frantz. In the Clark Building.

Mr. Barker. Clark Building?

Mr. Frantz. Yes, sir.

Mr. Barker. And what is the room number?

Mr. Frantz. 235.

Mr. Barker. Did you admit them to the office or did they push their way in?

Mr. Frantz. I opened the door, and they came in without waiting for any questions about that.

Mr. Barker. What did this deputy marshal, Arthur M. Ellis, Jr., say to you?

Mr. Frantz. He asked me where Mr. Hall was.

Mr. Barker. Is that all he said?

Mr. Frantz. No, that is not all he said. That is the first thing he said.

Mr. Barker. What else did he say?

Mr. Frantz. Well, most of the talking was done by the detectives. The marshal informed me that he was a deputy marshal. He told me his name. He told me he had a Dies committee subpena for Mr. Hall. The marshal asked me where Mr. Hall was, and I said I didn't know. I did tell him and the detective that Mr. Hall was out of town on a trip.

The marshal asked me whether I knew how he could get in touch with Mr. Hall and I said I didn't. He asked me whether I knew how he could, Mr. Hall, could be reached by long-distance phone. I said I didn't. I believe that is all I can think of at the moment that I am sure the marshal said to me rather than the detective. As I say, the detective did most of the talking.

Mr. BARKER. Were you arrested by the marshal or by the detective?

Mr. FRANTZ. By the detective.

Mr. BARKER. And he took you to the city jail?

Mr. FRANTZ. He took me first to the police headquarters and questioned me there. Then he had me booked at the desk sergeant's office.

Mr. BARKER. Now, if the marshal had made the arrest he would have taken you to the United States marshal's office, you presume, don't you?

The CHAIRMAN. Well, he made it clear that the city detective was the one that made the arrest.

Mr. BARKER. Let me ask you this, Mr. Frantz: Did the marshal participate in the arrest of you? Did he lay hands on you or state that you were under arrest or anything?

Mr. FRANTZ. No, sir. The marshal took place—took part in this questioning in Mr. Hall's office. The marshal—the three of us went together from Mr. Hall's office to the police headquarters. The marshal was present again when I was questioned at police headquarters. He knew that the detective was putting me under arrest because I was unable to give information which the marshal was seeking. And he made no protest. And he took part in both these questionings and he accompanied me to the police headquarters. He did not accompany me to the jail and neither did the detective.

Mr. BARKER. Now, Mr. Frantz, you have been arrested before, haven't you?

Mr. FLEISCHER. I object to the question. The fact that a person is arrested is no indication that he has been convicted of any crime.

Mr. BARKER. Mr. Chairman, I think that is a material question.

The CHAIRMAN. You have, no doubt, a particular reason for not saying——

Mr. FLEISCHER. For the reason, Mr. Chairman, that anybody possibly can be arrested, and the fact a person is arrested is no indication or reflection on his moral character.

The CHAIRMAN. Put the question this way——

Mr. FLEISCHER. "Has he ever been convicted," is another story.

The CHAIRMAN. Have you ever been indicted?

Mr. FRANTZ. No, sir.

Mr. FLEISCHER. I object to that.

The CHAIRMAN. You propose to ask him simply if he has been arrested?

Mr. BARKER. Yes.

Mr. FLEISCHER. We object to that.

The CHAIRMAN. Wait a minute.

Mr. BARKER. In connection with communistic activities?

The CHAIRMAN. Well, I don't think that the mere fact that a man is arrested, unless there is some conviction or trial or something else, would be a material question, because a man might be arrested—an innocent man might be arrested and still that would not be any evidence of his guilt.

Mr. BARKER. That is true, but in this particular instance——

The CHAIRMAN. Well, proceed with the questions. I hardly believe that, unless it becomes material in connection with some other testimony at this time, I don't see how the fact that a man is arrested, if it is not accompanied by an indictment or trial or conviction should be used against him, unless there is some evidence showing that he was actually, as a matter of fact, disturbing the peace or engaged in some riotous activities.

Mr. BARKER. Mr. Chairman, the purpose of the questions—the witness testified he was not a member of the Communist Party and that he had not attended any meetings of the Communist Party. The purpose of the question, Mr. Chairman, was to show that the witness had been arrested previously in connection with communistic activities, placed in jail, and held for investigation, and released.

The CHAIRMAN. Well, you mean that he was arrested at some Communist demonstration?

Mr. BARKER. No, sir. He was arrested while doing work for the Communist Party in Memphis, Tenn.

Mr. FLEISCHER. May I suggest Mr. Barker ask him whether or not he was ever convicted of a crime and whether or not he was functioning in the capacity of a Communist at the time arrested?

The CHAIRMAN. Well, this witness stated under oath that he was never at any meeting held under the auspices of the Communist Party. That is correct, is it, Mr. Frantz?

Mr. FRANTZ. That is right.

Mr. FLEISCHER. That is subject to a double interpretation, Mr. Chairman.

The CHAIRMAN. I am speaking now of the Communist Party. I use that word.

Mr. FLEISCHER. You mean a meeting where everybody attended was a member?

The CHAIRMAN. I said "under the auspices of the Communist Party, where the Communist leaders called the meeting." I am not speaking of a meeting at which Communists were present. He has testified he wasn't present at any time at such meeting; is that true?

Mr. FRANTZ. Well, I am not sure quite what you mean by "under the auspices of." You said in regard to this election meeting that Mr. Hall held at which I was present. You said that that didn't count because that was a meeting which was open to the public.

The CHAIRMAN. Well, that was called by the Communist Party?

Mr. FRANTZ. Well, it was a campaign rally for a Communist candidate. Presumably it was called by the Communist Party.

The CHAIRMAN. Well, was there any disturbance at the meeting?

Mr. FRANTZ. No, sir.

The CHAIRMAN. Nothing occurred at that time?

Mr. FRANTZ. I don't remember any occurrence.

Mr. FLEISCHER. May I point out to you, Mr. Chairman, even if such a meeting were held we must assume it was a legal meeting, properly—orderly.

The CHAIRMAN. Nobody questions the legality of it. What we are trying to do is inquire into the facts. The Communist Party under the existing situation is a legal party.

Mr. FLEISCHER. And anybody would have a right to attend a meeting.

The CHAIRMAN. No one disputes that.

Mr. FLEISCHER. That is what his question amounts to.

The CHAIRMAN. Proceed.

Mr. BARKER. Mr. Frantz, you are what—a citizen of the United States?

Mr. FRANTZ. I am.

Mr. BARKER. You were born in Tennessee?

Mr. FRANTZ. Yes, sir.

Mr. BARKER. Your father is a professor at the University of Tennessee?

Mr. FRANTZ. Yes, sir.

Mr. BARKER. Professor of Romance Languages at the University of Tennessee?

Mr. FRANTZ. That is right.

Mr. BARKER. And he lives at 3318 Woodhill Place in Knoxville; is that right?

Mr. FRANTZ. That is right.

Mr. BARKER. Do you know William Haines Spradling, also known as Wallace Haines Spradling, and also known as Wallace Spradley, of Independence, Kan., an organizer for the Communist Party?

Mr. FRANTZ. Mr. Chairman, it seems to me that this question has no reference to my activities. It is a question of do I know so and so.

The CHAIRMAN. We want to know the activities of the Communist Party in general and you are a witness and he asks you if you know the person. We are not here just to inquire solely of your own experience. We are asking you with reference to people in the movement that you know and that you have had contacts with. Do you know any such person as that?

Mr. FLEISCHER. Do you know him?

Mr. FRANTZ. Yes, sir.

The CHAIRMAN. You do?

Mr. FRANTZ. Yes, sir; I have met him.

Mr. BARKER. You know him?

Mr. FLEISCHER. He said he met him. He did not say he knew him.

The CHAIRMAN. He could hardly meet him unless he knew him, could he? Go ahead.

Mr. BARKER. Now, Mr. Frantz, you were a follow-up man for Mr. Spradling in trying to organize a union of the Communist Party in Shelby County at Memphis; is that right?

Mr. FRANTZ. No, sir.

Mr. FLEISCHER. I object to the form of the question. Well, it has been answered.

Mr. BARKER. I didn't hear you.

Mr. FRANTZ. No, sir; I was not.

Mr. BARKER. Do you know this gentleman when you see him? His picture? Would you know his picture, Mr. Spradley?

Mr. FRANTZ. I think so.

Mr. BARKER. [Handing photograph to the witness.]

Mr. FRANTZ. Yes, sir.

Mr. BARKER. Is that the gentleman?

Mr. FRANTZ. That is him.

Mr. BARKER. Mr. Chairman, Mr. Spradley was arrested in Memphis on October 19, 1937.

Mr. FLEISCHER. I object to any statements made by counsel. If he wants to testify, let him be sworn.

The CHAIRMAN. That is correct; don't make statements.

Mr. FLEISCHER. I ask it be stricken from the record.

The CHAIRMAN. Don't make statements. You can ask the witness questions.

Mr. BARKER. All right. Now, Mr. Frantz, at the time you were taken into custody at Memphis, was there found upon your person papers indicating that you were the follow-up agent for the Communist organizer, Mr. Spradley?

Mr. FLEISCHER. I object to that question because it assumes a state of facts which is not in the evidence. He said: "When you were arrested in Memphis, Tenn." There is no proof he was arrested in Memphis, Tenn.

The CHAIRMAN. Well, at any time were papers taken off of you indicating that you were associated with Spradley in any manner?

Mr. FRANTZ. I was not associated with Spradley.

The CHAIRMAN. I say at any time were papers taken from your person indicating or showing any connection between you and Spradley?

Mr. FRANTZ. I was—I was—I was in Memphis doing civil-rights work and one of the cases that I was interested in was the *Spradling case*.

Mr. FLEISCHER. As attorney?

The CHAIRMAN. And you had papers on your person showing a connection between you and Spradley?

Mr. FRANTZ. No. I don't understand what you mean by "connection."

The CHAIRMAN. Well, what were the papers about?

Mr. FRANTZ. I don't remember what I had on my person at that time, but I do know what I was doing in Memphis and I was——

The CHAIRMAN. I understand what you were doing in Memphis, but I am trying to inquire into whether or not you had any papers on your person at that time showing any kind of a connection between you and Spradling.

Mr. FLEISCHER. Mr. Chairman, will a date be fixed on that? Perhaps that will refresh his recollection.

The CHAIRMAN. Well, he has already testified about the occasion so he evidently is not in doubt about the date.

Mr. BARKER. I have a date, Mr. Chairman, if you want it.

The CHAIRMAN. What is the date?

Mr. BARKER. November 30, 1937.

Mr. FRANTZ. I came to Memphis with information in my possession about the *Spradling case*. If you call that a "connection with Mr. Spradling," then that is it.

The CHAIRMAN. I am not calling anything; I am just asking you.

Mr. VOORHIS. What organization were you connected with at that time?

Mr. FRANTZ. I was in Memphis for the National Committee for People's Rights.

The CHAIRMAN. What was your position in connection with that Committee?

Mr. FRANTZ. I was doing mostly legal research and other work for the southern representative of that Committee whose office was in Birmingham.

The CHAIRMAN. Who was that southern representative?

Mr. FRANTZ. That was Mr. Joseph Gelders.

The CHAIRMAN. Did this Mr. Gelders know—was he the one who employed you in connection with this work?

Mr. FRANTZ. Yes.

The CHAIRMAN. Did you know anyone else in the organization besides him?

(No answer.)

The CHAIRMAN. Any other official in the organization?

Mr. FRANTZ. No, sir. There were no officials of the organization in Birmingham except Mr. Gelders himself. I was working for him.

The CHAIRMAN. Did you meet any of the officials in any other section of the country?

Mr. FRANTZ. No, sir; I did not.

The CHAIRMAN. All your connections were with Mr. Gelders?

Mr. FRANTZ. That is right.

The CHAIRMAN. And he employed you in connection with this particular case?

Mr. FRANTZ. No, sir. He employed me in general as a sort of special assistant to do whatever work I was most needed on, and it was understood that the main body of that work would be legal research and other kinds of research, specially legal.

The CHAIRMAN. And was there some sort of proceeding against this man Spradling? Is that what I understand?

Mr. FRANTZ. This man Spradling had been arrested in his own room, as I remember the case, in his own room at the Memphis Y. M. C. A. and sent to the chain gang on a vagrancy charge. And the National Committee for People's Rights and Mr. Gelders considered that a violation of his civil liberties and that case was one of the violations of civil liberties in Memphis that we had in mind when Mr. Gelders sent me to Memphis.

The CHAIRMAN. What was Spradley? Was he an official in the Communist Party?

Mr. FRANTZ. I don't have personal knowledge of that, but I understand that he was.

The CHAIRMAN. Well, from your investigation and the papers you had and your connection with the case, was that generally known—that he was an official in the Communist Party?

Mr. FRANTZ. I don't know what was generally known, but my understanding was that he was arrested and charged with vagrancy—that he was working for the Communist Party.

The CHAIRMAN. Isn't it a fact that in the State of Alabama that Spradley was on the State committee of the Communist Party?

Mr. FRANTZ. I don't know.

The CHAIRMAN. You don't know that to be a fact?

(No answer.)

The CHAIRMAN. You know that Robert Hall is the district and State secretary, do you not?

Mr. FRANTZ. That is generally known.

The CHAIRMAN. Do you know Andy Brown?

Mr. FRANTZ. Yes. I think I have met him in Workers Alliance work.

The CHAIRMAN. In the Workers Alliance?

Mr. FRANTZ. Yes.

The CHAIRMAN. Were you active in the Workers Alliance?

Mr. FRANTZ. Yes.

The CHAIRMAN. What position did you hold?

Mr. FRANTZ. Well, I was mostly publicity director.

The CHAIRMAN. For the Workers Alliance at Birmingham?

Mr. FRANTZ. Yes, sir.

The CHAIRMAN. And you met Andy Brown, who was active in the Workers' Alliance, there?

Mr. FRANTZ. Yes.

The CHAIRMAN. What official position did Andy Brown hold in the Workers' Alliance?

Mr. FRANTZ. I don't think he held any.

The CHAIRMAN. You don't think he had any position in the Workers' Alliance?

Mr. FRANTZ. No.

The CHAIRMAN. He was just active in the work?

Mr. FRANTZ. Yes.

The CHAIRMAN. Did you meet Jim Mallory?

Mr. FLEISCHER. Mr. Chairman, I again press my objection. I think this is outside of the scope of the investigation of your committee. This witness will be glad to answer any question as to his particular activities with relationship to the matter under investigation by your committee.

The CHAIRMAN. This is his activity.

Mr. FLEISCHER. The fact that he knew somebody?

The CHAIRMAN. His activities in connection with Andy Brown. That is what I am asking about.

Mr. FLEISCHER. He testified that he was—he was active in the Workers Alliance. Now, as to whether any other person was active or involved, so far as this witness is concerned, I think is entirely irrelevant and immaterial.

The CHAIRMAN. Your exception is noted. Did you meet Jim Mallory?

Mr. FRANTZ. No; I don't know Jim Mallory.

The CHAIRMAN. Do you know John Parker?

Mr. FRANTZ. No.

The CHAIRMAN. Never met John Parker?

Mr. FRANTZ. I don't remember any John Parker.

The CHAIRMAN. Do you know Frank Curry?

Mr. FRANTZ. No.

The CHAIRMAN. Never met Frank Curry?

(No answer.)

The CHAIRMAN. Do you know Jane Speed?

Mr. FRANTZ. Yes.

The CHAIRMAN. Where did you meet Jane Speed?

Mr. FRANTZ. In Birmingham.

The CHAIRMAN. In connection with what did you meet her?

Mr. FRANTZ. I don't remember in what connection.

The CHAIRMAN. Didn't you meet her in the office of the Communist Party?

Mr. FRANTZ. No, sir; I don't think I did.

The CHAIRMAN. You don't recall where you met her?

Mr. FRANTZ. I don't recall with certainty where I met her; no. I think I met her first at her house.

The CHAIRMAN. You know that you met her at her house, you say?

Mr. FRANTZ. I don't remember with any certainty where I first met her.

The CHAIRMAN. I thought you said—you just said you thought you met her at her house.

Mr. FRANTZ. That is my impression.

The CHAIRMAN. That is your impression?

(No answer.)

The CHAIRMAN. Did you know Jane Speed to be a Communist?

Mr. FRANTZ. I knew that was her general reputation; yes, sir.

The CHAIRMAN. Did you know that Jane Speed was a member of the State committee of the Communist Party of Alabama?

Mr. FRANTZ. No.

The CHAIRMAN. All right; proceed.

Mr. BARKER. Mr. Frantz, do you recall a hosiery mill strike at the Rockwood Hosiery Mills at Roane County, Tenn., at Harriman, in April of 1935?

Mr. FRANTZ. In Harriman?

Mr. BARKER. Yes.

Mr. FRANTZ. Now, wait a minute. Harriman and Rockwood are two different places.

Mr. BARKER. The Rockwood Hosiery Mills are located in Harriman.

Mr. FRANTZ. I recall a strike in Harriman. I thought the name of it was the Harriman Hosiery Mills.

Mr. BARKER. Well, it might be. Your knowledge of that may be better than mine. Do you recall that strike in 1935?

Mr. FRANTZ. I think it was in 1934.

Mr. BARKER. 1934?

Mr. FRANTZ. I don't know what date it was. I think it was in 1934.

Mr. BARKER. Do you recall that the city water works at that time was dynamited?

Mr. FLEISCHER. I object.

The CHAIRMAN. What is it?

Mr. BARKER. I asked him if he knew the city waterworks at that time were dynamited?

Mr. FLEISCHER. Now, I object to this type of question. It is evidently an intent on the part of the examiner here to color the testimony of this witness and to create a picture as far as this defendant is concerned—this witness is concerned—which does not exist at all.

The CHAIRMAN. What is your purpose of asking that?

Mr. BARKER. I will ask another question.

Mr. FLEISCHER. I ask it be stricken from the record.

Mr. BARKER. Mr. Frantz, do you know Hilliard Bernstein?

Mr. FRANTZ. Yes, sir.

Mr. BARKER. You do know him?

Mr. FRANTZ. Yes, sir.

Mr. BARKER. Did you represent him when he was arrested at Rockwood?

Mr. FRANTZ. I did not.

Mr. BARKER. Did you represent him as a member of the bar when he was arrested?

Mr. FRANTZ. I did not.

Mr. BARKER. Did you know Hilliard Bernstein when he was arrested had a list of contacts where he was to contact you and several other individuals?

Mr. FRANTZ. I did not know that.

Mr. BARKER. Mr. Robert F. Hall is the district secretary of the Communist Party for Alabama, Georgia, and Mississippi; isn't that right?

Mr. FRANTZ. That is what I understand.

Mr. BARKER. He is also the southern representative of the national campaign committee of the Communist Party?

Mr. FRANTZ. That is right.

Mr. BARKER. Now, is Mr. Hall your only client that you have down in Birmingham or do you practice law down there generally?

Mr. FRANTZ. I was—neither one of those is quite true. Mr. Hall is not the only client, and I have never been engaged in full-time law practice.

Mr. BARKER. Now, at the time of your arrest by this city detective in Birmingham, Mr. Frantz, there was removed from your person some correspondence addressed to Mr. Hall, was there not?

Mr. FRANTZ. There was.

Mr. BARKER. Was there any connection between that correspondence and the Communist Party?

Mr. FLEISCHER. Explain it.

Mr. FRANTZ. That correspondence was from the department of justice in Mississippi with relation to the regulations regarding getting on the ballot in Mississippi.

Mr. BARKER. That was the correspondence?

Mr. FRANTZ. That is what it was.

Mr. BARKER. Well, how many clients have you had since you have been practicing law in Birmingham?

Mr. FRANTZ. I have had very few clients. I have been mostly engaged in work which had something to do with law yet was not the practice of law, such as this work that I did with Mr. Gelders.

Mr. BARKER. Do you know Paul Crouch?

Mr. FRANTZ. Yes.

Mr. BARKER. Is Mr. Crouch the secretary of the Communist Party for the State of Tennessee?

Mr. FRANTZ. I don't know.

Mr. BARKER. How long have you known Mr. Paul Crouch?

Mr. FRANTZ. A couple or 3 years.

Mr. BARKER. Have you ever attended any communistic meeting with Mr. Paul Crouch?

Mr. FRANTZ. No.

Mr. FLEISCHER. I object to that. The question has already been answered, Mr. Chairman. He testified at the beginning he never attended any Communist Party meetings.

The CHAIRMAN. Well, for the sake of the record, we want specific either affirmance or denial. If he did not attend any Communist meetings and did not attend this, he may so state.

Mr. FLEISCHER. His answer was "no," as I take it.

The CHAIRMAN. Is that right—your answer is "no"?

Mr. FRANTZ. My answer is "no"; yes, sir.

Mr. BARKER. Do you know Harold Ralston, alias Nathaniel Brown?

Mr. FRANTZ. No.

Mr. BARKER. Do you know Wirt Taylor?

Mr. FRANTZ. Yes.

Mr. BARKER. Also known as Wirt R. Taylor?

(No answer.)

Mr. BARKER. What position does Mr. Wirt R. Taylor hold in the Communist Party in Alabama, Mississippi, and Georgia?

Mr. FRANTZ. I don't know exactly. I think he is some kind of assistant to Hall.

The CHAIRMAN. One point right here. Now, you say Mr. Hall employed—did he employ you in behalf of the Communist Party of Alabama?

Mr. FRANTZ. He did not say. He asked me to do this work, and I agreed to do it.

The CHAIRMAN. What was the nature of the work he asked you to do?

Mr. FRANTZ. He asked me to study the election laws of 12 Southern States and furnish him a report on each State as to what was necessary to get the Communist Party on the ballot.

The CHAIRMAN. When did he employ you—what date did you say?

Mr. FRANTZ. It was about the middle of March.

The CHAIRMAN. About the middle of March?

Mr. FRANTZ. Yes.

The CHAIRMAN. Did you carry on your work in the office of the Communist Party?

Mr. FRANTZ. I carried on my work principally in the law library in Birmingham.

The CHAIRMAN. Did you carry on part of your work in the offices of the Communist Party in Birmingham?

Mr. FRANTZ. Yes, sir. When I completed the study on any State, why, I would come back to Mr. Hall's office, type up the information in the form that I thought would be most useful for him, and turned it over to him.

The CHAIRMAN. Did you represent anyone else during that period in the city of Birmingham?

Mr. FRANTZ. No.

The CHAIRMAN. Your only representation was Bob Hall, but it was in connection with the—it was for the Communist Party, was it not?

Mr. FRANTZ. Well, as I say, Mr. Hall asked me to do this work. I presume it was not just an individual whim of his, but that is all I know about it.

The CHAIRMAN. All right, proceed.

Mr. BARKER. Do you know Mr. Ted Wellman, also known as Theo F. Wellman?

Mr. FRANTZ. I know Ted Wellman. I don't know him by any other name.

Mr. BARKER. Was Ted Wellman a member of the Communist Party in Tennessee?

Mr. FRANTZ. Yes. He was well known as a member of the Communist Party.

Mr. BARKER. He was a candidate for Presidential elector on the Communist Party ticket in 1936, wasn't he?

Mr. FRANTZ. I don't know.

Mr. BARKER. Do you know where Mr. Ted Wellman is at this time?

Mr. FRANTZ. I do not.

Mr. BARKER. Do you know where Wirt Taylor is at this time?

Mr. FRANTZ. I do not.

Mr. BARKER. Is Mr. Wirt Taylor a member of the Communist Party?

Mr. FRANTZ. I believe I have seen his name on Communist Party material.

Mr. BARKER. Have you ever been out of the United States?

The CHAIRMAN. Have you ever attended any meetings of the Young Communist League?

Mr. FRANTZ. No.

The CHAIRMAN. All right, proceed.

Mr. BARKER. Mr. Frantz, have you assisted in the publication of a publication known as the New South?

Mr. FRANTZ. No, sir.

Mr. BARKER. Have you ever assisted in the publication of a publication issued in Knoxville under the name of the Volunteer?

Mr. FRANTZ. No.

Mr. BARKER. Mr. Frantz, while you were in Knoxville, were you also employed by W. P. A.?

Mr. FRANTZ. I was in a nonrelief capacity; yes.

Mr. BARKER. Sir?

Mr. FRANTZ. I was employed by the W. P. A. in Knoxville in a nonrelief capacity.

Mr. BARKER. Nonrelief capacity?

Mr. FRANTZ. Yes.

Mr. BARKER. You were supervisor there of a project to index all Federal archives?

Mr. FRANTZ. It was more like an inventory—survey of Federal archives is what it was called.

Mr. BARKER. Your office at that time was in room 306 of the Federal Building?

Mr. FRANTZ. It was.

Mr. BARKER. How long did that project last, Mr. Frantz?

Mr. FRANTZ. About 10 months.

Mr. BARKER. Do you recall Mr. Earl Browder, general secretary of the Communist Party, making an address in Chattanooga?

Mr. FRANTZ. Yes, sir.

Mr. BARKER. You attended that address?

Mr. FRANTZ. Yes; I did.

Mr. BARKER. You did?

Mr. FRANTZ. Yes.

Mr. BARKER. Mr. Frantz, this office that you worked in in Knoxville in the W. P. A. employed how many people?

Mr. FRANTZ. The most it ever employed was 10. We usually had 6.

Mr. BARKER. On the afternoon that Mr. Browder was to make this speech in Chattanooga, Mr. Frantz, the office closed out and all of you went down to Chattanooga to hear Mr. Browder, didn't you?

Mr. FRANTZ. I don't remember closing early that day; no. And I don't think it is true that all of us went down to hear Browder; no.

Mr. BARKER. Pardon?

Mr. FRANTZ. No; that statement is not true; no.

Mr. BARKER. You mean to say that not all of the employees—of the 10, went to Chattanooga; is that right?

Mr. FLEISCHER. Mr. Chairman, may I respectfully submit whether 1, 10, 15, or 50 people went to hear Earl Browder is not material as far as this witness is concerned.

The CHAIRMAN. We think it is, Mr. Attorney. Proceed.

Mr. BARKER. Mr. Frantz, state how many of the people employed in room 306 at Knoxville, under this project, W. P. A. project, of which you were supervisor, how many of those people went to Chattanooga with you to hear Mr. Earl Browder speak.

Mr. FRANTZ. I don't think any of them went to Chattanooga with me.

Mr. BARKER. You just went by yourself?

Mr. FRANTZ. I don't recall who went to Chattanooga with me. I went to Chattanooga; yes.

Mr. BARKER. Now, Mr. Frantz, you have a brother named John M. Frantz?

Mr. FRANTZ. I do.

Mr. BARKER. He is employed by the Tennessee Valley Authority?

Mr. FRANTZ. Yes.

Mr. BARKER. He is employed in mails and files in the New Spraukle Building in Knoxville; is that right?

Mr. FRANTZ. I believe he is employed in office service. I don't know what building.

Mr. BARKER. Did he accompany you to Chattanooga to hear Earl Browder speak?

Mr. FRANTZ. I think he did; yes.

Mr. BARKER. Did your father also go with you to Chattanooga to hear Browder?

Mr. FLEISCHER. I don't see what this has to do with the questioning of this witness.

The CHAIRMAN. You noted your exception.

Mr. FRANTZ. Mr. Chairman, I would like to add to that that I think Mr. Barker's questioning me about personal, private, and family affairs are not a proper subject for the inquiry and not within the scope of the investigation at all.

The CHAIRMAN. All right, proceed. You have already testified your brother went with you. The question is now: Did your father accompany you to hear Earl Browder speak?

Mr. FRANTZ. I don't think the question is material and I don't think it is within the scope of the investigation, Mr. Chairman.

The CHAIRMAN. You decline to answer the question?

Mr. FRANTZ. I decline to answer it for the grounds that I have just stated; yes, sir.

The CHAIRMAN. Well, go ahead.

Mr. BARKER. Mr. Frantz, do you know a lady by the name of Miss Dorothy Remine?

Mr. FLEISCHER. Mr. Chairman, I again press the same objection, whether he knew anybody else is not pertinent to the inquiry before this committee.

The CHAIRMAN. All right; your objection is overruled. Proceed.

Mr. BARKER. Answer the question.

Mr. FLEISCHER. Exception.

Mr. FRANTZ. Mr. Chairman, I don't wish to discuss my friends here under circumstances where their names will go out over the press wires under goodness knows what interpretation of the evidence, and with the possible result that these personal friends of mine might lose their jobs or be discriminated against in some way.

Mr. BARKER. Let me ask you this question then, Mr. Frantz. Is Miss Remine the wife of your brother John?

Mr. FRANTZ. Yes.

Mr. BARKER. Was she employed on this W. P. A. project under your supervision?

Mr. FRANTZ. She was—she was not at that time a wife of my brother.

Mr. BARKER. She was not?

Mr. FRANTZ. She was not.

Mr. BARKER. Did she go to Chattanooga to attend the Earl Browder speech?

Mr. FRANTZ. Mr. Chairman, I don't remember who went to Chattanooga.

The CHAIRMAN. You remembered your brother did.

Mr. FRANTZ. I—to the best of my recollection my brother was there. I am not positive of that. I answered that question to the best of my recollection.

The CHAIRMAN. Well, is your answer now that you don't remember whether this lady went to Chattanooga with you to hear this speech?

Mr. FLEISCHER. As far as you know, you don't remember.

Mr. FRANTZ. I don't have any clear recollection of who did and who did not go to Chattanooga.

The CHAIRMAN. All right.

Mr. BARKER. Do you know a woman by the name of Polly Carey?

Mr. FRANTZ. Mr. Chairman, I object to being asked continually: "Do I know this person and that person," because I don't wish these persons to be discriminated against or to suffer in any way for their having been personally acquainted with me.

Mr. STARNES. You don't think because somebody knows you that it is inimical to their welfare? You don't contend that?

Mr. FRANTZ. I think it is inimical to any person's welfare to have his name go out to the press from this committee.

Mr. STARNES. In other words, you—I would like to get your position. Do you mean to say that people who know you—it would be harmful for the country to know that people know you?

Mr. FRANTZ. No, sir. That is not my position.

Mr. STARNES. Well, that is the impression I am getting because you are refusing to answer because you say it will mean they will be discriminated against if you even know them and it will be harmful to them. I just want to get your position in my mind here. You mean to state that under your oath that if people know you and you so testify that you know them and they know you, here before this committee, it will be injurious to them just because they know you?

Mr. FLEISCHER. It is very clear, Mr. Committeeman, that the witness here has been subpenaed for the purpose of endeavoring to find out whether or not he is a member of the Communist Party.

Now, there is no proof that he is a member of the Communist Party.

Mr. STARNES. That is not, Mr. Counsel, what is bothering me. He is being asked certain pertinent questions here. No witness who ever came here has just been confined to questions as to whether he belonged to an organization or didn't, but his general knowledge about any of these organizations or people connected with them, and it is pertinent to this inquiry. But I just cannot get the witness' attitude here—just because people know him that it would be harmful to them in a business or professional way.

Mr. FLEISCHER. Because he is subpenaed here ostensibly as a member of the Communist Party, and people who may read the press may draw the wrong or incorrect conclusion or inference by virtue of the fact that he is here as a witness to testify as to his alleged connection with the Communist Party.

Mr. VOORHIS. Mr. Chairman, it seems to me this whole question depends on whether the committee is in possession of any evidence with regard to any of the persons concerning whom the questions are asked.

I am unfamiliar with it. I don't know whether it is or not. But if it isn't, I think the witness' objection is proper; but if these are persons concerning whom the committee does have evidence, that is a different matter.

Mr. BARKER. The purpose of the question is to find out if Polly Carey was his secretary while he was supervisor of this W. P. A. project.

Mr. FLEISCHER. Why not ask the question instead of asking whether or not he knew her?

Mr. BARKER. He did not give me an opportunity. Was she your secretary, Mr. Frantz?

Mr. FRANTZ. Before I answer that, may I make one more statement, Mr. Chairman? I would like to make one more statement and try to clarify my position to this committee member who asked me about it. Is that all right?

The CHAIRMAN. All right; go ahead.

Mr. FRANTZ. My position is this: I don't think that there is any reason, any legitimate reason, why anyone should suffer for being personally acquainted with me at all, but I do think that when Mr. Barker sits here and reads off names: "Do I know this person and do I know that person," that to say "Yes" under these circumstances and have their names go out in the record as mentioned here before the committee, will give an inference in the minds of the people who read these news reports that these persons were connected with some kind of activity that this committee is investigating. I don't think that is true of these people, and I don't want that inference to be made through the press accounts of this type of questioning. Is that clear?

Mr. STARNES. You don't mean to say you would attempt to censor the press, would you?

Mr. FRANTZ. I am not attempting to censor the press; no, sir.

Mr. STARNES. And not attempting to tell the press what it should or should not write.

Mr. FRANTZ. I am not.

Mr. FLEISCHER. It is the reading of the thing.

The CHAIRMAN. Proceed.

Mr. BARKER. Mr. Frantz, what happened to this W. P. A. project that you were working on in Knoxville?

Mr. FRANTZ. Nothing happened to it. The work was completed.

Mr. BARKER. The work was completed?

Mr. FRANTZ. Yes.

Mr. BARKER. At the time that this W. P. A. project was going in Knoxville, Mr. Frantz, were any fraction meetings of the Communist Party of Knoxville—of the Communist Party of Knox County—held in this office, room 306, in the Federal Building?

Mr. FRANTZ. No, sir.

Mr. BARKER. Mr. Frantz, did you hear anything about what caused this project to be closed up? Why it was closed? Were there any protests lodged here in Washington or with Col. Harry Bayer, in charge of the Tennessee W. P. A., about the activity of your office in Knoxville?

Mr. FRANTZ. I don't understand what you mean by "any protest." I don't know of any protest; no.

Mr. BARKER. You do not recall any protest being made?

Mr. FRANTZ. I don't know of any protest. I do know—well, I—well, what I am trying to get across is, I don't know of any protest, and that the project was closed down, to my knowledge, because the work was completed.

Mr. BARKER. Did Mr. Woodruff Booth, postmaster at Knoxville, and John D. Wine, custodian of the Federal Building at Knoxville, take the keys to this room away from you and impound the records?

Mr. FRANTZ. They did not; no, sir.

Mr. BARKER. Did not?

Mr. FRANTZ. No, sir.

Mr. BARKER. Who did you deliver the keys to, to this office?

Mr. FRANTZ. I was not on the project until right up until it closed. I was on the project until sometime in December. At that time my services were dispensed with, and the project was put in charge of someone else for a period of several weeks, and I gave the keys to my successor.

Mr. BARKER. And who was your successor?

Mr. FRANTZ. Miss Remine.

Mr. BARKER. Miss Dorothy Remine?

Mr. FRANTZ. Yes.

Mr. BARKER. R-e-m-i-n-e?

Mr. FRANTZ. Yes.

Mr. BARKER. Mr. Frantz, did you bring a speaker to Knoxville one time to address the student body at the University of Tennessee?

Mr. FLEISCHER. May I again press the same objection?

The CHAIRMAN. What was the question?

Mr. BARKER. I asked if he brought a speaker to Knoxville to address the student body at the University of Tennessee.

The CHAIRMAN. What speaker?

Mr. BARKER. I asked him if he brought a speaker.

Mr. FLEISCHER. I think the question is vague.

The CHAIRMAN. Wait a minute. Well, I don't think that would be a proper question—"bring a speaker" there for that purpose. You mean some Communist speaker?

Mr. BARKER. Well, I want him to state the name of the gentleman.

The CHAIRMAN. Just ask this question: Who is the man that you are inquiring about?

Mr. BARKER. I don't have his name, Mr. Chairman. I was asking the witness if he would state for the record the man he brought down to Knoxville.

The CHAIRMAN. To address a students' gathering there?

Mr. BARKER. Yes.

The CHAIRMAN. Where?

Mr. BARKER. At the University of Tennessee.

Mr. FLEISCHER. When?

Mr. BARKER. 1937.

Mr. FLEISCHER. What month?

Mr. BARKER. I don't have that date. It is during the year 1937.

Mr. FLEISCHER. Well, I object to the question, Mr. Chairman, on the ground it is vague, indefinite, and uncertain, and can have no bearing upon the scope or activities or functions of this committee.

The CHAIRMAN. I think the question in its present form would not be admissible. Go ahead.

Mr. STARNES. Let me get something in my mind. You say you were working with the W. P. A. in a nonrelief capacity in Knoxville?

Mr. FRANTZ. That is right.

Mr. STARNES. For a period of around 10 months?

Mr. FRANTZ. That is right.

Mr. STARNES. What year?

Mr. FRANTZ. 1936.

Mr. STARNES. Now, when did you go to Birmingham?

Mr. FRANTZ. 1937.

Mr. STARNES. 1937?

Mr. FRANTZ. Yes.

Mr. STARNES. How long were you there before you were connected with the Works Progress Administration anywhere?

Mr. FRANTZ. I made application to the Works Progress Administration in April 1938, after my work with Mr. Gelders and the National Committee for People's Rights had been terminated.

Mr. STARNES. Did you work on a relief or nonrelief capacity in Birmingham?

Mr. FRANTZ. On a relief capacity.

Mr. STARNES. How long had you been in Birmingham before you were accepted as a relief client?

Mr. FRANTZ. Well, I have been in Birmingham for something over a year.

Mr. STARNES. You were not there a year before you put in your application?

Mr. FRANTZ. Yes; I was.

Mr. STARNES. Did you meet Jack Donovan while you were in Birmingham?

Mr. FRANTZ. Yes; I did.

Mr. STARNES. How long had you been there before you met him?

Mr. FRANTZ. I don't remember exactly when he came there. It seems to be he came there last summer, but I am not sure about that.

Mr. STARNES. Did you have any conference with him with reference to the relief situation in the Birmingham area?

Mr. FRANTZ. I had frequent conferences with him; yes, sir.

Mr. STARNES. Did you ever have any conferences with Mr. Donovan in which either Mr. Dunn, the State welfare director, was present, and Mr. W. G. Henderson, the State administrator?

Mr. FRANTZ. No. I don't remember any conferences like that.

Mr. STARNES. Didn't have any conferences with those people?

(No answer.)

Mr. Starnes. Mr. Donovan is the direct organizer for the Workers' Alliance, was he not?

Mr. Frantz. He was a representative of the national office of the Workers' Alliance.

Mr. Starnes. Did you ever have any conference with Mr. Donovan at which Paul Crouch was present?

Mr. Frantz. I don't think so; no.

Mr. Starnes. Or with Jane Speed?

Mr. Frantz. No.

Mr. Starnes. How long did you stay on relief in Birmingham, Mr. Witness?

Mr. Frantz. I was on relief for about a year and a half with several breaks, two of which were for more than 30 days between projects.

Mr. Starnes. The 18-month provision, then, did not apply to you?

Mr. Frantz. It did not.

Mr. Starnes. What was the type of work that you did in Birmingham?

Mr. Frantz. I have already gone into that, I believe. I was—I did radio scripts for the health project. I was an editor on the writers' project, and I was an editor and then later principal editor on a national research project.

Mr. Starnes. How many did you have in your writers' project there, do you recall?

Mr. Frantz. Well, it seems to me there were about 8 in the State office.

Mr. Starnes. Eight in the State office, and the State office is located there in Birmingham?

Mr. Frantz. That is right.

Mr. Starnes. That is all.

Mr. Barker. Mr. Frantz, this office of Mr. Hall in Birmingham, room—I think you said—room 235 in the Clark Building, is that right?

Mr. Frantz. Yes.

Mr. Barker. That is Mr. Hall's office, his headquarters for the Communist Party, isn't it?

Mr. Frantz. Well, I don't know that it is. No; it is Mr. Hall's office, and he is an official.

Mr. Barker. Sir?

Mr. Fleischer. He already answered it.

Mr. Frantz. All I know is that it is Mr. Hall's office and that he is an official.

Mr. Barker. Official of the Communist Party?

Mr. Frantz. Yes.

Mr. Barker. Were there any records in that office, Mr. Frantz?

Mr. Frantz. I don't know of any records in that office. I am not in charge of the office, and if there were any records there I wouldn't be acquainted with them or have any business going into them.

Mr. Barker. How long has it been since you have seen Wirt Taylor?

Mr. Fleischer. Now, Mr. Chairman, I again press the same objection. I respectfully suggest the scope and activity of this committee is confined to matters pertaining to his activities and the relationship of the question of un-American activities. Anything outside of the scope of that is incompetent, irrelevant, and immaterial.

The CHAIRMAN. Well, with reference to Wirt Taylor, is he an official in the Communist Party?

Mr. FLEISCHER. There is no proof as to that.

The CHAIRMAN. I am asking that.

Mr. BARKER. Mr. Frantz identified Mr. Wirt Taylor as being an official in the Communist Party by stating that he saw his name on some material up there in that office, and a subpena has been issued for Mr. Wirt Taylor. He hasn't been located, and I wanted to know if Mr. Frantz——

The CHAIRMAN. Do you know Mr. Wirt Taylor to be—you understand him to be a member of the Communist Party?

Mr. FRANTZ. Yes, sir; I do.

The CHAIRMAN. He is a member of the Communist Party. Well, go ahead and ask your question.

Mr. FLEISCHER. Exception.

Mr. BARKER. How long has it been since you have seen Mr. Wirt Taylor?

Mr. FLEISCHER. I again press the objection. It seems the scope of this committee is to obtain information as to the whereabouts of this witness whom it is anxious to serve.

The CHAIRMAN. Would you be inclined to suppress any information?

Mr. FLEISCHER. Provided such type of questioning relates specifically to any activities or actions that his witness has carried on in the scope of un-American activities.

The CHAIRMAN. You would not have any objection to the committee finding this witness?

Mr. FLEISCHER. No; I wouldn't have any objection, but I still press the objection that such questioning is immaterial and irrelevant.

The CHAIRMAN. All right; proceed.

Mr. BARKER. Answer the question, Mr. Frantz.

Mr. FRANTZ. I saw him last Saturday.

Mr. BARKER. Last Saturday. Where did you see him?

Mr. FRANTZ. He took me to the train.

Mr. BARKER. He took you to the train?

Mr. FRANTZ. (No answer.)

Mr. BARKER. Have you been carrying on a general correspondence for Bob Hall, in addition to this work for the national campaign committee of the Communist Party?

Mr. FRANTZ. No.

Mr. BARKER. You did not handle any general correspondence?

Mr. FLEISCHER. I object to the question. It has already been answered. It is in the record.

The CHAIRMAN. You did not write any letters for Bob Hall or the Communist Party?

Mr. FLEISCHER. No.

The CHAIRMAN. Is that right?

Mr. FRANTZ. I did not.

The CHAIRMAN. Did you open any of the mail to Bob Hall or the Communist Party?

Mr. FRANTZ. This mail that was in my pocket at the time that I was arrested, while it was addressed to Mr. Hall, it was material regarding getting on the ballot, and Mr. Taylor turned it over to me to study in Mr. Hall's absence.

Mr. BARKER. Who else was in this room in the Clark Building when the city detective and the marshal came up there?

Mr. FRANTZ. No one.

Mr. BARKER. You were there?

Mr. FRANTZ. Yes.

Mr. BARKER. Did you have a key to the room, Mr. Frantz?

Mr. FRANTZ. I did.

Mr. VOORHIS. Could I ask one question. Were you retained by Mr. H   or by the party to make this study? Is that what I understand? all

Mr. FRANTZ. I was retained by Mr. Hall; yes.

Mr. VOORHIS. And he paid you a salary to do this work; is that right?

Mr. FRANTZ. That is right.

The CHAIRMAN. Did he pay you by check or in cash?

Mr. FRANTZ. He paid me by cash.

Mr. BARKER. Now, Mr. Frantz, this subpena that was served upon you by the United States marshal of Birmingham is a subpena duces tecum requiring you to bring all records of the Communist Party in your possession and custody, including correspondence, membership lists, and financial records. Did you bring the records with you, Mr. Frantz?

Mr. FRANTZ. I have never had any such records in my possession or custody.

Mr. BARKER. You had a key to Mr. Hall's office?

Mr. FRANTZ. Yes; but I didn't have custody of anything that was in Mr. Hall's office. I had the use of it—I had the use of the office.

Mr. BARKER. Have you been in communication since you were served with this subpena on April 11 with Mr. Bob Hall?

Mr. FRANTZ. I don't see how that is material, Mr. Chairman.

The CHAIRMAN. It is material.

Mr. FLEISCHER. In what way, Mr. Chairman.

The CHAIRMAN. Well, do you want me to disclose publicly the reasons he is being asked these questions? I am trying to be fair to the witness. We are not here just asking him questions to pass the time away. All of us have business to attend to and we are here asking questions because we have a definite reason for asking them. But I am not, in fairness to the witness, I am not disclosing such reasons. Proceed.

Mr. BARKER. Answer the question, Mr. Frantz. Were you in communication with Bob Hall after you had been served with the subpena on April 11?

Mr. FRANTZ. Yes, sir.

Mr. BARKER. You were?

Mr. FRANTZ. I was.

Mr. BARKER. At what place?

Mr. FRANTZ. At his office.

Mr. BARKER. In Birmingham?

Mr. FRANTZ. Yes.

Mr. BARKER. And what day was that?

Mr. FRANTZ. Well, I was in his office on Friday and also on Saturday of that week, which would be——

Mr. BARKER. April 12 and 13?

Mr. FRANTZ. Something like that.

Mr. BARKER. Were you in communication with Mr. Paul Crouch at any time after you were served with a subpena?

Mr. FRANTZ. No.

Mr. BARKER. Mr. Frantz, have you ever belonged to the American League Against War and Fascism or the American League for Peace and Democracy?

Mr. FRANTZ. No, sir.

Mr. BARKER. You have not?

Mr. FRANTZ. No.

The CHAIRMAN. When did you join the Workers' Alliance, Mr. Frantz?

Mr. FRANTZ. 1936.

The CHAIRMAN. You are still a member of the Workers' Alliance?

Mr. FRANTZ. Well, I would say, "No," because I haven't been active or paid my dues in some time.

The CHAIRMAN. Did you ever make any speeches in behalf of the Workers' Alliance?

Mr. FRANTZ. Yes.

The CHAIRMAN. Were you one of the organizers for the Workers' Alliance?

Mr. FRANTZ. No; I was the publicity director.

The CHAIRMAN. Were you ever approached by anyone to join the Communist Party?

Mr. FLEISCHER. He testified he was not a member of the Communist Party.

The CHAIRMAN. I am asking him if he was approached.

Mr. FLEISCHER. Would it make any difference? The fact is he is not a member of the Communist Party.

The CHAIRMAN. That is what we are inquiring into. Were you ever approached by anyone to join the Communist Party?

Mr. FRANTZ. I was never asked in so many words to join it; no.

The CHAIRMAN. Never asked in so many words to join the Communist Party. Bob Hall never solicited you to become a member?

Mr. FRANTZ. No.

Mr. STARNES. By the way, who assigned you to this writers' project and this publicity work on relief then in Birmingham, Mr. Frantz?

Mr. FRANTZ. Well, it was done through—I think you have got a little misunderstanding there. I—there was no publicity work on relief—on my relief employment.

Mr. STARNES. I understood you to say you were editor in chief of a writers' project. Maybe I didn't understand you.

Mr. FRANTZ. You did misunderstand me. I said I was editor. That doesn't mean of a publication. That means I was editing material sent in from the field.

Mr. STARNES. Who assigned you to that duty?

Mr. FRANTZ. Well, the—you mean who assigned me to the job that was done?

Mr. STARNES. Yes; who assigned you to the job?

Mr. FRANTZ. That was done through the W. P. A. assignment office.

Mr. STARNES. Did you make application for that kind of work and ask to be assigned to the writers' project?

Mr. FRANTZ. Yes, sir.

Mr. STARNES. To whom did you address the application?

Mr. Frantz. I made an application—I was on W. P. A.—I mean I was on the W. P. A. rolls at that time.

Mr. Starnes. Yes.

Mr. Frantz. And I had no assignment. I made an oral application, to the State director of the project.

Mr. Starnes. Who was the State director at that time?

Mr. Frantz. Miss Myrtle Miles.

Mr. Starnes. Miss Miles?

Mr. Frantz. Yes, sir.

Mr. Starnes. She lives in Birmingham?

Mr. Frantz. Her office was in Birmingham. She lives somewhere near there—not in the city.

Mr. Starnes. Now, how long had you lived in Birmingham before you applied for relief?

Mr. Frantz. (No answer.)

Mr. Starnes. You said you went down there, as I understand you, in 1937, sometime and that you were assigned to work about April 1938. Now, how long had you been there before you were assigned?

Mr. Frantz. I had been there for something over a year.

Mr. Starnes. But how long had you been there before you applied?

Mr. Frantz. Well, I was—it is the same thing. I was assigned almost immediately after I applied.

Mr. Starnes. You did not have any difficulty in getting on?

Mr. Frantz. Well, I got on about 1 week after my application.

Mr. Starnes. Did you apply through the Workers' Alliance or did they assist you in any way in getting your—did they expedite action on your application for relief?

Mr. Frantz. They did not; no.

Mr. Starnes. That is all.

The Chairman. Mr. Matthews.

Mr. Matthews. Mr. Frantz, how long did you work for the National Committee for People's Rights?

Mr. Frantz. I worked there for a little over a year.

Mr. Matthews. What was your salary—any?

Mr. Frantz. Well, it depended. It was somewhat—it varied a good deal. I got—I would say I got an average of $15 a week.

Mr. Matthews. What were you supposed to get in salary?

The Chairman. Speak a little louder, please.

Mr. Frantz. Well, I am trying to make clear that this was changed.

Mr. Matthews. Was there a fixed salary?

Mr. Frantz. There was at various times. It was changed frequently.

Mr. Matthews. What was the former name of this organization, Mr. Frantz?

Mr. Frantz. It was formerly known as the National Committee for the Defense of Political Prisoners.

Mr. Matthews. Who are the national officers of the National Committee for People's Rights?

Mr. Fleischer. I object to that, Mr. Chairman. I think it is not pertinent or relative.

The Chairman. If the witness knows.

Mr. Fleischer. Exception.

The Chairman. Do you want to state the purpose of going into this matter?

Mr. FLEISCHER. I wish you would.

The CHAIRMAN. I will state the purpose: Because this organization—the committee has evidence this organization is a Communist organization set up and controlled by the Communist Party. Proceed.

Mr. MATTHEWS. Who are the national officers of the organization?

Mr. FRANTZ. I don't know the organization at the present time.

Mr. MATTHEWS. When did you work for it?

Mr. FRANTZ. I worked for it in 1937—the early part of 1938.

Mr. MATTHEWS. Who were the national officers at that time?

Mr. FRANTZ. I haven't had occasion to think of their names for some time and offhand I don't remember their names.

Mr. MATTHEWS. Do you know?

Mr. FRANTZ. I had no dealings with them.

Mr. MATTHEWS. Do you know that a substantial majority of the members of this committee are publicly known Communists?

Mr. FRANTZ. I don't know anything about the members.

Mr. MATTHEWS. You worked for the organization, didn't you?

Mr. FRANTZ. I did.

Mr. MATTHEWS. Did you ever handle any of its letterheads?

Mr. FRANTZ. Yes; I think so.

Mr. VOORHIS. Mr. Chairman, I would just like to know whether you mean a substantial majority of the members of the committee—do you mean of the governing board or the membership of the whole committee?

Mr. MATTHEWS. So far as I know the organization is a national committee and the national committeemen are those listed on the letterhead.

Mr. VOORHIS. I see.

Mr. MATTHEWS. That is what I refer to.

Mr. FRANTZ. I don't know what the question is now.

Mr. MATTHEWS. Who were the national officers at the time you worked for the organization?

Mr. FRANTZ. I don't remember who they were. I would probably recognize their names.

The CHAIRMAN. What is your answer? You don't remember?

Mr. FRANTZ. I had no dealings whatever with the national officers or with the national office. All my dealings were with Mr. Gelders.

Mr. MATTHEWS. But you did have letterheads in your possession, you have stated?

Mr. FRANTZ. There were letterheads in the office; yes.

Mr. MATTHEWS. And did you conduct any correspondence at any time with reference to the affairs of the organization?

Mr. FRANTZ. Yes, I did.

Mr. MATTHEWS. You did use the letterheads then?

Mr. FRANTZ. I don't remember whether I used the letterheads or not. I think very probably I did.

Mr. MATTHEWS. You have seen the letterheads?

Mr. FRANTZ. Yes, sir.

Mr. MATTHEWS. And you did at one time know the names of the committee members?

Mr. FLEISCHER. Just for the sake of the record, let us get this clear. Are you referring to the National Committee for People's Rights or the National Committee for the Defense of Political Prisoners?

Mr. MATTHEWS. National Committee for People's Rights, the organization for which Mr. Frantz worked.

Mr. FRANTZ. I don't think I ever paid any special attention to the names on the letterhead. I certainly never memorized them.

Mr. MATTHEWS. I did not ask you if you had memorized them. Would it be a matter of interest to know who your sponsors or employers were?

Mr. FLEISCHER. I object to the question on the ground that it has already been answered. He testified he doesn't know.

Mr. MATTHEWS. Mr. Chairman, the witness has not answered any question that even remotely resembles that.

Mr. FLEISCHER. I submit the record speaks for itself, and he was asked whether he knew and he testified he did not—never had any dealings with them.

The CHAIRMAN. The record speaks for itself.

Mr. MATTHEWS. I ask the witness, too, if it isn't a fact—if it isn't a matter of interest to him to know for whom he is working.

Mr. FLEISCHER. I object to it on the further ground the question as put is argumentative and speculative and calls for the operation of the witness' mind.

The CHAIRMAN. If you had known the organization was a Communist organization, controlled by well-known Communists, would you have worked for the organization?

Mr. FLEISCHER. I object to that question on the ground it is highly speculative and hypothetical.

The CHAIRMAN. We are trying to get his viewpoint about it.

Mr. STARNES. Mr. Chairman, I don't think it is speculative because he testified he has been working for a man he knows to be a Communist.

Mr. FRANTZ. No, sir—oh, you mean Mr. Hall; I see.

Mr. STARNES. I thought you said you worked for Bob Hall.

Mr. FLEISCHER. He admits that.

Mr. STARNES. And he knew him to be a Communist.

Mr. FLEISCHER. He did not say he worked for him. He said he was retained there. There is a difference in working for and retained.

The CHAIRMAN. His work was for the Communist Party in order to get the names on the ticket.

Mr. FLEISCHER. As an attorney which he had a legal right to do.

The CHAIRMAN. And he has a legal right to belong to the Communist Party. On that theory we wouldn't have an investigation.

Mr. MATTHEWS. I show you a letterhead of the National Committee for People's Rights [handing document to the witness].

Mr. MATTHEWS. Have you ever seen letterheads like that?

Mr. FRANTZ. It looks like it.

Mr. MATTHEWS. I ask that this be marked as an exhibit.

The CHAIRMAN. Very well.

(The document referred to by Mr. Matthews was marked "Laurent B. Frantz, Exhibit No. 1.")

Mr. MATTHEWS. I should like to read the names of these committee members and ask the witness whether or not he knows of his own knowledge whether they were publicly known Communists.

Mr. FLEISCHER. I object to the introduction of the alleged exhibit into evidence on the ground there has been no identification by this witness. He said: "It looks like it." Didn't say it was a letterhead.

Mr. MATTHEWS. The witness said he had seen similar letterheads.

Mr. FLEISCHER. That does not mean it is a letterhead of the committee.

The CHAIRMAN. Proceed.

Mr. MATTHEWS. Rockwell Kent——

Mr. FLEISCHER. I press the same objection.

The CHAIRMAN. Do you know anything about him?

Mr. FLEISCHER. No.

Mr. FRANTZ. No.

Mr. MATTHEWS. Do you know Rockwell Kent, who is chairman for the Professional Groups for Browder and Ford?

Mr. FRANTZ. I don't know anything about it.

Mr. MATTHEWS. Did you ever hear of Ella Winter?

Mr. FRANTZ. What do you mean? I haven't met these people.

Mr. MATTHEWS. These are the people for whom you worked.

Mr. FLEISCHER. There is no proof in the record that he worked for these people and I object to Mr. Matthews assuming a state of facts that do not exist.

The CHAIRMAN. The evidence is, as I understand, that he worked for this committee.

Mr. FLEISCHER. For a local committee and that is a national committee.

The CHAIRMAN. But the local committee is under the control of the national committee.

Mr. FLEISCHER. Exactly.

The CHAIRMAN. A part of the same organization.

Mr. FLEISCHER. But Mr. Matthews put the question in the form that assumes a state of facts—that he worked for the national committee.

Mr. MATTHEWS. He testified he worked for the National Committee for the People's Rights. That is his language.

Mr. FLEISCHER. Suppose we ask a few questions as to the organizational set-up.

Did you work in New York City?

Mr. FRANTZ. No.

Mr. FLEISCHER. Did you work for the local territory?

Mr. MATTHEWS. Mr. Chairman——

The CHAIRMAN. Just a second. I will ask the questions.

Did you say that you were employed by this Mr. Gelders?

Mr. FRANTZ. Yes.

The CHAIRMAN. You were employed in behalf of what?

Mr. FRANTZ. Well, he was the southern representative of this organization.

The CHAIRMAN. And you were employed to work for the organization, were you not?

Mr. FRANTZ. I was employed to do whatever work he wanted done. He didn't describe it as "employed by the organization," no.

The CHAIRMAN. Well, you did not understand it was a personal work of his?

Mr. FRANTZ. No.

The CHAIRMAN. What did you understand when you were employed?

Mr. FRANTZ. I was—Mr. Gelders was the southern representative of this organization and I was employed by him to do research, special legal research and to do other things—what I could for him.

The CHAIRMAN. For whom were you to do the work?

Mr. FRANTZ. Well, the work, of course, was the work of the committee.

Mr. STARNES. Let him go ahead.

Mr. FLEISCHER. May I at this point ask one or two questions which I think will throw a little bit more light on this particular line of inquiry?

The CHAIRMAN. Tell me what you have in mind.

Mr. FLEISCHER. What I have in mind to show is this witness worked directly under the supervision and control of Mr. Gelders, and this witness never had any direct or indirect contact with the so-called National Committee of this particular committee, whose actions are now—we are seeking now to inquire into; that his only contact was with this Mr. Gelders under whom he worked. Therefore, any questions asked as to the composition or membership of the national committee, so far as this witness is concerned, is clearly irrelevant because he does not know.

The CHAIRMAN. If he doesn't know, he will have to say he doesn't know. Go ahead.

Mr. FLEISCHER. That is the purpose.

Mr. MATTHEWS. Mr. Frantz, did you ever have any correspondence of any kind with the national office of this organization?

Mr. FRANTZ. I don't remember any correspondence with the national office. Mr. Gelders dealt with the national office.

Mr. MATTHEWS. Will you state that you never did have any such correspondence?

Mr. FLEISCHER. I object to the question. It has already been answered.

Mr. MATTHEWS. The question has been answered by the attorney, not by the witness.

Mr. FLEISCHER. Answered by the witness, and I object to Mr. Matthews insinuating I am leading the witness.

The CHAIRMAN. You certainly can answer that question. Did you have any correspondence with the National Committee?

Mr. FRANTZ. I was not in correspondence with them. I couldn't sit here and tell you as a positive thing that I never wrote the National Committee a letter; no.

Mr. MATTHEWS. Mr. Chairman, the attorney has so stated——

The CHAIRMAN. So you don't remember whether you wrote a letter to the national office or had correspondence with the national offices; is that correct?

Mr. FRANTZ. I was—I do remember that I was not in regular communication with the national office. I do know that I was not supposed to be that. Mr. Gelders handled all relations with the national office.

Mr. STARNES. Mr. Chairman, he says he worked for Mr. Gelders, who is the southern representative of this National Committee. He was employed in that capacity. That makes him an employee of the National Committee because Gelders was—and got him to work for that purpose.

Mr. FLEISCHER. But that doesn't mean he knows who the member-ship of the National Committee is.

Mr. STARNES. He can say when asked the question whether he does or does not know.

The CHAIRMAN. Proceed.

Mr. MATTHEWS. Do you know who Ella Winters is?

Mr. FRANTZ. Mr. Chairman, I want to know how, when I am asked these questions, whether I am supposed to answer from what I personally know or from what I may perhaps have heard or read in the press.

The CHAIRMAN. Well, do you know?

Mr. FRANTZ. This question is, Have I ever heard of Ella Winters? I would like to answer——

Mr. STARNES. May I suggest, Dr. Matthews, "Do you know them personally or by reputation to be——

Mr. MATTHEWS. I think I can ask it in another form. Do you know Ella Winters, vice chairman of the National Committee for People's Rights was also a member of the Committee for Professional Groups for Browder and Ford?

Mr. FLEISCHER. I object because he assumes a state of facts not in the evidence.

The CHAIRMAN. He is asking if he knows Ella Winters as a member of the Professional Groups for Browder and Ford.

Mr. FLEISCHER. He asked if he knew whether Ella Winters, who is a member of the National Committee, is connected with another organization.

Mr. MATTHEWS. I would like to ask if you accepted this in evidence when I offered it in evidence, this letterhead?

The CHAIRMAN. That is true.

Mr. MATTHEWS. Then the document is in evidence?

The CHAIRMAN. Yes.

Mr. FLEISCHER. Subject to my objection.

The CHAIRMAN. Will you repeat the question?

Mr. MATTHEWS. Do you know whether or not Ella Winters, vice chairman of the Nation Committee for People's Rights, was also a member of the Committee of Professional Groups for Browder and Ford?

Mr. FRANTZ. I know nothing whatever of my own personal knowledge about Ella Winters—nothing whatever.

Mr. MATTHEWS. Do you know whether or not Sherwood Anderson is a member of the National Committee for People's Rights and was also a member of the Committee of Professional Groups for Browder and Ford?

Mr. FRANTZ. I never met Sherwood Anderson.

Mr. MATTHEWS. I did not ask you that.

Mr. FRANTZ. I am telling you I don't know anything about these people, as far as anything that I could testify to from my own personal knowledge.

Mr. MATTHEWS. Do you know whether or not Winifred Chappell is a member of the National Committee for People's Rights and also a member of the Committee of Professional Groups for Browder and Ford?

Mr. FRANTZ. I don't know anything about her either.

Mr. MATTHEWS. Do you know whether or not Lester Cohn is a member of the National Committee for People's Rights and also a member of the Committee of Professional Groups for Browder and Ford?

Mr. FRANTZ. I do not know anything about them.

Mr. FLEISCHER. In order to facilitate this type of questioning, may I suggest, Mr. Chairman, that as long as this is in evidence, subject to exception, that all—that the questions be phrased in this manner: That all the names on here, whether he knows they are in any way connected with any other organization.

The CHAIRMAN. As I understand he made the statement——

Mr. MATTHEWS. I will read the entire list of names and ask him the single question.

The CHAIRMAN. You saw the list of names there, didn't you, Mr. Frantz?

Mr. FLEISCHER. You saw the letterhead?

Mr. FRANTZ. I didn't read it down.

The CHAIRMAN. Read the list there. Pardon me, gentlemen, there is a roll call and vote.

Mr. FLEISCHER. May I at this point ask one or two questions that I think should be cleared up with reference to the service of the subpena?

The CHAIRMAN. Not at this point because we are going to have to suspend.

Mr. FLEISCHER. It is only two or three questions and will take 1 or 2 minutes to clear up. I think you haven't a clear picture as to what happened as far as the service of the subpena is concerned.

The CHAIRMAN. I think we have been very indulgent to permit you to ask these questions and step aside from the usual rule, because of the charges that were made, in order to clarify the issue. We have not only done that but the marshal and other people that he has made statements about will be brought here and the whole matter of his testimony, since he has made certain statements here under oath, I think that the whole matter should be referred to the district attorney's office.

Mr. VOORHIS. As I understand it you say when you were arrested they charged you with vagrancy?

Mr. FLEISCHER. Wasn't told of the charge until he was taken to the police station.

The CHAIRMAN. We will have to suspend for the time being.

Mr. FLEISCHER. May I make an offer of proof as to what this witness would testify to—as to some matters which I think will enlighten the committee on some matters?

The CHAIRMAN. You will have an opportunity to do that.

Mr. FLEISCHER. I would like to do it.

The CHAIRMAN. Before an appropriate grand jury because this witness made certain statements and certain charges that have been denied by the marshal and his office and by the investigator. I think the entire matter ought to go before the grand jury on the question of the whole question involved.

Mr. FLEISCHER. May I still make an offer of proof as to what this witness would testify to as to the manner of service?

The CHAIRMAN. The witness already testified.

Mr. FLEISCHER. No; he hasn't. If you remember, Mr. Chairman, that part of the inquiry was permitted and then we pursued another line of questioning.

The CHAIRMAN. We will have to suspend and if possible will meet again tomorrow morning at 10:30.

Mr. FLEISCHER. Not Saturday morning?

The CHAIRMAN. Well, we want to dispose of it so your witness can go. There is another witness here who wants to be heard. We will have to hear him in the morning.

Mr. FLEISCHER. Do I understand there will be no further committee hearing this afternoon?

The CHAIRMAN. We will suspend until 10:30 o'clock tomorrow morning.

(Whereupon at 3:30 p. m., the hearing was adjourned until 10:30 a. m., April 23, 1940.)

INVESTIGATION OF UN-AMERICAN PROPAGANDA ACTIVITIES IN THE UNITED STATES

TUESDAY, APRIL 23, 1940

House of Representatives,
Committee on Un-American Activities,
Washington, D. C.

The committee met at 10 a. m., Hon. Martin Dies (chairman), presiding.

T he Chairman. The committee will come to order.

The Chair announces a subcommittee composed of the chairman, the gentleman from Illinois, Mr. Mason, and the gentleman from California, Mr. Voorhis. Present are the chairman and Mr. Mason.

Call your first witness.

Mr. Matthews. Mr. O'Shea.

The Chairman. Raise your right hand and be sworn.

TESTIMONY OF THOMAS HUMPHREY O'SHEA

The Chairman. Do you solemnly swear to tell the truth, the whole truth, and nothing but the truth, so help you God?

Mr. O'Shea. Yes, sir.

The Chairman. Have a seat. Will you speak as distinctly and loudly as possible so we may hear you?

Mr. O'Shea. Certainly.

Mr. Matthews. Mr. O'Shea, will you give you full name for the record?

Mr. O'Shea. Thomas Humphrey O'Shea.

Mr. Matthews. Are you an American citizen?

Mr. O'Shea. Yes.

Mr. Matthews. Where were you born?

Mr. O'Shea. In Cobh, Ireland.

Mr. Matthews. C-o-b-h?

Mr. O'Shea. Cobh; yes.

Mr. Matthews. When?

Mr. O'Shea. October 21, 1897.

Mr. Matthews. When did you come to the United States?

Mr. O'Shea. In 1927.

Mr. Matthews. Where were you naturalized?

Mr. O'Shea. At the southern district court in New York City.

Mr. Matthews. When?

Mr. O'Shea. In 1933.

Mr. Matthews. Before you came to the United States what——

The Chairman. Just a second. I believe that is Mr. Onda.

Mr. Fleischer. Yes.

The CHAIRMAN. Will you step aside until we hear the other witness? He is here now.

(Witness excused.)

The CHAIRMAN. Raise your right hand before you sit down.

TESTIMONY OF ANDREW RUDOLPH ONDA

The CHAIRMAN. Do you solemnly swear to tell the truth, the whole truth, and nothing but the truth, so help you God?

Mr. ONDA. I do.

Mr. MATTHEWS. Please give your full name for the record.

Mr. ONDA. I just want to catch my breath. I have been walking up the stairs. Andrew Rudolph Onda.

Mr. MATTHEWS. What is your address?

Mr. ONDA. 3624 East One Hundred and Fifty-first Street, Cleveland, Ohio.

Mr. MATTHEWS. Are you an American citizen?

Mr. ONDA. I am.

Mr. MATTHEWS. Where were you born?

Mr. ONDA. Pittsburgh, Pa.

Mr. MATTHEWS. When?

Mr. ONDA. October 23, 1904.

Mr. MATTHEWS. What is your present occupation?

Mr. ONDA. I am the county secretary of the Communist Party, Cuyahoga County.

Mr. MATTHEWS. Is that in Ohio?

Mr. ONDA. That is.

Mr. MATTHEWS. Where are your headquarters?

Mr. ONDA. 1514 Prospect, room 305.

Mr. MATTHEWS. Cleveland, Ohio.

Mr. ONDA. Right.

Mr. MATTHEWS. How long have you occupied this position?

Mr. ONDA. December or November, I forget which, 1936.

Mr. MATTHEWS. How long have you been a member of the Communist Party?

Mr. ONDA. July 1932.

Mr. MATTHEWS. Where did you join the Communist Party?

Mr. ONDA. Cleveland, Ohio.

Mr. MATTHEWS. What positions have you held in the Communist Party since the time of your joining?

Mr. ONDA. Well, I am county secretary at the present time. I have held no position—that is, no position such as—outside of that one.

Mr. MATTHEWS. Have you ever been a member of any leading committees?

Mr. ONDA. Oh, yes.

Mr. MATTHEWS. Have you ever been a member of any factions in trade-unions?

Mr. ONDA. Oh, no.

Mr. MATTHEWS. Are you a member of a trade-union?

Mr. ONDA. Oh no.

Mr. MATTHEWS. Have you ever been a member of a trade-union?

Mr. FLEISCHER. Don't say "oh."

Mr. ONDA. No.

Mr. MATTHEWS. Have you held any positions of organizing besides the one you have now?

Mr. ONDA. No—yes; I have—yes; I have.

Mr. MATTHEWS. Please state what that was.

Mr. ONDA. I was the State secretary of the Unemployment Councils in 1933—I believe '34—somewhere along there.

Mr. MATTHEWS. Was that an organization under the national leadership of Herbert Benjamin?

Mr. ONDA. No. That is not. That organization was amalgamated with several other unemployment organizations, I believe, at least seven or eight other unemployed organizations, into what later became the Workers' Alliance—at the amalgamation—after the amalgamation it became the Workers' Alliance of America. I forget the year on that.

Mr. MATTHEWS. Well, who was the national leader of the Unemployed Councils?

Mr. ONDA. At that particular time?

Mr. MATTHEWS. Yes.

Mr. ONDA. Well, I was—I was national chairman of one of those years. I forget which one now.

Mr. MATTHEWS. Who was the national executive secretary?

Mr. ONDA. I think—I think—I am not sure—well, that is a matter of public record. You could look that up without any trouble.

Mr. MATTHEWS. Well, you have denied it was Herbert Benjamin. But, as a matter of fact, it was Herbert Benjamin?

Mr. ONDA. I am testifying here; you are not.

Mr. MATTHEWS. Yes; but you denied Herbert Benjamin was the leader of this Unemployed Council.

Mr. ONDA. I did not deny that Herbert Benjamin held a position or didn't hold a position. Now, let me testify. You ask the questions.

Mr. MATTHEWS. I would like to have the record read to the witness where the witness denied it and ask him if he persists in the denial.

The CHAIRMAN. You were asked the question whether or not Herbert Benjamin was leader of the Unemployed Councils. Do you know whether or not he was the leader at any time while you were connected with it?

Mr. ONDA. Of the Unemployed Councils? He was one—he was not the leader. Refer to the record and you will see.

The CHAIRMAN. What position did he hold?

Mr. MATTHEWS Was he national executive secretary?

Mr. ONDA. I could not tell you that. I don't know.

Mr. MATTHEWS. You were national chairman?

Mr. ONDA. One of those years.

Mr. MATTHEWS. Who was the national executive secretary while you were chairman—national executive chairman?

Mr. ONDA. I was under the impression Amter was.

Mr. MATTHEWS. Your recollection is faulty in that respect.

Mr. FLEISCHER. He has already answered the question, Mr. Chairman.

The CHAIRMAN. Just ask the question.

Mr. MATTHEWS. I want to know if the witness is sure that Amter was or was not, or just what it was.

Mr. FLEISCHER. He testified that he was under the impression that he was.

Mr. MATTHEWS. How long were you national chairman?

Mr. ONDA. I think for 1 year or thereabouts.

Mr. MATTHEWS. And what year was that?

Mr. ONDA. I think it was 1934.

Mr. MATTHEWS. Did you participate in any nationally organized demonstrations or marches in that connection?

Mr. ONDA. I did.

Mr. MATTHEWS. Will you please state what they were?

Mr. ONDA. In 1932, when Herbert Hoover was President, when there was no relief for the unemployed, although there were millions of us, I took part in what we called at that time a national hunger march, and I was in charge of the Ohio delegation to that march, where we had to sleep on New York Avenue, I believe it was, for a couple of days in the streets to petition——

The CHAIRMAN. Just answer the question.

Mr. ONDA. Well, I am trying to, the best I can.

The CHAIRMAN. The thing he is asking you is what demonstrations did you take part in. You took part in one. You just described it.

Mr. ONDA. Yes.

The CHAIRMAN. Any others?

Mr. ONDA. Yes; I did.

Mr. MATTHEWS. Nationally organized demonstrations?

Mr. ONDA. I think there was one in nineteen—not a demonstration; no. I wouldn't call it that. It was a convention more.

Mr. MATTHEWS. Do you know Arnold Johnson?

Mr. ONDA. I decline to answer that question. I know him, but I don't think that is the business here for me to say.

The CHAIRMAN. Now listen, it is a matter for the committee to determine on what ground. Do you decline to say whether you know Arnold Johnson?

Mr. ONDA. Well, I know that other names have been mentioned in this committee find it difficult to hold their jobs; and I know that other names mentioned before this committee—and names mentioned before this committee will find it harder to find jobs, Government or private. Now, I didn't want to become a partner to anything of that kind.

The CHAIRMAN. Well, it is very strange to the chairman that you and others belong to organizations that you consider legal, that you claim to be perfectly all right, and yet you decline to give the committee information on the grounds that someone who is connected with the organization may be injured or discriminated against. Now, we are here to get information, and it is vital information. We have tried to accord members of the Communist Party and its officials an opportunity to give us information. Now, we are asking you for important information, and the Chair expects you to answer the questions.

Mr. ONDA. That is right.

Mr. MATTHEWS. Whether or not you know this man?

Mr. ONDA. I want to help this committee.

The CHAIRMAN. All right; then answer the questions.

Mr. ONDA. Now, you made a statement, Mr. Chairman——

The CHAIRMAN. I don't care for any comment. I am asking you to answer the questions.

Mr. ONDA. But you made a comment to me.

The CHAIRMAN. That is all right. I am not asking for comment from you to the Chair.

Mr. FLEISCHER. Mr. Chairman.

The CHAIRMAN. Wait a minute. I am asking you if you will answer the question. Will you or will you not?

Mr. ONDA. Your question was on the reason, and you made comments on the reason, Mr. Chairman. You look at the record.

The CHAIRMAN. You made your statement as to the reason you decline to answer the question.

Mr. ONDA. And you stated that it seemed mighty—didn't seem right that a party called itself a legal party was afraid of having people discriminated. Now, it is a fact that not only Communists are discriminated for political reasons but also Democrats, under certain conditions, and you must be aware of those things.

The CHAIRMAN. That has absolutely nothing to do with this. Do you decline to answer the question?

Mr. ONDA. I do, for the reasons given.

The CHAIRMAN. All right; the Chair instructs you to do so, and you decline to do so?

Mr. ONDA. For the reasons stated.

The CHAIRMAN. You have stated the reasons. Ask the next question.

Mr. MATTHEWS. I understood the witness to say he did know Arnold Johnson.

The CHAIRMAN. He did say so and declined to say who he was.

Mr. MATTHEWS. Was Arnold Johnson one of the active leaders in the unemployed movement in the State of Ohio?

Mr. ONDA. When?

Mr. MATTHEWS. Now.

Mr. ONDA. I couldn't tell you now.

Mr. MATTHEWS. When did you know him in that capacity?

Mr. ONDA. Oh, I knew him for several years in the capacity of leader of unemployed organizations in Ohio.

Mr. MATTHEWS. Do you know him to be a member of the Communist Party?

Mr. ONDA. I decline to answer that.

The CHAIRMAN. The Chair instructs you to answer. Do you still decline to answer?

Mr. ONDA. I do decline.

The CHAIRMAN. Proceed.

Mr. MATTHEWS. Do you know Yetta Land?

Mr. ONDA. I do.

Mr. MATTHEWS. In what connection do you know Yetta Land?

Mr. ONDA. As the State chairman of the Communist Party of Ohio.

Mr. MATTHEWS. Do you know A. Ericson?

Mr. ONDA. Offhand I don't recall ever hearing the name.

Mr. MATTHEWS. Of Youngstown, Ohio.

Mr. ONDA. Don't know him.

Mr. MATTHEWS. Do you know Abe Lewis, of Youngstown, Ohio?

Mr. ONDA. I decline to answer, for the objections already given and for the reasons already given.

The CHAIRMAN. The Chair instructs you to answer the question. You decline to do so?

Mr. ONDA. I would like to make a statement on that. Mr. Chairman. It might help the committee.

Mr. THOMAS. Just a minute, please.

Mr. FLEISCHER. Now, I object to Mr. Thomas browbeating the witness.

The CHAIRMAN. No one is trying to browbeat the witness. The witness refuses to give this committee information that this committee is seeking.

Mr. FLEISCHER. For the reasons already stated in the record.

Mr. THOMAS. Mr. Chairman, it is not clear to me why the witness refuses to answer the questions about some of these people and yet is very frank to answer the questions about the others. That is all that I am trying to find out. Why is that, Mr. Witness?

Mr. ONDA. Well, you see, some of them are a matter of public record. As a matter of fact, Arnold Johnson's connection with unemployed organizations is a matter of public record. Yetta Land's chairmanship of the Communist Party is a matter of public record. Now, these things this committee could get with a 2-cent stamp—all that information.

Mr. THOMAS. Do I understand where it is a matter of public record and where we could get the information in other places you are willing to give that, but where we can't get the information from other places you are not willing to give that?

Mr. ONDA. No; I am not. I won't answer that question "yes" on either of your half of the questions because I don't think that is the purpose of this committee—in me was to get facts——

Mr. THOMAS. And that is what we are trying to do.

Mr. ONDA. About activities——

Mr. THOMAS. We are trying to get the facts, and we would like to have your assistance to give us the facts.

Mr. ONDA. I thought it was about my activities and facts about these activities. Now, this I am ready to give the committee.

Mr. THOMAS. Are you then going to say what the committee should have and what the committee should not have? Don't you think the committee should have some discretion in a matter like that?

Mr. ONDA. What is that? I don't challenge the right of the committee on any of these questions.

The CHAIRMAN. All right; let us proceed, gentlemen. We have other witnesses here.

Mr. MATTHEWS. Mr. Onda, you were subpenaed to appear before this committee and bring with you correspondence relating to your activities in the Communist Party. Did you bring that correspondence?

Mr. ONDA. What correspondence do you want, Mr. Matthews?

Mr. MATTHEWS. All correspondence dealing with your activities in the Communist Party or in your position in the Communist Party.

Mr. ONDA. I haven't got any—haven't kept any; therefore, I couldn't bring them.

Mr. MATTHEWS. Do you have correspondence in your office?

Mr. FLEISCHER. I object to the question. It has already been answered.

The CHAIRMAN. No; it has not been answered. He says he doesn't have now the correspondence, but that certainly doesn't preclude an inquiry whether he ever had any correspondence.

Mr. FLEISCHER. He didn't say that. He said he didn't have any.

The CHAIRMAN. What I want to know is, did you ever have any correspondence?

Mr. ONDA. Well, we get mail occasionally; yes.

The CHAIRMAN. What do you do with it? Destroy it?

Mr. ONDA. As I get through with it I throw it in the waste-paper basket.

The CHAIRMAN. In other words, when you get a letter you read it and then destroy it?

Mr. ONDA. That is right.

The CHAIRMAN. And when you write a letter you make no copy of the letter?

Mr. ONDA. That is right.

The CHAIRMAN. And, in turn, the person to whom you write is supposed to destroy it likewise?

Mr. ONDA. That is right. Most of the time I write the letter in longhand.

The CHAIRMAN. Is that the common practice in the Communist Party, as far as you know?

Mr. ONDA. Well, we are a little party in Cuyahoga County.

The CHAIRMAN. But you have quite a contact with other units of the party, do you not?

Mr. ONDA. I don't know, of units.

The CHAIRMAN. Of other branches of the party.

Mr. ONDA. Yes.

The CHAIRMAN. Other organizations?

Mr. ONDA. Yes..

The CHAIRMAN. Can you say whether or not that is the common practice of the party?

Mr. ONDA. I know it is in Cuyahoga County.

The CHAIRMAN. You don't know anywhere else?

Mr. ONDA. I don't.

Mr. MATTHEWS. How long has that been a practice in Cuyahoga County?

Mr. ONDA. Since I have been in the office.

Mr. MATTHEWS. For 4 years almost?

Mr. ONDA. Yes.

Mr. MATTHEWS. You have never kept any correspondence in that period?

Mr. ONDA. Never held them in the office; no.

Mr. MATTHEWS. Do you keep them anywhere else?

Mr. ONDA. No.

Mr. MATTHEWS. Have you ever kept them anywhere else?

Mr. ONDA. No.

Mr. MATTHEWS. Did you bring any membership lists or membership records with you, as instructed in the subpena which was served on you?

Mr. ONDA. I have no records, no membership records.

Mr. MATTHEWS. Are there any membership records in your district?

Mr. ONDA. Not in my county; there are no membership records.

Mr. MATTHEWS. How do you know who are the members of the Communist Party in Cuyahoga County?

Mr. ONDA. How do I know?

Mr. MATTHEWS. Yes.

Mr. ONDA. Well, it is not my job to know all of the members of the Communist Party.

Mr. MATTHEWS. Do you know any members of the Communist Party in Cuyahoga County?

Mr. ONDA. I do.

Mr. MATTHEWS. How many members of the Communist Party are there in your county?

Mr. ONDA. I would say about 1,800.

Mr. MATTHEWS. Approximately 1,800. How many of the 1,800 do you know?

Mr. ONDA. I wouldn't even want to make a guess. I never made a—I never tried to figure it out—how many I knew personally.

Mr. MATTHEWS. How do you know whether they are members of the Communist Party, or not?

Mr. ONDA. Well, I have no occasion to do any work where they have to prove to me they are members of the Communist Party or not.

Mr. MATTHEWS. Do they present books to you, or do you issue books to them, and thereby know they are members of the Communist Party?

Mr. ONDA. Well, I don't issue books. I sign their—when the cards come through for——

Mr. MATTHEWS. The application card?

Mr. ONDA. Yes, sir; as the county secretary I sign it.

Mr. MATTHEWS. What is done with that card after you sign it?

Mr. ONDA. I turn it over to the State man.

Mr. MATTHEWS. What does he do with it?

Mr. ONDA. I don't know. I know what he is supposed to do with it; but what he does, from my own knowledge, I don't know.

Mr. MATTHEWS. What is he supposed to do with it?

Mr. ONDA. He is supposed to send it on—get a book for it and so on.

Mr. MATTHEWS. Send it on where?

Mr. ONDA. That, I don't know.

Mr. MATTHEWS. To national headquarters?

Mr. ONDA. That, I wouldn't be able to tell you.

Mr. MATTHEWS. You have never heard where it is sent?

Mr. ONDA. I know it is supposed to be recorded. That is, just the number, you see, in our Daily Worker. Every once in a while there is a column tells how many were recruited in such and such a place. For example in this Daily Worker that I have here. That is all they need them for.

Mr. MATTHEWS. Only the numbers of the books are recorded, is that your meaning?

Mr. ONDA. The what?

Mr. MATTHEWS. Only the numbers in the books are recorded?

Mr. ONDA. Not to my knowledge—not in our county.

Mr. MATTHEWS. Did you bring with you the names and addresses of all branch and unit functionaries, as instructed in the subpena?

Mr. ONDA. I do not keep them.

Mr. MATTHEWS. Have you ever seen such a list of names and addresses of branch and unit functionaries?

Mr. ONDA. I have not seen such a list.

Mr. MATTHEWS. Under your jurisdiction?

Mr. ONDA. (No answer.)

Mr. MATTHEWS. Did you bring any financial records?

Mr. ONDA. I have none.

Mr. MATTHEWS. With you?

Mr. ONDA. I have none.

Mr. MATTHEWS. Are there any under your control?

Mr. ONDA. Any records?

Mr. MATTHEWS. Any financial records?

Mr. ONDA. No records.

Mr. MATTHEWS. Or in your custody?

Mr. ONDA. I have no records on it.

Mr. MATTHEWS. Does any one under your jurisdiction have custody of such records?

Mr. ONDA. Under me? As far as my instructions are concerned there are no records kept, so I wouldn't know.

Mr. MATTHEWS. No financial records, you are speaking of?

Mr. ONDA. That is right.

Mr. THOMAS. Mr. Chairman, right at this point—as I understand, you believe that you are part of a political party, isn't that true?

Mr. ONDA. That is right.

Mr. THOMAS. Don't you as a political party have to make any declaration in the State of Ohio as to revenue and expenses?

Mr. ONDA. For all election campaigns we do.

Mr. THOMAS. Then you have those records?

Mr. ONDA. I don't have them on hand. I was never in charge of the election campaigns. You see, I was never in charge of election campaigns.

Mr. THOMAS. But you kept the records of the revenues and expenses in political campaigns?

Mr. ONDA. If I recall correctly those records are with the State secretary of the State of Ohio, if I recall correctly.

Mr. THOMAS. That is all.

The CHAIRMAN. Now, you say you were born in Ohio, is that correct?

Mr. ONDA. No. I said I was born in Pittsburgh, Pa.

The CHAIRMAN. Did you graduate from high school?

Mr. ONDA. Sir?

The CHAIRMAN. Are you a graduate of a high school?

Mr. ONDA. No; I am not.

The CHAIRMAN. What was your education?

Mr. ONDA. What is that?

The CHAIRMAN. What did your education consist of?

Mr. ONDA. Well, I got most of my education right in the mills.

The CHAIRMAN. What mills did you work in?

Mr. ONDA. I worked for the National Tube in Pittsburgh. I worked for J. & L., Pittsburgh.

The CHAIRMAN. Now, after you became a member of the Communist Party in 1932, what work have you done since 1932?

Mr. ONDA. You know that was a tough time.

The CHAIRMAN. I am asking you if there was any work you did between '32 and the present time?

Mr. ONDA. Here and there, odd jobs.

The CHAIRMAN. What jobs were they?

Mr. ONDA. Well, I worked on the Bulkley Building tearing out walls at one time.

The CHAIRMAN. What is your trade?

Mr. ONDA. I am a miner, steel worker. I can do labor work of any kind.

The CHAIRMAN. Do you belong to the Steel Workers' Union?

Mr. ONDA. No; I don't. There wasn't any at that time.

The CHAIRMAN. I believe you stated you don't belong to any union?

Mr. ONDA. That is right.

The CHAIRMAN. So that from 1932 to the present, how much of that time have you worked—done anything?

Mr. ONDA. Well, I worked in '32–'33, quite a bit. I even washed dishes during that period. Anything I could lay my hands on, for that matter, and then I worked on W. P. A. from Thanksgiving Day—just before Thanksgiving Day, I believe it was 1935, now, I wouldn't know for sure, to about 1936.

The CHAIRMAN. What work did you do on W. P. A.?

Mr. ONDA. Oh, just digging a ditch.

The CHAIRMAN. Was that your job, digging a ditch?

Mr. ONDA. Yes: digging a ditch.

The CHAIRMAN. During the time that you worked there, you worked digging a ditch?

Mr. ONDA. Most of the time.

Mr. FLEISCHER. He means digging ditches, I suppose—not digging a ditch.

The CHAIRMAN. I imagine it would be more correct to say "a ditch."

Mr. FLEISCHER. I imagine more correct "ditches."

Mr. ONDA. I don't see the purpose——

The CHAIRMAN. Didn't you say "a ditch"?

Mr. THOMAS. I don't think that is important.

The CHAIRMAN. Of course it isn't.

Mr. THOMAS. What is the witness working at now? What is your present employment?

Mr. ONDA. I am the county secretary of Cuyahoga County.

Mr. THOMAS. You have no employment other than that?

Mr. ONDA. No.

Mr. MATTHEWS. What are your functions as county secretary of Cuyahoga County?

Mr. ONDA. Well, I am the head of the county executive—that is, my job is to prepare the agenda for county executives—prepare—I do some research work for the county executive, as such. My job is to check up on the various section organizers in the county and, to the best of my ability, to keep things going, you know.

Mr. MATTHEWS. How many section organizers are there under your jurisdiction?

Mr. ONDA. There are 6.

Mr. MATTHEWS. Will you please name them?

Mr. ONDA. For the reasons I already stated I will not give their names.

Mr. MATTHEWS. Do you know who they are?

Mr. ONDA. I do, of course.

The CHAIRMAN. Do you decline to answer?

Mr. ONDA. Yes.

The CHAIRMAN. The Chair instructs you to answer and you decline. Proceed.

Mr. MATTHEWS. In your work as county secretary do you make speeches?

Mr. ONDA. Yes.

Mr. MATTHEWS. Do you make speeches for organizations other than the Communist Party?

Mr. ONDA. Whenever I am invited, I do.

Mr MATTHEWS. In what or for what organizations have you made speeches recently?

The CHAIRMAN. The chairman wants to note that Mr. Thomas is present which constitutes a quorum composed of the chairman, Mr. Mason, Mr. Thomas, and Mr. Voorhis. Proceed.

Mr. ONDA. All right.

The CHAIRMAN. Yes.

Mr. FLEISCHER. What was the question?

Mr. MATTHEWS. For what organizations have you made speeches recently?

Mr. ONDA. Well, I spoke on the campus of the Ohio University.

Mr. MATTHEWS. At Columbus?

Mr. ONDA. At Columbus. Gee, I don't think——

Mr. MATTHEWS. Have you spoken before any meetings of the Workers' Alliance?

Mr. ONDA. Not in the last—oh, much more than a year, I think.

Mr. MATTHEWS. Have you spoken for any meetings of the American League for Peace and Democracy, prior to its demise in February?

Mr. ONDA. I don't think I ever spoke for them. I don't recall ever speaking before them.

Mr. MATTHEWS. Was there a chapter or local branch of the American League in Cleveland?

Mr. FLEISCHER. I don't see what this has to do with the questions and scope of his activities, as to whether or not there was a chapter of the American League. I think Mr. Matthews would be more familiar with that than the witness.

The CHAIRMAN. All right.

Mr. FLEISCHER. I object to the question on the ground it is incompetent, irrelevant, and immaterial.

Mr. MATTHEWS. Mr. Chairman, do you want the witness to answer the question?

The CHAIRMAN. If he knows. Do you know if there was a chapter?

Mr. ONDA. I know there was a mass meeting where Mr. Matthews spoke with Bishop Brown where I attended.

The CHAIRMAN. You know about that?

Mr. ONDA. Yes.

The CHAIRMAN. That is the only one you know about?

Mr. ONDA. That is the only one I attended.

Mr. MATTHEWS. Where was that?

Mr. ONDA. It was in the Moose Temple, I believe.

Mr. MATTHEWS. In what city?

Mr. ONDA. Cleveland, Ohio.

Mr. MATTHEWS. On what date?

Mr. ONDA. I don't remember that.

Mr. MATTHEWS. Are you testifying under oath now?

Mr. FLEISCHER. I object to that, Mr. Chairman.

The CHAIRMAN. Let us proceed.

Mr. FLEISCHER. And ask Mr. Matthews be admonished not to ask such type of questions.

Mr. THOMAS. I think, Mr. Chairman, the original question was whether there was a unit of the American League, and so forth.

Mr. FLEISCHER. That wasn't the question.

The CHAIRMAN. Whether there was a chapter in that town.

Mr. MATTHEWS. I would like to be called to the witness stand to refute the witness' testimony.

The CHAIRMAN. Well, I don't think——

Mr. FLEISCHER. And if he is called I would like to cross-examine him.

Mr. MATTHEWS. The witness has falsely stated——

Mr. FLEISCHER. I object to that. Mr. Matthews is testifying and he has not been sworn. If he wants to testify let him take the chair.

The CHAIRMAN. Just a minute.

Mr. FLEISCHER. I ask it be stricken from the record.

The CHAIRMAN. Let us proceed.

Mr. FLEISCHER. I ask it be stricken from the record.

Mr. MATTHEWS. Mr. Onda, is there a "Yanks Are Not Coming Committee"?

Mr. FLEISCHER. I object to that on the same ground.

The CHAIRMAN. Let him finish his question.

Mr. MATTHEWS. The question has been asked.

The CHAIRMAN. Has he asked you the question? Can you answer it?

Mr. ONDA. What is the question?

Mr. MATTHEWS. Is there a "Yanks Are Not Coming Committee"?

Mr. ONDA. Not to my knowledge.

Mr. MATTHEWS. Is there a "Keep America Out of Imperialistic War" in Cleveland?

Mr. ONDA. I have seen some articles in the papers but not to my personal knowledge.

Mr. MATTHEWS. Have you participated in any way in the organization of such a committee?

Mr. ONDA. No.

Mr. MATTHEWS. Did the Communist Party participate in the recent students' demonstration around the slogan "The Yanks Are Not Coming"?

Mr. ONDA. No.

Mr. MATTHEWS. Was there such a demonstration held, to your knowledge, in Cleveland last week?

Mr. ONDA. That I would not know. I was here last week, you see.

Mr. MATTHEWS. I have no more questions to ask the witness, Mr. Chairman.

The CHAIRMAN. Would you support the United States in case of war between the United States and Russia?

Mr. ONDA. Is there such a war?

The CHAIRMAN. Well, in the event there were such a war where would your allegiance lie? With the United States or Russia?

Mr. FLEISCHER. Ask him if there was a war between the North and South what he would do?

Mr. ONDA. If there was a war between the North and South what would you do?

The CHAIRMAN. I am the one that is doing the asking of the questions. I am asking you the question whether or not in the event of war between the United States and Russia whether you would support the United States? Now, do you decline to answer?

Mr. ONDA. I answered that question for you.

The CHAIRMAN. What is the answer?

Mr. ONDA. I said there is no such war.

The CHAIRMAN. Well, if there was such a war?

Mr. ONDA. And as far as the people of America are concerned I am sure the people will not have such a war.

The CHAIRMAN. Would you support the country in such a war?

Mr. ONDA. When that time comes you call me back and I will give you the answer.

Mr. THOMAS. In other words, you are dodging the question?

Mr. ONDA. And I asked the question whether Mr. Dies would support the North in a war against the South.

The CHAIRMAN. Mr. Dies, would support the United States.

Mr. THOMAS. You have dodged the same question the same as any other Communist dodges the question.

Mr. ONDA. What do you mean "dodge"?

Mr. THOMAS. You know what the word means.

Mr. ONDA. You are screwy.

Mr. VOORHIS. Can you conceive of a situation of international conflict in which you would feel called upon to give aid and comfort to an enemy of the United States?

Mr. FLEISCHER. Mr. Chairman, may I object to this type of question on the ground it is highly speculative and hypothetical? This witness is to be examined as to what he knows or specific acts or functions he has done. Any questions to disclose the operation of his mind is outside the scope of the committee. I except to Mr. Voorhis' question.

Mr. THOMAS. I don't think you can get anything from this type of witness.

Mr. FLEISCHER. I object to that remark by Mr. Thomas and ask it be stricken.

The CHAIRMAN. The witness is dismissed.

Come around, Mr. O'Shea.

Mr. FLEISCHER. Mr. Chairman, do you expect to call any other witnesses as far as the Communist Party is concerned for today?

The CHAIRMAN. Well, that is something that will have to be determined. We have a number of other witnesses but I don't presume we will call any of them today.

Mr. FLEISCHER. I would like to know where we stand on this so I will know whether we go ahead today.

The CHAIRMAN. There won't be any Communist witnesses called today.

Mr. FLEISCHER. That is definite?

The CHAIRMAN. That is definite. All right; let us proceed. I mean any witness that you would represent, you or Mr. Cohn would represent.

Mr. FLEISCHER. That is right. Not today?

The CHAIRMAN. That is right.

TESTIMONY OF THOMAS HUMPHREY O'SHEA—Resumed

The CHAIRMAN. Let us proceed, gentlemen.

Mr. MATTHEWS. We have your biographical sketch in the record already.

Before you came to the United States in 1927, Mr. O'Shea, did you participate in any political activities in Ireland?

Mr. O'SHEA. Yes. I was a member of the Irish Republican Army from approximately 1917 to 1924, while activities were in existence. Later then I was still a member of the Irish Republican Army.

Mr. MATTHEWS. Now, when you came to the United States what type of employment did you obtain?

Mr. O'SHEA. I was first employed at the New York Central. Later I was employed with the United States Lines in Hoboken and finally would up in the transit field—Interborough Rapid Transit Co., New York City.

Mr. MATTHEWS. Interborough Rapid Transit Co., of New York City?

Mr. O'SHEA. Yes, sir.

Mr. MATTHEWS. How long were you employed by the Interborough Rapid Transit Co.?

Mr. O'SHEA. Approximately 11 years.

Mr. MATTHEWS. In what capacity?

Mr. O'SHEA. As turnstile mechanic—maintenance man.

Mr. MATTHEWS. Is that your present employment?

Mr. O'SHEA. Well, at the present time I am a W. P. A. worker.

Mr. MATTHEWS. Now, in your work as an employee of the Interborough Rapid Transit Co., in New York City, did you come to know the Transport Workers' Union, which is a labor union in that field?

Mr. O'SHEA. Yes.

Mr. MATTHEWS. Will you please state, to the best of your knowledge, how many members there are in the Transport Workers' Union of New York?

Mr. O'SHEA. Well, the leadership of the Transport Workers' Union states that in New York City there were approximately 50,000. I say there were approximately 35,000.

Mr. MATTHEWS. Is the Transport Workers' Union nationally organized?

Mr. O'Shea. It is an international union.

Mr. MATTHEWS. An international union?

Mr. O'SHEA. Yes.

Mr. MATTHEWS. Is the largest local situated in New York City?

Mr. O'SHEA. Yes; it is. Largest local is New York.

Mr. MATTHEWS. Where else does the Transport Workers' Union have any appreciable organization?

Mr. O'SHEA. They have got a closed-shop contract in Juneau, Alaska.

Mr. MATTHEWS. Closed-shop contract?

Mr. O'SHEA. Yes. And have organizations in other cities but no contracts, with the exception, I think, of Kentucky, and a few small places.

Mr. MATTHEWS. Does the Transport Workers' Union have a closed-shop contract in New York?

Mr. O'SHEA. Yes. Practically everything on wheels in New York City with the exception of a few small bus lines that the Amalgamated Association has. That is the A. F. of L.

Mr. MATTHEWS. Do you know what the international membership of the union is?

Mr. O'SHEA. Well, according to the official figures and statements from time to time it is approximately 90,000 men.

Mr. MATTHEWS. About 90,000?

Mr. O'SHEA. About 90,000; yes.

Mr. MATTHEWS. Now, Mr. O'Shea, do you know Charles McGinnity?

Mr. O'SHEA. Yes; I know Charles McGinnity.

Mr. MATTHEWS. Will you please state when and how and under what circumstances you became acquainted with Charles McGinnity?

Mr. O'SHEA. My first contact with Charles McGinnity was during the activities for the Irish movement. I happened to meet him in Liverpool. He was working for the Irish Republican Army and I was on the same job. Later I met him in the city of New York when he was a member of the Irish Workers' Club.

Mr. MATTHEWS. Where were the headquarters of the Irish Workers' Club?

Mr. O'SHEA. Well, the Irish Workers' Club at that time had several branches. One branch was located where I live, in my locality, at St. Ann's Avenue in the Bronx. I happened to meet him at that particular time more or less by accident. I hadn't seen him for a number of years previously. Simply asked him what he was doing.

Mr. MATTHEWS. And what conversation did you have with Mr. McGinnity at that time?

Mr. O'SHEA. He then mentioned to me about those Irish Workers' Clubs, which I didn't know up to that time about, so I asked him what the purpose of the organization was, and many other questions. So he simply stated it was for the purpose of organizing the Irish in the United States and making them class conscious.

Mr. MATTHEWS. Making them "class conscious"?

Mr. O'SHEA. Yes.

Mr. MATTHEWS. Did he explain that any further?

Mr. O'SHEA. No, no; he did not.

Mr. MATTHEWS. Did he discuss with you the question of any trade-union organization?

Mr. O'SHEA. Well, as it so happened, it came—I drew his attention to the fact that I had already discussed in the transit field the possibility of organizing those workers, which for a number of years, or, as a matter of fact, for 20 years, had not been organized and I had contact with a number of men and I thought something might be done to the organization.

Then he stated to me, "Why, there is an organization already in the field."

Mr. MATTHEWS. Did he tell you what that was?

Mr. O'SHEA. No; he didn't explain it to me at all. But he just simply told me that there was an organizational group in the field and——

Mr. MATTHEWS. Did he suggest that you get in touch with that group?

Mr. O'SHEA. Yes. He suggested I should contact those people. So I arranged that this group should come to my home, which they did.

Mr. MATTHEWS. How many were in that group?

Mr. O'SHEA. There were—I don't know whether it was three or four. I know there were three.

Mr. MATTHEWS. Do you remember the names of the persons?

Mr. O'SHEA. Yes, sir.

Mr. MATTHEWS. Who came to your home?

Mr. O'SHEA. Yes, sir. The leader of the group was a man by the name of Peter Starr.

Mr. MATTHEWS. S-t-a-r-r?

Mr. O'SHEA. Yes. Another chap by the name of Adams and another chap by the name of Carr.

Mr. MATTHEWS. Do you know their first names?

Mr. O'SHEA. No. Peter Starr is the only one I knew by their first name.

Mr. MATTHEWS. What did you discuss with the group when they first met at your home?

Mr. O'SHEA. I asked the method of organization and what they intended to do and they had a more or less of a blueprint of the organizational set-up as they planned. They stated, of course, what they intended to set up—small groups of men, not more than 20, with an executive.

The purpose was, as they stated to me at the time, was to protect the men on the job so that in case that anything might go wrong with one group the other group would still function.

Mr. MATTHEWS. Now, what did you do after you had that first meeting with respect to organization?

Mr. O'SHEA. Then they asked me if I could contact anybody in a given territory of the Interborough Rapid Transit Co.—that was the uptown district for the county of Bronx—in the shops, barns, or terminals. So I said, "yes," I had contacts there in one of the principal shops, One Hundred and Seventy-ninth Street—inspection barn of the elevated division.

I arranged there to bring a group of men workers, approximately five or six, to a meeting to meet this organizational group, which was arranged some week or two later and held at One Hundred and Thirty-eighth Street in the Bronx around Cypress—between Cypress and Brook Avenue in an apartment.

Mr. MATTHEWS. Did you know at the time you were dealing with these men, Starr and Carr and Adams and McGinnity, whether or not they were members of the Communist Party?

Mr. O'SHEA. No, I didn't know at that time, but I learned later, of course, they were.

Mr. MATTHEWS. You learned later they were?

Mr. O'SHEA. Yes, sir.

Mr. MATTHEWS. Will you please state briefly the circumstances as they developed which lead you to the discovery that they were members of the Communist Party?

Mr. O'SHEA. After our first meeting, as I stated, between the employees of the Interborough Co. and the concentration group, the meetings flopped. It was due in a great measure to the question of nationality which had arisen between the two groups—the concentration group, which consisted mainly of Jewish fellows, and the union group, which consisted mainly of Irish. As you know, the Irish are extremely nationalistic and I was in a hotbed between the two forces to try and make them weld. The result was that our meetings were a flop, a failure; so I naturally warned Starr, who was the head of the concentration group, that if he continued the practice our organization would go up in smoke.

Mr. MATTHEWS. Before you go on will you explain what a "concentration group" or "unit" is?

Mr. O'SHEA. Well, for the information of the committee I would like to——

The CHAIRMAN. What is that? I did not get that.

Mr. O'SHEA. For the information of the committee I would like to explain what this "concentration group" is.

The CHAIRMAN. Don't talk too fast and talk as distinctly as possible so we can hear you.

Mr. O'SHEA. All right. In 1934 the Communist Party apparently had failed to make any headway in the trade-union movement of the United States and an extraordinary conference was called by the Communist Party of members from the United States and Canada, which was held in the Finnish Hall in New York City, and a definite program of action was adopted at this special conference.

It was arranged that what was known as an "Open Letter" should be prepared and sent to all secretaries of the Communist Party.

Mr. MATTHEWS. At this point, Mr. O'Shea, may I ask you to identify this document? Is this a copy of the Open Letter to which you refer?

(Handing document to the witness.)

Mr. O'SHEA. This is a copy of the Open Letter, gentlemen.

Mr. MATTHEWS. This is a supplement to the Daily Worker of July 13, 1933, entitled "An Open Letter to All Party Members." I ask that this be marked in evidence as "O'Shea Exhibit No. 1."

The CHAIRMAN. It will be so marked.

(The supplement to the Daily Worker, dated July 13, 1933, was marked "O'Shea Exhibit No. 1.")

Mr. MATTHEWS. Now, will you proceed with the explanation of this Open Letter?

Mr. O'SHEA. Well, this Open Letter was divided into various parts:

(a) The organization of a firm basis for our Party and the revolutionary trade-union movement among the decisive strata of the American workers in the most important industrial centers;

(b) The consolidation and strengthening of the revolutionary trade-unions, especially revolutionary unions of the miners, steel and metal, textile and marine workers, and systematic work in the reformist trade unions, above all among the reformist unions of miners and railroad workers, with a view to organizing a broad revolutionary trade-union opposition;

(c) The organization and mobilization of the millions of unemployed, together with the factory workers, for their most urgent needs and the organization of the struggle for unemployment insurance as the central immediate struggle of the party;

(d) The transformation of the Daily Worker into a really revolutionary mass paper, into an agitator and organizer of our work;

(e) The wide development of a new cadres of workers; the establishment of really collectively-working leading bodies of our movement; and the improvement of the work of these leading bodies by the drawing in of new capable working class elements.

In order to carry out these tasks, we worked out a concentration plan and pledged ourselves to transfer the center of our work to a number of selected most important large factories, subdistricts and districts. The entire work of the party and the best forces of the party were to be directed first of all to building up and consolidating the party and revolutionary trade-union movement in the most important industrial centers of the country, to effectively and systematically win the decisive sections of American workers, free them from the influence of the reformist and bourgeois parties, mobilize for the struggle against the bourgeoisie, and get our influence solidly established in these centers. We must do everything in our power to expose before the toiling masses of the entire country the utter bankruptcy and vacillating petty bourgeoisie, hence its inability to lead a consistent struggle against monopoly capitalism, it is our task to show to the petty bourgeoisie and nonproletarian masses of the country that they can hope for nothing under finance capitalism.

That is the complete contents of the Open Letter as was passed at this special conference which was to be acted upon by all those various sections.

The CHAIRMAN. That letter was to embrace the program that you all agreed to put into effect?

Mr. O'SHEA. That the Communist Party as a whole were to put into effect in all the major industries in the country.

The CHAIRMAN. That was what year?

Mr. O'SHEA. 1933.

Mr. MATTHEWS. Open Letter dated July 13, 1933?

Mr. O'SHEA. Yes.

Mr. MATTHEWS. Now, included in those major industries or fields of organization, was there the transit field?

Mr. O'SHEA. Yes. The transit field was one of the principal industries where the party had concentrated. As I have stated, I met a group of this concentration force which had already been established in the transit field to carry out the instructions of the Open Letter.

Mr. THOMAS. Mr. Matthews, what does the transit field include?

Mr. MATTHEWS. Will you answer that?

Mr. O'SHEA. The transit field includes all taxies, busses, all passenger vehicles on the streets, subways in the city of New York.

Mr. MATTHEWS. Now, Mr. O'Shea, I show you a photostatic copy of a portion of the Party Organizer for August–September 1933, the Party Organizer issued by the central committee of the Communist Party of the United States. Will you please state briefly what the Party Organizer was?

Mr. O'SHEA. Well, the Party Organizer was an official pamphlet issued particularly for the guidance of Communist organizers on mass work in the trade-union field or any other field, whatever the case may arise.

Mr. MATTHEWS. I wish to introduce that in evidence.

The CHAIRMAN. It is so ordered.

(The Party Organizer referred to by Mr. Matthews was received in evidence and made a part of the record.)

Mr. MATTHEWS. Now, on pages 24 and 25 of this particular issue of the Party Organizer, I wish to read you the following:

"Concentrate on Transportation." Next concentrate for New York: Railroad. On this we have done practically nothing, although the issues are there for us to mobilize the railroad workers.

Another point I think we should consider for concentration is city transport. Transport in all big cities plays a very important political role. I think it is a field that we must concentrate on. We have nothing there yet. In addition to concentrating on transport we can use the election campaign that we are now entering to put forward the proper issues, connecting the question of low fare, as it affects the workers generally, with the conditions of the transport workers.

Now I want to state that on the question of concentration the district leadership set the pace. Each and every one of us on the staff must give his major attention to a point of concentration. I don't mean the whole industry; I mean picking out certain points of concentration within the industries. We must set the pace.

Now, this article is by Charles Krumbein. Who was Charles Krumbein?

Mr. O'SHEA. Charles Krumbein, when I first met him, was secretary of the Communist Party of the State of New York and a member of the Communist national group.

Mr. MATTHEWS. Do you know what position Charles Krumbein occupies at the present time?

Mr. O'SHEA. At the present time I don't know. I haven't been interested.

Mr. MATTHEWS. I show you a copy of the Party Organizer or a portion of it, for March 1935. Have you ever seen that copy of the Party Organizer?

(Handing exhibit to the witness.)

Mr. O'SHEA. Yes, sir, I have seen this. Yes, I have seen this article.

Mr. MATTHEWS. On page 23 of this particular issue of Party Organizer there begins an article entitled: "Harlem Concentration on Transport, by Louis Sass, Harlem." I ask this be marked in evidence as O'Shea Exhibit No. 3.

(The document referred to by Mr. Matthews was marked "O'Shea Exhibit No. 3," and received in evidence.)

Will you please state briefly the gist of this article as you are familiar with it, Mr. O'Shea?

Mr. O'SHEA. This article, gentlemen, is dealing with the particular organizational job in one of the major shops of the transport industry in New York City, the Interborough Rapid Transit Co. The article is written by Louis Sass, who at that time, who when I first met him was section organizer of section 4 of district 2 in New York City, which was the Harlem section. This major shop of the Interborough Rapid Transit Co. is situated in the center of Harlem and has approximately 1,200 employees.

It was in this particular shop that this letter was specially written for, for concentration work and the building of the party and the building of the transport union.

Mr. MATTHEWS. I show you a photostatic copy of the portion of the Party Organizer for December 1933, Mr. O'Shea. Can you identify that?

(Handing exhibit to the witness.)

Mr. O'SHEA. Yes; I can identify this.

Mr. MATTHEWS. As a document with which you are familiar?

Mr. O'SHEA. Yes.

Mr. MATTHEWS. On page 21 of this issue of the Party Organizer there is an article entitled, "Communists Must Build Party During Strikes."

Was it your experience that the Communist Party utilized a strike for political as well as economic purposes?

Mr. O'SHEA. In my estimation it was purely for political purposes.

Mr. MATTHEWS. Now, on page 18 of this Party Organizer, there appears the following statement with reference to city transport:

City transport—last week's report shows that we have a group of about 40 workers in this industry, which is a step forward, although very little—four groups with some units concentrating on some of these shops. They do not know the best methods of work. We must teach them that.

Now, does this exhibit 4 represent this early stage of organization?

Mr. O'SHEA. Exactly.

Mr. MATTHEWS. Which you have begun to tell us about?

Mr. O'SHEA. Exactly.

Mr. MATTHEWS. Now, after these men met at your home on the first occasion and you found that the meetings were not successful because certain racial and nationalistic questions entered, what did you do?

Mr. O'SHEA. I, as I stated, of course, discussed this question with Starr, who was the leader of this concentration group, and warned him that it was dangerous if he continued that practice. He stated that he had no power to make any changes but would recommend to his superior, Mr. John Santo, and try and have this question rectified.

Mr. MATTHEWS. Now, who was John Santo?

Mr. O'SHEA. John Santo at this time was to my knowledge section organizer of section 15.

Mr. MATTHEWS. Of what?

Mr. O'SHEA. Of district 2 of the Communist Party in New York City.

Mr. MATTHEWS. And you had already learned now that Peter Starr was a member of the Communist Party?

Mr. O'SHEA. Well. I had no proof, but I suspected it and——

Mr. MATTHEWS. When he told you that he had to discuss the matter with his superior, was that information——

Mr. O'SHEA. Well, indirectly it was certain information.

Mr. MATTHEWS. Well, did he tell you who his superior was at that time?

Mr. O'SHEA. Yes. As a matter of fact he made an appointment with me to see the section organizer and discuss the whole question of organization.

Mr. MATTHEWS. You then met John Santo?

Mr. O'SHEA. I then met John Santo.

Mr. MATTHEWS. And what did you decide as a result of your conversation with John Santo?

Mr. O'SHEA. I drew his attention to the fact that I had met this McGinnity previously, who was a member of the Irish Workers' Club, and that in my estimation I felt it would be good policy if they had selected one or two of those Irish Workers, who were pretty well trained in the trade union field, and to give him some assistance in handling this Irish group, which consisted mainly in the transit field of New York City of 80 percent Irish, and you needed naturally an Irishman to handle an Irishman; so he arranged at that time that we would have a meeting and discuss this whole question.

Some few weeks later we did hold a meeting somewhere around Astor Place in New York, and I met Santo and he introduced me to a man at the time named Hogan.

Mr. MATTHEWS. Hogan?

Mr. O'SHEA. Hogan. He introduced me to a man by the name of Hogan.

Mr. MATTHEWS. What was Hogan's first name?

Mr. O'SHEA. Austin Hogan.

Mr. MATTHEWS. Did you have many of these meetings and how many attended?

Mr. O'SHEA. There were only four or five members attended. That is four or five from the industry plus Hogan and the other groups, Starr and a few of the other fellows.

Mr. MATTHEWS. Was Carr there?

Mr. O'SHEA. No, he wasn't there at the time.

Mr. MATTHEWS. Adams?

Mr. O'SHEA. No.

Mr. MATTHEWS. Santo?

Mr. O'SHEA. Santo, yes.

Mr. MATTHEWS. Well, then, did you have larger meetings later on?

Mr. O'SHEA. Oh, yes; we did.

Mr. MATTHEWS. Will you please describe them and what took place at these larger meetings in the earlier formative stages?

Mr. O'SHEA. Why, just before we pass from that there was one point there that it so happened when he introduced me to that chap, Hogan—I knew Hogan previously. Well, I would say 5 or 6 years before as Dilloughery and not as Hogan.

Mr. MATTHEWS. Will you please spell the name?

Mr. O'SHEA. D-i-l-l-o-u-g-h-e-r-y.

Mr. MATTHEWS. You had known him as Austin Dilloughery?

Mr. O'SHEA. Dilloughery.

Mr. MATTHEWS. And now introduced to you as Hogan?

Mr. O'SHEA. Yes.

Mr. MATTHEWS. Did you learn at the time why he was now using the name "Hogan"?

Mr. O'SHEA. Well, from the information I received he held a job in the P. W. A. at the time as an engineer in Bronx County and was speaking at Columbus Circle for the Irish Workers' Club and doing certain work which he felt would have put him on the spot or exposed him for the left-wing line.

Mr. MATTHEWS. Well, I wish to ask you some more about this change of names from Dilloughery to Hogan, but before we get to that, will you please state what the results of your first meetings were where you had the larger group present?

Mr. O'SHEA. Well, we continued from that particular meeting where I met Hogan, and he, of course, didn't know anything about the industry. He was absolutely ignorant of the whole situation. He never worked in the field, and it was no easy problem because this industry had approximately, as I say, 35,000 members, all in different departments, and he didn't know where to start.

Mr. MATTHEWS. That was Hogan?

Mr. O'SHEA. Yes, sir. So I had to lay out a campaign that covered the various departments, power, motor equipment, transportation, where the shops were, the times the men would be employed, the times of lunch hour, so that the schedule of meetings could be held and arrangements could be made for recruiting purposes.

Mr. MATTHEWS. Was Santo a worker in the transit industry?

Mr. O'SHEA. No. Santo was never a worker in the transit industry, and at that time, as I stated, to my knowledge was section organizer of Section 15. He had previously been in Cleveland editing a Hungarian paper, a language paper, as they call it, and I believe worked as a hairdresser—barber in his early time.

Mr. MATTHEWS. Do you know whether Santo has any position in the Transport Workers' Union?

Mr. O'SHEA. Yes. Santo now is holding the position of general secretary-treasurer of the Transport Workers' Union International.

Mr. HOGAN. I show you a photostatic copy of the Daily Worker for May 1, 1934, and an article entitled, "B. M. T. & I. R. T. Subway Workers Organize New Union to Fight Against the 1932 Slash in Wages," by John Santo. Are you acquainted with this article?

(Handing document to the witness.)

Mr. O'SHEA. Yes; that is right.

Mr. MATTHEWS. I offer this in evidence as O'Shea Exhibit No. 5.

The CHAIRMAN. That was an article by Santo in the Daily Worker?

Mr. MATTHEWS. That is correct.

The CHAIRMAN. It will be received.

(The document referred to by Mr. Matthews was marked "O'Shea Exhibit No. 5," and received in evidence.)

Mr. MATTHEWS. You say Santo was a barber?

Mr. O'SHEA. Barber; yes.

Mr. MATTHEWS. And he is now secretary, general secretary-treasurer of the Transport Workers' Union International?

Mr. O'SHEA. Yes.

The CHAIRMAN. There is a particular portion of this article that I should like to have incorporated in the record without reading it, the marked portion.

(The portion of the document referred to by Mr. Matthews is as follows:)

The Amalgamated Association of Street and Electric Railway Employees bureaucracy has very well earned the hatred and contempt of the transport workers of New York. They betrayed and sold out the strikes of 1920 and 1926 and laid the basis thereby for the establishment of company unions. Just recently they added to their black record of betrayal that of the bus drivers of the Fifth Avenue Coach Co. as well as the Bee Lines of Jamaica, Long Island. At both instances the National Recovery Act Labor Board was the solution offered by Mr. O'Shea, leader of the Amalgamated. No militant tactics, no mass picketing, no spreading of the organization and of struggle, but negotiations with Mrs. Herrick and trips to Washington. The results? About two dozen best union men of the Fifth Avenue Coach Co. fired, and in Jamaica, the strike of the Bee Lines is dying off by inches.

The road toward better wages and shorter hours in the transit industry lies over the dead body of the company unions as well as that of the Amalgamated Association through the building up of a new rank and file transport workers' union.

What was the date on which you first met Mr. Santo?

Mr. O'SHEA. Well, it was approximately the spring of 1934. I would not know the month. You know, it is so far back.

Mr. MATTHEWS. And you assured him, did you not, as I understand your testimony, that you considered it a dangerous practice to proceed as they had been proceeding in the work of organizing the Transport Workers' Union?

Mr. O'SHEA. Naturally, it would have been disastrous—wouldn't have made any headway.

Mr. MATTHEWS. Now, this first meeting which you had with Santo and others, was Arthur Anderson present?

Mr. O'SHEA. Yes; Arthur Anderson was present at those meetings.

Mr. MATTHEWS. Was James McGovern there?

Mr. O'SHEA. James McGovern was also present.

The CHAIRMAN. I wonder if it would interrupt the course of your examination if I asked the witness if he knows what was the purpose of placing men in these unions, in the transport union? What was the real purpose of the Communist Party in wanting to place men in strategic positions throughout the union?

Mr. O'SHEA. Naturally, to get control of the industry.

The CHAIRMAN. What did they want to do with the industry after they got control?

Mr. O'SHEA. Well, anybody knowing the Communist program— they are a revolutionary party, and as a revolutionary party they certainly were going to use the industry at a psychological moment for a revolution.

The CHAIRMAN. What use could they make of them?

Mr. O'SHEA. Well, anybody who had read the history of Russia and the revolution in 1917 should know that the strikes—that a strike situation usually preceded the final revolutionary set-up. In other words, the workers were pulled on the streets and everything was chaos. Military forces moved in and they simply combined and turned it into a complete revolutionary situation.

The CHAIRMAN. Does that interrupt you?

Mr. MATTHEWS. No; that is all right.

The CHAIRMAN. Did they discuss that phase of it in any of these meetings, the ability to cause a strike and tie up the entire transport system of New York?

Mr. O'SHEA. Well, of course, the Communists at all times do not come out to ordinary workers and say "revolution," but indirectly it is the duty of every Communist to advocate revolution in this way: When a Communist knows it all, he is sent out to recruit and he must always emphasize the fact that workers must depend purely on their economic strength. In other words, they can get nothing except through strike situations. In other words, that is carrying a revolutionary line.

The CHAIRMAN. And you understand that their purpose in formulating these plans and in seeking to infiltrate these organizations and get strategic positions was to be in a position at the psychological moment to tie up the entire transport industry in New York.

Mr. O'SHEA. Absolutely.

The CHAIRMAN. What effect would that have if they were able to do that?

Mr. O'SHEA. Well, it would naturally paralyze all trade and commerce. Every other industry would automatically be closed down. It would create a general strike situation.

The CHAIRMAN. Did they emphasize the necessity of going into key industries?

Mr. O'SHEA. Yes, sir. But the way they presented it to the workers, the non-Communists, was they would succeed much better by a general strike situation where the bosses would have to bend backward and give them their conditions.

The CHAIRMAN. That was the explanation to the workers?

Mr. O'SHEA. That was the explanation to the ordinary rank and file.

The CHAIRMAN. But the real explanation on the inside was the ability——

Mr. O'SHEA. To create a revolutionary situation.

The CHAIRMAN. Was to promote revolution?

Mr. O'SHEA. Yes, sir; that is right.

The CHAIRMAN. Or do whatever the Party might require at a particular moment?

Mr. O'SHEA. Exactly.

The CHAIRMAN. Well, I want to ask this: From your knowledge and experience and your activities in this Transport Workers' Union, are you in a position to say that the Communists can now paralyze the transport unions in New York if they so desire?

Mr. O'SHEA. Absolutely; yes; with the closed shops. They have got a closed shop today, practically, with all the major groups, even with the city of New York. They have it arranged when unification takes place, their contract will still be in existence; and even though the city controls, they can always find time to create a general strike situation.

The CHAIRMAN. So you think they now have the power to do it in New York?

Mr. O'SHEA. They have the absolute power at the present time.

The CHAIRMAN. If they see fit to exercise that power?

Mr. O'SHEA. They could use that power.

The CHAIRMAN. The Communists within the union?

Mr. O'SHEA. The Communist leadership with its control in all the different sections of the union is so powerful that they could stampede the men into a strike, and have it up, before the membership would know what is is all about.

Mr. THOMAS. Mr. O'Shea, isn't this the same Transport Union that threatened to strike in New York just a few weeks ago?

Mr. O'SHEA. Yes, sir; that is the same union.

Mr. THOMAS. And John L. Lewis came up to New York and had a meeting with Mike Quill and LaGuardia?

Mr. O'SHEA. Yes, sir.

Mr. THOMAS. The strike was called off because of an agreement entered into between John L. Lewis, Mike Quill, and LaGuardia?

Mr. O'SHEA. That is right.

Mr. MATTHEWS. Now, Mr. O'Shea, you spoke of the revolutionary objective of the Communists in their trade-union organization. Have you ever noticed any revolutionary activities or plans which seem to point to a revolutionary activity in the publications of the Transport Workers' Union?

Mr. O'SHEA. Yes, sir; as a matter of record they have established gun clubs.

Mr. MATTHEWS. You mean the Transport Union has gun clubs?

Mr. O'SHEA. Actual gun clubs formed in sections by motormen's groups, shop groups, and various groups. They meet on ranges on different days of the week regularly for target practice.

Mr. O'SHEA. Do they call these "rifle ranges"?

Mr. O'SHEA. Yes, sir.

Mr. MATTHEWS. Do they have real ammunition?

Mr. O'SHEA. Undoubtedly. You don't fire blanks on a rifle range.

Mr. MATTHEWS. I show you a copy of the Transport Bulletin. Will you identify that [handing paper to the witness]?

Mr. O'SHEA. Yes, sir. That is the official organ of the Transport Workers' Union.

Mr. MATTHEWS. This is dated December 1939. On page 15 there appears the following. Before reading this, I ask it be placed in evidence.

The CHAIRMAN. It is so ordered.

(The bulletin referred to by Mr. Matthews was marked "O'Shea Exhibit No. 6", and made a part of the record.)

Mr. MATTHEWS. On page 15 there appears the following:

Rifle ranges. Every member welcome. Rifles supplied. 148th Street Shop, Mondays, 7:15 to 10 p. m., Ranges. Surface Track, Tuesdays, 7:15 to 10 p. m., Ranges. Flatbush, Thursdays, 7:15 to 10 p. m., Ranges.

The rifles are supplied at the ranges according to this chart. Then there appears a note at the bottom:

Purchase your recreation card in the Transport Workers' Union offices. No additional charge for anything except cartridges for rifles.

Mr. THOMAS. Mr. O'Shea, what is the purpose of teaching these transport union men how to shoot?

Mr. O'SHEA. Well, I think it ought to be a foregone conclusion. A revolutionary party controlling a mass movement would certainly train—don't train men for target practice for the pleasure of it.

Mr. THOMAS. So in your mind they had guns for the same reasons that these 17——

Mr. O'SHEA. Absolutely.

Mr. THOMAS. Christian Front people had guns?

Mr. O'SHEA. Absolutely.

The CHAIRMAN. Let us go back. I believe we interrupted the chain of events from his last meeting showing his connection with it, and who he knew it, in and how he knows these facts to be true.

Mr. MATTHEWS. That is correct. Now, I wish to ask you, Mr. O'Shea, if you made an investigation of the change of name from Dilloughery to Hogan by Austin Hogan?

Mr. O'SHEA. Yes, sir; I did.

Mr. MATTHEWS. Did you find in the record of the Bronx County clerk's office that Austin Dilloughery had legally changed his name to Austin Hogan?

Mr. O'SHEA. Yes, sir.

Mr. MATTHEWS. Do you recall the approximate date of the order directing——

Mr. O'SHEA. Well, I would have to look it up again.

Mr. MATTHEWS. It was around April 1935, was it?

Mr. O'SHEA. April 1935.

Mr. MATTHEWS. And do you recall that the name to be assumed, Austin Hogan, was authorized on May 18, 1935?

Mr. O'SHEA. That is right.

Mr. MATTHEWS. After the publication of the order?

Mr. O'SHEA. That is right.

Mr. MATTHEWS. Was that order published in the Bronx Home News?

Mr. O'SHEA. Yes, sir; published in the Bronx Home News.

Mr. MATTHEWS. Published in the Bronx Home News?

Mr. O'SHEA. Yes, sir.

Mr. MATTHEWS. Did you ever see a copy of an affidavit made by Austin Hogan, stating that he was born on May 26, 1906, in Ennistymon County, Ireland?

Mr. O'SHEA. Yes, sir.

Mr. MATTHEWS. And did these records reveal that he was naturalized on August 6, 1931?

Mr. O'SHEA. Yes.

Mr. MATTHEWS. Do you know who the attorney was who handled these matters for Mr. Hogan in the change of his name?

Mr. O'SHEA. Mr. Harry Sacher.

Mr. MATTHEWS. Who is Mr. Harry Sacher?

Mr. O'SHEA. Mr. Harry Sacher is now general counsel for the Transport Workers' Union, C. I. O. He is also counsel, I understand, for the Musicians Local 802, A. F. of L., and district 9 of the Painters Union, all located in New York City—headquarters in New York City.

Mr. MATTHEWS. You have named the locals of three unions?

Mr. O'SHEA. Three unions; yes, sir.

Mr. MATTHEWS. Do you know of your own knowledge whether or not communists are powerful or entrenched in the leadership of these three locals that you have mentioned?

Mr. O'SHEA. Oh, absolutely, sure.

Mr. MATTHEWS. Is that a matter of general knowledge amongst trade unions in New York City?

Mr. O'SHEA. Among the left-wing groups it is general knowledge, but not among the membership as a whole.

Mr. MATTHEWS. I show you a photostat for June 1, 1934, issue of the Daily Worker, which has an article entitled: "Irish-American Workers Should Be Champions of Negro Liberation, says Murray at Farewell." Are you familiar with this article, Mr. O'Shea?

Mr. O'SHEA. Yes; I am familiar.

Mr. MATTHEWS. I wish to offer this in evidence.

The CHAIRMAN. It will be received.

(The photostat referred to by Mr. Matthews was marked "O'Shea Exhibit No. 7," and made a part of the record.)

Mr. MATTHEWS. Now, will you please state the significance of the Communist Party's approach to this Irish question?

Mr. O'SHEA. As you will note from the Daily Worker, this particular meeting was held as a farewell reception to the secretary of the Irish-Communist Party, who had come to the United States.

Mr. MATTHEWS. What was his name?

Mr. O'SHEA. Sean Murray. And his purpose was, of course, to stimulate amongst the Irish groups in the United States, and more or less encourage them to line up with the Communist Party in this country, and this farewell reception was given to him at the Irving Plaza.

In this, of course, you will note that Austin Hogan, who is the gentleman we have reference to, was present, and I quote:

Austin Hogan, active in the Irish Workers' Clubs of this city spoke and sang old traditional songs of Ireland.

Mr. MATTHEWS. Was Earl Browder one of the speakers on this occasion?

Mr. O'SHEA. Yes. Earl Browder was present at that meeting.

Mr. MATTHEWS. Was Hogan employed on a C. W. A. project?

Mr. O'SHEA. Yes. He was engineer at the time for Bronx County Gas & Electric on the project.

Mr. MATTHEWS. Is it according to your own personal knowledge and common practice for Communists to use aliases?

Mr. O'SHEA. Naturally.

Mr. MATTHEWS. Or to change their names?

Mr. O'SHEA. Yes, sir.

Mr. MATTHEWS. To conceal their identity for various purposes?

Mr. O'SHEA. Various purposes, yes.

The CHAIRMAN. Mr. Matthews, suppose we go back and have his further connection. All we have now is the early meetings with the concentration group. I thought it might be well to show first what his connections were with the Transport Union.

Mr. MATTHEWS. We are now in the period where they are just getting ready to organize the Transport Workers' Union and we will come immediately to Mr. O'Shea's official connection with the union.

The CHAIRMAN. All right.

Mr. MATTHEWS. Where did you first meet Michael Quill?

Mr. O'SHEA. I met him some weeks after we had the first small group meetings, as I stated, when we met Hogan.

Mr. MATTHEWS. Did you sign Michael Quill up?

Mr. O'SHEA. Yes.

Mr. MATTHEWS. For the new Transport Workers' Union?

Mr. O'SHEA. Yes, sir.

Mr. MATTHEWS. Did you make any arrangements for any meetings?

Mr. O'SHEA. Yes; I called a special meeting of Quill and all fellows who were really active, which was to be held at Fisher's Restaurant, Forty-second Street and Fourth Avenue in New York City. Quill attended that meeting, which was the first meeting, and approximately 15 other workers from the industry also attended.

Mr. MATTHEWS. Were Hogan and Santo there?

Mr. O'SHEA. I had arranged previously to bring them to this meeting but they failed to show up.

Mr. MATTHEWS. Now, did you do any business at that meeting where Quill attended for the first time?

Mr. O'SHEA. Yes; I described the organizational method and structure and supplied each man with application cards and instructed them, as Santo had previously instructed me, to form groups; that each individual going out was to take a number of cards, 10, 15, or 20, form a group and keep the group by itself and establish a secretary and chairman.

Mr. MATTHEWS. Did Quill form a group?

Mr. O'SHEA. Yes, sir; he formed a group on the west side. Seventh Avenue, of Interborough Rapid Transit Subway Division.

Mr. MATTHEWS. Now, subsequent to meetings of these groups were Santo and Hogan in attendance?

Mr. O'Shea. Yes, sir. Practically all the meetings they attended.

Mr. Matthews. After you had several groups formed, did you choose a delegates' council or set up a delegates' council?

Mr. O'Shea. Yes. That was the structure at the time. It was to form groups of sections and from those sections an executive would be formed known as the delegates' council, with a representative consisting of the secretary and chairman of each section.

Mr. Matthews. Where did those first delegates' council meet?

Mr. O'Shea. Well, we. met down on the East Side of New York City.

Mr. Matthews. Do you recall the persons who attended?

Mr. O'Shea. Yes; Santo attended; a conductor from the B. M. T. named William Suidema; a maintenance man from the lighting department of the Interborough Rapid Transit Co.

Mr. Matthews. What was his name?

Mr. O'Shea. James McGovern. Two other workers from the painting department. One was J. Sponza and the other worker was Holstrum.

Mr. Matthews. Herbert?

Mr. O'Shea. Herbert Holstrum.

Mr. Matthews. Who acted as the chairman of that delegates' council?

Mr. O'Shea. John Santo.

Mr. Matthews. What was the membership of the union at this time?

Mr. O'Shea. Well, figures given to me by Santo was approximately 100—about 100 men.

Mr. Matthews. Now, what year was this, to keep the story straight?

Mr. O'Shea. That was around—I would say around April of 1934—on or about April. I may be wrong in the month but I know it was within that time.

Mr. Matthews. Did you begin to publish any literature—leaflets, bulletins, or anything of that kind at this time?

Mr. O'Shea. Well, yes; we naturally discussed it at this meeting. We had to explain the situation in the industry and the necessity of putting out stuff, so he said: "Yes; we will take care of that; we will publish a bulletin."

Mr. Matthews. Now, what kind of a bulletin did you get out at this time?

Mr. O'Shea. Oh, it was just one of those six by four two-page bulletins.

Mr. Matthews. Who was the editor of the bulletin?

Mr. O'Shea. A man by the name of Forge.

Mr. Matthews. Is his first name Maurice?

Mr. O'Shea. Maurice Forge; yes.

Mr. Matthews. M-a-u-r-i-c-e?

Mr. O'Shea. Yes.

Mr. Matthews. Do you know now whether he is the editor of the Transport Workers' Bulletin?

Mr. O'Shea. Yes, sir. He is now editor of the Transport Workers' Bulletin.

Mr. Matthews. Does it so appear in the Transport Workers' Bulletin?

Mr. O'SHEA. Yes, sir; his name appears in the bulletin as the editor.

Mr. MATTHEWS. Did Forge work in the industry?

Mr. O'SHEA. No; Forge at that time was a member of the concentration unit at this shop in Harlem, which we discussed in the early part of the evidence. He was one of the seven men selected by Tass, who was the section organizer, to concentrate for the work and from this unit he still continued on and continued in a functionary capacity as an editor.

Mr. MATTHEWS. Do you know what section of the Communist Party he belonged to?

Mr. O'SHEA. Section 4. That was the Harlem section, New York City.

Mr. MATTHEWS. Do you know any further enlightening facts about Forge's connection or background?

Mr. O'SHEA. Well, Forge, from what I understood, he was what we used to call a "placard artist." He used to do some painting from time to time on dresses, I believe, and he had a job—the last job he had was a bus boy in some club on Park Avenue.

Mr. THOMAS. Mr. Matthews, right at that point I would like to know what proof the witness has that this man you are referring to is a member of the Communist Party. Why does he think he is a member of the Communist Party?

Mr. MATTHEWS. That is, Maurice Forge?

Mr. THOMAS. Yes.

Mr. MATTHEWS. Can you answer that, Mr. O'Shea?

Mr. O'SHEA. Well, I was going to come to that question later on. You see when we were going into the point of the structure of the Communist Party within the trade-unions I would have dealt with this particular question.

Mr. THOMAS. That is all right.

Mr. MATTHEWS. Now, I show you, Mr. O'Shea, a copy of the Transport Workers' Bulletin of July 1934 [handing paper to the witness].

Mr. O'SHEA. Yes.

Mr. MATTHEWS. Do you identify that?

Mr. O'SHEA. Yes, sir; that is one of our first bulletins.

Mr. MATTHEWS. I ask that this be made a part of the record.

The CHAIRMAN. It is so ordered.

(The document referred to by Mr. Matthews was marked "O'Shea Exhibit No. 8," and made a part of the record.)

Mr. MATTHEWS. Will you please state how this bulletin was financed? Who paid for its publication?

Mr. O'SHEA. The Communist Party.

Mr. MATTHEWS. How do you know the Communist Party paid for its publication?

Mr. O'SHEA. Certainly the union didn't pay for it, because the union didn't have any money—wasn't in existence, as a matter of fact.

Mr. MATTHEWS. Was 80 East Eleventh Street the address of the Transport Workers' Bulletin at that time?

Mr. O'SHEA. Yes; they had a room—we had a room, of course. When the thing began to start with the one hundred or so men, we had a room at 80 East Eleventh Street.

Mr. MATTHEWS. Do you know, Mr. O'Shea, where this Transport Workers' Bulletin was actually printed—what typographical union was connected with its printing?

Mr. O'SHEA. Well, I have some material here which is——

Mr. MATTHEWS. What is the union label on that?

Mr. O'SHEA. The number is 209. It is the union-label number, and I have some exhibits here which I will present to the committee—some closer connection. Here is the "Soviet-Finnish Peace—A Blow to the War Mongers." This also has union label No. 209.

Mr. THOMAS. May I ask were they both printed at the same place?

Mr. O'SHEA. Yes, sir.

Mr. THOMAS. Both of those pamphlets printed at the same place?

Mr. O'SHEA. Yes, sir. They have the same label, No. 209. That is a trade number.

Mr. MATTHEWS. And here is a pamphlet entitled "Captured by Franco," and published by the Friends of the Abraham Lincoln Brigade. Is that also——

Mr. O'SHEA. Also 209.

Mr. MATTHEWS. Bears union label 209?

Mr. O'SHEA. Yes, sir.

Mr. MATTHEWS. And here is a leaflet issued by the women's committee of the New York State Communist Party. Does that also bear the label 209?

Mr. O'SHEA. Yes; 209.

Mr. MATTHEWS. And an election campaign leaflet entitled "The People Versus Wall Street," published by the Communist Party and also has label 209?

Mr. O'SHEA. Yes.

Mr. MATTHEWS. If I have not offered exhibits 9, 10, 11, and this one as 12, I wish to do so.

The CHAIRMAN. They are admitted.

(The exhibits referred to by Mr. Matthews were marked "O'Shea Exhibits Nos. 9, 10, 11, and 12," and made a part of the record.)

Mr. MATTHEWS. Now, did you make any inquiries of the Allied Printing Trades Council as to the identity of union label 209?

Mr. O'SHEA. Yes, sir.

Mr. MATTHEWS. I will show you a letter——

Mr. O'SHEA. That is the letter; yes.

Mr. MATTHEWS. Can you identify this letter?

Mr. O'SHEA. Absolutely.

Mr. MATTHEWS. Dated June 13, 1939?

Mr. O'SHEA. Yes, sir.

Mr. MATTHEWS. The letter is from the Allied Printing Trades Council of Greater New York and is signed by Vincent J. Ferris. I wish to offer this in evidence.

The CHAIRMAN. It will be admitted.

(The letter referred to by Mr. Matthews was marked "O'Shea Exhibit No. 13," and made a part of the record.)

Mr. MATTHEWS. The letter states as follows:

Complying with the request contained in your letter of June 4, I hereby impart to you the following information:

The Prompt Press, now located at 113 Fourth Avenue has been the lessee of label 209 since 1933. The Printing Trades Bluebook gives the list of officers for 1939 as follows:

Frank Thistleton, president; Boris Cohen, secretary-treasurer and buyer.

Do you know what connection the Prompt Press has with the Communist Party or any of its organizations?

Mr. O'SHEA. Yes. You will find some documents here which will, I am sure, indicate that.

Mr. MATTHEWS. I show you a copy of the New York Post for August 8, 1939, with an article entitled: "Hathaway Uses Capitalist Dodge."

In this story it is stated that the Prompt Press, due to the judgment owed it by the Daily Worker, has become the receiver for the Daily Worker, is that correct?

Mr. O'SHEA. That is right.

Mr. MATTHEWS. Do you know if that is the legal situation of the Prompt Press and Daily Worker in New York?

Mr. O'SHEA. That is right.

Mr. MATTHEWS. Now, then, you understand from this and other information which was given to you, that the Communist Party paid for the publication of the first issues of the Transport Workers' Bulletin?

Mr. O'SHEA. Yes.

Mr. CASEY. Do I understand, Mr. Matthews, that the Prompt Press became receiver through judicial proceedings in court?

Mr. MATTHEWS. Is that right?

Mr. O'SHEA. As far as I understand, that is correct.

Mr. MATTHEWS. It is so stated in the article and as a result of an investigation. I checked that.

Now, what was your first position, Mr. O'Shea, in the Transport Workers' Union?

Mr. O'SHEA. President.

Mr. MATTHEWS. Were you the first president of the Transport Workers' Union?

Mr. O'SHEA. Yes, sir; I was the first president of the Transport Workers' Union.

Mr. MATTHEWS. And by whom were you elected president of the Transport Workers' Union?

Mr. O'SHEA. I wasn't elected president. I was appointed by Santo, who was the district representative of the party.

Mr. MATTHEWS. You were appointed president of the Transport Workers' Union by Santo?

Mr. O'SHEA. Yes.

Mr. MATTHEWS. Who was district organizer of the Communist Party in New York?

Mr. O'SHEA. District representative in the transit field?

Mr. MATTHEWS. Yes, district representative in the transit field?

Mr. O'SHEA. Yes, sir.

Mr. MATTHEWS. For the Communist Party?

Mr. O'SHEA. For the Communist Party; yes, sir.

Mr. MATTHEWS. Do you have any documentary evidence of your presidency of the Transport Workers' Union?

Mr. O'SHEA. Yes, sir. I think you will find it in the official organ, the bulletin.

Mr. MATTHEWS. I show you a copy of the Transport Workers' Bulletin for February 1935. which has a picture of yourself, is that correct?

(Handing paper to the witness.)

Mr. O'SHEA. Yes, sir.

Mr. MATTHEWS. And another copy of the Transport Workers' Bulletin for July 1935. Do you identify these as copies of the publication of your union?

Mr. O'SHEA. Yes.

Mr. MATTHEWS. I offer them in evidence.

The CHAIRMAN. They may be received.

(The Transport Workers' Bulletin dated February 1935 was marked "O'Shea Exhibit No. 15"; the Transport Workers' Bulletin dated July 1935 was marked "O'Shea No. 14," and made a part of the record.)

Mr. MATTHEWS. On page 1 of the Transport Workers' Bulletin for July 1935, there appears the following statement besides a photograph. Is that a photograph of yourself, Mr. O'Shea?

Mr. O'SHEA. That is right.

Mr. MATTHEWS (reading):

A few minutes before noon on Friday, June 21st, Tom O'Shea, fighting president of the Transport Workers' Union accompanied by two other union organizers, arrived at the 148th Street shop in preparation for the weekly shop-gate meeting—

and so forth.

I show you a Transport Workers' Union membership book.

Mr. O'SHEA. Yes, sir.

Mr. MATTHEWS. Mr. O'Shea, do you identify that?

Mr. O'SHEA. Yes, sir.

Mr. MATTHEWS. Does your signature appear as president of the Transport Workers' Union?

Mr. O'SHEA. Yes.

Mr. MATTHEWS. And the signature of Austin Hogan as secretary?

Mr. O'SHEA. Yes, sir.

Mr. MATTHEWS. Of the Transport Workers' Union?

Mr. O'SHEA. Yes, sir.

Mr. MATTHEWS. And this book was dated August 28, 1934?

Mr. O'SHEA. Yes, sir.

Mr. MATTHEWS. May we have this in evidence as O'Shea's exhibit 16?

The CHAIRMAN. It is admitted.

(The membership book referred to by Mr. Matthews was marked "O'Shea's exhibit No. 16" and made a part of the record.)

Mr. MATTHEWS. How long did you retain the position as president of the Transport Workers' Union?

Mr. O'SHEA. Until December 1935.

Mr. MATTHEWS. You held the position until December 1935?

Mr. O'SHEA. Held the position until December 1935; yes.

Mr. MATTHEWS. What were your instructions at that time with reference to the office of president?

Mr. O'SHEA. At that time I was instructed by Santo to resign, or not to oppose the future president at the election.

Mr. MATTHEWS. And did you follow those instructions?

Mr. O'SHEA. Absolutely.

Mr. MATTHEWS. And who was elected president of the Transport Workers' Union to succeed you?

Mr. O'SHEA. Quill was elected unopposed.

Mr. MATTHEWS. Michael Quill?

Mr. O'SHEA. Yes.

Mr. Matthews. And were you instructed to do that by Santo?

Mr. O'Shea. Yes, sir; by John Santo.

Mr. Matthews. Of the Communist Party?

Mr. O'Shea. Yes, sir.

Mr. Matthews. Was that in 1936?

Mr. O'Shea. No; at the end of November 1935. The election took place at the end of November 1935 and the officers were installed in January 1936.

Mr. Matthews. Now, were you ever approached to join the Communist Party, Mr. O'Shea?

Mr. O'Shea. Yes, sir; I was approached to join the Communist Party.

Mr. Matthews. Where was that and when?

Mr. O'Shea. I was asked to attend around 1934 at a house in Astoria, Long Island.

Mr. Matthews. Who was present at that meeting?

Mr. O'Shea. John Santo, Austin Hogan, and a chap by the name of James Garrison, who actually owned the apartment, a chap by the name of Arthur Anderson, a chap by the name of James Mc-Govern, and myself.

Mr. Matthews. Did you join the Communist Party at that time?

Mr. O'Shea. Yes; I joined the party at that time.

Mr. Matthews. This was in or around 1934?

Mr. O'Shea. May 1934; approximately that time.

Mr. Matthews. So that when you relinquished the presidency of the Transport Workers' Union in December of 1935 you were a member of the Communist Party?

Mr. O'Shea. Yes, sir; I was a member of the Communist Party.

Mr. Matthews. And you did, therefore, feel compelled to accept the instructions of the Communist Party with reference to your position in this union?

Mr. O'Shea. Yes, sir.

Mr. Casey. You mean when he was president of the Transport Workers' Union he joined the Communist Party?

Mr. Matthews. No. He had been a member of the Communist Party since May 1934.

Mr. Casey. Did he occupy a position then in the union?

Mr. Matthews. He occupied the position of president of the Transport Workers' Union from June 1934 to November 1935—about 18 months.

One month before you became president of the union you joined the Communist Party?

Mr. O'Shea. Approximately that time; yes.

Mr. Matthews. Did any of the other persons present at that meeting in Astoria join the Communist Party at the same time?

Mr. O'Shea. Yes. McGovern, Garrison, and Anderson. Anderson, as a matter of fact, rejoined the party.

Mr. Matthews. So you were present then at a meeting of the Communist Party and therefore knew from first-hand knowledge that these individuals became members?

Mr. O'Shea. Yes.

Mr. Matthews. Santo, Starr, Hogan, Garrison, Anderson, and McGovern; is that correct?

Mr. O'SHEA. Yes.

Mr. MATTHEWS. Now, from that time on did you attend regularly meetings of the party?

Mr. O'SHEA. Yes. The party then had scheduled regular what was known as "unit meetings." Established what was known as a "unit."

Mr. MATTHEWS. Where were those meetings held?

Mr. O'SHEA. We held quite a number of them at the Artist's Hall. I think it is around Twenty-third Street in New York City. We had some in the Metal Workers' Union, and later in the headquarters of the Transport Workers' Union.

Mr. CASEY. Before you go into that, Mr. Matthews, I am very curious to know how it happened that a good Corkman named O'Shea joined the Communist Party.

Mr. O'SHEA. Well, it so happened, conditions in the industry at that time were anything but hot. I worked as a maintenance man. My hours of work wasn't too bad. I had 48 hours a week—44. But I saw men working 84 hours a week. I was up in a booth, and after all a man is entitled to at least half-decent living conditions. I saw that there was absolutely no justice as far as the workingmen in the industry were concerned and I felt at the time it was absolutely necessary to have a union.

Now, I didn't see any activity on the part of the American Federation of Labor; and I have previously testified I made contact through this concentration group and they assured me they were interested in building a union. Now, the question was, was I going along with them? To my belief they were giving satisfaction. They were willing to spend money—pay for a bulletin, pay for lawyers, and give us as much protection as could be given. So I felt that really these people are interested in the working class. They were seriously interested in the working class so I said to myself, "Well, after all if these people are willing to come in here and make a Utopia and show nationally and internationally they are willing to do the same thing." Then naturally I read their material— Daily Worker pamphlets, bulletins, and various things, and from the contents of the material I believed that they were seriously interested in alleviating a lot of suffering.

This unemployment question and many other things were coming up from day to day and for that reason I felt I would join, so I did join.

Mr. MASON. May I ask a question. Following that, however, your eyes were opened to the fact that they were not particularly interested in the welfare of the workingman but had their political notions always to the fore and were using the working man as an excuse to get their political and revolutionary activities over, is that right?

Mr. O'SHEA. Sure. I realized that when I held that position as president, that I was simply nothing else but a Charlie McCarthy and it was a question not to have your own ideas on any question that arose, but simply do what you were told, right or wrong.

The CHAIRMAN. All right.

Mr. MATTHEWS. Now, Mr. O'Shea, you spoke of meeting with your unit of the Communist Party in various places in New York. I would like to ask you if Michael Quill was a member of the same unit of the Communist Party that you were?

Mr. O'Shea. Michael Quill was a member of the same unit of the Communist Party.

Mr. Matthews. Was that unit a part of section 28 of the Communist Party of New York?

Mr. O'Shea. Section 28.

Mr. Matthews. Who was the secretary of your unit?

Mr. O'Shea. Eddie Maguire was secretary.

Mr. Matthews. Did Quill hold any position in your unit?

Mr. O'Shea. Yes.

Mr. Matthews. In the Communist Party?

Mr. O'Shea. Yes. Quill was what was known as "literature agent."

Mr. Matthews. Did you hold any position?

Mr. O'Shea. Unit organizer.

Mr. Matthews. Do you recall the names of the other members of the unit?

Mr. O'Shea. Yes, sir. Austin Hogan, John Santo, Anderson, a chap by the name of McGovern from the industry, a chap by the name of Curran, and a chap by the name of Flemming, a John Murphy. A colored chap named King, who was a porter in the industry; a chap named Gunsen and Peter Starr.

Mr. Matthews. Was there a man named Garrison?

Mr. O'Shea. James Garrison; yes.

Mr. Matthews. These were in addition to yourself and Michael Quill?

Mr. O'Shea. Yes, sir. We were functionaries of the unit.

Mr. Matthews. And Ed Maguire?

Mr. O'Shea. Ed Maguire; yes.

Mr. Matthews. Did you ever have any prominent Communists attend your meetings?

Mr. O'Shea. Yes.

Mr. Matthews. Will you please state who they were?

Mr. O'Shea. Rose Wortis and George Siskind.

Mr. Matthews. Is that spelled W-o-r-t-i-s and S-i-s-k-i-n-d?

Mr. O'Shea. Yes.

Mr. Matthews. Why did George Siskind and Rose Wortis attend your meetings—they were unit meetings?

Mr. O'Shea. Yes. Our unit meetings were not long in existence at the time and a question arose as to the advisability of entering the company-union elections which were about to take place at the time, nominate candidates on the company-union slate and, if possible, get control of the company union from the inside.

At this particular unit meeting Quill could not see that policy and he went up in arms. He said it was a form of collaboration with the company; that he could not see that such a thing was possible.

Santo was unable at the time, at this meeting, to convince Quill, so he arranged for the following unit meeting to bring in somebody who would be able to explain the situation.

Mr. Matthews. You say Quill opposed entering——

Mr. O'Shea. The company union.

Mr. Matthews. In a Trojan Horse fashion?

Mr. O'Shea. Yes, sir.

Mr. Matthews. Because he said it was a form "of collaboration with the bosses"?

Mr. O'SHEA. Yes, sir.

Mr. MATTHEWS. Do you know whether or not that that attitude expressed by Quill at that time has been denounced by the Communist Party as "left-wing infantilism"?

Mr. O'SHEA. Absolutely.

Mr. MATTHEWS. Did Lenin write a book on that subject?

Mr. O'SHEA. That is true.

Mr. MATTHEWS. And is it the experience of the party that new recruits to the party sometimes fail to understand the importance of the Trojan Horse tactics?

Mr. O'SHEA. True.

Mr. MATTHEWS. On the ground that they are collaborating with reactionaries and bosses and what not?

Mr. O'SHEA. That is true.

Mr. MATTHEWS. And that was Quill's position at this time?

Mr. O'SHEA. That was Quill's position at that time.

Mr. MATTHEWS. And Siskind and Wortis were sent into your unit to discuss that subject with your unit?

Mr. O'SHEA. Yes.

Mr. MATTHEWS. And did they do more than discuss it with your unit?

Mr. O'SHEA. Oh, they went into the whole question of the party.

Mr. MATTHEWS. Did they lay down the party line for you?

Mr. O'SHEA. Absolutely. They said: "You understand the party's position. You have got to get inside and you have got to smash it down from the inside. It is the only way it can and must be done."

Mr. MATTHEWS. Did Quill yield after the instructions were laid down?

Mr. O'SHEA. Yes; he did yield.

Mr. MATTHEWS. What happened, do you know, to Siskind shortly after this meeting at your unit?

Mr. O'SHEA. Well, we had some later meetings with Siskind after that, you see, but I missed him from around the district. I was a frequent visitor at the headquarters of the district and——

Mr. MATTHEWS. Of the Communist Party?

Mr. O'SHEA. Of the Communist Party headquarters and naturally any question we had we would go and interview them on those things, and I was informed that he was gone—that he had gone to Russia.

Mr. MATTHEWS. Now, when Siskind was attending your meetings, do you know whether or not he was designated as the "agit prop"?

Mr. O'SHEA. He was.

Mr. MATTHEWS. Which I believe now is called "the educational director"?

Mr. O'SHEA. Yes, sir; the same thing.

Mr. MATTHEWS. Did you have a leading fraction formed at this time?

Mr. O'SHEA. Yes, sir. It is the practice with the Communist Party when they establish units within a given industry to also establish an executive which is known as a "fraction."

Mr. MATTHEWS. Now, what is the "leading fraction"?

Mr. O'SHEA. That is—a leading fraction, it usually consists of select men. They are not elected. But they are selected by the functionaries who are the full-time organizers of the party in the industry, who select maybe a half a dozen or a dozen men and place them in positions and they direct the activities or, in other words, carry the party line through the industry.

Mr. MATTHEWS. Isn't their responsibility to politicalize the union?

Mr. O'SHEA. Yes, sir; and responsible for recruiting.

Mr. MATTHEWS. Do you remember the names of the members of the leading fraction in the transit industry at this time?

Mr. O'SHEA. Yes, sir. Austin Hogan, Quill, and MacMahon.

Mr. MATTHEWS. Will you spell that?

Mr. O'SHEA. M-a-c-M-a-h-o-n. Forge, who was the editor of this bulletin.

Mr. MATTHEWS. He is the man we asked about before?

Mr. O'SHEA. He is the gentleman. Austin Hogan, James Garrison, Murphy—I mentioned Quill, did I?

Mr. MATTHEWS. Suidema?

Mr. O'SHEA. Yes; he was.

Mr. MATTHEWS. Santo a member of the fraction?

Mr. O'SHEA. Santo was a member of the fraction.

Mr. MATTHEWS. Were you a member of the fraction?

Mr. O'SHEA. Oh, yes; sure.

Mr. MATTHEWS. What about a man named Victor Bloswick?

Mr. O'SHEA. Yes, sir; Victor Bloswick. One Hundred and Forty-eighth Street. He was also a member.

Mr. MATTHEWS. Did you find that any friction or factionalism developed in your fraction?

Mr. O'SHEA. Yes, sir.

Mr. MATTHEWS. What was that due to?

Mr. O'SHEA. Well, during the course of organization Quill and I from time to time discussed this party thing, about the organization. We felt that they were not organizing properly and we drew this question to their attention from time to time, but we got no satisfaction. It seemed to be—weil, you just do as you are told, so we were opposed to the "bureaucracy," as we termed it, at the time—the dictatorial tactics of Santo and Hogan, with the result it got so hot that we were called to a special meeting.

Mr. MATTHEWS. Where was that meeting held?

Mr. O'SHEA. It was held in the home of Israel Amter.

Mr. MATTHEWS. Do you know who Israel Amter is?

Mr. O'SHEA. He is State chairman of the Communist Party for the New York district.

Mr. MATTHEWS. And where was his home at that time?

Mr. O'SHEA. On the East Side around—I couldn't say—around Fourth Street, but I would say on the East Side off of Third Avenue.

Mr. MATTHEWS. This was a meeting of your leading fraction in the transit industry at the home of Israel Amter?

Mr. O'SHEA. Yes.

Mr. MATTHEWS. For the purpose of dealing with the conflict that arose in the leading fraction?

Mr. O'SHEA. Yes, sir.

Mr. MATTHEWS. Were any charges brought against any particular individuals at the meeting at Israel Amter's home?

Mr. O'SHEA. It is usually discussed with the leaders of the district——

Mr. MATTHEWS. Were any charges brought?

Mr. O'SHEA. At this meeting?

Mr. MATTHEWS. Yes.

Mr. O'SHEA. Oh, yes. Anderson, who was one of our group from the industry, was charged at the meeting with being a stoolpigeon.

Mr. CASEY. For whom?

Mr. O'SHEA. Anderson.

Mr. CASEY. For whom?

Mr. O'SHEA. For the corporation. And to my knowledge there was no evidence presented to convince me that he was.

Mr. MATTHEWS. Now, who were some of the other persons present beside Amter and the members of your leading fraction on this occasion?

Mr. O'SHEA. Roy Hudson, a member of the central committee of the Communist Party who was responsible for this communistic activity in the maritime union; William Dunn, a member of the central committee and now district organizer in Butte, Mont.; James Ford, of Harlem, also a member of the central committee and now a member of the national committee of the Communist Party; and Rose Wortis, George Siskind, and Hogan, Santo, Forge, Quill, Garrison, Anderson, and myself.

Mr. MATTHEWS. Were Santo and Hogan reprimanded in any way at this meeting?

Mr. O'SHEA. Yes. Of course, at the meeting we brought up and presented our picture. We charged them with high-handed bureaucracy.

Mr. MATTHEWS. Were they found guilty of bureaucracy?

Mr. O'SHEA. They were found guilty—they found them guilty at the time to satisfy us of being bureaucratic—they were found guilty.

Mr. THOMAS. It is not clear to me what they were found guilty of?

Mr. O'SHEA. Bureaucracy.

Mr. MATTHEWS. Now, what happened after this meeting, immediately after?

Mr. O'SHEA. Immediately after the meeting, Santo, who naturally was—who was the district representative in our union—invited me to his home for dinner and during the meal he was trying to impress me with the fact that Anderson was a stooge.

The CHAIRMAN. Who was that?

Mr. O'SHEA. That this Anderson, who was charged at the meeting——

The CHAIRMAN. Who was trying to impress you?

Mr. O'SHEA. John Santo. I knew Anderson for years in the industry and I knew his activities in the industry and I knew there was some other motive for attacking Anderson. As I got more "developed," as they say in the Communist Party, I saw they wanted to isolate him because he was the brains of our group.

Mr. MATTHEWS. Have you observed, in your experience inside of the Communist Party, members who show too much independence or any independence or deviate from the party line are dealt with severely?

Mr. O'SHEA. Sure, and immediately isolated.

Mr. MATTHEWS. Is it customary to charge them with being stooges?

Mr. O'SHEA. That is the general practice. Naturally, it is something that they want to stick particularly among the membership. Using any other charge would not hold water with the men, but "stool pigeon," while it deals specifically with the men's economic condition, and for that particular reason they use that.

Mr. Casey. Just what does the term "isolate" mean?

Mr. O'Shea. Well. it so happened, as I showed at the time, there were four of us in a group. It was felt that if they could have influenced both Quill, Garrison, and me, we would have taken up against Anderson and believed their statements and put him by himself. In other words, he would lose his influence in the industry.

Mr. Matthews. Now, what happened after that meeting?

Mr. O'Shea. Well, after that meeting there was nothing to the party's satisfaction, so a second meeting was called and at this second meeting they introduced a resolution and they brought in approximately 100 members from the industry—party members—and the same question came up again, and it wasn't settled. I still maintained that there was some form of a frame-up, something being done—something that I could not see. There was no evidence submitted to me to prove this man was connected in any way with the corporation.

After this particular meeting the Communist Party sent to Boston for one of their members, active members, a man by the name of P. J. McCarthy, who happened to be an Irishman and also was a charter member of the Communist Party, as I later learned.

The purpose was to use McCarthy to neutralize this opposition that had developed, and that was the opposition of Quill, Anderson, and the other fellows against Santo and Hogan. They felt being Irish, he would be able to do that.

So when McCarthy did come he was assigned as an organizer; placed on the fraction and assigned as a union organizer for the Brooklyn-Manhattan division.

Mr. Matthews. Had McCarthy ever had any experience in the transit field?

Mr. O'Shea. No. He had trade-union experience. He was in many unions, you see, and he knew something about trade-unionism—more than Santo or Hogan.

Mr. Matthews. He was made an organizer immediately after being brought from Boston?

Mr. O'Shea. Yes, sir. The election I think took place 3 or 4 months later, and he was put on the slate as a business agent. We had then gone into the International Association of Machinists and he was made a business agent.

Mr. Matthews. Now, at that time you were still president of the union?

Mr. O'Shea. Yes, sir; I was still president.

Mr. Matthews. Who was the vice president of the union at this time?

Mr. O'Shea. Quill was vice president of the union at that time.

Mr. Matthew. Did any other meetings take place with reference to this issue of factionalism?

(No answer.)

Mr. Matthews. Do you recall any meetings that dealt with this question of factionalism subsequent to the one——

Mr. O'Shea. The one in Amter's home and the one following that on the East Side where the group of transit workers were brought in. It was at this meeting that McCarthy was introduced to the industry.

Mr. MATTHEWS. Now, I show you a copy of the Transport Workers' Bulletin for March 1, 1936. Can you identify that? (Handing paper to the witness.)

Mr. O'SHEA. Yes, sir.

Mr. MATTHEWS. I offer this Transport Workers' Bulletin for March 1, 1936, in evidence.

The CHAIRMAN. It is received.

(The Transport Workers' Bulletin referred to by Mr. Matthews was marked "O'Shea Exhibit No. 17" and made a part of the record.)

Mr. MATTHEWS. The list of officers includes the name of P. J. McCarthy as one of the business agents, is that correct?

Mr. O'SHEA. That is right. That is the man.

Mr. MATTHEWS. And John Santo was another?

Mr. O'SHEA. Yes, sir.

Mr. MATTHEWS. And Thomas H. O'Shea a third?

Mr. O'SHEA. Yes; I was the third.

Mr. MATTHEWS. You were the three business agents of the union at that time?

Mr. O'SHEA. Yes, sir.

Mr. MATTHEWS. Will you please explain how it was McCarthy was able to get elected to a position in the union after so short a time in the industry in New York?

Mr. O'SHEA. Well, as you know in communistic-controlled unions there is no such thing as democracy. The whole thing is planned inside by the fraction, and the unit members are placed on the floor to nominate their candidates, and the whole slate was put in a block—the whole party slate, with a few rank and filers thrown in as window dressing, and presented to the membership, and then if there were any nominations they would be individual and would not make the grade. Then, the official organ would play the thing up for a month or two in advance maybe. The issues would carry the pictures and records of the men, and the opposition was smothered down and had no chance at all.

Mr. THOMAS. In other words, the Communist Party dominated the elections in the Transit Workers' Union?

Mr. O'SHEA. Absolutely.

Mr. MATTHEWS. At this time, was the Transport Workers' Union affiliated with the American Federation of Labor?

Mr. O'SHEA. Yes; we were associated with the American Federation of Labor.

Mr. MATTHEWS. The Transport Workers' Union was?

Mr. O'SHEA. Yes.

Mr. MATTHEWS. What was its first affiliation?

Mr. O'SHEA. Its first affiliation was with the Trade Union Unity Council. That was when we were an independent union prior going into the American Federation of Labor.

Mr. MATTHEWS. Will you please explain briefly what the Trade Union Unity Council was?

Mr. O'SHEA. It is an organization of all Communist-controlled unions, similar to what the central trades of the A. F. of L. had. It was more or less a central body of all affiliated Communist-controlled unions.

Mr. MATTHEWS. That is, for the city of New York?

Mr. O'SHEA. City of New York. That was what was known as the Trade Union Unity Council. Then there was the Trade Union Unity League, which was affiliated with all the international "red" unions.

Mr. MATTHEWS. Was that the Red International Labor Union?

Mr. O'SHEA. Yes, sir; the Red International Labor Union.

Mr. MATTHEWS. Did you know of your own experience that the Trade Union Unity Council and the Trade Union Unity League were completely dominated by the Communist Party?

Mr. O'SHEA. Absolutely.

Mr. MATTHEWS. Was there any question about that in anybody's mind who knew the inside workings of the organization?

Mr. O'SHEA. No question about that; no question about that.

Mr. MATTHEWS. I show you a copy of a portion of the Daily Worker for June 11, 1934, an article entitled, "Trade Unions in Actions to Aid Thalmann—Mass T. U. U. C. Delegation to Visit Nazi Consul in New York Tomorrow." Have you seen this copy of the Daily Worker? [Handing paper to the witness.]

Mr. O'SHEA. Yes, sir.

Mr. MATTHEWS. I shall read a paragraph from this article, as follows:

A delegation has been elected by the T. U. U. C. to present this demand to the German consulate. The delegation consists of the following workers: G. Harrison, Rose Kuntsch, M. Perlow, J. Sirota, J. Hurling, Ross, William Bliss, J. Santo.

Is that the Santo?

Mr. O'SHEA. Same John Santo, yes, who is general secretary.

Mr. MATTHEWS (continuing):

Harry Cantor, Charlotte Todes, Fannie Golos, Sam Nesin.

Who were the executives or leaders of the Trade Union Unity Council in New York at that time?

Mr. O'SHEA. Overgaard was the secretary and Sam Nesin and Rose Wortis.

Mr. MATTHEWS. And who were the other two?

Mr. O'SHEA. Rose Wortis and Sam Nesin.

Mr. MATTHEWS. Where were the headquarters of the Trade Union Unity Council?

Mr. O'SHEA. 80 East Eleventh Street.

Mr. MATTHEWS. Was that the same building where the Transport Workers' Union headquarters were?

Mr. O'SHEA. Same building but different floor.

Mr. MATTHEWS. I have a copy of the Daily Worker for May 1, 1934, with an article: Transit Workers Are Seething Against Company Unions, Low Wages. Have you ever seen this article? [Handing paper to witness.]

Mr. O'SHEA. Yes, sir; I have seen this article.

Mr. MATTHEWS. This article describes the steps taken by the Trade Union Unity Council?

Mr. O'SHEA. Yes, sir.

Mr. MATTHEWS. To prepare for the next taxi strike?

Mr. O'SHEA. Yes, sir.

Mr. MATTHEWS. The Transport Workers' Union at this time was a member of the Trade Union Unity Council?

Mr. O'SHEA. Yes, sir.

Mr. MATTHEWS. Now, this is an article entitled: "By a Secretary of the Transport Workers' Union." And this page which concludes the article in an editor's note is signed by Andrew Overgaard, secretary, Trade Union Unity Council, is that correct?

Mr. O'SHEA. Yes, sir.

Mr. MATTHEWS. Now, will you please state briefly, Mr. O'Shea, how the affiliation with the Trade Union Unity League was abandoned?

(No response.)

Mr. MATTHEWS. The affiliation of the Transport Workers' Union?

Mr. O'SHEA. Well, after the decisions of the Seventh World Congress of the Communist International, orders were relayed to our fraction that the new policy of the party was the united-front policy. In other words, the Trojan Horse policy. We were ordered to make preparations and get inside of the American Federation of Labor.

The CHAIRMAN. What date was that?

Mr. MATTHEWS. August 1935.

Mr. O'SHEA. Yes, sir; August 1935, on or about August 5, 1935.

Mr. MATTHEWS. The Seventh World Congress was held in Moscow in 1935?

Mr. O'SHEA. And this was relayed to be put into effect in the United States.

Mr. MATTHEWS. And you were told then to get into the American Federation of Labor?

Mr. O'SHEA. Yes. "Get in it any way you possibly can do it, but just get into any branch."

Mr. MATTHEWS. And was the Trade Union Unity League entirely abandoned at that time by the Communist Party?

Mr. O'SHEA. Well, they still held together until such time as each group were able to get inside the various national and international unions of the American Federation of Labor.

Mr. MATTHEWS. Did the Transport Workers Union have an open, publicly known affiliation with the Trade Union Unity League at this time?

Mr. O'SHEA. No. It was kept completely in the dark. Any demonstration by the T. U. U. C.—we kept clear of it, because they felt at the time because of the group of Irish there that it would be dangerous for them—it would have linked them with the party. In other words, put them on the spot.

Mr. MATTHEWS. The sentiment among the Transport Workers Union was such they would not have looked kindly on an affiliation with a Communist-controlled labor federation?

Mr. O'SHEA. That is right.

Mr. MATTHEWS. When did you first make contact with the American Federation of Labor with a view to getting inside of the American Federation of Labor?

Mr. O'SHEA. As I stated, it was around August. We made an effort. We contacted a representative of the Amalgamated Association of Street, Electric Railway, and Motor Coach Employees of America, an A. F. of L. affiliate in New York City. And at a conference with him—his name was P. O'Shea, the same as myself, and he arranged that a delegation of our organization should go to Detroit and meet the executive board of the Amalgamated, which was then in session preparing for their convention.

Mr. MATTHEWS. Was such a delegation selected?

Mr. O'SHEA. Yes, sir. The delegation was selected.

Mr. MATTHEWS. Of whom was it composed?

Mr. O'SHEA. Hogan, Quill, Santo, and I.

Mr. MATTHEWS. Give their first names.

Mr. O'SHEA. This is the Santo that is now general secretary of the Transport Workers Union.

Mr. MATTHEWS. And Hogan who is vice president?

Mr. O'SHEA. Hogan is president of the New York local of the C. I. O., and he is also vice president of the State body of the C. I. O. body in the State of New York.

Mr. MATTHEWS. And Quill who is president of it.

Mr. O'SHEA. President of the Transport Workers Union.

Mr. MATTHEWS. Did you go to Detroit?

Mr. O'SHEA. Yes, sir; we went to Detroit.

Mr. MATTHEWS. How did you travel?

Mr. O'SHEA. By automobile.

Mr. MATTHEWS. Who paid the expenses of the trip to Detroit?

Mr. O'SHEA. Well, the question at the time—we had, as a matter of fact—we never seemed to have any money. It always seemed to go out in leaflets and stuff, but this trip involved quite some money—I believe it was something around three-hundred or three-hundred-and-fifty-odd dollars for the trip for a few days. We discussed this question with our fraction and tried to dig up dough, but it was impossible. We had already milked a lot of the members in the union for loans and things, so it was decided we would go to Amter, the State chairman of the Communist Party, and get cash.

We had a conference with Amter in the district office, and he came to the understanding that he would give us the cash provided that we would go to the Communist-controlled Nitgedaiget and Camp Unity. In other words, get some dough from the guests there and reimburse the party for a loan that they had given us. That was the understanding. So it was arranged that Quill and Hogan would go to those camps, which they did, and Santo and I were to follow them up the next day. They went up and they took Angelo Herndon along from each camp and made a big play and told them about the thing; and the result was, when the camp guests went home they left $1 apiece, and that was turned back to the party, but we got our cash from Amter.

We then proceeded in the automobile, after having a meal, to Detroit.

Mr. MATTHEWS. And what did you do when you reached Detroit?

Mr. O'SHEA. Well, we contacted the executive board members of the Amalgamated and had a conference. The next day the board was complete, and we discussed this whole transit situation about affiliation. Of course, the question did arise—they were rather skeptical of our group, and they decided that after their convention, which was to be held a few days later—they decided to send in an investigating committee to New York City and then asked for our membership list and many questions, and then they would see about the unification.

Mr. MATTHEWS. I show you a copy of the Motorman, Conductor, and Motor Coach Operator, a publication of the Amalgamated Association of Street, Electric Railway, and Motor Coach Employees of America.

Mr. O'SHEA. That is it.

Mr. MATTHEWS. For August 1937?

Mr. O'SHEA. Yes, sir.

Mr. MATTHEWS. You identify this as a document with which you are acquainted [handing pamphlet to the witness]?

Mr. O'SHEA. Yes, sir. That is the official organ of the Amalgamated Association of Street, Electric Railway, and Motor Coach Employees of America.

Mr. MATTHEWS. Does this explain the visit of your delegation?

Mr. O'SHEA. Yes, sir.

Mr. MATTHEWS. To Detroit at the time?

Mr. O'SHEA. Yes, sir.

Mr. MATTHEWS. This is the union into which you were trying to bore as a Trojan Horse under the directions of the Comintern.

Mr. O'SHEA. Yes; that is it.

Mr. MATTHEWS. On page 3 of this bulletin there appears a picture. Will you please identify these individuals?

Mr. O'SHEA. This is Austin Hogan [indicating].

Mr. MATTHEWS. On the left?

Mr. O'SHEA. Yes; and Quill and Santo.

Mr. MATTHEWS. And the caption above that is: Red Dictators of Transport Workers; is that correct?

Mr. O'SHEA. That is right.

Mr. MATTHEWS. Who are these persons on the back in the picture entitled "Birds of a Feather"?

Mr. O'SHEA. This is Quill and Thomas E. Murray, Federal receiver for the Interborough Rapid Transit Co., and this is John L. Lewis. This was when they were showing the closed-shop contract in 1937, taken in the head office of the Interborough Rapid Transit Co.

Mr. MATTHEWS. And this document also notes your membership in the delegation, does it not?

Mr. O'SHEA. Yes, sir. In here you will notice reference of the trip by the delegation to Detroit to appear before the executive board to lay down a proposition.

Mr. MATTHEWS [reading]:

Before Quill took over the presidency of the Transport Workers Union in 1935 he, Hogan, and Santo made overtures to the Amalgamated Association of Street, Electric Railway, and Motor Coach Employees. They came to Detroit and appeared before the general executive board to lay down a proposition.

The general executive board made a thorough investigation of the Transport Workers Union and came to the conclusion that there was no basis upon which the Amalgamated Association could accept the terms of their offer. At a later date Quill, Hogan, and Santo made further representations, but it was obvious the Amalgamated Association could not suspend its laws in favor of these men.

Mr. O'SHEA. Yes.

Mr. MATTHEWS. I ask that be marked as an exhibit.

(The pamphlet referred to by Mr. Matthews was marked "O'Shea Exhibit No. 20" and made a part of the record.)

Mr. MATTHEWS. Mr. Chairman, I am not certain that I offered the last two or three exhibits in evidence. If I did not, I wish at this time to offer O'Shea exhibits 18, 19, and the one just now marked "O'Shea Exhibit No. 20."

The CHAIRMAN. They may be received.

(The exhibits marked "O'Shea Exhibits Nos. 18, 19, and 20" were made a part of the record.)

Mr. MATTHEWS. Now, on your way back from Detroit, where you went to discuss the question of entering this American Federation of Labor Union, did you stop at Cleveland?

Mr. O'SHEA. Yes; we stopped at Cleveland.

Mr. MATTHEWS. Did you call on the Communist Party headquarters in Cleveland?

Mr. O'SHEA. Well, we called on the headquarters for the League for Peace and Democracy, and Santo apparently knew one of the New York Communists that was in the office, and we discussed the question. We discussed with them the transit situation in Cleveland. So we were informed there that the three delegates who were elected from the streetcars of Cleveland, or the busses, or whatever it was there, were also members for the League for Peace or League Against War and Fascism; and that if the occasion arose, that those three delegates could be used by the party on any questions that might arise with reference to our affiliation with the American Federation of Labor, if the question arose on the convention floor.

Mr. MATTHEWS. You mean these were three delegates from the local union who were going to the national convention in Detroit?

Mr. O'SHEA. That is right.

Mr. MATTHEWS. And you were told at the headquarters of the American League that these three men were all members of the American League Against War and Fascism?

Mr. O'SHEA. Yes.

Mr. MATTHEWS. And could be used by the Communist Party to represent its interest on the floor of the convention in Detroit?

Mr. O'SHEA. That is right.

Mr. MATTHEWS. Was it your own knowledge that the American League Against War and Fascism was a subsidiary of the Communist Party?

Mr. O'SHEA. Oh, yes, I knew that. Every Communist knows that. That is just a window dressing—the name is only a window dressing for the party.

Mr. MATTHEWS. When you arrived back in New York, did you make a report to the Communist Party headquarters on your trip to Detroit?

Mr. O'SHEA. Yes. When we returned we immediately went to the headquarters of the Communist Party and made a report to a member of the central committee.

Mr. MATTHEWS. Who was that?

Mr. O'SHEA. Jack Stachel.

Mr. MATTHEWS. Who was present and saw the report?

Mr. O'SHEA. Quill, Santo, Hogan, McCarthy, and I.

Mr. MATTHEWS. In addition to Jack Stachel to whom you made the report?

Mr. O'SHEA. Yes, sir.

Mr. MATTHEWS. Do you know whether Jack Stachel was at that time in charge of the trade union work for the Communist Party throughout the United States?

Mr. O'SHEA. Yes. I know he was in charge of the whole thing.

Mr. MATTHEWS. And subsequently was executive secretary of the Communist Party of the United States?

Mr. O'SHEA. Yes, sir.

Mr. MATTHEWS. You don't know where Jack Stachel is now, do you?

Mr. O'SHEA. No; I don't.

Mr. MATTHEWS. You know that a great many agencies would like to know where he is?

Mr. O'SHEA. Yes, sir; so I believe.

Mr. MATTHEWS. Now, what was the result of your conference with Jack Stachel on this occasion when you and Quill and Santo and Hogan presented your report on Detroit?

Mr. O'SHEA. The question arose—after, of course, the action of the executive board in Detroit we realized that we had a very shaky situation to deal with and we had discussed it in Detroit ourselves, so Santo had mentioned the fact that it would be a good policy if we had left somebody behind to make a contact with some party members who would attend the convention and have them bring up the question on the convention floor of the affiliation of the Transit Workers of New York City. And Santo reconsidered the question and went against it, but McCarthy, at this meeting with Stachel, was opposed. He said it should have been done—somebody should have been left there. So Stachel said: "No, it wouldn't be good policy; it was better to leave the thing go as it went and let the investigation go through and the easiest way was the best way. It wasn't the time for agitation on the convention floor. The proposition was too ticklish to fool around with." So Stachel agreed with Santo and that finished the situation. That was all.

Mr. MATTHEWS. Did the Amalgamated send some one to New York to investigate your union?

Mr. O'SHEA. Yes, sir. Some weeks later a delegation from the executive board appeared and we were met by a group consisting of Quill, Santo, Hogan, Douglas MacMahon, the general counsel and I, discussed the whole union question.

Mr. MATTHEWS. What did the investigating committee of the Amalgamated decide?

Mr. O'SHEA. They didn't make any decision but they asked for figures in the different departments and shops and various questions—a lot of questions and we were notified some weeks later through their representative that the thing was all blocked; that he did not know exactly what the situation was in Detroit and, of course, he wouldn't make any statements on it.

Mr. MATTHEWS. What advantage would it have been to the Communist Party to bring about this affiliation of the Transport Workers Union with the Amalgamated?

Mr. O'SHEA. Well, it was the policy of the party, particularly our group, to get inside of the Amalgamated particularly for this reason: that it was—that the Amalgamated is already established throughout the United States and Canada in the major cities, and their constitution was so written that it would give you a delegate for every 200 members. In other words, New York City with an approximate figure of 35,000 members working in conjunction with delegates who would be party members from the various other cities, would be sufficiently strong enough as a block to take over a convention floor the following year or two.

Mr. MATTHEWS. In other words through the size of your New York local which was already under the complete control of the Communist Party——

Mr. O'SHEA. Yes, sir.

Mr. MATTHEWS. You would be able to get into the Amalgamated and nominate the entire union, nationally—that was the hope of the party, wasn't it?

Mr. O'SHEA. Internationally, yes—Canada and the United States.

Mr. MATTHEWS. You mean that the Communist Party would have had complete control of the street cars, bus systems, in fact all transportation throughout the United States and——

Mr. O'SHEA. Yes, and Canada.

Mr. MATTHEWS. If this had been successful?

Mr. O'SHEA. If it had succeeded.

Mr. MATTHEWS. Now, you stated previously in your testimony the Communist Party paid the $300 for your trip to Detroit. Did this matter come before the membership of your union?

Mr. O'SHEA. Yes, sir. At that particular time we had our organization—our union organization on a section basis and we had section treasuries which was later abolished, but at that particular time one of our treasurers, who had happened to be in one of the major shops of the Interborough Rapid Transit Co. when the financial report was being read, questioned MacMahon, who was then financial secretary, on this item of the trip. MacMahon was, of course, taken off of his feet for the time being—didn't expect such a question, and he said that each delegate to Detroit had paid the money out of his own pocket and was to be reimbursed by the union when the union was sufficiently strong enough financially.

Mr. MATTHEWS. What were you doing at this time? Were you you on home relief?

Mr. O'SHEA. I was taken off the job for union activities and taken off the job about a year and was on home relief.

Mr. MATTHEWS. Was your home relief such as it would have been easy for you to repay these loans?

Mr. O'SHEA. Well, I certainly couldn't pay it out of my home-relief allowance.

Mr. MATTHEWS. These alleged loans?

Mr. O'SHEA. These alleged loans.

Mr. MATTHEWS. Is this man Laury still an officer of the Transport Workers Union?

Mr. O'SHEA. Yes, sir. He is a member of the executive One Hundred and Forty-eighth Street, I. R. T. repair shop.

Mr. MATTHEWS. This attempt to bore from within the Amalgamated by this Communist-controlled union, do you know whether the phrase "Trojan horse" is a part of the Communist Party's own literature and jargon?

Mr. O'SHEA. Oh, yes. They use that phrase.

Mr. MATTHEWS. They use the phrase?

Mr. O'SHEA. Yes.

Mr. MATTHEWS. Do you know whether or not Dimitroff in his e ch at the Seventh World Congress used the illustration of Trojan horse?

Mr. O'SHEA. Yes, sir. He really was the first to popularize it among the party members, after his speech.

Mr. MATTHEWS. And that was the tactics which he explained that the party must now specialize in for the purpose of getting into large organizations that were not Communist Party organized or controlled?

Mr. O'SHEA. Yes, sir. As a matter of fact, at that time they claimed that the American section of the Communist International was sectarian and was isolated from the masses; that they were not carrying out the Marxist theory of boring from within properly; that they were more or less taking a leftist position as the Communists would call it.

Mr. MATTHEWS. "Left-wing infantilism"?

Mr. O'SHEA. Yes, sir. They were more or less isolated from the masses. They wore the same kind of clothes and had red handkerchiefs and red ties and they said that should stop. They said they should dress like the other people and talk like the other people. That was the new line.

Mr. MATTHEWS. Were you publicly known as a member of the Communist Party?

Mr. O'SHEA. Oh, no.

Mr. MATTHEWS. At this time?

Mr. O'SHEA. Absolutely not; no.

Mr. MATTHEWS. Was Quill?

Mr. O'SHEA. No.

Mr. MATTHEWS. Was Hogan known as a member of the Communist Party?

Mr. O'SHEA. None of the officers were known as members of the Communist Party.

Mr. MATTHEWS. Did you ever have any explicit instructions as to what you should do if you were questioned under oath as to your membership in the Communist Party?

Mr. O'SHEA. I recall Rose Wortis and I were members of a fraction. If we ever happened to get locked up the only thing was to lie, lie, lie out of it—don't hesitate to lie; protect yourself and protect the party at all times.

Mr. MATTHEWS. Would it have been dangerous to the union?

Mr. O'SHEA. Well, naturally to expose the union at the time as a party organization would have caused it to collapse, no question about it.

Mr. MATTHEWS. Do you know whether or not Michael Quill has since admitted his membership in the Communist Party?

Mr. O'SHEA. No; he never has.

Mr. MATTHEWS. Hogan?

Mr. O'SHEA. No. Denied it, as a matter of fact.

Mr. MATTHEWS. Now, having failed to obtain a charter from the Amalgamated, what union did you try next?

Mr. O'SHEA. We made contact then with the International Association of Machinists.

Mr. MATTHEWS. Did you succeed in getting into that union?

Mr. O'SHEA. Yes, sir. Through one man named James Matles.

Mr. MATTHEWS. Was he a member of the Communist Party?

Mr. O'SHEA. He was also a member of the Communist Party and through his efforts—he had apparently made contact with the executives of the International Association of Machinists and arranged a conference with our group, with Santo and Quill, to appear at Washington and discuss affiliation with the machinists.

Mr. MATTHEWS. Is this the James Matles who is now a national organizer for the United Electrical, Radio Machine Workers of America?

Mr. O'SHEA. Yes, sir. He is what is known as the national director.

Mr. MATTHEWS. National director of the United Electrical, Radio and Machine Workers of America?

Mr. O'SHEA. Yes; national director of the United Electrical, Radio and Machine Workers of America.

Mr. MATTHEWS. Of which James Carey——

Mr. O'SHEA. James Carey is general secretary of the C. I. O.

Mr. MATTHEWS. Will you please describe how it was that Matles brought about your successful entering of the machinists' union?

Mr. O'SHEA. Well, Matles had, as I stated, went to Detroit and discussed with the machinists the large membership that could be brought into his organization and it was decided that our delegation should go to Washington and take up this whole question, which they did. And they issued a charter to us at the time and we became lodge 1547 of the International Association of Machinists.

Mr. MATTHEWS. That was the American Federation of Labor.

Mr. O'SHEA. American Federation of Labor; yes, sir.

Mr. MATTHEWS. When did you first meet James Matles?

Mr. O'SHEA. Well, I first met James Matles in the early days of organization at the fraction meetings.

The CHAIRMAN. When was that?

Mr. O'SHEA. That was at 80 East Eleventh Street.

The CHAIRMAN. What date?

Mr. O'SHEA. Oh, actually the first time I met him I would say would be around '35 when we were talking of the question of going in the American Federation of Labor. As a matter of fact Irving Potash of the Furriers union and James Matles attended one of our fraction meetings and they warned us, of course, "When you get into the American Federation of Labor it was a question of watching your step." And they explained what happened among the furriers and other groups.

The CHAIRMAN. When you say among the "furriers," do you mean that the Communist Party had in the manner in which you have described their control of the transport workers, that they also had control of the Furriers Union?

Mr. O'SHEA. Yes, sir. They were working in the Furriers Union at the time this question of Irving Potash had come up. He never worked in the industry and to get in he had to show that he was competent to work on furs and he described in detail of how he went to—apprenticed himself and learned the business and the American Federation of Labor executive couldn't keep him out.

The CHAIRMAN. What other union were they working in at that time to get control of?

Mr. O'SHEA. Oh, all the time—there was the food workers, laundry workers—oh, there was——

The CHAIRMAN. Which ones did they make the most progress in?

Mr. O'SHEA. The United Radio, Electrical, and Machine Workers became one of the strongest national groups. They had established themselves in machine shops in the New England States and I believe out in the Middle West. They went further really than the transport.

The CHAIRMAN. They got stronger control of the radio and electrical workers than they did the Transport Union?

Mr. O'SHEA. Yes, sir. As a matter of fact they controlled it from top to bottom and do today. As I say, James Matles is the director and Charlie McCarthy is the——

The CHAIRMAN. And they completely control the union?

Mr. O'SHEA. They completely control the union.

The CHAIRMAN. What power does that give them? What is their anxiety to become entrenched in that union?

Mr. O'SHEA. Well, I recall at one time William Foster discussed the question with us when we were going into the machinists, the importance of machine shops working with steel—that all products, all manufactured products from the steel industry had to pass through these machine shops. In other words the situation created in a machine shop industry would also paralyze the steel industry for the reason the stuff wouldn't be machined and therefore it was important to the party to have control of that particular industry.

The CHAIRMAN. Did the party work into the Maritime Union successfully?

Mr. O'SHEA. Yes. Roy Hudson is the man behind the scenes. He was the director of the forces in the Maritime Union.

The CHAIRMAN. Did they make much progress in the Maritime Union?

Mr. O'SHEA. On the west coast they had complete control. In New York they were making exceptionally strong headway and then in the South, I understand around New Orleans, they were digging in pretty strongly.

The CHAIRMAN. It is now 12:10. Will it be convenient to meet back here at 1 o'clock? If so, we will recess now until 1 o'clock.

(Whereupon, at 12:10 p. m., the hearing was recessed until 1 p. m., the same day.)

AFTER RECESS

The CHAIRMAN. The committee will resume. You may proceed.

TESTIMONY OF THOMAS HUMPHREY O'SHEA—Resumed

Mr. MATTHEWS. Mr. O'Shea, this morning I showed you a photostatic copy of a portion of the Daily Worker for May 1, 1934. I wish to read a paragraph of that article, "Transit Workers Are Seething Against Company Unions, Low Wages."

Capable comrades could be spared to write swell editorials, long articles analyzing the class struggle. Equally could they be spared for the organizing of workers in light industries, like pocketbook shops, millinery, furniture, and mattress makers. If all the workers in these industries, and, for good measure one may add Ben Gold's fur workers, would go on strike for 6 weeks, life in New York City would continue more or less the same.

But if the transit workers of New York should strike for 6 hours only, the life of the whole city would be upside down. With a little practical application of the Open Letter, the taxi strike might have been turned into a gigantic battle of New York transit workers against the Wall Street bankers; a battle the like of which New York has never seen, and which would knock a number of bricks off the capitalistic structure.

Is that the conception of the importance of the transit workers from the standpoint of the Communist Party strategy?

Mr. O'SHEA. Yes, sir. That is the strategy.

Mr. MATTHEWS. That has already been marked in evidence as "Exhibit No. 19." What are the important positions to be secured by the Communist Party in a trade or labor union?

Mr. O'SHEA. The principal positions in a trade and labor union is No. 1, secretary; No. 2, bulletin editor—the editor of whatever the official organ might be; and lawyer.

Mr. MATTHEWS. Will you please state briefly why these three particular positions, that of secretary, bulletin editor, and lawyer are so important from the standpoint of Communist control of a union?

Mr. O'SHEA. Well, you see the secretary, secretary-treasurer's position, which is usually held in national unions, gives complete control of minutes, financial reports, and all communications.

As for the editor of the paper he can prepare the ground work for any future problems that will arise. In other words, if they were planning a strike situation or wanted to create a particular situation, the ground work would be prepared by the bulletin through art and pictures and various things of that nature.

And a lawyer, of course, is really very important insofar as courts and testimony, and lots of things are given where men are arrested, and, of course, you know there is quite a lit of tabooing done from time to time and you must have the right man in the right place—can't afford to have a man except he is pretty well linked up with the party.

Mr. MATTHEWS. You mean the party engages in acts of sabotage in these key industries?

Mr. O'SHEA. Sure, absolutely.

Mr. MATTHEWS. In the key industries is it important to have a lawyer who accepts the party position on sabotage?

Mr. O'SHEA. Absolutely.

Mr. MATTHEWS. In order to——

Mr. O'SHEA. Present a good case.

Mr. MATTHEWS. Present a defense in court?

Mr. O'SHEA. To make a good case and protect the individuals involved.

Mr. MATTHEWS. What other positions can be used by the Communist Party for its purposes in a trade union?

Mr. O'SHEA. The secretary, as I say, is the most important. As a matter of record the now president of the Transport Workers' Union, who was in 1937 secretary of Lodge 1547, which was the Transport Workers' Union in the American Federation of Labor, played a very important role on this question of C. I. O. versus A. F. of L. split.

Mr. MATTHEWS. Well, let me ask you about some specific illustrations of that. I show you a copy of the Transport Workers' Bulletin, dated March 1, 1936. Will you identify that?

Mr. O'SHEA. Yes, sir. That is the official organ of the Transport Workers' Union.

Mr. MATTHEWS. And I show you a page from the Machinists' Monthly Journal for March 1936, page 154. Can you identify that [handing paper to witness]?

Mr. O'SHEA. Yes. This is the agreement signed between the Transport Workers' Union, independent, and the National Association of Machinists at the time of the affiliation.

Mr. MATTHEWS. Now, this was the affiliation that was brought about partly through the instrumentality of James Matles; is that correct?

Mr. O'SHEA. That is right.

Mr. MATTHEWS. Now, in reporting this agreement for affiliation, how——

The CHAIRMAN. Just one second. The Chair announces a subcommittee composed of Mr. Mason, of Illinois; Mr. Voorhis, of California, who is not present but who is on the subcommittee; and the chairman. Proceed.

Mr. MATTHEWS. You identify this page from the Machinists Journal [handing paper to the witness]?

Mr. O'SHEA. Yes.

Mr. MATTHEWS. Now, will you please show from these two publications, the one of the Transport Workers' Union and the other of the International Association of Machinists, how the bulletin editor was in a strategic position?

Mr. O'SHEA. Well, gentlemen of the committee, as you will note in this official organ dated March 1, 1936, an article is prepared in this dealing specifically with this agreement signed by the machinists. And I have marked off here "a charter grants jurisdiction over all employees in the transit industry of New York," under the caption of "Transit Employees in Wave of Organization Joining Transport Workers on News of American Federation of Labor Affiliation."

As you will note from this, the impression created was an industrial set-up. "All workers," it says, "in the transit system."

Mr. MATTHEWS. You mean an industrial union set-up as opposed to a craft union set-up?

Mr. O'SHEA. Craft union, and on the other hand we find signed actually at the same time by A. O. Wharton, international president of the machinists; E. C. Davison, general secretary-treasurer; and for the Transport Workers Union, Austin Hogan, general secretary; and Michael Quill, president; John Santo, general organizer; and Arthur Laury, member of the delegates' council.

Clause 6 of this agreement states:

In the event certain of the members come under the jurisdiction of other organizations and claim is made for such members, the matter will be worked out with the object in view of preserving unity of action between our organization and the organization making such claim. It not being our desire to segregate any of the membership involved in this amalgamation except to the extent we are obligated to do so and only when we believe no injury will result to the members directly concerned. Any adjustments of this kind to be made only after careful consideration.

Now, as you will note, the agreement actually signed is a craft agreement. The bulletin editor, on the other hand, in presenting it to the membership as a whole through this paper, which is given freely to all members of the union, gives an industrial phase.

In other words, that clause of the agreement was not written in and the full facts given to the membership.

Mr. MATTHEWS. In other words, a part of the agreement for affiliation was suppressed?

Mr. O'SHEA. Suppressed.

The CHAIRMAN. By the editor?

Mr. O'SHEA. By the editor.

Mr. MATTHEWS. Of the Transport Workers Bulletin?

Mr. O'SHEA. Yes, sir.

Mr. MATTHEWS. Does the Communist Party strongly favor the industrial type of union organization?

Mr. O'SHEA. Yes, sir. That is the party line.

Mr. MATTHEWS. As a matter of fact, it is opposed on principle to craft union organization?

Mr. O'SHEA. It is opposed to the craft unions on principle.

Mr. MATTHEWS. It would not hesitate to use craft organizations?

Mr. O'SHEA. No; to serve their purpose.

Mr. MATTHEWS. But it predicates its revolutionary theory on the large industrial union rather than craft unions?

Mr. O'SHEA. Yes, sir.

Mr. MATTHEWS. Now, is it true that the Communist Party propaganda in the Transport Workers Union in New York had led the members to believe that the Communist Party or the union itself were to favor only that industrial type of organization in the Transport?

Mr. O'SHEA. That was the situation.

Mr. MATTHEWS. So it was necessary not to disillusion the members?

Mr. O'SHEA. Exactly.

Mr. MATTHEWS. With respect to the actual agreement which was a craft agreement?

Mr. O'SHEA. Yes.

Mr. MATTHEWS. And to lead them to believe that they had got an industrial union type of organization?

Mr. O'SHEA. Yes.

Mr. MATTHEWS. And is that the kind of suppression and distortion that a party member who is the editor of a trades-union publication customarily practices?

Mr. O'SHEA. Yes, sir. That is the general policy of the party members in such capacity.

Mr. MATTHEWS. I wish to show you some documents, Mr. O'Shea, which are affidavits signed by various individuals. Can you identify these [handing papers to the witness]?

Mr. O'SHEA. Yes.

Mr. MATTHEWS. This is an affidavit: "State of New York, County of Bronx."

Mr. O'SHEA. Yes.

Mr. MATTHEWS. Made by William J. Halloran. And this is an affidavit: "State of New York, County of Bronx," made by Christopher Fin. and this is an affidavit: "State of New York, County of Bronx." made by John Cronin. You identify these?

Mr. O'SHEA. Yes, sir.

Mr. MATTHEWS. These affidavits?

Mr. O'SHEA. Yes, sir.

Mr. Matthews. What is the purport of these affidavits as they relate to this question?

Mr. O'Shea. We should take this first.

Mr. Matthews. You want to take the suppressed letter first?

Mr. O'Shea. Yes, sir.

Mr. Matthews. All right. Then I show you a communication addressed—this is a copy of a letter from the International Association of Machinists.

Mr. O'Shea. Yes, sir.

Mr. Matthews. Machinists Building, Washington, D. C., under date of May 10, 1937, addressed to Messrs. Michael J. Quill, Santo, Douglas, MacMahon, Joseph B. English, M. H. Forge, business representatives. Is this a true copy of an original which you have?

Mr. O'Shea. This is a true copy.

Mr. Matthews. Which you have seen?

Mr. O'Shea. Yes, sir.

Mr. Matthews. Now, will you please explain the contents of this letter [handing letter to witness]?

Mr. O'Shea. Well, gentlemen, at the time of the Transport Workers Union seceding from the American Federation of Labor and going into the C. I. O., at this particular period I didn't know the true situation, only that the question was coming up of breaking away. I sent a communication to Washington requesting information on the subject. Of course, I didn't hold any official capacity in the union at the time. I requested from Mr. Wharton information on the trouble which existed between the international office and the local, so he answered me; and I think I have a copy of the letter here. It is dated May 11, 1937. The letter is addressed to me:

DEAR SIR AND BROTHER: This will acknowledge receipt of your letter dated May 10, and I have forwarded copy of it to the vice president, Bowen, suggesting that he contact you at the first opportunity.

I have invited the officers of Lodge 1547 to meet with me at our headquarters in Washington, Wednesday, May 12, at 10 a. m., to discuss the situation which has developed. But I have no means of knowing at this time whether or not they will favorably respond. However, I assure you that it is my honest opinion that they have made a very serious mistake, and in the interest of the men who are so vitally affected I hope it will not prove disastrous to them.

The officers of the lodge have never communicated with me relative to any of the matters which may have contributed to the action taken, and I have no information from any other source. So you can readily understand that as far as headquarters is concerned we are completely in the dark except for information we secured through the medium of the press, which to say the least is not dependable.

I would like to suggest that you carefully read the press page in the May issue of our monthly journal, where I believe you will find information that should be of interest to those who are contemplating an affiliation with the C. I. O.

Fraternally yours,

A. O. WHARTON.
International President.

Mr. Matthews. What led you to make that inquiry of Mr. Wharton?

Mr. O'Shea. It was drawn to my attention by a chairman at the time that this question of C. I. O.-A. F. of L. was coming on the floor of the delegates' council meeting. I had no means, of course, of getting anything official without communicating with the national office, which I did, and this is the answer.

As you will note, he stated in his letter to me that he had communicated by special-delivery letter to the office of the Transport Union——

Mr. MATTHEWS. Now, is this a copy of that letter to which you refer?

Mr. O'SHEA. That is a copy of the letter which was sent from the national office of the machinists to Quill, Santo, MacMahon, and Forge, and the others.

Mr. MATTHEWS. Did this letter come to the attention of the union members?

Mr. O'SHEA. No. Not even to the Communist Party members on the executive board. It was absolutely kept out of the agenda and Hogan, who was the secretary at the time, made it his business to see it wasn't placed on the agenda.

What I am bringing out in this question is the importance of a position as secretary of concealing this document which undoubtedly would have clarified the whole situation on the C. I. O. versus A. F. of L. in this particular given situation.

Mr. MATTHEWS. In other words the secretary of the union, Austin Hogan, who was a member of the Communist Party, was suppressing correspondence that should have been brought to the attention of the entire membership of the union or its executive bodies, at least, to enable them to act with more information on this question of the withdrawal of the Transport Workers' Union from its A. F. of L. affiliation?

Mr. O'SHEA. Yes, sir.

Mr. MATTHEWS. And entering the C. I. O., is that correct?

Mr. O'SHEA. That is correct.

Mr. MATTHEWS. Now, these affidavits are in support of this question of the letter being suppressed, are they not?

Mr. O'SHEA. Yes. Well, I then made an investigation, as a matter of fact, it came to my attention by another man who presented one of his union books to me—as a matter of fact, I have the original here. This is the actual book of the member. In this book he presented to me, you will notice a signature where a stamp should be affixed. Well, this particular worker did not know the rules and regulations of the organization. In other words, he did not know his constitutional rights and he asked me was it in order. I said, "No, the constitution of the union specifically states that to be in good standing your book must be properly canceled and stamped with a stamp from the national office as a receipt for dues paid."

Mr. MATTHEWS. Now, will you please read that part of the constitution?

Mr. O'SHEA. Page 18 of the International Association of Machinists' constitution states here, page 18, lines 37 and 38:

The general secretary-treasurer shall furnish stamps as receipts.

Mr. MATTHEWS. In other words, he would not be allowed to merely sign the book without a stamp as a receipt for the payment of dues?

Mr. O'SHEA. Exactly.

Mr. MATTHEWS. Would that affect a man's death benefits in the union?

Mr. O'SHEA. Yes, sir. It is important for this reason.

Mr. MATTHEWS. In other words, if his book was not properly marked with a stamp——

Mr. O'SHEA. For 3 months he would lose all benefits. There was a death benefit for instance, maturing after 11 years of $300, and of his dues which he paid, a percentage of that was paid as per capita tax to put him in good standing. Now, what happened—I asked them from the national office of the Machinists when the last report was made on the financial question from the lodge. So I get an answer back from Washington, dated September 1, 1938:

Subject: Transport Workers Lodge 1547.

It is signed by H. W. Brown, general vice president.

The last report by the financial secretary of Lodge 1547 to the general secretary-treasurer's department was for January 1937, and said report indicated 4,714 members. Our former Lodge 1547, seceded to cast their lot with the C. I. O. during May of 1937, and at that time the said lodge had a debit balance with the grand lodge of $1,591.15.

Another point I want to bring out here is this. It was January 1937 when the last financial report was made. They seceded in May and became the C. I. O., which was 5 months later. In other words——

Mr. MATTHEWS. In a period of 5 months?

Mr. O'SHEA. No per capita tax was paid to the national office. All dues that were received from January until May was retained in the local office, and all those members who paid those dues were not in good standing. Now, then I went to some of the shop stewards and asked them what was the presentation given by the union on this question. One particular man was a shop steward. He collected the dues. And this is his affidavit. I will read it for you. It is rather short:

STATE OF NEW YORK,
    County of Bronx:
William J. Halloran, being duly sworn, deposes and says:
That since the 29th day of May 1929 he has been employed by the Interborough Rapid Transit Co. in the capacity of station agent.
That in January of 1937, up to and including May 1937, deponent was a member of the Transport Workers Lodge, No. 1547, International Association of Machinists, and was a duly authorized steward with authority to collect dues from the members and to pick up their union books as they paid their monthly dues. It was the procedure for deponent, as steward, to bring the union books, together with the dues of the various members, to union headquarters, where Michael Forge, as office manager, would insert in the books monthly stamps as receipts for dues paid.
That in March, April, and May of 1937, upon bringing the books of the members to union headquarters for the purpose of having dues receipt stamps inserted therein, deponent was informed by Michael Forge, as office manager for the Transport Workers Lodge, No. 1547, that there was a shortage of stamps in the national office of the International Association of Machinists and that, therefore, no stamp receipts could be placed in the books.
Accordingly, many of the men, for the months of March, April, and May of 1937, have membership books which are not properly stamped showing receipt by the Transport Workers Lodge, No. 1547, International Association of Machinists.

           WILLIAM JOSEPH HALLORAN.

Sworn to before me this 6th day of September 1938.
           DANIEL FLANNERY, *Notary Public.*

Mr. MATTHEWS. Now, let us get that picture perfectly clear. In other words here is a membership book which instead of having a stamp affixed as a receipt for the payment of dues, the square is initialed?

Mr. O'SHEA. Exactly.

Mr. MATTHEWS. Now, this means that the money was taken in but not forwarded to national headquarters in payment for a stamp?

Mr. O'SHEA. Exactly.

Mr. MATTHEWS. And the union gave to this man the explanation that there was a shortage of stamps?

Mr. O'SHEA. That is right.

Mr. MATTHEWS. Now, did the national headquarters agree there was a shortage of stamps?

Mr. O'SHEA. Well, in this communication which I previously read, under "financial report" I also asked this question: "Was there ever a shortage of stamps in the national office?" And following is the answer from the general vice president:

There never was a shortage of due stamps nor initiation and reinstatement stamps in our grand lodge headquarters.

Mr. MATTHEWS. In other words, there was a false explanation given to the members for not affixing a stamp and thereby depriving this member of the union of his death benefits?

Mr. O'SHEA. Exactly. I also have here affidavits from two men who were also employed in the industry of the transit field, but who were taken off the job at that particular time, to do work as temporary organizers, with the result that they had to go on the payroll of the union.

It so happened that at one particular time they were unable to draw their salaries and those affidavits will show exactly the situation as it was at that time. I will read one of them for you, and the other is simply more or less on the same style:

STATE OF NEW YORK,
County of Bronx,
Christopher Finn, being duly sworn, deposes and says:

That he is and has been since September 1929 employed by the Interborough Rapid Transit Co., in the capacity of station agent.

That on or about the 5th day of May 1937 he was vice president, Section 2, Transport Workers Lodge 1547 of the International Association of Machinists, affiliated with the American Federation of Labor, and was working as an organizer for the union.

That on or about that date, he accompanied John Cronin, another organizer to the offices of the Union, 153 West Sixty-fourth Street, New York City, for the purpose of drawing his pay as an organizer.

That he was present, and was informed along with John Cronin by Michael Forge, office manager for the union, that pay checks would be held up for 2 or 3 days due to the fact that funds of the union were being transferred to another bank account.

I was further informed by Michael Forge that the purpose of the withdrawal and the opening of the new account was to retain possession of some $25,000 which had been collected as the per capita tax of the International Association of Machinists, and that by putting it in another account the International Association of Machinists would not be able to claim it.

This is signed by Christopher Finn and sworn to "before me this 6th day of September, 1938, Daniel Flannery, notary public."

Mr. MATTHEWS. In other words, here was the sum of $25,000 which has been improperly kept back from national headquarters on payments of dues; is that the situation?

Mr. O'SHEA. That is exactly the situation.

Mr. MATTHEWS. And do you have any information as to why such funds are kept back by members of the Communist Party who hold positions of secretary-treasurer?

Mr. O'SHEA. Well, it is natural to expect that the party controlling the machine were going to utilize as much of funds as possible for propaganda work, for the purpose, in other words, to swell the general fund of their organization in any way that they could get a hold of money.

Mr. MATTHEWS. Do you know of any other organizations where the party has made it a principle to control the positions of secretary and treasurer?

Mr. O'SHEA. Yes. A similar situation developed, from what I understand, from investigations I made, with the Lodges 1548, 1549, and 1550 of the machinists at that time, which are now the International Radio, Electrical & Machine Workers of America, C. I. O. affiliate, of which James Matles is director and Carey is president. James Matles, of course, was also in this swim for the reason, you will note on the agreement signed between the Transport Workers' Union and the Machinists, that Maties sat in at a conference and his name appears and he also did the very same thing with those lodges. He grabbed all the per capita tax he could lay his hands on when the time, the psychological moment, arrived, and then shot them into the C. I. O.

Mr. MATTHEWS. The union funds, then, were misappropriated for party purposes?

Mr. O'SHEA. Yes; they actually committed fraud. They did not record the death benefits of the members.

Mr. MATTHEWS. Now, will you please explain, Mr. O'Shea, if that is the conclusion of that matter, how it was that the affiliation with the International Association of Machinists was planned some 6 months in advance, or the withdrawal from the affiliation was planned some 6 months in advance?

Mr. O'SHEA. Well, it was a political situation affecting the Communist Party as a whole. It so happened that the Communist International in 1935 laid down a definite policy for the American section of the Communist International. And it was a simple program of, No. 1, organizing the unorganized; No. 2, united front against fascism; No. 3, the Farmer-Labor Party. Now, in the situation we find when we went into the A. F. of L. we were carrying out the united-front policy and that was going inside of the A. F. of L. Now, No. 2 came along and that was organizing the unorganized. We already had completed a part of the program of the united front, but then the situation developed toward the United States. The C. I. O. became a mass movement. It began to sweep through industry, and the party was faced with the situation that for the moment they had to drop the united-front policy and secede from the A. F. of L. to organize the unorganized.

You see, with the purpose, of course, in mind of again returning to the A. F. of L. to fulfill the part of the program, the united-front policy by going back and taking over the labor movement, which, of course, records show and prove that members of the C. I. O., which incidentally the International president, Quill, was one of the delegates who appeared at Washington to negotiate with the American Federation of Labor on this question. You recall, of course, where these negotiations broke down. Well, that was the purpose at the time with the fulfilling the decision as laid down by the Seventh World Congress of the Communist International.

Mr. MATTHEWS. Do you mean to say the policies of the Transport Workers Union touching affiliations were determined not by the union but by the determining policy made in Moscow?

Mr. O'SHEA. Absolutely; Seventh World Congress.

Mr. MATTHEWS. You are sure of that?

Mr. O'SHEA. Absolutely. The policy of the Seventh World Congress——

Mr. MATTHEWS. Is it now the policy of the Communist International to bring about a reunion?

Mr. O'SHEA. Yes, sir. It is still the united-front policy as it exists—still the same. They have got to get back to the A. F. of L. How they are going to do it is a question. They also have to organize the unorganized, which is another part of the program. Now, the question of the united front as it appears in America, they are dealing not alone with the C. I. O. and the A. F. of L., but you have the four standard railroads—nearly 1,000,000 workers—and anybody reading the public press knows that a conference took place or, not a conference, but suggestions were made some time ago that the C. I. O.-A. F. of L. standard railroads should come together. It was intimated at the time that William Green and the secretary should resign and apparently John L. Lewis had agreed to leave the picture and that some other party should act as president to sort of solve this question.

Mr. MATTHEWS. Now, in the discussions that took place——

The CHAIRMAN. Just a moment. There was an effort made to unite the labor groups, but that doesn't mean that the effort was inspired by the Communist International. There are many people in this country who believe that ought to be done?

Mr. O'SHEA. That is true.

The CHAIRMAN. Who certainly are not in sympathy with the Communist program. I mean by that, the fact that that was suggested or the fact that that has been advocated by people in the United States does not even remotely leave the impression that it was inspired from abroad or by the Communist Party. Isn't that a fact?

Mr. O'SHEA. That is true.

The CHAIRMAN. What you mean to say is that that is the program of the Communist Party?

Mr. O'SHEA. Exactly.

The CHAIRMAN. And also the views of a great many people who are not Communists in any sense?

Mr. O'SHEA. Progressive people naturally believe you should have one labor body in the country, but the policy of the party is to see that those unions become one group; then they will have solved the united front policy in the trade-union field.

The CHAIRMAN. To what extent did the Communists leave or carry with them their unions and go to the C. I. O.? Did the majority of them leave?

Mr. O'SHEA. Well, I will tell you. Not in all cases—where it wasn't necessary—where they hadn't a question of organizing the unorganized, like, let us take for instance, the Musicians' Union in New York, Local 802. That is an A. F. of L. union. Communists control them. They didn't leave the A. F. of L. at the time. Why? Simply that New York was already organized in that field and it would not have been of any advantage to the party to come out and organize the unorganized and try to get back again. You see what I mean.

Now, secondly, in the Transport Union situation there was another question involved. The Transport Workers' Union at that time was only a lodge and confined to the New York district and as such could not branch out into other fields to organize the unorganized. To do so it was necessary to break from the A. F. of L., get into national status which gave them the right to go into Canada and the United States, and build up a mass movement; develop new cadres. That is all proof of their revolutionary tactics. Get into the American Federation of Labor with stronger forces and eventually destroy the leadership and take it over.

Mr. MATTHEWS. Now, Mr. O'Shea, would it be a correct statement of this policy to say that the Communist Party effects very rapidly reversals of its policy from one position to another?

Mr. O'SHEA. Oh, it is true. There is no question they will if it serves their purpose—any means justifies the end.

Mr. MATTHEWS. In other words, favoring at one moment and going into the A. F. of L., and very soon getting out of the A. F. of L., and then getting back into the A. F. of L.?

Mr. O'SHEA. Yes.

Mr. MATTHEWS. That is what you are saying?

Mr. O'SHEA. Yes, sir.

Mr. MATTHEWS. Not because the Communist Party desires a unified labor movement?

Mr. O'SHEA. No.

Mr. MATTHEWS. But because its interests at one moment, as it sees them, are served by going into one union and then getting out of it and next getting back into it; is that correct?

Mr. O'SHEA. That is correct.

Mr. MATTHEWS. Is it true that Quill and Hogan and Santo knew and planned 5 months in advance for taking the Transport Workers Union out of the A. F. of L. into the C. I. O.?

Mr. O'SHEA. No question about it.

The CHAIRMAN. That is merely a conclusion on your part. You are basing it upon the fact that the circumstances you have outlined indicate that?

Mr. O'SHEA. Yes.

The CHAIRMAN. Namely, that they had withheld payment of the per capita tax to the national office?

Mr. O'SHEA. Yes.

The CHAIRMAN. Is that the only information you have on which to base your statement?

Mr. O'SHEA. Well, I know myself the policy as laid down by the party from experience within the party.

The CHAIRMAN. You know it was the policy of the party that all Communists were to go into the C. I. O.?

Mr. O'SHEA. They were to organize the unorganized. I knew that they were also to create a united front wherever the situation warranted, and I knew that from the Communist point of view that it was correct, as far as they were concerned, of organizing the unorganized.

The CHAIRMAN. So that from your knowledge of the Communist policy and the fact that these funds were withheld——

Mr. O'SHEA. Yes, sir.

The CHAIRMAN. You base the statement that Quill and the others knew about this movement 5 months in advance and made preparations for withdrawal from the A. F. of L.?

Mr. O'SHEA. Well, as a matter of fact when we were going in the A. F. of L. the same ground that was prepared. Our bulletin had to show a different front because the policy at that time was, when we were an independent organization, was to attack the A. F. of L. Well, the bulletin—while you couldn't automatically change over night, it took months. You had to put in different articles about the A. F. of L.—maybe dealing with Frisco—about the organization, but when the time was ripe the men were already prepared to go in.

The CHAIRMAN. It took 4 or 5 months to make a sudden change in policy?

Mr. O'SHEA. Yes, sir; it took time.

The CHAIRMAN. And the ground work had to be laid?

Mr. O'SHEA. Yes. And the proper foundation laid and in going out the same thing had to be done.

Mr. MATTHEWS. Now, Mr. O'Shea, do you know a man named Sol Miles?

Mr. O'SHEA. Yes. Sol Miles was—I understand that he is—connected with the newspaper guild. He came to the Transport Union around about that time—about the time of the split, and he handled the publicity end of the union question. All press releases had to pass through his hands. He examined all press releases and saw that they were carrying the party line and the correct presentation was made to the press. He was on the rolls for a short time. I don't think he is at the present time in the organization. He only came in for some months to do that particular job of handling the publicity end for the party, being, of course, an experienced man in the newspaper field.

Mr. MATTHEWS. Was he a member of the Communist Party?

Mr. O'SHEA. Oh, yes; sure; a member of the Communist Party.

Mr. MATTHEWS. And he handled the publicity for the Transport Workers' Union in this question of shifting to the C. I. O.?

Mr. O'SHEA. Yes, sir. And arranging press releases.

The CHAIRMAN. Now, let me get back a little bit. From your experience in this union and your membership and experience in the Communist Party would you say that the policies of the union were directed by the Communist Party?

Mr. O'SHEA. Absolutely, from its very inception.

The CHAIRMAN. That the policy was determined in advance by Communist leadership and that policy was outlined to the leadership of the union and by the union carried out in the Transport Union?

Mr. O'SHEA. Exactly.

The CHAIRMAN. Is that right?

Mr. O'SHEA. That is right.

The CHAIRMAN. The Transport Workers' Union?

Mr. O'SHEA. Yes.

The CHAIRMAN. What other policies were outlined in addition to purely union matters?

Mr. O'SHEA. Well, the general policy, as I say, the Comintern organized the unorganized, the united front, and Farmer-Labor Party.

The CHAIRMAN. I am speaking with reference to the political field. Were there any instructions as to what was to be done with reference to local political fights or national political fights? Did they undertake to control the union for political purposes?

Mr. O'SHEA. Oh, of course they did. There was a definite line laid down for the party members to follow even with national questions in America.

The CHAIRMAN. Do you know of instances involving the leadership or the fraction that you belonged to?

Mr. O'SHEA. Well, I recall the national elections in the United States for the first time, I think, of President Roosevelt. This question came up and it was a burning question on the floor. The Communist Party went around to their sections and instructed them how they should act on this political question.

The CHAIRMAN. Did they do that with reference to the State elections, also, and local elections?

Mr. O'SHEA. Oh, yes. State and local elections, the same situation.

The CHAIRMAN. What about their own candidates? Were they concerned about building up any strength for the Communist candidates?

Mr. O'SHEA. Well, I will just give you an example. For instance, in New York City I was transferred from one unit to another—the transportation unit to section 5 of the Communist Party in the Bronx, and I was on the bureau of that section and the question came up of what stand the Communist Party would take on the national election—the question of President Roosevelt and Landon. So the position of the party now as Communists, we cannot vote for Landon. We must vote Communist, so the membership—well, if you do that you are voting—supporting Roosevelt. No, we are voting Communist, but you don't vote for Landon. That was the position of the party at the time. In other words—but they knew themselves what reaction of the membership would be. They couldn't get the masses of the people to vote for the purpose, but they didn't want Landon under any circumstances. So that was the party's position.

The CHAIRMAN. What other questions did they try to control outside of political questions?

Mr. MASON. On the political question I would like to ask a question. Did I understand Michael Quill was a candidate for the council in New York City?

Mr. O'SHEA. That is true. He had the office for 2 years.

Mr. MASON. He ran for the council in what year?

Mr. O'SHEA. 1935, I think it was; 1935 to 1937. Just last year he was defeated.

Mr. MASON. Do you know what action the Communist Party took in New York in regard to his candidacy?

Mr. O'SHEA. Well, as far as that was concerned—Quill, the ground work was prepared for Quill almost 2 years in advance.

Mr. MASON. But was the Communist Party active in advocating his candidacy?

Mr. O'SHEA. It was the Communist Party actually elected him. The Communist Party machine within the trade-union movement and the labor political field that were instrumental in actually putting Quill over.

Mr. MASON. It was also true of the Transport Union, wasn't it?

Mr. O'SHEA. Oh, yes. That is a Communist-controlled union.

The CHAIRMAN. Now, to what extent is a member of the party subject to party discipline—you yourself testified that you were appointed by representatives of the Communist Party when you became president of this union?

Mr. O'SHEA. Yes.

The CHAIRMAN. And that you relinquished that position upon instructions from the same authority. Does that degree of discipline obtain with reference to all members of the party?

Mr. O'SHEA. With the exception, of course, of new members. They are a little elastic as far as the rules are concerned. They consider they are not sufficiently developed, and they will allow a certain amount of give and take, but for those who are considered a year or 2 in the party, after they have been stewed in discipline and brought up in discipline, they are considered to be politically developed.

The CHAIRMAN. Then they have to follow the instructions of the party?

Mr. O'SHEA. Strictly.

The CHAIRMAN. Let us assume that the party wanted information with reference to a certain industry. Here is a member of the party working in a particular industry and the party wanted to obtain information with reference to that industry. Would it be the duty of the member of the party to give that information?

Mr. O'SHEA. Sure. Otherwise he would be due for expulsion if he refuses to get the information. He would be expelled from the party.

The CHAIRMAN. And if the Communist Party wanted the information to transmit it to a foreign power, then the members of the party would be acting as spies for the foreign power, would they not?

Mr. O'SHEA. Sure; absolutely—absolutely.

The CHAIRMAN. On the question of sabotage, if the party's instructions were to commit acts of sabotage to stop the shipment of any vital munitions of war material or anything of that sort, would it be the duties of the members of the party to carry out those instructions?

Mr. O'SHEA. All instructions of the party must be religiously followed at all times. Failure to do so means expulsion.

The CHAIRMAN. Do you know instances where they were expelled for failure to follow the party's instructions?

Mr. O'SHEA. Yes. There were numerous cases of members who didn't follow the party's position.

The CHAIRMAN. Now, is sabotage a definite part of the Communist program?

Mr. O'SHEA. Yes; absolutely.

The CHAIRMAN. In order if it becomes necessary to commit acts of sabotage to accomplish some policy of the party, then it is the duty of the members to commit the acts of sabotage; is that correct?

Mr. O'SHEA. Yes. As a matter of fact I can cite you an actual instance that occurred in the city of New York. The present treasurer of the New York local, which is approximately 35,000 strong, he is a responsible officer. During the threat of a partial strike in

1935 he was arrested for slashing tires of a taxicab on the street. He was tried at special sessions before three judges and convicted. He was an officer, one of the principal officers, of the New York local— the treasurer. I understand that he got approximately 60 days. It so happened, too, at that particular trial that the assistant district attorney questioned him—Mr. Faber, "Was he in the Communist Party?" and he admitted that he was a member of the Reichstag at one time before coming to the United States. And that is another public record. That can be gotten from the court files in the special sessions in New York City.

Mr. Mason. Is he a member of the Communist Party?

Mr. O'Shea. Absolutely, yes; a member of the Communist Party. I sat in Communist Party meetings with him.

The Chairman. Now, during the time that you were a member of the party were you fairly active?

Mr. O'Shea. Well, I happened to get fired twice in the I. R. T. and blackjacked once, so I think I did my share in the field. I was 2½ years off the job for union activities—and—

The Chairman. Did you meet with many Communist groups in New York?

Mr. O'Shea. Well, yes.

The Chairman. Did you have a fairly good idea of the type of people who were in the Communist Party?

Mr. O'Shea. Yes. You see you would naturally contact all the different groups. That is the furriers and the garment workers and laundry workers and at conventions and all different things from time to time.

The Chairman. Did you have many Irish in the Communist movement in New York?

Mr. O'Shea. Well, it is growing. They have got them in the Maritime Union, as a matter of fact, in the water front, and they have got some Irish fellows organizing.

The Chairman. What is the appeal that is made to the Irish people?

Mr. O'Shea. Well, that was a problem they were faced with. They were faced with a very serious problem dealing with the Irish. As you know they are nationalistic and extremely religious, and it was a question of how could they win those people over to their side. So the Communist Party decided, which appears in their official papers, that they should utilize the Irish revolutionary traditions. Of course everybody knows that for 600 years Ireland has been struggling for independence. A revolutionary situation always developed from century to century and the Irish race has a spirit of freedom. They felt at the time it would be easy to divert a national feeling to an international channel, and it was then plans were laid to utilize the Irish revolutionary traditions, and that all the literature possible, Daily Worker, official organ of the Transport Union, should carry as much material that would have an international complexion; that they had to be careful, too, on the national point.

I have some material here which will show that they are utilizing the one particular man—individual who happened to be in this country, at one time—he went back in 1913. His name is James Connolly. As a matter of fact—as a matter of record—he established the Transport Workers Union of Ireland and he was one of the leaders in the rebellion in 1916 with De Valera; and for his part in the rebellion, he was executed.

Now, Connolly, of course, has an international outlook besides his nationalistic outlook. Now, De Valera's position was different to Connolly's, he was purely a nationalist. Now, you notice here when they present this Irish stuff they deal specifically with Connolly—nothing else, nobody else—no other leader.

I show you in the Transport Workers bulletin of May 1938, we find a caption: "James Connolly, He Gave His Life in the Struggle for Economic and National Freedom." It shows his picture there; deals with the whole thing. And the Daily Worker of May 14, 1939, we find again James Connolly: "Irish Urged to Follow Connolly's Lead in Fight Against Anti-Semitism."

The CHAIRMAN. Was that one of their main appeals, to fight anti-Semitism?

Mr. O'SHEA. Well, they were appealing in this instance to the Irish to pull them closer to themselves. They were going to use any issue, anti-Semitism, the negro question—any question as a matter of fact. The anti-Semitic question—it wasn't that they were interested in the Jewish race but to use that issue to bring the Irish closer to themselves.

Now, again in the Party Organizer issued by the central committee of the Communist Party, April 1938, the Daily Worker—this is an actual letter written to the Daily Worker which is incorporated in the Party Builder. It will just show in this particular incident of how the Irish revolutionary traditions were used to recruit this man in the Communist Party. This is his letter:

In transportation we have a difficult task. Ninety percent of the workers are Irish. However in 1934 we had four members in the industry, and now we have a unit in every shop in transportation. The biggest problem in transportation is "red baiting." There is the Catholic Church which sends its priests into the precincts to help in the "red baiting," and at the present time they are forming every type of organization—the Holy Name, the Knights of Columbus, et cetera.

Communists have been in the front ranks in building the transportation union. But the most serious shortcoming is that there are not yet enough Communists among the transportation workers to fight this "red baiting" the way it's got to be fought.

I myself recruited 20 members. I think the Daily Worker gave me the first break, especially the Sunday Worker. I gave them out to some of the men, and after a while I was asked why I did not bring them the Daily Worker and Sunday Worker regularly. I did so, and I also got pamphlets to them, especially the one by our great revolutionary Irishman, James Connolly.

I have no more to say. I am not a speaker. The only thing I can do is carry on the truth.

And in this instance you see the effect of Connolly's propaganda used in that particular shop for this man. Now, again every effort is made to involve the Irish revolutionary situation. As a matter of fact a picture was made in Ireland showing the Black and Tans and the Irish fighting during that struggle before the Free State was established, and it was shown in the Transport Workers Union headquarters. And this is the heading: "Dawn Over Ireland." Now, the purpose of that was to bring as many Irish into the hall, even people not mixed up in the Transport Union, but to get them into the influence of the party.

The CHAIRMAN. In other words, whatever appeal is most effective to recruit members they use it regardless of the race. I mean, if a man happens to be in a particular race and there is a certain appeal that is most effective with him, they use that appeal, is that correct?

Mr. O'SHEA. Yes; but of course they apply a revolutionary line if possible.

Now, here is another excerpt of a mass meeting of I. R. A. clubs of greater New York: "To support the Irish Republican Army in their fight for Irish freedom. The principal speaker will be General Sean Russell, Chief of Staff, I. R. A., Thursday, June 15th, at the T. W. U. Hall at 153 West 64th Street." Now, the hall was given free without consulting the membership, whether it should be given or not. Sean Russell—the idea was that they know that the Clan-Na-Gael and the I. R. A. clubs are an organization in this country which are purely Irish national movements, and they are trying to work in amongst the membership to get them into the party.

Many of them have military training already, and can be useful for the revolution.

The CHAIRMAN. Now, did you come in contact with the communist effort in the maritime industry in New York while you were active in the Transport Workers Union? Did you come in contact with the same movement in the maritime industry?

Mr. O'SHEA. Yes; I recall having a long conversation with Roy Hudson at the time we had the meeting in Amter's home. After the session was over the question came up and he discussed the Maritime Union and the position on the west coast, and, in fact, he went into details where he himself had to be taken to Russia to be convinced of the communist set-up.

The CHAIRMAN. Had to be taken to Russia?

Mr. O'SHEA. Taken to Russia before he could accept the Communist line in the early days. In other words, he was trying to convince the men that, if certain things developed in the Communist Party, "we will forget them for the time being, everything comes all right." Of course, they were trying to settle the battle that was on at the time—this faction fight. He discussed, of course, the organization—the strength of the organization and how well they were entrenched and the importance, of course, of having collaboration between the forces.

In other words, transport and maritime. I recall Rose Wortis made a statement at a meeting which I attended—it would be around 1935 when we were attending. We were independent at the time. We were attending the Trade Union Unity Council meeting and we made a report on organization.

The CHAIRMAN. Who is that?

Mr. O'SHEA. We made a report to the Communist Party——

The CHAIRMAN. Roy Hudson did?

Mr. O'SHEA. We did, giving our stand in the trade-union field—that is the transport field. So Rose Wortis asked for a report of the shops, barns, and transportation position and how we were for a strike. She went on to explain a contract was coming up for the Maritime Union and the way it was possible to synchronize the two—it would be a good job. In other words, the transport situation strike and maritime strike pulled at the same time would probably have created, as they believed, a situation that happened on the west coast—paralyze the whole eastern seaboard—involve as many as possible other groups.

The CHAIRMAN. What meeting was it in which Roy Hudson described the control that the Communist Party was exercising over the maritime union?

Mr. O'SHEA. That was at Amter's home at the time we had this battle—the battle was on.

The CHAIRMAN. At Amter's home?

Mr. O'SHEA. Yes.

The CHAIRMAN. Israel Amter's home?

Mr. O'SHEA. Yes, sir; William Dunn was at the meeting and all the leading members of the committee of the Communist Party.

The CHAIRMAN. Well, did you have any other contacts that gave you information as to the progress of communistic control over the Maritime Union?

Mr. O'SHEA. Well, from time to time I happened to run across some of the fraction members or the active members in the concentration unit on the waterfront and they naturally would give you reports of how things were going in the shipping line, but of course at that time, as I say, my whole mind was more or less centered on the transit situation. We had a 24-hour job there.

The CHAIRMAN. But from the reports that you heard from faction members who were working on the waterfront and from Roy Hudson's report, what picture did you get of the progress of the Communists in the maritime union?

Mr. O'SHEA. That they were strong, and exceptionally strong, and it would be only a question of time when it was in the transport and utilities—in the maritime, that a general strike could be brought about very simply and, of course, a foundation for a complete change in the Government. In other words, a revolutionary situation could be developed from a strike.

The CHAIRMAN. What contact did you have with any of the officials in the Radio, Electrical, and Machine Workers Union?

Mr. O'SHEA. Well, Matles, as I say, attended all the meetings. He is the director. He is the Edgar Bergen, in other words, of the Radio and Electrical Workers.

The CHAIRMAN. What position does he occupy?

Mr. O'SHEA. Director.

The CHAIRMAN. And you attended fraction meetings of the Communist Party with him?

Mr. O'SHEA. Oh, yes.

The CHAIRMAN. When he was present?

Mr. O'SHEA. When he was—prior to the time he went to the machinists—the time when he was in the machinists and later.

The CHAIRMAN. Did he discuss at these meetings the progress that the Communists were making in the Radio and Electrical Union?

Mr. O'SHEA. Yes; it was an understood thing. As a matter of fact the principal officer of his group, for instance, in New York City, the director in New York City is a man by the name of Lustig. Now, Lustig was at one time organizer in the Bronx, one of the biggest sections, 1,500 Communists, prior to going in and becoming a functionary in the trade-union field.

Mr. MATTHEWS. You mean section organizer for the Communist Party?

Mr. O'SHEA. Section organizer for the Communist Party. And he had the official position—I think you will find that in the public records—and he is now regional director of New York. And there was another man, James Matles, and Lustig, and Rivers. Now, Rivers is in the machinists today, had control of Brooklyn. His office was around Borough Hall and he handled all of the groups in that territory—all the machine shops.

The CHAIRMAN. Was he a member of the Communist Party?

Mr. O'SHEA. Oh, yes; they are very important members. They are members of the district committee in New York.

The CHAIRMAN. What did you learn with reference to your conversations, with these men, the leaders in the Radio and Electrical Union, with reference to Communist control of that union?

Mr. O'SHEA. Well, it was always understood that they were really more left than we were. In other words, they had better party organization within the ranks—better developed elements.

The CHAIRMAN. What did the party derive from the control of that union?

Mr. O'SHEA. Well, you see they are already working in the machine shops, you see, and the machine industry is connected with steel. Well, if you tie up and paralyze the machinist end of the thing, steel is useless because the rough product has to be machined before it is manufactured.

The CHAIRMAN. What other unions, while you were active in the Transport Workers Union, did they control?

Mr. O'SHEA. They controlled the laundry workers union. There were so many of them. Their actual control, where the functionaries were completely Communist, is that what you mean?

The CHAIRMAN. Where they had positions of leadership similar to the Transport Workers Union that you learned from contact with the leaders in fraction meetings. Take the furriers union.

Mr. O'SHEA. Oh, yes; the furriers.

The CHAIRMAN. Is that controlled by the Communists?

Mr. O'SHEA. Well, it was understood to be controlled. Irving Potash was considered the leader of the furriers union and Ben Gold.

The CHAIRMAN. Both of them members of the Communist Party?

Mr. O'SHEA. Yes; sure.

The CHAIRMAN. Did you sit in fraction meetings with them?

Mr. O'SHEA. Yes, sir; I was with Irving Potash in many fraction meetings, and James Matles, as I previously testified. They came in an advisory capacity in all fraction meetings when we were going in the American Federation of Labor.

The CHAIRMAN. What about the Communication Association? Do you know any of the leaders?

Mr. O'SHEA. I don't know anything about them personally. I knew there was a link-up. The only unions I had personal contact with was the furriers through those meetings. You see what I mean, the radio and metal workers, because we had personal contact, and the utility workers—that is, the utilities in New York—Edison.

The CHAIRMAN. What leaders did they have in the utilities?

Mr. O'SHEA. Well, they had a fraction but the fraction at the time wasn't very strong. I recall in either 1934 or 1935, there was a strike threat called there, and a number of men were fired. The men called a strike but they didn't put it into effect and we were requested by the Communist Party groups, Santo and Hogan and I, to meet those leaders at the headquarters and advise them to stall on the strike—not to force the issue until such time as they had stronger membership.

The CHAIRMAN. Now, when you were active in the Communist Party, did you keep records of the members of the party?

Mr. O'SHEA. No; I didn't keep any records.

The CHAIRMAN. Do you know of any records being kept?

Mr. O'SHEA. The records are always kept, you see, by the district or by the sections. The instructions of the party is: Shop units are attached to sections, and section headquarters keep the records, and the section organizer keeps the records of all the units. The unit organizer don't keep any records. When he is getting his stamps he goes to his headquarters and he gets the stamps and brings them up to his unit meetings, which are held once a week. After the unit meeting is over he takes the books and gets them stamped and returns the stuff back to the headquarters.

The CHAIRMAN. Well, the party does keep detailed records?

Mr. O'SHEA. Oh, undoubtedly.

The CHAIRMAN. Of their financial condition and membership?

Mr. O'SHEA. They have to, because they have got to keep a record all the time. They wouldn't know exactly where they stood.

The CHAIRMAN. When you ceased to be active in the Communist Party, what was its membership in New York State? Did you get any idea of that?

Mr. O'SHEA. I wouldn't have any idea. I could not guess any figure on that.

The CHAIRMAN. What was the largest meeting you attended—strictly Communist meeting?

Mr. O'SHEA. Well, the largest meeting that I attended was the convention in 1936 held at St. Nicholas Arena. That was the district convention, and the convention—I would safely say there was approximately 600 delegates. That was four delegates from each section and 600 delegates and it all depended on the strength of a section. Some sections had 1,500 members and some had 200 and some had 300.

Mr. MATTHEWS. Were you a delegate?

Mr. O'SHEA. Yes, sir, I was one of the bureau members from section 5 in the Bronx.

Mr. MATTHEWS. Who addressed that convention you just mentioned?

Mr. O'SHEA. Well, Earl Browder addressed it. Rose Wortis, of course. I was more or less interested in her report, because she gave the trade union report. Quill reported a line on the transit situation, and there was a farmer—he happened to be the only man at the convention who was from the agricultural field.

Mr. MATTHEWS. Was Quill introduced openly?

Mr. O'SHEA. Yes, sir; openly introduced at the convention, yes. He spoke on the transit situation. As a matter of fact, I recall a statement he made: "That the Transport Union was to be the steam hammer for the transit industry, and as a steam hammer it would crush a mosquito and so would the Transport Union crush the barons of Wall Street when the time arrived." That was actually his quotation.

The CHAIRMAN. Do you know what the policy of the party has been since the alliance between Stalin and Hitler? Are you in a position to testify to that?

Mr. O'SHEA. Well, yes. You see, any means in Communist philosophy—any means justifies the end. It wasn't surprising to those in the Communist Party to expect a Stalin-Hitler pact because a similar situation developed in Russia in 1917 when Lenin collaborated with Germany—German imperialism. It was the Germans who really brought Lenin from Switzerland to Russia on a special armored train and put him in to form the revolution so as to withdraw their forces and send them to France in the big push of 1918. That situation was similar to what happened in Finland.

The CHAIRMAN. Well, do you know of your own knowledge or have you gained it through reliable information, and if so, what is the information, as to what policy the party is following since the alliance between Russia and Germany?

Mr. O'SHEA. Well, of course, it is hard to say. As I previously stated, any means justifies the end. Stalin and Hitler—I wouldn't be surprised to see if Stalin tomorrow turned on Hitler. As a matter of fact, I think there is something in the wind to that effect. Instructions have been issued to the various sections of the Communist International that a new phase must be put on the international situation owing to the Swedish position, that they must now go on record as being opposed to Germany pushing into Sweden. From my own observation it looks like they are afraid Germany is getting too strong and they eventually may come out on top and turn on Stalin.

The CHAIRMAN. Then if Stalin and Hitler break we can except the Communists to go back to its position of fighting fascism?

Mr. O'SHEA. That is exactly it. Reverting back to its original position.

Mr. MATTHEWS. At the convention at St. Nicholas Arena in 1936, was there a speaker named Archie Wright?

Mr. O'SHEA. Yes, sir; the farmer. He was the only man. They were always accustomed to needle workers and garment trades and all of that element——

Mr. MATTHEWS. Did he report on the organization of the Communist Party among the farmers in the State of New York?

Mr. O'SHEA. Yes, sir. He made a report with reference to the united-front policy as applied to the farmers of up-State New York and he stated that he was able to utilize a church and minister of religion to present the party's lines. In other words, take up economic questions and discuss them from a revolutionary angle.

Mr. MATTHEWS. Was this the Archie Wright who recently lead the milk strike in New York State?

Mr. O'SHEA. Yes, sir. I have seen his picture in the public press.

Mr. MATTHEWS. Can you identify this as a picture of Archie Wright. [Handing paper to the witness.]

Mr. O'SHEA. The same man.

Mr. MATTHEWS. Farmer delegate to the party convention?

Mr. O'SHEA. Farmer delegate to the party convention in 1936.

Mr. MATTHEWS. This is from the New York Post, Monday, August 21, 1939. Now, on the question of the exploitation of the Irish tradition among Irish workers in the Transport Workers Union, of the transit field, Mr. O'Shea, does Michael Quill himself try to make a great deal of his Irish revolutionary background?

Mr. O'SHEA. Well, the Communist Party propaganda machine certainly does. They realize, of course, as they state in their official papers, particularly, "We must now utilize the Irish revolutionary traditions," and they show, as a matter of fact, in the press—I think we find it in the Post and the Daily Worker and lots of other papers.

Mr. MATTHEWS. I show you for example an article from the New York World Telegram, June 5, 1937. Are they photographs of Michael Quill? [Handing paper to the witness.]

Mr. O'SHEA. Yes, sir; photographs of Michael Quill.

Mr. MATTHEWS. And is this a publicity story on Michael Quill which connects him with the fight for Irish freedom?

Mr. O'SHEA. Yes, sir; that is right.

Mr. MATTHEWS. Do you know whether or not the Communist Party has stated, or that Quill has stated, either one of them, that he was wounded in the Black and Tan Army in Ireland?

Mr. O'SHEA. Yes.

Mr. MATTHEWS. Is that a claim which Quill makes?

Mr. O'SHEA. It is right here in the paper. "He still limps and carries a cane from a Free State bullet in the left hip."

Mr. MATTHEWS. When was the fighting in Ireland?

Mr. O'SHEA. The fighting in Ireland originally started at least in 1916, the rebellion, and continued through in a small way until July 1921 when a truce was called and 9 months later a treaty was signed which established the Irish Free State. That was what was known as the Black and Tan period, July 1921.

Mr. MATTHEWS. In other words, the end of the Black and Tan period was in 1921?

Mr. O'SHEA. Yes, sir.

Mr. MATTHEWS. Do you know how old Michael Quill is?

Mr. O'SHEA. I understand he is around 32, 33, or 34.

Mr. MATTHEWS. Now, I show you a photostatic copy of his passport application, the passport application of Michael Quill, in which he gives as his birthdate September 18, 1905. That would have made Quill 16 years of age, would it not?

Mr. O'SHEA. Sixteen years of age, that is right.

Mr. MATTHEWS. Do you know whether or not in press publicity statements Quill now pretends to be 4 or 5 or 6 years older?

Mr. O'SHEA. Yes, sir.

Mr. MATTHEWS. Than this?

Mr. O'SHEA. Yes. In the public press I have noticed that they have made it particularly clear that they would put his age—advance it so it would link up with that period.

Mr. MATTHEWS. You were in the Black and Tan Army yourself?

Mr. O'SHEA. Yes, sir. I served through practically the whole movement from 1917 to 1924.

Mr. MATTHEWS. You didn't meet Quill in the ranks?

Mr. O'SHEA. No; I never met Quill.

Mr. MATTHEWS. In Ireland?

Mr. O'SHEA. No; I never met Quill. As a matter of fact the I. R. A. at that particular time, in 1918, it became the I. R. A. Previously it was the Irish Volunteers, but in 1918 they formed the Irish Republican Army of the groups of Irish Volunteers and at that time they established a constitution and held conventions every 2 years; and written into the constitution was that to become a member of the Irish Republican Army it was necessary to be at least 18 years of age—wouldn't be accepted otherwise.

Mr. MATTHEWS. Do you happen to know of your own knowledge whether Quill was injured in the rebellion?

Mr. O'SHEA. Naturally, when the union started originally I made a question "where he came from and who he was," and we discussed the Irish situation and I asked him at one time—his picture appeared in the bulletin. It was after the *Cole case* in New York, and he brought his passport in to show his picture—what he looked like— the changes that took place, and I glanced at his passport and I saw his age at the time and I said, "Mike, you were not connected with the movement; you couldn't possibly have been." And he said, "No; I wasn't." So I said, "What happened to your hip?" "Well," he said, "that was from infancy I have that." And he said, "I have just come back from Vienna. I was with Lorenz, the bloodless surgeon." It was a hip dislocation and he went to Vienna to have it put back in position. Well, of course, the party, as I say, is using Quill as a Charlie McCarthy—playing him up.

The CHAIRMAN. You have testified about the leaders. What about the rank and file in the Transport Workers Union? What percentage of the rank and file are members of the Communist Party?

Mr. O'SHEA. Well, I would safely say that the Communist structure—you see it is not like a bona fide union. New York, for instance, has a local of 37,000 or 40,000 members. One local is subdivided into 150 sections. Now, those sections, the most of the section chairmen, and the section secretaries are party members. You see, the most of the executives which come from this section group are, I would say, two-thirds party members and the executive board of the local is 90 percent. The international board is all 100 percent party controlled.

The party does not believe, of course, in big figures. They feel that if they can hold the key positions and with a number of men on the floor, a small organization of active men are much more effective than a big group that is hard to handle.

Mr. MASON. How many in the Transport Workers' Union in New York?

Mr. O'SHEA. They say about 90,000. I say about 35,000 would be the actual number. They give a figure of 90,000 but I would say 35,000.

Mr. MASON. How many would be Communists in the rank and file?

Mr. O'SHEA. I would safely say if you eliminate the—take the section leaders and executive officers, I would say, not 5 percent of the whole; but they have absolutely a strangle hold on the organization. They have a closed shop——

Mr. MASON. The Communist Party has only about 5 percent of the rank and file members in the Communist Party?

Mr. O'SHEA. And control——

Mr. MASON. And it has almost 90 percent of the leadership in the Communist Party?

Mr. O'SHEA. That is correct.

Mr. MATTHEWS. You have noticed the close proximity of Alaska to the Soviet Union and other centers of Europe, have you not?

Mr. O'SHEA. Yes, sir.

Mr. MATTHEWS. I will ask you if you can identify the Transport Workers' Bulletin for 1939? [Handing paper to the witness.]

Mr. O'SHEA. Yes, sir; that is the official organ.

Mr. MATTHEWS. On page 4 of this bulletin there appears a picture of Ervin H. Hill:

Ervin H. Hill, Transport Workers' delegate from Juneau, Alaska. T. W. U. Alaskan local has closed shop contracts and has organized "everything on wheels" in Juneau.

Do you have any information that bears upon the Alaskan situation?

Mr. O'SHEA. Well, I realize, as anybody who was ever connected with the Communist Party, the importance of such a position, as Communists and internationalists. They are subservient to Russia and holding a key position which in my estimation is a key position with another country, which is dominated by this same force. It is groundwork preparation. Its transportation is to be turned over at the psychological moment if in the event of difficulties arising between the United States and Russia. For instance, I don't think they would be worrying about the Navy in the Pacific Ocean or Atlantic. They would come through Alaska which is the shortest way in, particularly after having established a base.

Mr. MASON. Mr. O'Shea, is the Communist Party in control of the transport up in Alaska the same as in New York?

Mr. O'SHEA. No question about that.

Mr. MASON. When did they start to make inroads in the Transport Union up in Alaska? What year?

Mr. O'SHEA. Well, I couldn't give you the actual date on that question. I know that they have control now. When it actually started in my time, there was no organization there. We had no official organization there, you see, but I know that the party has used forces like in Frisco and other places—local section organizers and party members to do organizational work for them.

Mr. MASON. As I understand it, it is your opinion that the main reason for those inroads up in Alaska in the Transport Union is to carry on a campaign of sabotage, if this country should ever get into any sort of misunderstanding with the Soviet Government?

Mr. O'SHEA. No question about it.

Mr. MASON. Because of the proximity to the Soviet Union?

Mr. O'SHEA. Sure. For instance, in Norway during the invasion of Russia they had the groundwork prepared. As a matter of fact, they had American trucks immediately they landed—seized them on the docks and used them and pushed their army right ahead. Transportation in warfare is an important factor if you can get control of it at the psychological moment. If you can't, and the communication is destroyed, it isn't easy to move an armed force. So that is the importance of transportation from a revolutionary point of view.

Mr. MATTHEWS. Who is the general counsel for the Transportation Workers Union?

Mr. O'SHEA. Harry Sacher.

Mr. MATTHEWS. Do you know whether he is a member of the Communist Party or not?

Mr. O'SHEA. Yes, sir; he is a member of the Communist Party. I never actually sat in meetings with him, but from discussions with him—he handled a case for me in court and I discussed the union policy and everything with him.

Mr. MATTHEWS. I show you two pages from the Daily Worker, one of March 8—March 3, 1938, and the other, November 13, 1937. I ask these be introduced as exhibits.

The CHAIRMAN. They are received.

(The papers referred to by Mr. Matthews were marked "O'Shea Exhibits Nos. 21 and 22," and made a part of the record.)

Mr. MATTHEWS. Harry Sacher appears as a lecturer at the Workers' School of the Communist Party in New York City in both of these exhibits?

The CHAIRMAN. Attorney for the Transport Workers Union?

Mr. MATTHEWS. That is correct. That is all, Mr. Chairman.

The CHAIRMAN. Anything else?

Mr. MATTHEWS. We have another witness.

TESTIMONY OF E. C. DAVISON

The CHAIRMAN. Will you hold up your right hand, please. Do you solemnly swear to tell the truth, the whole truth, and nothing but the truth, so help you God?

Mr. DAVISON. I do.

Mr. MATTHEWS. Your name, please?

Mr. DAVISON. Emmett C. Davison, general secretary-treasurer of the International Association of Machinists.

Mr. MATTHEWS. You spell your name D-a-v-i-s-o-n?

Mr. DAVISON. Yes.

Mr. MATTHEWS. Mr. Davison, have you heard the testimony of Mr. Thomas O'SHEA. Yes, sir; I have.

Mr. MATTHEWS. Have you heard all of it?

Mr. DAVISON. Not all of it. I came in possibly 15 or 20 minutes after he had been speaking.

Mr. MATTHEWS. Did you hear the portion of his testimony which dealt with the affiliation of the Transport Workers Union with the International Association of Machinists?

Mr. DAVISON. Yes, sir.

Mr. MATTHEWS. What have you to say about that testimony? Will you state briefly?

Mr. DAVISON. Briefly, his testimony was correct in that the International Association of Machinists took the Transport Workers in in 1935 as a result of a conference between their representatives and the executive counsel of the International Association of Machinists.

He possibly did not lead up to the things that lead up to this amalgamation which he knew nothing whatever of.

Mr. MATTHEWS. But insofar as you heard his testimony, insofar as he testified?

Mr. DAVISON. Yes, sir; I think it is correct.

Mr. MATTHEWS. You can verify that as correct?

Mr. DAVISON. Yes, sir.

Mr. MATTHEWS. What do you have in the way of information about the James Matles who was a party to these negotiations?

Mr. DAVISON. James Matles came to us with a group in 1935, in the early part of 1935, as a representative of the Allied Metal Mechanics, which at that time, as was stated, was an independent group composed of men employed in machine shops and things of that nature.

The Radio and Electrical Workers—he claimed that he represented a number of them and the organization, I think, was known as the Allied Metal Association and Foundry Workers—some such organization as that, but he came to us in attendance at a meeting of our executive council in company with Mr. Quill, Mr. Lustig, Mr. Rivers, and Mr. Connolly.

Mr. MATTHEWS. Is that Eugene Connolly?

Mr. DAVISON. Yes, sir. I am trying to think of several other names. There were several there, possibly, who my memory don't recall.

Mr. MATTHEWS. Now, what have you discovered subsequently with reference to the political character of these men and their unions?

Mr. DAVISON. Well, when they appeared to us we presented them with our constitution, with the statement and a copy of a circular in which we have taken the position in 1925 that no Communist can be a member of the International Association of Machinists, and we have expelled quite a number. And they stated to us that they were not Communists; that they had two or three of them who had been Communists but because of some treatment they received inside they were now against the Communists, and so forth. That gave them the ground work. They denied being Communists. In fact they swore that they were not. Then they were presented with our constitution with the information that if we took them into our organization, in the amalgamation, they would have to agree to take such members as they then had and affiliate them with what ever trade or calling that particular group belonged to properly, the proper time. The answer to that was that there was an agitation going on for an independent union among the transport workers. We had some controversies over there in one of the power houses—with the machinists over there who were members of other local lodges and they assumed the protection of these men and they agreed to the proposition of segregation of the groups into the Amalgamated Street Railways—the helpers organizations of different types.

They claimed then to have a membership, I think it was 12,000. When we made our investigation we found that there were less than 6,000. But connected with the New York group were the groups in Philadelphia, in Ohio, and several other places that they supposedly represented, which represented a very small number of men.

They were with us, I think, about a year and then we discovered that Matles, who was on our staff, which was part of the agreement. was taking applications supposedly for the International Association of Machinists on machinist application blanks in New York, New Jersey, from the employes of the Worthington Pump Co. and turning them into a C. I. O. organization instead of the machinists.

We then made an investigation and sent an auditor in, which gave us considerable trouble, and fianlly we ran into court and got in their headquarters in New York and New Jersey and found there was about $900 collected through applications, these people thinking they were going into the machinists organization and found themselves in the C. I. O. We never recovered a great deal of the money. They left us owing us about $13,000—between $13,000 and $14,000 in the delayed payment of per capita tax. which they were excusing themselves by virtue of the fact that they were an unorganized group and they depended on us to work the whole situation out.

Mr. MATTHEWS. Let me get this straightened out. Do you refer to the Transport Workers Union or the United Electrical, Radio and Machine Workers?

Mr. DAVISON. I mean the whole group. When we dealt with them they were all in one group.

Mr. MATTHEWS. And they left together?

Mr. DAVISON. They all left together; yes. They joined or went out of the International Association of Machinists and we were told that they had gone with the C. I. O.—not all of the individual members. Numbers of them stayed with us and are still with us. That is the mechanics—the machinists except in the radio workers. They were then forced into the C. I. O. We notified all of the locals that had gone with the C. I. O. what our laws were in reference to the protection of the individual, recovery of property, and so forth, but as we got into it we found that that was playing their game. They wanted publicity and we just decided to abandon the whole proposition and let it stand as it was, because we were rather pleased with the fact that all of this group, after we discovered they were Communists, had left our organization in a group, like they came in.

Mr. MATTHEWS. Now, would these Communists in such a union be employed in powerhouses?

Mr. DAVISON. Oh, yes.

Mr. MATTHEWS. In airplane factories?

Mr. DAVISON. That is right.

Mr. MATTHEWS. In transportation?

Mr. DAVISON. That is right.

Mr. MATTHEWS. In navy yards?

Mr. DAVISON. Not to any great extent in navy yards except as individuals, because we were a little bit too strong in the navy yards to let them in, but there are some. I suppose in the navy yards, as individuals, but not as locals.

Mr. MATTHEWS. Do you have some documents or exhibits that you could supply the committee with——

Mr. DAVISON. Yes, sir.

Mr. MATTHEWS. To illustrate——

Mr. DAVISON. I have the records of some of these men in our organization whose names have been referred to here. One in that group which we would not agree to take in was Stephen Rubicky. He was expelled for being a member of the Communist Party, and then he furnished us with a statement stating that he was not and would not become a member of the Communist Party, and so forth. He was reinstated in the machinists and later on, of course, it developed that his words didn't mean anything. He was still a member although he had denied it. So he was expelled again. He was quite active in Lodge 1560.

Mr. MATTHEWS. Have you found it necessary to expel very many members?

Mr. DAVISON. Yes, sir. We have expelled quite a group, not only in New York but up in Minnesota.

Mr. MATTHEWS. Will you leave these with the committee as an exhibit?

Mr. DAVISON. If I can get them back. I may need them. We are having a convention very shortly.

Mr. MATTHEWS. I ask this be marked as an exhibit and we will make a copy of it.

The CHAIRMAN. And return it to him.

(The document referred to was marked "Davison exhibit No. 1," and made a part of the record.)

Mr. DAVISON. Now a letter from Andrew Overgaard, who was one of the men—which was one of the names mentioned here. That was given to our executive council on February 6, 1936. He had previously been expelled from the machinists in Pittsburgh for being an active member of the Communists, and he together with Hathaway, who is now the editor, I believe, of the Daily Worker, was expelled up in Minnesota. But on February 6, 1936, Overgaard wrote this letter:

FEBRUARY 6, 1936.

To the EXECUTIVE COUNCIL OF THE INTERNATIONAL ASSOCIATION OF MACHINISTS.

DEAR SIRS AND BROTHERS: I hereby wish to make application for reinstatement into the International Associations of Machinists.

Since my expulsion from the International Association of Machinists, I have done all in my power to spread the spirit of unionism among the machinists and metal workers. I have been an active member of the independent metal workers' organization since 1929. For the past year, I worked as secretary of the Connecticut district of the Federation of Metal and Allied Unions.

I wish to state to the executive council that during the past few years, I have realized, more than ever before, that only one united organization of machinists and metal workers can bring about decent working conditions in our industry. Due to this realization, I am not only in agreement with the decisions of our general executive board and the various locals to amalgamate with the International Association of Machinists, but I have been advocating full support for such step since the time our convention and General Executive Board decided to labor for such amalgamation.

Upon being reinstated into the International Association of Machinists and upon the amalgamation becoming effective, it is in good faith that I pledge myself to work loyally for the International Association of Machinists and live up to its constitution and bylaws.

I wish to declare that I have no other intentions in making this statement but to do my share to bring about a powerful International Association of Machinists in the industry.

Sincerely yours,

ANDREW OVERGAARD.

All the time he was working with this group.

Mr. MATTHEWS. Do you know anything about whether Andrew Overgaard went to Russia as a delegate of the Red International Labor Union?

Mr. DAVISON. From my personal knowledge I only know from the records that have been built in our organization of that visit he made. This was the trial that we gave him in the first instance. I don't know that.

Mr. MATTHEWS. And was Clarence Hathaway also expelled from your union in Minnesota?

Mr. DAVISON. Yes, sir. That happened in 1925.

Mr. MATTHEWS. On the ground of being a Communist?

Mr. DAVISON. A Communist; yes. At that time, in 1925 and 1926 and along in that period we were engaged in quite a battle with the Communists in Northwest United States and in Canada. And we were doing all in our power to eliminate this "boring from within," which at that time was rather prevalent in these unions. We succeeded, I think, very well in northwest Canada when they developed O. B. U.

At Winnipeg, at a later period when our conventions were in session, we took up this whole question on the trial of expelling a group of men there; and then decided to notify the entire membership that no Communist could become a member of the International Association of Machinists, and that if one was found and proven, he would be expelled. And we have followed that course ever since.

I have a document here that may be of some interest in furnishing a list of the officers of these unions that were taken over by our association, and it later developed in this circular we issued on the Communist Party. And at that time they were going under a different name like a "Trade Union Unity League," and "Educational Bureau" of some description. They had about as many names as I suppose they could coin. A list of these lodges in Philadelphia and New York, Brooklyn, Newark, together with the notices we sent them with reference to turning over the property and so forth to the organization.

Mr. MATTHEWS. We appreciate these documents, Mr. Davison.

Mr. DAVISON. I have a number of others that I have referred to and the reasons for their expulsion.

Mr. MATTHEWS. That is all for today.

The CHAIRMAN. Very well. We will meet tomorrow morning at 10 o'clock.

(Whereupon at 4:45 p. m., the hearing was adjourned until 10 a. m., Wednesday, April 24, 1940.)

INVESTIGATION OF UN-AMERICAN PROPAGANDA ACTIVITIES IN THE UNITED STATES

WEDNESDAY, APRIL 24, 1940

House of Representatives,
Committee on Un-American Activities,
Washington, D. C.

The committee met at 10 a. m., Hon. Martin Dies (chairman), presiding.

The CHAIRMAN. The committee will come to order. The Chair announces a subcommittee composed of the chairman, the gentleman from New Mexico, Mr. Dempsey, and the gentleman from New Jersey, Mr. Thomas. Let us proceed, gentlemen.

Mr. MATTHEWS. Our first witness is Fred M. Howe.

TESTIMONY OF FRED M. HOWE, SECRETARY, LOCAL 2, AMERICAN RADIO TELEGRAPHISTS' ASSOCIATION

The CHAIRMAN. Please rise and hold up your right hand. Do you solemnly swear to tell the truth, the whole truth, and nothing but the truth, so help you God?

Mr. HOWE. I do.

Mr. MATTHEWS. Your name is Fred Howe?

Mr. HOWE. My name is Fred M. Howe.

The CHAIRMAN. Will you speak as distinctly as possible so we may hear you.

Mr. MATTHEWS. Mr. Howe, where were you born?

Mr. HOWE. In the State of New Hampshire.

Mr. MATTHEWS. When?

Mr. HOWE. In the year 1888.

Mr. MATTHEWS. What is your profession or occupation, Mr. Howe?

Mr. HOWE. By profession I am a radio operator employed on ships.

Mr. MATTHEWS. How long have you been a radio operator?

Mr. HOWE. I learned the profession in 1918 in the Army.

Mr. MATTHEWS. Was that in the Signal Corps of the Army?

Mr. HOWE. It was.

Mr. MATTHEWS. What was the first union organization in the field of your profession?

Mr. HOWE. Well, I think the first one was referred to as the U. R. T. A.—United Radio Telegraphers' Association.

Mr. MATTHEWS. When was that founded?

Mr. HOWE. That was founded shortly after the World War.

Mr. MATTHEWS. Were you a member of that organization?

Mr. HOWE. No; I was not.

Mr. MATTHEWS. What was the first union in your field with which you were associated?

Mr. HOWE. The first union that I was affiliated with was the American Radio Association.

Mr. MATTHEWS. When was that organized?

Mr. HOWE. That was organized the 17th day of August, 1931.

Mr. MATTHEWS. Did you become a member of that union at once?

Mr. HOWE. I was a charter member and was there the first night it was organized.

Mr. MATTHEWS. Where was it organized?

Mr. HOWE. In New York City.

Mr. MATTHEWS. What was the subsequent development which led to the abandonment of that union and the setting up of the next one, if there was some transition?

Mr. HOWE. We called the association the American Radio Association. That was later changed to the American Radio Telegraphists' Association.

Mr. MATTHEWS. And is that known or was that known by the initials A. R. T. A.?

Mr. HOWE. It was.

Mr. MATTHEWS. And you carried over your membership into that organization?

Mr. HOWE. Yes, sir.

Mr. MATTHEWS. When did that change occur?

Mr. HOWE. The exact year I have forgotten, but I think in 1932.

Mr. MATTHEWS. And is the A. R. T. A. still in existence?

Mr. HOWE. Yes.

Mr. MATTHEWS. What relationship does the A. R. T. A. have to the American Communications Association?

Mr. HOWE. That is a rather complicated question. The parent organization is now known as the American Communications Association. I was elected when the maritime division of that parent organization was known as A. R. T. A., and we have maintained that name of A. R. T. A., Local 2. That was not changed.

Mr. MATTHEWS. You say when you were elected. To what were you elected?

Mr. HOWE. I was elected secretary-treasurer of A. R. T. A., Local 2. I might say in explanation that is referred to by some people as A. C. A. Local 2.

Mr. MATTHEWS. Are you still in possession of that office of secretary-treasurer of Local 2 of A. R. T. A. or A. C. A.?

Mr. HOWE. Legally, I believe that I am in possession of that office. Practically, I am not because I was thrown out physically by what we call in waterfront parlance a "goon squad," 2 months after I was elected to office.

Mr. MATTHEWS. When did that occur?

Mr. HOWE. That occurred on the 6th day of February 1939.

Mr. MATTHEWS. Will you please state the nature of your profession, Mr. Howe?

Mr. HOWE. The nature of my profession is radio operating on vessels of the American merchant marine and our duties aboard ship are to send and receive messages and take care of the apparatus in case it breaks down. Those are the general duties of my profession.

Mr. MATTHEWS. Would the radio operator on board ship be the one man who is responsible for maintaining connection with the shore?

Mr. HOWE. Yes. He is the sole communication officer.

The CHAIRMAN. The chairman wants to announce that a quorum of the full committee is present. We will go out of the subcommittee into the full committee. Present: The chairman, Mr. Mason, Mr. Thomas, and Mr. Dempsey. Please proceed.

Mr. MATTHEWS. Now, Mr. Howe, who are the officers of the American Communications Association?

Mr. HOWE. The president is Mervyn Rathborne.

Mr. MATTHEWS. Will you spell that?

Mr. HOWE. M-e-r-v-y-n R-a-t-h-b-o-r-n-e. And there are eight vice presidents, two from each division. Two from the maritime division, two from the broadcast division, two from the telegraph division, and two from the point-to-point.

Mr. MATTHEWS. Can you give us the names of the eight vice presidents of the American Communications Association?

Mr. HOWE. Yes, sir. The first vice president of the maritime division is Roy Pyle. The second vice president of the maritime division is James E. Croney. The first vice president of the broadcast division is Lenne Ohl. I forget the second vice president's name of that division.

Mr. MATTHEWS. Is that Ward?

Mr. HOWE. Douglas Ward is the first vice president of the telegraph division. Joseph P. Selly is the second vice president. I may have these reversed. I have forgotten how they stand.

Now, Michael Mignon is the first vice president of the point-to-point division. That is spelled M-i-g-n-o-n.

Mr. MATTHEWS. Roberts?

Mr. HOWE. Earnest Roberts is vice president—I have forgotten which division. He is one of the vice presidents but I have forgotten for which division.

Mr. MATTHEWS. Taylor?

Mr. HOWE. Howard Taylor is the vice president of the point-to-point division.

Mr. MATTHEWS. Is that Howard Taylor or Harold Taylor?

Mr. HOWE. I think it is Harold Taylor.

Mr. MATTHEWS. Harold?

Mr. HOWE. Harold, I believe.

Mr. MATTHEWS. Jordon?

Mr. HOWE. Chester Jordon is no longer a vice president of the A. C. A. He was first vice president.

Mr. MATTHEWS. I think you have named the vice presidents. Now, you are an official of the marine division?

Mr. HOWE. Yes, sir.

Mr. MATTHEWS. Of the marine division of the organization, are you not?

Mr. HOWE. Yes, sir.

Mr. MATTHEWS. And are your members employed on vessels operating to all parts of the world?

Mr. HOWE. Yes, sir.

Mr. MATTHEWS. Will you please describe briefly the nature of the equipment that you operate on board ship?

Mr. HOWE. Each vessel of the merchant marine is equipped with a transmitter and a receiving set. Transmitters vary in make-up and type but in general there is what we call the intermediate transmitter and also a short-wave transmitter.

The short-wave transmitter is you probably know, adapted for long distance and practically all of the passenger vessels today and many of the cargo and tanker vessels are equipped with short-wave apparatus which makes it possible for an operator at sea in any part of the world to communicate with practically any other part of the world. He can be off the coast of Australia and call up New York—Sidney, Australia, Shanghai, China, or Moscow, Russia. It is done every day on the majority of the vessels of the merchant marine.

Mr. MATTHEWS. Now, what is the largest or most powerful coast station in the world through which a great many of these messages from the ships all around the world go?

Mr. HOWE. I don't think there will be any dispute among radio operators as to the fact that WCC–WIM at Chatham, Mass., is the best, the largest, and the most efficient marine coastal station in the world.

Mr. MATTHEWS. By whom is that owned?

Mr. HOWE. It is owned by a subsidiary of the Radio Corporation of America.

Mr. MATTHEWS. Is it in constant touch with all parts of the world?

Mr. HOWE. It is in constant touch with all of the big passenger ships all over the world.

Mr. MATTHEWS. Will you please illustrate that from your own experiences as a radio operator aboard ship.

Mr. HOWE. Well, it is possible—I worked on a ship that went to the east coast of Africa, to Mombasa, and this ship was equipped with short-wave apparatus, and I was able at some time during the day or night, practically every day of that voyage, which lasted for 3 months and 20 days, to communicate directly with Chatham, Mass.

Mr. MATTHEWS. Did you ever have any experience aboard a ship that was not equipped with short wave?

Mr. HOWE. It is possible due to the fact that other ships are so equipped for a ship which is not equipped with short wave, to also work Chatham indirectly. I was off the coast of Pitcairn Island, and I received a message from New York, from the company's office, that by the way was not sent via Chatham, but was sent via KPH, San Francisco. It was relayed by that station to Sidney, Australia, and given to a British ship, which in turn gave it to me.

I received that message only a few hours after it was filed in New York. I was on a rusty old cargo vessel that was very poorly equipped with radio apparatus.

Mr. MATTHEWS. Now, Mr. Howe, have you ever known any Communist Party member who was employed at the Chatham, Mass., station about which you have been speaking?

Mr. HOWE. There was a man employed there who was one of the organizers of that station. He organized the men there or helped to organize them into the American Communications Association.

Mr. MATTHEWS. What was his name?

Mr. HOWE. His name, if I have not forgotten, is Hollis O. Fairchild.

Mr. THOMAS. Mr. Howe, do you know whether he is still employed there?

Mr. HOWE. He was discharged a few weeks ago due to the Neutrality Act that was passed by Congress, which made it unprofitable for the station to employ so many men. They discharged seven men and Mr. Fairchild, I have learned, was one of those discharged.

I know Mr. Fairchild was a Communist, is a Communist now, and was stationed at Chatham for a long period of time. He helped to organize the station. What other work he did, I don't know.

Mr. MATTHEWS. Can you name some of the other coastal stations on the Atlantic, Pacific, and Gulf coasts of the United States?

Mr. HOWE. There are stations located all along the Atlantic coast from Bar Harbor, Maine, clear up through to Alaska. They are stationed every few miles along the coast. Some are high-powered stations and some are low and some are medium; some are good and some are not so good.

The station at Bar Harbor, Maine, I believe that is where it is located, is owned by the Mackay Radio & Telegraph Co.

There is one in Boston owned by the Tropical Radio. The call is WBF. Stations around New York Harbor—we always go by their call letters—WSL, WSF, WNY. And another very powerful station down the coast, which works ships for New York Harbor, is WSC, located at Tuckerton, N. J.

There is a station in Philadelphia, WNW, privately owned by two men, which works ships going up the Delaware only.

Another station in Baltimore, WMH, is owned by the city of Baltimore.

The station at Norfolk, Va., is run by the Navy—NAM are the call letters. Stations all the way down the coast until we get to Miami. The station there is owned by the Tropical Radio. That is a subsidiary of the United Fruit Co. It is a very high-class, high-powered, very efficient station. There is also a station there owned by the Radio Corporation of America. The call letters are WOE.

Another one on the coast of Florida is owned by the Mackay Radio Co. Its call letters are WMR. There is another one in New Orleans which call letters are WNU. Another one in Port Arthur, Tex., WPA, and those on the west coast, San Pedro, Calif.—KSE, Radio Corporation of America. KOK, Los Angeles, owned by Mackay. WPH, San Francisco, the Radio Corporation. KFS by Mackay.

Station in Seattle owned by the city of Seattle and in the Panama Canal there are no privately owned stations. They are owned by the Navy Department. Vessels arriving or departing from the Canal Zone work this particular naval station.

The stations up in Alaska, I believe, are owned by the Army— Coast Guard Government stations.

Mr. MATTHEWS. Now, Mr. Howe, do you know whether or not members of the A. C. A. who are also members of the Communist Party have gone into Government service during the past few years?

Mr. HOWE. Yes. I know some that have gone into the Government service—C. A. A.—and also into the private airway companies.

I believe these men have been sent there with a purpose. They are well known Communists, and there is a move on foot right now to have these men get into key positions in the airways radio service.

I recall distinctly two men. One by the name of Walter Adams who went into a Government airways station in Kentucky. Another man by the name of Thomas C. Ault, a well-known Communist Party member, formerly an organizer for local 2, A. R. T. A., New York, a man who was arrested in Ecuador for distributing subversive literature.

Mr. MATTHEWS. Was that Communist literature?

Mr. HOWE. Yes; that is right.

Mr. MATTHEWS. And was this Ault who was arrested in Ecuador?

Mr. HOWE. That is right. He went into the Government airways service station at Camden, N. J., and later near Baltimore, Md.

Mr. THOMAS. Mr. Chairman, do I understand you, Mr. Howe, to say that the Communist Party had placed these gentlemen of theirs in these radio stations?

Mr. HOWE. That is what I said; yes. I didn't say "the Communist Party."

Mr. DEMPSEY. Did you say "placed" or "encouraged" them to go into it? How could they place them?

Mr. HOWE. Well, the party itself could not place them, but they could request these men to go into this particular service, and knowing as we do that they are required to do as they are ordered to do, we know that they do that.

Mr. MATTHEWS. I think you meant by the word "placed"——

Mr. THOMAS. I might have used that word. I don't say the witness used it. I might have used the word. I think Mr. Dempsey is correct.

The CHAIRMAN. That has been cleared up. Let us proceed.

Mr. MATTHEWS. Do you know a Ben Rosset?

Mr. HOWE. Yes; I know Ben Rosset very well. He is a Communist. He recently worked on the steamship *Cristobal,* owned by the Panama Railroad & Steamship Co., which is a Government corporation ship running from New York to Cristobal, C. Z.

Ben Rosset is a well-known Communist in local No. 2. He was employed aboard this ship until he was recently discharged. Now he is on another Government-owned ship named the *Mormacgull,* paid for by the Maritime Commission.

Mr. MATTHEWS. M-o-r-m-a-c-g-u-l-l?

Mr. HOWE. That is right.

Mr. MATTHEWS. Was Mr. Rosset, to your knowledge, ever arrested for distributing Communist literature?

Mr. HOWE. Mr. Rosset was arrested in Lisbon, Portugal, for distributing Communist literature and was discharged, as I understand, by the Export Steamship Corporation because he got in bad with the police in Lisbon.

Mr. MATTHEWS. Now, do you know whether or not any Communists occupy key positions on the largest and finest vessels of the American merhant marine?

Mr. HOWE. Yes, I know that to be a fact and it is an attempt of the Communist Party fraction in the American Communication Association to place good party members aboard the best of ships.

Mr. MATTHEWS. And by that you mean instruct them to get those positions if they can obtain them?

Mr. HOWE. They instruct them to get them and assist them in getting them. One man by the name of Joseph Belleza, of Portugese extraction, he was recently on the steamship *Manhattan*, one of the largest American passenger vessels. He is not on there at the present moment, however, because the company discharged him.

Another man by the name of Robert Kay on the *Washington*— a troublemaker of the first order and causes trouble aboard every ship that he goes on.

Mr. DEMPSEY. Is he Communist?

Mr. HOWE. As far as I know he is well known to be such in local No. 2, A. R. T. A. He follows the Communist Party line on all occasions.

Mr. MATTHEWS. Do you know Arthur Gobbles?

Mr. HOWE. I do.

Mr. MATTHEWS. Do you know what ship he is on?

Mr. HOWE. Arthur Gobbles has been on many ships. You would have to check up at the moment to find out exactly what ship he is on. Arthur Gobbles is slightly off in the upper story, as we say.

Mr. MATTHEWS. Do you know him to be a Communist?

Mr. HOWE. Yes, he is known to be a Communist.

Mr. MATTHEWS. Do you know Samuel Levin?

Mr. HOWE. Yes; I know Samuel Levin. He is radio-telephone operator on the *Washington*, steamship *Washington* owned·by the United States Lines.

Mr. MATTHEWS. Do you know him to be a Communist?

Mr. HOWE. Yes.

Mr. MATTHEWS. Do you know a Mr. Gottesfeld?

Mr. HOWE. I know Jack Gottesfeld quite well. He is a troublemaker and a Communist of the first order.

Mr. MATTHEWS. Do you know what ship he is on?

Mr. HOWE. The last I knew he was on the steamship *President Roosevelt* but he is not there at this time.

Mr. MATTHEWS. Do you know men on the steamship *Oriente*?

Mr. HOWE. Yes. That has been a Communist ship for the last 2 or 3 years. It runs to Havana, Cuba, from New York. The chief operator today is named Joseph de la Hunt.

The CHAIRMAN. How do you spell that?

Mr. HOWE. d-e l-a H-u-n-t.

Mr. MATTHEWS. Spelled with a capital H-u-n-t?

Mr. HOWE. That is right.

Mr. MATTHEWS. Do you know him to be a Communist?

Mr. HOWE. I know him to be a Communist. He always carries a Daily Worker in his pocket at all times and is well known in Arta local 2 to be a Communist.

Before he became the chief radio officer on that vessel they had a man by the name of Joseph Pearlman who was chief radio officer. He is well known to be a party member and a very radical Communist and a troublemaker. And I would like to say that the steamship *Oriente* is one of the finest class of its class in the American merchant marine. It is a famous excursion boat that runs between New York and Cuba.

Mr. MATTHEWS. Do you know Max Buch?

Mr. Howe. Max Buch is a New York radio operator, a Communist, and a member of the party, and also a troublemaker aboard ship.

Mr. Matthews. Do you know what ship he is on now?

Mr. Howe. I could not say at the moment. I believe he was on the *Monterey* of the New York & Cuba Mail Steamship Co.

Mr. Thomas. I think in the case of all these ships it would be helpful for the record if we also had the name of the steamship company at the time we get the name of the ship.

Mr. Howe. I would like to explain that these radiomen change their ships quite frequently, and it is difficult to say at any particular moment who is on what ship.

Mr. Thomas. My suggestion was that when you name a ship that you also name the company at the same time.

Mr. Howe. I will do that.

Mr. Matthews. You mentioned the *Manhattan*. We will go back over the ships and you give for the record the names of the companies.

Mr. Howe. The *Manhattan* is used by the United States Lines Steamship Co.

Mr. Matthews. The *Washington?*

Mr. Howe. That is owned by the same company.

Mr. Matthews. *Cristobal?*

Mr. Howe. The *Cristobal* is owned by the Panama Railroad & Steamship Co., a Government corporation.

Mr. Matthews. The *Oriente?*

Mr. Howe. That is owned by the New York & Cuba Mail Steamship Co.

Mr. Matthews. The *President Roosevelt?*

Mr. Howe. That is owned by the United States Lines Steamship Co.

Mr. Matthews. The *Monterey?*

Mr. Howe. The *Monterey* is owned by the New York & Cuba Mail.

Mr. Matthews. Now, do you know Howard Stroebel?

Mr. Howe. Howard Stroebel is a radio member—a member of A. R. T. A. local 2, and I believe a graduate of Columbia University—a Communist.

Mr. Matthews. Do you know what ship he has been on recently?

Mr. Howe. The last I knew he was on the *American Shipper*.

Mr. Matthews. Of what line?

Mr. Howe. The United States Lines.

Mr. Matthews. Do you know Harry Schlengier?

Mr. Howe. Harry Schlengier is a radio operator. I believe at present he is employed on the steamship *Annapella* of the Standard Fruit Co. It runs between New York and Honduras and Jamaica and other ports of the West Indies.

Mr. Matthews. Do you know Mr. Schlengier to be a Communist?

Mr. Howe. Mr. Schlengier told me that he had been a member of the party.

It was the policy of the party a short time ago to say that their members are ex-members of the party. Harry Schlengier told me a year ago that he was such an ex-member and proceeded to demonstrate to everyone in local 2 that he was still a good party member by backing up the Communists when they took possession of A. R. T. A., Local 2, and threw out the legally elected officials of that organization.

Mr. MATTHEWS. Do you know H. P. Jensen?

Mr. HOWE. H. P. Jensen is also a Communist and a troublemaker. The last I knew he was on the steamship *City of Rayville*. That is also a Government-owned vessel, owned by the United States Maritime Commission and was running at that time for the American Pioneer Line.

Mr. MATTHEWS. Do you know Vaetold Lamont?

Mr. HOWE. I know him very well. He is also a Communist, a member of the party and the last I knew he was working on the steamship *San Juan*. That is owned by the New York & Cuba Mail Steamship Co. The ship runs between New York and ports in Mexico. It was running to Puerto Rico.

Mr. THOMAS. Mr. Chairman, I would like to ask another question right there. On these various ships that you have named about what is the average number of radio operators they have on one of those ships?

Mr. HOWE. On cargo vessels there is always only one. On passenger vessels there are always three or more.

Mr. THOMAS. So on the ships that you have mentioned where they have Communists as radio operators, sometimes the lone operator is a member of the Communist Party?

Mr. HOWE. That is right; yes. There are only two ships that I recall at the moment that have more than three operators on board. Those two ships are the *Manhattan* and the *Washington*. Each of those has five; all of the others have three except the freight and tankers, and they have one.

Mr. MATTHEWS. Do you know Mr. Santo?

Mr. HOWE. Mr. Santo is a member of the A. R. T. A., Local 2, is a Communist and member of the party. The last time I saw him he was sitting in the radio room on the yacht *Sea Cloud*, owned by the Ambassador to Belgium. He copies and receives radiograms sent to and from the beautiful yacht *Sea Cloud* owned by Ambassador Davies of the United States, Ambassador to Belgium.

Mr. THOMAS. How many operators would they have on that particular yacht?

Mr. HOWE. He was the only man I found in the radio room at the time. He was chief, but I understand they carry three. However, there is no law governing the number that they carry on a yacht; it is purely up to the owner.

Mr. MATTHEWS. Mr. Howe, has it been your business as an official of the A. R. T. A. or the American Communication Association to know who are Communists and who are not?

Mr. HOWE. I made it my business to find out exactly who were and who were not Communists and members of the party.

Mr. MATTHEWS. Will you please state briefly how you are able to know in cases where a man does not show you his party membership book that he is a Communist?

Mr. HOWE. Well, you wouldn't need to get any inside information from the party itself to know exactly who they are.

You can always tell by the way they work; by the way they work in the union for the party.

The Communist Party, as we all know by reading its books and papers and magazines, tells their members that they must get control of all labor unions, and get into a labor union, and they work with that one object in view, to control that labor union; doesn't matter how they do it. They have no ethical standards whatsoever. If they can't do it by one means they will resort to any other means available, including physical force, and that is what the members of the international executive board of A. C. A. used in the case of A. R. T. A., Local 2.

You cannot attend a membership meeting, as I attended them for several years, without knowing exactly who these men are, because they follow what we all know to be the party line. We could always anticipate from one week to the other exactly what was coming up at the next meeting because we knew the party line, and we knew how they would line up. We could look over the meeting, and if we knew every man in there we could tell exactly how the vote was going to come out.

We anticipated every meeting. In addition to that, we also talked to members who do know that these men are members of the party. We receive personal letters. I have several here today that I would like to read from to prove that some of the higher officials of the American Communications Association are members of the Communist Party and have been for years. And they are in there for the sole purpose of getting control of communications and in time of war sew them up, tie them up, and help the party take over the United States and the industries in the United States and establish a soviet system. We do know who the Communists are in A. C. A., and everybody—every member there who has any intelligence—knows exactly who they are.

Mr. MATTHEWS. Who are the A. C. A. delegates in New York?

Mr. HOWE. What they call the international organizer. It is a high-sounding name, but the job is held by Murray Winnocur. He is now called the international organizer, and the reason he is so called is because he is being paid by what they call the international office of the A. C. A. He has a brother by the name of Jacob, who is also a delegate, or has been a delegate, and who attacked me physically on the street here last August and called me all kinds of insulting names, which he didn't get by with, by the way, and he is a delegate, and has been acting secretary of the Boston office of the marine division of A. C. A., and for the last 2 weeks he has been acting secretary of the New York office, marine division, of A. C. A.

These two men are Communists; members of the Communist Party, and they are vicious, and they will stop at nothing to accomplish their ends—a sit-down strike or slugging if necessary.

Mr. MATTHEWS. Do you know who the secretary of local 4 in Baltimore is?

Mr. HOWE. The secretary of local 4 in Baltimore is Paul Rothman, a well-known member of the party—has been for years. He has appeared here in Washington at various times before governmental committees—made himself ridiculous by his actions, and I believe that he has engaged in illegal activities in connection with W. P. A. in Baltimore.

Mr. MATTHEWS. Will you explain, please, what those activities were?

Mr. HOWE. He wrote me letters 2 years ago to send down as many of our unemployed members as we could spare to the city of Baltimore to go on W. P. A. I didn't know what the racket was. They were sent down. I later learned that they were put on W. P. A., I believe contrary to law. I understood later that the man had to swear that he quit a ship in Baltimore. If he had quit a ship in Baltimore the W. P. A. allowed him to go on their projects there, but these men that were sent down from New York at Rothman's request, did not quit ships in Baltimore—not within recent years. I think that should be investigated by somebody that is interested.

Mr. MATTHEWS. Do you know who the secretary of local 3 in San Francisco is?

Mr. HOWE. Secretary of local 3 in San Francisco is R. M. Hansen. He is a young fellow and is a very vicious one and an unreasonable Communist. He is very dangerous to the American Merchant Marine because from his point of view the shipowner and the Government and everyone in the world is wrong but Hansen is right. He uses Harry Bridges longshoremen and as many of the other maritime crafts as possible to gain his ends. He signs the most ridiculous agreements that could be imagined. They contain everything except taking the ships over.

Mr. MATTHEWS. You stated he was a Communist, did you?

Mr. HOWE. Yes.

Mr. MATTHEWS. Do you know who the secretary of local 6 in Seattle, Wash., is?

Mr. HOWE. Secretary of local 6 is T. J. Van Erman, a Communist, member of the party. He has been on the C. I. O. pay roll as an organizer in Seattle and also in Alaska. He has been an organizer in the Gulf of Mexico and is mixed up in all kinds of C. I. O.-communism as a radical organizer.

Mr. MATTHEWS. Do you know who is secretary of local 1 in Boston?

Mr. HOWE. The secretary of local 1 in Boston doesn't exist any more because of the fact that local 1 was taken over by local 2 in New York. The secretary of local 1 was Richard J. Golden. He resigned under fire of the Communists. The Communists went to Boston, a full automobile load of them. They put Golden on the spot and told him to resign or they would come down there and take over the same as they took over local 2. Golden was forced out and the New York local took over local 1 in Boston without any semblance of legality whatsoever.

Mr. MATTHEWS. Do you know who the secretary of local 20 in Cleveland is?

Mr. HOWE. The secretary of local 20 in Cleveland—his name was Leonard Anderson. I don't believe he is there any more. He was there a year or so ago. He was a well-known Communist and I might say he succeeded a man by the name of William Hathaway, who was killed in Spain fighting for Spanish democracy.

Mr. MATTHEWS. Do you know Kenneth Goss?

Mr. HOWE. Yes. Kenneth Goss was a member of local 1, A. C. A., in Boston, and he was employed on a fish trawler. I met Mr. Goss in Boston last July. Previous to that he was on one of the around-the-world American President Line boats, the name of which ship I have forgotten temporarily. Kenneth Goss is a well-known Communist and talks communism to everyone that will listen to him and he is therefore a dangerous character to have aboard any merchant ship, especially in time of war.

Mr. MATTHEWS. Do you know J. L. Fishbein?

Mr. HOWE. I don't know Fishbein in person. I have heard a lot about him. He was also a member of local 1, A. C. A., Boston, and is well known there to be a Communist.

I made inquiries when I was there from a great many men and they all told me the same story—that Fishbein was a Communist.

Mr. MATTHEWS. Do you know Karl Lundquist?

Mr. HOWE. Yes, I know Karl Lundquist very well, personally. Karl Lundquist is a Communist and is a member of the party and is also an agitator and a personal nuisance aboard every ship upon which he works. He is always mingling with the crew back aft and finding fault with the way the ship is run. He is one of these men who is never satisfied.

Mr. MATTHEWS. Do you know a man by the name of Antonacci?

Mr. HOWE. Yes, I know Mr. Antonacci very well.

Mr. MATTHEWS. Will you spell his name?

Mr. HOWE. A-n-t-o-n-a-c-c-i, I believe.

Mr. MATTHEWS. What do you know about Mr. Antonacci?

Mr. HOWE. He is a young fellow of Italian extraction, a Communist, a member of the party.

Mr. MATTHEWS. Do you know his first name?

Mr. HOWE. I think it is Antone. I wouldn't want to bet on that, though.

Mr. MATTHEWS. No; were you going to say something else about him?

Mr. HOWE. He is a typical Communist—a young fellow of enthusiasm. The world must be changed quickly. He wants the revolution to take place tomorrow if possible.

Mr. MATTHEWS. Now, Mr. Howe, do you know anything about the connection between the American Communications Association and the National Maritime Union, and the Transport Workers' Union, particularly the New York local?

Mr. HOWE. They are all linked up together. Of course that is the Communist Party line, as we all know, but the National Maritime Union is more closely linked up with the American Communications Association than any other union. As a matter of fact the old A. R. T. A. was the founder of the National Maritime Union.

When Joe Curran pulled his men off the steamship *California* in 1936, it was A. R. T. A., Local 2, that furnished the money and rented the hall, guaranteed the telephone bills for Joe Curran's so-called rank and file of the old I. S. U. We received a telephone bill in local 2 of almost $400 which was incurred by Curran's rank and file office at 164 11th Avenue, New York City, during the strike. Local 2, A. R. T. A., together with the national office of A. R. T. A. backed Curran's rank and file movement from its very inception. They worked very closely on all occasions.

One of the reasons why, perhaps, I was thrown out was because I refused to work with such kind of men as Joe Curran and Blackie Meyers and Jack Lawrence who are in there for some ulterior purpose other than the benefits to the radio officers or the seamen involved.

Mr. MATTHEWS. Now, what connections are there in the way of cooperation between the A. R. T. A. and the Transport Workers' Union of which Michael Quill is the head?

Mr. Howe. Well, they are all linked up together in this way: That the Communist Party desires to tie up communications and transportation. It so happens that the Transport Workers' Union is a land union and the Maritime Union, the National Maritime Union, is a water union, so to speak. One is engaged in organizing men on land and the other in organizing transport workers on the sea.

Mr. Matthews. Do you know anything about the situation with respect to Communist control in the Postal Telegraph?

Mr. Howe. It is very easily seen that the Communist faction in the A. C. A. controls the Postal Telegraph at least 99 percent. The Postal Telegraph Co. is organized by the American Communications Association. I attended the last two national conventions of that held in New York in 1937 and 1938, and the Communist Party got everything that it wanted. No question in my mind but what the Communist Party controls the A. C. A. 99 percent.

As a matter of fact they control in 100 percent but by 99—I mean about 99 percent of the officials are actually Communists, members of the party.

Mr. Matthews. Do you know of your own knowledge whether prominent labor leaders in the United States find it necessary to use other telegraph services because of their knowledge of the Communist Party's control?

Mr. Howe. I have heard that the officials of Postal Telegraph Co. themselves refuse to send messages via Postal Telegraph because they know very well the stooges who are employed by Postal Telegraph, who are members of A. C. A., may reveal the contents of the messages. I know that has been the case several times to my personal knowledge.

Mr. Matthews. What is the situation with respect to Communist Party control in the cables?

Mr. Howe. Well, the A. C. A. has an agreement with the French Cables Co. and it also has an agreement with R. C. A. C., which means the Radio Communications Corporation that has jurisdiction over the point-to-point radio services, such as between New York and Buenos Aires and New York and Moscow, New York and parts of England. In fact, all over the world. The A. C. A. has organized the communication workers that handle this point-to-point communication.

Mr. Matthews. Does the A. C. A. have a signed agreement with the Globe Wireless?

Mr. Howe. They have a signed agreement with the Globe Wireless which is an organization which communicates mainly with the American President Line vessels and also interoffice communication of the American President Line, formerly the Dollar Steamship Lines.

Mr. Matthews. Does the A. C. A. have a signed agreement with the Press Wireless?

Mr. Howe. They do for the west coast and Honolulu. They recently called a strike on the west coast and won their demands. They tied up the Wireless Press—the Press Wireless service for several weeks, I believe it was, and I believe they got everything that they asked for. The service in the meantime was completely at a standstill.

Mr. MATTHEWS. Now, what is a deadhead message?

Mr. HOWE. A deadhead message is usually one sent by someone who has a frank—doesn't cost him anything.

Mr. MATTHEWS. And what is the situation according to your information with reference to sending deadhead messages by cable via these stations where they have control?

Mr. HOWE. Well, I would like to explain that. The radio service on American ships is controlled to some extent by two major radio service companies and by that I mean that these companies manufacture or sell the radio equipment on board and they furnish the service and they furnish the radio operator on the vessel and when a company hires a man he must also be approved by the radio service company because the radio service company either rents that equipment to the company or owns it or they have a contract with the company.

So the radio service companies give the radio operator a frank and he can send anything from that ship to one of the company's land stations free of charge. The only charge he has to pay is a small land-line charge that is usually between 3 and 11 cents per word to all parts of the United States. Three cents to the city of the area in which the land station is located. So he could send a message for 30 cents which would cost anyone else $2 or $3.

Mr. THOMAS. Mr. Chairman, I would like to ask this question. Mr. Howe, what governmental agency has regulatory authority over communications?

Mr. HOWE. The Federal Communications Commission.

Mr. THOMAS. Do you know whether the Federal Communications Commission has taken any action in regard to these Communists who are radio operators in our ships?

Mr. HOWE. No. So far as I know no action was ever taken.

Mr. DEMPSEY. Does the Federal Communications Commission have any jurisdiction over personnel on ships?

Mr. HOWE. No; I don't believe they have, from what I have read of the act—I don't believe so.

The CHAIRMAN. They don't.

Mr. DEMPSEY. They have nothing to do with it?

The CHAIRMAN. They couldn't fire a man because he was a member of the Communist Party?

Mr. HOWE. No. The only time they could take action would be if this man had violated some rule of the Commission or some law which the Commission is charged with enforcing.

Mr. DEMPSEY. The Commission carries out the law that the Congress enacted and that is the only authority they have, isn't it?

Mr. HOWE. Yes, sir; so far as I know, that is.

The CHAIRMAN. Let us proceed.

Mr. THOMAS. Maybe it would be a good idea to change some of the laws.

Mr. DEMPSEY. And we are trying to get you to do it.

Mr. THOMAS. And I am willing to take it up at the next executive session.

The CHAIRMAN. Go ahead.

Mr. MATTHEWS. Mr. Howe, do you have personal knowledge of a slow-down strike on board ships, carried out by members of the——

The CHAIRMAN. Well, I don't believe you completed this deadhead message question—how they are able to transmit messages. Weren't you about to get down to that? Wasn't the question whether or not the Communists——

Mr. MATTHEWS. Are able to utilize their privilege for deadhead messages.

Mr. HOWE. There would be no charge as far as the ship was concerned. You must understand that when any man sends a message from ship to shore, the following charges prevail: Eight cents per word for the ship tax; for the land station which receives the land message the rate varies anywhere from 8 to 15 cents, depending on the station, the company and the country that controls the station. And then you have got the land-line charges which vary in various parts of the world. Some countries have a blanket rate for the whole country of 1 or 1½ cents a word or other countries like this country charge by zones.

As I said awhile ago, the rate is 3 cents minimum for the area in which the station is located, but if the message is received by a New York station, for example, and is transmitted by land line to San Francisco, there would be 11 cents per word charge for the land lines. So that would be 8 plus 10 for the coastal station charge, plus 11 for the land line.

Well, now, a Communist or anyone else for that matter, aboard the ship could save the 8 cents per word ship charge, the 10 cents per word land-line charge or coastal station charge would be only 8. He would be required to pay the land-line charge which would be 3 cents for New York or 11 cents across the country. I think that is about all.

Mr. DEMPSEY. Let me ask you this question: Do you send any messages from a ship that you do not keep a record of on board?

Mr. HOWE. No; you must according to the F. C. C. regulations keep a record of every message.

Mr. DEMPSEY. That is also true of the receiving station, isn't it?

Mr. HOWE. Yes.

Mr. DEMPSEY. They keep a record?

Mr. HOWE. They must.

Mr. DEMPSEY. Now, do you mean to tell the committee that a Communist or any employee having a frank is permitted to send any kind of a telegram or message they desire?

Mr. HOWE. Under the restrictions the law gives the master of the vessel the right to censor any message that is sent or received on board the vessel, but there is nothing to prevent the radio officer from sending anything that he wants to send when the captain is not in the room. And in fact it could be done if he were in the room because not knowing the code he could not tell what the man was sending.

Mr. DEMPSEY. What about the receiving station?

Mr. HOWE. Well, they would receive it.

Mr. DEMPSEY. There would be a record of it, wouldn't there?

Mr. THOMAS. The same thing could apply there. There need not be a record if they are both Communists.

Mr. HOWE. Yes. Two could arrange between themselves—supposing a man in Moscow was delegated to work someone on the steamship *Manhattan*. It would be prearranged that they would use false call letters. They would not use the call letters of the *Manhattan* and they would not use the call letters of the Moscow station. They would use some other call letters. They might use a Chinese call. So they call, and anyone hearing that would think that there was some Chinese ship and some Chinese land stations actually communicating with each other. No one could tell that it was the *Manhattan* and Moscow working each other.

So they could send their messages——

Mr. DEMPSEY. Do you know of any instances of that kind?

Mr. HOWE. Only to this extent: That it is so common among operators to work each other, especially from one ship to the other, that it is done thousands of times every day and those are not regular messages, although under the rules, under the law, they would require abstracting and a notation in the log, but it is not done. And I might also say that the coastal stations are so busy that they actually in practice do not make a notation of everything that they send. If they did they would never send much of anything. All they do is to make a notation every 15 minutes that they heard something; that they worked a certain ship. Although the rules require that every time they operate the transmitter they must make an entry in the log, but the ruling is so ridiculous that it can't be done.

Mr. THOMAS. You don't have to have a new law on that?

Mr. MATTHEWS. Mr. Howe, from your knowledge of the Communist Party members, and the Communist Party teachings, would it be your conclusion that the Communists would not hesitate to violate regulations of the kind that you describe?

Mr. HOWE. A Communist has positively no principles and no ethics. The better Communist he is the poorer are his ethics and principles. There is nothing that a good Communist will not do to further the aims and purposes of the party.

Mr. MATTHEWS. I asked you some time ago if you knew whether or not labor leaders in America found it inadvisable to use the Postal Telegraph and you did not answer my question directly. You spoke of the officials of the concern itself. Will you answer that question?

Mr. HOWE. I am sorry, I did not completely answer your question. The organization that I am now employed by, the Commercial Telegraphers' Union, Maritime Division, never uses Postal Telegraph. We would like to use Postal Telegraph because it is organized, but we can't do it because we don't trust the Communist members in the Postal Telegraph to deliver the messages promptly, efficiently, and accurately, and without revealing their contents to someone else. We know the Communists so well that we would not trust any message in their hands. We always use Western Union.

Mr. MATTHEWS. What do you know about the slow down?

Mr. HOWE. There was a slow down in Mackay Radio coastal stations only a few weeks ago. The operators at the Mackay coastal stations are the best operators in the world—second to none—40 to 45 words a minute is a common thing with them. And that is high speed in radio transmission and reception.

In order to win their demands, the demands which A. C. A. was making, they put themselves in the lowest class of the operating profession by means of a slow-down strike and advertised to all of the world that was listening in foreign ships of every nationality, that the Mackay Radio men were amateurs, and it took 2 hours to get a message through that should have been received in 2 minutes.

And that lasted for 2 or 3 weeks until the company was forced to give in to them. They didn't quit their jobs. They didn't go on strike. They merely refused to work. A ship would call up a Mackay coastal station and he would receive a reply: "Can hardly hear you, send slower." He was sending 10 words a minute then. And asked him to send still slower. That was a very bad—had a very bad advertising effect on thousands of foreign radio officers who listened in for weeks to the inefficiency of the Mackay coastal station radios.

Mr. DEMPSEY. What code do you use?

Mr. HOWE. It is called the International Morse Code. It is not exactly the same as the American land-line code but one-half of the letters are identical.

Mr. MATTHEWS. Mr. Howe, are you acquainted with the Communist Party teachings with respect to trade-unions?

Mr. HOWE. If I may—I did not finish my answer to that other question about the slow down; if I may complete that before I forget.

It is a practice on almost all of the ships of the Merchant Marine to send 2 weather messages daily to the United States Weather Bureau. One is sent at 7 a. m., Eastern Standard Time and the other at 7 p. m., Eastern Standard Time. During the hurricane season in the West Indies and the typhoon season in the Far East, they are sent several times a day at the request of the United States Weather Bureau.

A year ago last fall the radio operators on the Pacific coast, at the instigation of Roy A. Pyle, who is now the first vice president of A. C. A., at a certain specified time and at a certain specified date, these men refused to obey the lawful orders of the master of the vessel and refused to send these Weather Bureau messages to the Weather Bureau.

Now, I am sympathetic, greatly, with the men because I know what it means to get up at 4 o'clock in the morning as he has to do on the west coast. I said these were sent at 7 a. m., eastern standard time. On the Pacific coast that means 4 a. m. Pacific standard time. So he is forced to get up at 4 o'clock in the morning to send a weather message. But I don't approve of the means that were employed to straighten that matter out. They positively refused to accept the message from the captain; did not accept the message and did not send it and won their point by a refusal to obey the lawful orders of the master. And I would say that the F. C. C. would have a right under that matter to revoke the license of every man who refused to accept and send those messages.

Mr. THOMAS. Were the licenses revoked?

The CHAIRMAN. Yes. The F. C. C. has the right.

The CHAIRMAN. When did that happen?

Mr. HOWE. That happened a year ago last autumn.

The CHAIRMAN. You have no information that was ever brought to the attention of the F. C. C., do you?

Mr. HOWE. No; I don't know whether it was officially brought or not.

The CHAIRMAN. And if the company compromised with the men and reached another agreement, what could the F. C. C. do about it?

Mr. HOWE. If they could or any master should charge the operator with refusal to obey his orders, then the F. C. C. regulations provide that his license may be revoked.

The CHAIRMAN. The initiative would have to be taken by the master of the ship, would it not?

Mr. HOWE. By the master or company or possibly the Weather Bureau.

The CHAIRMAN. The F. C. C. could not take cognizance or judicial notice of it without somebody complaining?

Mr. HOWE. That is right.

The CHAIRMAN. You don't mean to imply the F. C. C. failed to perform its duty in any respect?

Mr. HOWE. No. I think it is an efficient body.

The CHAIRMAN. The object of an investigation of this kind is to bring to the attention of the Government conditions that exist throughout the country.

Mr. HOWE. I think, owing to the conditions that prevail on the west coast, that the companies themselves would not wish to have that done because it would probably mean the tying up of the entire Pacific coast. They have had so many tie-ups out there that the companies don't want to go through any more than are necessary.

Mr. MASON. But it only goes to prove the stranglehold that these Communists in the unions have upon the communications of the Government?

Mr. HOWE. Yes. And it also proves—and I believe it was put out for this purpose—it proves that they will obey orders. We know that the Communist Party's organization is based on the strictest kind of discipline, and they have to test these men out. They test out the members of the party by putting them to doing various menial tasks. They probably did this to see if the men would live up to the union rules, and they found that they would, so why wouldn't they refuse to do something in time of war?

Mr. MATTHEWS. Mr. Howe, you spoke some time ago of the Communist Party teachings with reference to the need for controlling labor unions?

Mr. HOWE. Yes, sir.

Mr. MATTHEWS. Are you acquainted with Communist Party literature on that subject?

Mr. HOWE. I have read quite a bit of it; yes.

Mr. MATTHEWS. I show you a copy of the program of the Communist International. Is that your own personal copy [handing paper to the witness]?

Mr. HOWE. Yes, sir; that is mine.

Mr. MATTHEWS. On page 77 of this booklet there appears the following:

It is particularly important for the purpose of winning over the majority of the proletariat to gain control of the trade unions which are genuine mass working class organizations, closely bound up with the everyday struggles of the working class; to work in reactionary trade unions and skillfully to gain control of them, to win the confidence of the broad masses of the industrially organized workers; to change and remove from their posts the reformist leaders represent important tasks in the preparatory period.

Has your experience in trade-union work indicated that the Communist Party members work precisely according to that program of the Communist International?

Mr. HOWE. Yes, sir. That has been my experience throughout.

Mr. MATTHEWS. You have seen the Communist Party maneuver to remove trade-union officials from their posts?

Mr. Howe. Yes, sir. I passed through that myself, and I know of many others that passed through the same thing. I might say that our organization was not organized by Communists. The sponsor of it was James Delaney, an Irishman, and he was not, is not, and probably never will be, a Communist. He organized the A. R. T. A.

When the Communist fraction discovered that there was a little money in it, there was a chance to get control, they came in and they threw James Delaney out, not exactly the same way they threw me out, but not much difference.

They took control and they kept control until a man by the name of Mark Burrow was elected as secretary of A. R. T. A., Local 2,. and I was his successor. When they had the purge a year ago last February the following results took place:

I was barred from the hall, barred from my own office. Local 2: was taken over by Mervyn Rathborne, Roy Pyle, and Chester Jordon. The assistant secretary was forced to resign. The Philadelphia delegate, who was elected by the membership, was summarily discharged—thrown out of his office and further payment of wages prohibited.

Then they went to work on the port of Boston. They sent six men down to Boston. The men were Roy A. Pyle, Chester Jordon, Van Erman, the two Winnocur brothers, and someone else. They went down there to put this little fellow on the spot. Tried to make him resign. He wouldn't resign. They got up a petition of 16 names only on it, and Roy A. Pyle called up the Boston office of A. C. A. by long-distance telephone and told Mr. Richard J. Golden that if he did not resign they would come down there and put him out the same as they put Howe out.

That frightened Golden and he resigned the marine division of A. C. A., and today it is controlled 100 percent by members of the Communist Party, and I don't mean maybe when I say they are known to any intelligent man in A. C. A., that these men are Communists, members of the party, and are using it for the benefit of the purpose and the objectives of the Communist Party.

And they did almost identical things in the National Maritime Union. I don't want to dwell on that because it is not my union, but I do know quite a bit about it. I know that a number of men were kicked out in about the same way that I was kicked out.

The Chairman. Tell me, Mr. Howe, how could the Communists and these unions, Maritime Union and the American Communication Association, Radio and Electrical Workers, and so on, and so forth, how could they use their position to serve the foreign policy of Moscow if that foreign policy decreed that the Communist Party of the United States was supposed to stop or was instructed to stop the sending of vital war materials to the Allies at the present time?

Mr. Howe. Well, it would be a very simple matter by the control of the longshoremen, such as they have on the west coast. They don't have it on the east coast; or by the control by the marine workers. If they didn't want to have this material go to a foreign country, they could have their men refuse to load the material on board the ships or have the men refuse to sail and that could be done, not directly—it probably would not be done directly. The Communists are too wise for that. They would have some other phoney beef.

They might ask for a 200 percent bonus, such as they asked here awhile ago when they asked for 250 percent. That was largely on account of the war. They did that—did the same thing during the Spanish crisis with the American Export Line—about the only line running over to Spain. They demanded 250 percent for passing through the Straits of Gibraltar—a bonus of 250 percent merely because the ship went near the war zone.

The CHAIRMAN. That was furnished as a pretext to carry out the party's line?

Mr. HOWE. Yes.

The CHAIRMAN. Party's instructions?

Mr. HOWE. Yes; they wanted to stop the ships from going over there. At least they wanted to stop the ships from carrying ammunition. They don't want to come out directly and say that possibly, so they call a strike for some other purpose, asking for an unreasonable increase in pay, which I think that was very unreasonable.

The CHAIRMAN. Well, what is the extent of their control or what could they do for instance if the party instructed them to do everything in their power to stop the shipment of war materials to the Allies? Could they stop it?

Mr. HOWE. On the east coast they could stop it on American vessels if they wanted to by calling a strike. Of course they couldn't stop it from being shipped on foreign vessels—vessels flying a foreign flag, but they could do that almost 100 percent on the west coast because Harry Bridges out there controls the stevedores—the longshoremen who load and unload the ships.

The CHAIRMAN. What could they utilize the communication associations for in time of war? Say in the event the United States entered the war on the other side of Russia, what use could they make of the control of these various unions?

Mr. HOWE. Well, they could use that for various purposes—to carry or transmit vital messages and there is no reason why they couldn't handle a great number of messages to any enemy nations.

They could reveal the position of convoys, battleships, submarines, if they happened to know them, and undoubtedly that is why they want to get control as much as possible of the maritime industry, so they could give the enemy information.

Mr. DEMPSEY. Since the listing of the arms embargo and the restriction of American vessels going into the combat zone, do you know of any American vessels carrying munitions of any kind?

Mr. HOWE. Well, of course under the Neutrality Act an American vessel cannot sail to belligerent ports.

Mr. DEMPSEY. So they don't carrying munitions?

Mr. HOWE. But they undoubtedly carry munitions or materials which would be classed as contraband—carry this material to countries adjoining belligerents. In fact it can be done even to belligerent nations. I believe the Export Line is calling at the port of Marseilles in southern France, which is really a violation of the Neutrality Act but I understand the State Department or some other department of the government has okayed that stop. So they do call that a belligerent port. They could carry any kind of material to any other port like Italy or any country adjoining any belligerent nation.

Mr. DEMPSEY. But not to a combat nation?

Mr. HOWE. No.

The CHAIRMAN. Now, suppose that the Communist dictatorship in Russia wanted to transmit messages to the Communist Party here or some agency of the Communist Government; Moscow wanted to transmit messages and they didn't want to do it in the regular way—through the way of cablegrams, would they be in a position to send instructions to the Communist Party of the United States in a secret way?

Mr. HOWE. Well, they could have that arranged between the party and the operators who were on various ships, such as the *Manhattan* and *Washington*—any ship that has a high-powered, efficient transmitter and sensitive receiving set could be delegated to receive these messages. Suppose the Manhattan is only a few hours from New York. bound for New York, and the Moscow Government wanted to send some vital information, so they call up the *Manhattan*, according to a prearranged schedule, transmit the messages. The operator makes no notation of them and he delivers them when he gets off the ship in New York. That could be done in a thousand ways. It could be done on several hundred ships.

Mr. THOMAS. In other words——

The CHAIRMAN. Wait just a second.

Mr. THOMAS. Right along that same line a good point to bring up, at the time Russia and Germany entered into its nonaggression pact, Earl Browder probably got some word from Moscow as to what to say. He waited a day or two. Then he got the word through that way. Isn't that true? That is possible, isn't it?

Mr. HOWE. Yes; that would be possible. In fact I think it is done.

The CHAIRMAN. As a matter of fact I think we have got the cablegrams—all the cablegrams between Russia and the Daily Worker outlining the various policies that the Daily Worker was to pursue and propaganda they were to spread, but there is no cablegram after the Soviet pact. There is nothing in that of record indicating how Moscow got the instructions to the Communist Party to the United States as to what line to take with reference to this new change of policy.

So whatever instructions that came would have had to come through the route that you have just described.

Mr. HOWE. That could be very easily done. It would be very difficult to find out who received it because there are probably around one hundred fifty, maybe, members of the Communist Party and good members I mean, who are working on ships and they could easily call up Moscow or any other station in Russia and get this important information, and they could even relay it to some other ship were they unable to deliver it in person. There is always some ship arriving in New York or Boston or some other port.

Mr. DEMPSEY. Would it not be possible for the station at Moscow to call up the *Manhattan*, as you say, a few hours out of New York?

Mr. HOWE. Oh, yes.

Mr. DEMPSEY. Without that message being intercepted by other ships?

Mr. Howe. Well, if the Moscow station would use its own call letters——

Mr. Dempsey. No matter what call letters.

Mr. Howe. I will explain that. If the Moscow station would use its own call letters and also the official call letters of the *Manhattan*, then if we were listening we would know that Moscow was working the *Manhattan*. But undoubtedly they wouldn't do it that way. As I said earlier in my testimony, they would probably use some false letters—a Chinese call. You understand that the international conventions of radio engineers have designated certain letters of the alphabet for each country.

For illustration, the United States has the letters "K" and "N."

Mr. Dempsey. The same as any telegraph station. They all have letters.

Mr. Howe. These are listed in books which are on board every ship. You can look in the books and look up the name of any ship and find out what its call letters are. But now if you are violating the law and you want to conceal your identity, you would not use that call letter. You would use some false call.

Mr. Dempsey. But the message itself could be heard by any one that might be listening in. There might be several hundred boats hearing the message?

Mr. Howe. That is right.

The Chairman. But suppose the message is a special code?

Mr. Howe. Then you would have to know the secret to the code to translate it.

The Chairman. So it would be possible if there was a secret code agreed upon between the radio operator and the Moscow sending station, it would be possible to transmit a message without any record being made or without anyone knowing what the message was?

Mr. Howe. I don't see why the Russian Government couldn't send a message to its Ambassador here. They undoubtedly——

The Chairman. The operator wouldn't have to know the code. The man that gets the message is the only man that needs to know the code?

Mr. Howe. Just so the letters are there—A, B, C, and D; doesn't matter what they mean. He can send or receive them.

Mr. Matthews. Mr. Howe, you stated a moment ago the Communist Party had something like 150 men aboard ships. Did you mean radio operators?

Mr. Howe. Yes, sir.

Mr. Matthews. One hundred and fifty radio operators?

Mr. Howe. One hundred and fifty operators; yes.

Mr. Matthews. With respect to the question the chairman asked you about the foreign policies of Moscow, being furthered by the Communist Party members who are in trade unions, I show you an official ballot. Can you identify that paper [handing paper to the witness]?

Mr. Howe. This is the official ballot of the marine division of the A. C. A. It was sent out to all members of the marine division in the fall of 1938.

Mr. Matthews. Now, underneath the place where the members vote for the national officers there appears a resolution entitled "Resolution on Spain, Resolution No. 27."

Mr. Howe. That is right. This resolution No. 27 was adopted by the fourth national convention of A. C. A. held in New York in 1938. during the month of August, I believe.

The resolution states that the A. C. A. will support the Spanish Loyalist Government.

"*Resolved.* That we extend our deepest sympathy to our brother unionists and democrats in the ranks of the people's army of the Spanish Loyalist Government, who are fighting against such great odds in defense of democracy, and the independence of their national freedom; against the aggressions of Italy and Germany.

That ballot was sent out to all the—I should say it was sent out to all the members of A. C. A.—15,000 members. This is the marine division ballot only. That was voted on. They have a place here where you could vote "yes" or "no" on it.

Mr. Matthews. I ask that be marked in evidence as an exhibit.

The Chairman. It is so ordered.

(The document referred to by Mr. Matthews was marked "Howe Exhibit No. 1," and made a part of the record.)

Mr. Matthews. Now, Mr. Howe, you are familiar with the various resolutions passed at the various conventions of the American Communications Association, are you not?

Mr. Howe. Yes; I am.

Mr. Matthews. I will read you some of these resolutions and ask you if you will please identify them.

In August 1937, the August 14 issue of the People's Press, there appears a report of the third national convention of the A. R. T. A., and this report states:

War and fascism were denounced. The delegates heard such speakers as John Brophy, Joe Curran, William Hinkley, of the American Youth Congress, and S. R. Solomonick, of the American League Against War and Fascism. And it voted unanimously to participate in the peace parade on Saturday.

Do you recall the adoption of that resolution?

Mr. Howe. That resolution was adopted and they voted to participate in the peace parade and they did participate in it. They adjourned the convention for that purpose.

Mr. Matthews. Was that peace parade under the auspices of the American League Against War and Fascism?

Mr. Howe. Yes; it was.

The Chairman. Now, is there any record that since Russia's invasion of Poland and Finland that this union or any other union affiliated with this group, has gone on record expressing the sympathy for the people of Poland or Finland who were invaded by Russia?

Mr. Howe. No; I haven't seen a single one. I don't think so.

The Chairman. Any record where the Communist Party or any of the unions controlled by the Communist Party have sought any relief funds to aid the people of Poland and Finland, who were the victims of aggression?

Mr. Howe. No. I haven't seen such thing. I don't think you will.

The Chairman. Or for the people of Norway or for the people of Sweden who are the victims of aggression—Denmark, rather, Denmark and Norway who are the victims of aggression by the Nazi-Germany? Have you seen any interest where the Communist Party are manifesting any sympathy for them.

Mr. Howe. I read the Daily Worker every night. That is the official daily organ of the Communist Party published in New York, and I haven't seen any sympathy expressed for Finland or Poland or Norway or Denmark. In fact they claim that Finland invaded Russia, I believe, and that Norway is to blame for Germany being in there.

The CHAIRMAN. And England was responsible for the invasion of Norway and Denmark?

Mr. Howe. The imperialists are the dirty scoundrels now.

The CHAIRMAN. In other words, it further illustrates what we have heard from the beginning here, that whatever the party line of Moscow, whatever the interest of Moscow is, that determines the entire policy of the Communist Party of the United States and every organization that it can control?

Mr. Howe. That is very true. I read the Pilot—I read the A. C. A. News and the Daily Worker and occasionally get a copy of the C. I. O. News. They take exactly the same position on everything.

They are against the Dies Committee. They are now against Mr. Hoover, the G-man, and they are silent about the Hitler-Stalin pact. They condemn Finland or else they keep silent about it, one or the other. They don't defend Finland and Norway. They take the same attitude on everything, including President Roosevelt.

When Browder changed his party line and came out against Roosevelt why the rest of them all followed suit. This is particularly true with the A. C. A. They passed a resolution against Roosevelt in Chicago a few days ago and at the same convention Mrs. Roosevelt made a speech.

The CHAIRMAN. So that we really have a situation of a foreign government dictating to a large group in the United States what their politics and activities must be?

Mr. Howe. That is exactly what it is.

The CHAIRMAN. And the absolute obedience on the part of these groups in such cases. In other words, no matter how much change of opinion it may involve, they are ready to turn about face whenever instructions are sent from Moscow to do that?

Mr. Howe. If Joe Stalin would tell them to commit suicide I really think they would all do it.

The CHAIRMAN. Might be well if he told them that.

Mr. THOMAS. Just a few days ago there was a public statement to the press praising the A. C. A. and the head of the A. C. A.

Mr. Howe. Who was that? Mrs. Roosevelt?

Mr. THOMAS. I am not going to mention any names but one of the people you mentioned. But in regard to your statement about the C. I. O., do you really believe that the C. I. O. News, the paper that you mentioned, follows the same line that is in the Daily Worker?

Mr. Howe. As far as I can see they have a writer—his name is Len De Caux, I believe. He writes for the Pilot, the A. C. A. News, and C. I. O. News. I believe he is also in the Daily Worker, but I have forgotten about that. I can't see any difference. It is the same old party line on everything.

The CHAIRMAN. All right. Have you been keeping up with some of the Nazi publications in the United States like the Weckruff?

Mr. Howe. No.

The CHAIRMAN. To observe the similarity between the line now, the arguments they use and the policy between the Daily Worker and the Weckruff. They are now using the same arguments. The Germans are talking about plutocratic countries and imperialists and the Daily Worker is using the same language?

Mr. HOWE. I haven't got that from the publications but I have from members who are—who claim to be Fascists and they do give the same story. It is difficult to tell a Communist from a Fascist or Nazi.

The CHAIRMAN. All right.

Mr. MATTHEWS. Mr. Howe, did you have some personal experiences with respect to the American League Against War and Fascism?

Mr. HOWE. I mention the name of S. R. Solomonick. He was an official of the American League for Peace and Democracy as also was Willard Bliss, who was executive vice president of A. C. A. They got in a fight with Rathborne and then went with the American League for Peace and Democracy and were there when that organization folded up during the winter of 1937. A. R. T. A., Local 2, voted to send a delegate to a Congress of the American League for Peace and Democracy and that was a very heated debate in Local 2 over that, and I was in favor of sending a delegate and I was elected to go to this convention.

So I went to see Mr. Solomonick before the Congress opened, to see what it was all about—what we were supposed to do. I met Mr. Solomonick in his office, and he offered to write my speech for me if I would come there and make a speech. I asked him what would be the nature of the speech or what could I say. "Well," he said, "you are a radio operator, aren't you? You work on ships." "Now," he said, "in time of war if this country gets into a war, what would be the first thing to do?" I said, "You can tell me that." "Well," he said, "naturally tie up the ships and stop the war." I said, "Mr. Solomonick, there are certain men in our organization that believe that this league is controlled by Communists." He said, "That was ridiculous." He showed me a list of around 200 names— there were two or three bishops and several preachers on the list. They were sponsors of the American League. I didn't tell Mr. Solomonick what I thought about him or his organization, but I went back to A. R. T. A., Local 2, and I resigned as a delegate to that Congress and no other delegate was elected.

I told the members what I had discussed with Mr. Solomonick; that I was certain that the American League was just as much a Communist organization as the Communist Party itself, and I would have nothing to do with it. But that American League sent speakers to A. R. T. A., Local 2, just as often as we would receive them.

They came there many times and talked about the May Day demonstration or the public trial of William Randolph Hearst, and were always taking up collections.

We frequently gave them money out of our treasury. And Mr. Solomonick spoke at the third and also the fourth A. C. A. national convention.

Mr. MATTHEWS. And he was an official of the American League for Peace and Democracy?

Mr. Howe. He was an official of the American League at that time and was invited there by Mervyn Rathborne, president of the A. C. A.

The Chairman. Now, before we go into the other phases of this witness' testimony, I think it would be well for us to adjourn for a while. I understand that you gentlemen were up nearly all night going over this material and getting ready for today. An early adjournment will give you an opportunity to rest for a while. Suppose we meet back here at 2 o'clock and complete this testimony.

(Whereupon, at 11:45 a. m., a recess was taken until 2 p. m., the same day.)

AFTER RECESS

The Chairman. The committee will please come to order. The witness will resume the stand.

TESTIMONY OF FRED M. HOWE—Resumed

The Chairman. For the benefit of the record, will you again state your name and the organization with which you are connected?

Mr. Howe. My name is Fred M. Howe; secretary of the American Radio Telegraphists' Association, Local No. 2, New York, affiliated with the C. I. O.

The Chairman. All right; proceed, Mr. Matthews.

Mr. Matthews. Mr. Howe, this morning you identified one of the resolutions passed at the convention of the A. R. T. A. I should like to read you some more resolutions passed at the various meetings and ask you to identify them:

Moved and seconded that the Communist Party be advised to refrain immediately from passing leaflets referring American Radio Telegraphers' Association.

Do you recall when that motion was introduced in Local 2?

Mr. Howe. That was passed by the membership of A. R. T. A., Local 2, some time during the strike—the seamen's strike which occurred during the winter of 1936 and 1937. The exact date I don't recall.

Mr. Matthews. Was the motion tabled?

Mr. Howe. Yes. That motion was tabled, to my recollection.

Mr. Matthews. Do you recall whether it was tabled by a vote of 33 to 14?

Mr. Howe. Well, I have forgotten about the details.

Pearlman, O. J. A., moved that those members who were not present at the last meeting and who desire to make it possible for the American Student Union to prevent students from scabbing, contribute to a collection to be taken up at this meeting and that a letter be sent to the American Student Union, to the local secretary, enclosing a check for the funds collected at this and the previous meeting.

Do you recall whether such a motion was passed or not?

Mr. Howe. Such a motion was introduced. I have just forgotten the disposition of it but I am quite certain that that was adopted by a majority of the members.

Mr. Matthews. July 21.

Moved and seconded that Mr. Van Taine of the American League Against War and Fascism be permitted to address the meeting. Carried unanimously.

Do you recall that motion?

Mr. Howe. I recall that and a great many others of that nature. Mr. Van Taine of the American League for Peace and Democracy at that time called the American League Against War and Fascism, came to the hall of Local 2 on a great many occasions and addressed the membership there for various purposes or causes. Sometimes it was a May Day demonstration. It may have been some kind of a peace meeting or parade or all the causes that the Communists usually sponsor. He came there many times.

Mr. Matthews. I will read you another motion of April 21.

Moved and seconded that a preparations committee be elected to make arrangements for the participation of ARTA in the May Day parade and to provide proper banners and to take care of all mechanics of participation.

Was that motion adopted?

Mr. Howe. I believe it was.

Mr. Matthews. Was that a May Day parade held in New York City?

Mr. Howe. Yes.

Mr. Matthews. Was it the May Day parade under the control of the Communist Party of New York City?

Mr. Howe. I think all of those parades are under the control of the Communist Party. About the only persons who participate in them are Communists and their stooges. Perhaps we should call them dupes.

Mr. Matthews. Mr. Howe, the water-front section of the Communist Party, located at 230 Seventh Avenue, New York, publish a ship paper. Did you ever see a copy of it?

Mr. Howe. I have a copy in my files at home.

Mr. Matthews. You have a copy?

Mr. Howe. Yes.

Mr. Matthews. Now, I would like to read you a paragraph from a certain issue:

This paper should be handwritten, type or mimeographed, depending on the ship's situation, length of trips and so forth. The paper should reflect the ship in company dues and should also raise issues for the crew. Establish contact with "sparks."

Now, what is "sparks"?

Mr. Howe. Sparks is the term given to the radio officer aboard ship. It dates back to the old type of transmitter where you could hear the sparkle all over the ship, so when the spark sounded they called the man who sent it "sparks."

Mr. Matthews. In other words, the Communist Party is here instructing its members to make contact with the ship operators?

Mr. Howe. Yes. That was put out to the seamen. Of course they told the seamen to contact sparks or the radio officer.

Mr. Matthews. Will you be good enough to furnish the committee a copy of that particular issue of this leaflet?

Mr. Howe. I will be very glad to.

Mr. Matthews. You are acquainted with Mervyn Rathborne, are you. Mr. Howe?

Mr. Howe. I know him very well.

Mr. Matthews. Mr. Chairman, for a minute I should like to have Mr. Frank B. Powers sworn to identify a communication.

The Chairman. Come around, Mr. Powers. Raise your right hand please.

TESTIMONY OF FRANK B. POWERS

The CHAIRMAN. Do you solemnly swear to tell the truth, the whole truth, and nothing but the truth soyhelp you God?

Mr. POWERS. Yes, sir.

Mr. MATTHEWS. It will not even be necessary for the witness to be seated, Mr. Chairman.

Mr. Powers, I show you a photostatic copy of a letter addressed to you and signed by Mervyn Rathborne. Can you identify that as a true copy of a letter you received from Mr. Rathborne [handing paper to the witness]?

Mr. POWERS. That is a true copy.

Mr. MATTHEWS. Thank you. This letter is dated February 4, 1931, and is addressed to Mr. Frank B. Powers, C. T. U. of N. A., the Commercial Telegraphers' Union of North America, 113 South Ashland Boulevard, Chicago, Ill.

DEAR SIR. Relative to my letter of January 20 I would appreciate some indication from you as to just what the officials of the CTU intend to do in regard to the Pacific Marine Radio Division. During the past two weeks two new members have joined. I had been working on these men for a long time and did not want to stop them from joining at the last moment while there was still a chance of settling the present difficulties in regard to support.

If the CTU is no longer interested in a radio division, please advise me at your earliest convenience so we make plans to establish an independent organization. Incidentally, the Communist Party in great contrast to the CTU, is eager and willing to organize the operators. Of course their idea is to cause a tie-up of American shipping and to make trouble, but one would think that an American organization, such as the American Federation of Labor, would be willing to do as much as a foreign outfit bent on making trouble.

I am still convinced that I can obtain a substantial number of new members if I were permitted to get out and organize. Results have proved this so far as each time I have been to the harbor I have obtained one member.

Trusting that I may hear from you in the near future, sincerely, Mervyn R. Rathborne.

TESTIMONY OF FRED M. HOWE—Resumed

Mr. MATTHEWS. Mr. Howe, you have seen a copy of this letter, have you not?

Mr. HOWE. Yes, sir.

Mr. MATTHEWS. I show you a photostatic copy of a page from the Daily Worker, dated January 4, 1935. Have you seen a copy of this particular page from the Daily Worker and particularly an article entitled "Red Scare Raised Among Telegraphists."

Mr. HOWE. I don't believe I have seen this particular issue of the paper, but I have seen that article reproduced.

Mr. MATTHEWS. This article reads in part as follows:

Bulletin against communists issued by candidate for president of the ARTA, Houston, Texas. There are certain elements in the American Radio Telegraphists' Association that are attempting to raise the Red scare as a means of splitting up our organization.

One of these birds by the name of Mervyn Rathborne, who ran for president of the ARTA in the election, has taken the initiative to issue the following slanderous bulletin, addressed to Dollar Line Radio Operators. Sections of the text follow:

"Judging from information received in New York it appears that our Association, the ARTA, is in danger of being dominated and run by a small but powerful group of communists.

"An indication of communist activity within our ranks is shown by an article entitled 'The Marine Strike', published on page 3 of the October issue of the ARTA Bulletin. This article mentions 'the United Front Strike Committee, composed of the New York Local of the ARTA, the Marine Workers Industrial Union, along with unorganized seamen, and the I. S. U. seamen who had gone over the heads of their leaders.' The existence of such a committee indicates definitely that close and active cooperation, if nothing more, exists between the ARTA and the M. W. I. U. Proof that the M. W. I. U. is a communist organization is given in the Official Program adopted by the M. W. I. U. National Convention. which states: 'The M. W. I. U. is affiliated with the Red International of Labor Unions which embraces over sixteen million workers organized in unions. Through the R. I. L. U., the M. W. I. U. is linked up with millions of revolutionary workers not only in Europe, Russia, but in China, Korea, Japan, Indonesia, Australia and Latin America.'

"Additional evidence that the ARTA is swinging very far to the left is shown in the minutes of the ARTA national convention held in New York last September. This meeting of ARTA representatives from all sections of the country adopted numerous resolutions endorsing or ordering active cooperation with the United States Congress Against War and Fascism. the Atlantic Unity Conference, the Telegraph Messengers Union. the United Telegraphers Association and others. At the Congress Against War and Fascism Earl Browder, Secretary-General of the Communist Party of America, stated, 'This congress was organized and called by the Communist Party.' "

This bulletin then goes on to urge the members to investigate who is responsible for these leftwing moves and vote accordingly in the election.

You have seen that statement put out by Mr. Rathborne in 1935?

Mr. Howe. Yes, sir.

Mr. Matthews. Do you know of your own knowledge that up until a date as late as January 1935, that Mr. Rathborne did so claim that the A. R. T. A. was in danger of being dominated by the Communist Party?

Mr. Howe. The exact date I am not certain about, but I do know that Rathborne at least ceased "red-baiting" about that time, and his stopping criticizing the "reds" is similar to that of a great many other officials and members of the A. R. T. A. and A. C. A., who have come under the influence of the party and suddenly stopped all criticism of it. because they were given a job or paid off or intimidated in some way.

Rathborne is a typical example. Another man is the vice president of the marine division of A. C. A.—J. E. Croney. Croney did the same thing. He suddenly stopped criticizing the "reds" at approximately April 2, 1939. My interpretation of that is that Rathborne was made an offer by the party—by the party faction in A. R. T. A.

Mr. Matthews. Your knowledge extends to the fact that since this date Mr. Rathborne has not criticized the Communist control?

Mr. Howe. Not once to my knowledge.

Mr. Matthews. But prior to that time he himself publicly stated that the A. R. T. A. was run——

Mr. Howe. Run by Communists.

Mr. Matthews. Under Communist domination?

Mr. Howe. Yes, sir.

Mr. Matthews. Or drifting in the direction of Communist domination?

Mr. Howe. Yes, sir.

Mr. Thomas. Mr. Matthews, it is not clear to me as to what date that is you are referring to?

Mr. Howe. It is the latter part of 1934 or the first part of 1935. Rathborne ran for the secretary-treasurership of A. R. T. A. on a "red baiting" ticket. He was elected and refused to serve and a deal was made by which he would give up that job to Willard Bliss. Bliss took the job, although he was not elected to it, with the understanding that Rathborne become the next president, which he did become, and then Bliss was to be Rathborne's successor, but Rathborne refused to give up the job. A fight occurred between Bliss and Rathborne. Bliss left the A. C. A. and went with the American League for Peace and Democracy and was with the American League for Peace and Democracy until it closed its doors here because of the exposure by the Dies committee.

Mr. MATTHEWS. Now, I want to read you another portion of a letter, and ask you if you can identify it, in which Rathborne was continuing to criticize the Communists. This letter was dated December 11, 1934. Rathborne wrote:

Your stand regarding outside influences in the ARTA is splendid. It reflects my opinion very well. You must remember that a good Communist cannot be a member of the ARTA and remain a C. P. man. The nature of the C. P. obliges him to carry on underhanded intrigue, plots, and plans in any other non-communistic organization.

I believe that it is impossible for a man to be a sincere and loyal communist and a good ARTA member at the same time.

Do you recall that?

Mr. HOWE. Yes. I have a photostatic copy of that letter at home.

Mr. MATTHEWS. Will you be good enough to supply the committee with a photostatic copy of the original of that letter?

Mr. HOWE. Yes, sir.

Mr. MATTHEWS. Do you recall any communication in which Rathborne stated that he was threatened if he did not withdraw from the race for the national secretary-treasurership of the A. R. T. A.?

Mr. HOWE. I have a copy of that letter—a photostatic copy, I should say—which Rathborne claimed that he was threatened with physical violence if he did not resign from the race for the secretary-treasurership.

Mr. MATTHEWS. I read you a quotation from the letter:

During the past 10 days I have been advised twice that my well-being and health will continue to be good only if I withdraw from the race for the secretary-treasurership.

Is that the language of the communication?

Mr. HOWE. Yes, sir.

Mr. MATTHEWS. Now, you say that after his election—that is, he did not withdraw, Rathborne resigned?

Mr. HOWE. Yes, sir.

Mr. MATTHEWS. Is that the fact?

Mr. HOWE. Yes. He did not accept the position.

Mr. MATTHEWS. Now, what magazine was he publishing at that time?

Mr. HOWE. The name of it was C. Q.

Mr. MATTHEWS. The letters C. Q.?

Mr. HOWE. C. Q., yes.

Mr. MATTHEWS. Did you notice a distinct change in the policy of C. Q., after Mr. Rathborne's resignation from his position?

Mr. HOWE. Yes; we all did. It was remarked upon.

Mr. MATTHEWS. Did he cease entirely his criticism of the Communists and the Communist Party.

Mr. Howe. As far as any of us can remember he never did criticize the party again and would object to anyone else criticizing the party. It stopped very suddenly at that particular time.

Mr. Matthews. Did C. Q. take on the political complexion of the Communist press at that time?

Mr. Howe. It practically followed the party line shortly thereafter.

Mr. Matthews. Now, was Rathborne subsequently and shortly made president of A. R. T. A.?

Mr. Howe. Yes; he was the next president of A. R. T. A. He succeeded Hoyt Haddock.

Mr. Matthews. And he defeated Bliss; is that correct?

Mr. Howe. Yes; Haddock defeated Bliss in the election for the secretary-treasurership.

Mr. Matthews. Now, will you please first answer the question and then give as definitely as you are able a reason for your answer. Is Rathborne a Communist?

Mr. Howe. Yes.

Mr. Matthews. Why do you make that statement, Mr. Howe?

Mr. Howe. I make that statement for a great variety of reasons, and if the committee wishes to hear them I will be pleased to give all the reasons.

Mr. Matthews. I think the evidence is important. Will you please.

Mr. Howe. I have some letters there, you have them in your possession, which I received from the second vice president of the marine division of A. C. A. His name is J. E. Croney. He lives in New Orleans. He is the secretary of A. C. A., Local No. 5, at the present time. And as I said second vice president of the marine division.

In these letters which he has written to me, to which he has signed his name, he states that Rathborne has been a member of the party for a considerable length of time, since 1935, I believe. But without looking at the letters we would still know that Rathborne is a Communist.

In the winter of 1937 we had a trial in local 2, a trial of the local secretary. His name was Frank W. Robinson, and he was a Communist and a member of the party and still is a member of the marine division of A. C. A.

Frank Robinson when asked by the trial committee whom he wished to defend him at the trial, stated that he would like to have Mr. Rathborne defend him. Mr. Rathborne was not known in New York by any of the members of local 2. He had just arrived in New York from San Francisco only the day before, and he was selected by Robinson to defend him.

During the course of his defense Rathborne stated as follows:

"I wish to quote from the Declaration of Independence," and he held up a book before him; the title of it was something like this:

"Communism by Earl Browder," and from that book he quoted the Declaration of Independence. It was the only place that Rathborne, apparently, knew where to find the Declaration of Independence—Earl Browder's book on communism.

Mr. Thomas. I would like to ask a question right there. Is this the same Mr. Rathborne who was just recently appointed by the President of the United States to the Board of the National Youth Administration?

Mr. Howe. Yes, sir; that is the same man.

Mr. Thomas. So this man Rathborne was appointed to aid in the development of our youth.

The Chairman. Wait a minute. That is a matter of public record.

Mr. Thomas. I want to have it in the record. I think it is very important it appear in this record because here is a man who was appointed to aid in the development of youth of this country, and you have had any amount of testimony that this man Rathborne is a Communist. It is just another flirtation of the New Deal with communism.

The Chairman. Well, that is a question that the witness, as I understand, cannot say on his personal knowledge that Rathborne is a member of the Communist Party. He is merely stating his conclusions based upon circumstances; is that right?

Mr. Howe. Well, I have never seen his membership card, naturally. Rathborne is said to hold——

The Chairman. Well, the only reason that you have for saying or believing that Rathborne is a member of the Communist Party is the fact that after 1935 he ceased to attack the party, ceased to criticize the party, and his publication followed the Communist line; is that right?

Mr. Howe. Yes; he followed the party line himself.

The Chairman. And in addition to that you state that another reason that you think he is a member of the Communist Party is that in a trial of some officer in the union he defended him. That would be entirely possible for a man to do without being a Communist himself, would it not?

Mr. Howe. It would seem that way, but when you know the Communists it is quite unthinkable.

Mr. Thomas. And there is an additional reason.

The Chairman. I may say in my judgment the only possible reason for admitting this type of testimony because of the circumstances that have arisen—the inability of the committee to get the membership lists of the Communist Party, their statement that they have no records, when the committee is fully advised that they do have records and in addition to that we have found records in certain places, detailed and complete records.

The committee has tried every possible way to secure an authentic list of the Communist Party members. We have secured lists but have been unable to get the lists that we think are authentic. We have been unable to get those lists proven in a satisfactory way. So in the face of the refusal of the Communist Party to make public their membership list so that the country may know who the members are we are compelled to resort to secondary evidence, but it should be recognized that it is secondary evidence. And as I interpret this testimony it is largely a conclusion of this witness based upon certain reasons that he has. But let us hear all the reasons.

Mr. Matthews. May I suggest the witness has not concluded his reasons?

The Chairman. I understand that is true, but I think when a witness says that a certain man is a Communist that there ought to be some tangible proof to support that statement.

Mr. Thomas. I would like to have the witness repeat the last reason which he gave, and that is about reading the Declaration of Independence from Earl Browder's book on communism. That is enough proof for me.

Mr. MASON. Go on with the hearing.

The CHAIRMAN. Go ahead.

Mr. MATTHEWS. Mr. Howe, have you ever openly in a meeting charged Mr. Rathborne with being a Communist?

Mr. HOWE. I have done that many times on the floor of Local 2.

Mr. MATTHEWS. And what happened when you did that?

Mr. HOWE. When Mr. Rathborne was present in a meeting he has never denied to the membership of Local 2 that he was a Communist; that he was a member of the party. I have read some of these letters that have been mentioned here. This one over here—Mr. Powers confirmed this one. I read that before the membership of Local 2, and accused Mr. Rathborne of being a Communist and a party member and he didn't get out of his seat to reply to that. I might say the same thing about Joe Curran, president of the National Maritime Union. He came down to Local 2 to put me on the spot several times, and I made that accusation to him and to Blackie Meyers and to Roy A. Pyle and none of them denied it point blank.

The CHAIRMAN. You mean by that that they were present at a public meeting of the union?

Mr. HOWE. Yes.

The CHAIRMAN. And that you charged Rathborne with being a Communist and read letters to show it and that he did not deny your charge?

Mr. HOWE. He did not deny it. He did not get up to defend himself by saying a single word and that was enough for me. It was enough for the membership of Local 2 to believe and they do so believe, nine-tenths of the members of the A. R. T. A., Local 2 right today believe that Mervyn Rathborne is not only a Communist, but that he is a member of the party because they were there at these various meetings when the charges were made and he failed to defend himself at all.

The CHAIRMAN. Well, was there any reason that he should fail to defend himself? I mean by that, did he undertake to treat it as a joke or did the members treat it that way. Were the charges treated seriously?

Mr. HOWE. Yes; they were with a serious meaning and it may have been due to the fact that I produced some of his old letters and he perhaps thought I had other things that I could produce also that he hesitated.

The CHAIRMAN. Any other reason?

Mr. MATTHEWS. Now, Mr. Howe, will you please answer this question: Who was it again who recommended Mr. Rathborne for the presidency?

Mr. HOWE. Mr. Rathborne was recommended to the membership of the Maritime Division of A. R. T. A. by Mr. Hoyt Haddock.

Mr. MATTHEWS. He was the retiring president, was he?

Mr. HOWE. Retiring president and took a job as labor adviser for the Standard Oil of New Jersey.

Mr. MATTHEWS. Now, was Haddock a known Communist?

Mr. HOWE. Haddock was a known Communist, the same as Rathborne is today and I have proof from Haddock's own words to me.

He invited me out to lunch. We had a discussion about the subject of communism and it became quite heated. Mr. Haddock told me that a man who was not a Communist—pardon me—"was a damn fool." They are the very words that Hoyt Haddock used to me.

Mr. MATTHEWS. Now, during the summer of 1937, did Rathborne receive any substantial sum of money from John L. Lewis for organizing purposes?

Mr. HOWE. Rathborne received more than $100,000 from John L. Lewis' organization for the purpose of organizing the communication workers, mainly in the Postal Telegraph, a little bit of Western Union, and a great deal for the longshoremen of the Atlantic coast and the Gulf.

Mr. MATTHEWS. Is that a matter of record in the publications of the A. C. A.?

Mr. HOWE. Yes, sir. That may be seen by reading the financial reports published in the A. C. A. News.

Mr. MATTHEWS. Now, did Rathborne engage organizers for organizing in accordance with the purpose of this donation?

Mr. HOWE. Yes. Rathborne hired a great many organizers.

Mr. MATTHEWS. Do you know any of the organizers that Rathborne engaged?

Mr. HOWE. I know most all of those who were engaged in the communications field.

Mr. MATTHEWS. Do you know that Rathborne did or did not make it a point to engage only organizers who were Communists or sympathetic to the Communist Party line?

Mr. HOWE. As far as we could determine he did not hire anyone who was not a Communist—all of his organizers were Communists.

The CHAIRMAN. The committee is now sitting as a subcommittee. I will make the statement for the sake of the record. We have been this afternoon as a subcommittee. I think that statement was made this morning. The subcommittee is composed of the chairman, Mr. Mason, the gentleman from New Mexico, Mr. Dempsey.

Proceed.

Mr. MATTHEWS. Will you please name some of the organizers whom you know to be Communists who were employed by Rathborne in this campaign of organization?

Mr. HOWE. Joseph Belleza, T. J. Van Erman.

Mr. MATTHEWS. Did he employ Al Lannon?

Mr. HOWE. Al Lannon, I believe was on his pay roll. Al Lannon is a Communist and writes for the Daily Worker frequently.

Mr. MATTHEWS. The previous witness testified he was a member of the Communist Party.

Mr. HOWE. Mr. Al Lannon was engaged in organizing the longshoremen mainly, and he was publishing a small paper called The Shape Up, for the benefit of the longshoremen and Local A. R. T. A. contributed money quite frequently to this shape-up—$5 and $10 at a time to keep it going.

Mr. MATTHEWS. Now, was Rathborne one of the chief organizers of the New York Maritime Council?

Mr. HOWE. Yes, sir. He was one of the chief organizers.

Mr. MATTHEWS. Who was the secretary of that Maritime Council?

Mr. HOWE. The secretary was Thomas Ray, of the National Maritime Union, and is well-known to be a Communist.

Mr. MATTHEWS. Is Thomas Ray generally known to be a Communist?

Mr. HOWE. I think everyone along the New York water front knows that he is. He doesn't deny that.

Mr. MATTHEWS. Well, was Ray compelled to resign from the secretaryship of the New York Maritime Council because of charges of being a Communist?

Mr. HOWE. I believe he resigned because of his failure to do anything. I opposed his reelection and voted against the continuation of the council and another delegate from the National Maritime Union did the same thing and he resigned, and we closed up the council.

Mr. MATTHEWS. Do you know who Rathborne's organizers are on the west coast at the present time?

Mr. HOWE. Douglas Ward is one. He is out in Frisco at the present time. Clare Brown is in Chicago. He is organizing for Western Union. He is a Communist and member of the party. Joseph Selly, I might say that I believe everyone of the vice presidents are on the pay roll as organizers.

Mr. MATTHEWS. Did Rathborne employ a publicity man by the name of Ted Sittell?

Mr. HOWE. Yes. Ted Sittell was quite popular among the Communist element. He was trying to convert non-Communists to the faith and he was hired by Rathborne to act as publicity agent. He was quite able to get Rathborne's name in the paper very often.

Mr. MATTHEWS. Now, you spoke of Roy A. Pyle, the first vice president of the Marine Division of the A. C. A. Did you identify him as a Communist this morning?

Mr. HOWE. I believe I did. He is one anyhow; if I didn't do it I will do it now.

Mr. MATTHEWS. Did Pyle have anything to say when you accused Rathborne and his international executive board of being Communists?

Mr. HOWE. I made a slip of the tongue one day while I was making a speech before the membership, and I accused the entire international executive board of being Communists. Pyle got up and said: "I would like to have you dare to accuse Lenne Ohl and Harold Taylor of being Communists." He only mentioned those two, leaving everyone to believe that all of the rest of them were Communists, including Pyle.

Mr. MATTHEWS. Were there seven others?

Mr. HOWE. There were nine members altogether. We called them the "nine old men."

Mr. MATTHEWS. When you said "the entire executive board were Communists" his reply was that he challenged you to accuse these two men of being Communists, is that correct?

Mr. HOWE. That is right. And he did not deny that he was a Communist.

Mr. MATTHEWS. Well, was there ever any occasion when Pyle was asked to sign an affidavit respecting his own political affiliations?

Mr. HOWE. We were trying to unite the C. I. O. radio officers' union with that of the A. F. of L., and we elected a committee to sit with a similar committee of the C. T. U. Pyle was elected as an alternate delegate. Not being a member of Local 2, he was not allowed to serve. He came to me and practically begged me to be allowed to go along and I told him that we all believed that he was a Communist, member of the party, and the C. T. U. would not meet with the Communists on the committee. So Pyle said: "Why, that is foolish; I am not a Communist." And I said, "Well, I will tell you what you do, Mr. Pyle. You go down to the next floor below before a notary public and make out an affidavit that you are not a Communist; that you are not a member of the party, that you never were such, sign that and swear to it and bring it back to me and I will do all I can to get you on this committee so that you can go along with us."

And Pyle refused to do that. Might also say that Hoyt Haddock only about 2 weeks ago refused to do that very thing in my presence—refused to put themselves on record that they are not such.

Mr. MATTHEWS. Have you frequently criticized the Communist Party and the Communists for their activities in the union?

Mr. HOWE. I was a severe critic of that all the time.

Mr. MATTHEWS. Have you been denounced by Rathborne for "red-baiting" because you criticized the Communist Party?

Mr. HOWE. Yes. I was denounced many times by him and by others for "red-baiting."

Mr. MATTHEWS. Now, Mr. Howe, I wish to show you some communications. Here is a letter dated June 2, 1938, addressed to "Dear Brother Howe," and signed by J. E. Croney. Did you receive that communication from J. E. Croney?

Mr. HOWE. Yes; I did.

Mr. MATTHEWS. And will you please identify it for the record?

Mr. HOWE. Mr. J. E. Croney is the second vice president of the Marine Division of A. C. A.

Mr. MATTHEWS. Then you received this communication in connection with your duties as secretary-treasurer of the A. R. T. A., did you?

Mr. HOWE. Yes.

Mr. MATTHEWS (reading):

The following is important: Safer informs me that Comrat Joe Thomas of Port Arthur fame is now in New York. He made one trip on a Lykes ship to Puerto Rico, and upon return to Beaumont the ship layed up. He hung around Port Arthur for a short while, and then disappeared from sight. There is a likelihood the C. P. has sent him to New York for a course of Commie intrigue in the workers' school and what next.

Now, I show you another letter dated June 9, 1938. Did you receive this communication from Croney?

(Handing paper to the witness.)

Mr. HOWE. Yes.

Mr. MATTHEWS. In connection with your duties as secretary-treasurer of Local 2?

Mr. HOWE. Yes.

Mr. MATTHEWS (reading):

Firstly, I want you to observe the Baltimore minutes of May 23rd. Observe the resolution blasting the membership of this Local for time worn Red-baiting. Observe the resolution blasting the members of Local No. 5 for being in the same category of the C. T. U. Well did you ever stop to realize that there never would have been any monstrosity such as the CTU if it had not been for the rule or ruin policy of the comrats? Did you ever stop to realize that the comrats run the unions by a small minority clique of commies and commie stooges. Now it certainly is very obvious who the Rathborne stooges are. Of course the most faithful are the old Commissars Van Erman and the man from Baltimore. There are two of the most venomous rats who have constantly indoctrinated the phoney commie policy to the small clique who quite complacently raise their hands to vote anything the clique puts over.

Now here is the situation. This local is spending every cent for the purpose of building a decent Local. With instructions from the membership we are not paying any more money to the national.

And what local does he refer to in that?

Mr. Howe. That is Local No. 5, New Orleans.

Mr. Matthews. "Did you ever stop to realize that we have never actually paid a bona fide per capita to our national." Now, why is that? Mr. Croney says that the Local in New Orleans has refused to pay to the national.

Mr. Howe. Well, he refused to pay because he thought the money was being spent for subversive purposes by the national office of A. C. A.

Mr. Matthews. I show you a communication dated—addressed to Brothers Howe and Barro.

Mr. Howe. That is right.

Mr. Matthews. Did you receive this communication from Mr. Croney?

Mr. Howe. That is right, I did.

Mr. Matthews. I read you a paragraph:

In conclusion let me tell you that I had a long talk with the Regional Director of the CIO for Alabama yesterday. He says John Lewis is fed up with the comrats. I asked him why the hell did he keep them on the payroll in non-elective positions. The only excuse is "it is a long range program."

I show you a communication dated only "Wednesday afternoon." Did you receive that letter from Mr. Croney?

(Handing paper to the witness.)

Mr. Howe. Yes.

Mr. Matthews. I quote a portion of the letter:

I am so damned mad today that I cannot think straight. I may as well tell you that I am reaching the end of my rope with the damned commie blanks. It is becoming too much for me. Personally I do not understand how decent people can carry along with them, but I am sending this in supplication that you do not resign at this time. You must realize that the real members of ARTA are on the ships and they will back you up. The comrats remain on shore; they live like rats in a sewer; wait to pack the meetings, and you will continue to have trouble as long as Rathburne remains in the national which, of course, he will. because there is no opposition to oust him.

Mr. Casey. Who is that letter from?

Mr. Matthews. This is from Mr. J. E. Croney, the secretary of local 5 of the American Communications Association, in New Orleans, addressed to Mr. Howe, secretary of local 2 in New York City.

If we are to just take them in to please the wishes of the Commissar chieftains, such as Curran. Please send me a letter to my house. For God's sake do not turn over the Local to the C. P. at this time. It is evident that the national will be in complete hands of the C. P. Jordan is a C. P. Selly and the rest of the gang.

I show you a letter dated August 1, 1938. Did you receive that communication from Mr. Croney [handing paper to the witness]?

Mr. Howe. Yes, sir; I did.

Mr. Matthews (reading):

I hope you fellows will not arouse the comrats to dupe you into any compromise. Their honor is that of a skunk and any terms they make will not be maintained. The mistake right along has not been to denounce the rats a long time ago. We have no intention of allowing Jordan to do any coordinating in this neck of the woods.

I show you another letter dated March 13, 1939. Did you receive this communication from Mr. Croney [handing paper to the witness]?

Mr. Howe. Yes, sir; I did.

Mr. Matthews (reading):

I want all of you to understand that there is no retreat so far as I am personally concerned, not even if the ACA gets control of the contracts. My decision is absolutely irrevocable. I shall never return to the ACA which is controlled by the worst kind of dictatorship that has ever been used in the American labor movement. It will take time for the members to realize the audacity of these comrat fakirs. These same rats who raved up and down the country a few years ago about the ISU dictatorship are even now worse than they. Their international executive board is the same thing as the ISU executive board. I cannot see the difference.

Here is a communication dated New Orleans, La., July 1, 1938. Did you receive this letter from Mr. Croney [handing paper to the witness]?

Mr. Howe. Yes, sir; I did.

Mr. Matthews (reading):

I am still suffering from the shock at reading your letter. To imagine you would waste any time with one of the most monstrous fakirs in the labor movement. One of the most dangerous comrats in this country. Sleek, hypocritical politician Comrade Hoyt Haddock. The curly haired boy of Standard Oil Company.

The Chairman. Just a second, please. Let me announce a change in the subcommittee. The subcommittee is now composed of the chairman, the gentleman from Massachusetts, Mr. Casey, and Mr. Mason. Proceed.

Mr. Matthews (reading):

Well, I will be darned. And this comrat is actually very perturbed and worried about the Gulf and ARTA in this Gulf.

And on page 2 of this letter:

You know damn well that CIO, ACA, C. P. was rammed down the throats of the members. You know that the boys on the ships are lead to do things that they know nothing about. I also see CIO as okay but not to be dominated and run by comrats, and there is no denying the fact that the whole damn sheebang is being run by them and the pie-card fakirs such as Brophy are just riding the gravy train.

On page 3 of the same letter:

If John Lewis continues to adhere to the policy of using the comrats to organize with the asinine idea in his head that he can throw them out, he is going to find himself holding the bag and it won't be very long either.

Here is a communication dated April 2, 1938, signed by J. E. Croney. Did you receive this communication from Mr. Croney [handing paper to the witness]?

Mr. Howe. Yes, sir; I did.

Mr. Matthews (reading):

From an unimpeachable source I know that he was kicked out from the grand and noble fraternity of Elks last summer.

What are the "Elks," Mr. Howe?

Mr. Howe. The Elks are the Communists.

Mr. Matthews. That was a slang way of referring to the Communists, was it?

Mr. Howe. Yes, sir.

Mr. Matthews. In your communications with Mr. Croney?

Mr. Howe. I never used that term.

The Chairman. Why did you use that term? If there was an anti-Communist organization, it is the Elks. Why did you use that term?

Mr. Howe. I never used it myself but it is used by men like Croney. That is what he meant.

Mr. Mason. In all probability it is used because the Elks is a great American institution and they wanted to ridicule that institution by perverting the use of that name.

Mr. Matthews. Quoting again from page 3 of this letter:

I warn you to be careful. There are more stooges in the Elks than Elks. The real truth is they do not care if you belong or not, so long as you pack the line and carry out the change of line whenever the great master desires to do so. At the present time the Elks are further to the right than any group. They are secretly sponsoring war. They are sponsoring collective security. They are Red Fascists and I go on record as denouncing them for being the most dangerous element in the labor unions today for the purpose of railroading us into a war which will mean the end of our democracy.

Mr. Mason. What is the date on that letter?

Mr. Matthews. That was dated April 2, 1938, at a period, obviously, when the Communist Party was in favor of collective security.

I show you another communication dated January 2, 1938. Did you receive this from Mr. Croney [handing paper to the witness]?

Mr. Howe. Yes, sir; I did.

Mr. Matthews (reading):

Now, here is something that might interest you: I have had several photostatic copies of letters exposing Mr. Pyle as a comrat since 1935 to 1936. At that time he was in the Communist Party with Haddock and Rathborne. Bliss was the big shot at that time. When Pyle on plans from the Communist Party made a damn mess in the 1935 east coast operators' strike, putting over one hundred fifty radio men on the bricks to no avail, and subsequently caused the loss of the entire UFCO membership, this little fakir Pyle was on the spot pretty bad. The Communist Party wanted Haddock, Bliss, Pyle to resign and Rathborne and Jordon were supposed to come east and take over. These were instructions from Earl Browder himself, but these good comrats would not obey orders. They refused to quit. Later Ratty was run for president. Haddock, becoming stale on the C. P. stuff, wormed his way into a stooge job with the Standard Oil Co., still keeping in C. P. good books. Haddock is the cagiest and most unscrupulous man among them, if you don't happen to know it. I had received this dope from a guy who was in the C. P. at that time but never really believed much of what this crackpot told me. It was with great surprise therefore when Jordon who came here last July and in the presence of his wife in a cafe told me that he was one of the boys who went to see Browder with Haddock, Pyle, and Bliss. Jordon told me he had just hooked up with the C. P. at that time but when Pyle, Haddock, and Bliss refused to resign upon advice of Browder, he never took any active part in the Communist Party from there on. He held a book but refused to go down the line at times. Had not held a Communist Party book since the early spring of 1938. I know it to be a fact the commies never trusted Jordon very much. Jordon, more of a rank and filer, and leaning more toward democracy would buck them at times with the result they called him an "opportunist." One well-known comrat who used to come here on a Swayne and Hoyt ship had lunch with me one day and he blasted the hell out of Jordon. Nevertheless things began to get so critical with the communists shortly before the 1936 to 1937 strike that they were careless with their trusted lieutenants. They started the system of using any man they could find as a stooge. In other words, they became careless. One brother, a rookie in the Communist Party who is now a member of this local, dropped into the national office one afternoon and found Roy Hudson, Haddock and Pyle working over the national's ledger. Roy Hudson, pencil in hand, was figuring out how they were going to cover up several hundred dollars of the money which had been spent. If my memory does not fail me I think there was a miscellaneous statement in the ARTA Bulletin for June 1935, showing something like $498.75 marked up to "Miscellaneous." This money was covered up by the unholy three: Haddock, Hudson, and Pyle. Believe Bliss was in on it also. This fellow as stated above is a member of local 5.

Will you please identify for the record at this point who Roy Hudson is?

Mr. Howe. Roy Hudson is an organizer for the Communist Party He did have charge of the waterfront section of the Communist Party.

Mr. Matthews. Now, I show you a communication dated March 7, 1939. Did you receive this from Mr. Croney [handing paper to the witness]?

Mr. Howe. Yes, sir; I did.

Mr. Matthews. I read a paragraph from page 1:

The following information is the truth and nothing but the truth. After the 1935 ARTA Convention held in December of that year, Mr. Haddock cancelled the ARTA New York charter, and from that time ARTA was a charterless organization, pending affiliation with the A. F. of L. by merger with the moribund Capital Commercial Telegraphers' Union. But the Communist Party line at that time, as you know, was to capture the A. F. of L. so the faithful followers of the Party decided that we should merge into the CTU as a part of that organization. In the spring of 1936 a referendum of ARTA was taken and by astute propaganda the majority of ARTA members voted to affiliate with the A. F. of L. by merger with the CTU. But in brief the CTU learning of our notorious communist officialdom arbitrarily refused to take the ARTA as a part of CTU. All through 1936 ARTA continued to operate as a charterless organization.

Was it true that the C. T. U. declined to accept the proposed merger?

Mr. Howe. That is right.

Mr. Matthews. I show you a letter dated July 23, without a year, addressed to "Brother Howe," and signed "J. E. C." Did you receive this from Mr. Croney [handing paper to the witness]?

Mr. Howe. I did.

Mr. Matthews. I read:

Earl Browder called Haddock, Pyle, Rathborne, Bliss, and myself to his office. We had quite a hot conference there. The decisions were that both Haddock and Pyle were to resign immediately and Rathborne and myself were to come east and take over.

I show you one final letter dated November 7, 1938. Is this a letter from Mr. Croney [handing paper to the witness]?

Mr. Howe. Yes, sir.

Mr. Matthews (reading):

In conclusion we come to the point. If the policy of our future is to be laid down by a Rathborne or a Rotham, or a Van Erman, it naturally will be the Communist Party line.

Mr. Chairman, I ask that these letters be accepted in evidence and marked as exhibits.

The Chairman. They will be received in evidence.

(The letters referred to by Mr. Matthews were marked "Howe Exhibits Nos. 1, 2, 3, 4, 5, 6, 7, 8, 9, 10, 11, 12, and 13," and made a part of the record.)

Mr. Matthews. From the New York Times of Sunday, May 9, 1937, I read a portion of an article entitled "Group hears plan to resist

United States war—Women Shoppers' League is told at luncheon maritime workers agree on course—Store union plans told—Mrs. Elinore Herrick emphasizes need of getting all facts on both sides of controversy."

Those are the headlines and the article follows:

Maritime workers throughout the country are opposed to war and if necessary will use their organized power to prevent this country from engaging in a foreign conflict. Mervyn Rathborne, president of the American Radio Telegraphists' Association, ship radio group, asserted yesterday.

Mr. Rathborne, who was active in the recent maritime strike on the west coast as secretary of the San Francisco Bay area district council of the Pacific Maritime Federation, spoke at the first annual luncheon of the League of Women Shoppers in the Town Hall Club.

Mr. Rathborne said the Pacific Maritime Federation has adopted a resolution opposing war and he predicted that all other maritime workers would endorse a similar course at a national maritime convention planned for this summer. They would agree not to handle war materials, he said.

Mr. Rathborne urged the women shoppers to refuse to sail on vessels whose employes' unions are not recognized by the shipowners. He asked also that the League of Women Shoppers support the unionized maritime workers politically.

Mary Hillyer, member of the league's board, who presided, assured Mr. Rathborne of the league's cooperation.

Mrs. Clarina Michelson, organizer of the Department Store Employes Union, Local 1250, expressed confidence that "in a very short while with the cooperation of consumers and workers, the 5- and 10-cent and department store workers will be organized 100 per cent." She said "the consumer has a decisive role to play" in organizing the store workers.

Mrs. Elinore M. Herrick, regional director of the National Labor Relations Board, said the Government's new powers with respect to labor "must be exercised wisely and with restraint." She said "it behooves any one going into the causes of industrial disputes to be careful and make an effort to get the facts on both sides."

Miss Leane Zugsmith, writer and member of the league's board, spoke on the need for a greater membership in the league.

Now, Mr. Howe, I should like to read you portions of a communication which this committee has received from a member of the A. C. A., and since he is not present, I will ask you if you can verify his statements or if you wish to correct them in any way in the light of your own information.

The CHAIRMAN. Why not just ask him certain questions based upon that—if he knows certain things were true.

Mr. MATTHEWS (reading):

To start with I am a ship radio operator and have been one for 12 years. I hold membership——

The CHAIRMAN. Just a second. There are certain communications which the committee receives which I do not think should be made public for various reasons so we will exclude that.

Mr. CASEY. He can use it as a base for questioning.

The CHAIRMAN. Yes, as a basis for questioning, but a great many people write this committee with the understanding that nothing they say will be made public or be used in any sense that might trace it to them.

Mr. MATTHEWS. Yes. This communication states that the opinion of the author——

The CHAIRMAN. Just ask him certain questions based on it. If it contains certain information, ask him if that information, without reading anything that might divulge who the man is or anything about it.

Mr. MATTHEWS. Well, you stated that the A. C. A. was 100-percent dominated by the Communist Party, is that correct?

Mr. HOWE. I forget whether I said 99 or 100, but it is very close to 100 percent.

Mr. MATTHEWS. Is your conviction based upon your connections with the A. C. A. and your knowledge of Communist tactics in the trade unions with which you have had experience for a number of years, that the A. C. A. being under the domination of the Communist Party represents a "Trojan horse" for the Communists in a field of vital concern to the national safety of this country?

Mr. HOWE. Yes. One cannot be inside of the A. C. A. or any similar organization any length of time without feeling that something is wrong somewhere. When you try to investigate what is wrong, you inevitably come to the fact that these men who do certain things, that the rest of us do not do, belong to the Communist Party.

Mr. MATTHEWS. Have you heard in your conversations with members of the union that the Communist Party maintains up and down the coasts of the United States short-wave receiving radio stations?

Mr. HOWE. I have heard it said that——

Mr. CASEY. We must not go into the field of what you have heard said. If you know something about it we would like to have it.

Mr. HOWE. To my knowledge I don't know of their existence.

Mr. MATTHEWS. Well, you would not be able to locate one in the light of your own connection, is that correct?

Mr. HOWE. No. My position in the union did not give me time to do such kind of work.

Mr. MATTHEWS. I think that is all the questions I have, Mr. Chairman.

Mr. CASEY. I wasn't here this morning, but I notice in the paper— you are Mr. Howe, aren't you?

Mr. HOWE. Yes, sir.

Mr. CASEY. I noticed in the paper a statement that you have seen a man named Stano—is that the way you pronounce his name—Stano?

Mr. HOWE. Yes; Stano.

Mr. CASEY. In the radio room of the yacht *Sea Cloud*, owned by Joseph B. Davies, and you identified him as a Communist.

Mr. HOWE. Yes; I stated that.

Mr. CASEY. How do you know he is a Communist?

Mr. HOWE. Well, I know it from the facts I have given here today.

Mr. CASEY. What?

Mr. HOWE. From the facts I have given here today—my testimony here today and based upon my experience in the A. R. T. A., Local 2; from my talks with Mr. Stano, his actions, what others have told me about him and also how he became a member of A. R. T. A., Local 2. He became a member in a very suspicious way and he was made a member without my knowledge or consent in my absence. He was placed upon the unemployed list by a man—I don't want to mention the man's name if I am not compelled to—by a man who I firmly believe is a member of the party—who was an official of the union at that time.

Mr. CASEY. Did you ever see Stano at a meeting of the Communist Party?

Mr. HOWE. Oh, yes—at the Communist Party, no. At the A. R. T. A. local.

Mr. CASEY. And did you handle his membership card?

Mr. HOWE. No. That was handled by someone else who took him in.

Mr. CASEY. Now, you said you knew by your talks with Stano. Will you tell us how those talks gave you the impression that he was a Communist?

Mr. HOWE. Well, I have just forgotten the exact nature of the conversation but I know that he stood for everything that Rathborne and Pyle and Jordan and those men stood for in the union, and was very much opposed to anything that I stood for. And there was a close division there in the union. We took sides. Every man belonged to one side or the other. He was either with us or against us.

Mr. CASEY. The fact that he opposed your faction in the union is what gave you the impression he was a Communist?

Mr. MASON. No; the fact that they opposed the anti-Communist faction in the union.

Mr. CASEY. Will you let me conduct this examination for a few minutes.

Mr. MASON. The fact of the matter is most of the testimony was given and the reasons were given this morning.

The CHAIRMAN. Mr. Casey is entirely within his rights in wanting to find out why the man says this fellow is a Communist—what reason.

Mr. HOWE. We learned in local 2 that men who were not Communists were not afraid to speak up and say they were not. We had meetings there when men got up and testified to that effect, that they were not Communists and they were proud to get up in the meeting and say that they were not. Other men, only a small minority, about 40 out of 500 who were Communists, refused to get up and say anything and they always voted the straight party ticket, so to speak.

Mr. CASEY. Now, that is a rather negative attitude. That is, if they did not disclaim being Communists you assumed they were.

Mr. HOWE. Well, everyone did assume that they were.

Mr. CASEY. By the fact that they did not say they were not?

Mr. HOWE. They would not say they were not.

Mr. CASEY. Well, now, have you anything positive that they ever— I know that they seek to hide the fact that they are Communists, but have you ever heard a statement directly from Mr. Stano which would give you the impression that he was a Communist?

Mr. HOWE. Well, yes. Many statements from him that gave me that impression.

Mr. CASEY. What were those statements?

Mr. HOWE. Well, it has been some time since I met Mr. Stano but one thing that struck me very much was that when I went aboard this *Sea Cloud* to see him; Mr. Stano and I never had any trouble—we never had an argument. There is no reason why Mr. Stano should not shake hands with me and speak to me like almost every other member of A. R. T. A., Local 2. I went aboard Mr. Stano's ship, and I was all but ushered off of the ship immediately without any discussion at all.

Now, that action for a man that has no reason to dislike me is strong indication of what the man really believes.

Mr. CASEY. You mean a person who changes his attitude toward you personally is evidence in your mind that he is a Communist?

Mr. HOWE. I wouldn't say that it proves that he was; no. But that is one of the many things that he did.

Mr. CASEY. Have you any other evidence that would lead you to the conclusion that he is a Communist?

Mr. HOWE. Well, I mentioned the way he was taken in.

Mr. CASEY. How was that—that is not clear in my mind.

Mr. HOWE. He was taken in without my knowledge or consent. I was the secretary-treasurer. I was the man that usually supervised the admission of men to membership or when members transferred from one local to another or when a man was placed upon what we called the beach list—the unemployed list.

One day I came in and I saw Stano's name on it and I inquired how he got on it and who he was and all about it, and the man that gave me the information, the man that placed him on the list didn't seem to want to come clean and tell me how he got on there, because I investigated every man that had his name placed upon this list. I wanted to be sure he was being put on the list in strict accordance with the rules of the local, and I am not sure whether Mr. Stano got on this list in accordance with the rules of the local. That is why they wanted to take him in when I wasn't there.

Mr. CASEY. Did you ever question Mr. Stano about his coming into your union in a way not in conformity with the rules of the local?

Mr. HOWE. No. I questioned the man that took him in.

Mr. CASEY. Did you ever question Mr. Stano directly to find out?

Mr. HOWE. Not why he got in; no. That would be improper, in my estimation. I should question the man that did actually let him come in and the man told me it was all right, that he was the right kind of a man.

The CHAIRMAN. Now, as I understand it, in your union there was a constant battle between the Communists and the non-Communists?

Mr. HOWE. That is right.

The CHAIRMAN. The lines were very sharply drawn?

Mr. HOWE. They were very sharply drawn.

The CHAIRMAN. And in the course of that battle between the two forces the non-Communists learned who the members—who the Communists were? They did not see their membership book but through their actions and their support of the party line and the general issues which they took, it became evident to the non-Communist members who the others were, is that true?

Mr. HOWE. That is right.

The CHAIRMAN. Over a long period of time?

Mr. HOWE. Yes.

The CHAIRMAN. I mean it was not just one incident?

Mr. HOWE. No.

The CHAIRMAN. But many incidents that supported the Communist line, is that right?

Mr. HOWE. That is right.

The CHAIRMAN. You knew you were one of the non-Communists in the group, is that right?

Mr. HOWE. Yes, sir; I can give a good illustration of that. We had a man by the name of Pearlman—Joe Pearlman, who is a well-known

Communist. He came into a meeting one day and not knowing what the issue was about, he took my side—spoke in support of what I was speaking for, and Tommie Ault—I mentioned his name this morning, he got up and turned around and looked at Pearlman and tried to tell him the best that he could that he was on the wrong side. Pearlman shifted over right in the middle of his talk and took the opposite when he knew what the party line was—what the faction of the A. R. T. A. was standing for. Every party member was supposed to get behind that bloc and vote for it and speak for it, and they did that.

The CHAIRMAN. Has a non-Communist in a labor organization any other manner of telling who the people are? They wouldn't tell themselves and often deny they are members of the party. They come before this committee and under oath deny membership in the party and refuse to give facts.

Now, in dealing with a situation within a union it is impossible for those who want to rid the union of the Communist influence and combat it, they can't ascertain by membership books or by records——

Mr. HOWE. No.

The CHAIRMAN. What is concealed from them. So the only way that union men generally in the movement can find out who are the Communists is largely through watching their tactics and their attitude and their positions with reference to the whole Communist Party line, is that true?

Mr. HOWE. That is the way we learned how they stood. And, of course, there is always someone that each Communist will tell. I was shown membership cards——

The CHAIRMAN. But there is always the possibility or always the danger that because some one disagrees—I mean you don't take the position because some one disagrees with you that that would necessarily mean he is a Communist?

Mr. HOWE. I did not wish to convey that impression.

The CHAIRMAN. What you did say, as I understand your testimony, and if it is not true I want you to correct me, as I understand you there was this fight within the union between the Communists and the non-Communists?

Mr. HOWE. I would like to say that I got a great deal of my definite information from an official of A. R. T. A., Local 2, whose name I would not like to mention here, but he was an elected official of A. R. T. A., Local 2, and while I am not certain that he was a party member, from his own statements he attended a great many meetings of the party higher fractions, boros, and so on, and he told me who the members were.

The CHAIRMAN. Now, why would he tell you who the members were if he was a member of the party?

Mr. HOWE. Because of the peculiar nature of this particular individual. He was one of what we call a fence rider—he was straddling both sides of the fence and he was giving me a certain amount of information and I presume he was doing the same to the other side.

Mr. CASEY. Why do you want to defend that particular individual here?

Mr. HOWE. Why do I favor it?

Mr. CASEY. No. Why do you want to defend him? Why so anxious to cloak his name with secrecy?

Mr. Howe. I would not like to disclose my reason unless I am compelled to.

Mr. Mason. Mr. Chairman, I would like to ask a question.

The Chairman. You should have some strong reason because you haven't had any hesitancy in designating other people as Communists. Unless you have some plausible and strong reason the chair is unable to understand why you would withhold this man's name.

Mr. Mason. Mr. Chairman, may I ask a question or two?

Mr. Howe, in your constant, persistent efforts over a long period of time to rid your union of the Communists and to block their program, you of course met violent opposition from certain members of your union, did you not?

Mr. Howe. Met violent opposition?

Mr. Mason. Yes.

Mr. Howe. Yes.

Mr. Mason. And naturally you would conclude that those who opposed your efforts to rid the union of its communism and its Communist element would naturally either be Communists or Communist sympathizers; is that right?

Mr. Howe. I don't think I ever took that view. I tried to take the broader view and if I thought the man was not a Communist I talked to him, and some men whom I suspected, after a discussion they came around to our way of thinking, and I no longer thought those men were Communists. But I always gave a man the benefit of the doubt.

Mr. Mason. Now I want to come to this man Stano. You, in your union meetings, at which these arguments pro and con over the Communist line, and so forth, met this man Stano in these union meetings before you went aboard that sloop? You met him constantly over a period of time, did you?

Mr. Howe. Well, I don't think I ever knew Stano very much. In fact, I don't know him very much now. Until he actually came into local 2, then he did attend a few meetings and he was around the hall waiting like other men did for jobs—for a job.

Mr. Mason. Now, in local 2 and in the meetings, what part did Stano take in these differences of opinion over this party controversy?

Mr. Howe. Well, I don't recall now any. He took part like the other members.

Mr. Mason. Did he line up with the minority group who were opposed to the Communist element, or did he line up with the other group?

Mr. Howe. He lined up with the Communists at all times.

Mr. Mason. With the Communists?

Mr. Howe. Yes, sir; at all times.

Mr. Mason. Then by his actions in these union meetings, lining up with the Communist group against those who wanted to eradicate those groups from the union, you would judge from his actions that he was one of that group, would you not?

Mr. Howe. Well, I wouldn't base my conclusions on that altogether. If I didn't have other reasons for believing it, which I told you about the man that took him in, gave me an idea that he was.

Mr. Mason. Well, all I can say is if you cannot get their cards and membership, and they lie about their membership, then the only thing you can do is to judge by their actions and their efforts and that is good enough for me.

Mr. Howe. Well, it is good enough for me. I don't suppose that would go in a court of law, but you can never get these men to admit that they are and if you would go on that alone there wouldn't be any Communist Party.

The Chairman. On the other hand, you had reasons for grievances of your own. You engaged in a fight and you were elected secretary. You say you are still the legally elected secretary, but you say you were forcibly thrown out of the union by this goon-squad method; you were expelled from the union. Therefore you have considerable feeling in the matter. Would you permit those feelings to influence you in your testimony? Would it be possible for you to naturally feel very much aggrieved with people who don't agree with you?

Mr. Howe. I would like to state that I got up on the floor of local 2 in the winter of 1937, during our strike, and after the strike was over, and actually defended the Communists. Others were "red-baiting" then when I was against "red-baiting," but I wasn't afraid to tell the membership that I was not a Communist. But I did say I believed a Communist had as much a right to be in a labor union as anyone else. But I didn't know when I said that, defending the Communists, that I was putting myself on the spot for the future because then there became a very definite degree of coolness toward me on the part of the Communists and they began to show that more and more as time went on and the more they showed it the more the other members supported me, so finally at the last election I got all the votes except 25—left only 25 real dyed-in-the-wool Communists who voted against me. But the fight became more and more bitter from that time on until I was finally thrown out by them.

Mr. Casey. Did Stano ever get up on the floor and speak in behalf of the Communists?

Mr. Howe. I don't recall that he ever did.

Mr. Casey. Did Stano or was Stano one of those 24 or 25 who voted against you?

Mr. Howe. I could not say that. The vote was secret. We don't know who voted.

Mr. Casey. You say Stano lined up with the Communists. Now, you say you don't recall that he ever spoke in favor of any measure they backed. You don't know whether he voted for any measures if it was a secret vote. What do you mean when you say "he lined up with the Communists"?

Mr. Howe. Well, when I say secret vote—when we elect officers we elect them by a referendum vote that takes 90 days, because we have to wait until our men get back from their foreign voyages, so they vote by mail or they can come in and place or go to the post office where these ballots were returned to a post-office box and deposit their ballot there. But at every membership meeting we also took up certain questions where the men voted. Every Tuesday we had a membership meeting but we didn't elect any officers there. We were discussing the policy of the local.

Supposing now the American League for Peace and Democracy came down there and Mr. Van Taine—it was done in this way. He would call me on the telephone and ask me if he could come down there Tuesday to make a speech. At first I told him that I wasn't running the union; if he wanted to come down there at a membership meeting, I would let the members vote on whether or not he could speak. So he would come down. He would get up there for a second and then the members would vote on whether they wanted him to speak. They might ask him to go outside while they debated the matter.

Well, those debates became hot over little things like that. So when everybody knew that the American League was a Communist front organization, any man who supported it when he should know that, know what it was, why, we suspected that he was inclined to be a Communist. Things like that. That is only one illustration. Had lots of other causes—Spanish democracy.

Mr. CASEY. I confess I don' see the connection between your nswer and my question.

Mr. HOWE. Perhaps I forget what the question was.

Mr. MATTHEWS. I think there was a misunderstanding about your question. When you asked Mr. Howe if they voted against him did that mean they were men being voted on for elective office or on the question of resolutions.

Mr. HOWE. I am talking about the policy of the local.

Mr. CASEY. My question was: In what way did Stano line up with the Comunists, because you use that phrase.

Mr. HOWE. Well, at the membership meetings where the policies of the local were framed—

Mr. MATTHEWS. And the voting was not secret on those policies.

Mr. CASEY. And the voting was not secret?

Mr. HOWE. No. They voted by a show of hands.

Mr. CASEY. You saw him raise his hands in opposition or in support of policies supported by the Communist Party?

Mr. HOWE. He always followed the Communist Party line.

Mr. CASEY. Now, do you recall any prominent measures that were communistic that he supported? I don't want to go back through it all. Give us the outstanding one in your mind.

Mr. HOWE. Nothing in particular, but there were many things that came up during that period when he was there. One I think was the famous auditing committee report which was prepared by Roy Robinson, Wayne Pascal. That was brought up for the purpose of trying to put me on the spot. They tried to make it look like I had stolen about $2,000 of the money. They didn't actually say I had stolen it but they inferred it had been spent—strike-fund money had been spent for general purposes including salaries, but that was thoroughly explained by two certified public accountants.

Mr. CASEY. You were cleared of that?

Mr. HOWE. I was.

Mr. CASEY. But what was the resolution? A resolution to investigate your activities, was it?

Mr. HOWE. No. This was a resolution that was passed to elect an auditing committee to audit the books. So they audited the books and they made their report.

Mr. CASEY. Had a committee audit your books?

Mr. HOWE. Yes, sir.

Mr. CASEY. And Stano voted in favor of that resolution?

Mr. Howe. I would not say about that. I am just bringing this up as typical of one of the many questions that were brought up during that period. They were trying to frame me so they could kick me out and they could never do it. And the Communists or the men lined up to do that were considered by everybody as being Communists or fellow travelers.

The Chairman. Was there ever a vote of the union expelling you?

Mr. Howe. There was a vote of one membership meeting which was attended by around 20 or 21 members, only. We had 500 members in the local but under a provision of the constitution they could—they didn't have to submit that to the entire membership if they didn't want to. But that was 3 months after I was thrown out.

The Chairman. You explained the circumstances of being thrown out. You say you were physically removed?

Mr. Howe. I was physically barred from entering the hall and office. I came to the office at 9:40 in the morning and when I went to open the door I was stopped from doing so by a big, six-foot, husk sailor and wasn't allowed to enter the hall or office of local No. 2.

The international executive board had passed a resolution on the previous day suspending me from office, which was entirely illegal, without calling a membership meeting or submitting this to any member of the local. It was done entirely by the international officers.

I would like to say we have a case coming up in about a week in the courts of New York City in which this whole matter will be tried. We still have $3,000 of the local's funds tied up which the comrades haven't got so far.

The Chairman. Any other questions?

Mr. Matthews. No.

Mr. Mason. No questions.

The Chairman. All right, the committee will stand adjourned until tomorrow morning a 10 o'clock.

(Whereupon at 3:45 p. m., a recess was taken until 10 a. m., Thursday, April 25, 1940.)

INVESTIGATION OF UN-AMERICAN PROPAGANDA ACTIVITIES IN THE UNITED STATES

THURSDAY, APRIL 25, 1940

House of Representatives,
Special Committee to Investigate Un-American Activities,
Washington, D. C.

The committee met at 10 a. m., Hon. Martin Dies (chairman), presiding.

The CHAIRMAN. Gentlemen, the committee will come to order. The Chair announces a subcommittee composed of the chairman, Mr. Dempsey, of New Mexico, and Mr. Mason, of Illinois. All right, proceed. Who is your first witness?

Mr. MATTHEWS. Mr. Chase. Will you take the stand, please?

TESTIMONY OF EZRA F. CHASE

The CHAIRMAN. Raise your right hand. Do you solemnly swear to tell the truth, the whole truth, and nothing but the truth, so help you God?

Mr. CHASE. I do.

The CHAIRMAN. All right, Mr. Matthews, you may proceed.

Mr. MATTHEWS. Please give your full make for the record.

Mr. CHASE. Ezra F. Chase.

Mr. MATTHEWS. What is your present address?

Mr. CHASE. Los Angeles.

Mr. MATTHEWS. Where were you born?

Mr. CHASE. Idaho Falls, Idaho.

Mr. MATTHEWS. When?

Mr. CHASE. February 12, 1896.

Mr. MATTHEWS. Have you ever been a member of the Communist Party?

Mr. CHASE. Yes.

Mr. MATTHEWS. When did you join the Communist Party?

Mr. CHASE. 1931.

Mr. MATTHEWS. Will you please give a brief outline of the positions which you held in the Communist Party?

Mr. CHASE. During the early part of my connection in the Communist Party I was the organizer of the unemployed work in Los Angeles. I was an organizer for the Communist Party. I was at one time the secretary of the Los Angeles branch of the American League Against War and Fascism. I was later the organizer of the Upholstering International Union, Local 15. I was also the floor leader of the Communist Party—that is, one of the floor leaders in the Los Angeles

Central Labor Council. I was also an officer of the Workers Ex-Servicemen's League and held various functions from time to time in innumerable mass organizations controlled by the Communist Party.

Mr. MATTHEWS. When you were a member of the Communist Party did your own name appear on your party membership book?

Mr. CHASE. Never.

Mr. MATTHEWS. What names did you use as a member of the Communist Party?

Mr. CHASE. One of the names that I used was F. E. Shrader.

Mr. MATTHEWS. Will you spell that, please?

Mr. CHASE. S-h-r-a-d-e-r.

Mr. MATTHEWS. Did you use another name?

Mr. CHASE. I also used the name of Jose Valez.

Mr. MATTHEWS. What was the last party name you used?

Mr. CHASE. That was the last.

Mr. MATTHEWS. Was it a practice for members of the Communist Party to use aliases or party names?

Mr. CHASE. Yes; it was.

Mr. MATTHEWS. Was that a general practice?

Mr. CHASE. Yes; it was.

Mr. MATTHEWS. Were you ever arrested in connection with your activities as a Communist?

Mr. CHASE. Yes; a number of times.

Mr. MATTHEWS. Will you please state some of the occasions and describe the incidents of your arrest in connection with your Communist Party activities?

Mr. CHASE. My first arrest took place in 1932 in Long Beach, Calif. That was a section convention of the Communist Party. My next arrest was when William Z. Foster and myself attempted to speak at the Plaza in Los Angeles. I was later arrested while conducting a meeting of the Workers' Exservicemen's League. I was arrested a number of times in leading groups of unemployed before the relief organizations in Los Angeles. Some of these resulted in quite serious fights. I was arrested several times while speaking on street corners in the city of Los Angeles. I was also arrested in connection with the turning on of electricity and gas where it had been disconnected.

Mr. MATTHEWS. You said "turning on"?

Mr. CHASE. Turning on.

Mr. MATTHEWS. Was that in connection with your work as an organizer for the Unemployed Councils?

Mr. CHASE. Yes; that is right.

Mr. MATTHEWS. Was the organization known as the Unemployed Councils under the control of the Communist Party?

Mr. CHASE. It was.

Mr. MATTHEWS. Completely so?

Mr. CHASE. Completely.

Mr. MATTHEWS. Were you under instructions, as a member of the Communist Party, in the work which you did in the Unemployed Councils?

Mr. CHASE. Yes.

Mr. MATTHEWS. Were you under instructions to turn on gas and electricity?

Mr. CHASE. Yes.

Mr. MATTHEWS. Will you please state the results of your arrest in that case?

Mr. CHASE. I was sent by the Communist Party into the Unemployed Cooperative Relief Organization, which was an unemployed organization of the unemployed themselves. My function in that organization was to colonize in that group and to convert this unemployed organization into a more militant organization, carrying forth the program of the unemployed.

This organization, the Unemployed Cooperative Relief, had been founded upon the basis of exchanging their work with various farmers for vegetables. My function was to put an end to that sort of thing and to make the organization an organization with militant demands—to demand upon the county of Los Angeles and upon the State of California and upon the Nation that they take care of this problem. At this time there was considerable turn-off of the utilities on the unemployed, and it was our purpose in that to show this organization that these utilities and things were the property of the people, and that through their inability to pay for them that they must have them just the same. And where the utility companies turned off the meters they were to be organized for the turning on of the meters and again using those facilities. I was arrested in this connection. I was charged with one count of theft of illuminating gas and one count of electricity, and upon my conviction I served a sentence of 6 months in the Los Angeles County jail.

Mr. MATTHEWS. Your conviction in this case was the direct result of instructions which you received from the Communist Party; is that correct?

Mr. CHASE. That is correct.

Mr. MATTHEWS. I show you a mimeographed pamphlet and ask you if you have ever seen a copy of this [handing pamphlet to the witness].

Mr. CHASE. Yes.

Mr. MATTHEWS. That is the "Fighting Methods and Organization Forms of the Unemployed Councils"?

Mr. CHASE. That is right.

Mr. MATTHEWS. Issued by the national committee, Unemployed Councils of the United States?

Mr. CHASE. Yes.

Mr. MATTHEWS. I offer this pamphlet in evidence.

The CHAIRMAN. It will be received.

(The pamphlet referred to by Mr. Matthews was marked "Chase Exhibit 1" and made a part of the record.)

Mr. MATTHEWS. Do you know who the national officers of this organization were?

Mr. CHASE. At the time?

Mr. MATTHEWS. At the time.

Mr. CHASE. At the time that this was issued, Herbert Benjamin was the national secretary along with Emanuel Levin, Israel Amter, and others who were active in it at that time.

Mr. MATTHEWS. On page 4 of this pamphlet I read the following:

We do not negotiate, request, plead or beg. *We organize and Demand! We demand and Fight.* In order to be able to demand and fight, we must have the greatest possible force behind our demands and in our fight.

Will you please explain how that is a part of the Communists' approach to questions which involve the daily needs and interests of working people?

Mr. CHASE. Yes. Our plan at that time was to begin with small committees and failing to effect what we wanted with the smaller committees, we would move upon the relief offices with the largest possible committees that we could organize. Our purpose was to get what we demanded in there and in the event the police or law enforcement bodies were brought in there, why, it invariably went into a fight.

Mr. MATTHEWS. You mean that there was no disposition to negotiate anything on behalf of the needy unemployed, is that correct?

Mr. CHASE. Well, we went in with a set of demands. We would be demanding things in conformity to the program of the national unemployed councils.

Of course, failing to realize those demands and upon the refusal by the relief authority, then we would make it known that our intent was to remain there in the offices until such time as those demands were granted. Invariably the police would be called and a riot would take place.

Mr. MATTHEWS. On page 13 of this same pamphlet there appears an outline of the duties of what is described as a self-defense corps. Was there organized such a self-defense corps under the auspices of the unemployed councils?

Mr. CHASE. Yes. We at all times had a defense corps. The function of the defense corps was to protect their leader in taking these committees before the various relief offices and also in the holding of street meetings, demonstrations, and so forth.

Mr. MATTHEWS. Was it a function of the defense corps to prevent by physical means or force evictions?

Mr. CHASE. Yes. When an unemployed member was evicted by the law, their furniture and their belongings were picked up and placed back in their house. This happened on many occasions.

Mr. MATTHEWS. Now, will you please give some outline of your activities in connection with trade union work while you were a member of the Communist Party and acting under its instructions?

Mr. CHASE. I went to work in the furniture industry in Los Angeles and at the same time I joined the Upholsterers International Union.

Mr. MATTHEWS. When did you go to work in the furniture industry?

Mr. CHASE. In 1925.

Mr. MATTHEWS. Did you go into that as a Communist Party member or under instructions from the Communist Party?

Mr. CHASE. Well, I had been instructed, along with the others, to seek employment in any of the factories in Los Angeles, and I did enter into the furniture industry and joined the union having jurisdiction over that work.

Mr. MATTHEWS. Did you become an organizer in that union?

Mr. CHASE. Yes. Less than a year after I became a member of that union I was the organizer of it.

Mr. MATTHEWS. Was it a part of your obligation as a member of the Communist Party to carry out the Communist Party instructions in that union?

Mr. CHASE. Yes. We controlled that union from the top to the bottom.

Mr. MATTHEWS. Did you have ony other connections with trade-union activities while you were a member of the Communist Party?

Mr. CHASE. While I was the organizer of that union and even before that, I was the speaker—one of the speakers of the Communist Party on the floor of the Los Angeles Central Labor Council.

Mr. MATTHEWS. Will you please describe how the Communist Party functioned in the Central Labor Council?

Mr. CHASE. We had what was styled as a progressive bloc, and our purpose there was to have the various local unions elect as many Commununist delegates as possible into the central body of the American Federation of Labor, which was the Labor Council. And once the Communist became a delegate to that body he then entered in so-called progressive bloc where he would meet in fraction. We would meet from time to time, and we would also have enlarged caucus meetings, as we called them, where we would draw in other non-Communist delegates who were partially sympathetic to the program that we were putting forth.

This group became known as the "progressive bloc." That was so styled by the Communist Party themselves. And in this bloc we elected a group of floor leaders which was known as the steering committee. I was one of the floor leaders in this group.

Mr. MATTHEWS. Approximately how many members were there of the self-styled progressive bloc which was under the control of the Communist Party in the Central Labor Council?

Mr. CHASE. There was actually about 25 or 30 of us, but we usually controlled somewhere about 100 votes.

Mr. MATTHEWS. Out of how many members in the entire council?

Mr. CHASE. The usual attendance would be something over 200 members—possibly something close to 300.

The CHAIRMAN. The chair wants to announce the presence of a quorum of the full committee: Mr. Casey, Mr. Dempsey, Mr. Mason, and the chairman. We will now proceed as a quorum of the full committtee.

Mr. MATTHEWS. Did this bloc under the discipline of the Communist Party, even though a minority, act in such cohesion it was able to put over the party's views at times?

Mr. CHASE. Oh, yes. We were successful any number of times in carrying out our resolutions and motions.

Mr. MATTHEWS. Was the bloc ever charged by non-Communists or anti-Communists in the Central Labor Council with being communistic?

Mr. CHASE. Oh, innumerable times. It was well known.

Mr. MATTHEWS. Did members of the bloc who were members of the Communist Party deny their Communist Party membership?

Mr. CHASE. Practically always.

Mr. MATTHEWS. Were you known openly as a member of the Communist Party?

Mr. CHASE. I was known to be a Communist in there. There was not point in my denying it.

Mr. MATTHEWS. Were there other members who were not known as Communists?

Mr. CHASE. Oh, yes.

Mr. MATTHEWS. But who were?

Mr. CHASE. Yes.

Mr. MATTHEWS. And were they under instructions to deny their Communist Party membership?

Mr. CHASE. Yes, sir.

Mr. MATTHEWS. Were they under obligation to deny their Communist Party membership in their discipline of the Communist Party?

Mr. CHASE. Will you state that again?

Mr. MATTHEWS. Were they under rigid obligation to deny their party membership?

Mr. CHASE. The Communist uses every available means to cover up the identity and the connections with the party of some of its members while on the other hand there will be those who are instructed to openly assert their membership in the Communist Party and to openly defend its policy.

Mr. MATTHEWS. Were you required, as a member of the Communist Party, in the Furniture Workers' Union, to make reports to the Communist Party?

Mr. CHASE. Yes, sir.

Mr. MATTHEWS. Are Communist members of trade unions required to report, as a rule, on the state of things in the union?

Mr. CHASE. Well, I would say without exception.

Mr. MATTHEWS. What is a "top fraction"?

Mr. CHASE. Wherever a group of Communists are working inside of an organization, all of the Communists in there become a "fraction" and out of that general fraction the outstanding ones, those with greater capabilities and greater loyalty to the party, become a "top fraction."

Mr. MATTHEWS. Were you a member of a top fraction?

Mr. CHASE. Yes.

Mr. MATTHEWS. I show you a mimeographed document entitled "Resolutions and proposals adopted at Los Angeles County Convention, March 27–28, 1937." Have you ever seen that document [handing document to witness]?

Mr. CHASE. Yes; I have.

Mr. MATTHEWS. Can you identify that as the resolutions and proposals of the Los Angeles County Convention of the Communist Party for the dates specified?

Mr. CHASE. Yes; this is correct.

Mr. MATTHEWS. It is?

Mr. CHASE. That is the resolutions and their report as made up by the county committee.

Mr. MATTHEWS. This is signed "Los Angeles County Committee." Does that mean the Los Angeles County Committee of the Communist Party?

Mr. CHASE. That means the Los Angeles County Committee.

Mr. MATTHEWS. The first report is to the California State Committee of the Communist Party, to the central committee.

DEAR COMRADES.

Mr. CHASE. That is right.

Mr. MATTHEWS. Now, I notice on page 3 of this document that one of the convention's decisions was to "organize the progressive caucus in the Central Labor Council." That is the progressive bloc that you spoke of?

Mr. CHASE. That was the group of which I was a part.

Mr. MATTHEWS. And of which you were a floor leader?

Mr. CHASE. That is right.

Mr. MATTHEWS. Another one of the decisions passed at the convention was—

To organize the C. L. C. fraction; C. I. O. committee fraction and assign the necessary forces to the C. I. O. committee; to organize the progressive caucus in the Central Labor Council.

Mr. CHASE. In the Central Labor Council; yes.

Mr. MATTHEWS. Resolution 8 on page 3:

To carry through of assignments of eligible comrades to trade unions, especially to CIO unions and factories where organizational drives are beginning.

Mr. CHASE. Yes.

Mr. MATTHEWS. Was that a part of the campaign of the Communist Party to get into the C. I. O. and control it as far as possible?

Mr. CHASE. It was.

Mr. MATTHEWS. Resolution 4 on page 3 reads:

To assign all county committee members to shop and industrial units, and certain selected branches; to see that all section committee members are held responsible for a unit; and that every section selects one unit for concentration.

Mr. CHASE. That is correct.

Mr. MATTHEWS. Resolution 6 on page 3 reads:

On the basis of registration to assist units in better distribution of forces, with special assignments to bourgeois organizations. This to be started in major sections and rotate. A minimum of 100 assignments to be made.

Can you explain briefly what that means?

Mr. CHASE. Well, that would mean going outside of the trade-union field and delegating them into the various political organizations, such as the Young Democrats or the Republican organizations; into church groups, student bodies, and in innumerable other organizations made up of what they called the bourgeois society.

Mr. MATTHEWS. I notice that this is to be started in major sections and rotate. What does that mean, "to rotate"?

(No answer.)

Mr. MATTHEWS. Does that mean that a member is to be placed in one organization for a certain period and then put into another organization and someone else to take his place?

Mr. CHASE. Yes; it would mean that.

Mr. MATTHEWS. Now, on page 5 of this report there appears the statement——

The CHAIRMAN. Mr. Matthews, have you sufficiently identified that report?

Mr. MATTHEWS. Yes. I would like to offer it in evidence.

The CHAIRMAN. It is received.

(The report referred to by Mr. Matthews was marked "Chase Exhibit 2" and made a part of the record.)

Mr. MATTHEWS. This has been identified as the resolutions and proposals adopted at the Los Angeles County Convention of the Communist Party.

The CHAIRMAN. All right.

Mr. MATTHEWS. On page 5 there appears the following statement:

The main activity of the Party must be directed towards rallying the entire population of Los Angeles behind the trade union organization drive, particularly in those basic industries now being tackled by the CIO. Organization of these basic industries, like rubber, auto, oil, steel, aircraft, etc., will be the most effective force making for unity of the organized labor movement.

Now, did the Communist Party have as a part of its strategy the special concentration of its work in basic industries?

Mr. CHASE. Yes; they did.

Mr. MATTHEWS. Did it aim to specialize in the mass-production industries as contrasted with what interest it might have in small industries?

Mr. CHASE. Yes; they had made great efforts to build the most effective organization possible in the basic industries, which they considered steel, automobiles, aircraft, communication, such as that—transportation.

Mr. MATTHEWS. Will you please give as briefly as possible the Communist Party's theory which underlies the special interest in the basic industries?

Mr. CHASE. The Communist Party is an organization having revolutionary intent. Their purpose is to take over this form of government and institute one of their own. And their interest in the industries of the country is simply this: Through organization, if they can control the employees in the basic industries throughout the country, then they are in a position at their will to declare a general strike throughout the Nation, and in a general strike they can paralyze the industries, communication, transportation, manufacturing, and so on. And out of that situation they are able to create that situation leading to civil war, and from civil war is a simple matter to convert that into revolutionary war for the overthrow of this system. That is, basically, their interest in trade-unions.

Mr. MATTHEWS. Let me ask you a question which you may be able to answer with respect to the party's interest in the basic industries. Have you found in your experience as a Communist that if a group of workers in a light or small industry were even more underprivileged or had poorer working conditions than a group in a basic industry, that the party would be more interested in the workers in the basic industry than they would in the former?

Mr. CHASE. Undoubtedly so. The Communist Party, among ourselves, we seldom talked about hours, wages, and conditions. We saved that to be used on the floor of the union hall. But among ourselves we were interested in organizational work that would be the most beneficial to the ultimate aims of the Communist Party.

Mr. MATTHEWS. In other words, the Communist Party's interest in basic industries was a political rather than an economic interest?

Mr. CHASE. Yes; that is right.

Mr. MATTHEWS. That is, instead of being concerned solely with the economic interests of working people, the Party is primarily concerned with the political advantage to accrue to the party by its strength in a basic industry?

Mr. CHASE. A good, economic condition in the country would not serve the means of the Communist Party. The Communist Party, I again state, is interested in the building of a revolutionary situation.

Mr. CASEY. Mr. Witness, do I understand you to mean that the Communist Party is not interested in better working conditions or relief for the unemployed; they are not sincerely interested but merely use those as a weapon with which to gain entrance to these labor groups?

Mr. CHASE. The Communist Party is interested in them to this extent: That they realize that a revolutionary movement can only be built among the people who have a grievance, real or imagined, or invented, or otherwise, and by playing upon the wages, the hours, and conditions, or the treatment, and such as that for the unemployed. It is only there that they can gain the organizational— strictly and actually the Communist Party knows that good working conditions throughout the country and a good economic condition would not contribute substantially to the overthrow of the capitalist system, but by putting forth Utopian demands for the unemployed and increased wages and shorter hours for the worker, they realized that they can put capitalism through a certain preparation. In other words, they can exact during this period of struggle a great many demands from the capitalist system and thus weaken them and prepare them for the final conflict and the destruction of this system.

Mr. MATTHEWS. Now, on page 5 there appear two references to the party's special interests in aircraft, is that correct?

Mr. CHASE. Yes.

Mr. MATTHEWS. And again on page 8 there appears reference to the party's need to build a shop unit in aircraft, is that correct?

Mr. CHASE. Aircraft, rubber, oil, steel—such as those things have long been concentration centers in Los Angeles.

Mr. CASEY. You mentioned the aircraft industry. My understanding is the aircraft industry pays high wages and have decent working conditions, is that correct?

Mr. CHASE. No. The aircraft industry does not pay high wages.

Mr. CASEY. I have been misinformed.

Mr. CHASE. The bulk of the employees in there are in the small-wage class and it does present a good opportunity for the Communist Party to build an organization.

Mr. MATTHEWS. Now, again on page 12 the party expresses its especial interest in aircraft, is that correct?

Mr. CHASE. Yes.

Mr. MATTHEWS. And again on page 12 appears the sentence:

In the immediate future the party must help establish Y. C. L. branches in aircraft.

Mr. CHASE. That is right.

Mr. MATTHEWS. Is that correct?

Mr. CHASE. Yes.

Mr. MATTHEWS. And again on page 16:

Building up the party in a number of important factories, rubber, aircraft, oil refineries, etc., and make every comrade eligible a member of a union.

Is that correct?

Mr. CHASE. That is right.

Mr. MATTHEWS. And again on page 18—

with emphasis on mass recruitment especially in important factories and industries—aircraft, oil, maritime, auto, rubber, railroad, etc.

Is that correct?

Mr. CHASE. That is correct.

Mr. MATTHEWS. Again aircraft is emphasized?

Mr. CHASE. That is correct.

Mr. MATTHEWS. And again on page 19—

Establishing Y. C. L. units in important industries and factories (aircraft)?

Mr. CHASE. That is right.

Mr. MATTHEWS. Do you notice, Mr. Chase, that in all of these references nothing is said about the industries where the greatest need exists for the workers?

Mr. CHASE. That is right.

Mr. MATTHEWS. But these are described as important for what purpose? Why are these factories important?

Mr. CHASE. Because those are the basic—they are the basic industries.

Mr. MATTHEWS. That is. they are important politically?

Mr. MATTHEWS. Yes. Politically, yes; and economically.

Mr. MATTHEWS. And again on page 23 we find the statement: "Red builders should be established." What are "red builders"?

Mr. CHASE. Red builders are those workers that are active circulating literature, propaganda, and visiting and calling upon workers whom they intend to recruit.

Mr. MATTHEWS. And it is stated here that "red" builders should be established at the Douglas plant. What is that? An aircraft plant?

Mr. CHASE. That is an aircraft plant; yes.

Mr. MATTHEWS. At Lockheed. Is that an aircraft plant?

Mr. CHASE. That is another aircraft plant.

Mr. MATTHEWS. And again on page 24:

AIRCRAFT—To pay careful attention to the newly organized shop unit in aircraft, establishing a functioning leadership, giving assistance to the issuance of a shop paper. All other comrades in the industry shall be combined in one unit to concentrate the building of a shop unit in the N. Plant.

What was the "N. Plant"?

Mr. CHASE. North American.

Mr. MATTHEWS. That is also an aircraft plant?

Mr. CHASE. That is right.

Mr. MATTHEWS. Now, I show you another document entitled:

Proceedings of the California Convention. May 14–15, 1938, Communist Party.

Have you seen this report [handing exhibit to the witness]?

Mr. CHASE. Yes. This covers the period that I was in the party. I left the party in December of 1937 and this would cover the activities of the year 1937. I am familiar with that.

Mr. MATTHEWS. Are you familiar with this report?

Mr. CHASE. Yes, sir.

Mr. MATTHEWS. Have you ever seen it?

Mr. CHASE. Yes; I have seen this report.

Mr. MATTHEWS. On page 43 of this report there appears a summary of 1938 registration and there is a break-down, Mr. Chairman, of the Communist Party membership into the various unions and industries in Los Angeles County, or the State of California, this is.

The CHAIRMAN. Will you read that for the benefit of the record?

Mr. MATTHEWS. The number registered is 4,751. Seamen and agricultural workers, 300; number of counties, 22; number of shop units, 22; number of industrial units, 86; number of neighborhood and professional units, 146.

There is a break-down under the head of "Union affiliation," in American Federation of Labor unions, 698; in C. I. O. unions, 1,457; in independent unions, 166; and in company unions, 15. A total union affiliation of Communist Party members of 2,336.

The CHAIRMAN. Out of a membership of approximately 4,000?

Mr. MATTHEWS. Four thousand seven hundred and fifty-one.

The CHAIRMAN. Is that for the entire State of California?

Mr. MATTHEWS. That is for the entire State of California, is it not, Mr. Chase?

Mr. CHASE. Yes. That would be the entire State.

Mr. MATTHEWS. Was that the approximate membership of the Communist Party in California when you were last in the party?

Mr. CHASE. Yes.

Mr. MATTHEWS. Then there is a break-down of membership into unions and occupations of major importance, and under that heading we have "aircraft, 42."

Did you know of your own knowledge, Mr. Chase, that the Communist Party had members in the aircraft plants in California?

Mr. CHASE. Yes; I knew about it.

Mr. CASEY. What were the 42?

Mr. MATTHEWS. Forty-two Communist Party members in the aircraft plants.

The CHAIRMAN. In California.

Mr. MATTHEWS. Under the same schedule there appears "Electrical, 29." Would that be approximately correct, according to your information of the Communist Party members in the electrical industry?

Mr. CHASE. I wasn't too well acquainted in that part—distinctly in the electric part.

Mr. MATTHEWS. Marine, 388. Was the Communist Party numerically strongest in the maritime industry in the State of California?

Mr. CHASE. Yes. The Maritime Federation is their strongest hold.

Mr. MATTHEWS. Does the Communist Party in California control the Maritime Federation?

Mr. CHASE. Yes, they do.

Mr. MATTHEWS. Completely?

Mr. CHASE. Yes.

Mr. MATTHEWS. Canning, 35; longshoremen, 74; metal, 30; oil, 19; office. 297. That seems to have been the second strongest section of the Communist Party membership in the occupations in California, is that correct?

Mr. CHASE. Yes. There was no organization of office workers there until the Communists took that over.

The CHAIRMAN. What would that include—office workers?

Mr. CHASE. That includes stenographers, office clerks, and white-collared workers, working in various offices, such as insurance offices and bank offices and offices of various industries.

The purpose is not only to organize the worker on the bench or on the assembly line but to organize the clerical staff as well.

The CHAIRMAN. An office worker would in many instances be in a position to get more information than a worker on an assembly line in a plant, wouldn't he?

Mr. CHASE. Yes; they would, and they are under the same obligation that a worker on the line would be.

Mr. MATTHEWS. Is a Communist Party member who works in an office under discipline to obey what instructions the party might give with reference to getting information from the office?

Mr. CHASE. Yes, they would be.

Mr. MATTHEWS. Including correspondence?

Mr. CHASE. Yes.

Mr. MATTHEWS. Confidential material of any kind?

Mr. CHASE. Yes, they would.

Mr. MATTHEWS. There is also a schedule of the party membership here, according to countries of birth. Out of a total of 4,751 members in California, 2,801 are indicated as having been born in the United States, something slightly less than 2,000 being indicated as born abroad. Russia, 446. One-tenth of the membership of the State of California having been Russian born. Poland, 93. Mexico, 174, and Spain, 64. Canada, 61; the Philippines, 61, and England, 46. Germany, 45; Japan, 38; Slavonian, 42; Italy, 28; China, 20; and Ireland, 15.

Mr. DEMPSEY. Mr. Matthews, would the witness have any information as to the foreign-born, as to whether they were citizens or aliens?

Mr. MATTHEWS. Do you have any information on that, Mr. Chase?

Mr. CHASE. Well, I would question the accuracy of that report. There are many of the foreign born inside of the California party— inside of the Communist Party in California who will claim their birth here in the United States and there can be no doubt that a great many of them get away with it. We had an earthquake in San Francisco in 1936 and many records were destroyed. The Communists have, in many instances, used that for stating that they were born in this country and when asked, stated they were born in San Francisco.

Mr. DEMPSEY. Do you have any knowledge as to whether those foreign-born are aliens or American citizens?

Mr. CHASE. Many of them are aliens; yes.

Mr. MATTHEWS. They have not yet been naturalized?

Mr. CHASE. That is right. I know personally a number of them that have not been naturalized or are only in the process of being so.

Mr. MATTHEWS. There is also a schedule here which indicates the length of time in the party. Less than 1 year, 2,230. A little less than half of the entire membership has been in the party 1 year, according to this schedule.

Mr. Chase, do you know of your own experience whether the Communist Party has had a pretty high turn-over in membership?

Mr. CHASE. Yes. The Communist Party has had an exceedingly high turn-over. That is a problem that they have devoted a great deal of thought and energy of trying to correct—the enormous turn-over in the membership.

Mr. MATTHEWS. Can you state briefly the reason for this tremeudous turn-over in the Communist Party?

Mr. CHASE. Yes. The manner in which workers are recruited— thousands upon thousands of workers are recruited from out of the trade-union field, in their feeling that they can better serve the American workingman's interest in it; with the feeling they can improve the economic conditions of the people throughout the country as a whole. They are not approached and haven't been since about 1934 or 1935 on a revolutionary basis, but strictly upon a basis of local issues, of correcting disorders of a local nature. But upon entering into the party they sooner or later find out that they are a part of a revolutionary group. In many instances, they object to the fact that everything is under the leadership, in most instances, of people whom we don't readily consider as Americans—people of foreign birth—some of them known to be aliens, and such as that. That furnishes a great deal of objection· on the part of American workers and it accounts, no doubt, for a·great deal of the turn-over.

Mr. MATTHEWS. Now, Mr. Chase, according to this schedule, out of 4,751 members in the party only 91 had been in the party 7 years. Would that be in accordance with your own understanding of the tremendous turn-over in the Communist Party or do you think that is a mistake in the report? You see the gradual decrease there.

Mr. CHASE. I would say there are far more than 91, in my opinion, yes, that have been in more than 7 years.

Mr. CASEY. You are talking about California, now.

Mr. CHASE. Out in California alone, yes, there is more than 91 that have been in more than 7 years.

Mr. CASEY. Where did you get the figures?

Mr. MATTHEWS. This is the Communist Party's own report.

Mr. CASEY. Do you doubt the accuracy of the report?

Mr. CHASE. In that instance I would. Their object in there is to show a rapid growth of the party.

Mr. MATTHEWS. But on the contrary this would show a pretty rapid turn-over, wouldn't it?

Mr. CHASE. Yes, sir, it would.

Mr. MATTHEWS. Two thousand, two hundred and thirty in the party less than 1 year; 558 in the party less than 2 years; and 281 less than 3 years; 253 less than 4 years; and so on.

The CHAIRMAN. But, as a matter of fact, it is true, is it not, that during along about that period the Communist Party enjoyed its greatest growth?

Mr. CHASE. The growth of the Communist Party really started to take hold in a big way in 1934 and 1935.

Mr. CASEY. Was that due then to their increased activity or to the economic conditions, or both?

Mr. CHASE. Well, that can be due to a number of things—the C. I. O., the launching of the C. I. O. program and the new trade-union policies started skyrocketing the Communists on to a very rapid growth. That gave them their entrance then into the place that they had been striving for a number of years. They were striving to gain a foothold in the basic industries. The C. I. O. gave them that.

Mr. CASEY. They attached themselves to the increased unionization of new plants?

Mr. CHASE. That is right.

Mr. MATTHEWS. Now, Mr. Chase, it is true, is it not, that these reports, both of them, were not intended for the public?

Mr. CHASE. Those were intended for the State committee and for the national committee.

Mr. MATTHEWS. In other words, would you assume, in view of the fact that these reports were not intended for public release, that the statements generally would be more accurate than reports that might be intended for public release?

Mr. CHASE. Yes, sir. It is a serious breach of discipline in the Communist Party for any functionary to make an exaggerated or untruthful report to a higher committee. They would make them accurate to the best of their ability.

Mr. CASEY. In the face of that, what have you to say now as to your skepticism regarding the figure 91?

Mr. CHASE. My general impression is that there are more than that. There may not be, but it seems to me that I could almost name that many.

Mr. MATTHEWS. You joined the party 9 years ago; is that correct?

Mr. CHASE. Yes. It would be about 9 years ago.

Mr. MATTHEWS. Now, on page 2 of the proceedings of the California convention there appears the results of the elections to the offices of the convention on the honorary presidium. It appears that Joseph Stalin was elected to the honorary presidium of the California State Convention of the Communist Party. Is that in line with the Communist Party's attitude toward Stalin?

Mr. CHASE. Yes. It is a common procedure for them to pay homage to some outstanding Communist somewhere in the world, someone who has devoted a great deal of time to their cause, to give them that honor of making them an honorary member of some organization or group that they have organized.

Mr. CASEY. Is Stalin the most frequently honored person?

Mr. CHASE. Well, Stalin—he is their god, you might say.

Mr. MATTHEWS. Georgi Dimitrov was also a member of the honorary presidium of the California State Convention of the Communist Party?

Mr. CHASE. Yes. Dimitrov—yes; that is correct. He is held in very high esteem.

Mr. MATTHEWS. And Otto Kuusinen?

Mr. CHASE. Yes. He is the Finnish leader.

Mr. MATTHEWS. And various other persons from other countries—Spain, Germany, Brazil, and Mexico.

Mr. CHASE. Yes. There are other names.

Mr. MATTHEWS. China.

Mr. CHASE. These names, the greater part of them—it happens very frequently—it is almost a matter of form to elect them as honorary members.

Mr. CASEY. Are they ever notified of the distinction?

Mr. CHASE. Well, they receive these reports. There can be no doubt about that.

The CHAIRMAN. You say this Kuusinen was the Finnish leader?

Mr. CHASE. Kuusinen?

The CHAIRMAN. Yes.

Mr. CHASE. Yes. He has been for some years the outstanding leader of the Communists active in Finland. He was named the head——

The CHAIRMAN. Did he have any place in the provisional government that the Communists set up in Finland?

Mr. CHASE. Yes. He was appointed to head their provisional government when the Communists invaded Finland.

The CHAIRMAN. He was a citizen of Finland?

Mr. CHASE. Yes.

Mr. MATTHEWS. You don't mean that he has lived in Finland for the past 20 years, do you?

Mr. CHASE. I don't now that definitely.

Mr. MATTHEWS. As a matter of fact, hasn't he been a secretary of the Communist International in Moscow?

Mr. CHASE. He has been a part of the Communist International; yes.

Mr. MATTHEWS. Now, on page 5 of the resolutions and proposals there appears the statement that the party is to engage in its campaign for building the party by colonizing party and nonparty forces from mass organizations, such as the Workers' Alliance, International Workers' Order, and so forth, into the strategic shops in Los Angeles in order to guarantee a successful organization drive by the C. I. O. "This must be the task of the faction in these organizations."

Mr. CHASE. That is correct.

Mr. MATTHEWS. Now, will you please describe briefly what is meant by "colonizing party forces from mass organizations into the strategic shops"?

Mr. CHASE. Yes. I believe I could give you this illustration that would possibly make that quite clear. You know if a person had a systemic disorder—in other words, a disease that takes place in the human body—it seems to be Nature's habit of flooding that disease with a bacteria to sort of carry it away. Well, the Communists, in building a colony, would set about it in the same way, in effect. That would amount to substantially the same thing.

Mr. MATTHEWS. Well, do you know any medical phraseology? As a matter of fact, those bacteria are called "colonies" in medicine, are they not?

Mr. CHASE. I believe they are. I have never studied medicine.

The CHAIRMAN. The Communist Party calls members sent into these factories "colonists"; is that correct?

Mr. CHASE. It is; yes, sir; distinctly a colony. It couldn't be anything else.

Mr. MATTHEWS. Now, how would you distinguish between the party's effort to recruit in a shop and to colonize in a shop? What would be the difference?

Mr. CHASE. Well, there would be this distinction: We take, for instance, a large group of the unemployed——

Mr. MATTHEWS. I am talking about a shop now. Please distinguish between the party's effort to recruit in a shop and to colonize in a shop.

Mr. CHASE. To colonize in a shop would be to make that shop a concentration center where various members of the party who are unemployed are able to make a change in employment—would seek employment in a factory or in an industry for the purpose of building a colony in there. The recruiting would follow.

Mr. MATTHEWS. Well, I wonder if I may suggest and ask you to contradict it, if you please, that the difference is simply this: When the party colonizes in a shop it takes a person who is already a member of the party and instructs him to seek employment in that shop. Is that correct?

Mr. CHASE. That is correct.

Mr. MATTHEWS. And when the party recruits in the shop it goes to a person who is already working there and attempts to win him for membership in the Communist Party?

Mr. CHASE. That is correct.

Mr. MATTHEWS. Do you know of many actual instances where the Communist Party has colonized in shops?

Mr. CHASE. The Goodyear Tire & Rubber Co. has long been a concentration center. It took some years before penetration could be made. Douglas Aircraft is a shop that could be pointed to as an excellent example of colonizing by Communists. They seized upon the recent strike at the Douglas Aircraft and came out of that with something over 40 members from a very small colony in the beginning.

Mr. MATTHEWS. Does the party colonize in other organizations than trade unions or in other places than shops?

Mr. CHASE. Yes; extensively so in churches, student groups, and political organizations.

Mr. MATTHEWS. Were you a member of the Communist Party in 1935?

Mr. CHASE. Yes.

Mr. MATTHEWS. That was the time when the Seventh World Congress met in Moscow, was it?

Mr. CHASE. Yes.

Mr. MATTHEWS. In August?

Mr. CHASE. Yes; that is right.

Mr. MATTHEWS. Do you recall a resolution adopted at the Seventh World Congress instructing members of the Young Communist League to colonize themselves in religious organizations?

The CHAIRMAN. Just one second. You say that that is a definite part of their policy, to colonize in these industries. What would be the purpose of colonizing in the Douglas Aircraft industry? For instance, assuming you get a membership in there of 40 members, in the aircraft factory, would it be the duty of those members to supply any information required by the party leadership with reference to that factory and with reference to airplanes, new methods, and so on and so forth?

Mr. CHASE. Wherever a Communist is working in any factory, aircraft or any other factory, it is the duty and obligation of a Communist to report any information that he is able to obtain back to the party.

The CHAIRMAN. The reason I asked that is because we had the secretary, James Dolson, here, and I asked him specifically the question: If it was the duty of a Communist to give information, any information required by his leader to the leader, and he said it was. So that is in line with your statement to the effect that it would be the positive obligation of a Communist working in a basic industry, including airplane factories, naval yards, or wherever they are, to give any information that the party leadership might require.

Mr. CHASE. Yes. And any party member will give that without hesitancy.

The CHAIRMAN. With reference to the aircraft factories. You say there are 40 men working in them. Suppose that the Soviet Union wants certain information with reference to American manufacture or improvement of airplanes, and instructions came from Moscow to the Communist Party of the United States that all such information should be obtained. Then the party leadership in turn would contact the 40 members who are employed in the airplane factories and instruct them to submit certain information. Then would it be the duty and obligation of those 40 members to get that information, if they can, and submit it to the party leadership?

Mr. CHASE. That is absolutely correct.

The CHAIRMAN. And isn't it a fact that one of the chief purposes of maintaining the Communists or the immediate purpose, not the long-range purpose, but one of the immediate objectives of the Communist Party in the United States is to secure valuable military and industrial secrets to transmit to Moscow.

Mr. CHASE. Yes.

The CHAIRMAN. So that they have a potential espionage system maintained in this country that they wouldn't have to pay for; they wouldn't have to finance in the usual way in which governments finance espionage systems in foreign lands, is that true?

Mr. CHASE. That is correct.

Mr. CASEY. You said it was the duty of a Communist working in any industry to furnish information. Does that duty rest upon a request by Communist leaders, or is this a general duty? If they happen to notice anything that they deem particularly important, is it their general duty to report that voluntarily?

Mr. CHASE. A Communist would not have to be urged. You must remember that Communist members are in there with the definite purpose of promoting revolution; that they have become enemies of the system that prevails in this country. They are ambitious to replace this system with the workers and farmers or a proletariat dictatorship, as it is more generally known, and they will readily, without any urge, look for anything that they can use to their—what they consider their own advantage. That information would readily be furnished upon their part even without a request.

Mr. CASEY. Then the information, I suppose, is sifted by the leaders to determine what is important and what is relatively unimportant?

Mr. CHASE. That is right.

Mr. CASEY. The workers themselves furnish everything which they think is relevant or important?

Mr. CHASE. Yes. Things of a local nature that were not of any great importance would probably rest right with the committee in the territory, but things of such importance would be forwarded to the central committee in New York and in turn, if they considered it of sufficient importance, it would be forwarded on to Moscow.

Mr. CASEY. Let me see if I follow the channel of progress that this information takes. The worker forwards information to whom in California? A man works in a factory in California, to whom does he give his information?

Mr. CHASE. He is attached to a unit of the Communist Party, and he is responsible to his organizer. The organizer of that particular unit will carry forth the program of the organizing committee, which is the program of the controlling body in that particular locality.

Mr. CASEY. The organizer gets the worker's report?

Mr. CHASE. That is right. Right in the meeting, and he carries force—he brings to that meeting the decisions of the higher bodies, and the members are assigned the particular tasks which they are expected to perform, and the results of these things are reported. The usual procedure would be to the unit organizer, but in many instances the most capable worker in the unit will not be the organizer. He will oftentimes hold no particular office in that unit. He may be working in confidence directly with a State committee or with a county committee, and in that event his reports would not be passed through the unit but would go beyond that. He would make his report in confidence and direct to a higher body.

Mr. CASEY. Before the report is sent to the central body in New York, who passes upon it to determine whether it should be forwarded to New York?

Mr. CHASE. The county secretary or the State secretary.

Mr. CASEY. That is not done by a vote, or by debating, or anything of that sort? There is a person delegated to that job?

Mr. CHASE. That is right. There would be no debate or no discussion around it. If they had anything of importance they would take it to the county organizer and he in turn would submit it either to the State secretary or forward it on to the central committee.

Mr. CASEY. If he thinks it is merely local?

Mr. CHASE. He would take action, whatever action he decided upon himself there, and it would rest there.

Mr. CASEY. Now, if it is of a national characteristic or international characteristic, he would forward it to New York, is that right?

Mr. CHASE. That is right.

Mr. CASEY. And over in New York who determines whether it should be forwarded? Is it forwarded to the Comintern, did you say?

Mr. CHASE. To the Comintern; yes.

Mr. CASEY. Who determines that in New York?

Mr. CHASE. That would be the central committee or some member of it.

Mr. CASEY. That is all.

The CHAIRMAN. Now, following that line of inquiry, Earl Browder testified before this committee that the Communist Party of the United States has 100,000 members. Since then the committee has secured a Communist Party membership book numbered one-hundred-eighteen-thousand-seven-hundred-and-something. Assuming that there are 118,000 members in the Communist Party in the United States. Browder said that more than 50 percent of them were working in industries—in unions. Assuming that you had 60,000 Communists scattered throughout the industries in America, from your knowledge and experience in the work you did as a Communist, would you say that out of this 60,000 and through the 60,000 members, that Moscow would have practically complete sources of information with reference to everything that takes place industrially in the United States?

Mr. CHASE. Yes; the support would go much farther than the 60,000 or the 100,000 members that they acknowledge, because the actual membership in the Communist Party is only a small portion of their influence.

We must remember this, that the International Workers or the C. I. O. could be mentioned, and Friends of the Soviet Union, Friends of the Chinese people, Friends of the Abraham Lincoln Battalion, and organizations too numerous to mention, which are not made up of people that are entirely communistic; who either wholly or in part do believe in the Communist program. Many of them are considered faithful, reliable, and loyal to the cause of the Communist Party, so the influence from that 100,000 members would extend much farther.

It would be more reasonable to say possibly a couple of million people.

The CHAIRMAN. In other words, if there are 40 Communists in an airplane factory they have contact among non-Communists who are sympathetic with them in that factory, is that true?

Mr. CHASE. It is the belief of the Communist Party that every Communist should have around him not less than 10 persons who will follow his leadership in any period of crisis or difficulty.

The CHAIRMAN. Well, of course, the whole theory of the party is that the Communist Party proper is the vanguard—the general staff?

Mr. CHASE. That is right.

The CHAIRMAN. Of the others? So that each Communist is looked upon as an officer and he is supposed to surround himself with followers, is that true?

Mr. CHASE. That is right, followers who are not themselves a member of the Communist Party.

The CHAIRMAN. So if Moscow wanted information in a given country then they have not only the members of the party in those countries, but also sympathizers through whom they can work to secure that information?

Mr. CHASE. That is accurate and correct.

The CHAIRMAN. And where Russia is in alliance with another country the information would not be only for Russia, but would be transmitted or made available to that other country?

Mr. CHASE. That is right; yes.

The CHAIRMAN. You know, for instance, in the Los Angeles area the number of men who belong to the German-American Bund, for instance?

Mr. CHASE. No, I don't know their membership there. I am not very familiar with that.

The CHAIRMAN. Isn't it a fact that in Los Angeles there was at one time around 1,500 members—the German-American Bund?

Mr. CHASE. I do know that their mass meetings are well attended.

The CHAIRMAN. Well, do you know that most of them work as skilled workers, and that a number of them are in the basic industries—as a matter of fact, most of them are in basic industries.

Mr. CHASE. Yes; I do know that.

The CHAIRMAN. So that two governments working together, like Germany and Russia, have facilities for obtaining military and industrial secrets in the United States for any purpose they see fit. As I say, they have today the greatest facilities for that purpose. They have the greatest idealogical set-up that has ever been known in the history of the world. I mean they have a spy system that masquerades as a political party that is unrivaled anywhere else in the world right here in the United States.

Mr. CHASE. There is no doubt about that, not only the United States, but in many countries throughout the world there exists the greatest political and economic conspiracy, I believe, within the history of all times. It has long been the declared purpose of the Communist Party—they have not mentioned a word about it; they have made this very clear on numerous occasions, over a period of years, that in the event that the United States or any other capitalistic country should be bold as to declare war upon the Soviet

Union it is their purpose not only to paralyze the industry of this Nation but to sabotage it in every way that it is possible, and to preserve the fatherland. Time and again they have raised that slogan: "Hands off the Soviet Union, the Workers' Fatherland."

The CHAIRMAN. Now, what percentage of the Communists are known among the workers as Communists? Take, for instance, in the average industry, would you say that the majority of the Communists conceal their identity and are unknown as members of the Communist Party?

Mr. CHASE. Oh, those that would be known as Communists would be a very small percentage. I could only speculate on that, but it would be very small.

The CHAIRMAN. But the majority of them are kept absolutely in the background so far as their identity in the party is concerned, so that they can work more effectively; is that true?

Mr. CHASE. That is true.

The CHAIRMAN. The ones who are designated to come out in the front are the few that are necessary to provide both a legal organization and an illegal organization, isn't that right?

Mr. CHASE. The Communists maintain two distinct organizations. They maintain an underground movement at all times, because they are constantly aware that some change in a political administration in a country may necessitate them going immediately underground.

The CHAIRMAN. Well, isn't it a fact that the constitution of the Communist International requires every unit of the Communist Party to have both a legal and an illegal organization?

Mr. CHASE. That is right.

The CHAIRMAN. And they maintain the legal organizations in countries where they are authorized to do so and where they are not outlawed?

Mr. CHASE. Yes.

The CHAIRMAN. And then, of course, if they are outlawed, they set up their illegal organization?

Mr. CHASE. That is right. And we must realize that those who are active in the illegal work in the underground movement of the Communist Party are certainly not going to be silly enough to stand up and say that they are members of the Communist Party.

The CHAIRMAN. Well, what is the teaching with respect to a member of the Communist Party who is not openly known? Take the case of a Communist who is not known, who hasn't been designated to go into the open and make known the fact that he is a Communist, and he is brought before a committee or the court and is asked the question: "Are you a member of the Communist Party?" What will be his answer under the party's rules?

Mr. CHASE. His answer would be "No."

The CHAIRMAN. Would he hesitate to perjure himself to conceal his identity?

Mr. CHASE. The Communist doesn't regard that as perjury. They regard these laws as laws that have been made by capitalists for the preservation of the capitalist system, and where the rights or the intent of the worker is involved those laws should be totally disregarded.

The CHAIRMAN. And they get that directly from the teachings of Lenin with respect to religion?

Mr. CHASE. Yes.

The CHAIRMAN. And his ethics and morals in which he denies that Communists have any morals, insofar as morals are understood throughout the world. I mean by that, isn't that part of the whole communistic doctrine?

Mr. CHASE. Lenin states that substantially in these terms: That the Communist program must be an elastic program; it may be this way today and it may be another way tomorrow. He states very plainly that they must resort to chicanery and trickery in order to outwit and to fool the bourgeois.

The CHAIRMAN. All right, Mr. Matthews.

Mr. CASEY. Just one question. Have you any evidence of any cooperation between the Communist Party and the German-American Bund in California?

Mr. CHASE. I have seen no evidence of them cooperating there locally.

Mr. CASEY. Well, do you keep up with their publications? Have you read since the Soviet pact or have you had occasion to read the Communist publications and the publication of the German-American Bund and the publications of certain other groups that work with thm?

Mr. CHASE. I have read some of those things; yes.

Mr. CASEY. Have you noticed any similarity in the phraseology since that pact and the arguments that they have advanced in support of the fact and in support of the alliance between Russia and Germany?

Mr. CHASE. Yes; I have heard some of the arguments. I have discussed it with some of them.

Mr. CASEY. Have you noticed in the bund publications that they no longer attack the Communists; that they no longer use the words "plutocratic" and "gangster," and that there is no longer in the publications of the respective organizations that constant bombardment?

Mr. CHASE. I am perfectly aware that because of this alliance between Russia and Germany that the Communist Party is to cease attacking the Nazis and the Nazis are to cease attacking the Communists.

Mr. CASEY. Are you aware of the fact that since the invasion of Norway the Communist publications lay the blame on England and practically defended the Nazi seizure and control of Norway?

Mr. CHASE. Yes; I am familiar with that.

Mr. CASEY. So that when an alliance takes place across the waters the new situation is immediately reflected in the attitude not only of Communist groups but of Nazi groups in the United States?

Mr. CHASE. That is correct.

Mr. CASEY. While there wouldn't be any evidence of any outward cooperation, since they would be too smart for that, the very fact that the whole party line, if both of them change and they cease to be antagonistic, would take up other issues.

Mr. CHASE. The struggle of both of them at this time without a doubt is to attack Great Britain and France.

Mr. CASEY. And in the publications of both of them when you read them now, instead of the Communists talking about Nazi aggression and Nazi imperialism, and so on and so forth, they are talking now about the British imperialism.

Mr. CHASE. Yes. They have made a complete about face on that issue.

Mr. CASEY. Is that in accordance with Stalin's so-called elastic program?

Mr. CHASE. Yes. And the Communists defend that because they revert back to the bible, which is the teaching of Lenin, and Lenin made that issue very clear years ago.

Mr. CASEY. So it would be an elastic program, which means subject to change without notice.

Mr. CHASE. They have no scruples against forming an alliance with the bourgeois wherever they can do that to advantage.

Mr. CASEY. Then the Communists in America have no discretion. They must follow blindly whatever comes out of Russia?

Mr. CHASE. Yes; the policy is laid down in Russia.

The CHAIRMAN. All right, Mr. Matthews.

Mr. MATTHEWS. Mr. Chase. with reference to the alien members of the Communist Party in the State of California you said you did not know exactly what proportion of the membership there has failed to take out citizenship. Is it true that the Communist Party has no hesitation to take into membership persons who are ineligible for citizenship in the United States?

Mr. CHASE. They have always held as part of their program the defense of the aliens, and that has been their program right along.

Mr. MATTHEWS. I am referring to such individuals who would be ineligible for citizenship—Japanese and Chinese, for example?

Mr. CHASE. Oh, yes; they take them as members.

Mr. MATTHEWS. Does that indicate to some extent that the Communist Party is not a political party in the ordinary sense of the word?

Mr. CHASE. That certainly indicates that. May I elaborate on that?

Mr. CASEY. Sure.

Mr. CHASE. The Communist Party should not be considered a political party in the sense that other parties are considered political. Now. the Republican Party, the Democratic Party, or their equivalent in other countries would be limited to the affairs and the activities of that nation and its members would pledge loyalty to that particular nation. In the instance of the Democratic Party or the Republican Party their loyalty would be pledged to the United States Government. But the Communist Party differs with them on this point. They recognize no boundary lines. In fact, Karl Marx stated "This world belongs to the workers. There is no room for a boundary line." They were the words that he used. The Communist Party pledges allegiance to no country other than the Soviet Union and the program of the Communist International.

Mr. DEMPSEY. But they pledge allegiance to one country.

Mr. CHASE. To the Soviet Union.

Mr. MATTHEWS. That is because they consider that the source of the Comintern or the Communist Party?

Mr. CHASE. Yes.

Mr. MATTHEWS. And the home, you might say. of the Communist Party.

Mr. CHASE. Their allegiance wouldn't be pledged to Russia. It would be pledged to the Soviet Union. That is the way they would phrase that because the Soviet Union is made up of a number of countries.

The CHAIRMAN. Or, isn't the entire structure of the Communist Party designed for the purpose of covering up one fact, namely, that the Communist Party is an agency of the Soviet Union? I mean when you get down to the proposition while they pretend their officers are elected by the membership and that it is a democratic organization, isn't it a fact that the whole structure and the pretense of a democratic organization is for the purpose of concealing the fact that Russia has in the United States an agency to do its bidding, whatever its bidding may be?

Mr. CHASE. That is correct.

The CHAIRMAN. And in the case of the Communist International, the Communist Party of the United States, and of other countries are sections of it?

Mr. CHASE. That is right.

The CHAIRMAN. But isn't it a fact that since the Communist Party of Russia has 1,800,000 members, as compared with the rest of the countries, that gives the Communist Party of Russia a complete control of the Communist International?

Mr. CHASE. I want to make this point. The Communist International—there was a gap of 7 or 8 years that no conventions whatever were held. Now, the Communist International is made up of delegates from the Communist Party in the various countries throughout the world. But naturally Russia, having by far the largest membership, would naturally have the greater number of delegates. Now, inside of the Communist International is the presidium. The presidium acts upon problems between conventions. Now, this presidium is practically all made up of Russians and those that are not Russians are usually taking care of problems in their own countries. The result is that a quorum will act between conventions made up entirely of Russians and, therefore, the entire program of the Communist International can truthfully be said to be dictated by the Russian Communists.

The CHAIRMAN. It is just a clever way for a foreign country to build up an espionage system in another country without having to pay for it and without any danger of that other foreign country treating it as an espionage system?

Mr. CHASE. Yes, sir. It is that in every sense of the word.

Mr. MATTHEWS. Mr. Chase, in the event that a Communist Party member is instructed to obtain highly confidential information in a plant such as an aircraft plant, isn't it true that that information would not be transmitted to his unit organizer or section organizer or, as a matter of fact, to anybody else in the Communist Party as such, but wouldn't that be transmitted to the other agency of the Communist conspiracy, the Soviet military intelligence or the Ogpu?

Mr. CHASE. All Communists belong to the unit, of course, but a member that has the ability and is in the position to render some particular service would be assigned to some other part of the Communist Party, to some other group, some individual or for some particular duty that they have, and he would work in confidence and he would make his report accordingly.

Mr. MATTHEWS. Do you know anything about the existence of the secret organization which is commonly described now as the Ogpu?

Mr. CHASE. Wherever there is a Communist Party they have it.

Mr. MATTHEWS. That is under what is now called the Commissariat of Internal Affairs of the Soviet Union, is it not?

Mr. CHASE. Yes. That is the correct name for it now.

Mr. MATTHEWS. And that is an espionage organization wherever it exists, outside of the Soviet Union as well as inside?

Mr. CHASE. That is a secret-police department.

Mr. MATTHEWS. Now, in addition to the——

The CHAIRMAN. Right there, Mr. Matthews, the ability to engage in espionage work or, rather, the opportunity for it without being apprehended by the authorities is greatly enhanced by the attitude of a government treating the Communist Party as a political organization, is that not true? I mean you see very prominent men occasionally who would speak of the fact they don't inquire into a person's political affiliations. They are under the impression that the Communist Party is just another political party so that that makes it much easier for the Communist Party to carry on its espionage work in a given country, isn't that true?

Mr. CHASE. Yes. There has been a great deal said here lately about maintaining a democratic condition throughout the country. Now, the Communists have made themselves the greatest champions— that is, they have made themselves champions of democracy in this country, and they have done that for a distinct purpose, because the Communist has placed upon democracy the burden of giving them the privilege to carry on any sort of activity that they wish, and the Communist friendship and his loyalty to democracy is only to this extent, that by carrying forth that program then they can maintain a condition under the framework of which the Communist Party can carry on their activities without any kind of legal resistance whatever, and that is exactly what they are doing.

Mr. MATTHEWS. Now, in addition to this Commissariat of Internal Affairs, which was formerly known as the Ogpu, there is also the fourth division of the Red Army which is known as the Soviet Military Intelligence. Does that operate in countries where the Communist Party also exists?

Mr. CHASE. Yes. Their agents would be present.

Mr. MATTHEWS. Now, isn't it true that highly confidential information of an industrial or military character would be transmitted to Moscow, not through the regular party channels, but through one of these other channels?

Mr. CHASE. The Communists are always going to use the safest possible channels that they can use for communication purposes, certainly.

Mr. MATTHEWS. You mentioned a moment ago that under the influence or control or both, of the Communist Party in this country, there were approximately 2,000,000 individuals. That is your estimation of the situation?

Mr. CHASE. Yes. That figure could only be estimated, and I believe that would be conservative.

Mr. MATTHEWS. Do you recall that Earl Browder wrote an article in the Communist, which is the official monthly publication of the party, that the party had under its control 2,000,000 individuals who were sympathetic to its program?

Mr. CHASE. I did not read any article.

The CHAIRMAN. Well, now, getting back to California. Have you any other questions, Mr. Matthews?

Mr. MATTHEWS. I have a question to ask about California in that connection.

The CHAIRMAN. Very well, go ahead.

Mr. MATTHEWS. You spoke of the underground organization of the party by which I take it you meant that there are actual committees formed, as well as individuals, who are not known to the public at large as Communists, is that correct?

Mr. CHASE. That is correct.

Mr. MATTHEWS. For example, in the State of California was there an underground central committee which differed in its personnel from the central committee such as would be reported to the secretary of the state of California?

Mr. CHASE. The central committee of the Communist Party in no instance would be those that are known to us as the central committee. The real control of the Communist Party is in the hands of the underground movement.

Mr. MATTHEWS. Now, the Communist Party of California is required to report to the secretary of state of California, is it not, the personnel of its leading body?

Mr. CHASE. I don't know that they are.

Mr. MATTHEWS. For purposes of the ballot.

Mr. CHASE. Oh, yes; that is correct, for the purpose of the ballot.

Mr. MATTHEWS. Now, in reporting that personnel of that party is it your information or knowledge that that would differ from the actual governing body of the Communist Party?

Mr. CHASE. Yes; it would differ.

Mr. MATTHEWS. So that that further evidences the fact that the Communist Party is not a political party in the ordinary sense of the word?

Mr. CHASE. I can say this definitely, I have been a member of the top faction of the Communist Party, which is supposed to run that, and my own observations showed to me very plainly that inside of that top faction there was a top faction.

The CHAIRMAN. Now, of course, a great difficulty that this committee has is the fact that this is not just another political party. The committee has the difficulty of convincing people in positions of authority, people in unions, that this is not just another political party. You will notice that the invariable answer we get here is "Well, our organization does not inquire into a man's political belief. We take people independently of their political belief," and until the country can understand, people in authority can understand that this is not a political party but an espionage system of a foreign government that is masquerading under slogans of democracy and under the framework of a democratic organization, then it is impossible ever to deal with it in the way that it has to be dealt with as an espionage agency of a foreign government.

Mr. CHASE. Well, I could easily recognize your difficulty in getting that across. I have encountered that experience in innumerable instances.

The CHAIRMAN. Now, you made the statement here that the Maritime Union is "completely controlled by the Communist Party." What do you base that statement on? First, because you were in the party for 7 years?

Mr. CHASE. Yes.

The CHAIRMAN. Now, did you come in contact with the Maritime Union officials and workers along the west coast as a Communist yourself?

Mr. CHASE. Yes. I came in contact with them. The fact that the Maritime Union so persistently and so capably carries forth the program of the Communist Party at all times——

The CHAIRMAN. Did you know yourself of Communists who had leadership in the union?

Mr. CHASE. Oh, yes; I have known numbers of them.

The CHAIRMAN. You mean leaders in the Maritime Union that you have met with in the Communist Party and whom you know are members of the Communist Party?

Mr. CHASE. Yes. One of the outstanding ones is Chester Jordan.

The CHAIRMAN. What is his position in the Maritime Union?

Mr. CHASE. His position in there—he was a member of the Radio Telegraphists' Union. He later became the secretary of the Industrial Council of the C. I .O.

The CHAIRMAN. Do you know that he is a member of the Communist Party?

Mr. CHASE. I have been in a lot of meetings with him. I know it definitely.

The CHAIRMAN. That he is a member of the Communist Party?'

Mr. CHASE. Yes.

The CHAIRMAN. Does he occupy a strong or important position in the Maritime Union?

Mr. CHASE. Yes. He has been a leader in that union on the west coast for quite some time.

The CHAIRMAN. Do you know any other leaders?

Mr. MATTHEWS. Just a minute. Were you here yesterday, Mr. Chase?

Mr. CHASE. No; I was not.

Mr. MATTHEWS. The witness yesterday identified Chester Jordan as the vice president of the A. R. T. A.

The CHAIRMAN. Yes.

Mr. MATTHEWS. Is that the same Chester Jordan?

Mr. CHASE. Yes.

Mr. MATTHEWS. Vice president of the American Radio and Telegraphists' Association?

Mr. CHASE. Yes.

The CHAIRMAN. And you know he is a member of the Communist Party?

Mr. CHASE. Yes.

The CHAIRMAN. Can you give us any more in the Maritime Union that you have personal knowledge of and have sat with in Communist meetings?

Mr. CHASE. Not of officials; no. He is the only one that I have actually sat in meetings with.

The CHAIRMAN. Do you have any information with reference to others who were members of the party, who were leaders in the Communist Party in the Maritime Union?

Mr. CHASE. There are numbers of them that I know but I have never been in meetings with them.

The CHAIRMAN. How would you know it if you were not in meetings with them?

Mr. CHASE. Well, it is not difficult for one Communist to recognize another.

Mr. MATTHEWS. When you speak of the Maritime Union, you don't mean there is a union known by that name?

Mr. CHASE. I am speaking of the maritime industry. I am speaking now of the Maritime Federation, the union which makes that up, of which there are a number.

The CHAIRMAN. I was using it in a general sense. Several unions that make it up.

Mr. CHASE. The Maritime Federation embraces the entire shipping and seagoing industry.

The CHAIRMAN. Who is the head of the whole Federation?

Mr. CHASE. Harry Bridges.

The CHAIRMAN. Did you ever sit with Harry Bridges in a Communist meeting?

Mr. CHASE. Not where they were everyone Communists. There was a meeting—a few meetings there where there were some that were not Communists. They were not made up solidly of Communists.

The CHAIRMAN. Do you have any information, any dependable information or sound grounds, to believe that Harry Bridges was a member of the party?

Mr. CHASE. I have never doubted it, and neither has any other Communist among themselves.

The CHAIRMAN. Well, on what would you base such a belief?

Mr. CHASE. The accuracy with which he carries the Communist programs and other points. That makes it seem very strong. Harry Bridges came to Los Angeles to lay down the party policy to guide the conduct and the activities of the Communists in the American Federation of Labor unions and in the C. I. O. unions as well. This meeting took place on West Washington Boulevard in Los Angeles in the early part of 1937.

I was called to the telephone in the union headquarters, and Lou Barron was speaking on the other end. Lou Barron at that time was the organizer of the trade-union section of the Communist Party. Lou Barron told me that Harry was in town and he said, "Harry is holding a meeting at 1210½ West Washington Boulevard" and he said, "You, yourself, and Walter Westphal and Joe Sylva are to go there as the representatives of your union." He says, "And Bridges is going to lay down the policy, the new policy, with which we are to follow in regard to taking of A. F. of L. unions over to the C. I. O." And I attended that meeting.

Mr. CASEY. Now, that policy was not a Communist policy but a union policy?

Mr. CHASE. That was a Communist policy. That was the program of the Communist Party for Communist Party members in trade-unions, but they were to bring into that meeting to hear Bridges others that had been working or traveling along with them in carrying forth this trade-union program.

Mr. CASEY. I thought you and your associates were told over the telephone to go as representatives of your labor union.

Mr. CHASE. We were; yes. We were going to represent the labor union, but we were going as Communists under instructions from the Communist Party, but to represent our unions which we got to the meeting.

Mr. MATTHEWS. Now, you have identified Lou Barron as a member of the Communist Party and you stated he was head of the trade-union section of the party at that time.

Mr. CHASE. At that time; yes. He was the organizer of the trade-union section of the Communist Party.

Mr. MATTHEWS. And you mentioned Walter Westphal.

Mr. CHASE. Walter Westphal was the business agent of the Upholsterers Union, Local 15.

Mr. MATTHEWS. And did you identify him as a Communist?

Mr. CHASE. He is a Communist.

Mr. MATTHEWS. Have you sat with him in meetings?

Mr. CHASE. Yes.

Mr. MATTHEWS. Have you worked with him on this trade-union commission?

Mr. CHASE. We belonged in the same trade-union and belonged to the same unit for a long while.

Mr. MATTHEWS. Who was Joe Sylva whom you named?

Mr. CHASE. Joe Sylva was a member of the Communist Party and he was the president of Local 15 of the Upholsterers' International Union.

Mr. MATTHEWS. That was the union to which you belonged?

Mr. CHASE. That is right.

Mr. MATTHEWS. Did you know anyone in the Automobile Workers Union who is a Communist?

Mr. CHASE. Yes; I know quite a few of them in there.

Mr. MATTHEWS. Did you know Ed Sugar?

Mr. CHASE. Yes; I know Eddie.

Mr. MATTHEWS. Is he a Communist?

Mr. CASEY. Eddie what?

Mr. CHASE. Sugar, S-u-g-a-r.

Mr. MATTHEWS. Was he a Communist?

Mr. CHASE. Yes.

The CHAIRMAN. What position did he hold?

Mr. CHASE. Well, he is sort of a free-lance organizer. Then in the latter part of 1937 he was on the pay roll, I believe, as an organizer.

Mr. MATTHEWS. Did you know a man by the name of Pelman?

Mr. CHASE. Yes.

Mr. MATTHEWS. Was he a Communist?

Mr. CHASE. Yes.

Mr. MATTHEWS. What was his trade-union connection?

Mr. CHASE. He was a member of the Trade Union Commission and he was also one of the speakers of this so-called progressive bloc in the Central Labor Council.

Mr. MATTHEWS. When you say of a trade-union commission do you mean of the Communist Party?

Mr. CHASE. Of the Communist Party, yes—the Trade Union Commission; yes. That is of the Communist Party entirely.

Mr. MATTHEWS. Did you know Hugh Campbell?

Mr. CHASE. Yes; I know Hugh Campbell.

Mr. MATTHEWS. Was he a Communist?

Mr. Chase. Yes.

Mr. Matthews. What was his trade-union connection?

Mr. Chase. He is secretary of the District Council of the Painters in Los Angeles.

Mr. Matthews. Was he a member of the central council?

Mr. Chase. No.

Mr. Matthews. Do you know Don Healy?

Mr. Chase. Yes.

Mr. Matthews. Was he a Communist?

Mr. Chase. Yes. Don Healy is a Communist.

Mr. Matthews. What was his trade-union connection, if any?

Mr. Chase. Don Healy was a member of the Painters' Union and he became the secretary of Labor's Nonpartisan League and he was a delegate to the Central Labor Council.

Mr. Casey. Is that the State Nonpartisan League?

Mr. Chase. Labor's Nonpartisan League. It is a national organization.

Mr. Casey. National secretary?

Mr. Chase. No; not national secretary. He was the local, southern California secretary. I misunderstood your question.

Mr. Matthews. Did you know Dorothy Ray?

Mr. Chase. Yes.

Mr. Matthews. Did you know her as a Communist?

Mr. Chase. Yes.

Mr. Matthews. Was she vice president of the United Cannery, Agricultural, Packing, and Allied Workers?

Mr. Chase. Yes.

Mr. Matthews. Of which Don Henderson is the head for the United States?

Mr. Chase. That is right.

Mr. Matthews. Is that a picture of Dorothy Ray [handing photograph to witness].

Mr. Chase. Yes; that is right.

Mr. Matthews. I would like to introduce this in evidence.

The Chairman. It is received.

(The photograph referred to by Mr. Matthews was marked "Chase Exhibit 4" and made a part of the record.)

Mr. Matthews. When you said that Harry Bridges laid down the party line at this meeting which you and Westphal and Sylva and others attended, what party line was it that he laid down?

Mr. Chase. There had been considerable confusion as to just what treatment the Party members were going to give to A. F. of L. unions and A. F. of L. members that were sympathetic and desirous of affiliating themselves with the C. I. O. There was quite a high fever among these unions and many of them wanted to just pick up their local union and bring it away from the A. F. of L. and move it right on over to the C. I. O. And the part that Bridges was to lay down there was a new national policy to guide our conduct and coordinate it with unions throughout the United States.

Mr. Casey. California is rather a hotbed of pension plans. Has the Communist Party any policy with respect to these pension plans?

Mr. Chase. Confidentially and among themselves, the Communist Party does not have any sympathy toward any of the old-age pension plans, but they look upon them as more or less ridiculous and an impossibility, but for the purpose of undermining and extending their influence into the pension organizers, in the People's World and other publications they have given them considerable favorable publicity and have always sent speakers before these organizations. But the Communist Party looks upon old-age pension movements as an impossible thing and a very ridiculous movement.

Mr. CASEY. Outwardly they give lip service and support.

Mr. CHASE. They give lip service knowing that these movements are doomed to ultimate failure. And then it will be the purpose of the Communist Party to point out to these organizations the impossibility of adequate old-age pensions under a system of capitalism; that it would be only in the destruction of the capitalist system and the setting up of the proletarian dictatorship that these people would be able to gain security.

The CHAIRMAN. We will adjourn at this time subject to the call of the chairman.

(Whereupon, at 11:40 a. m., the hearing was adjourned.)

INVESTIGATION OF UN-AMERICAN PROPAGANDA ACTIVITIES IN THE UNITED STATES

MONDAY, MAY 6, 1940

House of Representatives,
Committee on Un-American Activities,
Washington, D. C.

The committee met at 10 a. m., Hon. Martin Dies (chairman) presiding.

The Chairman. The committee will come to order.

Mr. Innes, will you please hold up your right hand and be sworn.

TESTIMONY OF PETER J. INNES, JR., FORMER MEMBER, NATIONAL MARITIME UNION

The Chairman. Do you solemnly swear to tell the truth, the whole truth, and nothing but the truth, so help you God?

Mr. Innes. I do.

Mr. Matthews. Will you please state your full name?

r. Innes. Peter J. Innes, Jr., 892 Hallet Street, Bridgeport, Conn.

Mr. Matthews. Mr. Innes, will you please outline briefly your connection with the National Maritime Union?

Mr. Innes. I joined the National Maritime Union when it was first formed, following the dissolution of the International Seamen's Union.

The Chairman. Let me note here in the absence of a full committee, there is a subcommittee consisting of the chairman and Mr. Thomas and Mr. Voorhis of California. Proceed.

Mr. Innes. Following the dissolution of the International Seamen's Union, I held various positions. I was organizer for the port of New York in the engine division, and the last position I held was that of national purchasing agent.

Mr. Matthews. Now, what year did you join the National Maritime Union?

Mr. Innes. Well, I joined it on the day of its formation but I joined the union first in January 1936—the International Seamen's Union—the Marine Firemen, Oilers, and Watertenders' Union of the Atlantic and Gulf, which later became the engine division of the Maritime Union.

Mr. Matthews. Are you a seaman?

Mr. Innes. I am.

Mr. Matthews. In what capacity?

Mr. Innes. Oiler in the engine room.

Mr. Matthews. How long have you followed that occupation?

Mr. INNES. In the merchant marine since 1935.

Mr. MATTHEWS. Have you been working during the past year?

Mr. INNES. I have.

Mr. MATTHEWS. Where?

Mr. INNES. Well, after I left New York I was under the doctor's care until July of 1939, and—at which time I went to work as a fireman on the automobile ferry operating between Bridgeport, Conn., and Long Island.

Mr. MATTHEWS. And up to what time did you engage in that work?

Mr. INNES. Well, the close of the season in October last year, at which time I then went to work for the Peppenstahl Forge Co.. in Bridgeport, where I remained employed until subpenaed by this committee.

Mr. MATTHEWS. And when were you subpenaed by this committee?

Mr. INNES. April 20.

Mr. MATTHEWS. 1940?

Mr. INNES. 1940.

Mr. MATTHEWS. Will you explain, please, the union affiliation that you had throughout?

Mr. INNES. Throughout?

Mr. MATTHEWS. Yes.

Mr. INNES. I joined the union in 1936, and at that time I was employed on board the steamship *Santa Paula* of the Grace Line on the return trip from San Francisco which started in January and ended in April. The outlaw strike of 1936 was taking place in the port of New York.

Mr. THOMAS. I did not hear what strike that was.

Mr. INNES. The outlaw strike, as it was called, of 1936 was taking place in the port of New York, ostensibly lead by Joseph Curran of the steamship *California.*

The ship's crew, previous to the day of our arrival in New York, voted that the delegates, of which I was one, were to go ashore and get the score of the strike.

When we went ashore we found that the strike was more of a sympathy strike and concentrated against the United States Lines and the Grace Line.

We came back and reported that fact to the crew, and they voted that they would strike provided that the entire port of New York was placed on strike. So the entire crew came off with the exception of two men and I was elected their representative to the strike committee in the port of New York.

At that time the strike committee designated me as chief picket dispatcher for the entire strike, and I remained in that capacity throughout the entire period of the strike.

Mr. MATTHEWS. Will you please explain briefly what the chief picket dispatcher's functions were?

Mr. INNES. The chief picket dispatcher's functions were—he was responsible for the placing of pickets at various piers, the formation and execution of mass picket lines, informing the legal department with reference to men who were arrested, and to actively participate in all picketing.

Mr. MATTHEWS. Did you have to sign cards for the pickets?

Mr. INNES. My signature appears on all the strike cards that were issued during the spring of 1936.

At the close of the strike the committee of nine men were elected, composed of three of the deck department, three of the steward's department and three of the engine department who were to carry on the rank and file work of reorganizing the seamen during the summer in preparation for the fall of 1936 when a strike was supposed to take place on the Pacific coast. That committee was given power to cooperate with any other persons that they saw fit.

In other words, to make subcommittees of them.

I was selected as a member of the cooperative committee for the engine department and was elected secretary-treasurer of the M. F. O. W. appeal fund, as the Marine Firemen, Oilers, and Watertenders' Union at that time was in court attempting to get their constitution overridden by the courts.

Mr. MATTHEWS. Now, will you please state what the M. F. O. W. is?

Mr. INNES. Marine Firemen, Oilers, and Watertenders' Union. That was our division of the American Federation of Labor.

This committee ran a strike or ran a dance, I mean, to raise funds for this appeal, and all told I think we raised around $1,200. I participated actively in that committee until July 13, I believe it was, of 1936. On the afternoon of that date I came into the office—the strike headquarters, the defense committee office at 146 Eleventh Avenue, and there I met Joe Curran and Tommy Ray, who told me they had another job for me. I asked them what that was. I told them I had my hands pretty filled up with what I had. They said: "You can drop all that, we are sending you to the west coast."

Mr. LYNCH. What date was that, Mr. Innes?

Mr. INNES. I believe that was July 13. I don't know. A copy of my resignation will show.

Mr. LYNCH. July 13 of what year?

Mr. INNES. 1936.

Mr. LYNCH. Did you go to the Pacific coast then?

Mr. INNES. Following the instructions of Tommy Ray I went over to the steamship *President Taft* in search of a man by the name of Al Yates. When I found him—his job was that of engineer's yeoman. He took me to the chief engineer and told me that I was his relief. Yates then got off the ship. I took his place. We made the triangle run—that is the run between New York, Boston, and back to New York, and then I departed for San Francisco, where I arrived on August 16. I believe, of 1936, and Mr. Yates was on the dock waiting for his job back.

Mr. LYNCH. Now, wait a minute. In regard to this switching of positions on this boat; what boat was that?

Mr. INNES. The steamship *President Taft* of the Dollar Line.

Mr. LYNCH. And who is Tommy Yates?

Mr. INNES. Al Yates. He was the engineer's yeoman. He is, in fact, a well-known Communist who has been thrown in jail several times in Japan for carrying on subversive activities over there.

Mr. LYNCH. And who is Tommy Ray?

Mr. INNES. At that time Roy Hudson's right-hand man in charge of marine labor. He is now in charge of the marine fraction of the Communist Party, and I believe a member of the central committee in charge of marine.

Mr. LYNCH. Was Tommy Ray a Communist at the time, in 1936, when he arranged this switch on this boat for you?

Mr. INNES. He was.

Mr. LYNCH. Now, while you were on this ship or had some connection with this *President Taft*, did you have any information or knowledge with regard to receiving messages?

Mr. INNES. At that time—the time that I was going on board the ship, as I stated, I had been working on this firemen's committee and one of our functions was the getting out of ballots to the membership of the Firemen's Union. As we had an election of officers going on, I was very interested in the outcome, so before I left New York I asked Ray how I was going to get any dope on the results of the elections as they were due in another week. His orders to me were that any time I wanted any dope to take my credentials which I had been given, and go to the radio operator and show them to him and he would get me any information that I wanted.

When we arrived in the Canal Zone in August, I believe it was in Balboa, I wanted to find out who had been elected in the firemen's union, so I went to the radio operator in accordance with my instructions. I showed him my credentials and he said: "Well, I can't do anything about it now, but as soon as we get out to sea I will get your dope for you."

In about 6 hours later he came down with a little typewritten slip that told me that Phillips had been elected; the rank and file slate was in, and that a wire would await me in San Francisco pending my arrival, which would confirm this radio report.

Mr. LYNCH. And that definitely indicated to you that the radio operator on the ship was getting messages from shore or from other ships without the knowledge of the captain.

Mr. INNES. Well, in order for a radio operator to get a message—legally and technically—the captain is the censor of all messages aboard ship and all messages are supposed to have his approval and a copy of all messages sent and received are supposed to be supplied the captain, but he didn't see the message, because when I got to San Francisco the wire was waiting for me.

Mr. LYNCH. What wire?

Mr. INNES. Confirming the election of officers.

Mr. LYNCH. Did you go to see the captain of the *President Taft* to get his approval for sending this message?

Mr. INNES. No sir.

Mr. LYNCH. And that was Tommy Ray who told you to go and show your credentials to the radioman?

Mr. INNES. That is correct.

Mr. LYNCH. And those credentials were what?

Mr. INNES. Credentials from the Seamen's Defense Committee signed by Joseph Curran as chairman and Ralph Emerson as secretary, designating me as the representative of the Seamen's Defense Committee on the Pacific coast.

Mr. LYNCH. When you left that ship, the *President Taft*, you say this fellow Yates was there to take over this job again?

Mr. INNES. Yates was on the dock waiting for the ship when we arrived; yes, sir.

Mr. LYNCH. And that was all arranged by Curran and Tommy Ray?

Mr. INNES. That is correct.

Mr. THOMAS. Mr. Chairman, I would like to ask the witness a question. As I understand it this job that Mr. Curran wanted you to take over was to become a member of the Seamen's Defense Committee out on the Pacific coast or was there some other job in addition to that?

Mr. INNES. No sir. It was to represent the Seamen's Defense Committee on the Pacific coast.

Mr. THOMAS. To represent the Seamen's Defense Committee on the Pacific coast?

Mr. INNES. That is correct.

Mr. THOMAS. That was the particular job that Joe Curran wanted you to take over?

Mr. INNES. Possibly a word of explanation is due you there. During the strike there had been a mix-up and a cross-up—of course, everybody was writing to everybody else and the result was nobody knew just exactly what was taking place and as this new strike was in the making it was decided that they would have one source of communication and I was to be it.

Mr. LYNCH. In other words, you were to be the clearing house for the east-coast seamen?

Mr. INNES. On the Pacific coast.

Mr. LYNCH. On the Pacific coast?

Mr. INNES. Yes, sir.

Mr. LYNCH. Who did you deal with on the Pacific coast?

Mr. INNES. Before leaving New York I had asked that question: Who I was to see, and Ray told me that I would be put in touch with the proper members of the party who were all right, on the Pacific coast.

Mr. LYNCH. What party did he have reference to when he said the "proper members of the party"?

Mr. INNES. Well, that goes back a little bit to May of 1936. I received an invitation to attend a dinner. I believe it was at the Spartacus Club on Twenty-fifth Street and Eighth Avenue in New York. And I went. I didn't know what the dinner was about, but when I arrived all the higher lights of the Communist Party from Roy Hudson, Amter, on down were there to give a welcome-home dinner to Charlie Krumbein, who had just gotten out of jail.

Mr. LYNCH. Is Charlie Krumbein a Communist, to your knowledge?

Mr. INNES. Yes, sir; he is.

Mr. LYNCH. Go ahead.

Mr. INNES. So after that particular dinner I went hunting for Patrick Whalen—the next night I went hunting for Whalen, who was the chairman of the particular subcommittee that I belonged to and I found him in the Communist Party headquarters on Thirteenth Street between Fourth Avenue and Irving Place, I believe, and at that meeting—it was a meeting of the firemen's fraction of the Communist Party. Tommy Ray was presiding and they were designating delegates to attend the Communist Party convention.

That was my second experience with Ray, so, therefore, when he told me that "the proper members of the party" I knew exactly what he meant, because at that fraction meeting he had asked me if I had desired to join the party.

Mr. LYNCH. That was when he referred to "the party" he referred to the Communist Party?

Mr. INNES. That is correct.

Mr. MATTHEWS. What was the Spartacus Club?

Mr. INNES. The Spartacus Club, I believe, was a Greek club—a Communist Party club—but I believe it was one of the foreign-language clubs.

Mr. MATTHEWS. Charles Krumbein, whom you mentioned, is State secretary of the Communist Part for New York State, is he not?

Mr. INNES. I believe he was. I don't know what he is now, because I haven't seen him in a couple of years.

Mr. LYNCH. Mr. Innes, before you take up in detail this west coast matter, I show you a letter dated August 6, 1936, from you to Joseph Curran, and I will ask you if that confirms in writing the testimony that you just gave a few minutes ago with regard to the sending and receiving illegal messages from a United States boat—from the liner *Taft?*

Mr. INNES. Yes, sir. This is from the *President Taft* on August 6, 1936, and is signed by me, and it states that I had the radio operator contact the New York office for information regarding the election.

Mr. LYNCH. I would like to put this in the record.

The CHAIRMAN. It is so ordered.

(The document referred to by Mr. Lynch was marked "Innes Exhibit No. 1," and made a part of the record.)

Mr. MATTHEWS. What is the date of the letter?

Mr. INNES. August 6, 1936.

Mr. THOMAS. May I ask right there how many radio operators would they have on the *President Taft?*

Mr. INNES. I believe the *President Taft* had two at that time.

Mr. LYNCH. The first paragraph, Mr. Chairman——

Mr. INNES. They may have had three, Mr. Thomas.

Mr. LYNCH. "Dear Joe"—this is sent from the *President Taft*— "the trip is so far uneventful." And—

I did get a couple of scabs here off the *Santa Clara* which will probably be good news to you. Have not had any word concerning the M. F. O. elections although I had "sparks" contact ARTA in New York last night and there is a possibility that I may have word tonight. In any event I hope that everything will come out okay for the rank and file.

Now, what is the A.R.T.A.?

Mr. INNES. At that time it was the American Radio Telegraphists' Association, which is now the American Communications Association.

Mr. LYNCH. And who is "Sparks"?

Mr. INNES. "Sparks" is a seaman's term for radio operator.

Mr. LYNCH. All right. And this was written after you had asked the radio operator to get the information?

Mr. INNES. That is correct.

Mr. LYNCH. And then you did get the information?

Mr. INNES. I got the information; yes, sir.

Mr. THOMAS. Now, for the record, may I ask the witness a couple of questions? Is the *President Taft* still in service?

Mr. INNES. I don't believe so. I think she is out of service now, sir.

Mr. THOMAS. And what was the name of this particular radio operator?

Mr. INNES. I don't recall that. That can be found out very easily from the ship's articles.

Mr. THOMAS. Do you know whether he is still a radio operator on one of the United States Line ships?

Mr. INNES. No doubt he is. That could be ascertained from the Maritime Commission's records.

Mr. MATTHEWS. The date of this run was in August 1936?

Mr. INNES. I have the discharge here. I can give you the exact dates. Departed New York on July 29, 1936. That was after the triangle run, and arrived in San Francisco—the date of discharge August 16, 1936.

Mr. MATTHEWS. On board the *President Taft?*

Mr. INNES. On board the *President Taft;* yes, sir.

Mr. LYNCH. I will show you a report of yours to Joseph Curran. It does not seem to be dated, Mr. Innes. I will ask you if you also mentioned in that report, apparently after you arrived on the Pacific coast, information with regard to the receiving of word from the radio operator of the *President Taft* concerning the elections?

Mr. INNES. This report I would state roughly, was written on August 21 and it states here at the beginning of it: "Arrived at"—it is a daily report—

Arrived San Francisco August 16th, Sunday. No activities. Monday, August 17, reported to the secretary of the Pacific Coast M. F. O. W. and with Brother Earl King, and presented my credentials. He showed me the wire from New York confirming information that I had received from ARTA New York by radio aboard ship on results of the firemen's elections on the east coast—

and that is my signature on the bottom.

Mr. LYNCH. Now, Mr. Innes, after you arrived on the west coast, who did you contact out there?

Mr. INNES. I went to the marine firemen's office at 58 Commercial Street, I believe it was, and reported to Earl King on Monday.

Mr. LYNCH. And who is Earl King?

Mr. INNES. Earl King was the secretary of the Marine Firemen's Union of the International Seamen's Union on the Pacific coast, and he is now doing a life sentence in San Quentin Penitentiary for murder.

Mr. LYNCH. By the way, you spoke of Krumbein a few moments ago as having met him in New York at a dinner?

Mr. INNES. Yes, sir.

Mr. LYNCH. Had he then been convicted of a passport violation or since then was he convicted of a passport violation?

Mr. INNES. The dinner I attended was a welcome-home dinner to him after he got out of jail. He just got out of jail. What the crime was I don't know. I believe it was a passport violation or something of that nature.

Mr. MATTHEWS. Do you know whether the prison where he was incarcerated was Lewisburg, Pa.?

Mr. INNES. That is something I could not tell you.

Mr. LYNCH. After you talked to the people on the west coast, what did you learn was their policy with regard to the impending strike?

Mr. INNES. As I stated before, I reported to King and then he took me to Harry Bridges' office at 112 Market Street, where I was, in turn, introduced to Bridges, Mervyn Rathborne, who was in the same office with him—that is in the same suite. There were three rooms to the suite.   Bridges on one side and him on the other and a stenographer in the room between.   Roy Pyle, who at that time was secretary of the local of Radio Operators' Union in San Francisco.   Rathborne was secretary of the Maritime Federation of the Pacific coast, and then I went to the district council No. 2 meeting of the Maritime Federation of the Pacific in San Francisco, where I presented my credentials officially and was officially seated as a fraternal delegate on the council, and I actively participated in meetings of their negotiations committee and was therefore in position to know their policies as they took place from day to day.

Mr. LYNCH. Now, you went to Bridges, Rathborne, and Pyle first and had a conversation with them?

Mr. INNES. That is correct.

Mr. LYNCH. Do you know whether or not they had contacted the persons who would be in charge of the union to tell them what to do when you presented your credentials?

Mr. INNES. They were the persons who were designated for me to contact.   I believe some place in them files you will find a letter stating to that effect.   I was supplied with a list of names from Curran upon my arrival in San Francisco and heading the list was Pyle, then Bridges, Rathborne, Walter Stack, and Jim O'Neil, Henry Schmidt, and several others.

Mr. MATTHEWS. Chester Jordan?

Mr. INNES. Jordan was mentioned later.

Mr. LYNCH. Is Mervyn Rathborne a Communist?

Mr. INNES. Is he a Communist?

Mr. LYNCH. Yes, sir.

Mr. INNES. Yes, sir.

Mr. LYNCH. What about Harry Bridges?

Mr. INNES. He is a Communist.

Mr. VOORHIS. I would like to ask the witness how he knows those two are Communists?

Mr. INNES. Because I attended fraction meetings with them.

Mr. VOORHIS. Both of them?

Mr. INNES. Yes; both of them.

Mr. VOORHIS. Can you give the committee the dates and other people who were there and things of that sort?

Mr. INNES. Well, I attended many of them, Mr. Congressman, where we discussed policies that were to be presented at various committee meetings—where I received instructions to transmit to New York.   I attended fraction meetings with Harry Bridges, Mervyn Rathborne, Joe Curran, Roy Pyle, Roy Hudson, and——

Mr. VOORHIS. All of them together?

Mr. INNES. All together; yes, sir; prior——

Mr. VOORHIS. You mean at one meeting?

Mr. INNES. At one meeting; yes, sir.

Mr. VOORHIS. Can you tell us or do you know where that meeting took place, the date, and everything like that?

Mr. INNES. The meeting took place in San Francisco prior to the strike.   It was in the latter part of October 1936 when Joe Curran had come to the coast upon my instructions for him to come there.

Mr. THOMAS. Was there only one meeting or more than one meeting?

Mr. INNES. One that I attended.   That was when Curran and Hudson were present.   There were various other meetings when I attended with Bridges, Rathborne, Stack, and Piye and others, later on during the strike.

Mr. THOMAS. About how many meetings—Communist fraction meetings—did you attend at which Harry Bridges was present?

Mr. INNES. Well, roughly stating, I should judge 10 or 12 or possibly 15. I wouldn't be accurate on that unless I gave it deep thought.

Mr. LYNCH. But in the conversations, irrespective of the meetings that you attended at which they were, but the conversations which you had with them and the instructions that they gave you, was it clearly evident to you that they were Communists?

Mr. INNES. Well, it was evident from the line the party was following at the time.

Mr. LYNCH. And what line was the party following at the time?

Mr. INNES. The line varied from day to day according to the situation on the Atlantic coast and it was also evident when Tommy Ray can give orders to Harry Bridges and Ray is a known and admitted member. Bridges is also a Communist.

Mr. LYNCH. And did Ray give orders to Bridges?

Mr. INNES. He absolutely did.

Mr. LYNCH. And Bridges would relay the orders to somebody else?

Mr. INNES. The particular order that I am thinking of was the order to Bridges that he had to come to New York to attend the Madison Square Garden meeting and those orders were transmitted to him through me, as the record will prove.

Mr. LYNCH. What date was that?

Mr. INNES. That was in December 1936. I think it was around the 5th or 6th. I think the conversations started in the latter part of November. I may be wrong but I have teletype messages in the file here.

Mr. THOMAS. Now, will you develop those orders? I mean by that, tell the committee exactly what those orders consisted of and who you received them from and who you gave them to?

Mr. INNES. The program on communications, as it had been worked out, were that any official messages from the Pacific coast to the Atlantic coast were to go through me.

We had several small code words worked out where we would know a message was authentic and any message from the Atlantic coast for the Pacific coast was transmitted through me also.

Mr. MATTHEWS. Did you transmit them by teletype?

Mr. INNES. Both teletype, telephone, and telegraph. I have the complete files.

Mr. THOMAS. I am interested in this particular order.

Mr. MATTHEWS. The witness has the actual messages here.

Mr. LYNCH. Showing the code also that was existing between Curran and this witness.

Let me ask you one question while you are looking for that, Mr. Innes. Did you have a conversation or are there letters here which will prove the fact that Curran stated to you and you confirmed it, that unless these letters or code letters were given you were to disregard a communication?

Mr. INNES. That is correct. That was the first part of the time I was out there.

Mr. MATTHEWS. Did you attend fraction meetings at any other \ce besides San Francisco?

Mr. INNES. Well, I attended the one I spoke of here in New York. I attended minor fraction meetings in Portland, Oreg., and also in San Pedro prior to our trip into Mexico. We had a fraction meeting over that. The arrangements were made for the Garden meeting. I transmitted——

Mr. THOMAS. Have you got the date of the Garden meeting?

Mr. INNES. The Garden meeting was held on December—I have a flyer on it here somewhere; I have it right here.

Mr. VOORHIS. You mean the Madison Square Garden?

Mr. INNES. Yes. December 16, 1936. It has Bridges' picture on it.

Mr. THOMAS. Harry Bridges was the chief speaker there?

Mr. INNES. Him and Vito Marcantonio.

Mr. LYNCH. What was the other fellow?

Mr. INNES. That was Curran.

Mr. LYNCH. Now, may I ask you a question before you go into this? Was a teletype system installed between the Pacific coast and New York?

Mr. INNES. The teletype arrangement. There was a teletype in Bridges' office in San Francisco, there was one in Seattle, there was one in Portland, one in San Pedro, and then I paid to have one put in the office in New York so we could have conference calls on it and all get on the wire together.

Mr. LYNCH. In other words, this is one of the teletypes which was used?

Mr. INNES. That is correct.

Mr. LYNCH. By you from the Pacific coast to New York?

Mr. INNES. That is correct.

Mr. LYNCH. And from New York to the Pacific coast?

Mr. INNES. Yes, sir.

Mr. LYNCH. Now, is this the one that has to do with the instructions with regard to Bridges coming east?

Mr. INNES. When this message was sent it was sent to Bridges, but as it states later on he wasn't there and it was given to him. And then I have others where he confirmed the date of arrival in New York. This one is dated—there is no date on it, but it is from San Pedro, Calif., to the District Council No. 2, San Francisco, 104, on the teletype, attention Rathborne, and it states:

Due to phone call from here I had to leave without seeing you again. Talked to New York on phone this a. m. They desire to know whether Bridges will come to New York, expenses paid, to be on the platform, Madison Square Garden, December 14th. They desire he notify them yes or no immediately as John L. Lewis is to be there. The above is strictly confidential. Ask him to notify Joe in New York in writing as they also have made arrangements for Francis J. Gorman to be there also.

And it is signed by me. Rathborne's answer:

Okay. Have already discussed question with H. B. re going back to New York. Think perhaps he can go. Confirm date December 14.

And that is signed by Rathborne.

Mr. MATTHEWS. Mr. Innes, do you know whether or not the Communist Party paid for the Madison Square Garden for that meeting?

Mr. INNES. They did pay for it.

Mr. MATTHEWS. At this point, Mr. Chairman, there has been introduced in the record here a letter from the Madison Square Garden

Corporation stating that the rental of $3,500 for Madison Square Garden on this occasion was paid by certified check drawn by D. Leeds, and Mr. Leeds has been identified already as the treasurer of the Communist Party of the State of New York up until last May, when William Browder was the treasurer.

The CHAIRMAN. So they paid the $3,500 for rental of the hall at which Harry Bridges and these other people spoke?

Mr. VOORHIS. Was the meeting held under the auspices of the Communist Party or under whose auspices?

Mr. INNES. Why, absolutely it wasn't held under the auspices of the Communist Party because the seamen as soon as they found out actively to their own knowledge the Communists were involved they had nothing to do with it. It was held under the auspices of the strike committee which a that time was practically controlled by the Communist Party.

Mr. LYNCH. Mr. Voorhis, we have a great deal more testimony with regard to this Madison Square Garden incident which I thought we would come to a little later, if that is agreeable to the committee.

The CHAIRMAN. The Chair wants to note that a quorum is present, consisting of Mr. Voorhis, Mr. Casey, Mr. Thomas, and the chairman. The committee is now acting as a full committee. Proceed.

Mr. LYNCH. Mr. Innes, going back to the Pacific coast. After you arrived there and had the conferences you have indicated, were there any instructions given you or any decisions come to with regard to your going to Mexico in relation to a Grace Line ship, *Santa Elena?*

Mr. INNES. That was in the first month of the strike in November of 1936 when the matter of an expedition into Mexico was discussed.

Mr. LYNCH. And what date or what month was that?

Mr. INNES. In November 1936.

Mr. LYNCH. And did you go to Mexico?

Mr. INNES. I did.

Mr. LYNCH. And who did you go with?

Mr. INNES. I went with Chester Jordan, the secretary of the Radio Operators' Union in San Pedro and was also secretary of the strike committee in San Pedro. Donnelley, who was president of the International Longshoremen's Association local in San Pedro; Farrell, who represented the Marine Firemen's Union in San Pedro, and myself as the representative of the east coast striking seamen because it was really one of our ships that we went down there about.

Mr. LYNCH. Now, this Jordan has previously been identified as a known Communist in the record. Now, where did you go in Mexico—what place?

Mr. Innes. Went to Ensenada in Mexico in Baja—lower California.

Mr. LYNCH. And you had received word that one of the Grace Line ships, the *Santa Elena*, was going to attempt to dock there?

Mr. INNES. Yes.

Mr. MATTHEWS. And do you know how that information was received?

Mr. INNES. Was received—information was received by me by telephone from New York.

Mr. LYNCH. And do you know how New York received that information? Whether legally or illegally?

Mr. INNES. Well, no doubt they received it legally as the Grace Line docks were right across the street from strike headquarters.

Mr. LYNCH. And when you arrived at this point in Mexico had the ship arrived there?

Mr. INNES. The ship had not arrived; no, sir.

Mr. LYNCH. Tell what you did and what the others did before the arrival of the ship and after the arrival of the ship.

Mr. INNES. Well, I received the—if I may be given the privilege of going back a little bit. When I received the information about the ship leaving, we had heard, or at least I had heard, a lot about this international solidarity, as they call it, so I thought it would be a good idea to try some of it out. So I contacted Bridges in San Francisco and he says: "I have already beat you to it," he said, "I have made arrangements for us to go to Mexico," and he says, "We will leave Sunday." So while the matter was being discussed it appears that Bridges changed his mind because his attorney had advised him that him being an alien he could not cross the border and get back again unless he got over there without somebody finding out about it. So that was all out so far as his going over was concerned. Then it was decided on the committee that I have just spoken about.

Mr. THOMAS. Did he tell you that?

Mr. INNES. Yes, sir. That he was an alien and he could not get a permit to cross the border and come back again. So we left for Ensenada, and if I might be allowed I have a report here that I made at the time—if I can just read a paragraph from it it will bring it back to my mind exactly the way we went.

Mr. CASEY. Who did you make the report to?

Mr. INNES. To the strike committee in New York on November 24:

We left for Ensenada, Mexico, on Sunday, November 21st, at 9 a. m. We stopped at Bay Harbor, California, and picked up the secretary of the Los Angeles Local of the Confederation of Mexican Workers.

We arrived in Tia Juana at 1:20 p. m., where we immediately met the Secretary-General of the Confederation of Mexican Workers of lower California, who immediately called a special meeting of the C. R. O. M., which is the equivalent of our Central Labor Council. We presented our case to them and they, after discussion on the matter from every angle, elected a committee of five, including the secretary to accompany us to Ensenada. We arrived at Ensenada at 6:30 p. m., where we immediately went into session with the heads of the various unions.

As I say, we arrived in Ensenada around half past six at night, and the police met us there and accompanied us to headquarters of the C. R. O. M., which was one labor section, and the C. T. M., which was another labor faction.

Mr. LYNCH. Had the fellows in Tia Juana arranged for the police to meet you and escort you to the various places?

Mr. INNES. I would assume that had been arranged in Tia Juana, because the policy as you enter those Mexican towns, there seems to be one of these immigration places where you would have to stop and identify yourself to the police to get in there. This was during some of the unrest they had down there. But when we stopped there the police were waiting for us, and they took us right to the heads of these labor unions and we talked well into the night with them—

talked the situation over, and they called a meeting of the long-shoremen of the harbor the next morning for around 5 o'clock.

While the meeting was going on the ship arrived and the long-shoremen voted that they would not handle the ship in any way, shape, or form, so there was one outfit, one fellow down there who had two or three motorboats who used to go out to the Japanese ships that put in there and bring people ashore. You could not dock in the town on account of the shore line. You had to anchor out and they went to him and told him not to go out and bring anybody off of the ship. So he went into a long harrangue with them and he finally decided he was going anyway, and they sunk his motorboats where they were at. He didn't get away from the docks.

Mr. LYNCH. How many did they sink?

Mr. INNES. Two to my knowledge. I don't know how many more they got outside of that, but I know two of them were sunk and all we could see then was the one government launch. It was a minia-ture tugboat. So with that happening Mr. Ford, the vice president of the Grace Line on the Pacific coast arrived in town and up until his arrival we got along fine with everybody, but when he arrived things took another change.

They turned the garrison out—I should judge about four squads of soldiers, and they lined up in front of this dock where this tugboat was. It seemed funny after it was over, but it was no laughing matter when it was going on.

So we had the Mexican longshoremen on one side of us and the troops in front of us and we were in the big Packard in between them.

Mr. LYNCH. Did you have the police on your side?

Mr. INNES. We had them up until the soldiers turned out, and the police called it quits and went back to the police station.

Mr. LYNCH. So Mr. Ford, the president of the Grace Lines, by some means arranged that the garrison of soldiers go there and protect the docks?

Mr. INNES. That was the way it was. There was only one dock—a little jetty. The ship was anchored in the harbor.

Mr. CASEY. Did you ever learn how you accomplished what you did there?

Mr. INNES. I can give my opinion. Of course opinions don't count. I know we passed out around $300 in gold. I don't know how much he passed out, but I assume he passed it out. We prob-ably got to the wrong people.

Mr. LYNCH. Or maybe he had more.

Mr. INNES. Of course that is just my opinion.

Mr. LYNCH. In any event the soldiers were the stronger of the two powers and they took charge from then on?

Mr. INNES. They did. And that is what made me decide I wanted to get out of there. We were sitting in our car—that is the car that I had, and this fellow in civilian clothes came over and spoke good English and identified himself as the immigration officer and stated he wanted our visitor's permits. So we told him we didn't have any permits. He said: "Well, then, I am very sorry, I will have to ask you to leave immediately for the border."

So with that these secretaries of these different labor unions told him "nothing doing," they said we had not finished what we were down there for. We didn't enter that argument at all. As far as I was concerned I was ready to leave right then.

So he took us over to the immigration office, and I then demanded to see the American Consul. I didn't like the looks of things, and I was ready to holler for help. We sent to the consul's office where I protested at the attempted landing of the United States mails from this boat. When we left there in front of the consulate, the Mexican longshoremen had lined up, and it seemed they had sent out via the grapevine route. I imagine, a call and the peasants from the surrounding country had started to arrive in town and they naturally took the part of the longshoremen. The longshoremen told us we were not to leave town at all; they would take care of us. So we went with them to the telegraph office where we dispatched wires to President Cardenas, Vincente Toledano, and another one—Treviano I believe was another one. He was the secretary of the Regional Mexican Confederation. Sent another one to the secretary of labor's outfit in Tia Juana. That was the Governor General or whatever you call it of the State we were in, and I dispatched a wire to New York to Curran. stating we had arrived there and so far we had the ship stopped.

So when the wires were sent I wanted to get out. We didn't have any choice in the matter. They brought a truckload of soldiers up and told us to leave town; they were going to escort us to the border. We had 100 or more miles of mountain territory to go through. The Mexican longshoremen designated a carload of Mexicans to go with us—that is, the peons—so they got off their donkeys that they were on and put their rifles in the back with them, and we were in between the two of them.

As soon as we got by the outlying police station I pulled the Packard to one side and left them both in the dust. I didn't wait for them. So Felix, the secretary of the Tia Juana Labor Council that accompanied us in our car, when we got to Tia Juana, told us we could stop there and have another meeting. No; I was ready to go for the border. It was only a couple of minutes away. So he turned out an escort in Tia Juana to take care of us while we were there.

Jordan got on the telephone, and he called—I don't know where he called, but he came back and he said it would be a good idea to get out an edition of the local paper there.

Mr. LYNCH. That was in Tia Juana?

Mr. VOORHIS. Who is Jordan?

Mr. INNES. Jordan is now a vice president of the American Communications Association and at that time secretary of the strike committee in San Pedro.

Mr. VOORHIS. He was with you all this time?

Mr. INNES. That is correct. He was part of the committee.

Mr. MATTHEWS. His first name is Chester?

Mr. INNES. Yes, sir.

Mr. LYNCH. Do you know whether he is a Communist or not?

Mr. INNES. If he wasn't he joined the party when Pyle laid the law down to him in Pedro; I know that.

Mr. LYNCH. What is his present position?

Mr. INNES. Vice president of the American Communications Association. At this time I believe he is in New York.

Mr. LYNCH. What was done after Jordan telephoned?

Mr. INNES. So Jordan and I went with Felix to the local print shop, and they had a little newspaper that they put out—four pages, about the size of the Congressional Record, or I mean in dimension—and for $18 bought up the whole edition—that was the three papers. We wrote our own story through our interpreter and we told the workers in Ensenada what the story was, and the papers were delivered down there to them.

So we left then for San Pedro, and we got to the border, and the immigration officers informed us that President Cardenas had wired we were to stay in Mexico.

Donnelley was all for turning around and going back, and Jordan and I said, "No." I said: "One look of the soldiers is enough, and we might go to jail for starting a revolution."

Mr. VOORHIS. What was Jordan's position at that time?

Mr. INNES. His official position in the union—he was the secretary of the local of A. R. T. A., the American Radio and Telegraphists' Association in San Pedro, and his position in the strike was that as secretary of the strike committee—the joint strike committee in San Pedro, of which I was a member.

Mr. VOORHIS. You said you knew he joined the Communist Party?

Mr. INNES. I said if he wasn't then a member of the party I know that he joined the party when Pyle came down.

Mr. VOORHIS. How did you know that?

Mr. INNES. It was on a Sunday morning, and Pyle came down and Jordan was not following his instructions out, and he told Jordan to obey the orders from the higher-ups or get out.

Mr. VOORHIS. You heard him say that?

Mr. INNES. I was there present when it happened.

Mr. LYNCH. When you returned to San Francisco——

Mr. INNES. San Pedro——

Mr. LYNCH. Who did you confer with there as to what happened in Mexico?

Mr. INNES. I don't quite understand you.

Mr. LYNCH. Did you talk to Bridges?

Mr. INNES. We got on the telephone and told him what happened there. so the next day Jordan received a wire from Toledano—Toledano was the secretary general of the C. T. M.—just a moment, I will give it to you—Confederation of Mexican Workers. I have the whole list of them.

Mr. MATTHEWS. His first name is Lombardo, is it?

Mr. INNES. Vincente Lombardo Toledano.

The wire that Jordan received was from Toledano. It states:

Telegrams Carillo and myself received. Have wired instructions that American ships bound your ports be prevented to discharge passengers, cargo, Mexican west coast. Confederation Mexican Workers has declared boycott against such boats. Please inform us of specific instances of unfair American ships so our cooperation can be more effective.

Fraternally,

VINCENTE LOMBARDO TOLEDANO.

Mr. LYNCH. Mr. Innes, the various meetings that you had with these committees and the seamen out on the West coast, would you get instructions or would instructions or policy be informed prior to the actual meeting of the men?

Mr. INNES. We would—that is the general policy, anyway.

Mr. LYNCH. And was that followed out there on the West coast?

Mr. INNES. It was followed to a great extent. It was followed in every instance as far as the strike committee or policy making was concerned.

Mr. VOORHIS. Could I ask a couple of questions just to help me follow this?

Mr. Innes, at this time and during the period that you are testifying about, what was your own position—what were you at that time?

Mr. INNES. Well, I had many titles, as far as that went. I was the representative of the Joint Marine Strike Council of the Atlantic and Gulf for the past——

Mr. VOORHIS. You were a representative of what?

Mr. INNES. I was representative of the Joint Marine Strike Council of the Atlantic and Gulf for the Pacific coast.

Mr. VOORHIS. In other words, you were the ambassador at large?

Mr. INNES. I was the ambassador at large on the Pacific coast; that is correct.

I was also a member of the—I was chairman of the East Coast Seamen on the Pacific coast—that is, chairman of their own strike committee. I was a member of the joint port strike committee in San Pedro. I was delegate on the joint coast policy committee of the Pacific coast, where the policy for the strike was formulated.

Mr. VOORHIS. Just a moment. What were your relations with Harry Lundeberg?

Mr. INNES. Lundeberg, as far as I was concerned, was just another delegate on a committee.

Mr. VOORHIS. On the same committee that you were on?

Mr. INNES. That is correct; on the policy committee. I represented his outfit, and I represented mine on the policy committee.

Mr. VOORHIS. But you were representing a different organization?

Mr. INNES. My credentials, of course, were also addressed to his organization. If there was a dispute of any sort between the organization I represented and his, why, I would naturally go to him with it, the same as I would to Bridges or to Pyle or to anyone else, if a particular argument arose between our organizations.

Mr. VOORHIS. Was Lundeberg cooperating with Bridges at that time?

Mr. INNES. Abosolutely not.

Mr. VOORHIS. That is what I am trying to get at. You were representing the Seamen's Union, is that right? Of the Atlantic coast?

Mr. INNES. That is right.

Mr. VOORHIS. What was the relation between the Seamen's Union and the Atlantic Coast Seamen's Union?

Mr. INNES. And myself?

Mr. VOORHIS. Yes.

Mr. INNES. Well, relations were quite strained, but at the same time we didn't break into open warfare, if that is what you are trying to arrive at.

Mr. VOORHIS. What was your political affiliation at that time?

Mr. INNES. I was a registered Democrat and still am.

Mr. Voorhis. Never were anything else?

Mr. Innes. No, sir.

Mr. Voorhis. Then how did they let you into all these meetings?

Mr. Innes. I have been expecting that question. I often wondered myself just how this came about, but as I smartened up—of course, when I first got into the labor movement I was just like a fish out of water; I didn't know what it was all about and entered into it with both feet—but as time went along and I attended these various meetings and watched the fighting on both sides between the different factions, I learned quickly, and I came to the conclusion, as facts later bore out, that I would possibly make good party material in the eyes of some of them, and I was a very good friend of Curran.

Mr. Casey. You came to that conclusion yourself?

Mr. Innes. No. I came to the conclusion that that was their viewpoint, that I possibly would make good party material, and of course all the party figures on the Atlantic coast were well known on the Pacific coast and there were factional fights in all the unions out there at the time, although the party had dominant control in the radio operators and the longshoremen, the Masters, Mates, and Pilots Association, the Marine Engineers' Beneficial Association, the Cooks and Stewards, the Marine Firemen, Oilers, and Watertenders' Union, and a very strong minority in the Sailors' Union, and they couldn't send any well-known party figures out there.

At the same time, if they did not send somebody out that didn't know what it was all about he probably would not learn too much, and if he did he would forget about it, but it so happened after a couple of weeks with Curran I began to get suspicious of his attitude and everybody else around me, so instead of following his instructions of destroying things, I kept them, and this is the result. [Indicating several files of documents.]

Mr. Voorhis. Destroy things? What do you mean?

Mr. Innes. I was told to destroy our communications between us, but I didn't do that. I kept them, and I have a complete record of the period out there.

Mr. Voorhis. You said you knew Curran very well at that time. Was Curran a Communist, in your opinion?

Mr. Innes. At that time?

Mr. Voorhis. Yes.

Mr. Innes. No. At that time Curran was looking for a "pie card," as we would call it. He didn't belong to anything. He belonged to whoever could supply him with the wherewithal to live.

Mr. Voorhis. He wasn't a Communist?

Mr. Innes. At that particular time he wasn't; no, sir; at the date we are talking about here in August——

Mr. Voorhis. August of 1936?

Mr. Innes. August of 1936; yes.

Mr. Lynch. I have a letter on that point. I just wanted to get how he entered——

Mr. Innes. When I say he wasn't—I mean at this particular time Mr. Lynch was alluding to.

Mr. Lynch. Will you refer to the letter of August 23, 1936, written in pen and ink to you from Joseph Curran, and read it into the record, please. Read it slowly so we can get it.

Mr. INNES. It is from the Seamen's Defense Committee, 164 Eleventh Avenue, New York City. [Reading:]

NEW YORK CITY, *August 23, 1936.*

DEAR PETE: I have written you one letter today and I forgot a few things, so I am writing them now.

After carefully studying the situation here today I find that we have nothing but a lot of factional fights. Everybody is fighting for leadership and no one is helping the real fight, the M. F. O. W. Fight is terrible. The elected officials, Byne and Phillips have not guts and are being lead along by the Parties out for their own ends. Whalen is a sort of chief and does a lot of talking. Mulderig also does a lot of talking and no one does any constructive work. They had a meeting tonight at the M. F. O. W. hall on Tenth Avenue and I had to tell them about the size of the job they had undertaken and how the entire marine industry's eyes were on them and that they better get to work.

Today they couldn't get enough firemen together to keep Carlson from getting all the records out of the office on West Street, so you see there is too much talk and no action. If we lose this fight we might as well fold up.

I intend to take up the question of disbanding the Defense Committee altogether as they are getting further and further away from the Union.

The trip I made to the Gulf was great. They down there are really fighting and then I have to come home to a faction fight here all the time. It is disgusting. I want you to take up the question of me coming out to the coast and staying there as I frankly do not believe there is anything here, as I believe the Communist Party have broken all our chances up. See if you can get the Federation and the S. U. P. to bring me out on the basis of the Fink Book Campaign and write all your letters and wires to 460 West 23rd Street, New York. And treat this letter as confidential.

Fraternally yours,

JOE CURRAN.

Mr. LYNCH. Mr. Innes, while you were on the west coast did Mr. Rathborne arrange a speaking engagement for you at the University of California?

Mr. INNES. That is correct.

Mr. LYNCH. When was that and what was it?

Mr. INNES. That was in September, I believe, of 1936. It was relative to what we then called the fink-book campaign. It was at that time that Senator Copeland had the continuous discharge book bill in Congress, and I was to go to the University of California in Oakland to address a meeting of the student body on this particular question. And also, as we were having a strike coming up, I was to speak to them regarding the prevalence of students that went out and scabbed in order to see the world when a strike was on.

So I attended that meeting, and I addressed around 250 or possibly 300 students at the university.

Mr. LYNCH. Did Rathborne ever tell you how he was able to arrange that speaking engagement for you?

Mr. INNES. I don't know how he arranged it, but I know the engagement was held—or the rally, or whatever you would want to call it—the meeting was held under the auspices of the American Student Union.

Mr. LYNCH. And Rathborne, the man that you have identified a few moments ago, is the one who made all the arrangements for that?

Mr. INNES. That is correct.

Mr. VOORHIS. What did the university have to do with it?

Mr. INNES. It was the student body of the university, and the meeting was held on the university grounds.

Mr. Voorhis. Was it the student body or the American Students' Union?

Mr. Innes. I was held under—well, now, maybe I did not make myself clear, but the persons I addressed were members of the student body. The meeting was held under the auspices of the American Student Union—not under the auspices of the university.

Mr. Voorhis. Nor under the auspices of the student body?

Mr. Innes. I don't know the difference.

Mr. Vcorhis. Of course, they would be students; but what I mean is, did the official organization of the student body of the university have you speak or did the——

Mr. Innes. Mervyn Rathborne had me speak. I know the flyers were put out by the American Student Union.

The Chairman. The American Student Union did not represent the whole student body? They represented the members of that particular organization?

Mr. Innes. I would assume that.

Mr. Voorhis. You say there were about 250 students present?

Mr. Innes. Two hundred and fifty to three hundred.

The Chairman. The university has considerably more than that?

Mr. Innes. I don't know what the number.

Mr. Lynch. Mr. Innes, do you know of any activities of the Communist Party in September 1936 to get control of the firemen's newspaper? That is, a newspaper published by the firemen's organization?

Mr. Innes. On the Atlantic coast?

Mr. Lynch. Atlantic or Pacific.

Mr. Innes. Well, the firemen on the Pacific had a newspaper. They called it the Black Gang News. That was put out by—that is, the editor wrote it, and it was run off on what we used to call the Moscow Mill—mimeograph machine—press the button and they roll out by the hundreds. That was put out by Thomas Selly, who is a member of the Communist Party.

The east coast firemen having gained control of their union—that is, through the elections—decided to publish a journal of their own, and it was called the M. F. O. W. Journal, I believe. And at a meeting—the first meeting, first official meeting, of the membership at headquarters in New York of the Firemen's Union—two members of the Communist Party introduced a motion to elect an editorial board to run the newspaper, and I believe somewhere here I have the minutes of that particular meeting.

Mr. Lynch. Irrespective of the minutes, do you know who they attempted to get on the board?

Mr. Innes. Well, the motion was introduced and seconded by members of the Communist Party, and I would say, naturally, from that, the party's move was to put three members of the party on the editorial board to run the newspaper.

Mr. Lynch. Control its policies also?

Mr. Innes. That is correct.

Mr. Lynch. Do you recall the seamen's march on Washington at or about this time?

Mr. Innes. In September?

Mr. Lynch. September or October?

Mr. Innes. Well, the seamen's march on Washington, although it wasn't held then—it was held in January 1937. That was on the same continuous-discharge-book campaign. The march was held by east coast men and lead by Joe Curran, who got all the publicity for starting it, but the march never originated on the east coast.

Mr. LYNCH. Where did it originate?

Mr. INNES. Originated in Harry Bridges' office in San Francisco.

Mr. LYNCH. When?

Mr. INNES. September 1936.

Mr. LYNCH. The march actually took place in January 1937?

Mr. INNES. Yes, sir.

Mr. LYNCH. Who agreed to pay for the expenses of the men and the marchers, and so forth?

Mr. INNES. On this coast the busses were paid for by Tommy Ray and Al Lannon.

Mr. LYNCH. And were never paid for out of the union itself?

Mr. INNES. No, sir.

Mr. THOMAS. I would like to ask a question. How did you know the plans for this march on Washington originated in Harry Bridges' office?

Mr. INNES. Because I was there and transmitted the orders to New York from San Francisco, and I believe I have wires or letters here where I gave the orders to Curran to start formulating the march.

Mr. THOMAS. Who else were present at that time?

Mr. INNES. Rathborne, Pyle, and Bridges.

Mr. LYNCH. I could probably find that, Mr. Thomas, and get the actual minutes on it.

Mr. THOMAS. Who paid for the busses?

Mr. INNES. Tommy Ray and Al Lannon.

Mr. THOMAS. How much was spent?

Mr. INNES. At the time I saw Lannon was when the march was really contemplated—in December of 1936, when I came back to the coast, and then I saw him again when I finally arrived back for good in February 1937. He told me then that it probably cost around $500, and that he was making arrangements then with the Daily Worker to get the money to put it across.

Mr. THOMAS. He got the money from the Daily Worker?

Mr. INNES. I would not say that, but he said he was making arrangements with the Daily Worker to get the money.

Mr. THOMAS. But you did get the $500?

Mr. INNES. Yes, sir; he did pay for it. He told me later he paid for it.

Mr. LYNCH. And Al Lannon is a known Communist?

Mr. INNES. An avowed Communist.

Mr. MATTHEWS. He is a member of the national committee of the national party of the United States, according to Mr. Browder's own statement.

Mr. CASEY. We have gotten a long way from the Mexico situation. I never did hear what happened to the cargo on board the Grace liner. Did they unload it?

Mr. INNES. No, sir; as I stated, we got back to San Pedro, and we got Felix on the wire. This Felix was secretary of the labor council in Tia Juana, and he stated that the ship was still tied up; that the passengers were coming ashore in the soldiers' launch under a soldier escort. They put up in a hotel there in town, and, as I recall now, they were there, I believe, the better part of a day as the Mexican Chauffeurs' Union would not chauffeur them to the border. They were trying to get these sightseeing busses from Los Angeles to go down across the border to get them, and they wouldn't go down there because of threats made by the C. T. M. and the C. R. O. M. in Tia Juana, and it was the truth.

They had about 100 miles of mountains to go down there, and I told them I didn't like the look of the soldiers behind us, and they said: "One stick of dynamite, no more soldiers," and the soldiers didn't go down. They went as far as the border at San Diego.

Mr. LYNCH. Did they threaten to run the busses off the road into the ravines?

Mr. INNES. It was along that general line.

Mr. MATTHEWS. What happened to the passengers?

Mr. INNES. They came up under soldier escort to the border and were taken on up the Pacific coast.

Mr. LYNCH. How long did you stay on the west coast altogether, the first trip?

Mr. INNES. From August 1936 to February 1937.

Mr. LYNCH. And then you came East in February?

Mr. INNES. You mean——

Mr. LYNCH. The first time?

Mr. INNES. I stayed there from August to December 10, I believe it is.

Mr. LYNCH. Nineteen hundred and thirty-six?

Mr. INNES. That is correct.

Mr. LYNCH. Then you came East?

Mr. INNES. That is correct.

Mr. LYNCH. To the Madison Square Garden?

Mr. INNES. That is correct.

Mr. LYNCH. From New York, where did you go next?

Mr. INNES. I went first to Boston.

Mr. LYNCH. Then where?

Mr. INNES. Then to Baltimore.

Mr. LYNCH. Then where?

Mr. INNES. Then to Washington Airport.

Mr. LYNCH. You were here in Washington how long?

Mr. INNES. I was here in Washington about an hour.

Mr. LYNCH. You came from Baltimore?

Mr. INNES. That is correct.

Mr. LYNCH. Then left Washington and went back to the coast?

Mr. INNES. That is right.

Mr. LYNCH. What were you doing in Baltimore?

Mr. INNES. I was attending the strike rally. I accompanied Bridges and Curran in Baltimore.

Mr. LYNCH. What date was that?

Mr. INNES. December 17, 1936.

Mr. LYNCH. And what strike rally was it?

Mr. INNES. That was the rally under the auspices of the strike committee in Baltimore held in the State Armory there.

Mr. LYNCH. And was Bridges with you?

Mr. INNES. Bridges accompanied me from New York.

Mr. LYNCH. He was with you in New York and also in Boston?

Mr. INNES. That is right.

Mr. LYNCH. And came down to Baltimore?

Mr. INNES. That is right.

Mr. LYNCH. How long were you in Baltimore?

Mr. INNES. We arrived in Baltimore in the afternoon and left Baltimore around 3 o'clock the following morning for Washington.

Mr. LYNCH. Who arranged the meeting in Baltimore?

Mr. INNES. Patrick Whalen.

Mr. LYNCH. And who is Patrick Whalen?

Mr. INNES. Patrick Whalen is a member of the firemen's division of the National Maritime Union. He is now an official and an admitted and avowed member of the Communist Party.

Mr. LYNCH. And do you know whether or not at the time the meeting in Baltimore occurred—the rally occurred there—whether or not that was paid for by the Communist Party or by some outstanding Communist, as it was in New York?

Mr. INNES. As I gathered, Whalen arranged for the armory, I believe rent free, with the exception of paying the cost of cleaning it up. I believe he arranged that through the Governor's secretary or something of that nature in the State of Maryland; at least that is the report he put out.

Mr. LYNCH. Now, who was with you in Baltimore—who composed your party? Bridges, yourself, and who else?

Mr. INNES. Curran. We arrived in Baltimore by train.

Mr. LYNCH. After arriving in Baltimore by train, what did you do?

Mr. INNES. Well, we arrived in Baltimore by train, and Bridges said he had to meet—had to make a telephone call.

Mr. LYNCH. Did he make a telephone call?

Mr. INNES. He did.

Mr. LYNCH. Did he tell you at that time to whom it was?

Mr. INNES. No, sir; except he said he was making arrangements—making arrangements for an appointment after the meeting.

Mr. LYNCH. Did they have a meeting that night?

Mr. INNES. Yes, sir; we had the rally and a parade that night.

Mr. LYNCH. After the meeting, did you have an appointment with anyone?

Mr. INNES. After the meeting he had an appointment with three gentlemen in the back of the armory—that is, in the back entrance of the armory. He met them on the street.

Mr. LYNCH. Who were they? Were you introduced to them?

Mr. INNES. I was. Bridges was talking to me when these three gentlemen came over, and Bridges stepped to one side, and he came over to me and he said, "I am leaving for Washington." And I said, "So am I, and my orders are to stay with you."

Mr. LYNCH. Had you planned to come to Washington before this time?

Mr. INNES. I had planned; yes, sir; because I called the airport to make reservations. He said, "Well, I have an appointment with these gentlemen." Incidentally, he said, "This is Mr. Edwin Smith, of the National Labor Relations Board, who made an appointment with me and two of his assistants."

Mr. LYNCH. Do you know the names of the assistants?

Mr. INNES. I don't know. I was only introduced to Mr. Smith.

Mr. LYNCH. Do you know whether it was Edwin Smith or not?

Mr. INNES. I know him, certainly. I have seen his pictures many times since.

Mr. LYNCH. And what happened then? Was there a conference there?

Mr. INNES. Yes, sir.

Mr. LYNCH. Did you confer with Mr. Smith or anybody else confer with him?

Mr. INNES. We left the armory. I had one car that Whalen had assigned to Bridges and myself with a bodyguard, so I got in the car with this bodyguard. His name as I recall it was "Broken-Nose" Burns. He is over in the penitentiary here in Maryland. Anyway Bridges got in the car with Mr. Smith and the other two gentlemen, and we followed them. That is, we went in line to an office building in Baltimore. What the name of the building was, I don't know.

Mr. LYNCH. Downtown Baltimore?

Mr. INNES. Yes, sir; downtown Baltimore.

Mr. LYNCH. What happened there?

Mr. INNES. When this Smith rapped at the door a watchman let us in the building, and we went up to one of the upper floors. I don't recall the number of it. And Bridges and Smith and the other two fellows that were with him went in the room. The room had no name on the door. And I stayed in the corridor. They were in there from a half to three quarters of an hour when Bridges came out with Smith and we stood talking in the lobby of the building and Bridges said: "I think we have arranged for the elections on the Atlantic coast for you."

Mr. LYNCH. What elections were going to take place then?

Mr. INNES. They were elections that we were trying to get under the Labor Relations Board. That is with their machinery elections within the framework of the American Federation of Labor constitution in the Sailors and Cooks and Stewards' Union, and it was also the problem of conducting Labor Board elections in some way among the men on strike, with the steamship companies. The steamship companies were hollering they didn't know who to negotiate with and that was what the discussion was at that time, about holding elections in the steamship companies and this one within the union itself to decide on a bargaining agent.

Mr. VOORHIS. Let me get this straight. After this meeting, did you go along with them after they had this meeting in the office building?

Mr. INNES. What was said—I went in the building with them; yes, sir. What was said inside this office, I don't know; I wasn't there. All I know is what was said to me when they came out.

Mr. VOORHIS. Who was in the office?

Mr. INNES. Bridges, this Edwin Smith, and two other men whom Smith said were his assistants.

Mr. VOORHIS. Do you remember the date on which this took place?

Mr. INNES. That took place, I believe, shortly after midnight on the 17th. It was around midnight when we got out of the armory, so it was the early morning of the 18th—probably 1 or 2 o'clock in the morning.

Mr. VOORHIS. Then what did Bridges tell you after he came out?

Mr. INNES. The statements that I made I mean were made in front of Smith. There was no denial. Bridges said: "I believe we have arranged for the elections on the Atlantic coast," and then Mr. Smith wanted to know what elections were pending, and I told him elections within the unions under the framework of the union constitution, but with the machinery of the Labor Board. And I believe I have here in my papers somewhere stuff relating to that—and elections between the men on strike in the steamship companies.

Mr. VOORHIS. What was this strike about, leaving other things aside for the moment? In your judgment was the strike justified?

Mr. INNES. On the Atlantic coast?

Mr. VOORHIS. Yes; and Pacific?

Mr. INNES. Very much so. The strike was justified.

Mr. VOORHIS. In other words there were real grievances?

Mr. INNES. Yes, sir.

Mr. VOORHIS. And conditions needed to be improved?

Mr. INNES. That is correct.

Mr. VOORHIS. Was the same thing true on the Pacific coast?

Mr. INNES. The Pacific coast strike was what we would call a Federation strike. The longshoremen had gotten everything that they wanted. That is the employers agreed to everything but the cooks and stewards and sailors and firemen and others had grievances and the longshoremen went on strike with them.

Mr. VOORHIS. You think the grievances were real grievances?

Mr. INNES. Oh, yes; absolutely. The one on the Atlantic coast was a grievance to the extent that the year previous, in January, when the contract that the operators wanted to give the union officials that we had at the time—that was given to them and they agreed to sign it—and the steamship officials demanded that an election or vote be taken on the contract and the contract was turned down eight to one, yet the officials signed it anyway and that was what we were striking for—more to clean house within the union than anything else.

Mr. VOORHIS. Do you believe there is any way to correct those problems that the seamen and other maritime workers have except by legitimate union organization?

Mr. INNES. No, sir; there isn't—that is legitimate unions.

Mr. VOORHIS. That is what I say.

Mr. LYNCH. How long did this meeting last in the lobby of this office building in Baltimore?

Mr. INNES. I should judge we probably stayed there talking for 10 or 15 minutes—that is when I was present.

Mr. LYNCH. And this election which you spoke about a moment ago, it was an election within the union—it was not to determine whether they would be affiliated——

Mr. INNES. That it wasn't affiliated—the firemen of course already held an election. There were three unions you might say within a union in the International Seamen's Union—the firemen and cooks and sailors. The firemen's union conducted their election and won it. The sailors and cooks and stewards were demanding elections within their union, so the Federation of Labor agreed to hold it.

Mr. LYNCH. You mean the American Federation of Labor?

Mr. INNES. The American Federation of Labor executive board. Their executive council had taken—you might say the executive council had taken control of the whole works, and they agreed to hold an election while the strike committee in New York would not agree to that unless the machinery for the election was impartially handled and that was what this particular subject was that Bridges referred to at that time, plus the one that we were trying to get with the steamship operators.

Mr. LYNCH. Any question of whether or not the unions were to be controlled or be affiliated with the C. I. O. or A. F. of L.?

Mr. INNES. Not at that time; no, sir.

Mr. THOMAS. I would like to ask a question. From what you saw that night did it appear to you that Mr. Smith and Harry Bridges were on intimate and friendly terms?

Mr. INNES. Very intimate because they walked up and shook hands with one another and went off in the car. Bridges tried to duck me, and I wouldn't be ducked.

Mr. VOORHIS. He tried to duck you?

Mr. INNES. Well, he told me: "I can get to Washington all right, I know these fellows," and introduced me to them then.

Mr. VOORHIS. But you went alone?

Mr. INNES. I said, "You are not going to Washington without me," and that was that and so he didn't raise any more uproar and then we followed his car down and went in the building with him.

Mr. THOMAS. Did they call each other by their first names, like "Harry" and "Ed"?

Mr. INNES. Well, that I can't tell you.

Mr. THOMAS. But they did seem to be on intimate terms?

Mr. INNES. Yes; they had met before I would assume from the way they met because there was no one there to introduce them to one another. Just walked up and shook hands and proceeded to talk.

Mr. VOORHIS. You don't have any idea who the other two men were that were there?

Mr. INNES. No, sir; I don't know. I know one of them was a little short fellow.

The CHAIRMAN. Well, the fact that Mr. Smith knew Mr. Bridges is not important. He would naturally know all the labor leaders, and Mr. Bridges was in charge of one of the largest unions in the country, so I would not think that particular fact would have anything to do with Mr. Smith in his capacity as a member of the National Labor Relations Board. He would naturally know all the labor leaders.

Mr. INNES. Not if Bridges had not been to the Atlantic coast since the Board was formed.

Mr. THOMAS. It is a little odd that the head of the National Labor Relations Board should go out and meet one of these labor leaders at 1 o'clock in the morning in the back of some hall out in Baltimore.

The CHAIRMAN. That is a different question.

Mr. CASEY. The meeting wasn't over until 1 o'clock in the morning.

Mr. INNES. The meeting ended around midnight and it was after midnight when we were in this office building because Bridges and I left immediately after the meeting and arrived in the airport here around 6 o'clock in the morning—in Washington.

Mr. LYNCH. Did you drive over to Washington?

Mr. INNES. Drove over from Baltimore, that is right.

Mr. LYNCH. After staying in Washington for a few hours you took a plane for California?

Mr. INNES. No, sir; I put Bridges on the plane, and I went back to New York for my final instructions and went from there to San Francisco. I did not go by plane because there was only one seat and I gave that to Bridges.

Mr. LYNCH. Now, have you knowledge or information as to the direction of the activities of both the east coast and west coast by Bridges from California?

Mr. INNES. I don't quite get what you mean.

Mr. LYNCH. In other words, whether or not Bridges would give directions to Curran as to what to do and what statements to make and then Curran would actually make those statements?

Mr. INNES. Yes, sir; for instance I know that during the strike I wired Curran that I wanted him to send certain wires to me and the wires would come right back.

This march on Washington was one of the instances where Bridges issued instructions and Curran followed them out. That was in September—September 25, 1936.

Mr. LYNCH. I will also ask you whether on September 23, 1936, Mr. Rathborne made a speech to the seamen in California.

Mr. INNES. Yes, sir; it was part of my job at that time to hold meetings of the crews of east-coast ships in San Francisco to disseminate information and other things to them, and the first one I held was on the date that you speak of and Mr. Rathborne addressed that meeting as the secretary of the Maritime Federation of the Pacific, I believe it was.

Mr. LYNCH. You have definite knowledge of that fact, Mr. Innes?

Mr. INNES. Yes, sir; because I called the meeting to order, and I have the minutes of the meeting. They show him present and making the speech.

Mr. LYNCH. Now, what about the Lawrence Simpson case? Lawrence Simpson was taken into custody in Germany, was he not?

Mr. INNES. I was shipmates with Lawrence Simpson on the *Manhattan* in 1935, I believe it was, and Simpson had a great habit of taking communistic stickers and Daily Workers ashore in Hamburg—smuggled them ashore in radio sets and in different articles of food. So while I was on the Pacific coast, I believe it was, or probably just prior to that, Simpson had been arrested for this same activity on board the *Manhattan*, and there was a great hullabaloo about it.

Mr. LYNCH. Do you know whether or not Simpson was a Communist?

Mr. INNES. He was a member of the Communist Party; yes, sir.

Mr. LYNCH. What occurred in regard to Curran and the union?

Mr. INNES. In an effort to get Simpson released over there in Germany, Curran through the defense committee called or attempted to call a 1-day strike in New York, but at the same time he stated that he had to be pretty cagey about it.

The CHAIRMAN. Are those all original copies of letters that you wrote and kept?

Mr. INNES. Original and copies. Well, Mr. Chairman, I have practically all of the originals of my own letters. It may seem funny to the committee how I happened to get them, but when I came back from the coast I got orders from Joe—he told Walter Coney and myself to go up to the apartment, up to where he was living and destroy the papers that were up there.

They were all personal correspondence and the spring strike records and a lot of the financial records from the fall strike, so I asked him, I said, "How did all this stuff get up there, Joe," and he said, "You know how it is whenever I want to get things out of here, why I just get a rumor that the F. B. I. is going to make a raid and I just purge the files and send them to my house."

So when I went up there and I went through it and found all my correspondence, so I purged the originals and put them with my carbon copies, and so I have them both.

Mr. LYNCH. Do you have the memorandum with regard to the Simpson case?

Mr. INNES. Here it is. September 28.

Mr. LYNCH. This is a letter from Joe Curran to you on the stationery of the Seamen's Defense Committee, September 28, 1936. Will you read that paragraph relating to the Simpson case?

Mr. INNES (reading):

New York City, September 28, 1936. Today, as you know, was the day that Lawrence Simpson was to be tried. We tried to get the ships to stage a sitdown and had a small degree of success.

A committee of two seamen, Joe Cain and Jimmie Gavin, along with some trade union delegates went to Washington and saw the Secretary of State while we had picket lines on the consulate of the German government, so all in all we did the best we could and I think we did pretty well and now we must be very careful how we are identified with the case from now on as we know it smells of communism and the only things we are interested in is that he was an American seaman.

and that is all. There is a last paragraph on the same matter.

Enclosed you will find a clipping on the Simpson case and you will notice why I say we must be careful how far we are involved in this mess.

Mr. LYNCH. That was a newspaper clipping?

Mr. INNES. Yes; newspaper clipping.

Mr. LYNCH. Did it play up his communistic activities?

Mr. INNES. It played up his communistic activities along the line that the seamen were getting into deep water by being involved in this thing, and it is signed by Joe Curran, and there is a postscript in his original handwriting.

Mr. LYNCH. Was that about the time, Mr. Innes, when you received word from Curran that letters would have a code mark on them?

Mr. INNES. No, sir; that arrangement was made after Curran went in—right after Curran came out to the coast.

Mr. LYNCH. Did you receive also on the same day another letter from Curran with regard to strike activities and so forth—what they would do with crews that were found——

Mr. INNES. At time there was a sit-down strike on the *President Roosevelt*, the steamship *American Trader* and the *Pennsylvania*, called by the defense committee for recognition of the rank and file officials of the Firemen's Union in an attempt to coerce Federal Judge Hulbert, of the New York bench, New York district, into rendering a decision in their favor, and when the strike came on the Judge went down to the water front to the defense committee office, and he said:

Well, now, it seems funny we don't know whether the American Federation of Labor officials, the ones they designate are the officials or you. Let us see who can move the ships.

So the defense committee released the *President Roosevelt*, and kept the *American Trader* and *Pennsylvania* tied up to the docks. So Curran wrote a letter that date, September 28, 1936. He states in part to me:

If the ships should get out with scab crews in the event the striking crews are forced off, we will let you know what happens immediately so you can see that the proper reception is prepared for the crews.

Mr. LYNCH. What does he mean, proper reception for the crews?

Mr. INNES. So the *Pennsylvania*, if she arrived on the Pacific coast with a scab crew aboard, I was to arrange to have a strong-arm squad there and take care of them and see they didn't get back when they came ashore.

Mr. LYNCH. Didn't get back to the ship?

Mr. INNES. That is right.

Mr. LYNCH. What would happen when they got ashore?

Mr. INNES. Break a few heads and send them to the hospital.

Mr. LYNCH. And physically prevent them from going on the ship?

Mr. INNES. That is correct.

Mr. LYNCH. Do you have a letter from Tommy Ray——

Mr. INNES. Here is the code you were asking about.

Mr. LYNCH. This is the code established between you and Curran on September 29, 1936; is that correct?

Mr. INNES. The strike was originally scheduled to be called September 30, so in order there would be no slip-up on the exact calling of the strike or no false word get out. In a conference with Bridges and Rathborne, and I state here:

In the event of trouble and if there is a strike or lock-out you will receive the following wire: "John is dead." If the continuance is granted: "John is better."

Bridges also suggests that we arrange a code word to use in all correspondence that takes place between us in the event of trouble. He wrote me:

I suggest that in the event of trouble you receive your mail at an altogether different address and even under a different name and that the following code word be used as part of the first sentence in each and every letter that takes place between us: "Unity." If you can think of something different let me know immediately.

Then he goes on to say—

Enclosed is report to Phillips and signed by myself.

Mr. LYNCH. Was that plan followed?

Mr. INNES. All letters from there use the word "unity" until Curran arrived on the coast when we arranged a new procedure.

Mr. LYNCH. Did you also have a code with regard to the date that——

Mr. INNES. That was arranged after Curran arrived on the coast.

Mr. LYNCH. Now, with regard to the letter from—Tommy Ray's letter of October 2, 1936. Whom was that addressed to?

Mr. INNES. The letter was addressed to me on the Pacific coast.

Mr. LYNCH. And what was the purport of that letter with regard to the control of candidates to be selected by Tommy Ray?

Mr. INNES. Well, to start with, the letter was not written in the union hall. Ray was not a member of the Firemen's Union, so he was not even a member of the defense committee. The letter was written in Attorney Standard's office. The letter arrived to me in an envelope from his office.

Mr. LYNCH. And on legal paper?

Mr. INNES. And on legal paper and addressed to "Dear Comrade Innes."

Mr. LYNCH. By the way who is that Standard?

Mr. INNES. William H. Standard, who is now counsel for the National Maritime Union and who at that time was counsel for the Firemen's Union, carrying on their court fight.

Mr. THOMAS. Where does he keep his offices?

Mr. INNES. It used to be, if I recall correctly, I think 328 Broadway. I know it is over the River Savings Bank.

Mr. LYNCH. Was he on the west coast at this time, however?

Mr. INNES. No, sir; he was in New York.

Mr. LYNCH. Tommy Ray was in New York and wrote this letter to you?

Mr. INNES. From Standard's office. Ray wasn't even a member of the Firemen's Union but he starts off anyway—it is dated October 2, 1936:

DEAR COMRADE INNES: Enclosed is a copy of the agreement entered into between the I. S. U., the Carlson group and Phillips and Byne. The agreement is self-explanatory.

We here feel that this agreement is a splendid victory for the rank and file. The details of the agreement will be worked out within the next few days, in regard to credentials for delegates who the officials are to be who will represent the Carlson group and all other matters pertaining to the carrying out of the agreement.

This agreement makes it possible for us to have an election and to make a clean sweep of all the old officials of the M. F. O. W., provided of course that a correct and energetic campaign is carried through. The first prerequisite is to see that we have sufficient candidates to nominate for every office at the time of the nominations meeting.

So far we haven't enough and we expect you in the ports to make a check-up among the membership aboard the ships as well as ashore in a search for qualified candidates. In the search for candidates we must make a double check-up to be sure that they qualify in every respect with regard to the constitutional provisions of three years membership in the Union and the last year in continuous good standing. It is not so important that they be active and well known rank and filers.

The CHAIRMAN. He is speaking now about the Communists within the union; is that right?

Mr. INNES: Well, "rank and filers" at that time were supposed to be the general run of the membership.

Mr. LYNCH. And the letter did not make any difference whether the man was well known or active in the union or whether he was a good man or not provided he was a "right man"?

Mr. INNES. That is right.

Mr. LYNCH. And you knew of course that Ray was a Communist at that time, didn't you?

Mr. INNES. Oh, yes; I knew it before I went out there.

Mr. LYNCH. And was the whole tone of the letter and the inference it was to carry, you were to get persons, members of the Communist Party, to become officers of the union?

Mr. INNES. The inference that I got out of it at that time was that if possible to pick members of the party, but if you couldn't get them—there were very few members of the party who were qualified to run for office or they would have been run in the first election. The thing was to get people, active rank and filers all right, or the general run of the membership, but people who didn't have any brains of their own. That was the general requirement for candidates for office at that time.

Mr. LYNCH. To be controlled by somebody?

Mr. INNES. That is correct.

Mr. LYNCH. Now, on October 2, 1936, did you receive another letter from Curran with regard to the manner in which you should operate— that is in regard to the code and the sending of the mail to a secret address?

Mr. INNES. Yes, sir.

Mr. LYNCH. Will you refer to that and that part of it and also those code words which were used?

Mr. INNES. The letter is dated October 2, 1936, and is addressed to me at room 145, 268 Market Street, where I had at that time established an office next door to the American Radio and Telegraphists' Association. He states:

DEAR BROTHER INNES: Received your letter dated September 30th at 11 a. m., in which you state that you have not received any letters since the 17th. I sent two letters since the 17th, one through the ARTA connection and one direct to you. Will suggest that if you haven't got letters that you see Pyle about it personally.

The matter of the sit-down strike settled satisfactorily so far. So much for that. In regards to the code word. The word that you suggest is a very good one and we will use it until I arrange for a box at the main post office. Suggest you send letters to same home address.

I have an important job for you to carry out. I understand that you received an official letter from Phillips a few days ago and immediately afterwards you received a telegram from either Mulderig or King, stating that you were to ignore the letter sent by Phillips. It is important that I have a copy of both the letter and the telegram. This, of course, is in strict confidence between you and I. Am unable to give explanation at present why I want these letters but will be able to explain later.

Mr. LYNCH. Now, who was Phillips?

Mr. INNES. Phillips at that time was the duly elected secretary of the Marine Firemen, Oilers, and Watertenders' Union of the Atlantic and Gulf.

Mr. LYNCH. Who was King?

Mr. INNES. Elected assistant secretary of the Marine Firemen, Oilers, and Watertenders Union. They were both officers duly elected by the membership.

The objective in obtaining these letters—the Communist Party, through Ray, had succeeded in putting a Communist stenographer by the name of Dorothy Snyder, who is now private secretary to Joe Curran, in Phillips' office, to do his paper work.

Phillips, at an odd moment when nobody was around, had written a letter and sent a telegram of which he kept no copy and all that they knew was that the letter had come out and the party was anxious to find what he was saying that they didn't know about. Well, there was nothing in the letter anyway——

Mr. LYNCH. This girl would apparently get all other information?

Mr. INNES. She would write the letters and have the information.

Mr. LYNCH. And give it to anybody who asked for it in the Communist Party?

Mr. INNES. That is right.

Mr. THOMAS. How do you know Dorothy Snyder was a Communist?

Mr. INNES. She was arrested in the Communist Party headquarters on Seventh Avenue. The seamen hang out up there and Dorothy Snyder also participates actively in the Communist fraction of the U. O. P. W. A.—the office workers' union—and I believe at one time she was also a member of the executive board of that union.

Dorothy Synder was accused at meetings in New York among the membership and, in fact, was the cause of several riots in union headquarters in New York, including the baseball-bat raid, and so forth, that took place during the elections, all because of Dorothy Snyder.

Mr. VOORHIS. What union headquarters?

Mr. INNES. National Maritime Union headquarters.

Mr. LYNCH. What name did Curran sign on that letter?

Mr. INNES. Signed it "Joseph Curran, yours for unity and harmony."

Mr. LYNCH. Did he later take up a different name to use in signing his letters?

Mr. INNES. Later the new address for the new name he used was "John Moran, 460 West Twenty-third Street, New York City."

Mr. LYNCH. Did you also have correspondence with Curran with regard to the right of the men to pass upon the question of the strike on the east coast?

Mr. INNES. While negotiations were going on in September of 1936, I had been introduced to Edward McGrady, who was one of the conciliators sent to San Francisco by the Secretary of Labor to see if they couldn't have the strike date extended, and it was through his activities that the strike was extended from September 30. to October 15.

At a conference attended by McGrady, Bridges, and myself, I was introduced to him as a representative of the east-coast men and he asked what we were going to do on the Atlantic coast, so I told him that if the west coast went on strike we are going on strike too.

So with that Rathborne came in and was present and they sent for Pyle—that is Bridges did, so Mr. McGrady offered several suggestions for me to transmit to the Atlantic coast and the suggestions were agreed to by Bridges, Pyle, and Rathborne, and that was that the east-coast Seamen's Defense Committee conduct a referendum vote along the Atlantic coast, a secret-ballot vote, to determine whether or not the membership along the Atlantic coast would go on strike and what they would go on strike for.

In other words, to practice the democracy they were preaching and still preach.

From his conversation I made several notes which I sent to Curran, and he stated that the referendum would be a way for them to act without having to be called outlaws like they were in the spring, and it would give them a chance to show that the membership themselves were behind the defense committee, if such a thing was true.

Bridges agreed to it. Rathborne agreed to it, and McGrady asked that Curran write him a letter to Washington—to his Washington office stating that he was going to do this. And Curran in his letter of October 2 states that he did that. But around the 12th of October the policy changed again, and the matter of referendum vote was thrown completely overboard by the same people who had agreed to it in the first place.

Mr. LYNCH. And who were those people?

Mr. INNES. Bridges, Pyle, and Rathborne.

Mr. LYNCH. Why did they throw it overboard?

Mr. INNES. Because they were leery as to whether or not the men would actually go for it—would go on strike. After all there was no union to speak of at the time. Out of 40-odd thousand men sailing the ocean there was probably at the very most eight or ten thousand members of the union. Even at the peak of the strike with 25,000 men out there were less than 10,000 union members out.

Mr. LYNCH. So it was questionable whether or not they would go for the strike?

Mr. INNES. That is the thing of it, and the party didn't want to take any chance of losing out on the control that they had.

Mr. LYNCH. I will show you a letter dated October 8, 1936, addressed to you and signed by Joseph Curran and ask you whether or not there is any statement in that letter regarding the control by the Communist Party of the union?

Mr. INNES. The letter is on the letterhead of the defense committee and dated October 8 and addressed to me.

Curran states:

I am going to see that you get a money order sent to you if it is at all possible. I know what you are up against there on the coast and the firemen here now with the exception of Jerry King are all pie-cards. They have credentials from Hunter and they think that they are big shots now the Communist Party has about got control of the outfit now with Tommy Ray director of operations here in New York.

Mr. LYNCH. When was the strike supposed to be called on the west coast?

Mr. INNES. The original date was September 30 and then advanced to the 15th at the request of the Labor Department.

Mr. LYNCH. Of October?

Mr. INNES. Yes, sir. And then later advanced to the 29th at midnight.

Mr. LYNCH. Do you know whether or not Bridges or Rathborne were communicating with Tommy Ray on the east coast?

Mr. INNES. Whether or not they were?

Mr. LYNCH. Yes.

Mr. INNES. As far as I know, at that time the only direct communication that Bridges had with the Atlantic coast was all carried on through me. As I later surmised when I got things together and started to work it out in my own mind, in the event the strike blew up the only people that would be actually involved or incriminated when the seamen would not be members of the Communist Party, it would be myself and Curran at the time if it blew up and the men didn't come out on strike—we would be the fall guys.

Mr. LYNCH. Now, the fact that there was a countermand of that agreement which was made with McGrady, would that indicate to you that there were private conversations had between Bridges and

Rathborne with the east coast directing them what to do?

Mr. INNES. I would assume that Mr. Ray overruled the matter of a referendum.

Mr. LYNCH. Somebody overruled it, didn't they?

Mr. INNES. That is correct.

Mr. LYNCH. And you did not know who overruled it?

Mr. INNES. No, sir.

Mr. LYNCH. Until you were advised of it later by Curran?

Mr. INNES. That is correct.

Mr. LYNCH. Did you also have a letter from Joseph Curran dated October 13, 1936, to you on the stationery of the Seamen's Defense Committee, with regard to his inability to get a ship and why?

Mr. INNES. Well, as Curran stated before, Ray was the big shot on the Atlantic coast. At the time he was being shoved in the background. He states on October 13:

If there is an extension of time on the coast I intend to come out there and get the real picture and possibly I may have to stay out there as there are not possibilities of my getting a ship here on this coast.

The pressure was being put on him. He was being made to take orders whether he liked it or not from the party on the Atlantic coast through Ray and that was when he didn't know whether to go overboard or what to do. That is signed by Joseph Curran "in unity." It has the code word on it.

Mr. LYNCH. Now, did you get instructions from Bridges to Curran through you—all those instructions?

Mr. INNES. Yes, sir. A letter from me, myself, to Curran on October 13. I state in part:

Had quite a lengthy conference with Harry Bridges yesterday and he asked whether or not you were on your way to the coast. I read to him that part of your letter covering that. He stated that he did not think it advisable for you to come out here after the 15th as it would be better for you to be on the scene of operations when things broke loose, if they did. That he thought it would have a great effect on every one concerned, if you had been able to have gotten here prior to that date as it would have definitely left the ship owners and the Maritime Commission know we were not kidding when we were saying the entire Atlantic and Pacific coast would be involved.

That is signed by myself and also uses the code word.

Mr. LYNCH. I will show you a letter addressed to you and dated October 14, 1936, signed by C. H. Jordan, Secretary, on the stationery of the Maritime Federation of the Pacific coast. What was that Maritime Federation?

Mr. INNES. The Maritime Federation was a sort of council with representatives from all the component marine organizations on the Pacific coast, from the cannery workers to the shipyard men, including longshoremen, seamen, firemen, and cooks and stewards, and what have you.

Mr. LYNCH. Had no definite connection with maritime unions?

Mr. INNES. It was composed of maritime unions?

Mr. LYNCH. But it represented other unions, too?

Mr. INNES. It was at that time.

Mr. LYNCH. What is that letter about?

Mr. INNES. It is dated October 14, 1936, and addressed to me as Pacific coast representative of the Marine Firemen, Oilers, and Watertenders of Atlantic and Gulf, and Seamen's Defense Committee.

Dear Sir and Brother.

In behalf of Southern California District Council No. 4 of the Maritime Federation of the Pacific, I wish to express our thanks for your telegram of support in case of a lock-out or a strike on the Pacific Coast.

Yours fraternally,

C. H. Jordan, *Secretary.*

That was in reply to telegrams that I had sent to Aberdeen, Seattle, Portland, and San Pedro, informing them that the strike committee on the Atlantic coast had voted unanimously to support them in the event of a strike or lock-out on the Pacific coast.

Mr. Lynch. And the reply to that—to those telegrams was written by Jordan?

Mr. Innes. The reply to the one from San Pedro was written by Jordan, that is correct.

Mr. Lynch. I will show you a letter dated October 15, 1936, and signed by Patrick Whalen. It is on the stationery of the Marine Firemen, Oilers, and Watertenders' Union and sent to you on the Pacific coast. I call your attention to that part near the bottom of the first page. Will you please state what that means?

Mr. Innes. At that time the Calmer Line had a ship by the name of *Penmar* which sailed from Philadelphia to Baltimore with a scab crew on it. The crew had had some argument of some nature—I don't recall now exactly what it was, and the entire crew walked off the ship and the company hired a new one. So I had received a wire from Whalen, notifying me that the full crew of the *Penmar* was scabs, so I wired him back and asked him what the status of the ship was—to find out the score on it so I could handle it from the Frisco end when she arrived there. He says here:

After the 3rd day two tugboats moved her to Sparrows Point which is, as you know, the United States Steel Trust's property, where with the help of the international officials they did get a crew of scabs from New York. With this scab crew she proceeded to Philly, where they got rid of the steward all right, but the company refused to pay the scabs all off because they would have to give them one months' pay. With the scab crew still aboard leaving Philly for the West Coast, the scab quartermaster ran her on the mud where she remained another 24 hours. This ship is one hundred per cent hot, rat, scabby, and so forth, which includes the entire crew from captain on down. Dump them all. This is the only way we can teach these rats not to take ships out when one department is on strike. So hoping you treat these people as they should be treated, I am relying on this.

And it is signed by Pat Whalen, agent at Baltimore.

Mr. Lynch. What did they mean by "dump them all"?

Mr. Innes. Why, to dump them ashore, and they were not to return back to the ship no matter what happened to them.

Mr. Voorhis. What did happen?

Mr. Innes. I went to Usher, the general manager for the Calmer Line in San Francisco, and told him very bluntly and plainly he had to take the crew off when it arrived on the Pacific coast or I would throw a picket line in front of it and he wouldn't be able to work his ship. He called Bridges up and he, Bridges, said if I put a picket line there, there would be one there, and the longshoremen would not work the ship. So Usher said: "I don't know what the status of the crew is but how about us bringing the ship here to San Francisco?" I said, "All right." So I sent word to San Pedro to work the ship in San Pedro and let her come to Frisco.

When she arrived in Frisco Curran had arrived the night before. He and I went down to the ship and the captain paid the entire crew off—the whole works. So then Usher turned to me to get a crew to him to take his ship on up the line. I tried to get a crew but the West Coast Union would not supply a crew, even though they had promised me they would, because there was a difference in wages and hours and overtime.

There had just been a bunch of Filipinos come off the ship and they refused to fumigate it and the ship was in a generally lousy condition. So, in order to make my word good to the company, I then went to the steamboat inspector's office and demanded a survey of the ship, and it was made and she went into the shipyard and she stayed there until the ship was in—she was tied up about 5 months.

Mr. MATTHEWS. Isn't the word "dump" an expression which indicates a very definite type of handling?

Mr. INNES. It means to take them out and beat their ears off.

Mr. LYNCH. About this time did you get a new word from Curran, a new name for Curran, that he was using in his correspondence?

Mr. INNES. Yes, sir. The name that had been arranged when Curran arrived on the Pacific coast, that all wires from thereon from him or letters from him to me would be signed "Jacy" instead of Curran.

Mr. LYNCH. Now, about this time that you just indicated that Mr. Curran arrived on the Pacific coast, do you recall the precise date of his arrival?

Mr. INNES. Yes, sir; October 20, 1936.

Mr. LYNCH. Did you have conferences with him?

Mr. INNES. Joe arrived in San Francisco around 7 o'clock at night, I judge. I took him to a hotel where we had quite a long talk, and and I asked him what he meant by these letters, that the Communist Party had about assumed control of the work in New York and that Tommy Ray was the big shot. He said: "Well, let us don't kid ourselves." He said: "I can't get a ship any more and neither can you." He said: "I got to have a job so I did the best thing there was. I have joined the party and I advise you to do the same thing."

Mr. LYNCH. That was in October 1936?

Mr. INNES. Yes.

Mr. LYNCH. Did you also talk to him about the general strike situation, or had the strike been called on the 15th?

Mr. INNES. Had been called. The strike at the request of the Labor Board had been extended.

Mr. LYNCH. Labor Department?

Mr. INNES. Labor Department; had been extended until October 28.

Mr. LYNCH. And so Curran arrived before the calling of the strike?

Mr. INNES. That is correct.

Mr. LYNCH. You had conferences with Curran and Bridges together?

Mr. INNES. I took Curran then to the District Council No. 2 meeting of the Maritime Federation of the Pacific where I introduced him to Roy Pyle, Mervyne Rathborne, Harry Bridges, Walter Stack,

Jim O'Neil, Revels Cayton, and the whole shooting match because the policy committee at that time constituted the whole board.

Mr. LYNCH. Hudson?

Mr. INNES. He wasn't present at that meeting.

Mr. LYNCH. All those persons whom you have named, were they all avowed Communists?

Mr. INNES. The ones I have named right now are; yes, sir.

Mr. LYNCH. During the time when Curran was in California, did Bridges make a speech to any particular union or class of workers there?

Mr. INNES. On October 21, 1936, I called a meeting of the east coast seamen in the Marine Firemen, Oilers, and Watertenders' hall in San Francisco. Bridges and Curran both attended the meeting and both spoke. There was 347 men present when the meeting adjourned.

Mr. LYNCH. Did you preside over the meeting?

Mr. INNES. I was chairman of the meeting; yes, sir.

Mr. LYNCH. Do you have a record of the speech made by Bridges at that time and at that meeting?

Mr. INNES. I have the verbatim speech here.

Mr. LYNCH. Will you read the last part of it?

The CHAIRMAN. Is that a speech of Bridges to the meeting?

Mr. INNES. That is correct, at a closed membership meeting of the east coast seamen.

Mr. MATTHEWS. And you were chairman of the meeting?

Mr. INNES. Yes, sir. And I signed the minutes, and this is the minutes of the entire meeting. Bridges said in conclusion:

> I am proud to be here and talk to you along with Brother Joe Curran, whose work I have watched and I realize the tremendous job he has tackled back there and the success he made of it. If we had a few more the same as Joe the troubles on the east coast would be over.
>
> I will conclude and give Joe a chance. I must leave shortly to attend another meeting, but all I can say is that I am optimistic. When I see the workers sticking together and know they are going forward with a solid program, that is all you can expect until the workers take charge of this world, and some day we are going to do that too.

Mr. LYNCH. Did you ever talk to Curran as to that particular phase of Bridges' speech where the "workers were going to take over the world"?

Mr. INNES. No.

Mr. MATTHEWS. As to whether he agreed with it or not?

Mr. INNES. No, sir; I never discussed it.

Mr. CASEY. What was meant by the statement of Curran to you or what was your inference "that you can't get a ship and neither could he"?

Mr. INNES. Well, at that time, as I have tried to make clear, there was a factional fight going on on the Atlantic coast between the rank and file membership of the three unions and the officials of the unions. The American Federation of Labor and the International Executive Board of our own particular International—it was a whole humdrum mess. We were in court and out of court and everything else and the strike was really based on our argument with these union officials more so than the steamship companies and as a result we were blacklisted in the union. We were expelled—that is Joe was expelled. I wasn't, because my own particular union—we had already gained control of it. We were blacklisted with the steamship companies and what he meant was that neither of us could get a job on the Atlantic coast, that we were out as far as going to sea any more was concerned.

Mr. Casey. That was merely a figure of speech, "couldn't get a job anywhere"?

Mr. Innes. That is right.

Mr. Casey. Now, which faction did the Communists have control of?

Mr. Innes. The Communists had control with the faction that was leading the fight against the steamship operators. The A. F. of L. and the International Union, that was the Seamen's Defense Committee, was composed of representatives from all three crafts.

Mr. Casey. They held the whip hand?

Mr. Innes. That is correct. The strike committee at that time, I think out of seven members on the strike council, they had five of the seven—five of the seven were Communists, if I recall offhand. I can tell later on.

Mr. Casey. So what happened was that Curran took the attitude if "we can't beat them may as well join them"?

Mr. Innes. That is the idea. In other words, as I stated previously, Curran was out for a pie card, and he did not care where he got it.

Mr. Casey. Out for a what?

Mr. Innes. Pie card, as we call it. It is a seaman's term—something for nothing in other words.

Mr. Lynch. Mr. Innes, how long was Curran on the west coast?

Mr. Innes. Curran was on the west coast from October 20, I believe, until the 28th, at which time I bought him a plane ticket and he came east.

Mr. Lynch. What cities did he visit besides San Francisco?

Mr. Innes. Just San Francisco—no; he went across the Bay to one ship—Alameda, I believe it was, or Oakland.

Mr. Lynch. And during those 8 days that he was there did he have frequent conferences with Bridges and Rathborne and Pyle and Hudson, and the others that you have mentioned?

Mr. Innes. We had one conference that I attended at Mervyn Rathborne's house on Pine Street, I believe it was, in San Francisco. At that conference Roy Hudson was present, Mervyn Rathborne, Walter Stack, Harry Bridges, Jim O'Neil, and Revels Cayton.

Mr. Lynch. Who is Revels Cayton?

Mr. Innes. At this time secretary of the Maritime Federation of the Pacific Coast.

Mr. Lynch. Is he a Communist or not?

Mr. Innes. He is a Communist and an admitted Communist.

Mr. Lynch. And was then?

Mr. Innes. He was then.

Mr. Lynch. Now, was everyone else at the conference a Communist, and admittedly so?

Mr. Innes. Admittedly so.

Mr. Matthews. Not by themselves?

Mr. Innes. No, sir.

Mr. Lynch. Rathborne admitted it?

Mr. INNES. They were admitted Communists to me by Tommy Ray because of my instructions to report to them.

Mr. CASEY. Did the shipowners cooperate with the Communists to the extent the Communists got control?

Mr. INNES. Did the shipowners cooperate?

Mr. CASEY. Yes.

Mr. INNES. Well, I would say that as events developed later on the shipowners had no other choice. It was a case they didn't sail their ships unless they did cooperate, but that was long after this period. That was in 1937. When a captain got his crew and his passengers and mail aboard he never knew that he would actually sail until he dropped his pilot off outside the breakwater. Five minutes before sailing time it was nothing to go aboard a ship and tell the crew to squat, and you didn't sail.

Mr. CASEY. Tell the crew to squat?

Mr. INNES. Sit down; not do any work.

Mr. LYNCH. Did that happen frequently?

Mr. INNES. That was the predominate organizing feature of the National Maritime Union after its formation until, well, in the fall of 1937, because I was organizing at the time.

Mr. LYNCH. And was that practice and tactics developed by the Communist influence in the union?

Mr. INNES. Correct. It was imported from France—is where it was imported from.

The CHAIRMAN. We will adjourn at this time until 1: 30.

(Whereupon, at 12: 10, a recess was had until 1: 30 p. m.)

AFTER RECESS

The CHAIRMAN. The committee will come to order.

TESTIMONY OF PETER J. INNES, JR.—Resumed

Mr. LYNCH. Mr. Innes, I show you a sample ballot for 1940 for the National Maritime Union of America and ask you if you have checked over the names of the persons who are running for positions and offices in that union?

Mr. INNES. I have checked them over; yes, sir.

Mr. LYNCH. How many, approximately, would you say are Communists?

Mr. INNES. From 90 to 95 percent of the men running on the ballot are Communists.

Mr. LYNCH. And will you state whether or not in May 1936 there was a fraction meeting held in New York in which it was determined what to do with the members of the union or anyone else who wouldn't go along with the policy laid down in that meeting?

Mr. INNES. Just prior to the dinner in the Spartacus Club that was given for Krumbein there was a fraction meeting held at 208 West Fourteenth Street in a rooming house run by a Communist by the name of MacDonald; and present at that meeting, fraction meeting, were Roy Hudson, Jack Lawrenson, Tommy Ray, Al Lannon, Bill McCuisiton, myself, and Pat Whalen, where Hudson told them that the newspaper publicity was beginning to turn against the seamen due to the Communist-front organizations that were appearing on the seamen's picket lines on the water front, including the League of Women Shoppers; the American Student Union; the Citizens' Committee, run by Gene Connolly, of Mike Quill's outfit—I think he is an organizer in the Transport Workers now—and many others along the same line. And told Ray he would have to stop having those people down on the water front and that in the matter of firemen who were raising so much cain along the front about these Communists and Communist organizations being present, that they would have to be purged; in other words, through adverse publicity in the union publications and by whispering campaigns and word of mouth, in order to stop the disruptive tactics they were carrying on at the various meetings.

Mr. LYNCH. In other words, if a member of the Firemen's Union or any other union would object to the control by the Communist Party that member would be destroyed as a member of the union?

Mr. INNES. As a member of the union or his usefulness to the union itself would be destroyed by the ridicule they would heap upon him.

Mr. LYNCH. Now, you speak about the publications. What publications would be read by the members of the National Maritime Union seamen and the firemen, and so forth?

Mr. INNES. Well, at that time on the Atlantic coast we had a paper which was known as the I. S. U. Pilot. On the Pacific coast there was the Voice of the Federation, and in the Hawaiian Islands at that time they had a publication which I believe was called the Voice of Labor, which was run by Corby Paxton.

Mr. LYNCH. Who controlled those three papers?

Mr. INNES. The Communist Party, through its control of the editorial board.

Mr. LYNCH. Have you checked those various publications with the articles which would appear in the Daily Worker?

Mr. INNES. If you checked them they would run—many, many of them would run—verbatim. In fact, the prevalent cry among the average seamen at the time and later was that the publications, instead of giving union news, were giving the news about how well the capitalist class had been downtrodden in Russia and what was going on in Siberia, and everything else except what the men wanted to read.

Mr. LYNCH. While you were on the west coast did you have access to get on board ships whenever you wished?

Mr. INNES. I did.

Mr. LYNCH. And how was that arranged for you?

Mr. INNES. Well, when I first arrived and had order to start organizing the men I didn't have passes to get aboard the ships or docks. I had no legal standing with the steamship companies where I could get the passes. So I went to Bridges, and he said, "We can arrange that very easily"; and he stepped into the next office, to Rathborne's office, and told Rathborne what I was up against, and Rathborne says, "Well, I will fix that," and he reached in and pulled his wallet out, and he had passes issued to him as secretary of his organization aboard the docks and ships and gave me the passes, and I got aboard any dock I wanted to.

Mr. LYNCH. Now, this strike committee—how many of them on that strike committee were Communists, or can you say it was definitely controlled by the Communists?

Mr. INNES. Pacific coast or Atlantic coast?

Mr. LYNCH. Pacific coast.

Mr. INNES. On the Pacific coast the committee was called a policy committee. Each port had its own strike committee and each union was represented on the coast, the policy committee, by representatives that they had elected to negotiate with the operators, and on the night that the strike was called the negotiating committee dissolved as such and resolved itself into a coastwise policy committee to lay down the policy for the carrying out the strike; and roughly, in figures, I would not be able to tell you how many Communists there were, but all organizations, the various units of each organization, was represented—that is, the component organizations—if they had five of their particular unit on the strike committee, of course they only had one vote. It was by unit vote and the Communist Party controlled sufficient votes in each unit to cast the vote the way the party wanted it, with the exception of the Sailors' Union of the Pacific.

That was the only one that they did not control outright.

Mr. LYNCH. Was Jack Lawrenson on that committee?

Mr. INNES. Jack Lawrenson was not. He was on the Atlantic coast committee.

Mr. LYNCH. He was not, however, a member of any union, was he?

Mr. INNES. Lawrenson was a member of the Firemen's Union on the Atlantic coast. Tommy Ray was not a member of the Firemen's Union.

Mr. LYNCH. Was he on that committee?

Mr. INNES. Tommy Ray officially was not on the committee; no, sir; but he issued orders in the name of the committee.

Mr. LYNCH. This code you speak about with Curran, who else knew the code except you and Curran?

Mr. INNES. Bridges, Rathborne, and myself.

Mr. LYNCH. Who is Walter Carney?

Mr. INNES. Walter Carney in 1936 was Joe Curran's bodyguard and leader of what we called the "educational squad."

Mr. LYNCH. And what was the "educational squad"?

Mr. INNES. That was the dumping or goon squad that went out to collect dough for the strike fund.

Mr. LYNCH. And do you have a letter on that?

Mr. INNES. I have. It was sent to me on the Pacific coast. It states "that I am Joe's personal secretary and trouble shooter," and he states that he is head of the educational squad and that the room rent for Joe and himself and a few others is due and they expect the scabs on the *Washington* to contribute. It is signed by the bo'sun's mate, Walter Carney, and, incidentally, he is now doing time in the New York State Penitentiary.

Mr. LYNCH. Refreshing your recollection, Mr. Innes, with regard to telegrams and correspondence, who controlled the orders and outlined the demands which would be made for the east-coast strikers?

Mr. INNES. The demands for east-coast strikers, the policy, was outlined in Bridges' office in San Francisco between Mervyn Rathborne, Bridges, and myself, and was transmitted to New York.

Mr. LYNCH. By telephone?

Mr. INNES. By telegram and teletype both, and by telephone.

Mr. LYNCH. And was the arrangement for Bridges to go to New York also made by telegram and teletype? ..

Mr. INNES. Teletype.

Mr. LYNCH. And Bridges went to New York, and did you go with him?

Mr. INNES. I did.

Mr. LYNCH. And you met him where?

Mr. INNES. I met Bridges—well, I left the Pacific coast prior to Bridges' leaving.

Mr. LYNCH. Where did you meet him in New York?

Mr. INNES. I met him at the airport the next time I saw him.

Mr. LYNCH. Who was there at the airport with him?

Mr. INNES. We went over in three automobiles.

Mr. LYNCH. Just who was there?

Mr. INNES. Charlie Krumbein, a fellow by the name of Leeds, Tommy Ray, Al Rothbart, Al Lannon, Joe Curran, and myself.

Mr. LYNCH. And then did you have a meeting in New York before the actual meeting in Madison Square Garden?

Mr. INNES. We did.

Mr. LYNCH. Where?

Mr. INNES. In the Victoria Hotel.

Mr. LYNCH. Were substantially the same persons present that you just mentioned?

Mr. INNES. That is correct.

Mr. LYNCH. And during that rally at the Madison Square Garden, was anyone taking up funds—collections?

Mr. INNES. A collection from the platform speech was made by Bill McCuistion and the money was taken up by people passing through the aisles with pans. I received the pans, together with individual donations that were sent up with slips. Those donations—that is, the slips—I handed to the chairman, who was Bill McCuistion. The money was dumped into a sack.

Mr. LYNCH. Go ahead. Were those names read off as to who was making the contributions?

Mr. INNES. That is correct, and so many donations were coming in—that is, small donations of a dollar or two or three dollars and odd pennies—from various units of the Communist Party and McCuistion was calling them off over the loudspeaker in the Garden, and Al Lannon came to me and told me to tell McCuistion to stop calling out any contributions from the Communist Party.

Mr. LYNCH. After you got through with New York you and Bridges went to Boston. Did he speak up there?

Mr. INNES. The night before the Garden meeting Bridges went to Philadelphia. I stayed to attend a coastwise conference in New York.

Mr. LYNCH. Did he also speak in Boston?

Mr. INNES. He went to Boston the night following the Garden meeting.

Mr. LYNCH. And also spoke in Baltimore, which you have already covered?

Mr. INNES. That is right.

Mr. LYNCH. When he went to the west coast did you return there afterward?

Mr. INNES. I did .

Mr. LYNCH. How long, after he left?

Mr. INNES. He went back by plane, and I went back by train.

Mr. LYNCH. Now, did there come a time when there was informa-tion brought to you with regard to the tie-in with the seamen in France and Germany with regard to an American boat?

Mr. INNES. Yes, sir. I received letters on that tie-up prior to my going East.

Mr. LYNCH. What was that?

Mr. INNES. That the longshoremen in Le Havre, France, through a request of the Seamen's Defense Committee in New York, had coop-erated to the extent that they refused to handle any part of the cargo or anything else of the steamship *Washington.* When that happened the ship went to Hamburg, Germany, where the German longshore-men did likewise, although under a different guise than the one in France, due to the difference in governments.

The ship returned to New York with her initial cargo still on board.

Mr. LYNCH. Did you learn as to who controlled the instructions to the seamen in France and the seamen in Germany as to the fact that they would not unload the vessel?

Mr. INNES. When I arrived in New York in December to attend the coastwise conference, I spoke of the matter to Ray, and he told me that he had made the arrangements directly with the French longshoremen's union and they, in turn, through the underground route in Europe, had made arrangements with the longshoremen in Hamburg, Germany, which was, and still is, known as a hotbed for communism.

Mr. LYNCH. How about Roy Hudson at the time of the east-coast speeches? Was Roy Hudson active?

Mr. INNES. Roy Hudson was in New York at the time; yes, sir.

Mr. LYNCH. Any conferences with him, so far as you know?

Mr. INNES. The conference—the first conference that we had with him was in the back room of the Garden after the meeting and after the newspaper men had left, in one of the dressing rooms there. There was Roy Hudson and this Leeds, the treasurer of the Com-munist Party, who was given the entire take—all the money that was taken in. He received that, and Hudson, Leeds, Ray, Lannon, Rothbart, McCuistion, Bridges, Curran, and myself.

Mr. LYNCH. Now, when you were up in Boston, who met you up there?

Mr. INNES. In Boston—we went from New York to Boston by plane. We were met at the airport by Marty Flaherty, together with Ann Burlap or Burlak.

Mr. LYNCH. Is Marty Flaherty a Communist?

Mr. INNES. Marty Flaherty is definitely a Communist.

Mr. LYNCH. And Ann Burlak was also?

Hr. INNES. She was secretary of the Communist Party in either Rhode Island or Massachusetts, I am not sure which, at the time.

Mr. LYNCH. Who would give orders and tell Bridges what to do and where he was to go next?

Mr. INNES. Tommy Ray.

Mr. LYNCH. Now, when did you—what date did you return to California?

Mr. INNES. I arrived back in Los Angeles on December 23.

Mr. LYNCH. And what was the date of the strike or was the strike then on?

Mr. INNES. The strike was still on.

Mr. LYNCH. When was the strike finally settled?

Mr. INNES. The strike was settled on the coast on January 24, 1937. It was settled as far as the Pacific coast unions were concerned on February 4, 1937, and the sixteen-hundred-odd men that I had in my particular group, we settled our end of it on February 6, 1937.

Mr. THOMAS. Mr. Chairman, may I ask a couple of questions?

Mr. Innes, you told us this morning how you had sat in with Harry Bridges at some 10 Communist faction meetings?

Mr. INNES. Yes, sir.

Mr. THOMAS. You probably got to know Harry Bridges pretty well—entered into various conversations with him about various subjects. I am wondering if you can recall any statements that Harry Bridges might have made about his friendliness with any Government officials?

Mr. INNES. No, sir. The only statements that I know that Bridges made the statements before we left the Atlantic coast and came or, before we left the Pacific coast. It came up several times in the talk of these negotiations that he was going to arrange for that and in the Labor Department conciliations he said he could pretty nearly get what he wanted.

Mr. THOMAS. Now, you distinctly recall that, do you?

Mr. INNES. That is correct.

Mr. THOMAS. That he told you or you heard him tell other people that you could get what?

Mr. INNES. He could arrange for the elections; that he would arrange for them and that as far as Labor Department conciliation went on on the Atlantic coast that he would take care of that; that he could get what he wanted there.

Mr. THOMAS. When he said that was he referring to the National Labor Relations Board or the Department of Labor?

Mr. INNES. I would assume it was the Labor Board he was talking about.

Mr. THOMAS. Do you recall him making any statements about the Department of Labor?

Mr. INNES. No, sir; outside of the agreement we had made with McGrady and he threw that overboard himself; that is, Bridges did.

Mr. THOMAS. That is all. I might ask a couple of questions right there. Now, did he say or did he make any comments about his deportation case?

Mr. INNES. Only the particular time that I spoke about when we were to go to Mexico; that he had advice of his attorney that he did not dare leave the country or he wouldn't be able to get back in again. But there was no comment about his deportation at the time. I think that he was served with the warrant I believe when we were here or one warrant while we were over here on the Atlantic coast at that time where he had to put up the bond.

Mr. THOMAS. Do you recall any statements he made in regard to that?

Mr. INNES. Except the "reactionary so and so's were after him again." That was all. He never made any statement regarding the case itself.

Mr. THOMAS. Did he intimate that he would be able to get out of it all right?

Mr. INNES. Well, he hoped so, but he never made any statements to me about it.

Mr. THOMAS. That is all.

Mr. LYNCH. While you were on the west coast and this tele-type that you had with New York and the other cities, have you refreshed your recollection during the lunch hour as to whether or not you were advised by Curran to keep in touch with the people who were the head of the Communist Party out there and to cooperate with them?

Mr. INNES. That matter was discussed with me and Curran when I was in New York. As I stated, Curran had told me in San Francisco—he advised me to join the party the same as he had in order to get a job and the way the strike was going I began to get a little suspicious of Curran and everybody else involved, including Bridges and the rest of them, because when the east coast men first struck on my orders to them, they had left their ships. They came ashore in San Pedro, and the first batch of them I think was about 800, and they were the largest single group of men in the port of San Pedro excepting the longshoremen, and they were being knocked from pillar to post, the idea being to run them out of the port of San Pedro, so I went to San Pedro and we formed a component and separate organization entirely composed of nothing but east-coast men.

This did not meet with the party line and I was called on the telephone, teletype, and by letter from both Rathborne on the teletype, Bridges on the telephone and New York by letter and telegraph and everything else to break up this outfit that I had and let them go into the different unions. The policy, as I found from my observation attending the different meetings was that inasmuch as the Communist Party had active control of the unions on the Pacific coast, namely, the cooks and stewards and the firemen and had a very strong minority in the S. U. P., that they would then be in a position to force the east coast operators who operated intercoastal ships and whose ships were tied up on the Pacific coast into signing contracts with those unions and thus being able to spread their domination definitely to the east coast by opening subbranches of their Pacific coast unions on the east coast to carry out their contracts, thus forcing the legitimate east coast seamen out into the cold entirely, unless they went along with the party line.

By my forming the separate organization I set up a party that, or a body that the east coast shipper could deal with on the Pacific coast and when the party ordered the men back to the ships I refused to deliver the orders to them and we stayed out and the result was I did negotiate contracts with the Atlantic coast operators who operated intercoastal, and that is when I had my falling out with the party, all over this business of maintaining a separate organization on the Pacific coast.

Mr. LYNCH. In other words, you were unwilling that they would control the east coast men?

Mr. INNES. That is correct.

Mr. LYNCH. And the pressure from all sides was on you, too?

Mr. INNES. To discredit me and to throw me out.

Mr. LYNCH. Disband them and throw them entirely in the west coast unit?

Mr. INNES. That is correct.

Mr. LYNCH. Which was controlled as you have stated by the Communist Party?

Mr. INNES. That is right.

Mr. LYNCH. And the ultimate result was that these men were kept separate and separate contracts were made with the east coast shippers?

Mr. INNES. That is right.

Mr. LYNCH. Now, I want to put in the record also the list of the various persons that you were told to get in touch with in Mexico in case of the development of trouble.

Mr. INNES. I transmitted this list to the Atlantic coast for their information. It included the President of Mexico, the general secretaries of three unions and the secretary of the C. R. O. M. and the C. T. M. in Ensenada and Tia Juana, Mexico.

Mr. LYNCH. Who gave you this list?

Mr. INNES. It was given to me by A. Felix of the C. R. O. M. in Tia Juana, Mexico.

Mr. LYNCH. Did Bridges and the other persons that you have mentioned on the west coast have knowledge of this list?

Mr. INNES. They received copies of them through Jordan.

The CHAIRMAN. Did you have an opportunity to find out the strength of the Communist Party in Mexico while you were down there?

Mr. INNES. Yes, sir; from the two particular places that I was in. The secretary of the C. T. M., I believe it was in Ensenada, was wearing a Star of Lenin and several other members of the Central Labor Council in Tia Juana had just returned from a course in trade-unionism in Moscow and altogether I met about three different people that were decorated with the highest order of the Soviet Republic.

The Mexican people in Mexico, in Ensenada, of course, were carrying arms that had been distributed among them during the revolution down there by Cardenas, who is now President, when he was first elected and they were very much on the Communist side with the exception of the eastern portions of Mexico. The west portion that I happened to be in was very definitely communistic and Marxist because you would go down the street and find regular billboards with the pictures of Lenin and the Communist salute and Marxist material on them.

Mr. THOMAS. Isn't it true the C. T. M. is the largest union in Mexico?

Mr. INNES. There are two of them—the Toledano outfit is the largest component part. There is from my observations there, what I gathered from the way Felix had told me, the C. T. M. and the C. R. O. M. are very similar to our American Federation of Labor and C. I. O. squabble, only more so. They are the political bodies in the country. If a man enters politics there he forms a labor union.

Mr. THOMAS. Have you ever seen any of the letterheads of the C. T. M.?

Mr. INNES. I have the letters here.

The CHAIRMAN. Do they have the hammer and sickle on them?

Mr. INNES. I can tell you in a moment, if I look at it.. This particular letterhead I have is the union, Marine Union, affiliated with the C. T. M. It has nothing on here excepting the picture of a steamship.

Mr. THOMAS. We have some letterheads of the C. T. M. with the hammer and sickle on them.

Mr. INNES. Well, I would not doubt that a bit.

Mr. LYNCH. It was evident to you, was it, Mr. Innes, from your contact with these people in Mexico and Ensenada where you were for several days, that it was completely controlled by the Communist Party trade union?

Mr. INNES. The trade unions are the political parties in Mexico.

The CHAIRMAN. Was there much contact between the Communists in Mexico and the Communists in California?

Mr. INNES. Our contacts that we made were made by people in the United States—the original contact was made by Bridges with this fellow in Los Angeles—a division of the, I believe it is the C. T. M. that has an office in Bar Harbor, Calif.

It is the field workers—the Mexican field workers, cannery workers, or whatever you want to call them. They didn't at that time belong to an American trade union. They belonged to a Mexican trade union with headquarters or a division of their headquarters in the United States in Bar Harbor, I believe it was.

Mr. VOORHIS. Where is Bar Harbor?

Mr. INNES. That is one of the outskirts of Los Angeles. It is Bar Harbor, Calif.

Mr. LYNCH. Were you there?

Mr. INNES. I was there. We stopped and picked this fellow up and he is the one that took us to Tia Juana.

Mr. LYNCH. How far from Los Angeles?

Mr. INNES. Well, just like driving from here across the bridge to Arlington, but it is all out in the—it is in the peon quarters out there.

Mr. LYNCH. And the contact was first made by Bridges with this party?

Mr. INNES. That is correct.

Mr. LYNCH. In Bar Harbor?

Mr. INNES. Yes.

Mr. LYNCH. And then you went there?

Mr. INNES. Picked him up and he took us south and introduced us to the various people in Mexico.

The CHAIRMAN. What other information did you get with reference to the tie-up of the Communists in the United States and Mexico? Was there any other evidence besides what you have related?

Mr. INNES. Well, excepting that Toledano, or rather part of his outfit in Mazatlan, when I made a complaint to them—I wrote to Mazatlan—that was the Seamen's Union of Mazatlan. They received orders from Toledano that they were to do as we asked. And the Mexicans that were on board the *Santa Rosa*, which I had tied up in San Pedro, didn't do any more work. And if I recall correctly there were no more American ships handled in Vera Cruz or Tampico after we made our trip there.

The CHAIRMAN. Now, you say that the people were pretty well armed?

Mr. INNES. Yes, sir.

The CHAIRMAN. They had guns that had been distributed to them sometime before?

Mr. INNES. After Cardenas went into office.

The CHAIRMAN. And they were openly communistic? No question about that?

Mr. INNES. When the troops came out against us the labor leaders in the town sent word out to the outlying districts, the farms—the peons and the farmers came into town and brought their guns with them.

The CHAIRMAN. Do you know what the contact is between the Mexicans on the United States side and the Mexicans in Mexico? Is there a close relationship?

Mr. INNES. Very much so. They go back and forth across the border without any hindrance whatsoever. I know we brought this fellow back into the United States—whether he was a citizen or not I don't know, but there was nothing done except the car was searched back and forth across the border. We were not stopped going down for a passport or anything by the Mexican authorities and coming back it was the same way.

The CHAIRMAN. You say these labor leaders in Mexico that you met had received their instructions at the Lenin University in Moscow?

Mr. INNES. That is right.

The CHAIRMAN. Where they got their instructions on trade-union activities and one of them was decorated with the Star of Lenin?

Mr. INNES. Yes, sir; that is correct.

Mr. VOORHIS. When you say that the Mexican labor movement is communistic, what do you mean by that? I mean that is a pretty big mouthful, isn't it?

The CHAIRMAN. He is talking, as I understand it, about the ones he came in contact with in Tia Juana and Ensenada.

Mr. INNES. That is a big mouthful, as the Congressman says, but knowing that we went there and that I was actually with Communist leaders in the labor movement, and they sent word to Toledano and the result was the word went all over the country that the American ships were not to be handled. That definitely shows that the Communists controlled Toledano's outfit and he represented the Government party at the time and I believe he still does.

Mr. VOORHIS. I don't want to argue about it, but I do think this is a matter of such importance we ought to be sure. Does that show the definite influence of Communists or Toledano or does it show he was willing to play ball with the Americans—what he considered to be an American union? I mean why does it show one instead of the other?

Mr. INNES. Well, it shows this much, that the schools, the traveling schools in Mexico which I ran into a couple of times in Ensenada—they hand out pamphlets. You can go down here to any Communist store and for a penny here or there you buy them.

For instance, the seamen used to be able to buy the "red" flag for a couple of cents. That is openly taught in the schools there—they have books on Marxism and Stalin——

Mr. VOORHIS. What schools?

Mr. INNES. Government-owned schools. There is only one set of schools down there now, and that is the one the Government runs.

Mr. VOORHIS. You saw that happen?

Mr. INNES. I definitely saw that.

Mr. VOORHIS. I mean you saw them in the schools?

Mr. INNES. I saw these traveling schoolhouses like we have in our rural districts—the traveling libraries—the traveling schoolhouses with a teacher comes down and holds the school right in the outlying peon districts where they come in from the farms and hold a school session in the public square, as you would call it.

The CHAIRMAN. As a matter of fact, Pathe News had a rather long news reel showing the same thing in Mexico about 8 or 9 months ago. It was here in Washington. It showed all the scenes in Mexico with the hammer and sickle and distribution of Lenin's works, and so on and so forth.

Mr. VOORHIS. Do these activities in Mexico come within the scope of this committee's investigation? I mean to say we are supposed to investigate un-American activities in the United States. How does this Mexican situation come within the scope of this committee's work?

Mr. INNES. Mr. Congressman, that is something I could not answer. I was summoned here to answer questions, and that is all I can do.

The CHAIRMAN. Well, he is not testifying primarily about Mexico. He is testifying as to his activities in connection with the maritime union on the Pacific coast which involved, incidentally, his trip into Mexico.

Mr. VOORHIS. That is what I am trying to get at. That is what I am inquiring about.

The CHAIRMAN. I don't think the witness is qualified to testify whether Toledano or the C. T. M. is communistic. All he knows, as I understand it, is that in two or three sections that he visited he saw certain things. I agree that that evidence would not be sufficient to show that the labor organizations in Mexico were under the control of the Communist Party. All he knows is that in the places he visited he knew the labor leaders were definitely Communists.

Mr. INNES. The particular outfit——

The CHAIRMAN. Open and aboveboard Communists.

Mr. INNES. Yes, sir.

The CHAIRMAN. But whether they were in other sections you don't know?

Mr. INNES. That is right.

The CHAIRMAN. And the fact that they did get in touch with Toledano is the only circumstance you have to indicate that his organization is communistic?

Mr. INNES. All I have is the wire that we received from Toledano.

Mr. VOORHIS. What did that say?

Mr. INNES. To let them know the list of hot ships that left the United States, and we would be assured of 100-percent cooperation. That wire was sent to Jordan and a copy of it as a member of the committee that went south was given to me. The number on it if you want the whole thing is S–2150–NL, Mexico City, Mexico, November 25, 1936, addressed to C. H. Jordan, secretary, Southern California Council, Maritime Federation Pacific Coast.

The telegram is:

Telegrams Carillo and myself received. Have wired instructions that American ships bound your ports be prevented to discharge passengers and cargo. Mexican west coast. Confederation Mexican Workers has declared boycott against such boats. Please inform us of specific instances of unfair American ships so our cooperation can be more effective. Fraternally Vincente Lombardo Toledano.

The CHAIRMAN. Of course the Mexican situation along the border involving the close workings and interrelationship between the Communist Party of the United States and the Communist Party of Mexico certainly comes within the jurisdiction of this committee; not that we are concerned with what is going on in Mexico—that is none of our concern—but where the Communist Party of Mexico cooperates and maintains a very close contact with the Communist Party of the United States comes within the scope of this committee's work and is imporant. They are involving themselves in American Affairs and not us. And if they do involve themselves in an interchange or exchange of information by reason of a common program in the two countries and are using Mexico as a base for their propaganda work in the United States and for the promotion of the Communist Party in this country, then it becomes a matter I think of great concern to the United States, but only insofar as their activities are in conjunction or in cooperation with the activities of the Communist Party in the United States.

Mr. VOORHIS. Well, I think the whole matter might be a matter of concern to us, but I don't see how our committee can go beyond the point where there is definite evidence that affects directly things in the United States.

The CHAIRMAN. But it is important that we have a definite understanding about that phase of it because that is going to become increasingly important in the next 2 months, since a great deal of the work of this committee will be concerned with the close interlocking associations and the cooperative efforts between Communists in Mexico; and not only Communists in Mexico but also representatives of the Comintern working over there in conjunction with Communists in the United States.

For instance, we just had evidence of certain Communist leaders who have been in Mexico for sometime actively at work, among whom was James W. Ford and Krumbein and others who have been in Mexico from time to time. That becomes a matter of great importance to us. It is important to us to what extent the Mexican Communists are participating in it, but we are not involving the Mexican Government; nor will we permit any testimony involving the internal affairs of Mexico.

Mr. LYNCH. Did you make a report by telegram to Mr. Curran in New York of the activities in Mexico and what the situation was there with regard to your ability to get around and stop the ships from unloading?

Mr. INNES. The day after our return I sent a day letter to Joe Curran, that possibly might answer the Congressman's question to a certain extent, to 164 Eleventh Avenue, New York, with the code words:

Telephone conversation Mexican Federation secretary Tia Juana reveals Santa Elena's passengers still at border. Mexican chauffeurs refuse transport Ensenada. Mexican government requests unions transport passengers, baggage. States after that unions will not be requested to handle cargo or mail. President Cardenas wires permission Tia Juana. Deported delegation return Mexico, release press.

That is signed "Innes."

Mr. LYNCH. Mr. Innes, did you also have knowledge, both verbally and by documents, that the Communist Party was attempting and did successfully get their representatives on the various committees and in the various unions?

Mr. INNES. The reason I came to New York was to attend a coast-wise conference for every port that had a strike committee. They elected men to come to New York to elect trustees for the Cooks' and Stewards' Union of the Atlantic and Gulf and the Eastern and Gulf Sailors' Association. I participated in that conference and the trustees that we elected for the Cooks' and Stewards' Union were Phillip Mantlebano, a Negro from Mobile, Ala.; Gaithen Lyons, from New York; and G. M. Monabalo, another Negro from New York. The three were Communists.

Mr. LYNCH. Without going into the various names all through the various unions.

Mr. INNES. There was one known Communist out of three elected by the sailors. The firemen designated three of their elected officials, one of whom was a Communist, to sit on the district committee, which made the district committee three to four or three out of nine that gave the Communist Party control of six out of the nine.

The two Negroes that were originally elected to the trusteeships the cooks and stewards resigned by party pressure, as they were too dumb to advocate anything, and Frank Jones and Ferdinand Smith, both officials in the National Maritime Union and both members of the Communist Party, were designated by a meeting of 18 men in the port of New York to take their places.

Mr. THOMAS. Before you go on, I don't know whether you are reading from something or whether that is your own opinion or not.

Mr. INNES. I am not reading from anything; no, sir.

Mr. THOMAS. When you say, "Two Negroes had to resign because they were too dumb"——

Mr. INNES. That was the explanation used.

Mr. THOMAS. That was the explanation that you heard?

Mr. INNES. I was there when it was done.

Mr. LYNCH. Let me ask you, are these the records of the meetings or what are these records you are referring to?

Mr. INNES. This here—I am reading the names—the report of the conference where they were elected. In other words, the men that had been elected by the representatives of the membership were dumped overboard on instructions from Tommy Ray because they were too dumb to follow the party line even if they were members of the party.

Mr. THOMAS. That was Tommy Ray's organization?

Mr. INNES. That was his organization.

Mr. THOMAS. And that is the explanation he gave?

Mr. INNES. That is correct. The two Negroes resigned. They were told to resign and they did so and one Negro, Ferdinand Smith, was placed there and Frank Jones was placed there by a meeting of 18 men. In the sailors' end of it Curran, because he didn't hold a union book at the time—he was an expelled member of the union—he was not eligible under the union's constitution to hold office, was designated as general organizer. Desmond, who had been elected a trustee had so much pressure put on him through wrangling and fighting that he didn't resign—he just got on a ship and shipped out and Curran sat in and sat in ever since in his place. Even though he was never elected by anybody to take the job.

Mr. VOORHIS. Who were the 18 men? I don't mean their names but what kind of meeting was this?

Mr. INNES. That was the supreme governing body of the union on the Atlantic and Gulf coast—the district committee.

The CHAIRMAN. Do you have any evidence of the way in which Tommy Ray's orders were handed down? What I mean is how do you know that happened?

Mr. INNES. The orders were handed down at a fraction meeting in New York.

The CHAIRMAN. Were you there?

Mr. INNES. I was not present; no, sir; but I came back from the coast and Curran told me how the thing worked from the time he returned to the Pacific coast and got back to the Atlantic coast. These two men were out of the picture entirely and then after I really broke with the party I started checking back through the records and that is how I found 18 men at a meeting had elected these other two.

The CHAIRMAN. To these two fellows' places?

Mr. INNES. Which wasn't even a quorum according to the union's constitution to take these other two places. Desmond shipped out and Curran moved in on his seat. Meyers resigned for so-called ill health. He went to the Communist Party school in upper New York State and Murray Stein, I think his name is Stone now, took his place. He is up in the Great Lakes. He is running for office on the union ballot now. When Meyers came out of school Stein resigned and Meyers took his job back and that is how that worked.

Mr. LYNCH. This paper right here, without reading it all, is the recommendation of Rathborne as to the terms of settlement that should be demanded by Curran on the east coast?

Mr. INNES. When the east coast men struck they struck strictly in sympathy with the Pacific coast. The resolution of the strike was that they would go back to work when the Pacific coast strike was settled. Then when the original policy was set out by the coast policy committee, the request for support was on intercoastal ships only; that each of the intercoastal ships was to return to its respective home port before being struck.

In other words, if a west coast ship was in New York and belonged in San Francisco they would not strike. They would bring the ship home before they struck and the same way on the Pacific coast. Well, the men did not go for that at all. The west coast men could not understand why they should sail out and the result was the policy was then changed to sit-down strikes along the Atlantic coast.

Mr. LYNCH. Who set that policy?

Mr. INNES. That was Bridges, Rathborne, Pyle, Walter Stack, and myself.

Mr. LYNCH. That was carried over the teletype to Curran in New York?

Mr. INNES. Well, it was decided by us first at Rathborne's office, and then we went in the coast policy committee with it and Bridges advocated it and naturally the rest followed right along and their orders were to vote the way he voted. Then the policy was set down.

So I transmitted the orders from Bridges to Curran and it was sit-down strikes all up and down the coast and when the party saw that the men were actually sitting down on the ships that is when they gave the orders for them to come out, but they came out with the understanding they would go back to work when the Pacific coast had signed their agreement. It was a sympathy strike. Then Bridges decided as long as the strike was going so well on the Atlantic coast, he called me in and gave me a list and he says, "this is the terms for the east coast"; and that was that we were to ask for identically the same things as the Pacific coast unions. In other words, an entirely different strike proposition altogether.

Mr. LYNCH. Did you visit the Communist Party book shops in San Francisco with regard to selling literature of the Maritime Union?

Mr. INNES. I went to the International Workers book shops in San Francisco and in San Pedro both and they were selling the I. S. U. Pilot, which was our official publication at the time, together with the time the Harbor Workers Voice and the Western Worker and all the rest of the Communist periodicals.

Mr. LYNCH. Now, Mr. Innes, did there come a time when you finally had a definite disagreement with the policy makers on the West Coast in which it was clear that you could not go along with them anymore; there would have to be a definite break?

Mr. INNES. Well, as I stated before the break started prior to my departure for New York in December.

Mr. LYNCH. What date was the final break?

Mr. INNES. The final break came in January 1937 while I was making my coast tour. There were to my recollection about 25 or 30 east coast men in San Pedro proper and the east coast men or, I mean in San Francisco, rather, instead of San Pedro. The east coast men in San Pedro had established a strike fund of around $3,000 themselves. It was their own money and they had their own committee administering it. The bunch in San Francisco wondered why they couldn't get a hold of some of it so they set up a set of charges to send to New York and when the charges didn't hold because the east coast men in San Pedro wouldn't stand for it, and they said regardless of what New York said that that was their outfit and they were keeping it, but they did have some effect on the bunch in New York, because I called Curran on the telephone January 24, after receiving a letter from him stating that the men in San Pedro may run the affairs there but in New York they still run the affairs as far as intercoastal things were concerned and that my credentials were going to be listed if the charges they received were true.

So I asked Joe what about it and he said, "Why, I am on charges myself." I said, "What charges," and he said, "For advocating the Fink book and the pressure is on me right and left here. They don't like your independent strike," and so forth.

So I told him I was going to read it off to the men and he says, "I know you can read that letter," and I said, "If I read it I have got to submit my resignation," and he says, "All right, you can explain it.' There are a lot of letters here from individual members," so I asked him to name one and he named a fellow by the name of Fishman, who was a stooge from San Francisco—was traveling between San Francisco and San Pedro at the time.

So Joe and I ironed that out. He said as far as he was concerned the credentials still stood, but that he was in trouble in New York and he wanted a resolution from the men in San Pedro endorsing him again and that I was to send the resolution to Stuyvesant High School on Fifteenth Street, which was done. Then the east coast men—they were in meeting at the time and I brought up the telephone conversation and read it to them. So they definitely threw New York overboard at that time themselves in a body and we elected our own negotiating committee and I was told to go to San Francisco and regardless of Bridges or anybody else negotiate contracts for them, which was done, although they stayed out on strike for several days after the strike was over.

Mr. Lynch. That is all, Mr. Chairman.

The Chairman. Do you have any questions?

Mr. Matthews. I have one or two matter here, Mr. Chairman.

Mr. Innes, did you ever hear that Communist Party members of the crews on American ships had thrown the ship libraries overboard so as to compel the crew to read only Communist Party literature?

Mr. Innes. I know of several instances where that happened on freighters that were going—on two or three ships. The ship libraries would be in little chests, and they would be thrown overboard.

Mr. Matthews. I have here a copy of the Daily Worker for Thursday, May 30, 1935. There is a column entitled "Party Life." It is by the central organization department and there appears a letter entitled: "Voyage Letter, Activities Aboard Ship Building the Party," and a portion of that letter reads:

S and I threw the ship's library overboard. They are now devoted to reading "red" literature.

Mr. Matthews. I ask that that be marked in evidence for the record.

The Chairman. It is so ordered.

(The Daily Worker referred to by Mr. Matthews was marked as "Innes Exhibit No. 2" and made a part of the record.)

Mr. Matthews. You have known of similar instances, have you?

Mr. Innes. Yes, sir.

Mr. Matthews. Do you know whether or not there was a marine training school operated by the Communist Party for seamen, Mr. Innes?

Mr. Innes. Yes, sir. There is and still is, I believe, in upper New York State.

Mr. Matthews. In the Washington Post, Washington, D. C., for Saturday, November 6, 1937, there appears an article entitled: "Soviet Camp in United States Training Red Seamen," and there is a reproduction of a subscription blank for Red Annapolis, and the blank reads:

Develop marine leaders, $1. Billed the Marine Training School, Waterfront Section, Communist Party, 35 East Twelfth Street, New York City.

and there is a picture of the hammer and sickle, with a picture of a seaman superimposed on the hammer and sickle. You knew about this school, did you?

Mr. INNES. That school is at Camp——

Mr. MATTHEWS. Nitdiget, N. Y.?

Mr. INNES. That is where it is at.

Mr. MATTHEWS. Was the existence of this school generally known?

Mr. INNES. It was common knowledge after those tickets were on sale around the front; yes, sir; but you had to be recommended by a party faction to go to it.

Mr. MATTHEWS. Did you know that Joseph Curran, when he was on the stand before this committee, testified that he did not know of this training school?

Mr. INNES. I did not know that, but I don't know why he shouldn't, because the delegates of the union were openly selling the blanks up and down the streets, and in fact union officials were buying the blanks—had to buy them.

Mr. LYNCH. Did you refer a few moments ago to somebody going up to a certain school for training?

Mr. INNES. I know several who went there.

Mr. LYNCH. This fellow named Stein, was it?

Mr. INNES. No; Meyers went to that school, and a fellow by the name of Saunders from Philadelphia went to the school.

Mr. VOORHIS. Went to this school where? In New York?

Mr. INNES. In New York; yes, sir; up in New York State.

The CHAIRMAN. Any other questions, gentlemen?

Mr. THOMAS. Mr. Chairman. Mr. Innes, you said that libraries, the books of the libraries, were thrown overboard, and all they had to read then was the Communist literature. You mean to infer that those libraries contained Communist literature as well as other literature?

Mr. INNES. No, sir; I did not mean to infer that, if I did. The American Merchant Marine Library Association in New York at the start of every voyage of a vessel puts aboard several chests of books, according to how long the voyage is going to take, and you most assuredly won't find any Communist literature in them. But the Communist Party members, in accordance with their instructions that were put out by the Communist Party for party work aboard a ship—there was a pamphlet—I have seen a copy of it, where the Communist Party members before they sailed are duty bound to go to the waterfront fraction headquarters and pick up party literature which they carry aboard the ship and put it in their lockers.

The last ship I made to China our forecastle was full of it until we caught up with it and caught up with the guy that was putting it out, and we cleaned out his locker and dumped it overboard. If you walked out in the recreation room or alleyway you find the stickers, and on the bulletin board you find the clippings, and on the mess table you find the pamphlets. Well, fellows going on a 35-day run from New York to Port Said with nothing to read—it gets monotonous—and after awhile they will read anything they get their hands on.

Mr. VOORHIS. Take a ship where, for example, the library is dumped overboard, what percentage of that crew would be Communist Party members?

Mr. INNES. Well, you wouldn't need but one in a small crew.

Mr. VOORHIS. What would the rest of them think about it?

Mr. INNES. Well, I don't know whether the Congressman knows how it works aboard one of those particular ships, the type I am talking about. We will say for instance a motor ship with six men in the engine room and three on deck and you would only have four of those men up at the same time, and at night it is easy for the men when everybody is asleep to come back and scatter anything they want to around the ship and you never know where it comes from.

The CHAIRMAN. What percentage of the men working in the American Merchant Marine do you estimate are Communist?

Mr. INNES. The percentage of men in the Merchant Marine?

The CHAIRMAN. Yes.

Mr. INNES. If you have got ten percent you have got a pretty tall figure, but now the Communists have control of the unions by flooding the unions with young men just getting out of school.

The CHAIRMAN. In your opinion what percentage of the leadership is Communist?

Mr. INNES. The leadership is 90 to 95 percent and in some ports 100 percent.

The CHAIRMAN. In other words, here is a group with a small minority in its membership that have managed in one way or another to gain control over the organizations, is that right?

Mr. INNES. That is correct. They maintain their control through their domination of the shore-side meetings. Now, there used to be provisions in the union constitutions, but I understand they are not there any more and when they are they are not strictly enforced, that a man on the beach over 6 months had to retire from the union. Well, under your union membership you can attend to meeting anywhere in the country that you want to where the union maintains an office. There is nothing to prevent the party with 25 men in Baltimore and 25 in Marcus Hook, and 25 or 50 in Philadelphia and Boston to hire a bus and pay for that whole works and come into New York and attend a meeting there together with the party fraction there and actually control the meeting of bona fide members with union books, because the majority of men, after they come from a trip, they won't go near the union hall anyway.

Mr. VOORHIS. Do you mean there is nothing to prevent a fellow whose home port is Baltimore from attending a meeting in New York?

Mr. INNES. Anywhere he wants to his union book is good—it is good anywhere in the country.

Mr. VOORHIS. Is that a part of the constitution?

Mr. INNES. Yes, sir; there is no such thing as a local. Wherever I drop my hat I can go in there. There is nothing to stop me.

The CHAIRMAN. Is that all?

Mr. VOORHIS. That is all as far as I am concerned.

The CHAIRMAN. The committee will recess until Wednesday morning at 10 o'clock.

(Whereupon at 2:30 p. m., the hearing was adjourned until 10 a. m., Wednesday, May 8, 1940.)

INVESTIGATION OF UN-AMERICAN PROPAGANDA ACTIVITIES IN THE UNITED STATES

WEDNESDAY, MAY 8, 1940

House of Representatives,
Committee on Un-American Activities,
Washington, D. C.

The committee met at 10 a. m., Hon. Martin Dies (chairman) presiding.

The CHAIRMAN. The Chair announces a committee composed of Mr. Voorhis, Mr. Dempsey, Mr. Casey, Mr. Thomas, and the chairman.

As I understand the first witness is Mr. Quill. Please come around, Mr. Quill. But may I say to you gentlemen first, that the committee is faced with this situation:

We have several votes on the floor of the House this morning, one vote immediately upon the convening of the House. In addition to that the agricultural appropriation bill is coming up. There are some 18 or 19 matters in the transportation bill tomorrow. We will do the best we can, but we will have to interrupt these proceedings from time to time because members of the committee will have to be on the floor of the House to vote. I am afraid we will have that all this week to contend with.

However, you gentlemen are here and we will do the best we can. It is possible we will have to go to the floor of the House and suspend proceedings here. It is going to make it rather inconvenient for everybody but I know of nothing else we can do.

All right, Mr. Quill, will you stand and be sworn?

TESTIMONY OF MICHAEL J. QUILL

The CHAIRMAN. Do you solemnly swear to tell the truth, the whole truth, and nothing but the truth, so help you God?

Mr. QUILL. I do.

The CHAIRMAN. Have a seat, Mr. Quill. You are Mr. Quill's attorney (addressing Harry Sacher)?

Mr. SACHER. Yes; I am.

The CHAIRMAN. What is your name?

Mr. SACHER. Harry Sacher.

The CHAIRMAN. You reside in New York?

Mr. SACHER. I am from New York, 342 Madison Avenue, New York City.

The CHAIRMAN. All right, Mr. Matthews, you may proceed with the examination.

Mr. MATTHEWS. Mr. Quill, will you please give your full name for the record?

Mr. QUILL. Michael J. Quill.

Mr. MATTHEWS. Where were you born?

Mr. QUILL. I was born in County Kerry, Ireland.

Mr. MATTHEWS. When?

Mr. QUILL. In 1905, September.

Mr. MATTHEWS. What was the date?

Mr. QUILL. September 18, I am told.

Mr. MATTHEWS. September 18, 1905?

Mr. QUILL. That is right.

Mr. MATTHEWS. What is your present occupation?

Mr. QUILL. President of the Transport Workers Union of America.

Mr. MATTHEWS. Will you please state briefly the crafts covered by this union?

Mr. QUILL. We are not a craft organization; we are an industrial union of employees of all passenger transportation in and around cities throughout the United States.

Mr. MATTHEWS. What occupations are included in your industrial organization?

Mr. QUILL. We take in bus drivers, taxi drivers, maintenance men, subway motormen, streetcar conductors, track structure—drainage department. All the various departments of transit.

Mr. DEMPSEY. Mr. Matthews, will you ask Mr. Quill in connection with the subway motormen, those belonging to the Brotherhood of Locomotive Engineers?

Mr. QUILL. The motormen of the B. M. T. system are not in our organization; motormen of all other systems are.

Mr. DEMPSEY. They are with the Brotherhood of Locomotive Engineers?

Mr. QUILL. That is right.

Mr. MATTHEWS. How any members are there in the Transport Workers Union?

Mr. QUILL. We have under contract in New York some 44,000 members. Throughout the United States, in and around New York, we have the remainder of around about 85 to 90.

Mr. CASEY. I did not understand how many in New York?

Mr. QUILL. 44,000 members under contract in New York City, sir.

Mr. CASEY. How many country-wide?

Mr. QUILL. Roughly 50,000 throughout the United States.

Mr. CASEY. That is the total figure, 50,000?

Mr. QUILL. The total figure would be about eighty-six to eighty-seven thousand members.

Mr. MATTHEWS. What is the affiliation of the Transport Workers Union?

Mr. QUILL. We are affiliated with the Congress for Industrial Organizations.

Mr. MATTHEWS. How long have you been president of the Transport Workers Union?

Mr. QUILL. Since 1936 in January.

Mr. MATTHEWS. January 1936?

Mr. QUILL. Yes.

Mr. MATTHEWS. Who was your predecessor as president of the Transport Workers Union?

Mr. QUILL. There was no elected predecessor ahead of me in the Transport Workers Union.

Mr. MATTHEWS. Was there a president of the Transport Workers Union?

Mr. QUILL. Yes; there was a president in name.

Mr. MATTHEWS. What was his name?

Mr. QUILL. He was your stool pigeon. You brought him in here a week ago.

The CHAIRMAN. Now, let us have an understanding about this——

Mr. QUILL. All right, sir, we will have it.

The CHAIRMAN. You are to answer the questions.

Mr. QUILL. All right.

The CHAIRMAN. Responsively. When a question is asked you answer the question.

Mr. QUILL. All right, I will do that.

The CHAIRMAN. There is no occasion for anything but a courteous and agreeable examination here if you will just answer the questions.

Mr. QUILL. I expect, Mr. Chairman, that will go both ways.

The CHAIRMAN. We will determine the questions with reference to procedure.

Mr. THOMAS. Mr. Chairman, before we proceed I think that that last statement of Mr. Quill's should be stricken from the record—that this committee had a stool pigeon. There is no place for that in the record. The committee hasn't had any stool pigeons at any time.

Mr. QUILL. Well, would you change the name to "lunatic"?

The CHAIRMAN. Now, you are not called upon to volunteer your opinions. Proceed.

Mr. THOMAS. Just a minute. I want to know whether the committee——

The CHAIRMAN. Let us take that up later. Go ahead; proceed. As far as I am concerned, I don't care whether it is in the record or out. Go ahead.

Mr. MATTHEWS. Are you a member of the governing body of the Congress of Industrial Organizations?

Mr. QUILL. Yes; I am a member of the national board for the Congress of Industrial Organizations.

Mr. MATTHEWS. When you were elected president of the Transport Workers' Union in January 1936 were you elected without opposition?

Mr. QUILL. I was; yes.

Mr. MATTHEWS. At the present time you are 34 years of age; is that correct?

Mr. QUILL. I am almost 35, in September.

Mr. MATTHEWS. Have you seen an article in the magazine Friday for March 22, 1940, Mr. Quill, about the Transport Workers' Union and yourself?

Mr. QUILL. I don't remember the article that you speak of, although I read the magazine Friday. It is possible that I have seen it.

Mr. MATTHEWS. I show you a copy of Friday magazine dated March 22, 1940, volume 1, No. 2—an article beginning on page 9 of this issue. Have you seen this article?

(Handing magazine to the witness.)

Mr. QUILL. Yes; I have seen that article. That is the one where the picture and the name of Laura Law is on the front page that you haven't investigated yet.

The CHAIRMAN. All right; can't you answer the question?

Mr. QUILL. I am answering too well.

The CHAIRMAN. You have asked the right to be heard here.

Mr. QUILL. Of course I have asked the right to be heard, and as an American I have a right to be heard.

The CHAIRMAN. You have asked for that right and you are going to show ordinary respect for this committee.

Mr. QUILL. I have respect for the committee, but I have no respect for the stool pigeons of this committee. You don't want to hear the truth.

Mr. THOMAS. He doesn't want to be heard.

Mr. QUILL. I insist on getting my side into the record.

The CHAIRMAN. There is no need to continue with this man. He came here with the purpose of trying to insult the committee. I have a speech you made in New York in which you attacked the chairman of this committee and the committee as stool pigeons. That is the respect you have for this committee. I thought you wanted to come here and give the committee the benefit of any information you might have.

Mr. QUILL. I want to be heard.

The CHAIRMAN. And it is very evident——

Mr. QUILL. You don't want to get my story in the record. You are afraid to hear the truth.

Mr. CASEY. Let us see if we can proceed with the questions and answers. I think we will get much further that way.

Mr. SACHER. May I make a suggestion, Mr. Chairman, that I think will prove helpful to the committee. I think if you will permit Mr. Quill to make a statement of his side of the case and reserve questions for cross examination perhaps you will expedite the hearing.

The CHAIRMAN. We have a rule that does not permit us to do that. We have not accorded that privilege to any other witness and we are not going to make any exception here at this time.

Now, the questions will be asked him and there is no reason why this witness cannot answer the questions without indulging in personal attacks and volunteering statements.

He would not undertake to do that nor would you permit him to do that in a court, would you?

Mr. SACHER. If Mr. Quill can get the assurance that questions or no questions he will get an adequate opportunity to present his side of the case——

The CHAIRMAN. This committee has afforded every witness—

Mr. SACHER. And I think Mr. Quill will act accordingly.

The CHAIRMAN. This committee has accorded every witness who has appeared before it the privilege of stating his side of the case. In fact we have been overindulgent. We have permitted them to say things and enjoy a latitude that they couldn't enjoy in any court in the land.

Mr. SACHER. That we are impressed with——

The CHAIRMAN. It is a simple proposition. This witness wants to be heard and if he is willing to answer the questions specifically and to show some degree of courtesy, that is one thing; but if he is going to persist in his present attitude, so far as I am concerned, as chairman of the committee, I decline to hear him. That is all there is to it. I don't care who he is or anything else. He owes respect to this committee. Whether he likes the individual members is another matter and immaterial to most of the members and immaterial so far as I am concerned. But we certainly have given him a fair proposition. If he wants to be heard, we simply ask that he answer the questions responsively and courteously; and if he has an explanation that he wants to offer in connection with any question or any answer where an explanation is in order, the Chair will grant him that opportunity.

Mr. QUILL. Provided I get that opportunity then we will go ahead.

The CHAIRMAN. You are not going to assume that attitude. You are going to answer questions propounded to you. If in the course of the examination the necessity for an explanation arises, the chairman will give you the privilege of making that explanation. The committee wants to be perfectly fair with you. Do you think we can proceed on that basis?

Mr. SACHER. I think so.

Mr. DEMPSEY. In addition to that I think if there have been any statements made here reflecting upon Mr. Quill, I think he should have the right to make a proper explanation but it must be in proper form.

The CHAIRMAN. But the hearing must proceed by questions and answers for the present.

The rule of the committee has been without exception that every witness answer questions and does not volunteer statements. That rule came into existence at the insistence of the members. The question now is whether that procedure will be followed in the case of this man or whether an exception is to be made. As far as the Chair is concerned, this man should be dealt with exactly as everyone else. All right, proceed. We will try it again.

Mr. MATTHEWS. Mr. Quill, you stated that you had seen this article in the Friday magazine on page 11. The author of the article describes you as "the first and only president of the Transport Workers' Union." Is that an incorrect statement?

Mr. QUILL. That is a true statement.

Mr. MATTHEWS. You have already testified, I believe, that Mr. Thomas Humphrey O'Shea was your predecessor as president of the Transport Workers' Union?

Mr. QUILL. As president in name only. He was never elected by the membership.

Mr. MATTHEWS. I did not ask you whether or not he was elected.

Mr. QUILL. I thought you wouldn't.

Mr. MATTHEWS. But whether or not he was president.

Mr. DEMPSEY. Now, Mr. Matthews, if he wasn't elected I think he should say so. If this other man had not been duly elected I think it is all right for the record to show that.

Mr. MATTHEWS. The other man testified that he was not elected but that he was appointed by the Communist Party as president of the union.

The CHAIRMAN. All right, let us proceed.

Mr. MATTHEWS. Again in this article on page 11, it is stated that you are 36 years of age. That is an incorrect statement?

Mr. QUILL. That is incorrect.

Mr. MATTHEWS. When did you join the Transport Workers' Union?

Mr. QUILL. In the month of May 1933. We formed the first small group. It wasn't a union at the time. We didn't even name it.

Mr. MATTHEWS. What was your position in the union prior to your assumption of the presidency?

Mr. QUILL. I was a member of the governing body of that small group called the "delegates' council."

Mr. MATTHEWS. Was that the only office you held up until the time you were elected president in January 1936?

Mr. QUILL. That was the only office; yes.

Mr. MATTHEWS. The author of the article referred to, Mr. Chairman, is Ruth McKenney, one of the editors of the New Masses.

Mr. Quill, you sent greetings to Friday magazine published in this issue, did you not?

Mr. QUILL. Yes.

Mr. MATTHEWS. Do you recall sending the greetings?

Mr. QUILL. Yes.

Mr. MATTHEWS. On page 21 there appears a greeting from Michael Quill, president of the Transport Workers' Union of New York City, and also a greeting from Rockwell Kent, of the American Artists' Congress, and Joe Curren, president of the National Maritime Union, New York City; one from Marc Blitzstein, and one or two others.

On page 22 of the magizine appears the statement——

Mr. SACHER. Just a moment, Mr Chairman. May I interrupt, Mr. Chairman, and ask the same limitations be placed around the examiner that are placed around the witness?

The CHAIRMAN. To ask questions?

Mr. SACHER. Mr. Matthews made a statement of people who were there. That is not testimony, and I request that that be stricken from the record.

The CHAIRMAN. Confine the examination to questions. All right, let us proceed.

Mr. MATTHEWS. Did you notice on page 22 of this issue of Friday magazine the following statement:

We are pretty proud of our two cartoonists, Fred Ellis and Bill Gropper.

Mr. QUILL. No; I did not notice that.

Mr. MATTHEWS. You know that Fred Ellis and Bill Gropper are very well-known Communist cartoonists, do you not?

Mr. QUILL. I don't know any of the two people that you mention.

Mr. MATTHEWS. You mean you do not know them personally or do not know them by reputation?

Mr. QUILL. I do not know them personally or by reputation. I have been too busy in the last 5 years to go snooping around looking for people.

Mr. MATTHEWS. I offer this copy of Friday magazine and ask that it be marked in evidence as an exhibit.

The CHAIRMAN. It will be received.

(The document referred to by Mr. Matthews was marked "Quill Exhibit No. 1," and made a part of the record.)

Mr. MATTHEWS. Mr. Quill, before you came to the United States were you enlisted in the I. R. A. ?

Mr. QUILL. Yes.

Mr. MATTHEWS. Did you see active service?

Mr. QUILL. I did.

Mr. MATTHEWS. Bearing arms?

Mr. QUILL. Yes.

Mr. MATTHEWS. In the I. R. A.?

Mr. QUILL. That is right.

Mr. MATTHEWS. What were the dates of your service?

Mr. QUILL. I joined the Irish Republican Army in the month of November 1920. I was transferred to the Irish Republican Army, to the active service, from the Boy Scout movement. I joined in the month of November 1920. I saw service until July 11, 1921. I fought in the civil war starting in 1922 that ended on the 28th of April 1923.

Mr. MATTHEWS. You were 15 years of age at the time of your enlistment?

Mr. QUILL. I was 15 years of age at the time; that is right.

Mr. MATTHEWS. And were you wounded in action?

Mr. QUILL. No; I was not wounded in action by a gunshot. I hurt my left hip joint in the winter of 1920 while in active service.

Mr. MATTHEWS. I show you a copy of a membership book of the Transport Workers Union. Have you ever seen one of these books?

(Handing document to witness.)

Mr. QUILL. Yes.

Mr. MATTHEWS. You have seen one of these books, Mr. Quill?

Mr. QUILL. That is right; I have.

Mr. MATTHEWS. You can identify that as an authentic copy, can you, of a membership book?

Mr. QUILL. If you will show me the front page I may be able to do that.

Mr. MATTHEWS. "Transport Workers Union Independent, New York City."

Mr. QUILL. That is right.

Mr. MATTHEWS. This book has already been marked in evidence as "O'Shea Exhibit No. 16." The book is made out in the name of M. J. McNichols and is signed "Thomas H. O'Shea, president; Austin Hogan, secretary."

Mr. SACHER. What is the date of that?

Mr. MATTHEWS. The date of the book is August 28, 1934. You know Mr. Hogan, do you, Mr. Quill?

Mr. QUILL. Austin Hogan; yes, sir.

Mr. MATTHEWS. What was his name when you first knew him?

Mr. QUILL. When I first knew him his name was Dilloughry.

Mr. MATTHEWS. Was it Austin Dilloughry or Gustave?

Mr. QUILL. Gus Dilloughry.

Mr. MATTHEWS. Gus Dilloughry?

Mr. QUILL. That is right.

Mr. MATTHEWS. D-i-l-l-o-u-g-h-r-y ?

Mr. QUILL. Yes. He changed his name the same as Mr. Thomas Parnell Feeney, et cetera, but for a different purpose.

Mr. MATTHEWS. I show you a photostatic copy of a page from the Transport Workers' Bulletin for March 1, 1936, page 4. Can you identify that as a true photostatic copy of a page of the bulletin of the Transport Workers' Union?

[Handing exhibit to the witness.]

Mr. QUILL. Yes; I am sure I can. Yes.

Mr. MATTHEWS. This has already been marked in evidence as "O'Shea Exhibit No. 17." Can you identify these as the officers of the union in 1936, Mr. Quill?

Mr. QUILL. Yes; just a moment, that is correct.

Mr. MATTHEWS Austin Hogan was general secretary of the union at that time; is that correct?

Mr. QUILL. That is right.

Mr. MATTHEWS. Is Austin Hogan still an official of the Transport Workers' Union?

Mr. QUILL. He is president of the New York local—that is the greater New York area of the Transport Workers' Union.

Mr. MATTHEWS. At this time, in March 1936, Thomas H. O'Shea was a business agent of the union. That is also correct; is it not?

(No answer.)

Mr. MATTHEWS. You have identified this. Would you like to look at it again?

Mr. QUILL. Yes; that is all right.

Mr. MATTHEWS. Was John Santo also a business agent of the union at that time?

Mr. QUILL. That is right.

Mr. MATTHEWS. Is John Santo still an official of the Transport Workers' Union?

Mr. QUILL. John Santo is secretary-treasurer of the Transport Workers' Union.

Mr. MATTHEWS. That is for the International?

Mr. QUILL. For the International; yes.

Mr. MATTHEWS. Do you know John Santo as a member of the Communist Party?

Mr. QUILL. No; I do not know John Santo as a member of the Communist Party.

Mr. MATTHEWS. Do you know him by reputation as a member of the Communist Party?

Mr. QUILL. No; I do not, except by the word of stool pigeons.

Mr. MATTHEWS. Do you know Austin Hogan, by reputation or otherwise, as a member of the Communist Party?

Mr. QUILL. I do not know Austin Hogan to be a member of the Communist Party by reputation or otherwise.

Mr. MATTHEWS. I will show you a photostatic copy of a portion of a page from the Daily Worker of June 1, 1934. Do you recall ever having seen this particular copy of the Daily Worker?

[Handing paper to the witness.]

Mr. QUILL. No; I do not.

Mr. MATTHEWS. Do you know whether or not there was a meeting for the Irish-American workers in Irving Plaza in May—May 31, 1934—at which meeting Sean Murray spoke?

Mr. CASEY. Sean Murray?

Mr. QUILL. No; I don't recall that meeting.

Mr. MATTHEWS. In the article which has already been introduced as an exhibit in the record of the hearings of this committee, O'Shea Exhibit No. 7, there appears this statement:

Sean Murray, general secretary of the Irish Communist Party, was the speaker at this gathering, and the statement to which I referred follows: "Earl Browder, secretary of the Communist Party in this country, greeted Comrade Murray and pledged solidarity with the Irish workers." Did you ever hear of that particular occasion when Mr. Browder greeted Mr. Murray?

Mr. QUILL. No; I never heard of that particular occasion.

Mr. MATTHEWS. And following in the same article there appears the statement: "Austin Hogan, active in the Irish Workers Club of this city, spoke and sang old traditional songs of Ireland. Charles Krumbein and Charles Newell also spoke."

Did Mr. Hogan ever tell you about speaking and singing at any meeting which was addressed by Earl Browder?

Mr. DEMPSEY. Now, Mr. Chairman, I don't see any objection to singing Irish songs any place you want to sing them. He has a perfect right to sing Irish songs.

Mr. QUILL. I didn't know that Mr. Hogan was a singer.

Mr. DEMPSEY. Well, most Irish are, I think.

Mr. QUILL. We have many qualities in our executive board, I see.

The CHAIRMAN. All right.

Mr. MATTHEWS. He never told you about such a meeting?

Mr. QUILL. He never told me he sang at the meeing; no.

Mr. MATTHEWS. Or where he spoke with Earl Browder and Sean Murray?

Mr. QUILL. No; he never did.

Mr. MATTHEWS. Under the auspices of the Communist Party?

Mr. QUILL. No; never mentioned it to me.

Mr. MATTHEWS. In the Daily Worker for June 11, 1934, Mr. Quill, there appears an article headed "A Trade Union in Action to Aid Thalmann," and at the end of this article appears the following statement:

The delegation has been elected by the T. U. U. C. to present this demand to the German consulate. The delegation consists of the following workers—

And among those named is J. Santo. Were you ever acquainted with the T. U. U. C. or the Trade Union Unity Council?

Mr. QUILL. I am sorry, Mr. Matthews, but I only speak good English and you are speaking Greek and German to me now. If you are interested in Thalmann, go ahead and ask the German Government about him. I know nothing about the meeting that you speak of or the article that you speak of.

Mr. MATTHEWS. I am asking you now about the Trade Union Unity Council.

Mr. QUILL. I know nothing about the Trade Union Unity Council. I have no connection with them. I don't know them.

Mr. MATTHEWS. Did you ever hear Mr. Santo speak on any of the Communist affiliations?

Mr. QUIL. I never heard Mr. Santo speak of communism or Communist affiliations.

Mr. MATTHEWS. But you do know that the Trade Union Unity Council was under the control of the Communist Party, do you not?

Mr. QUILL. I do not know anything about the Trade Union Unity Council.

Mr. MATTHEWS. The article to which reference has been made has already been introduced as O'Shea Exhibit No. 18 in the record of the hearings of this committee.

Mr. Chairman, I have here a document headed "District 2 Control Tasks Adopted at Enlarged District Committee Meeting, March 8, 1936," which is an eight-page document, setting forth the work of the Communist Party in district 2, which has been identified before this committee as the New York district.

On page 7 of this document there appears a list of the comrades who are designated as district "reps.," meaning representatives, in the 29 sections of the Communist Party in district 2.

Now, Mr. Quill, the person set down in this document as the district representative for the Communist Party for section 22, district 2, is Santo. Do you know whether or not John Santo was ever a district representative of section 22 of the Communist Party for the city of New York?

Mr. QUILL. No. To my knowledge John Santo had no connection then or now with the Communist Party, and I challenge any agency of the Federal Government to show one line of documentary evidence that any member of the Transport Workers' Union is connected with the Communist Party.

Mr. MATTHEWS. Mr. Chairman, here is documentary evidence and I ask it be offered in evidence as an exhibit.

Mr. QUILL. Mr. Chairman, before it is offered I want him to show it in writing because he does not have one line—this is a lot of stool-pigeon bunk.

Mr. MATTHEWS. All right.

Mr. QUILL. I want to get that in the record.

The CHAIRMAN. Are you going to comply in some degree of courtesy in connection with this committee or are you going to continue in such outbursts?

Mr. QUILL. I am going to defend my organization from slanderous attacks. If there is one line of documentary evidence, I want it shown.

The CHAIRMAN. All right.

Mr. CASEY. What is that document?

The CHAIRMAN. He has an attorney here. If the attorney wants to object to the document, he may do so. It has not been received in evidence yet.

(Mr. Matthews handing paper to Mr. Casey.)

Mr. MATTHEWS. Mr. Quill, on page 1 of the document in question, from which I have just taken a reference to Santo, there appears the following statement:

Especially did we make headway in the trade-union field of the concentration industries, such as Marine, where the influence of our party was extended considerably, and the rank and file movement is developing most rapidly; in Traction, where the union, built and lead by our comrades, has grown to the strength of 5,000 members, and now being in the A. F. of L., stands out as the only trade-union recognized by the workers in the entire industry.

Now, in 1936, did the Transport Workers' Union have approximately 5,000 members?

Mr. QUILL. No.

Mr. MATTHEWS. How many members did it have?

Mr. QUILL. In 1936 we didn't have dues-paying members more than 1,100.

Mr. MATTHEWS. What other classes of members did you have than dues-paying members?

Mr. QUILL. Borderline people who were sympathetic—who were waiting to get a little warmer to jump in.

Mr. MATTHEWS. Including them, how many members did you have?

Mr. QUILL. Oh, I wouldn't put it more than 1,500.

Mr. MATTHEWS. In this copy of Friday magazine, which has already been marked in evidence. the author, Ruth McKenney, states on page 10:

In 1935 Mike Quill added up 3,500 on the membership rolls.

Is that an untrue statement?

Mr. QUILL. I don't know Ruth McKenney and she is not a member of our organization and we take no responsibility for this paper.

Mr. MATTHEWS. I am asking you about the fact.

Mr. QUILL. That is not true.

Mr. MATTHEWS. That is not true?

Mr. QUILL. No. I would appreciate getting a look at this document if you don't mind.

Mr. MATTHEWS. Sure.

(Handing document to the witness.)

Mr. QUILL. I would like to see Mr. Santo's handwriting. This, Mr. Chairman. is a typewritten or mimeographed propaganda sheet. We have no connection with it. We don't know anything about it.

Mr. SACHER. May I see that a moment, please?

The CHAIRMAN. All right.

Mr. SACHER. There is a "Santo" on this paper which does not seem to be anything. There is no identification. There are a million "Santos" in the world.

Mr. THOMAS. I suggest we suspend for a few minutes until the chairman comes back.

Mr. DEMPSEY. No; go ahead.

Mr. THOMAS. Are you going to act as the chairman?

Mr. DEMPSEY. I agree with the attorney and I agree with him that does not prove that is John Santo.

Mr. MATTHEWS. None of the first names are set forth here.

Mr. DEMPSEY. I don't think you can identify John Santo as the man you are talking about.

Mr. MATTHEWS. Mr. Santo has been identified by six witnesses who have appeared before this committee as a district organizer for the Communist Party and this is only offered for substantiation by asking Mr. Quill if he is aware of this fact.

Mr. DEMPSEY. He can state whether he was aware of it but I don't see how you can identify it as the particular man. Would you tell us where the document came from?

Mr. MATTHEWS. Yes; this document is from files of the Workers Alliance of New York City and bears the signature at the upper left hand corner of S. Wiesman. It is either "W-e-i" or "W-i-e," I am not sure which, who has been identified before this committee as a member of the Communist Party and formerly head of the Unemployment Councils of New York City and later connected with the Workers Alliance. This signature has been checked with letters signed by Mr. Wiesman.

Mr. DEMPSEY. That is all right.

Mr. QUILL. May I ask a question?

Mr. Casey. One moment. I think the only possible use that document. can have with respect to Mr. Quill here is not that it should be introduced in evidence because there is no foundation laid for it being introduced in evidence. If there is some question that you wish to ask and use it for the purpose of contradicting the witness, I think that is perfectly proper to use it for that purpose, but certainly the witness cannot be charged with responsibility for a document which he denies knowing the existence of or which doesn't bear his signature or which isn't connected with him.

Mr. Matthews. I offered it only for the purpose of introducing contrary testimony in support of previous testimony before this committee and not for any other purpose.

Mr. Quill. Mr. Chairman, I would like to ask a question. I hate like anything to make all this noise here but I thought I came here to clear the name of the Transport Workers Union from lying propaganda and now he is dealing with everything but—he is not dealing with the Transport Workers Union.

Mr. Dempsey. We are going to give you that opportunity.

Mr. Quill. Thank you.

Mr. Matthews. You would prefer not to have this introduced in evidence?

Mr. Dempsey. I think we ought to wait on that.

Mr. Matthews. Then I will hold it.

Mr. Quill, I show you a photostatic copy of page 1 of the Transport Workers bulletin for July 1935. Can you identify that as a true photostatic copy (handing paper to the witness)?

Mr. Quill. Yes; that is correct.

Mr. Matthews. This has already been introduced in evidence as exhibit 14 during the testimony of Mr. Thomas Humphrey O'Shea.

On page 1 there appears a photograph. Is that a photograph of Mr. O'Shea, Mr. Quill?

Mr. Quill. That is him, all right; that is him.

Mr. Matthews. And in connection with that photograph there appears an article entitled or subheaded "President Thomas H. O'Shea speaks 5 minutes after assault by Brotherhood." and in the body of the article appears the following statement:

A few minutes before noon on Friday, June 21, Tom O'Shea, fighting president of the T. W. U., accompanied by two other union organizers, arrived at the 148th Street shop in preparation for the weekly shop meeting.

Mr. Quill, in July 1935, Mr. O'Shea was known as the "fighting president of the Transport Workers Union," was he?

Mr. Quill. Yes; there is some mistake there though, because that is the first time I ever knew O'Shea to speak 5 minutes. That fellow can go on for hours.

Mr. Matthews. But he was known as the "fighting president"?

Mr. Quill. Oh, yes; very much so.

Mr. Matthews. Of the Transport Workers Union?

Mr. Quill. Very much so.

Mr. Matthews. I show you another photostatic copy of a page of the Transport Workers bulletin for February 1936. Can you identify that as a true photostatic copy of a page of the Transport Workers bulletin (handing document to the witness)?

Mr. Quill. Well, yes that is; although I had a little more hair than I have now.

Mr. MATTHEWS. That is your picture on the first page?

Mr. QUILL. Yes; I am sure it is.

Mr. MATTHEWS. And to the left of your photograph is one of Thomas H. O'Shea and to the left of Mr. O'Shea is Mr. Machado?

Mr. QUILL. That is right. That is not the former president of Cuba. He is a worker in the transit lines—Machado.

Mr. MATTHEWS. This has already been marked in evidence as "Exhibit 15" during the testimony of Mr. O'Shea.

Mr. CASEY. Is this Mr. O'Shea still a member of the Transport Workers' Union?

Mr. QUILL. No, sir; he is not a worker of the Transport Workers' Union.

Mr. CASEY. When did his membership expire?

Mr. QUILL. In 1938. He was tried by the trial committee of the Transport Workers' Union and expelled for stool-pigeon activities and for playing ball with the bosses in the transit lines and double crossing the Transport Workers' Union.

He tried to get reinstated in the courts. The case went to many courts in New York State, and the courts refused to reinstate him.

The CHAIRMAN. Let us proceed.

Mr. MATTHEWS. I show you a photostatic copy of a page from the Transport Workers' Bulletin, page 15, for December 1939, Mr. Quill, and ask you if you can identify that as a page from the Transport Workers' Bulletin [handing paper to the witness]?

Mr. QUILL. Yes; that is.

Mr. MATTHEWS. This has already been marked in evidence as "Exhibit 6" during the testimony of Mr. O'Shea. Now, Mr. Quill, has the Transport Workers' Union ever maintained rifle ranges?

Mr. QUILL. No; the Transport Workers' Union never maintained rifle ranges.

Mr. MATTHEWS. Did it ever invite or suggest that its members take recreation at rifle ranges?

Mr. QUILL. Yes, sir; the sports division of the Transport Workers' Union is affiliated to the Trade Union Athletic League—of the Trade Union Athletic League Association, and we have invited our membership to take part in the games there. As far as the rifle range is concerned, that is a lot of bunk. The rifle range is a .22-rifle range. It wouldn't kill a cat. It is supervised by the board of education and under the supervision of the New York police department.

We suggest, sir, you ask Commissioner Valentine for a statement on that.

Mr. MATTHEWS. On page 15, which you have just identified, there appears a list of three rifle ranges: One at the One Hundred and Forty-eighth Street shop, I. R. T.; one at the surface track, B. M. T.; and one designated "Flatbush motormen." They were three of the places where rifle practice was carried on.

Mr. QUILL. They were not three of the places where rifle practice was carried on. They are large shops, and the men there are invited to come to the schools supervised by the board of education way downtown.

Mr. MATTHEWS. This designation meant that particular section of the union?

Mr. QUILL. That is correct.

Mr. MATTHEWS. Could have rifle practice?

Mr. QUILL. Yes.

Mr. MATTHEWS. On these particular days and hours stated here?

Mr. QUILL. Yes.

Mr. MATTHEWS. You will see where the apparent confusion arose in that the rifle ranges are designated below as those shops?

Mr. QUILL. Yes; that is like the fairy story of the Alaska revolution.

The CHAIRMAN. All right.

Mr. MATTHEWS. That is an incorrect heading, is it?

Mr. QUILL. Of course, it is incorrect.

Mr. MATTHEWS. There appears——

Mr. QUILL. But if you took the trouble to investigate you would find out very soon——

The CHAIRMAN. All right, how many times does the Chair have to admonish you.

Mr. QUILL. You don't have to admonish me.

The CHAIRMAN. You made the statement once.

Mr. QUILL. I want to clear our union.

The CHAIRMAN. Well, you are having an opportunity to do it.

Mr. QUILL. And I am doing it now.

The CHAIRMAN. All right.

Mr. MATTHEWS. Mr. Quill, are you a member of the American Labor Party?

Mr. QUILL. Yes.

Mr. MATTHEWS. How long have you been a member of the American Labor Party?

Mr. QUILL. I am a member of the American Labor Party since 1937, in June, I believe.

Mr. MATTHEWS. And you were a member of the New York City Council, were you not?

Mr. QUILL. Yes.

Mr. MATTHEWS. As an elected member of the American Labor Party?

Mr. QUILL. That is right.

Mr. MATTHEWS. What years did you occupy that position in the Council?

Mr. QUILL. From the first of the year 1938 to the later days of 1939—two years.

Mr. MATTHEWS. Did you stand for re-election?

Mr. QUILL. I did.

Mr. MATTHEWS. As councilman?

Mr. QUILL. That is right.

Mr. MATTHEWS. With the support or without the support of the American Labor Party?

Mr. QUILL. With the support of the membership of the American Labor Party and without the support of the official top leadership.

Mr. MATTHEWS. Will you please state briefly why the American Labor Party did not support your candidacy?

Mr. QUILL. Because I advocated the building of a real American Labor Party where the membership would have a right to speak for themselves; where they would have a right to organize the youth, the tenants, the consumers, the white collar and professional workers, the organized and unorganized workers, and the aged people; but the small group leadership of the American Labor Party wanted to keep control, and they didn't like me for that.

Mr. MATTHEWS. What was the reason assigned by the American Labor Party itself for refusing to support your candidacy?

Mr. QUILL. Oh, the same as yourself. They are digging up some phony idea about the Soviet-German pact. I don't know what it had to do with building sewers in Bronx County, New York, but they wanted me to take a stand in it and support the war policy of Chamberlain. We don't support that by anybody. We in the labor movement are against war and anybody who causes war.

Mr. MATTHEWS. Did you refuse to comply with the instructions of the American Labor Party with reference to repudiating the Soviet-Nazi pact?

Mr. QUILL. I did; and as an Irishman I refuse anytime to pat Mr. Chamberlain in the back.

Mr. MATTHEWS. This was the Soviet-Nazi pact.

Mr. QUILL. Yes; and they asked me to support the war policy of the western democracies. And if you can show any democracy in England—well, it is all right, I would not rather say it, Mr. Chairman.

Mr. MATTHEWS. Did you maintain your membership in the American Labor Party?

Mr. QUILL. Oh, yes, yes.

Mr. MATTHEWS. And are you a member of the progressive committee?

Mr. QUILL. Yes.

Mr. MATTHEWS. To rebuild the American Labor Party?

Mr. QUILL. Very much so; that is correct.

Mr. MATTHEWS. Can you identify this as a copy of a leaflet put out by the Progressive Committee of the American Labor Party (handing paper to the witness)?

Mr. QUILL. No; I can't identify it. It is quite possible that it is. They put those out by the thousands.

Mr. MATTHEWS. But you are a member of the committee?

Mr. QUILL. Oh, yes.

Mr. MATTHEWS. You have no doubts about the authenticity of it?

Mr. QUILL. I don't have any doubts, no.

Mr. MATTHEWS. I ask this be marked in evidence as an exhibit: "Progressive Committee to Rebuild the American Labor Party." This has not yet been received in evidence.

The CHAIRMAN. It may be admitted.

(The document referred to by Mr. Matthews was marked "Quill Exhibit No. 2," and made a part of the record.)

Mr. MATTHEWS. Has there been pressure of any kind put upon the members of the American Labor Party, and upon yourself in particular, Mr. Quill, to make any public statement with respect to the Soviet invasion of Finland?

Mr. QUILL. Oh, no. I don't yield to pressure. Nobody asked me to touch the Finnish situation.

Mr. MATTHEWS. I did not ask you if you would yield, but if that pressure had been brought to bear upon the members of the Party?

Mr. QUILL. No; not that I know of.

Mr. MATTHEWS. Including yourself?

Mr. QUILL. No.

Mr. MATTHEWS. Have you made any public statement with respect to the Soviet invasion of Finland?

Mr. QUILL. No; not that I can recall.

Mr. MATTHEWS. The American Labor Party has had a great deal to say about it, have they not?

Mr. QUILL. They say quite a lot of things but I don't know what they said about Finland. I had nothing to do with it. I don't put the words in their mouths.

Mr. MATTHEWS. You have not participated in the proclamation or manifestoes of the American Party on the subject?

Mr. QUILL. No. I am too busy fighting for better conditions for the transport workers so they can have an American standard of living.

Mr. THOMAS. I would like to ask a question if I may. Mr. Quill, did the Communist Party support your candidacy for the council?

Mr. QUILL. Will you repeat the question, sir?

Mr. THOMAS. Did the Communist Party support your candidacy for the city council?

Mr. QUILL. I don't know. I did not seek support from anybody but the American Labor Party.

Mr. THOMAS. I did not ask you whether you sought support. I asked you whether the Communist Party supported your candidacy or not.

Mr. QUILL. I don't know, sir. You should ask the Communist Party for that.

Mr. THOMAS. Well, you should know who supported you and who didn't.

Mr. QUILL. Well, I got some 41,000 votes. I don't really know who voted and who did.

Mr. THOMAS. The Communist Party did support your candidacy?

Mr. QUILL. If they did they had the full right to do so, but I did not seek their support. I will take support from anybody.

Mr. THOMAS. I did not ask you whether you sought support or not. I asked whether the Communist Party did support your candidacy, and you admitted they did.

Mr. QUILL. You tried, Mr. Feeney Parnell Thomas, to put it in a streamlined manner, but you did not get away with it.

Mr. MATTHEWS. Mr. Quill, has it been a consistent policy of yours that you were too busy with union matters to make public statements with reference to the invasion of one country by another?

Mr. QUILL. Oh, no, no. I am an Irishman, you know. You would not suspect it but I came from the other side, you see, and I am very much interested in what happens on the other side, because what will affect the workers of Europe will also affect the workers of America. But I believe our place in the labor movement is bettering the standards for American workers.

Mr. MATTHEWS. But you have made statements in other situations where other governments were involved in persecutions and invasion, have you not?

Mr. QUILL. That is quite possible. I am against persecution in all lands no matter for what reason.

Mr. MATTHEWS. Have you ever made any statements with respect to persecutions in the Soviet Union?

Mr. QUILL. I probably have if there are persecutions in the Soviet Union. If they are in Germany, England, or Ireland, I probably have made statements. If they are in America I have made them, and there are some persecutions here, too.

Mr. MATTHEWS. You say you have not made any statement with respect to the Soviet invasion of Finland?

Mr. QUILL. I don't remember, but if you bring it to my attention—if you show me proof of it, then we will look it over.

Mr. MATTHEWS. Did you address a meeting in Pittsburgh on November 17, 1938, under the auspices of the American League for Peace and Democracy?

Mr. QUILL. I don't remember addressing such a meeting.

Mr. MATTHEWS. In the Daily Worker for November 18, 1938, there appears a statement:

A large mass meeting to protest Nazi atrocities under the auspices of the American League for Peace and Democracy was addressed among others by Michael Quill.

Does that refresh your recollection?

Mr. QUILL. Well, I make many meetings. I just can't remember that one. But I am still out on a limb here. I cannot understand why you don't come back to the Transport Workers Union. What are you beating around the bush for?

Mr. THOMAS. Mr. Matthews asked you a very fair question.

The CHAIRMAN. Let us proceed.

Mr. MATTHEWS. Do you recall that you addressed a meeting under the auspices of the American League for Peace and Democracy in Pittsburgh at which Ben Gold was also a speaker with you?

Mr. QUILL. I don't remember but it is quite possible. I have spoken with Ben Gold many times.

Mr. MATTHEWS. And you know that Ben Gold is a member of the Communist Party, do you not?

Mr. QUILL. I am told he is.

Mr. MATTHEWS. And do you recall whether or not Lewis Merrill, president of the Office Workers' Union was a speaker on any occasions where you addressed a rally on the subject of Nazi persecutions?

Mr. QUILL. I don't remember that either.

Mr. MATTHEWS. I show you a copy or photostatic reproduction of a copy of a throw-away under the auspices of the American Labor Party, announcing a rally in New York City. Do you recall ever having seen that statement?

Mr. QUILL. No; I don't recall that.

Mr. MATTHEWS. Among the sponsors, Mr. Quill, appears your name: "Michael J. Quill."

Mr. QUILL. Yes.

Mr. MATTHEWS. Do you recall having sponsored such a mass rally?

Mr. QUILL. No; I do not recall it but the correspondence in my office in New York should show whether or not I did.

Mr. MATTHEWS. Probably you did, would you say on the basis of this?

Mr. QUILL. It is quite possible.

Mr. MATTHEWS. On the basis of the document here?

Mr. QUILL. Yes, it is quite possible.

Mr. MATTHEWS. Do you know Eugene P. Connolly?

Mr. QUILL. Yes; very well.

Mr. MATTHEWS. Is his name listed as one of the speakers representing the Transport Workers Union?

Mr. QUILL. That is right.

Mr. MATTHEWS. And Thomas O'Leary?

Mr. QUILL. He is from Ethiopia.

Mr. MATTHEWS. Is he an official in the Transport Workers Union?

Mr. QUILL. Yes, sir.

Mr. MATTHEWS. And you think that you probably did join in this protest against the Nazis on this particular occasion?

Mr. QUILL. It is quite possible that I did; yes.

Mr. MATTHEWS. But you did decline to follow the American Labor Party in the repudiation of the Soviet-Nazi pact?

Mr. QUILL. What is that?

Mr. MATTHEWS. But you did decline to follow the American Labor Party in the repudiation of the Soviet-Nazi pact?

Mr. QUILL. Yes. But you don't put the question properly. They asked me to repudiate the Soviet-Nazi pact and support the western democracies at one time.

The CHAIRMAN. Just a moment.

Mr. THOMAS. He has no right to make that statement.

The CHAIRMAN. Let him explain. As I understand you say you had refused to join in the condemnation of the Soviet-Nazi pact. Now, you want to explain that, is that right?

Mr. QUILL. What is that?

The CHAIRMAN. I say as I understand your answer, you had refused to join in the condemnation of the Soviet-Nazi pact, is that right?

Mr. QUILL. Yes. When it was brought into the political situation in New York I did.

The CHAIRMAN. Now, you want to explain why you refused?

Mr. QUILL. I refused to bring it into New York politics. I refused to bring it into my election campaign because in one resolution they wanted me to condemn the Soviet-Nazi pact and to applaud Mr. Chamberlain and the western democracies all in one resolution. It was a double-barrel proposition and I just didn't take it from them.

The CHAIRMAN. You did, as a matter of fact, condemn it, independently of Mr. Chamberlain? You were opposed to the Soviet-Nazi pact?

Mr. QUILL. I don't know anything about the Soviet-Nazi pact. I didn't happen to be in Berlin or Munich when this went on, either before or after. I insist in staying in America. If you enter into American politics—but you don't do that, Mr. Dies.

The CHAIRMAN. I am asking you. You said you wanted an opportunity to explain.

Mr. QUILL. That is what I do. I came here to explain and I don't want to be hampered.

The CHAIRMAN. And I have given you an opportunity to explain.

Mr. QUILL. Well, we will see. I have a little evidence I want to introduce.

The CHAIRMAN. The reason I asked you that question is because you said you refused to join in that resolution and the reason you refused to join in the resolution was because they coupled the condemnation of the Soviet-Nazi pact with a praise of Mr. Chamberlain. I asked you independently if you were opposed to the Soviet-Nazi pact and as I understand you are not opposed to it, is that right?

Mr. QUILL. I am not expressing ideas in European pacts. The more American people keep out of Europe the better.

Mr. THOMAS. I would like to ask Mr. Quill a question.

Mr. Quill, if this country should get into a war with Soviet Russia, and I hope that never comes about, but if it should get into a war with Soviet Russia, would you be willing to take up arms for this country against Soviet Russia?

Mr. QUILL. Sir, I am an American citizen and if this country was invaded by any country——

Mr. THOMAS. That is not the question. It is a very simple question. It is a question that we have asked many other witnesses and some of them have been very free in their answers. My question is: If this country should ever get into a war with Soviet Russia, would you be willing to take up arms in defense of this country againstySoviet Russia?

Mr. QUILL. And my answer is very direct, Mr. Chairman, or Mr. Parnell Thomas Feeney——

The CHAIRMAN. Wait just a minute.

Mr. QUILL. If this country should ever get into a war with Soviet Russia or any other country, I am first of all an American citizen and would defend this country's flag.

Mr. THOMAS. Then you would be very willing to join the Army of this country against Soviet Russia even though we had to go over there to fight on their soil?

Mr. QUILL. I am opposed to going overseas and leaving America. And I believe that this is what is being done here under your leadership, Mr. Chairman. You are trying to bring about a war hysteria to stampede the American people into war.

The CHAIRMAN. I think the witness should be held in contempt for that statement.

Mr. QUILL. You are not frightening me. You can put me in jail but the cause will go on. You are not frightening me.

Mr. VOORHIS. Well, Mr. Quill——

Mr. THOMAS. Let us go into executive session.

Mr. VOORHIS. Just a minute. Mr. Quill, you answered the question and made your statement. Now, do you want to insist upon making that additional statement about the committee?

Mr. QUILL. What is that?

Mr. VOORHIS. What good is it going to do you? I say, do you insist upon making that additional statement about the committee?

Mr. QUILL. Mr. Chairman, I came here with evidence to clear my union, and I want to produce it, and the chairman is not giving me a chance to do it.

Mr. VOORHIS. That is a different matter. We are going to get to that.

Mr. QUILL. Because you are afraid to hear the truth from me. I want to clear my union. I brought evidence here of sabotage in the New York subways and I want to present it here.

The CHAIRMAN. So far as the Chair is concerned, we are not going to proceed any further. This witness has deliberately come here for the purpose of insulting this committee. You are not going to get by with that insofar as this Chair is concerned. You have been treated courteously and you have been warned. I think the committee should determine whether it will hear this witness.

Mr. QUILL. I want to be heard and you are afraid to hear the truth.

The CHAIRMAN. You will be in order.

Mr. VOORHIS. Mr. Quill, I think perhaps all the members of the committee—I know I speak for myself when I say this, that I am anxious to hear you on these points, but you are making it difficult because of the fact that it is not an explanation of your answer to a question, but you are gratuitously adding things about the work of the committee that I don't think have anything to do with either the defense of the Transport Workers Union or the answers to the question. It will make it that much easier if you don't do that.

The CHAIRMAN. The question is now whether the committee will go into executive session and determine what we shall do about this matter.

Mr. QUILL. I want to get this in the record.

The CHAIRMAN. The committee is going into executive session.

Mr. QUILL. You are afraid to hear the defense of our union. Our union is not controlled by the Communist Party and I am going to put this in the record.

The CHAIRMAN. You are going to have some respect for a congressional committee. You are not going to come here and insult it.

Mr. QUILL. You are afraid to hear the truth, but the labor movement will live.

The CHAIRMAN. Clear the room.

(Whereupon, at 11:20 a. m., the hearing room was cleared and the committee went into executive session, to meet at 2 p. m., the same day.)

AFTER RECESS

The CHAIRMAN. The committee will come to order.

Mr. SACHER. Mr. Chairman, Mr. Quill would like to be accorded the opportunity to present his side of the case in regard to the testimony of Thomas H. O'Shea.

The CHAIRMAN. Well, the Chair will state that upon the request of Mr. Quill, he was accorded an opportunity to appear before this committee with the understanding that he was to answer questions.

The committee wished to afford him full and complete opportunity to answer any and all charges that have been made before this committee with respect to Mr. Quill or the union that he represents. Notwithstanding that fact and the fact that it was made known to Mr. Quill that it was the established policy of this committee to conduct its investigations by questions and answers, and to require witnesses to be responsive in their answers to the questions propounded, Mr. Quill refused to comply with that policy of the committee, and although repeatedly admonished to do so, persisted in his refusal to comply with the rules of this committee. In view of that fact this committee is not going to continue Mr. Quill, or as a matter of fact to hear any witness who requests to be heard unless such witness is willing to come here courteously and answer questions responsively and to comply with the rules of the committee.

Now, as to whether or not Mr. Quill is willing to comply with such rules, willing to be responsive in his answers and where an explanation is pertinent or material, in fairness to the witness or any witness he should be allowed to make such explanation.

· If Mr. Quill is not willing to proceed on that basis, or any other witness, then this committee declines to afford them an opportunity to appear before it.

I don't believe that any one can question the fairness of that character of procedure, and I want to make it plain that that applies to every witness who appears before the committee.

Mr. Rathborne has been notified that he would be heard at 2 o'clock and he will be. Your request will be referred to the committee for decision.

· Do I understand, speaking for Mr. Quill, you give that assurance to the committee that in his conduct throughout the rest of his examination he will be responsive?

Mr. SACHER. I do.

The CHAIRMAN. And comply with the rules as I have outlined the rules in our procedure?

Mr. SACHER. I do give you that assurance.

The CHAIRMAN. All right. The other members of the committee are not here and we will proceed for the time being with Mr. Rathborne.

The chairman will have to designate a subcommittee composed of the chairman and the gentleman from New Jersey, Mr. Thomas, and the gentleman from California, Mr. Voorhis, until the other members of the committee appear.

Mr. Rathborne, will you stand and be sworn?

TESTIMONY OF MERVYN RATHBORNE

The CHAIRMAN. Do you solemnly swear to tell the truth, the whole truth, and nothing but the truth, so help you God?

Mr. RATHBORNE. I do.

The CHAIRMAN. Let the record show Congressman Vito Marcantonio is appearing as counsel for the witness.

May I make this statement. In the course of the questions that will be asked you, Mr. Rathborne, you will have an opportunity to deny, as will be the procedure with respect to every witness,· every charge that has been made against you. We cannot permit witnesses to read statements or make general statements.

The committee established that policy unanimously sometime ago and we have had to refuse witnesses the opportunity to do so. However, in the course of the examination, questions will be framed that will enable you to enter a denial of any charge that you see fit to deny, and make any appropriate or material explanation where a direct question would not afford you such an opportunity.

Mr. THOMAS. Mr. Chairman, may I interject here for a moment? I understand that Mr. Rathborne has already sent a statement to the press in connection with his appearance here today. I am wondering if Mr. Matthews, who is going to ask the questions, has a copy of the statement. Do you have such a copy, Mr. Matthews?

Mr. MATTHEWS. I haven't seen it.

The CHAIRMAN. As far as the Chair is concerned, he is not interested in what any witness may say with respect to his views in any other place. But in the course of this hearing that is an entirely different matter. What any witness may think or say in any public forum, or to the press, or otherwise, is a matter for the witness himself, and this chair is not concerned with it.

Mr. THOMAS. I agree with that, but at the same time——

The CHAIRMAN. I am only speaking now with reference to what goes on in the course of the investigation.

Mr. THOMAS. At the same time there may be a couple of questions Mr. Matthews might want to ask in regard to the statement.

Mr. MARCANTONIO. May I interpose an objection at this point to questioning this witness with regard to the statement he issued to the press. I don't think that comes within the purview of this investigation, and I don't see what it has to do with it.

The CHAIRMAN. We haven't read the statement.

Mr. MARCANTONIO. Although we haven't any objection to the committee having a copy of the statement. If you want it we will offer it for the record. It is extraneous.

The CHAIRMAN. Let us proceed.

Mr. MATTHEWS. Will you please state your full name for the record, Mr. Rathborne?

Mr. RATHBORNE. My name is Mervyn Rathborne.

Mr. MATTHEWS. What is your address?

Mr. RATHBORNE. 10 Bridge Street, New York City.

Mr. MATTHEWS. What is your present occupation?

Mr. RATHBORNE. At the present time I am president of the American Communications Association, a labor organization affiliated with the Congress of Industrial Organizations.

Mr. MATTHEWS. Will you please describe briefly the extent of that union with respect to the crafts or occupations covered by it?

Mr. RATHBORNE. The American Communications Association is an industrial unit which embraces in its membership employees of all communication companies such as telegraph, radio, and telephone companies which operate in the continental United States, United States possessions, and the Dominion of Canada.

Mr. MATTHEWS. How many members are there in the American Communications Association?

Mr. RATHBORNE. At the present time 20,000, approximately.

Mr. MATTHEWS. When was the union first organized?

Mr. RATHBORNE. The union was first organized in August of 1931 and was known at that time as the American Radio Telegraphers' Association.

Mr. MATTHEWS. Is there any local or section of the American Communications Association still known as the American Radio and Telegraphers Association?

Mr. RATHBORNE. No; there is not.

Mr. MATTHEWS. Mr. Rathborne, previous witnesses before this committee have made statements which involved you. I should like to read those statements or at least to give the purport of them where they are lengthy and ask for your comment on them.

Mr. MARCANTONIO. Just a moment. May I interject here and say that the witness would like to answer those statements by statements. In other words, if the interrogator refers to a few statements, then I submit that the witness should be given an opportunity to take up every statement—charge—that has been made by the previous witnesses so he can have an opportunity to answer it.

The CHAIRMAN. Let us go along. You are certainly not interested in some immaterial thing.

Mr. MARCANTONIO. Nothing immaterial. But my idea is if he doesn't cover all the charges the witness should be given an opportunity to answer whatever charges have not been covered.

The CHAIRMAN. We will develop that all right.

Mr. MATTHEWS. In August of 1939 Mr. John P. Frey appeared before this committee and on page 104 of the printed hearings of this committee there appears the following statement made by Mr. Frey:

With regard to American Communications Association, a few days ago Richard D. Hallett, chairman of the Washington local of the American Communications Association, resigned because he declared that the organization has too much of a tie-up with the Communist Party. The president of this organization is Mervyn Rathborne, a Communist.

He goes on to say: "There has been considerable argument in regard to the status of this man, but so much information has come in in the past 6 months in regard to his communistic connections that one cannot be in doubt as to how he stands."

That is the end of the statement that refers to you.

Mr. RATHBORNE. Well, the comment that I have to make on it is that it is not a true statement and I see nothing in the statement made by Mr. Frey that is any—conclusive evidence. It is just merely a general opinion on his part that that may be the case and Mr. Frey was incorrect in his assumption.

Mr. MATTHEWS. In respect to the matter of stating that you were a Communist?

Mr. RATHBORNE. That is correct; yes.

Mr. MARCANTONIO. Just a moment. I wish the witness would be given an opportunity to say in what respect that statement is incorrect. You are limiting him to just one respect. There are various elements.

Mr. MATTHEWS. I am going to ask some more questions about the statement.

Mr. MARCANTONIO. I think we should have it at this time.

The CHAIRMAN. We will give you an opportunity to answer.

Mr. MATTHEWS. I am going to give him that opportunity now.

Mr. Frey also stated that Richard D. Hallett, chairman of the Washington local of the American Communications Association, resigned because he declared that the organization has "too much of a tie-up with the Communist Party."

Was Mr. Hallett at one time chairman of the Washington local of the American Communications Association?

Mr. RATHBORNE. Yes, sir; he was.

Mr. MATTHEWS. Did he resign?

Mr. RATHBORNE. Yes; he did.

Mr. MATTHEWS. From the union?

Mr. RATHBORNE. He did.

Mr. MATTHEWS. As well as from the chairmanship of the local?

Mr. RATHBORNE. Yes.

Mr. MATTHEWS. Did he state, as his reason for resigning, that there was "too much of a tie-up between the American Communications Association and the Communist Party"?

Mr. RATHBORNE. I never heard directly what Mr. Hallett's reasons were. I was merely advised that he had resigned from the chairmanship of the Washington local and what his specific reasons were—his specific reasons were not communicated to me.

Mr. MATTHEWS. Assuming that this was his own stated reason, do you wish to comment upon the statement of Mr. Frey?

Mr. RATHBORNE. Well, the statement I would like to make in that connection, if Mr. Hallett did resign and stated—did resign for those reasons, I don't know why he gave that particular reason as wanting to resign with the exception of the fact that Mr. Hallett later on went over to a rival organization and helped them organize and it was my opinion at the time that Mr. Hallett was interested in establishing another dual organization under a different affiliation in Washington, D. C.

Mr. MATTHEWS. Was that dual union of which you speak, or dual organization, the Commercial Telegraphers Association?

Mr. RATHBORNE. Yes, sir.

Mr. MATTHEWS. Affiliated with the American Federation of Labor?

Mr. RATHBORNE. Yes, sir.

Mr. MATTHEWS. Was it in existence prior to the organization of the American Communications Association?

Mr. RATHBORNE. To my knowledge it was not in existence in Washington, D. C. It was in existence in other places.

Mr. MATTHEWS. That is, it had been established elsewhere?

Mr. RATHBORNE. That is right.

Mr. MATTHEWS. Prior to the American Communications Association?

Mr. RATHBORNE. Yes.

Mr. MATTHEWS. Did the American Communications Association ever establish a local in any place where the Commercial Telegraphers Association had already been in existence?

Mr. RATHBORNE. Not until 1937.

Mr. MATTHEWS. It did at that time?

Mr. RATHBORNE. After 1937 it did; yes.

Mr. MATTHEWS. In other words, what you refer to as a "dual organization" in Washington then would have made the American Communications Association a dual organization in these other places, is that correct?

Mr. RATHBORNE. Yes. I mean—I suppose that the American Federation of Labor has the same reasons for calling us a "dual organization" as we have for calling them.

Mr. MATTHEWS. Is there any other statement you wish to make with reference to this particular passage which I have read from Mr. Frey's testimony?

The CHAIRMAN. Well, he has answered it pretty fully. You have a great many other things to cover.

Mr. MARCANTONIO. About his being a Communist.

The CHAIRMAN. He denied that. He said it was incorrect.

Mr. RATHBORNE. I would like to emphasize the fact from Mr. Frey's own testimony he says that he believes. There is no concrete evidence there. It is merely an opinion that he stated on the basis of information that he had received and he says that some of the information is not to the effect that—that some of the explanation is not too reliable.

Mr. MATTHEWS. Now, on page 134 of the hearings of this committee, there is further testimony given by Mr. John P. Frey which reproduces an open letter addressed to Mr. Mervyn Rathborne, president of the American Communications Association, C. I. O., New York, N. Y., and that communication was stated to be from Mr. Hallett. The communication is not dated here. Do you recall having received such a communication from Mr. Hallett—an open letter?

Mr. RATHBORNE. No, sir.

Mr. MATTHEWS. That was given to you and the press?

Mr. RATHBORNE. No. sir; I do not. I do not recall seeing a letter.. I recall reading some comment in the press with respect to this incident but to my knowledge I never received the letter.

Mr. MATTHEWS. First, I will read the introductive paragraph in Mr. Frey's own language and then read from the letter:

The American Communications Association is not made up of a Communist membership, although they have Communist members. The trouble is that the control, that is, of ship radio, has come under the Communist group.

In this city there is a man named Hallett, Richard D. Hallett. When he discovered what this organization was, he resigned; and I want to put in the record Mr. Hallett's letter of resignation. which is addressed to Mr. Rathborne, the president of the association. whom I am informed, so far as the evidence indicates. outside of the Communist records themselves, is a member of the party.

When Mr. Hallett gave this letter to the press, the press did not reproduce all of it, and I want to put all of it into this record. I want the committee to have the full letter. It reads:

"DEAR SIR: Consider this my resignation, not only as chairman but also as member of the American Communications Association, effective immediately.

"Since I have been active in the interest of American Communications Association since the very beginning of its organizing campaign in Washington, D. C., and since I was the second Western Union man in the entire country to join American Communications Association. this action calls for some explanation.

"When I signed my application for membership in American Communications Association on April 23, 1937. I bargained for unionism and unionism only. I definitely did not bargain to aid or comfort or to support in any way, financially or otherwise. communism or any communistic agencies. However, during the 14 months of my chairmanship of Local 35–b, American Communications Association, I have not only received communications from numerous pseudo-patriotic organizations asking support, but have been strongly urged by numerous representatives of national office of American Communications Association to support these organizations. These aforementioned representatives of American Communications Association include Messrs. John Austin, William Pomerance, Ted Zittel, Joseph Kehoe, and Dan Driesen.

"The 'pseudo-patriotic organizations' previously referred to include the American League for Peace and Democracy. formerly known as the American League Against War and Fascism, which organization, by its very name, which conspicuously admits communism, appears to be of necessity, communistic. Moreover. among the national officers of this organization, are prominently mentioned the names of Earl Browder, Presidential candidate of the Communist Party of America, and Clarence Hathaway, editor of the Daily Worker, official organ of the Communist Party of America.

"Another organization with which we are urged to closely cooperate is the Workers Alliance of America, whose president and secretary are David Lasser and Herbert Benjamin, both well-known Communists.

"Yet another group with which we are urged to be friendly, is the International Labor Defense, the president of which is Vito Marcantonio, former Democratic t?) Congressman from New York, who has contributed much material to the Daily Worker. and who is the author of Labor's Martyrs, a booklet which undertakes to extol the virtues of the notorious Sacco and Vanzetti. Communists, who were executed some years ago. The introduction to Labor's Martyrs is. written by William Z Foster, former Communist Party candidate for President of the United States.

"Still other organizations, which I place in the same category as the aforementioned Communist-lead groups include the Washington Friends of the Spanish Democracy, the New Theatre Group, and others, all of which would have us support what they quaintly choose to call 'Spanish Democracy,' as exemplified by Loyalist Spain.

"Any informed person knows full well that the current war in Spain is nothing more or less than a struggle between communism and fascism and I consider communism much the greater of the two evils.

"Communism, as you are probably well aware, Mr. Rathborne, is built around the program of Karl Marx, its founder, which program sets forth as one of its major objectives, government control of communications, which corresponds to the letter with the ultimate program of American Communication's Association; and in view of the above-mentioned communistic tendencies of American Communications Association, I hardly feel that it can be termed a 'mere coincidence.'

"It is incorrect to assume that I have only recently become aware of these tendencies toward communism on the part of American Communications Association. I have opposed them from the very inception of the organizing campaign, and have on numerous occasions been taken to task by American Communications Association organizers for doing so.

"One particular occasion which comes to mind in connection with my being taken to task because of my anticommunistic attitude is that occasion some months ago, when I stayed until 5 o'clock in the morning, in the room in the Ambassador Hotel, of Mr. Ted Zittel, former editor and whistle blower of the American Communications Association, editor of the Peoples Press, arguing on the subject of communism—he in favor of it, and I myself against it. During the discussion he warmly defended every communistic point brought up by me, but concluded the discussion by advising me that I was not to think of him as a Communist, but only as a 'student' of Communism. My own opinion is that he is not only a 'student' but a 'graduate cum laude' of communism, and I wish to state that although I cannot agree with any Communist, I have infinitely greater respect for a real honest to goodness arm-waving capitalist-hating Communist who proudly admits his identity, than I can possibly maintain for a left-wing radical, who to all intents and purposes, is a Communist, but who, because of his ulterior motives doesn't dare to sail under his true colors.

"As I have previously stated, I have known these things for some time, but have not disclosed them, simply because I felt that if I ignored the attempts of the aforementioned organizations to sow the seeds of radicalism in Local 35–B, and struck strictly to unionism, along really democratic lines, then we, in Local 35–B, could make progress and radicalism could not take root.

"However, I have found that my beliefs with regard to holding radicalism in check were erroneous, as witness the case of Mr. C. W. Gravely, financial secretary of Local 35–B, who has been the object of the rabble-rousing abilities of Mr. Dan Driesen, legislative representatives of American Communications Association, to such an extent that I now believe him to be a fanatic on the subject of unionism and the American Communications Association brand.

"Mr. Gravely has for months been conducting a whispering campaign within Local 35–B against me, and making statements inspired by Mr. Driesen to the effect that I am too conservative to be chairman of the American Communications Association, Local 35–B, and has opposed me and my policies to such an extent that I am convinced he tried to 'fix' our recent election of delegates to the American Communications Association convention which will open in New York, July 18, 1938. The circumstances are as follows:

"After we decided to hold the election at a meeting to be held on June 24, Mr. Gravely, prior to the meeting, actively campaigned for another member to run against me, for the delegateship. I do not quarrel over his right to campaign for the election of another member whom he sees fit to support, but I most certainly do question his tactics, in canvassing the membership as to how they intended voting, and, having discovered that many members intended to vote for me, in opposition to his wishes, seeing to it that these members did not receive a notice advising them when and where the meeting was to be held, thereby denying them their right to vote.

"It is significant to note, that of our entire membership only eight people attended the meeting. I was defeated in the election by a vote of 5 to 3. When the results of the election became known, many of the members who had not been notified of the meeting registered complaints, both verbal and written.

"Being at a loss as to what procedure to follow in ordering a new election held. I wrote to Mr. Dan Driesen, explaining the situation in full.

"His answer of July 5, condones Mr. Gravely's tactics, and describes them as 'an old American custom.' Mr. Driesen's letter also states, and I quote him verbatim. 'According to these same (national office) records, you have not paid your dues for November, December, January, February, March, May, and June. You have only paid dues for the month of April of this year. Your own standing therefore is deficient and I do not see how, under these circumstances you could have been a candidate. The rules governing this are very strict and the credentials committee at the convention certainly would not have seated you as an accredited delegate.'

"One quick glance at my union card reveals that I am in good standing, and that I have actually paid up six of the seven dollars which national office records show that I still owe. For your information, should you desire to check this statement, my membership card for 1937 shows me as paid up for November and December, and carries stamps Numbers 3358 and 3359 for these months. My 1938 card shows me as paid up for January, February, March, and April, and carries stamp Numbers 7065, 7860, 9824, and 9854.

"Briefly then, Mr. Gravely's tactics and Mr. Driesen's letter were the final straws that broke the camel's back, and I feel that I can no longer continue either as local chairman or member of the American Communications Association, hence my action."

Do you recall now having received that communication, Mr. Rathborne?

Mr. RATHBORNE. No; I don't recall having received it. The only thing I recall is reading parts of it in the press.

Mr. MARCANTONIO. May I ask, Mr. Chairman, was it testified by anybody before this committee that that letter was sent to Mr. Rathborne?

The CHAIRMAN. Yes.

Mr. MARCANTONIO. Is that what the records show?

Mr. MATTHEWS. That is correct.

The CHAIRMAN. Do you have any comment to make on the letter independent of whether it reached you or not, but on the contents of the letter?

Mr. RATHBORNE. I am not denying the letter may have been sent or may not have reached my office because I am out of town quite a bit and correspondence quite frequently is answered by my secretary and I don't see it, but as far as the letter itself is concerned it raises a question of control of our organization and with the permission of the chairman I would like to explain how our organization is controlled so that the allegations made in this letter can be refuted.

Mr. CASEY. You say the allegations with respect to the control of your organization by Communists as set forth in the letter is true or false?

Mr. RATHBORNE. I say it is false.

Mr. CASEY. I think he ought to have an opportunity of explaining that.

Mr. RATHBORNE. I would like to read a brief excerpt from the constitution of our union. Article 6, section 1, states:

The supreme authority of the international union shall be in the general membership which from time to time through referenda and convention may delegate such powers as it deems proper, necessary, and desirable, to the international executive board, the president, or any other officers or officer of the international union.

In practice that is the way our organization functions and in the first place all of the officers are nominated by petition signed by the members. For example any member of our union who has been a member for 2 years and obtains 250 signatures on a petition may have his name put on the ballot to run for president. And the requirements for other officers are 1 year's service and 100 signatures. The officers are elected by direct secret referendum of the membership. The international officers of the union, of which there are 9, constitutes the international executive board which sets the policies of the union between conventions.

The conventions are attended by delegates who are elected by secret referendum vote of the members of the various local unions. These delegates gather together in a convention and the policies and program of the union are set forth and determined at these international conventions of ours. And it is the people directly elected by our 20,000 members who gather together in conference, who determine the policies of our organization, and who run the union and who elect the officers. And with that kind of a set-up it is obvious to any fair-thinking person that any small group could not be running the union because it is very easy for the members of the union to recall the officers if they violate the constitution or if they go contrary to the policies and programs set down by our international conventions. And the major decisions of the convention are always submitted to referendum vote for approval by the membership before they become effective.

So, in connection with the control of our organization, it is controlled by the membership acting through their directly elected representatives, either by conventions or on our international executive board and the membership of our union chooses its officers—their officers.

That is all I have to say with respect to the control of the organization.

To me, Mr. Hallett appears to be a rather disgruntled person, and I think that is borne out by the fact that at the present time Mr. Hallett is acting as an organizer for the American Federation of Labor in the Commercial Telegraphers Union, an organization with which we are—we have—controversies from time to time. And as far as Mr. Hallett is concerned, I cannot see any real basis to controvert the statements I have made here with respect to how our organization is controlled or run.

Mr. MATTHEWS. Now, as far as the main part of it, namely, that the American Communications Association has been working too closely with the Communists, you stated that that was untrue. May I ask you a few questions with respect to separate items? Do you know whether or not the allegation that members of the American Communications Association had been urged to cooperate with the American League for Peace and Democracy is true?

Mr. RATHBORNE. I know that we had a convention in New York City in 1938, and a representative of the American League for Peace and Democracy was there—requested the right to appear before the convention delegates. The question was brought to a vote, and the delegates voted to let him appear and he spoke and presented his point of view to the convention.

Subsequently, the representatives from other organizations were permitted to appear in the same manner on the basis that our organization is a democratic organization, and we believe in letting anybody have the right to appear before a representative group of our members and say what he has in his mind, whether we agree with him or not.

Mr. MATTHEWS. Did you, Mr. Rathborne, at any time ever have any official connection with the American League for Peace and Democracy?

Mr. RATHBORNE. No; I had no official connection with them; no.

Mr. MATTHEWS. Now, with respect to the allegation that the members of the American Communications Association had been urged to cooperate closely with the Workers Alliance, do you have any information as to whether or not that was true?

Mr. RATHBORNE. Well, the same thing applies in that case as in the case of the American League for Peace and Democracy. At various times representatives of the Workers Alliance have appeared before representative groups and members of our union and spoken and presented their point of view.

Mr. MATTHEWS. And was that also true of the International Labor Defense?

Mr. RATHBORNE. Yes. We received several communications from Mr. Marcantonio requesting support for the International Labor Defense on various issues.

Mr. MATTHEWS. And you have responded favorably to those requests?

Mr. RATHBORNE. In some cases, yes; and other cases, no.

Mr. MATTHEWS. And what about the Washington Friends of the Spanish Democracy? Do you know whether or not there was any cooperation with that group?

Mr. RATHBORNE. I am not familiar with what that organization is at all.

Mr. MATTHEWS. The New Theater Group—did you know about that?

Mr. RATHBORNE. No; I don't.

Mr. MATTHEWS. Do you know whether or not Mr. Ted Zitell is or was a Communist?

Mr. RATHBORNE. I don't know, but I believe not.

Mr. MATTHEWS. In the latter part of 1938 there appeared before this committee as a witness one John E. Ferguson, of Portland, Oreg. A portion of his testimony appears on page 2922 of the hearings of this committee. I read you the statement which has to do with you, Mr. Rathborne:

Mr. STARNES. Who was Lawrence Rose?

Mr. FERGUSON. Lawrence Rose at the time I knew him was the editor of the Western Worker.

Mr. STARNES. Is he a Communist?

Mr. FERGUSON. He is.

Mr. STARNES. Did you ever sit in a meeting with Lawrence Rose?

Mr. FERGUSON. I did.

Mr. STARNES. Who sat in the meeting with you?

Mr. FERGUSON. There are quite a number, Mr. Chairman. If you care for the names, I could recall most of them.

Mr. STARNES. Name some of them.

Mr. FERGUSON. There was Aubrey Grossman, an attorney.

Mr. STARNES. Is that the same Grossman you mentioned a while ago?

Mr. FERGUSON. No, sir. The other one was Gross. This is Aubrey Grossman, an attorney who defended the accused in the *King-Ramsey-Conner case.* There was Mervyn Rathborne, secretary of the American Radio Telegraphists Association.

Do you know Mr. Ferguson, Mr. Rathborne?

Mr. RATHBORNE. I believe, if that is the same person, he was at one time connected with the Marine Firemen's Union on the Pacific coast.

Mr. MATTHEWS. I think he is so identified in this record in other places. Did you ever meet him personally?

Mr. RATHBORNE. I have met with Mr. Ferguson or I have been at meetings at which Mr. Ferguson was present—meetings of the Maritime Federation of the Pacific Coast, and I believe Mr. Ferguson was a representative of the Marine Firemen's Union at several of those meetings.

Mr. MATTHEWS. He states here that he was business agent for the Pacific coast for the Marine Firemen, Oilers & Water Tenders & Wipers Association.

Mr. RATHBORNE. That would be the same one.

Mr. MATTHEWS. You say you have attended meetings with Mr. Ferguson?

Mr. RATHBORNE. Yes. I have been at meetings of various bodies of the Maritime Federation of the Pacific when Mr. Ferguson was present representing the Marine Firemen's Union.

Mr. MATTHEWS. Did you ever sit in any meetings that could be called a Communist Party meeting with Mr. Ferguson?

Mr. RATHBORNE. No. The only meetings I sat with Mr. Ferguson in were meetings of the district council of the Maritime Federation at San Francisco, meetings of the executive committee of that council or meetings of the coastwise council of the federation.

Mr. MATTHEWS. Did you of your own knowledge know whether Mr. Ferguson himself was a member of the Communist Party?

Mr. RATHBORNE. I knew very little about Mr. Ferguson. I met him only casually at these meetings, so obviously I did not know any connection he may have had.

Mr. MATTHEWS. Did you know Aubrey Grossman?

Mr. RATHBORNE. Yes. I know Aubrey Grossman.

Mr. MATTHEWS. Did you know him as a Communist?

Mr. RATHBORNE. No, sir.

Mr. MATTHEWS. Do you have any other statement to make with respect to this statement of Mr. Ferguson?

Mr. RATHBORNE. The only additional statement I have to make is that I have never heard or never met the other gentleman referred to in there—what was his name again?

Mr. MATTHEWS. Gross.

Mr. RATHBORNE. No; that wasn't it.

Mr. MATTHEWS. Lawrence Rose?

Mr. RATHBORNE. Lawrence Rose. I have never heard of him or never met him.

Mr. MATTHEWS. Others mentioned in this connection are Henry Schmidt. Do you know Henry Schmidt?

Mr. RATHBORNE. Yes, sir; I know Henry Schmidt. He was the president of the Longshoremen's Union in San Francisco.

Mr. MATTHEWS. And Walter Stack?

Mr. RATHBORNE. Yes; I know Walter Stack.

Mr. MATTHEWS. And Al Quittenton?

Mr. RATHBORNE. I think he was connected with the Sailor's Union of the Pacific. I am not sure.

Mr. MATTHEWS. He is designated here as the secretary of the Sailors' Union of the Pacific. Crabtree of the Masters, Mates & Pilots Union?

Mr. RATHBORNE. No; I never met him that I recall.

Mr. MATTHEWS. And William Sondheim?

Mr. RATHBORNE. I don't know him.

The CHAIRMAN. Did you answer that question or did you just shake your head?

Mr. RATHBORNE. I said, "I don't know him," Mr. Chairman.

Mr. MATTHEWS. On page 2930 in a further portion of the testimony of Mr. Ferguson there appears the following:

Mr. STARNES. Do you know any other Communists holding key positions or top positions in the labor movement on the Pacific coast other than Harry Bridges?

Mr. FERGUSON. Yes, sir; I do.

Mr. STARNES. Who are they?

Mr. FERGUSON. Mervyn Rathborne.

Mr. STARNES. Spell that name for us, Mr. Ferguson?

Mr. FERGUSON (spelling the name). He is now president of the ARTA. That is the American Radio Telegraphists Association affiliated with the Congress for Industrial Organizations.

Do you wish to make a comment on that statement?

Mr. RATHBORNE. Well, the same comment I made before, that I am not a Communist and that this is a statement—a gratuitous statement by Mr. Ferguson of his opinion and it is an incorrect opinion.

The CHAIRMAN. Well, that is not quite accurate. Mr. Ferguson said that he sat in a fraction meeting of the Communist Party with you. That is not an opinion insofar as he is concerned. It may not be true, but it is not an opinion. He says that he sat in a fraction meeting of the Communist Party with you. The answer is, as I understand it, that is not true.

Mr. RATHBORNE. No. The only meetings I sat with Mr. Ferguson were meetings of the official union body.

The CHAIRMAN. And you deny his statement?

Mr. RATHBORNE. That is right.

Mr. THOMAS. Mr. Chairman, I would like to ask a question.

Mr. MARCANTONIO. I wish he would be permitted to complete the answer.

The CHAIRMAN. Go ahead.

Mr. RATHBORNE. The only meetings I sat in with Mr. Ferguson were meetings of the official union body of the Maritime Union on the Pacific coast known as the Maritime Federation of the Pacific.

The CHAIRMAN. That wouldn't include any meetings of Communist groups?

Mr. RATHBORNE. No. It is a union group.

Mr. THOMAS. Mr. Rathborne, have you ever at any time sat in on any Communist fraction meetings?

Mr. RATHBORNE. No, sir.

Mr. CASEY. Now, that last question has not been answered. I wish Mr. Matthews would repeat it. It was in connection with Mr. Bridges and Mr. Rathborne. That wasn't sitting in at a meeting. He asked if he knew some labor leaders on the Pacific coast that were Communists besides Mr. Bridges, as I understand, and he said "Yes, he did; Mr. Rathborne."

Mr. MATTHEWS. But he named others because it was——

Mr. CASEY. I would like to get the witness' answer to that.

The CHAIRMAN. I thought he answered it. He said he wasn't a Communist. Didn't you?

Mr. RATHBORNE. Yes, sir.

The CHAIRMAN. And you never have been a member of the Communist Party?

Mr. RATHBORNE. No, sir.

The CHAIRMAN. Never have been affiliated in any respect with the Communist Party, have you?

Mr. RATHBORNE. No, sir; I haven't.

Mr. CASEY. Was that what you had in mind when you said it was his opinion and his opinion was incorrect?

Mr. RATHBORNE. I say that was Mr. Ferguson's opinion and if that is his opinion, it is an incorrect opinion.

The CHAIRMAN. A fraction meeting was not a question of opinion. The witness testified he sat in a fraction meeting.

Mr. VOORHIS. Did Mr. Ferguson so testify?

Mr. MATTHEWS. There were two statements. The first was at a meeting and the second does not state the connection in which he claims to know about Mr. Rathborne.

Mr. VOORHIS. Does he say the meeting was a Communist fraction meeting?

Mr. MATTHEWS. He doesn't say a fraction meeting. He said a Communist meeting.

The CHAIRMAN. Let us proceed.

Mr. MARCANTONIO. If I may interrupt, Mr. Chairman, so as we can have the record clear. I don't want to have any confusion on this point as to the meetings, whether he sat in a fraction meeting or any kind of a Communist meeting at all, if that is what was in my colleague's from Massachusetts mind. Is that correct?

Mr. CASEY. That is correct.

Mr. MARCANTONIO. I think Mr. Rathborne ought to be permitted to answer that question.

The CHAIRMAN. He answered it.

Mr. MARCANTONIO. I believe he has, but at the same time——

The CHAIRMAN. He said he had not.

Mr. RATHBORNE. If that is what Mr. Ferguson says, he was not telling the truth.

The CHAIRMAN. All right, go ahead.

Mr. MATTHEWS. Mr. Maurice Malkin appeared before this committee as a witness and on page 5767 of the record of the committee there appears the following:

The CHAIRMAN. Are there any other unions you know that are under the control of the Communist Party?

Mr. MALKIN. I have got a list of the unions here.

The CHAIRMAN. Suppose you let him give us the names of them.

Mr. MALKIN. Yes.

The CHAIRMAN. I want to get the complete list.

Mr. MALKIN. Of course, I have mentioned the Furrier Workers and the Transportation Workers and the Communications Association.

The CHAIRMAN. Let me ask you about the Communications; is that under the control of the Communists?

Mr. MALKIN. Absolutely; under Rathborne.

Mr. MATTHEWS. How do you know he is a Communist?

Mr. MALKIN. I have seen him down at the office of the Communist Party dozens of times.

Do you know Mr. Maurice Malkin?

Mr. RATHBORNE. No. I would like to ask who the gentleman is. I have never heard of him.

Mr. MATTHEWS. He was a witness before this committee. At one time he was an organizer for the International Labor Defense and at another time he was an active——

Mr. MARCANTONIO. I want to interpose an objection. Mr. Malkin, to my own knowledge, was never an organizer for the International Labor Defense. He was a clerk and forged a check and was fired for forgery.

The CHAIRMAN. He is asking from the record as to what the witness testified.

Mr. MARCANTONIO. He made a statement. Mr. Matthews made a statement that his man was an organizer.

The CHAIRMAN. But identifying him from the witness' testimony.

Mr. MATTHEWS. I shall be very glad to read from the witness' own testimony on that particular point.

The CHAIRMAN. He is identifying the witness so Mr. Rathborne may know who he is.

Mr. MATTHEWS. The witness introduced originals as exhibits before this committee and copies of the originals are printed here in the record. On page 5744 appear the credentials issued to Mr. Malkin [reading]:

CREDENTIAL

To Whom It May Concern:

This will introduce Comrade M. Malkin, who has been appointed as special organizer for the International Labor Defense to do field organization work in the Albany section. Please give him every assistance possible.

And again :

To Whom It May Concern:

This is to certify that the bearer is authorized to act in the name of the International Labor Defense. Any courtesy extended to him will be appreciated.
Thanking you,
Fraternally yours,

CARL HACKER,
International Labor Defense, District Organizer.

Mr. MARCANTONIO. What date was that?

Mr. MATTHEWS. Dated October 1, 1931.

Mr. MARCANTONIO. And since then he worked as a shipping clerk and was fired for forging a check.

Mr. MATTHEWS. I only stated "at one time he was an organizer for the International Labor Defense." Mr. Marcantonio said he wasn't. There are five or six other credentials of the International Labor Defense.

The CHAIRMAN. Let us not get into a dispute about Mr. Malkin. The point is he made certain statements. What is the question you asked the witness about Mr. Malkin? We have not had an answer on that.

Mr. RATHBORNE. On that statement, Mr. Chairman, I would like to say in the first place I have never heard of Mr. Malkin. He has no connection with our organization whatsoever and any statement he may have made about our union, I don't know where he got the information because I know he didn't get it from the union and so from my point of view it is based on very poor sources and the statement that he made in the record there, is incorrect. It is not true.

Mr. CASEY. The statement is that he had seen you in Communist headquarters 12 times, I think it was.

Mr. MATTHEWS. "Dozens of times." Have you ever been to Communist headquarters in New York, Mr. Rathborne?

Mr. RATHBORNE. I have been down town to the book store—downstairs a couple of times.

Mr. MATTHEWS. On Thirteenth Street?

Mr. RATHBORNE. That is correct.

Mr. MATTHEWS. But not in the headquarters of the party upstairs?

Mr. RATHBORNE. No, sir.

Mr. THOMAS. Have you ever been in any other Communist headquarters in New York City?

Mr. RATHBORNE. No, sir.

The CHAIRMAN. Well, let us stick now to the statement that he had seen you at Communist headquarters "dozens of times." Is that true or false?

Mr. RATHBORNE. That is not a true statement.

Mr. MATTHEWS. On April 24, 1940, Mr. Fred Howe appeared before this committee as a witness and I have here before me a transcript of Mr. Howe's testimony, which has not as yet been printed.

The CHAIRMAN. The witness has had an opportunity to see a copy of that transcript. You have a copy of the testimony furnished you by our committee?

Mr. RATHBORNE. Yes, sir. The committee furnished me a copy, Mr. Chairman.

Mr. CASEY. A copy of whose testimony?

Mr. RATHBORNE. Mr. Howe's testimony?

Mr. CASEY. Have you read that testimony?

Mr. RATHBORNE. Yes, sir; I have.

Mr. CASEY. I suggest, in the interest of expedition, he read over the things he objects to in Mr. Howe's testimony and tell why he objects to it.

The CHAIRMAN. You don't mean objects to it. You mean deny it?

Mr. CASEY. Deny or affirm.

The CHAIRMAN. Well, I don't know about that. In order to follow the rules of the committee I suggest that you ask him questions.

Mr. MATTHEWS. On page 58 of the transcript——

Mr. MARCANTONIO. Excuse me, with the reservation, of course, Mr. Chairman, that on those matters that Mr. Matthews does not inquire about, that the witness be permitted to discuss.

The CHAIRMAN. Will you suggest them to the Chair?

Mr. MARCANTONIO. We certainly shall. The witness will do that as we go along.

Mr. MATTHEWS. On page 58, line 4:

> Mr. MATTHEWS. Now, will you please first answer the question and then give as definite, as you are able, a reason for your answer: Is Rathborne a Communist?
> Mr. HOWE. Yes.

And then for quite a number of pages there follows Mr. Howe's complete answer or explanation of his answer. Do you wish to comment on his answer in brief?

Mr. RATHBORNE. I would like to comment on the answer and also comment as to why I believe it was given, because later in this testimony Mr. Howe makes a statement to the effect that everybody that was opposed to him was a Communist and certainly I was one of those who was opposed to Mr. Howe when he was in the American Communications Association, and the reason I was opposed——

Mr. MATTHEWS. Can you cite the page where he said "everybody opposed to him was a Communist"?

Mr. RATHBORNE. I don't know exactly what page it is on but—he didn't make that exact statement.

Mr. MATTHEWS. He did not make that exact statement?

Mr. RATHBORNE. I am not quoting his words.

The CHAIRMAN. Let us get to that when we come to that part. The first thing is you have read his statement to the effect you are a Communist. Now, is that true or false?

Mr. RATHBORNE. Well, I have denied that several times and I will deny it again for the record.

The CHAIRMAN. All right. Now, do you want to state why in your opinion Mr. Howe made that statement? Is that what I understand?

Mr. RATHBORNE. If I may.

The CHAIRMAN. All right.

Mr. RATHBORNE. Mr. Howe was an official of our organization and during his term of his office he carried on a campaign which was detrimental to the union, which was in opposition to the program of the union adopted by the membership, which was in violation of the constitution of our organization.

The CHAIRMAN. All right. Will you tell me what sort of campaign that was? You say it was in violation of the constitution.

Mr. RATHBORNE. Specifically, the activities that Mr. Howe engaged in were—he defied the international officers. He refused to permit international officers to participate in negotiations for contracts as provided by the constitution of the union. He persisted in using the name "ARTA"—American Radio Telegraphers' Association—in defiance of the decision of the fourth national convention that the name of the organization be changed to American Communications Association, C. I. O., which decision was approved by a referendum vote of the entire membership of the organization. He repeatedly accepted membership dues without issuing official dues stamp receipts.

Mr. CASEY. What was his position then?

Mr. RATHBORNE. He was the secretary of Local No. 2, our marine local in New York City, and as secretary he was responsible for carrying out the duties under the constitution.

The CHAIRMAN. Elected secretary and removed by whom?

Mr. RATHBORNE. He was suspended on February 4, 1939, by vote of our international executive board and later in May of 1939 was expelled from membership in the union by the members of his own local.

The CHAIRMAN. By a secret referendum?

Mr. RATHBORNE. No; at a membership meeting that was held by a duly elected trial committee of his own members. The trial committee presented the charges, furnished Mr. Howe with them and heard all the evidence and then brought in a report to a membership meeting. The membership meeting voted in accordance with the provisions of our constitution that he be expelled and that the question not be submitted to referendum vote, and the meeting had that right under the provisions of our constitution.

Mr. MATTHEWS. Was Mr. Howe present at this meeting?

Mr. RATHBORNE. Mr. Howe refused to attend the meeting. He was furnished by registered mail, return receipt, with copies of the charges. He was requested to appear and the trial was postponed twice, due to his failure to appear.

Mr. MARCANTONIO. May I suggest the witness be permitted to read into the record the resolution with regard to Mr. Howe. It is a resolution of expulsion. It is an official record of the union and the witness has that with him. Other witnesses have been permitted to read letters.

The CHAIRMAN. Wait a minute. Now, don't get into an argument.

Mr. MARCANTONIO. I am making my argument for my motion.

The CHAIRMAN. You have a resolution of the committee.

Mr. RATHBORNE. I have here a resolution which was adopted by the international executive board of our union, which is the highest body, suspending him from office, and I also have here the transcript of the trial proceedings at which he was expelled in the membership meeting. In the transcript it lists the specific charges that he was brought up on and expelled on; and if the chairman would permit me I would like to put in the record—read into the record the resolution and the enumerated specific charges, which are 8 or 10, that he was brought up on trial for.

The CHAIRMAN. All right.

Mr. THOMAS. Mr. Rathborne, at that meeting where his expulsion took place, how many members were present at that time?

Mr. RATHBORNE. I don't know positively. I think it was about 30.

The CHAIRMAN. How many members are there in the local?

Mr. RATHBORNE. Four-hundred-sixty-some.

The CHAIRMAN. Thirty members were present out of four-hundred-sixty-odd that voted to expel him. Is that right?

Mr. RATHBORNE. That is right. I would like to add a point that other members have the right, under our constitution, if they disagreed with the action of those 30 members, to submit the question to referendum vote by petitions signed by 15 percent of the local.

The CHAIRMAN. Why didn't the committee submit it to referendum and permit the entire membership to pass on it?

Mr. RATHBORNE. I am sorry, Mr. Chairman, I don't know the answer to that question. Under the constitution they have a right to do it either way.

The CHAIRMAN. Didn't you say a moment ago the committee voted not to submit it to referendum?

Mr. RATHBORNE. Yes, sir, they did; but I do not know their reasons.

The CHAIRMAN. All right.

Mr. VOORHIS. One question. Could the committee have submitted it to referendum if they had chosen to do so?

Mr. RATHBORNE. The committee could have submitted the question to referendum if it had chosen to do so. In addition, 15 percent of the members of the local could have done so if they desired to have a referendum on that particular question; and if they had signed a petition and presented it to the local they could have had a referendum on the expulsion of Mr. Howe. But 15 percent of the members—a petition was started—but 15 percent of the members did not sign it.

Mr. Casey. Was Mr. Howe given a notice of this meeting?

Mr. Rathborne. Mr. Howe was served notice by registered mail, return receipt requested. The notice contained specific charges against Mr. Howe, and the date on which the trial—the date and place on which the trial would be held.

Mr. Casey. Was he present?

Mr. Rathborne. He did not attend.

Mr. Casey. Did he have counsel?

Mr. Rathborne. I will have to look in the record for that. No. He was requested to send a representative and he declined to do so.

Mr. Thomas. Mr. Rathborne, isn't it very strange that at a meeting where action was to be taken to expel the secretary of the local that out of 450 members only 30 should be present?

Mr. Rathborne. Not in this particular situation because that is a marine local and many of the members are at sea and our membership meetings are normally attended from between 30 and 40 people.

Mr. Thomas. But this was a very important action you took there, to suspend an officer of the local, and out of 450 members there certainly must have been more than 30 in this country that could have attended.

Mr. Casey. That isn't so strange as is the fact the accused himself did not appear.

Mr. Thomas. I am not addressing the question to you. I am addressing my question to the witness and I would like to have the witness answer it.

Mr. Rathborne. I would say that that is a marine local and most of the members are normally at sea and the average attendance at membership meetings over a period of years has been 30 or 40 people. So this was a normally attended meeting.

Mr. Thomas. But at your average meeting you don't expel somebody, particularly an officer.

Mr. Rathborne. Well, that is true.

Mr. Voorhis. What were the substantial charges against Mr. Howe?

Mr. Marcantonio. May I say this, that the witness was given permission to read into the record the resolution containing the charges plus the specific charges that were presented to him.

Mr. Thomas. And Mr. Marcantonio, I am very much in agreement with that idea. I think it should be put into the record.

Mr. Rathborne. On February 4, 1939, the international executive board of our union met and adopted the following resolution:

Whereas Fred M. Howe, secretary of Local No. 2, has, for a period of months past, openly violated the constitution of the American Communications Association, C. I. O., and defied the international officers, has refused to permit the international officers to participate in the negotiation of contracts with employers, as provided by the constitution; has persisted in using the name Arta in defiance of the decision of the fourth national convention that the name of the organization be changed to American Communications Association, C. I. O., which decision was approved by a referendum vote of the entire membership of the organization; has repeatedly accepted membership dues without issuing official dues stamp receipts, as required by the constitution, and otherwise violated its provisions and failed to keep proper financial accounts; and

Whereas at the meeting of Local No. 2 held on January 24, 1939, the said Fred M. Howe procured the adoption of a resolution by the local refusing to pay any per capita tax in the future to the American Communications Association, C. I. O., and has recommended and advocated a resolution of secession from the American Communications Association, C. I. O., and is now endeavoring to have the said recommendation adopted by a minority of the members of said Local No. 2 in the name of the majority; and

Whereas the large majority of the members of the said local is now at sea and the local meetings will be attended by a small minority of the said membership, and there is danger that those who will attend may be under the improper influence of said Fred M. Howe and take action which will be injurious to the membership of the said local as well as the international as a whole;

Now, therefore, in pursuance to the provision of the constitution of the American Communications Association, C. I. O., which enjoins upon the international executive board the duty of carrying out the wishes of the members of the association and to protect the property and interests of the association, and in order to prevent the carrying out of the said treasonable designs to disrupt Local No. 2, or to procure its secession from the American Communications Association, C. I. O., be it

Resolved, That this board hereby suspends the Fred N. Howe from his office as secretary of Local No. 2, as an emergency measure, pending the preferring and hearing of charges against him under the constitution; and it is hereby further

Resolved, That Chester H. Jordan and Roy A. Pyle, vice presidents of the marine division, be, and they are hereby appointed joint administrators of Local No. 2, and they are hereby directed to take possession of the office of said local, its books, records, papers, and effects, money in bank, and all other property, and they keep, preserve, and administer the same, as well as the contracts of said local with employers, and otherwise carry on the functions of the said local and preserve and protect the interests of the members thereof, pending further action by the membership of this international as well as of the said Local No. 2.

That was the resolution adopted.

The CHAIRMAN. Let me see that resolution, if you don't mind.

Mr. THOMAS. As I understand, Mr. Rathborne, a copy of those charges were sent to Mr. Howe, were they not?

Mr. RATHBORNE. Yes, sir.

Mr. THOMAS. Before this meeting?

Mr. RATHBORNE. Yes, sir.

Mr. THOMAS. Have you got a copy of the letter that was sent to Mr. Howe?

Mr. RATHBORNE. Perhaps it is in this record. Will you give me a minute to look it over?

The CHAIRMAN. Do you have the return receipt or any evidence from the Post Office Department that such a letter was sent?

Mr. RATHBORNE. I have the return receipt; yes, sir. I don't know that I have it with me, but I can make it available to the committee.

The CHAIRMAN. If you have it, will you furnish the committee the return receipt or the registered notice or whatever you have. You sent it under registered mail?

Mr. RATHBORNE. Registered mail and return receipt requested.

The CHAIRMAN. You would have two records of it—the registry and the return receipt.

Mr. RATHBORNE. Yes.

Mr. THOMAS. Will you turn those over to the committee?

Mr. CASEY. Mr. Howe testified he did not get a notice, so that would be very important if you have a return receipt.

Mr. THOMAS. How soon do you think you can turn it over to the committee?

Mr. RATHBORNE. I am returning Friday——

Mr. MARCANTONIO. I will give it to you Monday or Tuesday, at the latest.

The CHAIRMAN. Isn't this unusual [reading].

Whereas, a large majority of the members of the said local is now at sea and the local meetings will be attended by a small minority of the said membership; and there is danger that those who will attend may be under the improper influence of said Fred M. Howe and take action which will be injurious to the membership of the said local as well as the international as a whole—

What justification would there be for the international officers to assume they cannot trust the men who are present and therefore proceed to the trial of a man that involves whether or not he will continue in his duly elected office. This is a very serious charge. There are very serious consequences.

What justification would there be for the officers to say: "We can't trust the members who would be present because they may be under the improper influence of Fred Howe and therefore we will deal with the matter" in the way in which they did?

Mr. RATHBORNE. Very easily explained. It happens that our marine locals—they hand out jobs—that is, with our contracts with the employers, the shipping is done through the union hall; and the improper influence referred to is Mr. Howe attempting to give his friends jobs—those that supported him—and those that opposed him, to refuse them the opportunity of obtaining employment.

The CHAIRMAN. But doesn't that involve a distrust of democratic processes? Here you say that most of your meetings are conducted by 30 members being present.

Mr. RATHBORNE. Yes, sir.

The CHAIRMAN. Thirty or forty?

Mr. RATHBORNE. Yes, sir.

The CHAIRMAN. And that is because most of them are at sea?

Mr. RATHBORNE. That is right.

The CHAIRMAN. Here you have a union, and you are going to try your secretary on serious charges which involve his expulsion from the union, and you are not willing to trust the 30 members who are present because you fear that they might be under the improper influence of Fred M. Howe.

Mr. RATHBORNE. Well, that was the case, Mr. Chairman.

The CHAIRMAN. Do you do that often? I mean, is that a regular procedure?

Mr. RATHBORNE. No, sir; it is not. This was a case in this particular situation—Howe was violating the shipping rules of the local which were approved by the membership. The shipping rules provided the members do their own handing out of their jobs. If you took away that right from the members and he set himself up as the one to pass on all people who got the jobs, as a result he was able to set up a machine there where his friends got the jobs and people that were opposing him were denied the opportunity to work, and so in the membership meetings—he was able to put over any program he wanted to whether it was good or bad just through the threat of withholding employment from the members.

The CHAIRMAN. Well, didn't you say that a moment ago, approximately? Or wasn't it unanimous on the part of the 30 who were present in voting to expel him? Or did you say that?

Mr. RATHBORNE. That was after he was suspended. He was suspended in February. The trial took place for his expulsion in May.

The CHAIRMAN. And it was unanimous on the part of the 30 present?

Mr. RATHBORNE. I believe it was; yes, sir. I don't know whether it was exactly unanimous, but it was a very large majority. I have the record here. I can look it up, if you like.

Mr. THOMAS. What did you do, wait until such time as you could find 30 members who would be against him?

Mr. RATHBORNE. Mr. Howe was advocating—was openly advocating—secession of a section of our union from our organization—taking it away in violation of the constitution. In order to prevent him splitting away a part of our union, he was suspended from membership, which the international executive board—and his influence toward secession was thereby taken away and later on, after the requirements of the constitution were fulfilled, Mr. Howe was brought to trial by his own members in accordance with the constitution adopted by the membership of our union and tried strictly according to that constitution.

Mr. THOMAS. How often does that local meet?

Mr. RATHBORNE. Once a week.

Mr. THOMAS. And why did you wait 3 months before you had this trial?

Mr. RATHBORNE. I don't know exactly why the long delay. There were court cases, and Mr. Howe went to court, and the court found that the action of the international was within the provisions of the constitution, and also it was necessary to circulate a petition preferring the charges against Mr. Howe, which were signed by 15 percent of the membership, and there were other actions that were taken in the meantime.

Mr. CASEY. Did Mr. Howe protest the manner of his expulsion?

Mr. RATHBORNE. He protested the manner of his suspension.

The CHAIRMAN. As a matter of fact, he has a lawsuit now involving this whole question?

Mr. RATHBORNE. That is right; yes, sir.

Mr. MARCANTONIO. Now, will you read the specific charges into the record?

Mr. RATHBORNE. Charge No. 1 states:

Fred M. Howe has for months past deliberately and willfully violated section 15 of article 6 of the constitution of the American Communications Association, in that he has entered into secret agreements with shipowners; and has refused to permit duly elected members of the international executive board, who are vice presidents of the marine divisions, to attend and participate in negotiations with shipowners.

Then it quotes the article of the constitution.

Mr. THOMAS. You were looking for the copy of the letter you sent to Mr. Howe?

Mr. RATHBORNE. Do you want that first?

Mr. THOMAS. Did you find it?

Mr. MARCANTONIO. Wait a moment. The agreement was he was going to read that statement first—the charges—and then he will come to that letter.

The CHAIRMAN. Yes; continue with the charges.

Mr. RATHBORNE. Charge No. 2 [continuing]:

The said Fred M. Howe has violated the provisions of article 11, sections 28 to 34 of said constitution, in that he has collected moneys from various members of the American Communications Association and had refused to issue official receipts therefor, but has retained this money and refused to pay per capita tax to the American Communications Association; and has failed to render a proper account of same, thereby jeopardizing the good standing membership of members of the American Communications Association in the international and in the C. I. O. and has further caused to be printed illegal receipt books in place and stead of the official American Communications Association receipt book.

Mr. VOORHIS. Did you have complaints from individual members of the local on that point, Mr. Rathborne?

Mr. RATHBORNE. Yes, sir; we did. We had many complaints from members that they were not receiving proper receipts and thereby their standing was jeopardized as members of our union.

The CHAIRMAN. Well, now, it seems to me—I am not absolutely certain, and I don't want to interrupt you, but in connection with that charge it seems to me that the testimony of Mr. Howe was to the effect that the international office ceased supplying the secretaries with the stamps necessary to place upon these receipts.

Mr. MATTHEWS. That was with respect to Mr. O'Shea's testimony.

The CHAIRMAN. I may be mistaken in that.

Mr. RATHBORNE. I want to say that stamps were available at all times if Mr. Howe had cared to get them.

The CHAIRMAN. Now, I notice in connection with that [reading]:

Whereas at the meeting of Local No. 2 held on January 24, 1939, the said Fred H. Howe procured the adoption of a resolution by the local refusing to pay any per capita tax in the future to the American Communications Association, C. I. O.

Do you mean that the local at a meeting voted not to pay the per capita tax?

Mr. RATHBORNE. That is correct, but that motion was in violation of the constitution that was adopted by all the members, the same thing as if one of the States adopted a law that is unconstitutional.

The CHAIRMAN. Wouldn't the members who voted for it be just as guilty as Mr. Howe was?

Mr. RATHBORNE. He was the one who advocated it.

The CHAIRMAN. Well, I understand that; but if the members voted for it, wouldn't they be just as guilty as Mr. Howe so far as the union was concerned?

Mr. RATHBORNE. It was our purpose, Mr. Chairman, not to wreck the union, but to try to preserve the union as much as possible, and to get rid of the influence that was causing these illegal and unconstitutional activities, and Mr. Howe was the ringleader. He was the one that was leading the parade, and when he quit that ended it.

Mr. THOMAS. Was that why he was suspended and expelled—because he was the ringleader in this union—this local?

Mr. RATHBORNE. He was a ringleader in a move to cause Local No. 2 to secede from our organization—to swing it over to another organization—and to violate the constitution, negotiate secret agreements with the shipowners, and to collaborate with the labor spies working in the N. M. U.

The CHAIRMAN. We will suspend at this time until 10 o'clock tomorrow morning.

(Whereupon, at 3:30 p. m., the hearing was adjourned until 10 a. m., May 9, 1940.)

INVESTIGATION OF UN-AMERICAN PROPAGANDA ACTIVITIES IN THE UNITED STATES

THURSDAY, MAY 9, 1940

House of Representatives,
Committee on Un-American Activities,
Washington, D. C.

The committee met at 10 a. m., Hon. Martin Dies (chairman) presiding.

The CHAIRMAN. The committee will come to order.

The chairman is sitting as a subcommittee of one until the other members arrive.

Mr. Rathborne, will you please come forward?

Mr. MARCANTONIO. Mr. Chairman, I anr sorry Mr. Rathborne is not here yet.

The CHAIRMAN. Very well, we will recess until he comes.

(Whereupon, at 10: 05 a. m., a recess was taken until 10: 30 a. m., the same day.)

AFTER RECESS

The CHAIRMAN. The Chair wants to announce that at 11 o'clock the House begins consideration of the transportation bill and that that will be followed immediately by the agricultural appropriation bill, and my understanding of the program is that the House is going to run until tonight.

In view of that fact, we would have such a short time to proceed that the Chair thinks it is advisable to defer this hearing until a further date, to be determined upon the basis of the legislative program of the House. Many Members feel that it is of vital interest to be present at the debate that is going to begin at 11 o'clock.

We only have a few minutes now, and I have consulted Mr. Marcantonio, counsel for Mr. Rathborne, and he agrees with me that that is, perhaps, the best procedure.

Therefore, we shall not hold the hearing today.

Mr. MARCANTONIO. You don't propose to hold any hearings tomorrow, do you, Mr. Chairman?

The CHAIRMAN. No; not this week. In other words, when the committee resumes its hearings Mr. Rathborne will be the first witness, and we will choose a day when there is no heavy legislative program and we can continue the hearing. It is very inconvenient to be running backward and forward and losing the chain of the examination. We can't meet tomorrow, because the Smith committee has asked for the caucus room.

So the committee will stand adjourned, subject to the call of the chairman.

(Whereupon, at 10: 35 a. m., the hearing was adjourned without date.)

INVESTIGATION OF UN-AMERICAN PROPAGANDA ACTIVITIES IN THE UNITED STATES

TUESDAY, MAY 21, 1940

HOUSE OF REPRESENTATIVES,
COMMITTEE OF UN-AMERICAN ACTIVITIES,
Washington, D. C.

The committee met at 10 a. m., Hon. Martin Dies (chairman), presiding.

Present: Messrs. Dies, Dempsey, Mason, and Thomas.

Present also: J. B. Matthews, Director of Research for the committee.

TESTIMONY OF NICHOLAS DOZENBERG

The CHAIRMAN. The committee will come to order. The witness is Nicholas Dozenberg.

Will you please stand and raise your right hand? Do you solemnly swear to tell the truth, the whole truth, and nothing but the truth, so help you God?

Mr. DOZENBERG. I do.

The CHAIRMAN. Give your full name to the reporter, please.

Mr. DOZENBERG. Nicholas Dozenberg.

The CHAIRMAN. You may proceed, Dr. Matthews.

Mr. MATTHEWS. Do you use a middle initial, Mr. Dozenberg?

Mr. DOZENBERG. No.

Mr. MATTHEWS. You have in the past used a middle initial, have you not?

Mr. DOZENBERG. I have in connection with N. L. Dallant.

Mr. MATTHEWS. The initial was "L"?

Mr. DOZENBERG. L.

Mr. MATTHEWS. What did the "L" stand for?

Mr. DOZENBERG. Ludwig.

Mr. MATTHEWS. Where were you born, Mr. Dozenberg?

Mr. DOZENBERG. For all practical purposes I suppose I was born in Riga, Latvia, but there is a contention I was born in this country.

Mr. MATTHEWS. There was a contention you say?

Mr. DOZENBERG. There is a contention that I was born in this country.

Mr. MATTHEWS. When were you born?

Mr. DOZENBERG. November 15, 1882.

Mr. MATTHEWS. What do you mean by "there being a contention that you were born in this country"?

Mr. DOZENBERG. Now, Mr. Chairman, may I request that no pictures be taken. I strenuously object to it.

The CHAIRMAN (addressing several photographers). Well, gentlemen, refrain from taking pictures.

Mr. DOZENBERG. When I saw my mother the last time she told me a story which, according to her, was a secret, to the effect that I was born here in this country during the time when she made a trip to this country seeking for her sister and brother-in-law who at one time had run away with a pay roll—a pay roll representing about seven or eight hundred men's pay, monthly pay, and that I was born in this country during that trip, at Bismarck, N. Dak. That is the contention.

The CHAIRMAN. That is what your mother told you?

Mr. DOZENBERG. That is what my mother told me.

The CHAIRMAN. Have you ever found any record of entry of your mother to the United States or any evidence that she was here at that time?

Mr. DOZENBERG. Mr. Chairman, I didn't pay the least attention to it because my status as a citizen was satisfactory to me. I had been naturalized in 1911 and I simply did not pay any attention to it at all.

Mr. MATTHEWS. When did your mother tell you this story of your birth in this country?

Mr. DOZENBERG. In 1919.

Mr. MATTHEWS. Where was she at that time?

Mr. DOZENBERG. In Prince Albert, Saskatchewan, Canada.

Mr. MATTHEWS. Is your mother alive?

Mr. DOZENBERG. No; she is not.

Mr. MATTHEWS. How long has she been deceased?

Mr. DOZENBERG. Oh, for 15 or 16 years now.

Mr. MATTHEWS. Is it the understanding that you yourself do not claim that this is a correct story of your birth?

Mr. DOZENBERG. I have not formally claimed it; no.

Mr. MATTHEWS. You were naturalized, were you not, in the United States?

Mr. DOZENBERG. Yes.

Mr. MATTHEWS. When?

Mr. DOZENBERG. On February 6, 1911.

Mr. MATTHEWS. Where were you naturalized?

Mr. DOZENBERG. United States district court in Boston, Mass.

Mr. MATTHEWS. When did you come to the United States, Mr. Dozenberg, neglecting for the moment this story of your mother's?

Mr. DOZENBERG. In June 1904.

Mr. MATTHEWS. You were at that time 22 years of age, approximately?

Mr. DOZENBERG. No. I was just a little over 20—I would have been 21 in November.

Mr. MATTHEWS. You would have been 22 in November?

Mr. DOZENBERG. No.

Mr. MATTHEWS. You were born November 15, 1882?

Mr. DOZENBERG. 1882.

Mr. MATTHEWS. Then you were already 21, were you not?

The CHAIRMAN. Well, the record speaks for itself.

Mr. DOZENBERG. I won't dispute that. I may be wrong. But my impression was that I was 20 and would have been 21 but perhaps I was 21 and would have been 22.

Mr. MATTHEWS. You would have been 22 on November 15, 1904, or 5 months after your arrival in this country.

Where did you land in the United States?

Mr. DOZENBERG. From what I remember, I landed in New York.

Mr. MATTHEWS. What steamer did you cross the Atlantic on?

Mr. DOZENBERG. *Norge.*

Mr. MATTHEWS. Was that a ship of the Norwegian Line?

Mr. DOZENBERG. I think they call it the Norwegian-American Line, if I am not mistaken, but I would not say for sure.

Mr. MATTHEWS. Where was your first residence in the United States?

Mr. DOZENBERG. In Boston, Mass.

Mr. MATTHEWS. Did you go immediately from New York to Boston?

Mr. DOZENBERG. If I remember correctly, I immediately went over there.

Mr. MATTHEWS. Where did you reside in Boston?

Mr. DOZENBERG. Several places. Principally in the section of Boston called Roxbury.

Mr. MATTHEWS. R-o-x-b-u-r-y?

Mr. DOZENBERG. Yes.

Mr. MATTHEWS. How long did you reside in Boston?

Mr. DOZENBERG. It must have been 17 or 18 years—something of that sort.

Mr. MATTHEWS. From 1904 until about 1921 or 1922.

Mr. DOZENBERG. 1920—16 years.

Mr. MATTHEWS. Until 1920?

Mr. DOZENBERG. Yes.

Mr. MATTHEWS. What occupations were you engaged in during your residence in Boston?

Mr. DOZENBERG. For the major part I was a railroad locomotive machinist.

Mr. MATTHEWS. How long after you came to this country did you obtain employment?

Mr. DOZENBERG. I could not recollect now.

Mr. MATTHEWS. Did you have relatives in Boston?

Mr. DOZENBERG. I had my brother-in-law here.

Mr. MATTHEWS. In this country; and was he residing in Boston?

Mr. DOZENBERG. He was residing in Boston.

Mr. MATTHEWS. Did you live with him when you first arrived?

Mr. DOZENBERG. I think I did.

Mr. MATTHEWS. Was it some weeks or months after you came to this country that you obtained employment?

Mr. DOZENBERG. I wouldn't even try to make an attempt to remember. That is 36 or 37 years ago.

Mr. MATTHEWS. Well, don't you remember whether you were employed or unemployed, say, for a period of 6 months or a year after your arrival?

Mr. DOZENBERG. I do not remember definitely. I may have been, and I may not have been.

Mr. MATTHEWS. Where was your first job?

Mr. DOZENBERG. My first job was with the firm making artificial marble—Meyers & Co., if I remember correctly.

Mr. MATTHEWS. M-e-y-e-r-s?

Mr. DOZENBERG. Yes.

Mr. MATTHEWS. And was that in Boston?

Mr. DOZENBERG. Boston.

Mr. MATTHEWS. And how long did you work for Meyers & Co.?

Mr. DOZENBERG. I do not remember, but I remember that my next job was with the Voss Piano Co.

Mr. MATTHEWS. V-o-s-s?

Mr. DOZENBERG. Yes.

Mr. MATTHEWS. Do you recall how long you worked for the Voss Piano Co?

Mr. DOZENBERG. I do not.

Mr. MATTHEWS. What was your next employment?

Mr. DOZENBERG. My next employment was with Kressler & Co. Iron Works.

Mr. MATTHEWS. Will you please spell that?

Mr. DOZENBERG. K-r-e-s-s-l-e-r?

Mr. MATTHEWS. Kressler & Co. Iron Works?

Mr. DOZENBERG. Yes, sir.

Mr. MATTHEWS. Do you recall how long you were employed there?

Mr. DOZENBERG. I do not recall, but I will make a guess, for about a year or so.

Mr. MATTHEWS. And what was your next place of employment?

Mr. DOZENBERG. Then I obtained employment as a machinist with the New York, New Haven & Hartford Railroad Co.

Mr. MATTHEWS. In what year did you obtain employment there?

Mr. DOZENBERG. I think it was in 1906 or 1907. Most likely 1906.

Mr. MATTHEWS. And how long did you work for the New York, New Haven & Hartford Railroad Co.?

Mr. DOZENBERG. All this time, until 1920.

Mr. MATTHEWS. For approximately 14 years?

Mr. DOZENBERG. Yes, sir.

Mr. MATTHEWS. And you were working as a machinist during that entire period?

Mr. DOZENBERG. Machinist.

Mr. MATTHEWS. You were never unemployed during that period?

Mr. DOZENBERG. Unemployed? No.

Mr. MATTHEWS. That period also covered the World War, is that correct?

Mr. DOZENBERG. That is correct.

Mr. MATTHEWS. Did you see service during the World War?

Mr. DOZENBERG. I did not.

Mr. MATTHEWS. Were you exempted for any special reason?

Mr. DOZENBERG. I was at the age of 32 or 33 years of age at that time, and I understood my classification was not called—the draft had not reached that stage.

Mr. MATTHEWS. Were you married at that time?

Mr. DOZENBERG. I was married at that time.

Mr. MATTHEWS. What was your wife's name?

Mr. DOZENBERG. Catherine Dozenberg.

Mr. MATTHEWS. Were you married in this country?

Mr. DOZENBERG. Yes.

Mr. MATTHEWS. In what year?

Mr. DOZENBERG. In 1906.

Mr. MATTHEWS. Mr. Dozenberg, in an issue of the Daily Worker for October 6, 1923, there is a notation of a subscription to the Daily Worker by Nicholas and Anita Dozenberg. Who was Anita Dozenberg?

Mr. DOZENBERG. Well, there is no such person. That was my first wife's nickname. Her name was Ancit and some people who did not know figured it must have been Anita.

Mr. MATTHEWS. Did you become a member of the International Machinists' Association while you were employed for the New York, New Haven & Hartford Railroad Co.?

Mr. DOZENBERG. Yes.

Mr. MATTHEWS. When did you join that union?

Mr. DOZENBERG. Soon after I obtained employment with the New York, New Haven & Hartford Railroad Co.

Mr. MATTHEWS. In 1906?

Mr. DOZENBERG. 1906.

Mr. MATTHEWS. Did you continue your membership in that union until——

Mr. DOZENBERG. I continued my membership even after that.

Mr. MATTHEWS. Did you ever hold any official position in the International Machinists' Association?

Mr. DOZENBERG. In the local union; yes.

Mr. MATTHEWS. What positions did you hold?

Mr. DOZENBERG. I was president, I was secretary, I was treasurer, and I was chairman of the shop committee. I think I held all the positions that the local union could give.

Mr. MATTHEWS. Was that Local 391?

Mr. DOZENBERG. Correct.

Mr. MATTHEWS. In Boston?   •

Mr. DOZENBERG. Well, they met in Hyde Park—now Boston.

Mr. MATTHEWS. A suburb of Boston at that time?

Mr. DOZENBERG. It was not at that time—at the beginning. It became a suburb of Boston in later years.

Mr. MATTHEWS. Did you, during this period of your employment with the New York, New Haven & Hartford Railroad Co., join the Socialist Party?

Mr. DOZENBERG. Not as an individual. The joining of the Socialist Party became a group question.

Mr. MATTHEWS. Was that the Lettish Federation of Boston, the group that you refer to?

Mr. DOZENBERG. It was the Lettish Workmen's Association and it became the Lettish Federation afterwards, after the federation or the association had joined the Socialist Party and the Socialist Party had grouped its language groups according to languages. They then came to be known as the Lettish Federation—Lettish Federation, Finnish Federation, Jewish Federation, and so forth.

Mr. MATTHEWS. But you were a member of the Lettish Workers Association?

Mr. DOZENBERG. Yes, sir.

Mr. MATTHEWS. Did you join that shortly after your arrival in this country?

Mr. DOZENBERG. I suppose it must have been 3 or 4 years afterwards.

Mr. MATTHEWS. And that body as a whole joined the Socialist Party?

Mr. DOZENBERG. Yes; that party joined the Socialist Party.

Mr. MATTHEWS. Is that the way you became a member?

Mr. DOZENBERG. That is the way we became members; yes, sir.

Mr. MATTHEWS. And do you remember what year that was?

Mr. DOZENBERG. I could not say for sure.

Mr. MATTHEWS. Was it entirely agreeable to you for the Lettish Workers or the Workmen's Association to join the Socialist Party?

Mr. DOZENBERG. Oh, I suppose it is fair for me to say that it was.

Mr. MATTHEWS. You were a party to the action, were you?

Mr. DOZENBERG. (No answer.)

Mr. MATTHEWS. Did you favor the vote for it?

Mr. DOZENBERG. I am pretty sure that I favored voting and voted for it.

Mr. MATTHEWS. Were you a member of the Socialist Party continuously, until the time that the organization became the Lettish Federation and joined the Communist Party?

Mr. DOZENBERG. If I remember correctly the joining of the Communist Party was not any more a matter of Federations joining or not.

Mr. MATTHEWS. Well, did you retain your membership in the Socialist Party through your membership in the Lettish Workmen's Association?

Mr. DOZENBERG. Yes.

Mr. MATTHEWS. Until the time that you joined the Communist Party?

Mr. DOZENBERG. The joining of the Communist Party also became a matter of the same procedure nearly. That is, the same form there occurred, if I remember correctly. There occurred a split in the Socialist Party and one fraction of it later on developed or became as the nucleus of the—which later became the Communist Party.

Mr. MATTHEWS. I understood you to say the same procedure was not followed, and it was a matter of the individual joining the Communist Party.

Mr. DOZENBERG. Now, if you had told me beforehand to prepare or to kind of refresh my memory I might be able to tell you in more detail as to dates and how and so forth, but this comes as a complete surprise.

Mr. MATTHEWS. All right, Mr. Dozenberg, were you a member of the Socialist Party during the period of the World War?

Mr. DOZENBERG. Yes.

Mr. MATTHEWS. Did you, as a Socialist, oppose the entrance and participation of the United States into the World War?

Mr. DOZENBERG. I did not. The whole Socialist Party, as such, did not oppose except, if I remember correctly, except as the party's sentiments were expressed at the St. Louis convention, where Eugene V. Debs made a speech against the United States entering the World War.

Mr. MATTHEWS. Yes; the party as a whole did go on record at the St. Louis convention as opposed to the participation of the United States in the World War.

Mr. DOZENBERG. That is my recollection.

Mr. MATTHEWS. But you in no way actively engaged in opposition to it?

Mr. DOZENBERG. No.

Mr. MATTHEWS. To the participation of this country in the World War.

Mr. DOZENBERG. No. Just the opposite as a matter of fact. I became chairman of a liberty sales committee among the Letts at Roxbury, Mass.

Mr. MATTHEWS. Now, this split in the Socialist Party occurred in the year 1919, did it not?

Mr. DOZENBERG. There is nothing to lose, or anything to gain, either, if I would say yes. Perhaps it was 1918 or 1919 or 1920.

Mr. MATTHEWS. Well, at the time of the split in the Socialist Party you went with the part——

Mr. DOZENBERG. With the left wing. That came later on——

Mr. MATTHEWS. And that later on became the Communist Party?

Mr. DOZENBERG. And later on became the Communist Party; yes, sir.

Mr. MATTHEWS. And you did that immediately?

Mr. DOZENBERG. I beg your pardon?

Mr. MATTHEWS. You went with the left-wing group immediately?

Mr. DOZENBERG. No; not immediately, because I was in Canada at the time when the actual split took place.

Mr. MATTHEWS. How long had you been in Canada?

Mr. DOZENBERG. I was in Canada nearly a year.

Mr. MATTHEWS. Now, that was in 1919. What were you doing in Canada a year?

Mr. DOZENBERG. Well, you see, my sister—my brother-in-law had a general store there and I was working for them, taking care of the general store.

Mr. MATTHEWS. Now, you may have slipped on your dates. You said you were employed by the New York, New Haven & Hartford Railroad Co. without any interruption up to that time.

Mr. DOZENBERG. I was on leave as far as the employment was concerned.

Mr. MATTHEWS. That was during the year 1919?

Mr. DOZENBERG. 1919; yes, sir.

Mr. MATTHEWS. Now, when you returned from Canada, did you go back to work for the New York, New Haven & Hartford Railroad Co.?

Mr. DOZENBERG. I did not.

Mr. MATTHEWS. Then your employment there did not extend down to 1920 as you previously testified?

Mr. DOZENBERG. It just so happened that the termination of my employment with the New York, New Haven & Hartford Railroad Co. came in this way:

They were not necessarily short of any type of labor at that time, and they permitted sort of a leeway to a large extent, and I enjoyed the privilege of using the railroad pass which I had earned because of having worked for so many years. Now, then, when the company—when I was to renew my request for the extension of the railroad pass, then naturally I had to disclose the fact that I had—that I intended to be employed in something else, and that is how my termination of employment came about.

Mr. MATTHEWS. What time did you return from Canada? Do you recall that?

(No answer.)

Mr. MATTHEWS. Was it in the year 1920 or 1919?

Mr. DOZENBERG. I think it must have been in 1919.

Mr. MATTHEWS. You were there approximately 1 year?

Mr. DOZENBERG. Yes.

Mr. MATTHEWS. Where did you go on your return from Canada?

Mr. DOZENBERG. To New York.

Mr. MATTHEWS. And how long did you remain in New York at this time?

Mr. DOZENBERG. I think for about 3 or 4 months or so.

Mr. MATTHEWS. Now, during this period of employment up until 1919 in this country, did you come in possession of any property—did you purchase any property?

Mr. DOZENBERG. No.

Mr. MATTHEWS. Were you able to put aside any savings of any appreciable sum?

Mr. DOZENBERG. I had at one time a small account with the Tremont Trust Co., but it didn't amount to much.

Mr. MATTHEWS. When you came back to New York after your sojourn in Canada for a period of a year, did you get in touch with the left-wing faction of the Socialist Party?

Mr. DOZENBERG. Yes.

Mr. MATTHEWS. And was it at that time that you joined the left-wing faction?

Mr. DOZENBERG. No. It was not a question of joining again. I suppose it was—it must have been just a matter of paying up your dues.

Mr. MATTHEWS. Had the split already occurred in the Socialist Party?

Mr. DOZENBERG. Yes.

Mr. MATTHEWS. When you returned from Canada?

Mr. DOZENBERG. Yes.

Mr. MATTHEWS. So that it was a matter of paying up your dues in the organization which later became the Communist Party?

Mr. DOZENBERG. That is the idea.

Mr. MATTHEWS. In other words, was your membership in the Communist Party continuous from that date, say, down until 1927?

Mr. DOZENBERG. Correct.

Mr. MATTHEWS. When you left New York after a period of 3 or 4 months on your return from Canada where did you go?

Mr. DOZENBERG. I went to Chicago.

Mr. MATTHEWS. And that was in 1920 some time?

Mr. DOZENBERG. I think that was in 1920.

Mr. MATTHEWS. Why did you go to Chicago?

Mr. DOZENBERG. I was offered a job there to become the business manager of a labor publication called The Voice of Labor.

Mr. MATTHEWS. Was that publication a Communist Party publication?

Mr. DOZENBERG. No. It was a left-wing publication. It was a trade-union publication. As a matter of fact there was no Communist Party at that time in the United States at all.

Mr. MATTHEWS. Well, there was a Workers' Party, was there not?

Mr. DOZENBERG. There was a Workers' Party; yes.

Mr. MATTHEWS. And the Workers' Party later changed its name to the Communist Party, did it not?

Mr. DOZENBERG. Yes. That was a number of years later.

Mr. MATTHEWS. But it would be correct to say that the Workers' Party was a communist party, spelling the word "communist" with a small "c"?

Mr. DOZENBERG. No; I don't think it is correct, because you must understand also all the different phases that the final formulation of the order—the final crystallization of the party took place. There could not have been the Communist Party from the very beginning although their aims may have been the same thing or their beliefs or convictions, but in my estimation the whole movement had not crystallized itself to any extent to call it the Communist Party and consequently they didn't——

Mr. MATTHEWS. But the Workers' Party immediately affiliated with the Third International?

Mr. DOZENBERG. So did other organizations which were not Communist organizations at all.

Mr. MATTHEWS. Did the Third International admit into membership parties that it did not consider Communist?

Mr. DOZENBERG. According to my understanding or recollection there was a time when they did admit them.

Mr. MATTHEWS. Was not the split in the Socialist Party over the affiliation with the Third International?

Mr. DOZENBERG. Absolutely not, to the best of my recollection.

Mr. MATTHEWS. Don't you recall that the debate which split the Socialist Party was over the acceptance or rejection of the terms of affiliation offered by the Third International?

Mr. DOZENBERG. I will not dispute your statement because as I said, I am not well versed after so many years, what it may have been and what it may not have been.

Mr. MATTHEWS. I show you some bound volumes of the "Voice of Labor" and ask you if you can identify these as the publication?

(Handing books to the witness.)

Mr. DOZENBERG. Yes.

Mr. MATTHEWS. With which you obtained employment when you left New York to go to Chicago?

Mr. DOZENBERG. Yes; correct, correct.

Mr. MATTHEWS. You recall these?

Mr. DOZENBERG. Yes; sure.

Mr. MATTHEWS. These are bound volumes——

Mr. DOZENBERG. I did not know they were in existence.

Mr. MATTHEWS. You are satisfied as to the identity of these?

Mr. DOZENBERG. Yes. Those are the ones; yes.

Mr. MATTHEWS. These are bound volumes of the Voice of Labor for the year 1921 and for the first half of 1922 and for July 7, 1922, and until the first part of 1923. What was your employment with this publication, the Voice of Labor?

Mr. DOZENBERG. If you will turn——

Mr. MATTHEWS. What was your employment with this publication?

Mr. DOZENBERG. If you will turn to the editorial page you will see that I am there as the business manager.

Mr. MATTHEWS. I think that will appear in a later issue.

Mr. DOZENBERG. Oh, that may have been so. Perhaps they did not publish the names of the editor or the business manager.

Mr. MATTHEWS. In the year 1922 they appear to have begun to publish names in the issue of April 28, 1922—Jack Carney is listed as editor and N. Dozenberg as the business manager.

Mr. DOZENBERG. Yes, sir.

Mr. MATTHEWS. How long were you the business manager of the publication?

Mr. DOZENBERG. All the time while it was issued.

Mr. MATTHEWS. Now, was this publication in fact the publication of the Workers' Party?

Mr. DOZENBERG. It was not.

Mr. MATTHEWS. Of the United States?

Mr. DOZENBERG. It was not.

Mr. MATTHEWS. Would you not say that its editorial policy was——

Mr. DOZENBERG. The editorial policy?

Mr. MATTHEWS. Entirely in line with the policy of the Workers' Party?

Mr. DOZENBERG. The editorial policy, yes; I would say that.

Mr. MATTHEWS. You were a member of the Workers' Party at that time?

Mr. DOZENBERG. I was.

Mr. MATTHEWS. Was Mr. Carney a member of the Workers' Party?

Mr. DOZENBERG. To the best of my knowledge and belief he was.

Mr. MATTHEWS. And the paper consistently supported the revolution of the Soviet Union; did it not?

Mr. DOZENBERG. If I remember correctly, although I didn't have much to say about the editorial policy——

Mr. MATTHEWS. Your employment began in 1920 at some time; is that correct?

Mr. DOZENBERG. It must have been 1920; yes.

Mr. MATTHEWS. The publication began in the year 1920?

Mr. DOZENBERG. Yes.

Mr. MATTHEWS. And you were employed by this publication until it ceased——

Mr. DOZENBERG. Yes, sir.

Mr. MATTHEWS. Publication in 1923?

Mr. DOZENBERG. No; it did not cease publication in 1923 just because you don't have the other copies. It did not cease. It kept on going for several years longer.

Mr. MATTHEWS. And were you still the business agent?

Mr. DOZENBERG. All the time.

Mr. MATTHEWS. Still the business agent of the publication—still the business manager of the publication?

Mr. DOZENBERG. All the time.

Mr. MATTHEWS. Do you recall what year it ceased publication?

Mr. DOZENBERG. To the best of my recollection it ceased in 1926 or 1925. It ceased at a time when the Workers' Party headquarters was moved from New York to Chicago.

Mr. MATTHEWS. Well, now, is that true of the publication known as the Voice of Labor, or was its name changed to something else?

Mr. DOZENBERG. After the Workers' Party headquarters was moved to Chicago then the two papers were amalgamated. The subscription list was turned over to the Worker, which was published before then here in New York and continued publication in Chicago. So the Voice of Labor was, it can be said, absorbed by the Worker, which was a weekly publication.

Mr. MATTHEWS. Do you recall having given your biographical sketch to the editors or publishers of a volume entitled "The American Labor Who's Who"?

Mr. DOZENBERG. I have a very slight recollection.

Mr. MATTHEWS. Edited by Solon de Leon?

(No answer.)

Mr. MATTHEWS. Do you recall that volume?

Mr. DOZENBERG. No. I don't. Possibly I have seen the volume myself.

Mr. MATTHEWS. The biographical sketch of Nicholas Dozenberg on page 62 of this volume lists your employment as business manager of the Voice of Labor for 1921 to 1923.

Mr. DOZENBERG. Well, I may be mistaken. I am not disputing the dates at all.

Mr. MATTHEWS. You are not quite—absolutely sure, are you?

Mr. DOZENBERG. No, I am not.

Mr. MATTHEWS. That the publication continued publication down to 1926?

Mr. DOZENBERG. No, I am not. I am just impressed that way, that it did continue longer.

Mr. MATTHEWS. Now, during your editorship, that is, your business managership of the Voice of Labor, where were the headquarters of the publication?

Mr. DOZENBERG. Eighteen something—some number on North California Avenue in Chicago.

Mr. MATTHEWS. Wasn't it 2003 North California?

Mr. DOZENBERG. Oh, yes, yes. You have the publication there so you can see the number.

Mr. MATTHEWS. Now, where were the headquarters of the Workers' Party in Chicago at that time?

Mr. DOZENBERG. I could not tell you at this time. I don't really remember.

Mr. MATTHEWS. Well, you were in close touch with the headquarters of the Workers' Party in Chicago at that time, were you not?

Mr. DOZENBERG. Well, it all depends on what you would consider "in close touch." I suppose it is reasonable that I was, because after all it was the members of the party who supported the Voice of Labor and so I must have been in touch.

Mr. MATTHEWS. Do you remember the events of June 15, 1922?

Mr. DOZENBERG. I have no idea what you are referring to.

Mr. MATTHEWS. I am referring to the events that took place at Herrin, Ill., on June 15, 1922.

Mr. DOZENBERG. Oh, yes, yes. I remember now.

Mr. MATTHEWS. You remember there was considerable bloodshed at Herrin, Ill., now?

Mr. DOZENBERG. Yes.

Mr. MATTHEWS. On June 15, 1922?

Mr. DOZENBERG. Yes, sir.

Mr. MATTHEWS. In connection with a strike in the mines at Herrin?

Mr. DOZENBERG. Well, the papers had quite a lot of publicity on that.

Mr. MATTHEWS. Will you please describe your connections with the events of the Herrin, Ill., mine strike?

Mr. DOZENBERG. None whatsoever.

Mr. MATTHEWS. You were interested in that strike, were you not?

Mr. DOZENBERG. I was not. I had nothing to do with it.

I was no more interested than any other individual was who was reading the papers.

Mr. MATTHEWS. The Voice of Labor carried a good deal of publicity about the Herrin strike, did it not?

Mr. DOZENBERG. I don't suppose the Voice of Labor carried any more than the Chicago Tribune did.

Mr. MATTHEWS. Did the Voice of Labor very actively support those who captured and killed the so-called "scabs" who were at work at the Herrin mines?

Mr. DOZENBERG. Well, now, I do not recollect just exactly what happened in reference to that—as to the moral support. It stands to reason that the Voice of Labor could have done that and did do that, but I am sure that the Voice of Labor wasn't the only publication doing that. And then you must understand that, as far as any of the editorial policies are concerned, I had nothing to say in the matter.

Mr. MATTHEWS. In the Voice of Labor for June 26, 1922, there is a front-page article entitled "Miners Kill Scabs."

Mr. DOZENBERG. Yes.

Mr. MATTHEWS. Do you recall that?

Mr. DOZENBERG. I do not recall, but you are showing it to me. It is there.

Mr. MATTHEWS. In the issue of the Voice of Labor for June 30, 1922, there is a front-page headline entitled: "Miners Avenge Their Dead." Does this refresh your recollection that the Voice of Labor did actively support those——

Mr. DOZENBERG. I am not entering into a dispute. You see you are showing me publications—the fact of the matter is, it is there; but I am telling you I had nothing to say or do about it.

Mr. MATTHEWS. Mr. Dozenberg, do you recall the fact that Mr. John L. Lewis' organization, the United Mine Workers of America, published a series of articles for newspaper publication on the events of the Herrin tragedy?

Mr. DOZENBERG. I have a slight recollection of having—that something of that sort had been done and had been offered for publication, or something of that sort, but what was published I could not say.

Mr. MATTHEWS. Did you know that on January 3, 1924, Senator Henry Cabot Lodge introduced those articles in the records of the United States Senate and that they were published as Document No. 14 of the Sixty-eighth Congress, first session?

Mr. DOZENBERG. I did not; no.

Mr. MATTHEWS. Reading from the Senate document on page 18:

With the local Lithuanian miners as a nuclei, a Communist Party chapter was organized in Herrin, holding its meetings secretly in the Lithuanian language, but taking its instructions from the agents of Dozenberg in the office of Carney at Chicago. Quietly and stealthily they work among the idle miners at Herrin, preaching insurrection and armed attack upon the strip mine, where coal was being produced.

In June a query as to the status of the men employed in the strip mine was made of President Lewis. He replied to this query, classifying the situation as one of strike breaking. This telegram was immediately pounced upon by the Communist agents in the vicinity and distorted into an excuse for an armed attack upon the strip mine.

The workers there were captured, and under the leadership of the 19 Communist agents who, according to Dozenberg, had been imported for the purpose of starting armed insurrection and revolution, the men were shot down.

That night and the next day there was rejoicing in the office of the Voice of Labor in Chicago. The armed insurrection that had been carefully planned was at hand—it had actually started. Dozenberg proclaimed that the new Communists at Herrin had proven that they were real Communists, and that now the revolutionary work must be spread to Indiana and Ohio.

Dozenberg expressed confidence that no one would be punished for the crime, for the Communist grip was strong in Herrin, and "our people working among the miners used clever tactics in assisting them, and are using the party tactics to influence the public officials."

"Our great advantage is," said Dozenberg, "that the head of the mine workers, Lewis, sent a telegram there. This was used as an opportunity by our people by which they easily could be covered in their action."

Dozenberg then went to the center of the affair.

"We have 67 members of the Communist Party in Herrin," he said. "They are all Lithuanians, besides the 19 sent down from here. The 19 sent down from here represent the Lithuanian Bureau of the Communist Party. They are all members of the Lithuanian Federation of the Bolshevik faction of the Communist Party."

Did you know that Mr. John L. Lewis had made these charges?

Mr. Dozenberg. I did not.

Mr. Matthews. Even though this was published in 1924, this had not come to your attention until today?

Mr. Dozenberg. No, no.

Mr. Matthews. But you were associated with Mr. Carney in the office of the Voice of Labor as business manager of the publication?

Mr. Dozenberg. Yes.

Mr. Matthews. Did you know Arnie Swabeck?

Mr. Dozenberg. If I remember it correctly he was a Swede and he was the editor of a Swedish publication that was published or printed at the same place where the Voice of Labor was published.

Mr. Matthews. And you knew Mr. Swaback, therefore?

Mr. Dozenberg. I knew him; yes.

Mr. Mathews. And did you know a man named Frankel?

Mr. Dozenberg. I do not remember him.

Mr. Matthews. Now, did you not know that Mr. Swabeck spent most of his time on the scene in Herrin during these events?

Mr. Dozenberg. I did not know that. It is news to me.

Mr. Matthews. Didn't Mr. Swabeck ever give you any reports as to how——

Mr. Dozenberg. Never.

Mr. Matthews. —things were going?

Mr. Dozenberg. He was not supposed to give me any reports.

Mr. Matthews. In Herrin?

Mr. Dozenberg. And he never gave me any reports.

Mr. Matthews. I don't mean formal reports but a verbal account of what was taking place?

Mr. Dozenberg. No, no.

Mr. Matthews. After hearing this statement included in this document published by Mr. Lewis of the United Mine Workers of America, what recollections do you have concerning your own interest and activities in connection with this Herrin affair?

Mr. Dozenberg. It is absolutely from one end to the other, as far as I am concerned, just 100 percent lies, from one end to the other.

Mr. Matthews. Did the Communist Party have an organization in Herrin?

Mr. Dozenberg. If the Communist Party did have an organization there it would not have been to my knowledge.

Mr. Matthews. And, of course, when I use the name "Communist Party" I mean the name under which it went at that time, the "Workers' Party"?

Mr. Dozenberg. Now, for instance that article mentions about a Lithuanian branch or those being Lithuanians I am inclined to believe. I am not speaking Lithuanian; I am not a Lithuanian.

Mr. Matthews. You are a Lett?

Mr. Dozenberg. A Lett and that is a distinctly different language.

Mr. Matthews. Well, you are not credited here with speaking the Lithuanian language, Mr. Dozenberg; only the Lithuanians themselves.

Mr. Dozenberg. May I make a suggestion, if you are really placing any value on that story at all other than just a story written up for publicity purposes or for sale, as some of those things are done, why don't you get ahold of the court records of the trials and everything else before the courts of the State of Illinois? Why do you have to resort to anything of this sort as to bringing in the record of the Herrin miners trials, and so forth.

Mr. Matthews. Well, this is a record made by the organization of which Mr. John L. Lewis was head and he was very much involved in the situation, inasmuch as his telegram had been used as the occasion for the outbreak.

Mr. Dozenberg. But you don't—all of those things came up before the court trying the cases. Don't you think that there were witnesses and a jury and everything else? Why spend your time about something that some one has said or written? Why don't you——

The Chairman. Well, the important thing, Mr. Dozenberg, is whether or not it is true. Now, you have denied that those statements are true.

Mr. Dozenberg. Mr. Dies, I can assure you that as far as I am concerned, it is a lie and a write-up publicity stunt from one end to the other; and it simply occurred to me that an organization of yours should not waste your time because you have the real source in the court records of the trial itself.

The Chairman. Well, the document speaks for itself. Here is a document that has been in circulation since 1924 and which was prepared by one of the large unions in the United States, and the examiner is simply asking you if the statements made by that organization with reference to you and your alleged activities in the strike are true.

Mr. Dozenberg. They are not true, Mr. Chairman, absolutely not one iota.

The Chairman. All right.

Mr. Matthews. Now, Mr. Dozenberg, were you ever questioned by the authorities with reference to what took place at Herrin?

Mr. Dozenberg. Never, not a single instance, never.

Mr. MATTHEWS. Did the Voice of Labor, during the time that you were business manager of the publication, advocate measures that corresponded with what took place at Herrin, namely, the killing of these so-called scabs and mine guards by the striking workers?

Mr. DOZENBERG. I would say no, but if the editorial policy was such that it would advocate that, I surely did not have anything to say or to do with it.

Mr. MATTHEWS. Did the Voice of Labor advocate workers arming themselves to meet such situations?

Mr. DOZENBERG. I doubt it.

Mr. MATTHEWS. Now, you were acquainted with the publication. You did not ignore its contents, did you?

Mr. DOZENBERG. Mr. Counsel, if you would only have an inkling of an idea as to what I was up against to keep the publication going, you would appreciate the fact that I did not have 1 minute of time to read this or tell the editor what is what or what is not what.

Mr. DEMPSEY. If you were so interested in keeping the publication going, you certainly had an interest in its objects—in what it was doing; isn't that true?

Mr. DOZENBERG. Yes.

Mr. DEMPSEY. So you were in sympathy with the editorial policy of your paper?

Mr. DOZENBERG. Oh, yes; no question about that. The purpose was to reach the trade-union movement.

Mr. MATTHEWS. Now, Mr. Dozenberg, on August 11, 1922, a few weeks after the Herrin incident, there appeared an editorial on page 4 of the Voice of Labor, which reads in part as follows:

Let us purge our movement of those who talk peace in the hour when brute force is the only law. Let us go forward agitating and preparing the working class for the day when it can assume power and thus dictate to those who now dictate conditions,

and so forth, and again in the issue of the Voice of Labor dated August 18, 1922, on page 2, a few weeks after the Herrin incident, the following statement:

The time has come for the United Mine Workers and the Western Federation of Miners to levy a special monthly assessment to create a gunmen defense fund. This fund should be sufficient to provide each member with the latest high-powered rifle, the same as used by the corporation gunmen, and 500 rounds of cartridges.

In addition to this, every district should purchase, and equip, and man enough gatling and machine guns to match the equipment of Rockefeller's private army of assassins. This suggestion is made advisedly.

Do you recall that sort of statement appearing in your publication?

Mr. DOZENBERG. I do not recall it.

Mr. MATTHEWS. Don't you recall that throughout the Voice of Labor during the entire period of its publication, such principles were set forth?

Mr. DOZENBERG. I would say this, if it is permissible, that I did know it and that I agreed to it; but the other side of the story is, as the article itself says, that the employer has the money to buy these things with, has bought them, has an army and is the one attacking the trade unionists; and therefore, the logic seems to follow that if the other fellow is doing it why should you lie down and not do the same thing.

Even as late as 1938 or 1939, I remember reading in the papers that the La Follette committee was investigating, and the "little steel" corporation had a dozen machine guns and 20,000 rounds of ammunition. Now, if any trade unionist had known that beforehand, the chances are they would have advocated the same thing. If the "little steel" people are permitted to do it, why shouldn't the unions do it?

Mr. MATTHEWS. Have you ever read any of the trade-union publications of the United Mine Workers where they have advocated arming men in that fashion?

Mr. DOZENBERG. I don't remember having read it.

Mr. MATTHEWS. You said that any trade-union leader would have done the same thing, or would have agitated the same thing.

Mr. DOZENBERG. If they had known the employer was doing it; I qualify that thing.

Mr. MATTHEWS. Well, isn't it well known that there are guards who guard the plants of American industry in many places?

Mr. DOZENBERG. But it is not known generally that they have acquired machine guns with so many thousands of rounds of ammunition. That evidently also was disclosed by a congressional committee.

Mr. MATTHEWS. Now, Mr. Dozenberg, I read you the names of some of the contributors to the Voice of Labor:

"C. E. Ruthenberg, secretary, Workers' Party of America." He was the secretary of the Communist Party, as it was named at that time, was he not?

Mr. DOZENBERG. Well, you see the Communist Party was not in existence.

Mr. MATTHEWS. I am not speaking of the party bearing the name "Communist" but the Workers' Party.

Mr. DOZENBERG. Yes.

Mr. MATTHEWS. Ruthenberg has been looked upon as having been the secretary of the Communist Party at that time?

Mr. DOZENBERG. Yes, yes.

Mr. MATTHEWS. The next signed article that I see here is by Harry Gannes?

Mr. DOZENBERG. Yes, sir.

Mr. MATTHEWS. Did you know Harry Gannes?

Mr. DOZENBERG. I knew him.

Mr. MATTHEWS. He wrote a regular column for the Voice of Labor, didn't he?

Mr. DOZENBERG. I don't suppose he did a regular one. but I understand that he was one of the contributors.

Mr. MATTHEWS. He was at that time secretary of the Young Workers' League?

Mr. DOZENBERG. Yes.

Mr. MATTHEWS. Which later became the Young Communist League?

Mr. DOZENBERG. Yes.

Mr. MATTHEWS. And more recently he has been a columnist on the Daily Worker?

Mr. DOZENBERG. That is also news to me. I haven't seen the Daily Worker for 12 years, so I don't know who is who.

Mr. MATTHEWS. You know Mr. Gannes is under indictment for traveling on a fraudulent passport?

Mr. DOZENBERG. I have been so told.

Mr. MATTHEWS. You have no doubt about his having been a member of the Communist Party through this period when it had different names?

Mr. DOZENBERG. Mister, I did not know that he has had different names, but I don't doubt that he has been a member of the Communist Party.

Mr. MATTHEWS. I don't say whether he had a different name; when the party had different names.

Mr. DOZENBERG. I would not say for sure just exactly when he joined the party.

Mr. MATTHEWS. I see here a contributed article by Earl Browder. You knew Mr. Browder at that time, didn't you?

Mr. DOZENBERG. I doubt it very much whether I knew Browder. My recollection goes to Browder back to 19—I would not say just exactly what year it was—at the time when I remember having seen Browder the first time and that was when the Workers' Party headquarters was in Chicago.

Mr. MATTHEWS. Well, the Workers' Party headquarters were in Chicago at that time?

Mr. DOZENBERG. Not while this was—I mean the national headquarters of the Workers' Party.

Mr. MATTHEWS. They were in Chicago at this time, were they not?

Mr. DOZENBERG. Not while the Voice of Labor was published.

Mr. MATTHEWS. This is in the year 1922?

Mr. DOZENBERG. The headquarters of the Workers Party was in New York.

Mr. MATTHEWS. You knew Mr. Browder in Chicago during this period, did you not?

Mr. DOZENBERG. I just learned to know him. I did not know him before.

Mr. MATTHEWS. You have no doubts about his having been a Communist from this period down to the present time?

Mr. DOZENBERG. I have doubts.

Mr. MATTHEWS. You have doubts?

Mr. DOZENBERG. Yes.

Mr. MATTHEWS. You have no doubt about his having been a member of the Communist Party?

Mr. DOZENBERG. Yes.

Mr. MATTHEWS. You have doubts about that?

Mr. DOZENBERG. Yes, sir; I have doubts.

Mr. MATTHEWS. What are those doubts, Mr. Dozenberg?

Mr. DOZENBERG. I don't think that Browder joined the Communist movement any sooner, or the party, than 1924 or 1925, according to my beliefs and recollections.

Mr. MATTHEWS. That doesn't conform to Mr. Browder's testimony.

Mr. DOZENBERG. No; no.

Mr. MATTHEWS. Here is a contributed article by Zinoviev.

Mr. DOZENBERG. Yes.

Mr. MATTHEWS. He was at that time secretary of the Communist International, was he not?

Mr. DOZENBERG. To the best of my recollection; yes. Whether he was the secretary—he was known as one of the theoreticians of the Communist International.

Mr. MATTHEWS. Mr. Benjamin Gitlow is named on page 6 of the July 21, 1922, edition. Did you know Mr. Benjamin Gitlow?

Mr. DOZENBERG. I did.

Mr. MATTHEWS. And you knew him as a Communist, did you not?

Mr. DOZENBERG. Yes.

Mr. MATTHEWS. Did you know Mr. William Z. Foster at this time?

Mr. DOZENBERG. Well, I learned to know him. I met Mr. Foster the first time a year or so after the Voice of Labor was published or had started publication.

Mr. MATTHEWS. Mr. Foster contributed to the Voice of Labor, did he not?

Mr. DOZENBERG. Yes, sir.

Mr. MATTHEWS. And you knew him as a Communist at that time?

Mr. DOZENBERG. No; he was not.

Mr. MATTHEWS. When did he become a Communist?

Mr. DOZENBERG. I don't suppose Foster became a member of the Communist Party or the party, by whatever name, any sooner than 1926 or 1925.

Mr. MATTHEWS. In his autobiography Mr. Foster says he became a member of the Communist Party in 1921. You doubt that, do you?

Mr. DOZENBERG. I doubt that, although I do not profess of knowing all the "ins" and "outs." I am speaking to the best of my recollection and beliefs.

Mr. MATTHEWS. Now, in another issue we have the name of Ella Reeve Bloor.

Mr. DOZENBERG. Yes, sir; an old lady.

Mr. MATTHEWS. You have known her for some years?

Mr. DOZENBERG. Yes, sir.

Mr. MATTHEWS. You know her?

Mr. DOZENBERG. Yes, sir; I know her.

Mr. MATTHEWS. You know her as a Communist?

Mr. DOZENBERG. I took it for granted she was.

Mr. MATTHEWS. As a matter of fact, Mr. Dozenberg, isn't it true that every contributor, maybe with a few exceptions, to the Voice of Labor during your business managership was publicly known as a Communist?

Mr. DOZENBERG. Publicly known individuals but I did not know them personally. For instance, you mentioned Zinoviev. I never met Zinoviev in my life.

Mr. MATTHEWS. My point was this: You stated earlier in your testimony that the Voice of Labor was not a Communist publication.

Mr. DOZENBERG. Well, from the editorial point of view I suppose it was, as far as the Communist movement went in those days.

Mr. MATTHEWS. Could it have been any more of a Communist publication in the real sense than if it had designated itself as the official organ of the Workers' Party?

Mr. DOZENBERG. I think that it would be a different one—not like the Voice of Labor was then.

Mr. MATTHEWS. Now, after your work as business manager of the Voice of Labor, did you become connected with the Worker, or during your business managership?

Mr. DOZENBERG. No. After the Voice of Labor was discontinued then I was given the manager of the literature department position with the Workers' Party in Chicago.

Mr. MATTHEWS. Now, the Weekly Worker was the predecessor of the Daily Worker, was it not?

Mr. DOZENBERG. It was all transferred——

Mr. MATTHEWS. I asked you if the Weekly Worker was not the predecessor of the Daily Worker?

Mr. DOZENBERG. Yes, sir.

Mr. MATTHEWS. And you were at one time business manager of the Weekly Worker, were you not?

Mr. DOZENBERG. I don't think so.

Mr. MATTHEWS. This will probably refresh your recollection, Mr. Dozenberg.

Mr. DOZENBERG. Perhaps so.

Mr. MATTHEWS. I show you a bound volume of the Worker. This is for Saturday, September 22, 1923.

Mr. DOZENBERG. Yes, sir.

Mr. MATTHEWS. "Nicholas Dozenberg, Business Manager."

Mr. DOZENBERG. How many issues is that, may I ask?

Mr. MATTHEWS. I don't know, but you were business manager?

Mr. DOZENBERG. No; it must have been some insignificant—you are telling me news—I have forgotten all about it.

Mr. MATTHEWS. You have no doubt about the correctness of this, have you?

Mr. DOZENBERG. No; I have no doubt, but it may have been for one or two issues and consequently it hasn't left any impression on my mind at all.

Mr. MATTHEWS. Now, the managing editor at that time was J. Lewis Engdahl.

Mr. DOZENBERG. Correct.

Mr. MATTHEWS. And Robert Minor was cartoonist for the publication?

Mr. DOZENBERG. Yes.

Mr. MATTHEWS. Now, turning to the end of this bound volume, which is dated December—that is a period of four months, you are still listed as "Nicholas Dozenberg, Business Manager."

Mr. DOZENBERG. Well, you see those things have simply dropped from my mind.

Mr. MATTHEWS. Do you have your recollection refreshed now that for a period of at least four months——

Mr. DOZENBERG. If you had not shown me I would still insist upon I never was manager of the Worker.

Mr. MATTHEWS. Now, the Worker was published in Chicago at that time and you were still——

Mr. DOZENBERG. You see those little details I have completely forgotten, even just exactly what happened after the Voice of Labor was discontinued; whether I also for any time became the business manager of the Worker or not. My recollection goes that after the Voice of Labor was discontinued that I became the manager of the literature department of the Workers' Party. Now, there may be a period while the Worker was continued in Chicago and the Voice of Labor done away with that I was formally also the business manager of the Worker.

Mr. MATTHEWS. Well, for 4 months you are listed as that. You say you have forgotten that completely?

M. DOZENBERG. Four months. That is quite a number of years ago, and that simply dropped from my mind also.

Mr. MATTHEWS. Is it possible you may have forgotten your connection with the Herrin incident also?

Mr. DOZENBERG. No; it is not possible.

Mr. MATTHEWS. Well, that was less than 4 months, and that was even longer ago.

Mr. DOZENBERG. No; but that is altogether a different phase. If you are accused of having played a role in murder and advocating murder that is a different story altogether.

Mr. MATTHEWS. Did you ever have any connection with the publication known as the Liberator?

Mr. DOZENBERG. The Liberator was also published from the same office, and if I remember correctly, Engdahl's wife was the business manager of the Liberator; and then the Liberator, again, if I remember correctly, was discontinued.

Mr. MATTHEWS. Well, were you ever business manager of the Liberator?

Mr. DOZENBERG. I could not say for sure. I doubt it very much.

Mr. MATTHEWS. Do you recall having given in your biographical sketch——

Mr. DOZENBERG. Oh, please, that is a publicity stunt. Don't pay any attention to that.

Mr. MATTHEWS. Did you supply these details?

Mr. DOZENBERG. I don't think I did.

Mr. MATTHEWS. Then who would have known your birthday besides yourself?

Mr. DOZENBERG. That is easy enough for anyone to find out.

The CHAIRMAN. Well, you gave the information for all of that.

Mr. DOZENBERG. The chances are, Mr. Dies, that I have given it.

Mr. MATTHEWS. He would know you attended grammar school in Latvia, if you did not supply the information?

Mr. DOZENBERG. That is possible.

Mr. MATTHEWS. And how would any one know that you went to work at the age of 10 years?

Mr. DOZENBERG. This is publicity stuff.

Mr. MATTHEWS. If you stated here you were business manager of the Liberator—I want to know if you supplied the information, and if it is a fact and is correct?

Mr. DOZENBERG. It may be correct, and it may be incorrect.

Mr. MATTHEWS. You don't recall whether you were business manager of that publication or not?

Mr. DOZENBERG. I do not recall. I doubt it. Personally, I doubt it very much.

The CHAIRMAN. You would not have falsely supplied that information for the purposes of publicity, would you?

Mr. DOZENBERG. Honorable Dies, it is reasonable I would not have, but I am honest in telling you that I do not recollect.

The CHAIRMAN. All right.

Mr. MATTHEWS. Do you recollect that the Worker, which was published weekly, became a daily publication?

Mr. DOZENBERG. Yes.

Mr. Matthews. On instructions by cable from Zinoviev in Moscow?

Mr. Dozenberg. No.

Mr. Matthews. You don't recall that?

Mr. Dozenberg. I don't recall that. I had nothing to do with it.

Now, may I mention this, Mr. Dies? I have been told that Benjamin Gitlow, whom I learned to know quite well because he was at the headquarters ever so often, has written a book called I Confess, and my name is not mentioned once in the whole book.

The Chairman. What has that got to do with it?

Mr. Dozenberg. It shows that I had played such an insignificant role in matters of this sort that the attorney refers to. I was instrumental in carrying out some, they say, certain technical work.

Mr. Matthews. You would not consider the business managership of the Voice of Labor insignificant, would you?

Mr. Dozenberg. From a certain point of view it is.

Mr. Matthews. Would you consider the business managership of the Worker insignificant?

Mr. Dozenberg. Well, if you understood just exactly what the business managership of publications of that sort is doing, you would consider it insignificant.

Mr. Matthews. Now, you say you became head of the literature department of the Workers' Party?

Mr. Dozenberg. Yes.

Mr. Matthews. Would you consider that insignificant?

Mr. Dozenberg. Well, it was a sales organization. My work was to promote sales.

Mr. Matthews. Wasn't it extremely important to distribute literature?

Mr. Dozenberg. I was not doing the distributing. . I was doing the selling. It was a means of making money for the party as far as I was concerned.

Mr. Matthews. The Worker, dated August 25, 1923, on page 1, carries a message from G. Zinoviev, instructing the Workers' Party of America to make a daily publication out of the Worker, which was a weekly publication. Do you recall that?

Mr. Dozenberg. I don't recall. I never had anything to do with receiving any telegrams from Zinoviev or anyone else whatever. Anything that appeared in the paper had nothing to do with me attending to certain technical sides of publication.

Mr. Matthews. As head of the literature department of the Workers' Party. Mr. Dozenberg, you were acquainted with the literature published by the party, of course.

Mr. Dozenberg. I can frankly tell you that I was instrumental in having seen that it is printed, that it is bound, that the people working around be paid off; but as to its contents, I had nothing to do or nothing to say one iota about it.

Mr. Matthews. I did not ask you if you had any decisive vote in such matters, but you were acquainted with the literature.

Mr. Dozenberg. I doubt very much, even if I had time to read the contents while it was published.

Mr. Matthews. How long did you hold the position as head of the literature department of the Workers' Party?

Mr. Dozenberg. Until the time the Workers' Party headquarters was moved back to New York.

Mr. MATTHEWS. And what year was that?

Mr. DOZENBERG. I could not say.

Mr. MATTHEWS. In 1926?

Mr. DOZENBERG. It is either 1926 or 1927. I am not sure which. But you have that record.

Mr. MATTHEWS. During the period of your leadership in the literature work of the Workers' Party, the communists began the publication of what they called the Lenin Library. You recall that, don't you?

Mr. DOZENBERG. Yes; I recall that.

Mr. MATTHEWS. And the first volume of the Lenin Library was a book entitled "Lenin On Organization." You recall that, don't you?

Mr. DOZENBERG. I do not recall it but I do not dispute it. You are showing it to me.

Mr. MATTHEWS. You were a member of the organization at that time?

Mr. DOZENBERG. I was a member of the Workers' Publishing Society.

Mr. MATTHEWS. As a member of the Society you subscribed to its principles?

Mr. DOZENBERG. Correct.

Mr. MATTHEWS. And you accepted the teachings of Lenin?

Mr. DOZENBERG. Correct.

Mr. MATTHEWS. You had to, in order to be a member of the party?

Mr. DOZENBERG. Exactly.

Mr. MATTHEWS. Lenin is considered the highest authority of the Communist Party?

Mr. DOZENBERG. On the theoretical side of it; yes, sir.

Mr. MATTHEWS. Now, in this book which was published during your own active leadership in the literature work of the Workers' Party, on page 64, Lenin is describing the nature of a Communist Party when it is correctly organized. He says:

Such an organization must of necessity be not too extensive.

You recall the theories of the Communist Party regarding the vanguard of the proletariat, that the party is not to be a party which includes a majority of the voting population but is to be merely the general staff or the vanguard of the proletariat?

Mr. DOZENBERG. I shall leave it to you to expound it all.

Mr. MATTHEWS. But you understand that?

Mr. DOZENBERG. I understand that, but you must understand I haven't had anything to do for 12 years with it and a lot of those things have dropped from my mind completely. I leave it to you to expound the theories. I think you can do it better than I can.

Mr. MATTHEWS. You accept some measure of responsibility for this literature; don't you?

Mr. DOZENBERG. No; I do not.

Mr. MATTHEWS. Having been head of the literature department of the party.

Mr. DOZENBERG. I was instrumental in carrying out certain technical work in that connection and that is the finish of it, in that sense. You can also hold the same thing about the publishers of Professor

Russell's works, where he is advocating certain theories, as being responsible for holding similar theories.

Mr. MATTHEWS. Now, continuing that quotation:

Such an organization must of necessity be not too extensive and as conspiratorial as possible.

And again on page 74 of the same volume, Lenin describes the party as follows:

A small tight kernel consisting of reliable, experienced, and steeled workers with responsible agents in the chief districts, and connected by all the rules of strict conspiracy.

Mr. DOZENBERG. He speaks a typical trade-union language. He speaks a typical trade-union language.

Mr. MATTHEWS. And again on page 111 through page 125, Lenin describes in more detail the conspiratorial nature of a Communist Party when it is properly organized, and he says:

For instance, the disputing groups require—

This is on page 117—

require the utmost conspiratorialness and military discipline.

And finally on page 124, Lenin says:

In the same way, and after the type of branch department of the Committee or Committee institution, all the other groups serving the movement should be organized—the university students and high-school students groups, the groups, let us say, for assisting Government officials, transport groups, printing groups, passport groups, groups for arranging conspiratorial meeting places, groups for tracking spies, military groups, groups for procuring arms, organization groups, such as for running income-producing enterprises, etc. The whole art of conspiratorial organization consists in making use of everything and everybody.

Now, you were a member of the Communist Party until what year, Mr. Dozenberg?

Mr. DOZENBERG. 1928, I think.

Mr. MATTHEWS. In other words, for a period of approximately 8 years?

Mr. DOZENBERG. Yes.

Mr. MATTHEWS. At least you were a member of the Communist Party?

Mr. DOZENBERG. Yes.

Mr. MATTHEWS. You haven't forgotten the nature of the Communist Party during that period, have you?

Mr. DOZENBERG. (No answer.)

Mr. MATTHEWS. You know that it was a conspiratorial organization?

Mr. DOZENBERG. It was not.

Mr. MATTHEWS. Why did the party publish Lenin's advice on organization emphasizing the necessity for being conspiratorial if the party was not going to take any cognizance of that advice?

Mr. DOZENBERG. You are asking me why. Well, those were Lenin's theories. There may be a time when someone else will be publishing a book about you that you are also a conspirator.

Mr. MATTHEWS. And you have also stated that Lenin is considered the highest authority in theory.

Mr. DOZENBERG. That he is considered the highest authority as far as certain theories are concerned.

Mr. MATTHEWS. Now, on page 114 of this book we read:

We must get the workers to understand that while the killing of spies, provocateurs, and traitors may sometimes, of course, be absolutely unavoidable, it is highly undesirable and mistaken to make a system of it.

In other words, you knew that Lenin did advocate the killing if unavoidable, of those who were considered traitors by the Communist Party.

Mr. DOZENBERG. If that is your interpretation, I have no objection to it. I have never understood it that way as far as I am concerned.

Mr. MATTHEWS. That is what took place at Herrin, isn't it?

Mr. DOZENBERG. I don't think that you are a conspirator, but there may be people on the outside calling you a conspirator against other people, and if someone would write a theory about it, I would not accuse someone else, responsible for publishing it, also being a conspirator.

Mr. MATTHEWS. Now, Mr. Dozenberg, you were head of the literature department of the party down until what date, again, please?

Mr. DOZENBERG. Until the party headquarters was moved from Chicago to New York. I don't remember the date.

Mr. MATTHEWS. And what did you engage in then when the party moved its headquarters to New York? What became of your position?

Mr. DOZENBERG. I became the manager of the Workers' Publishing Society.

Mr. MATTHEWS. Where was that located?

Mr. DOZENBERG. One Hundred and Twenty-fifth Street; I don't remember the number.

Mr. MATTHEWS. In New York?

Mr. DOZENBERG. In New York.

Mr. MATTHEWS. And how long did you hold that position?

Mr. DOZENBERG. I think for a year, more or less. I am not sure.

Mr. MATTHEWS. And was that the last position you held in the Workers' Party?

Mr. DOZENBERG. That was the last position.

Mr. MATTHEWS. And that was done until about the end of 1927, was it not?

Mr. DOZENBERG. It is either 1927 or 1928.

Mr. MATTHEWS. And then it was the end of 1927, was it not, that you enlisted in the work of the Soviet Military Intelligence?

Mr. DOZENBERG. I do not remember anything of the sort.

Mr. MATTHEWS. Well, what was it? Early in 1938?

Mr. DOZENBERG. I have never enlisted in the Soviet employ.

Mr. MATTHEWS. How do you describe your work under the Soviet Military Intelligence?

Mr. DOZENBERG. Mr. Chairman, may I address a request?

The CHAIRMAN. Certainly.

Mr. DOZENBERG. If you wish me to make any statements along those lines at all, I would suggest an executive session. I am not going to make any public statements, and I want you to understand that, irrespective of what the committee might decide to do with me; because I figure that a question of my welfare is at stake.

The CHAIRMAN. You mean in answering any questions dealing with yourself?

Mr. Dozenberg. With a foreign power.

The Chairman. Well, if the committee holds an executive session, will you be thoroughly frank with the committee?

Mr. Dozenberg. I will.

The Chairman. And tell the committee your whole connection in this matter, if any, and your knowledge of others in it?

Mr. Dozenberg. I have confidence in the committee that if I tell them something in confidence for the use of the Government that I will do so, but I do not wish to make any public statements.

The Chairman. You are no longer connected with the Communist Party, are you?

Mr. Dozenberg. I am not.

The Chairman. You have repudiated the Communist Party and you no longer believe in the Communist Party?

Mr. Dozenberg. Exactly.

The Chairman. Is that right?

Mr. Dozenberg. That is right.

The Chairman. And you realize the danger of this thing to the United States, don't you?

Mr. Dozenberg. I do.

The Chairman. And you want to help protect this Government and this country, do you not?

Mr. Dozenberg. I want to protect myself as well, Mr. Dies.

The Chairman. I think that the request is reasonable.

The committee will go into executive session. Will you please clear the room, everyone?

(Whereupon the hearing room was cleared of all spectators.)